Believers Church
Bible Commentary

Elmer A. Martens and Willard M. Swartley, Editors

BELIEVERS CHURCH BIBLE COMMENTARY

Old Testament
Genesis, by Eugene F. Roop, 1987
Exodus, by Waldemar Janzen, 2000
Judges, by Terry L. Brensinger, 1999
Ruth, Jonah, Esther, by Eugene F. Roop, 2002
Psalms, by James H. Waltner, 2006
Proverbs, by John W. Miller, 2004
Ecclesiastes, by Douglas B. Miller, 2010
Isaiah, by Ivan D. Friesen, 2009
Jeremiah, by Elmer A. Martens, 1986
Ezekiel, by Millard C. Lind, 1996
Daniel, by Paul M. Lederach, 1994
Hosea, Amos, by Allen R. Guenther, 1998

New Testament
Matthew, by Richard B. Gardner, 1991
Mark, by Timothy J. Geddert, 2001
Acts, by Chalmer E. Faw, 1993
Romans, by John E. Toews, 2004
2 Corinthians, by V. George Shillington, 1998
Ephesians, by Thomas R. Yoder Neufeld, 2002
Colossians, Philemon, by Ernest D. Martin, 1993
1-2 Thessalonians, by Jacob W. Elias, 1995
1-2 Timothy, Titus, by Paul M. Zehr, 2010
1-2 Peter, Jude, by Erland Waltner and J. Daryl Charles, 1999
Revelation, by John R. Yeatts, 2003

Old Testament Editors
Elmer A. Martens, Mennonite Brethren Biblical Seminary, Fresno, California
Douglas B. Miller, Tabor College, Hillsboro, Kansas

New Testament Editors
Willard M. Swartley, Associated Mennonite Biblical Seminary, Elkhart, Indiana
Loren L. Johns, Associated Mennonite Biblical Seminary, Elkhart, Indiana

Editorial Council
David W. Baker, Brethren Church
Derek Suderman, Mennonite Church Canada
Christina A. Bucher, Church of the Brethren
Eric A. Seibert, Brethren in Christ Church
Gordon H. Matties, Mennonite Brethren Church
Paul M. Zehr (chair), Mennonite Church USA

Believers Church Bible Commentary

Psalms

James H. Waltner

HERALD PRESS
Scottdale, Pennsylvania
Waterloo, Ontario

Library of Congress Cataloging-in-Publication Data
Waltner, James H., 1931-
  Psalms / by James H. Waltner.
      p. cm. — (Believers church Bible commentary)
  Includes bibliographical references and index.
  ISBN 0-8361-9337-7 (pbk. : alk. paper)
  1. Bible. O.T. Psalms—Commentaries. I. Title. II. Series.
  BS1430.53.W35 2006
  223'.207—dc22
                              2006009226

Bible text is mostly from *New Revised Standard Version Bible,* copyright 1989 by the Division of Christian Education of the National Council of the Churches of Christ in the USA, and used by permission. Abbreviations listed on page 6 identify other versions briefly compared.

BELIEVERS CHURCH BIBLE COMMENTARY: PSALMS
Copyright © 2006 by Herald Press, Scottdale, PA 15683
  Released simultaneously in Canada by Herald Press,
  Waterloo, Ont. N2L 6H7. All rights reserved
Library of Congress Control Number: 2006009226
International Standard Book Number: 978-0-8361-9337-4
Printed in the United States of America
Cover by Merrill R. Miller

14 13 12 11 10   10 9 8 7 6 5 4 3

To order or request information please call 1-800-245-7894 or visit www.heraldpress.com.

To my wife, Lenore,
companion and partner in life and ministry,
whose love, encouragement, and help sustained me
in this journey through the Psalms

Abbreviations/Several Ancient Sources

//	parallels
AB	Anchor Bible
ABD	*Anchor Bible Dictionary.* Edited by David Noel Freedman. 6 vols. New York, 1992
AD	anno Domini, in the year of the Lord, present era
ANET	*Ancient Near Eastern Texts Relating to the Old Testament.* Edited by James P. Pritchard. 3d ed. Princeton, 1969
ASV	American Standard Version
BC	before Christ
ca.	circa, approximately, about
cf.	compare
e.g.	for example
esp.	especially
Heb.	Hebrew text or word (for transliteration, see below)
IDB	*The Interpreter's Dictionary of the Bible.* Vols. 1-4 edited by G. A. Buttrick. Nashville, 1962. Vol. 5 (= *Supplementary Volume*) edited by K. Crim. 1976
JB	Jerusalem Bible
lit.	literally
LXX	the Septuagint: an ancient Greek version of the Hebrew Bible
ME	*The Mennonite Encyclopedia.* Vols. 1-4 edited by H. S. Bender et al. Scottdale, PA, 1955-59. Vol. 5 edited by C. J. Dyck and D. D. Martin. 1990
MT	Masoretic Text of the Hebrew Bible, via the Masoretes (6th to 9th centuries AD)
n	note/footnote, as in NRSV n
NASB	New American Standard Bible
NEB	New English Bible
NIB	*The New Interpreter's Bible.* 13 vols. Nashville, 1994-2004
NIV	New International Version
NJPS	*The New JPS Translation of Tanakh: The Holy Scriptures.* 1999
NKJV	New King James Version
NRSV	New Revised Standard Version
NT	New Testament
OT	Old Testament
Ps/Pss	Psalm/Psalms
REB	Revised English Bible
RSV	Revised Standard Version
TEV	Today's English Version
[Torah]	sample reference to appended essay, first word/s of title
v./vv.	verse/verses
midrash	Traditional Jewish scriptural exegesis, partly legal, but mostly homiletical
Mishnah	Early third-century AD compendium, with traditional regulations and beliefs foundational for rabbinic Judaism and later Jewish thought
Septuagint	A Greek version of the Hebrew Bible made before the time of Christ (LXX)
Talmud	Compilations of commentary on the Mishnah; core for Jewish legal and moral thought
Targum	Ancient Aramaic paraphrases of the Hebrew Bible

Contents

Abbreviations, Transliteration, Ancient Sources 6
Series Foreword 13
Author's Preface 15

Introduction to Psalms 17
Encountering God in the Psalms 17
Finding One's Way Through the Psalms 18
The Message of the Psalms: Theological Themes 19
The Psalms and the New Testament 24
Suggestions for Use of the Commentary 26

Commentary on Psalms 29
Book One (Psalms 1–41)
Psalm 1   Blessed—the Way of the Righteous 30
Psalm 2   The LORD and His Anointed 35
Psalm 3   How Many Are My Foes! 41
Psalm 4   Evening Prayer to the Giver of Peaceful Sleep . . .45
Psalm 5   Morning Prayer to the God of Righteousness 49
Psalm 6   The LORD Has Heard My Weeping 53
Psalm 7   Prayer to God, the Righteous Judge 57
Psalm 8   The Wonder of Creation: Creature and 61
                Creator
Psalms 9–10   Thanksgiving and Prayer for God's Justice 66
Psalm 11   In the LORD I Take Refuge 72
Psalm 12   Destructive Words and the Saving Word 76
Psalm 13   How Long, O LORD? .80
Psalm 14   Prayer for Deliverance in a Corrupt Age 84
Psalm 15   Admission to the Temple 88

Psalm 16	The LORD, a Goodly Heritage	92
Psalm 17	Plea of the Innocent to the Savior of Fugitives	96
Psalm 18	A King's Thanksgiving Hymn for Deliverance and Victory	101
Psalm 19	In Praise of God's Creating and Redeeming Word	107
Psalm 20	Prayer for the King	112
Psalm 21	Thanksgiving Prayer for a King	116
Psalm 22	My God, My God, Why Have You Forsaken Me?	120
Psalm 23	The LORD as Shepherd and Host	127
Psalm 24	The King of Glory	132
Psalm 25	To You, O LORD, I Lift Up My Soul	137
Psalm 26	To Walk in Integrity and God's Faithfulness	142
Psalm 27	The LORD Is My Light and My Salvation	146
Psalm 28	Petition and Thanksgiving	151
Psalm 29	The Voice of the LORD in the Storm	155
Psalm 30	You Have Turned My Mourning into Dancing	160
Psalm 31	My Times Are in Your Hand	164
Psalm 32	The Blessing of Confession and Forgiveness	169
Psalm 33	Hymn to the LORD, Whose Steadfast Love Fills the Earth	174
Psalm 34	O Taste and See That the LORD Is Good	179
Psalm 35	Plea from One of the Quiet in the Land	184
Psalm 36	With You Is the Fountain of Life	188
Psalm 37	Commit Your Way to the LORD	192
Psalm 38	Do Not Forsake Me, O LORD!	197
Psalm 39	I Am Your Passing Guest	202
Psalm 40	The Lord Takes Thought for Me	206
Psalm 41	O LORD, Be Gracious to Me	211

Book Two (Psalms 42–72) 217

Psalms 42–43	The Cry of the Soul for God	218
Psalm 44	Israel Cries Out for Help in a Time of National Crisis	223
Psalm 45	Royal Wedding Song	228
Psalm 46	God Is Our Refuge and Strength	233
Psalm 47	Call to Joyful Praise of the God Who Reigns over All the Earth	238
Psalm 48	Zion, City of Our GOD	242
Psalm 49	Not Wealth, but God	246
Psalm 50	The Judge Speaks	251

Psalm 51	Have Mercy on Me, O God. . . . . .256 I Have Sinned	
Psalm 52	To Boast, or to Thank? 263	
Psalm 53	God, the Deliverer, in a Corrupt World 267	
Psalm 54	Confidence in God's Name 269	
Psalm 55	Betrayed by a Friend 273	
Psalm 56	In God I Trust 278	
Psalm 57	Be Exalted, O God 282	
Psalm 58	A God Who Judges on Earth 285	
Psalm 59	Deliver Me, O God of Steadfast Love 289	
Psalm 60	With God, . . . for Human Help Is Worthless . .294	
Psalm 61	God, a Refuge in Time of Trouble 298	
Psalm 62	For God Alone My Soul Waits in Silence 302	
Psalm 63	Your Steadfast Love Is Better Than Life 306	
Psalm 64	Wicked Tongues and Tongues of Witness 310	
Psalm 65	Thanks for God-given Bounty 314	
Psalm 66	Come and See. . . . Come and Hear! 319	
Psalm 67	The Blessing—for All Nations 324	
Psalm 68	Procession Hymn of Praise to the . . . . .328 Ascended God	
Psalm 69	The Desperate Cry of God's Suffering Servant . .335	
Psalm 70	O LORD, Make Haste to Help Me! 341	
Psalm 71	Do Not Cast Me Off in Old Age 344	
Psalm 72	Prayer for the King: May Righteousness . . . . . 349 Flourish and Peace Abound!	

Book Three (Psalms 73–89) 355

Psalm 73	Nevertheless—the Great Affirmation 356
Psalm 74	Remember Your Congregation 362
Psalm 75	God Executes Judgment, . . . Eventually 367
Psalm 76	The Awesome God 371
Psalm 77	Questions About the God Who Works . . . . .376 Wonders
Psalm 78	That the Next Generation Might Know 380
Psalm 79	Help Us, O God of Our Salvation 387
Psalm 80	Restore Us, O God 391
Psalm 81	If You Want to Live, Listen! 395
Psalm 82	Rise Up, O God, and Judge the Earth! 399
Psalm 83	Prayer Against the Enemies of God 403
Psalm 84	How Lovely Is Your Dwelling Place, O LORD . . . .408 of Hosts!
Psalm 85	Surely His Salvation Is at Hand 413

Psalm 86	Incline Your Ear, . . . for You Alone Are God	.418
Psalm 87	Zion, Glorious City of God	.423
Psalm 88	Like One Forsaken Among the Dead	.428
Psalm 89	Where Is the Steadfast Love You Swore to David?	.433

Book Four (Psalms 90–106) 441

Psalm 90	Our God, from Everlasting to Everlasting	.442
Psalm 91	Abiding in the Shadow of the Almighty	.446
Psalm 92	Praise for the LORD's Righteous Rule	.451
Psalm 93	The LORD Reigns!	.455
Psalm 94	Rise Up, O Judge of the Earth	.459
Psalm 95	O That Today You Would Listen!	.463
Psalm 96	Proclaim Among the Nations, "The LORD Reigns!"	467
Psalm 97	Rejoice in the LORD's Reign of Righteousness and Justice!	.472
Psalm 98	A New Song to the LORD as Savior, King, and Judge	.476
Psalm 99	A Hymn to the God of Holiness	.480
Psalm 100	Make a Joyful Noise to the LORD	.485
Psalm 101	A King's Vow to the Way That Is Blameless	.488
Psalm 102	Prayer to the Everlasting God by One Afflicted	.492
Psalm 103	Praise to the God Abounding in Steadfast Love	.497
Psalm 104	O LORD, How Manifold Are Your Works!	.502
Psalm 105	Remember the Wonders God Has Done	.507
Psalm 106	Both We and Our Ancestors Have Sinned	.514

Book Five (Psalms 107–150) 521

Psalm 107	Let the Redeemed Thank the LORD for His Steadfast Love and Wonderful Works	.522
Psalm 108	Liturgy of Thanksgiving and Petition	.528
Psalm 109	Accusations, Curses, and the Steadfast Love of the LORD	.530
Psalm 110	The Priest-King at the Right Hand of God	.536
Psalm 111	Great Are the Works of the LORD	.542
Psalm 112	The Blessedness of Fearing the LORD	.546
Psalm 113	God's Majesty in Mercy	.550
Psalm 114	When Israel Came Out of Egypt	.553
Psalm 115	Not to Us, O LORD, but to Your Name Give Glory	.557

Psalm 116	Thank You, God!	562
Psalm 117	Let All People Praise!	566
Psalm 118	A Processional Liturgy of Thanksgiving	568
Psalm 119	How I Love Your Word, O LORD!	575
Psalm 120	People of Peace in a World of War	589
Psalm 121	The LORD Is Your Keeper	593
Psalm 122	Pray for the Peace of Jerusalem	597
Psalm 123	Our Eyes Look to the LORD Our God	600
Psalm 124	Deliverance from a Close Call	603
Psalm 125	Protector of Those Who Trust in the LORD	607
Psalm 126	Joy Remembered and Joy Anticipated	611
Psalm 127	Everything Depends on God's Blessing	615
Psalm 128	Blessed Are Those Who Fear the LORD	618
Psalm 129	Often Have They Attacked Me, . . .Yet They Have Not Prevailed	621
Psalm 130	Out of the Depths	624
Psalm 131	Calmed and Quieted Like a Weaned Child	628
Psalm 132	God's Choice of David and Zion	631
Psalm 133	When Sisters and Brothers Live in Unity	636
Psalm 134	To Bless and to Be Blessed	639
Psalm 135	Hallelujah to the LORD Above All Gods!	642
Psalm 136	Litany of Thanksgiving: "For His Steadfast Love Endures Forever"	646
Psalm 137	By the Rivers of Babylon	651
Psalm 138	I Give Thanks, O LORD, with My Whole Heart	656
Psalm 139	O LORD, You Have Searched Me and Know Me	661
Psalm 140	Protect Me from the Violent	668
Psalm 141	With Hands, Heart, and Eyes Toward You, O God	672
Psalm 142	Cry to the LORD, My Refuge and My Portion	676
Psalm 143	Prayer of a Penitent in Distress	680
Psalm 144	A New Song to the God Who Rescues and Blesses	685
Psalm 145	In Praise of God's Greatness and Goodness	690
Psalm 146	Praise the LORD, the One True Helper	695
Psalm 147	How Good It Is to Sing Praises to Our God	699
Psalm 148	Let All Praise the Name of the LORD	704
Psalm 149	Glory for All His Faithful Ones	709
Psalm 150	Praise the LORD!	714

Outline of Psalms	719
Essays	745
Anointed, Anointed One	745
Asaph	746
Composition of the Book of Psalms	746
Enemies	750
Hebrew Poetry	751
Holiness, Holy	753
Imprecation	755
Judge, Judgment, Justice	757
Korah	758
Musical Terms	758
Names of God	759
Oracle	761
Penitential Psalms	762
Psalm Genres	762
Righteous, Righteousness	767
Selah	768
Sheol	769
Sin	769
Steadfast Love	771
Superscriptions	772
Theophany	774
Torah	775
Vengeance	776
War and War Images	777
Ways of Reading the Psalms	779
Wicked	782
Wrath of God	782
Zion	783
Map of Palestine	785
Map of the Ancient Near East	786
Appendix I. The Psalms Arranged by Literary Genre (Type)	787
Appendix II. Index of Psalms According to Genre (Type)	789
Bibliography of Works Cited	793
Selected Resources	805
Index of Ancient Sources	811
The Author	833

Series Foreword

The Believers Church Bible Commentary series makes available a new tool for basic Bible study. It is published for all who seek to understand more fully the original message of Scripture and its meaning for today—Sunday school teachers, members of Bible study groups, students, pastors, or other seekers. The series is based on the conviction that God is still speaking to all who will hear him, and that the Holy Spirit makes the Word a living and authoritative guide for all who want to know and do God's will.

The desire to be of help to as wide a range of readers as possible has determined the approach of the writers. No printed biblical text has been provided so that readers might continue to use the translation with which they are most familiar. The writers of the series have used the *New Revised Standard Version,* the *Revised Standard Version*, the *New International Version*, and the *Today's New International Version* on a comparative basis. They indicate which text they follow most closely, as well as where they have made their own translations. The writers have not worked alone, but in consultation with select counselors, the series' editors, and the Editorial Council.

Every volume illuminates the Scriptures; provides necessary theological, sociological, and ethical meanings; and in general makes "the rough places plain." Critical issues are not avoided, but neither are they moved into the foreground as debates among scholars. Each section offers explanatory notes, followed by focused articles in "The Text in Biblical Context" and "The Text in the Life of the Church." This commentary aids the interpretive process but does not try to supersede the authority of the Word and Spirit as discerned in the gathered church.

The term *believers church* has often been used in the history of the church. Since the sixteenth century, it has frequently been applied to the Anabaptists and later the Mennonites, as well as to the Church of the Brethren and similar groups. As a descriptive term, it includes more than Mennonites and Brethren. *Believers church* now represents specific theological understandings, such as believers baptism, commitment to the Rule of Christ in Matthew 18:15-20 as crucial for church membership, belief in the power of love in all relationships, and willingness to follow Christ in the way of the cross. The writers chosen for the series stand in this tradition.

Believers church people have always been known for their emphasis on obedience to the simple meaning of Scripture. Because of this, they do not have a long history of deep historical-critical biblical scholarship. This series attempts to be faithful to the Scriptures while also taking archaeology and current biblical studies seriously. Doing this means that at many points the writers will not differ greatly from interpretations found in many other good commentaries. Yet basic presuppositions about Christ, the church and its mission, God and history, human nature, the Christian life, and other doctrines do shape a writer's interpretation of Scripture. Thus this series, like all other commentaries, stands within a specific historical church tradition.

Many in this stream of the church have expressed a need for help in Bible study. This is justification enough to produce the Believers Church Bible Commentary. Nevertheless, the Holy Spirit is not bound to any tradition. May this series be an instrument in breaking down walls between Christians in North America and around the world, bringing new joy in obedience through a fuller understanding of the Word.

—*The Editorial Council*

Author's Preface

The opportunity to write a commentary on the book of Psalms is a high privilege. It is also a heavy burden, for the published product will necessarily be incomplete and fall short of what it might have been. Thus, as writer, I must take comfort in a process that has enriched my life for a quarter century, and I trust that what is now handed over to others will be received as a process that continues.

As I began the commentary writing project, I was aware that the Psalter had become prayer book, hymnbook, and instruction book for people of faith in the Jewish tradition and in the Christian church. As a pastor, I have been intrigued by the mystery of the divine word as it continues to come to us through many inspired writers. The psalms bear compelling witness to the vitality of the worship of God's people. It is my hope that this commentary will serve as an aid to further study and hearing of God's word and will enhance congregational worship.

Early memories of the Psalms in my life include memorizing Psalms 1, 19, 23, and 100 during vacation Bible school. During my first year at Freeman Junior College (SD), an Old Testament (OT) survey course, taught by Orlando J. Goering, sparked my interest in biblical studies and became part of my call to prepare for pastoral ministry. Jacob J. Enz, my formative Bible professor at Mennonite Biblical Seminary (then in Chicago), passionately introduced me to the Psalms as a rich treasure of faith for God's people. Rolf Knierem, my major professor at Claremont School of Theology (CA), helped me see the role of the psalms in OT theology and their value for preaching. An invitation to teach a course in Psalms to students at Bethel College (KS) in 1976 engaged me much more personally in studying the psalms and recognizing their contemporary message.

However, it is through a lifetime of pastoral ministry that I became most involved with the psalms as biblical resource for preaching, teaching, pastoral care, prayer, and hymnody, as well as for personal spiritual growth. Consequently, my study and writing has fed into my ministry for nearly three decades, even as life in the midst of the congregation has informed my work in the book of Psalms.

Writing a commentary involves engagement with other interpreters, past and present, as the bibliographical references indicate. My initial formal training emphasized inductive Bible study methods, but it was also influenced by form-critical study of Psalms. Only later did I become more appreciative of the literary and poetic character of the psalms, and the more recent canonical approach, which takes seriously the editorial shaping of the Psalter and the intertextual connections [Ways of Reading].

Yet it has been most of all through the life of the congregation that this commentary has been shaped. Throughout the writing, my stance has been that of a pastor. Consequently, I have given attention to the possibilities of preaching from the psalms and using them in prayer, hymnody, and the worship of the congregation. I hope that the commentary can be a helpful guide for readers, to lead them deeper into faith through the use of the psalms for their inspiration and obedience, their hope and praise of the God of steadfast love.

Specific thanks must be expressed to the former BCBC OT editor, Elmer A. Martens, who patiently walked with me through several drafts, providing positive encouragement, useful resources, and many insightful revisions. I am grateful also for the support and helpful ideas shared by the present OT editor, Douglas B. Miller, and specific suggestions proposed by Gordon H. Matties, Derek Suderman, and Paul M. Zehr. The critical reviews offered by Editorial Council members, along with their generous and constructive feedback, has significantly strengthened the commentary and the essays. Peer reader, Professor Craig C. Broyles, Trinity Western University, Canada (Langley, BC), offered a helpful assessment. Special thanks go to Levi Miller, director of Herald Press, and to S. David Garber, copy editor, who has contributed much to improve the manuscript. In addition, some of my pastoral colleagues, fellow church members, Sunday school classes, family, and other friends have read my comments on given psalms, frequently inquired about this seemingly endless project, and offered prayer support. Thank you all.

Finally, from beginning to end, my wife, Lenore, has been my constant support, even when "The Psalms" occupied time that rightfully belonged to her. Nevertheless, she read through several drafts and often alerted me to better ways of communicating the message. For her unfailing devotion, I dedicate this work to her.

—James H. Waltner
Goshen, Indiana

Introduction to Psalms

Encountering God in the Psalms

The influence of the book of Psalms on Jewish and Christian traditions, both in terms of the worship of the community and the spiritual experience of countless individuals, is immense. Some psalms had a fixed place in the great Jewish festivals. The daily morning service in the synagogue today includes Psalms 145–150, and the Sabbath morning service contains a sequence of psalms culminating in 92 and 93 (Davidson, 1998:1).

The Gospels tell of Jesus and the disciples singing "hymns," likely the so-called Hallel psalms at the beginning of the Passover meal (113–114) and at the end (115–118). The early church was enjoined to "sing psalms, hymns, and spiritual songs to God" (Col 3:16). Within Christian tradition, many different churches have nurtured worship through the psalms, spoken or sung as invocation, adoration, confession, hymns, chants, and responses.

Beyond the liturgies of synagogue and church, the psalms have been woven into the richly varied experience of countless men and women across the centuries. Martin Luther referred to the Psalter as "a little Bible." Thomas Merton, a Roman Catholic, wrote that the psalms are more than language. "They contain within themselves the silence of high mountains and the silence of heaven. . . . The Psalter only truly begins to speak and sing within us when we have been led by God and lifted up by Him, and have ascended into its silences" (Merton: 160).

This grand collection of psalms is a treasured *hymnbook* inviting and expressing the people's praise to their sovereign God. Here is also a *prayer book*, voicing the needs of individuals and the community in times of trouble. Finally, the book of Psalms serves as *instruction book*, as indicated in the opening psalm's invitation to "meditate day and night" on the life-giving word of God's instruction for living (1:2; cf. Pss 19; 119).

The reader of these sacred poems soon discovers that a psalm speaks for itself. While the commentary may provide some helpful background, alert the reader to linkage with words and themes, and stimulate the imagination for application, it will not replace repeated readings of a psalm in order to hear God speak through the psalm's own distinctive structure and world of words. Only through reading the psalms, slowly and reflectively, will we find ourselves in these ancient Hebrew Scriptures, which draw us into the presence of the sovereign God. As these texts become our prayers and heart-songs, we will come to know ourselves more fully and to know God more surely.

The psalms, in their rich diversity, confessional uncertainties, and perplexities, invite us to join Israel in worship. The psalms invite us also to draw on the rich experience of their use in the Christian church through the years. The utilization of the psalms in liturgical settings is not well-known in believers church congregations that generally eschew prescribed rituals. Psalms for specified liturgies are included in this commentary in order to help readers appreciate the diverse and highly meaningful use of psalms in private or public worship in the long history of the church.

Finding One's Way Through the Psalms

Of the Old Testament (OT) books, Psalms has a special place in the hearts of Christians. Many copies of the combined New Testament (NT) and Psalms are sold each year. Every believer has a favorite psalm or two. Nevertheless, for many the Psalter is a complex and even foreboding book. Its words convey a wide range of moods, contradictory feelings, and even angry outbursts. Many psalms appear to be haphazardly placed. Some psalms give evidence of worship leaders reworking them to fit new situations. Many images and expressions are difficult to understand. What help is there to guide us through this anthology of ancient poems, which may span a period of eight hundred years?

The word *psalm* is from Greek *psalmos*, "song accompanied by a stringed instrument; song." This is the term used by the Septuagint (LXX, early Greek translation of the OT) for the Hebrew word *mizmôr*, a "melody, song, psalm." The Psalter is made up of 150 of these psalms in five books (1–41; 42–72; 73–89; 90–106;

Introduction to Psalms 19

107–150). But there are clues to other subcollections and a complex history of psalm writing, collecting, and editing. The psalms were not produced by poets sitting down to create poems after the fashion of modern poets. The origin of the biblical psalms lies, rather, in the cultic, the liturgical life of a community of faith (Guthrie: 15). In this process, the community often took over and expanded individual prayers for its own use (cf. Ps 130). Many of the psalms come from the time of the monarchy in Israel (David to Josiah, ca. 1000–600 BC). Community laments, some reflecting the destruction of the temple and the fall of Jerusalem in 587 (or 586) BC, are prominent in book III of the Psalter. Books IV and V proclaim the sovereignty of God even though the Davidic dynasty had ended. Current psalm studies ascribe significance to the Psalter's shaping, some taking place after the exile. For further background to psalm studies and a brief history of interpretation of the psalms, see relevant essays in the back of this book [Composition; Hebrew Poetry; Psalm Genres; Superscriptions; Ways of Reading].

Among the many aids to study of the psalms are commentaries such as this volume in the Believers Church Bible Commentary series. A common definition of commentary is "the treatment of individual psalm verses in their specific context" (Keel: 12). Commentaries provide a broader perspective, such as looking at verses in the context of the whole psalm, as well as the psalm's place in the Psalter and all the Scriptures. Context is important, implying that we take a particular passage as a "text," a piece of writing with a meaning to be discovered. Often multiple meanings await us. The amazing gift of the Word is that as we bring it to bear on the spiritual experience of persons, it opens new insights for living. This commentary is offered as an invitation to let the Word encounter us. As the Psalter comes from the life of God's people, so may it point us to the sovereign God and inspire us to greater faithfulness.

The Message of the Psalms: Theological Themes

The book of Psalms is not a systematic theology. Rather, it is a treasury of experiences accumulated by generations of people who nourished their hopes and anxieties as they clung to their values and their faith in God. As such, the psalms contain and reflect on a wide range of topics. One may find lists of major theological themes in the psalms in Kraus' *Theology of the Psalms* (1986), Allen's *Psalms* (1987), Limburg's article "Psalms, Book of" (*ABD* 5:534-36), and Mays' *Psalms* (1994b:29-36).

The following brief description identifies several themes relating to

God, the human situation, and the people of God, including worship, Scripture, and obedience. The Psalter, as a book about God, extols the LORD as refuge, the incomparable God, and God the King.

The LORD as Refuge

Psalms 1 and 2 provide an introduction to the Psalter as a whole. According to Psalm 1, "happiness" derives from the complete orientation of life to God, including perpetual openness to God's instruction. Psalm 2 concludes with the reminder that happiness lies in taking refuge in the LORD (2:11). This appeal to entrust one's whole self, existence, and future to God runs throughout the Psalter (31:1, 4, 6, 14, 19; 52:7-8; 62:7-8; 71:1, 3, 5; 91:2, 4, 9; 143:8-9). The appeal is based on the assurance that the LORD is "my rock and my redeemer" (19:14). These metaphors, particularly prevalent in the psalms of lament, trust, and thanksgiving, assert that God protects and provides security for the individual, and God delivers those who are hurting in situations of crisis.

God as "rock" and "refuge" asserts the trustworthiness of God (62:2, 6-7; 91:2). God as "shepherd" and "host" (Ps 23) conveys the comfort and guidance of the LORD. Many prayer psalms request God's help. When deliverance comes, the psalms of praise and thanksgiving tell the story of what God has done and invite others to discover God's goodness (30:2, 11-12; 34:4, 8).

The Incomparable God

Worshippers offer psalms of prayer and praise to the God whose name is *Yahweh*, the name translated in many English versions as LORD (printed in all capital letters to distinguish the name from the title *Lord*) [Names of God]. They understand the LORD to be the God of Israel who made his way known to the people from the exodus to land occupancy, through exile and the return. Israel sometimes asked, "Has God forgotten to be gracious?" (77:9; 89:49). These times became occasions to retell the deeds of the LORD during the exodus, and God's leading through sea and wilderness in proclamation of their God as incomparable and above all gods (77:13-15, 19-20). The LORD has control over nature, turning back the sea, sending rain, thunder, lightning, and earthquake (77:16-18). The psalms emphasize the work of God the creator (8; 19:1-6; 104; 148) and celebrate God's saving acts in history (78; 105; 106). Numerous psalms portray God as acting in both nature and history (33; 65; 66; 114; 135; 136; 146; 147).

The liturgical cry "the LORD reigns" (47; 95; 96; 97; 99; 103:19-

22) asserts the sovereignty of the LORD as king over the whole earth. The LORD rules over all nations and is active in their histories as well. To live under God's rule is to live in harmony with all other species of creatures and with the earth itself (8; 19; 29; 104; 107; 148). The LORD will judge the whole earth (96:13; 98:9). The judgments are the providential interventions of the LORD to maintain his sovereignty.

The psalms tell of the attributes of the LORD as "the great king over all the earth." "His greatness is unsearchable" (145:3) and includes his awesome majesty (97), irresistible power (76), and holiness (99). Righteousness and justice are the foundation of his rule (48:11). Righteousness is rooted in the LORD's saving actions (7:9-11; 33:5; 99:4). Psalms call the LORD "lover of justice" (37:28; 99:4) and regard him as the source and guardian of justice because justice and righteousness are his very nature (33:5; 72:2; 97:2). They portray God as having a special concern to restore the lost rights of the oppressed (10:17-18; 76:9; 82:1-4; 109:16; 113:4-9; 146:7-9) *[Judge; Righteous]*.

Steadfast love and faithfulness accompany the LORD's actions (85:10-11; 89:1). Steadfast love (ḥesed) is the characteristic of the LORD that informs all the others and constitutes the goodness of the LORD (36; 103; 107; 136). Steadfast love means "the reliable helpfulness of the LORD to any and all that are dependent on him" (Mays, 1994b:33) *[Steadfast]*.

God the King

The royal psalms, beginning with Psalm 2, are scattered throughout the Psalter and serve to articulate God's sovereignty. The regent on earth of the LORD's reign is the Davidic king, designated as the "anointed" by the LORD's covenant (89; 132). The king is to represent the divine rule to the people of the LORD and to the nations (2; 18; 20; 21; 45; 72; 110). Peace is the basic theme involved in the activity of the king (72:1-7). The royal psalms and songs of Zion make it clear that God's rule is constantly opposed (46:6; 48:4-5; 76:7-9).

Israel asserted "the LORD is king" (93; 95–99), emphasizing God's universal reign amid circumstances that seemed to deny it. Thus the psalms affirm God's reign as a present reality. At the same time, the royal psalms, which speak of the king as being "the anointed" (2:2; 18:50; 20:6; 89:38, 51; 132:10, 17), became the seedbed out of which grew Israel's messianic hope as articulated by the prophets (Isa 9:1-7; 11:1-10; Jer 23:1-8; Mic 5:2-6; Zech 9:9-10; Limburg, *ABD*, 5:536). The NT declares that these promises find their fulfillment in Jesus of Nazareth (Matt 16:13-20; Mark 8:27-30; Luke 9:18-22). See "Royal" and "The LORD is King" in the essay *Psalm Genres*.

The Human Situation

The Psalter, a book about God, also contains themes relating to the human situation. Many of the psalms, particularly the wisdom psalms, deal with the mysteries of life and death. Some are pessimistic about the human situation, expressing the view that "mortals . . . are like the beasts that perish" (49:12). Bemoaning human frailty (90:3-10), they nevertheless point toward hope. If humans cannot ransom themselves from death's power, God can and will do so (49:15).

Reflections on life's mysteries wrestle with the problem of the success of the wicked (37; 73). Wisdom psalms, however, also comment on the blessing of life in the midst of the family and the community of worshippers (127; 128; 133). The psalms express amazement at the significance of human life as God's creation and gift (8; 104; 139).

Yet the human predicament is ever present. The people in the psalms are affected "by finitude and fallibility, by mortality and vulnerability and sinfulness" (Mays, 1994b:34). God's people encounter the opposition of nations and rulers and people whose gods and power and autonomy are rebuked by the reign of God (Pss 9–10). The servant of the LORD encounters the hostility of enemies. The servants and the enemies are frequently called the "righteous" and the "wicked" to characterize them in terms of conduct. In the vocabulary of the psalms, "the faithful" (85:8; 86:1-4; 116:15) are "those who fear the LORD" (85:9; 135:20). The righteous are persons who acknowledge their dependence upon God and preserve the peace and wholeness of the community by fulfilling the demands of communal living (15:1-5; 24:3-6). Righteousness is the standard not only for a person's relationship to God, but also for interrelationships with one another (Rad, 1962:370). However, this ongoing conflict gives rise to the many prayers for refuge, deliverance, and salvation [Enemies; Sin; Wicked].

The Community of the People of God

Beyond the cry of individuals, the psalms are also the expression of the community. The people speaking in the psalms call themselves "the people of his pasture, and the sheep of his hand" (95:7). The LORD redeemed them to be the tribe of his heritage (74:2). God's way with them in the past provides the key to God's continuing presence (44; 74; 77; 78; 80; 105; 106).

The community is related to the understanding of God's justice, implying that the psalms are not simply individualistic or otherworldly. The psalms "insist upon equity, power and freedom enough to live one's life humanely," but in solidarity with all those who hope for justice and liberation (Brueggemann, 1984:175-76). Throughout the psalms we hear God's will for peace, shalom (šālôm). The people pray for, hope for, and await peace for the land and for the whole earth (29:11; 34:14; 85:8, 10; 120:6-7; 122:6-8; 147:14). The community of God's people, through its members with their different gifts and callings, can lead the life that constitutes the human response to God. The psalms give witness to the reality of Israel, a people chosen and caught up in community and in faithfulness to the covenant, people who have a mission to all peoples and nations (57:9-11; 67:1-7; 96:1-4; 108:3-4).

The Vitality of Worship

The psalms are rooted in worship and shaped by worship. Worship is the community's response to God and what God has been doing. The cultic community of Israel gathered at the holy place in Jerusalem (84:1-4; 122:1-5). "Out of Zion, the perfection of beauty, God shines forth" (50:2). Israel, assembled in worship at the holy place, is the answering community (148:14). Here the prayers of God's people arise anew (80:4; 118:1-4; 124:1; 129:1).

Central to worship are hymns of praise (Pss 100; 103; 113) and thanksgiving (30:4-5; 116:5, 12; 118:26-29; 136). But so also are the laments that call forth petition (22:1-2; 77:7-9; 130:1-2). These cries, out of the depths of suffering, often move to praise for past deliverance (22:23-24; 28:6-7; 86:5, 15). To praise God is the destiny of God's people, because praise includes the confession that they are dependent upon the LORD, and that everything they have received or will receive is the result of his goodness as creator.

The worshipping community expects and prays for blessing from the LORD (3:8; 29:11; 67:1, 6-7; 118:26; 128:5; 129:8). Gathering in worship renews hope (96:1; 98:1; 115:9; 130:7-8; 149:1). The doxologies of God's people testify that wonders have not ceased and that hope is authentic.

The Psalms as Scripture

To differentiate, bless, and govern his people, the LORD has given them his torah (tôrâ) (instruction/law) in word, decrees, commandments, and statutes (Pss 1; 19; 119). The torah is an instrument of salvation (94:12-15). The LORD's law is the norm of their faithfulness (25:10; 50:16-17; 103:17-18; 112:1). "Your word is a lamp to my feet and a light to my path" (119:105).

Psalm 1, as introduction to the Psalter, invests the book of Psalms with distinctive authority, commending it for meditation as God's word. As prayers of God's people, the faithful now present psalms as God-centered compositions. The NT received the Psalms as part of the Jewish Scriptures, introducing psalm references with the biblical formula "as it is written" (Rom 3:10; 15:9-11) or "he [God] says" (Heb 1:7, 8, 10, 13).

As Scripture, the psalms move beyond song and prayer; they become instruction in the way of life (Pss 1; 39; 49; 53; 90). Typical homiletical forms of speech developed in communal worship, with descriptive, meditative, and exhortative overtones, often focusing on the "Word of God" or his marvelous deeds (34; 37; 52; 58; 78; 95; 105). Such instructive discourse became part of synagogue and Christian worship (Gerstenberger: 251).

Instruction and Obedience

The psalms leave no doubt that Israel's worship is to result in "justice" and "righteousness" (37:28; 50:16-23; 82:3-4; 103:6; 119:5-7; 146:7; 147:19). The psalm writers warn that the Israelites did not obey the voice of the LORD and interpret the wilderness experience as the result of disobedience (95:7c-11; 106:24-27). In Israelite worship, the LORD speaks to the assembled people (85:8-9). Readiness to hear a prophetic message shows the significance attached to the word of God in Israel's worship (50:7-15; 81:8-13).

In the Psalter, the LORD is the guardian and promoter of life; death is the constant challenge to the psalmists (39; 88; 139). But life is not authentic without justice. "Equity" and "solidarity" are key theological concepts in Israel's worship. Social justice is an integral part of the psalmist's understanding of God's faithfulness and of human responsibility (9:8; 45:6-7a; 67:4; 72:1-4; 75:2; 96:10; 98:9; 99:4).

In praise and adoration, the worshipping community is fully committed to the LORD, looks away from itself, and fulfills its destiny as the "people of the LORD" (79:13; 95:7; 100:3).

In addition to these clusters of themes, we could add others. This commentary identifies theological themes in individual psalms and frequently relates them to other biblical texts and their use in the church. Two sections, "The Text in Biblical Context" and "The Text in the Life of the Church," customary features in the Believers Church Bible Commentary, are conflated in this commentary.

The Psalms and the New Testament

The Psalms and its prophetic companion, Isaiah, are the two OT books most quoted in the NT. Jesus quoted more often from the

Introduction to Psalms

Psalms than from any other OT book. In the NT are some ninety-three quotations from over sixty psalms, amounting to one-third of the OT quotations. The frequency of the use of Psalms highlights the importance of the Psalter for the early church.

Although there are citations from many psalms, Psalms 2, 22, 31, 69, 110, and 118 are particularly important. In the Gospel accounts, Jesus is recognized at his baptism with a quotation, "You are my son" (Ps 2:7; Matt 3:17; Luke 3:22), which is also related to Jesus' transfiguration (Matt 17:5; Luke 9:35). Several times the NT applies two verses from another royal psalm to Jesus (Ps 110:1, 4; Mark 14:62; Heb 5:6, 10; 6:20; 7:11, 15, 17, 21).

The Gospels narrate the passion with quotations and motifs from Psalms 22; 31; and 69. All four Gospels let Psalm 22 shape the account of the crucifixion. The words Jesus spoke from the cross are a quotation of 22:1 (Matt 27:46; Mark 15:34). This psalm, which ends on a note of vindication and the universal coming of the kingdom of God (22:22-31), is echoed in the passion story as passersby deride Jesus and wag their heads at him (22:7; Matt 27:39; Mark 15:29; Luke 23:35). The division of Jesus' garments and casting lots for them (Matt 27:35; Mark 15:24; Luke 23:34; John 19:24) recall Psalm 22:18, and the demand that God deliver him (Matt 27:43) is like Psalm 22:8.

In Luke, Jesus' final words from the cross are a quotation of Psalm 31:5 (Luke 23:46), and in John, Jesus' final words appear to allude to Psalm 31:5 (John 19:30). Psalm 69:21 is in another individual lament that is reflected in the passion narrative (Matt 27:34; Mark 15:36; Luke 23:36; John 19:29). The Gospel writers drew upon the three longest laments of an individual in order to relate the story of Jesus' suffering. Thus, the Gospels (and the whole NT) present Jesus as "the ultimate paradigm of the faithful sufferer," and it is precisely "Jesus' faithful suffering on behalf of others that reveals what God is like" (McCann, 1996:674-75).

"The stone that the builders rejected has become the chief cornerstone" (Ps 118:22) are words cited to refer to Jesus' rejection and vindication (Matt 21:42; Mark 12:10-11; Luke 20:17; Acts 4:11; 1 Pet 2:6-8). The messianic overtones are clear in the citation at the time of Jesus' triumphal entry into Jerusalem (Ps 118:25-27; Matt 21:9; Mark 11:9-10; Luke 19:38; John 12:13).

Peter's first recorded sermon (Acts 2:17-36) bases important aspects of the proclamation on Psalms 16:8-11; 110:1; and 132:11. Paul's sermon (Acts 13:16-41) draws on Psalms 2:7; 16:10; and 89:20. The book of Revelation shares the Psalter's conviction that

God rules the world (11:15; 12:10; 15:3), and the mention of "a new song" (5:9; 14:3) recalls Psalms 96; 98; and 149, all of which assert God's reign.

This commentary will give attention to additional quotations and allusions in the NT as we encounter individual psalms. These links are important because the theology of the psalms is congruent with the core of Jesus' preaching and teaching. The theological heart of the Psalter—God reigns—is the good news that Jesus announced from the beginning of his public ministry (Mark 1:14-15; McCann, 1996:672).

Suggestions for Use of the Commentary

This commentary has been prepared in the awareness that many scholarly as well as nontechnical commentaries and introductions to the Psalms are available. Yet, we still need to write Bible commentaries: we always see with some new insights even as we draw on the work of many who have gone before us. The aim of this commentary is to serve as a help for the study of the psalms by pastors, Sunday school teachers, and others who simply want to read the psalms to gain greater understanding of this rich treasury of the ways of God with his people. It is the writer's hope that readers will encounter God again and again through the psalms.

The commentary uses the New Revised Standard Version (NRSV) as the primary English text. It also gives attention to readings in the New International Version (NIV) and other English versions.

Ideas for Study of a Psalm

1. Make it a habit to read the text of the psalm before studying the commentary. Reading the text aloud is encouraged.
2. After reading the PREVIEW and noting the OUTLINE, reread the text in order to become more deeply appreciative of the word of God in the Bible. Note the rhetorical form, spot the words that carry the freight (use of the names of God, verbs, repetition), and sense the mood.
3. After reviewing the EXPLANATORY NOTES, read the psalm again. Check the biblical references cited, thus seeing how the larger patterns of biblical theology enrich the psalm and its key phrases. Ask: Who is talking in this psalm? What issues does it raise? What circumstances call forth the faith statements of this psalm? What do I learn about God, creation, and humanity in this psalm?

Introduction to Psalms 27

4. After reviewing THE TEXT IN THE BIBLICAL CONTEXT AND LIFE OF THE CHURCH, think of how the psalm applies to your own needs and aspirations. Read the psalm carefully and prayerfully again, asking: Who would find this psalm appropriate today? What is God saying to me and/or those around me through this psalm?
5. As a further step, you may wish to write your own psalm as response to God. The psalms we write may be as simple as this verse of adoration that a college student wrote on a piece of eucalyptus bark, one Sunday morning by the Sea of Galilee:

> The lapping of the water makes me quiet;
>   the hills around give me strength.
> The cooling breeze calms my spirit;
>   I am at peace. Shalom.

Or our cry out of distress may voice a petition, such as this one inspired by Psalm 80:1-3 (Haas: 54):

> God, turn to us;
>   we need to see your saving face.
> Shepherd of our lives,
>   shine forth with the power of your angels
>   and save us now!

Using the Psalms

The church has a long tradition of using suggested psalms for seasons and days in the Christian Year. Examples include Christmas Eve and Christmas Day (Pss 96; 97; 98); Epiphany (72); Baptism of Jesus (29); Lent (51; 130); Palm Sunday and Good Friday (22; 31); Maundy Thursday (116); Easter Day (118); Ascension Day (110); and Pentecost (104). The commentary will report other similar connections.

Lectionaries, such as the *Revised Common Lectionary*, provide a list of psalms that worshippers can use each Sunday over a three-year cycle. These psalms are usually related in theme to the other prescribed Scripture texts. Pastors can profitably use these texts for preaching or for the congregation's meditation or devotional reading during the week.

Psalms form the basis for many hymns used by congregations and choirs. This commentary will identify some hymns relating to a particular psalm. Most hymnals include an index of "scriptural allusions or references," which is useful in finding hymns relating to a particular psalm for worship planning or personal reflection.

Prayer psalms provide wording that one can use or adapt for personal or corporate prayers. Reflection on the experience of saying a prayer psalm as one's own prayer can lead to insights and consideration of the practice of prayer. Examples include Psalms 13; 25; 30; 34; 39; 116; and 130. Eugene Peterson's *Answering God* illustrates use of the Psalms as tools for prayer. David Haas in *Psalm Prayers* has written prayers based on specific psalms. Among many excellent Catholic Church publications encouraging daily prayer based on psalms are Huck's *Proclaim Praise* and *Psalms for Morning and Evening Prayer*.

Finally, the psalms are a rich resource for pastoral care. Examples include meditating on who and what we are before God (8; 49; 90; 139) and on God as creator, provider, and savior (103; 104); crying out in times of distress (3–6; 13; 51; 88; 130); and trusting in God as our help (16; 23; 27; 42–43; 62; 63; 73; 121).

The psalm texts are open and speak to a wide variety of situations in every generation. Here people can hear God's Word coming to them amid their own needs and joys. Here are the words through which God's people can continue to offer prayer and praise.

Book One
Psalms 1-41

Psalm 1

Blessed—the Way of the Righteous

PREVIEW

The first psalm reflects Hebrew wisdom literature from its opening word *Happy*, "Blessed" (NIV, RSV) and by the message contrasting the character and fate of the wicked and the righteous. The psalm's focus on the law (torah, *tôrâ*) sounds a strong teaching note. The world is organized in such a way that conduct matters. Placed as introduction, the psalm presents the Psalter as a study and prayer book, essential for the ordering of life to God's purposes.

Psalm 1 commends joyous and continuous engagement with the law of the LORD. Shunning the counsel and influence of the wicked, the person who allows the instruction of the LORD (Yahweh) to nurture life will prosper like the fruit-bearing tree. Striking contrasts abound from the first word, *happy* (blessed), to the last emphatic word, *perish*! The psalm uses two powerful similes: a *tree* that has its roots in the water and therefore bears fruit abundantly as intended, and *chaff*, the light, flaky refuse that in threshing the grain is blown away as useless!

Book I of Psalms (1–41) may have been assembled under influence of the wisdom writers since both Psalms 1 and 41 are "blessed" psalms, introduced by a beatitude. Likely not part of the original collection, Psalm 1 was placed to open the Psalter following the exile and the work of Ezra, when the law (torah) became a unifying force for the Hebrew people *[Composition]*.

Psalm 1

OUTLINE

Portrait of the Righteous, 1:1-3
Portrait of the Wicked, 1:4-6

EXPLANATORY NOTES

Portrait of the Righteous 1:1-3

An emphatic *Happy* (*'ašrê*) describes the righteous person. The meaning is "O the blessedness, the joy, the good fortune!" The shift by translators from "man" (v. 1 Heb, RSV, NIV) to *those* (NRSV) represents the attempt to employ phraseology for human beings that is not gender specific. The psalm warns against the evil counsel of the wicked. Note the progression "walks," "stands," "sits" (v. 1 RSV). Here too, a translation such as NRSV has moved to convey how the verbs are used metaphorically since "walk" and "way" in Hebrew often imply a lifestyle and how to live. Sinners can increasingly lead a person down the wrong path so that the wrong people become one's company and counsel.

In contrast, the blessed one's *delight is in the law of the LORD* (v. 2). For the Hebrews, the *torah* (translated into English inadequately as "law") meant teaching, guidance. The torah was the instruction revealing the covenant story of God's dealing with his people. Torah referred to the Ten Commandments as a summary of God's basic instruction for community living. Eventually Torah (capitalized) was/is used to speak of the first five books of the OT. In later times, it came to mean all of Jewish learning and sacred literature *[Torah]*.

We commonly think of law in the sense of "Thou shalt not . . ." as oppressive and restrictive, as ought and as burden. But the Hebrews looked on torah as a guide to life, as that God-given structure and order that was freeing. The psalm invites people to meditate (*hāgāh*), which implies murmuring and mumbling. Isaiah uses the word for the growling sound a lion makes over its prey (Isa 31:4). Psalm 1 tells of reciting words of the torah throughout the day and during waking moments of the night. Other torah Psalms are 19 and 119, though in Psalm 1 *torah* likely also refers to the teaching of all of the psalms that follow. If so, then the first psalm offers a specific orientation to the reader for the entire Psalter.

High regard for the law implies not only singing its virtues, but also obeying. The Torah at the center "reminds us that the primal mode of faithfulness and knowing God is obedience. . . . Life has a moral coherence on which we can rely" (Brueggemann, 1982:56). What kind of success in life is implied by the word *prosper* (v. 3; Josh 1:8)?

Belief in the link between obedience to God and worldly, material prosperity was widespread (Pss 37:25; 128:3; 144:12-14). To *prosper* may also mean that as the tree fulfills the purpose for which it was created, so the nature and value of an obedient life are to be found in the fulfillment of the divine will.

Portrait of the Wicked 1:4-6

"Not so the wicked!" (NIV) catches the emphatic Hebrew in contrast to verse 1. The way of the wicked is a dead-end street. When called to account either by due legal process in society or spiritually by God here and now, the wicked have no valid defense (v. 5). For those who opt out of the covenant way, how often their way of life becomes destructive. The wicked—often viewed as those who accuse the innocent, afflict the lowly, and undermine the trust of the faithful (Pss 3:7; 10:2; 11:2)—represent the incongruence between the will of God and the will of human beings (Mays, 1994b:43) [Wicked].

The final verse summarizes the two ways. The LORD *watches over*, "knows," or "approves, has regard to" the righteous (NASB). "To know" in Hebrew implies a relationship, not just perceiving. Constant meditation on torah nurtures life for fruit-bearing, *but the way of the wicked will perish.*

A Comparison Between Two Contrasting Groups

Verses	Subject	Characterization	Focus	Like	Fate
1:1-3	righteous	Blessed!	law	tree	prosper
1:4-6	wicked	Not so!	counsel of wicked	chaff	perish

THE TEXT IN THE BIBLICAL CONTEXT AND LIFE OF THE CHURCH

Two Ways

The language of Psalm 1 is reminiscent of the opening chapter of Joshua (1:7-8), and brings to mind the story of finding the "book of the law" (Deuteronomy) in the temple (2 Kings 22:8-23:3). Note also Psalms 32; 41; 112; and 128 as beginning with the emphatic Hebrew word *'ašrê*, "happy." Later Jesus echoes this language: "Blessed . . . are those who hear the word of God and obey it!" (Luke 11:28). In the Sermon on the Mount, Jesus uses the Beatitudes to teach about true righteousness (Matt 5:3-12). In this sermon Jesus also refers to the Law (Torah) and the Prophets, and his coming "not to abolish but to fulfill" (5:17). In concluding his sermon, Jesus refers to the two ways: "the road is easy that leads to destruction" (7:13), and "the road is hard that leads to life" (7:14). The Sermon on the Mount ends with powerful images of the "wise man who built his house on rock" and the "foolish man who built his house on sand" (7:24-27). One stood; the other perished.

In the life of the early church, followers of Jesus came to be called people of "the Way" (Acts 9:2; 19:9, 23; 22:4). Through the centuries believers have thus identified themselves. In Thieleman J. van Braght's great collection of martyr stories, many imprisoned for their faith took courage in Psalm 1, frequently quoting verses in their letters to encourage family and friends: "Abide with God, and mingle not with the wicked." "Give yourself up to the Lord, and always join yourself to those who fear the Lord." "Weary not in the ways of the Lord; have your delight therein day and night" (549, 468, 1053).

Invitation to Dialogue

If the way of the wicked will perish, then why do the wicked sometimes appear to thrive (Ps 73:3-12)? If the righteous are to *prosper* in all they do, what of those who experience life differently? Famine, ethnic cleansing, the destruction of war and terrorist activity do not distinguish between the just and the unjust. Psalm 1 provides an introduction to the entire Psalter. Many of the psalms that follow seem to enter into dialogue with it, questioning and searching for meaning in the midst of life's wide range of experiences, including the dark night of the soul (Davidson, 1998:13-14).

This sharp contrast between the righteous and the wicked is not always evident. A mixture of good and bad is found in everyone, and the two ways may not seem that clear. But at every moment people move along one way or the other. It is important to be reminded what the end of each road is. The psalms will tell of a powerful companion along the one road, but along the other people walk alone.

Invitation to Put Our Roots Down

On what do Christians focus their life's attention? Who are their people? From whom do they get their bearings? What will give stability and fruit-bearing nurture to their soul? The first psalm invites us to put our roots down in the instruction and relationship to God offered us in the word of torah. By reading and praying these psalms, by delighting in them, we are invited to make these Scriptures part of our life of faith. Through these words from the worship life of God's people, we too can learn to cry out to God in the personal and corporate crises of life. We can learn to place trust in the God of steadfast love and faithfulness. The hymns of thanksgiving and praise can help us voice doxologies that declare hope. An exciting adventure awaits the reader of the Psalms.

Psalm 2

The LORD and His Anointed

PREVIEW

This royal psalm may have been composed for the coronation of a king of Judah, at Jerusalem in the time after David. We cannot identify the specific historic setting. The liturgy celebrates the accession to the throne and the vital place of the king in the life of the community.

The psalm's recital by the king at enthronement, or at an annual ceremony reenacting the coronation, expressed confidence at a time often marked by political unrest both from within and outside the nation. Its message lies in the clear focus, not on the struggle of earthly powers for their existence, but on God as Lord of the earth, as the King of kings, with whom all nations must reckon. Psalm 2 addresses the question of power: Where does power to control world history ultimately reside? The psalm's resounding answer: Power resides in the LORD of the heavens, and his anointed set as king on Zion's holy hill.

The later identification of this psalm with Jesus as the Messiah, the extensive quoting of this psalm in the NT, and its striking message for today—all suggest that the psalm writers often wrote more than they knew. That is the remarkable timelessness of these ancient writings!

OUTLINE

Astonishment at the Rebellion of the Nations, 2:1-3
The LORD's Response from the Heavens, 2:4-6
The King's Report of the Decree of the LORD, 2:7-9
Admonition and Invitation, 2:10-12

EXPLANATORY NOTES

Astonishment at the Rebellion of the Nations   2:1-3

If the psalm is viewed as liturgy, it is helpful to know who is speaking. A possible outline of the psalm's speakers may include: verses 1-2, priest; 3, rebel kings; 4-5, priest; 6, God; 7, God's king; 8-9, God; and 10-12, priest.

The psalm opens with the question of why nations plot against *the LORD and his anointed* (vv. 1-2). The verb that dominates the action of Psalm 1, *meditate* (*hāgāh*), appears in 2:1 but is translated *plot* in the sense of devising and scheming. The earthly scene involves conspiracy, troop assembly, and the taunt of those plotting rebellion (v. 3). The immediate reference to *his anointed* (v. 2) is the newly crowned king. Anointing with oil as a sign of consecration to some function or office was common (Exod 28:41; 1 Kings 19:16; Ps 105:15). Frequently it refers to the king (1 Sam 24:6, 10), who was seen as the LORD's earthly regent. From *anointed* (*māšîaḥ*) comes the English word "messiah," a title later used to express the hope of one whom God would send, and a name given to Jesus *[Anointed]*.

The tone of these opening verses is incredulity. How can anyone, even the most powerful earthly rulers, hope to break free from the sovereign LORD and his anointed?

The LORD's Response from the Heavens   2:4-6

Now the scene changes. From the heavens, from God's perspective, the clamor of the nations and the assembling of their troops is laughable (v. 4)! They have no sense of what the fury of God's wrath unleashed could mean! In his good time God will come face-to-face with the rebellious forces. The wicked will not escape when the LORD speaks (v. 5; Ps 50:3, 16, 22). In the quotation from the LORD about Zion as his holy mountain (v. 6; 3:4; 15:1; 43:3; 87:1; 99:9), the king's installation in Jerusalem is declared a divine act. This is not just any city, but the city of the great King (48:1-2), the city of the house of the LORD (122:1, 9) *[Zion]*.

The King's Report of the Decree of the LORD   2:7-9

The third stanza, which shifts the focus from the high heavens to the royal palace on earth, begins with the king's statement of intention (v. 7a), followed by quotation of the LORD's word (vv. 7b-9). Here are the words legitimizing the king's reign by the LORD's *decree* (*ḥōq*), a term from sacral royal law. In the Hebrew understanding of kingship, the ruler was seen as adopted by God (v. 7; 2 Sam 7:14; Ps 89:26-27). The ruler is declared to be the *son of God* (v. 7), with the king's authority including inheritance, possession, and administration (vv. 8-9). The *rod of iron* may refer to a royal scepter, symbol of the king's power. We know about dashing pottery to pieces from Egyptian coronation rituals: the king demonstrated his worldwide power by smashing earthen vessels bearing the names of foreign nations.

The language seems boastful and extravagant. At no time in Hebrew history was the nation so great and powerful as envisioned here! In these lofty descriptions of the king in Psalms 2 and 110, some see the influence of pre-Israelite Canaanite rituals, while Psalm 89 describes a more specifically Israelite concept of kingship (Westermann, 1980:106). For Judean kings, the model of world empire was the reign of David. "The logic of the psalm is not historical but theological. . . . The psalm is based on the faith that the LORD throned in heaven is the ultimate power" (Mays, 1994b:47).

Admonition and Invitation   2:10-12

The final stanza declares a warning to kings and rulers that God's reign is invincible, and it offers an alternative to rebellion. The four Hebrew words that span the verse division of 11-12 have given rise to a variety of translations because of an uncertain Hebrew text. Translations include "kiss the Son" (NIV), "do homage to the Son" (NASB), and "kiss the king" (NEB). However, A. Bertholet's "Kiss his feet with trembling" has been widely accepted (Gerstenberger: 48). The sense is that of a call to submit to the LORD and his anointed with the kiss of homage. The kissing of the feet is a well-known act of self-humiliation and homage. This psalm calls attention to God as Lord. In these final verses there is no further mention of the king of Zion. The question is, Will the Lord be recognized and acknowledged? Not in kings, but in "the fear of the LORD" is true refuge!

Words used in verse 12 echo Psalm 1, *perish, the way, happy.* The message of Psalm 2 is clear. The LORD's incomparable ridicule falls upon rebellious powers and his wrath upon his foes (v. 12; 110:5). The spotlight shines on God's representative, and warning gives way to invitation. An alternative to defying God lies in accepting the invitation to *take refuge in him* (5:11; 7:1; 11:1). That is the way to happiness and well-being.

THE TEXT IN THE BIBLICAL CONTEXT AND LIFE OF THE CHURCH

Psalm 2 as Introduction to the Psalter

The placement of the first two psalms is not by accident. Some early Hebrew manuscripts have Psalms 1 and 2 written as a single psalm. Some have Psalm 2 as the first psalm, with Psalm 1 as the prologue. Regarding the placement of Psalms 1 and 2, B. W. Anderson writes: "These two themes—the revelation of God's will in the Torah and the hope for the coming of the Messiah to inaugurate God's kingdom—constituted the two cardinal beliefs of the Jewish people at the time the Psalter was given its final form" (1983:23).

In looking at book I of the Psalter, almost all the psalms from Psalm 3 to Psalm 41 carry a superscription of attribution to David. The exceptions, Psalms 10 and 33, may each be linked to the preceding psalm. Psalm 2, affirming the covenant made with David at his coronation, may have been prefixed to the sequence of "Davidic" psalms (3–41) as the LORD's assurance of continued protection for David against his scheming enemies (Holladay: 77) *[Composition; Superscriptions]*.

As introduction to the Psalter, Psalm 2 identifies themes found throughout the psalms. God is enthroned in the heavens. The king, made holy by divine choice and anointed regent, represents God's rule in the world. All nations and people with their rulers belong to his dominion. The nations appear as opponents. They are under the wrath of God, but they are offered the service of the LORD as a better way. The invitation to the readers is to "take refuge in him." Psalm 2 points forward to all the following prayers as the liturgy of those who take refuge in the LORD amid all that threatens life (Mays, 1994b:48). In its context, Psalm 2 is a royal psalm that points up the ideology of a divinely appointed king, and so functions as an introductory psalm to have the reader view the psalms from an eschatological viewpoint.

Psalm 2 as Reinterpreted in the New Testament

Originating with the promises of the prophet Nathan in 2 Samuel 7, the hope of an ideal anointed one was nurtured by the eleven royal

Psalm 2

psalms (2; 18; 20; 21; 45; 72; 89; 101; 110; 132; 144) *[Psalm Genres]*. These psalms, focusing on the king, speak in hopeful and extravagant language. Yet king after king was a disappointment. After Judah fell to the Babylonians, there were no more kings. Yet the Jews still used royal psalms, expressing the people's hope for an ideal king. Thus, the royal psalms became seedbed for messianic hope (Limburg, 2000:7).

The early Christians came to believe that in Jesus the Messiah had come. They read the royal psalms in that belief. The NT often quotes or refers to Psalm 2. It is quoted in connection with the baptism of Jesus and his transfiguration. At Jesus' baptism the heavenly voice declares: "This is my Son, the Beloved" (Matt 3:17; Mark 1:11; Luke 3:22). At the transfiguration the affirmation comes: "This is my Son, the Beloved. . . . Listen to him!" (Matt 17:5; Mark 9:7; Luke 9:35). A nuance already implicit in Psalm 2:7 (2 Sam 7:14; Ps 89:26-27) is that the son is chosen by God and that God is "well pleased" with his son.

On his first mission journey Paul preaches a sermon at Antioch in Pisidia. In telling the story of Jesus, he draws on this psalm, "You are my Son; today I have begotten you" (Acts 13:33), to refer to the resurrection of Jesus. Psalm 2:7 is quoted also in Hebrews 1:5 and 5:5 in support of Christ's divine sonship and exaltation.

Other NT quotations of Psalm 2 include verses 1-2 in Acts 4:25-26, where the enemies conspiring in vain against the Lord and his anointed are identified as Herod, Pilate, and those set against Jesus and his followers; verses 8-9 in Revelation 2:26-27, regarding authority over the nations to the one "who conquers and continues to do my works," and in Revelation 19:15, on how the Word of God will rule the nations. Some also see Psalm 2:8 as foreshadowing the Great Commission (Matt 28:19-20; Acts 1:8).

Use of Psalm 2 by the Church

Since the NT gave a messianic interpretation to Psalm 2, it is also extensively quoted by early church writers, beginning with Clement, bishop of Rome, at the end of the first century AD (*1 Clement* 36.4). Justin Martyr (ca. 150) understood Psalm 2 as a testimony of Herod, the Jews, and Pilate conspiring against Christ. Origen of Alexandria (ca. 185-254) took it for granted that the psalm deals with Jesus Christ; he proposed that in 2:3 Christ addressed the angels. Jerome (ca. 342-420) also saw Psalm 2 as referring to Jesus Christ, and Christ's opponents as all the kings of the world mentioned at Christ's temptation in the wilderness. Theodore of Mopsuestia (ca. 350-428) identified "the Lord and his anointed" as the Father and the Son, and the "rulers" as the scribes and Pharisees (Holladay: 162-63, 169-70, 172, 174).

Martin Luther (1483-1546) spoke of David as author of the psalm and that the psalm speaks of Christ. He identified the "rod of iron" (v. 9) as "the holy Gospel which is Christ's royal scepter in his Church" (Luther, 1974:35). In this psalm John Calvin (1509-1564) saw David describing his own kingship. He also viewed David as a "type" for Christ, who prophesied concerning Christ (J. Anderson, 1:9).

Psalm 2 plays a prominent role in lectionaries, prayer books, and hymnals of the church. Perhaps most striking is the musical setting by G. F. Handel. Who can forget the thundering bass solo of *The Messiah:* "Why do the nations so furiously rage together?" Handel's oratorio then follows with a chorus, "Let us break their bonds asunder," and the tenor solo, "Thou shalt dash them in pieces like a potter's vessel." After these songs comes the magnificent "Hallelujah" chorus. The "messianic" character of Psalm 2 is well established!

Learning from Nationalistic Poetry Today

The royal psalms are nationalistic poetry. Jacob J. Enz has called attention to how the NT writers appear to have deliberately ripped these metaphors out of their context of nationalism, earthly power, and brutality "and used them to compose a new hymn of imperialism, the imperialism of love and truth and righteousness and judgment" (Enz: 72) [Hebrew Poetry].

Does the NT's broad use of this psalm as a pointer to Jesus as the Messiah deliberately invite the reader to go back and read the whole psalm? What is the Messiah's way? Is it not ultimately the way of humility and suffering, as revealed in Jesus, the heaven-approved Messiah?

How do the squabbles among the nations look from God's perspective? How foolish the politics of cold war or preemptive war must appear! How devastating will unchecked military buildup be? What if God's sovereign lordship over the earth is not to be mocked? Will an unbridled militarism become the means of God's wrath on the rebellion of humanity to his lordship? Will human power and military hardware decide the history of people and nations, or is there another way to security and fullness of life?

This psalm, possibly written for the coronation of a king, kept hope alive after the exile for the "coming one" who would rule with righteousness and justice. For the Christian church, the psalm spoke of Jesus as the Messiah. Psalm 2 thus takes on a mission message for followers of the King of kings and Lord of lords. God's sovereignty is over all peoples and nations.

Psalm 3

How Many Are My Foes!

PREVIEW

This lament introduces the first of 73 psalms given the title *A Psalm of David [Superscriptions]*. The specific reference in the title, *when he fled from his son Absalom,* has sometimes been seen as a later designation of the setting. That story, told in 2 Samuel 15–19, reminds the reader of David's foes, including Saul, his father-in-law, and Absalom, his beloved son. David knew what it was to be a minority in his own kingdom (2 Sam 15:6, 13).

The psalm, despite its heading, does not refer specifically to David or to Absalom. It expresses the plight of one (a king or other leader) facing a formidable adversary (vv. 1, 6) whose ridicule strikes at the person's honor and credibility (v. 2). But it is also an expression of confidence and trust in the LORD, who has power to deliver. Following Psalms 1–2, this psalm proclaims that happiness/blessedness consists of the good news that God's help is forthcoming (v. 8). Many can identify with the mood and content of this individual's lament.

OUTLINE

Invocation and Complaint, 3:1-2
Affirmation of Confidence, 3:3-6
Petition and Vow of Trust, 3:7-8

EXPLANATORY NOTES

Invocation and Complaint   3:1-2

Laments come out of the low moments of life. When foes surround, when ridicule strikes, the situation may seem hopeless. Prayer begins with the elemental cry "Help!" The psalmist calls on the name of the LORD and describes the trouble. The threefold repetition of *many* (vv. 1-2) underscores the desperate situation of multiple foes and their ridicule. Their charge, *no help*, translates the Hebrew word *yāšaʻ*, the word for "save." The word *yāšaʻ* appears again in the petition *Deliver me* (v. 7) and in the affirmation *Deliverance belongs to the LORD* (v. 8).

Selah, at the end of verses 2, 4, and 8, is a marginal note, likely having to do with musical instruction. *Selah* possibly represents some kind of rise or strengthening, the joining in of the orchestra, or a transition to forte. However, the precise meaning is not known *[Selah]*.

Affirmation of Confidence   3:3-6

Note the mood shift with the emphatic *But you, O LORD!* In striking metaphors, the psalmist asserts the LORD's protective strength and aid as a *shield* (v. 3; 7:10; 18:2). *Glory* has to do with a surrounding presence, with what people on earth perceive of God. God can help persons to hold their head high again rather than be bowed in shame or despair! God *answers* the human cry. *Holy hill* refers to Mt. Zion (Jerusalem), the site not only of the ark of the covenant and the temple; it also was considered a sacred mountain, where the deity met the people (v. 4; 2:6; 15:1; 99:9).

Having the LORD as ally, the psalmist can now fearlessly face whatever comes! Verses 5-6 reflect supreme confidence—to sleep, to awaken, and to meet whatever the day brings! The usual translation *ten thousands of people* suggests the image of warfare, a metaphor sometimes used for the sarcastic arrows and insults of the foe (27:2-3; 55:18; 56:1-2; 59:1-3).

Petition and Vow of Trust   3:7-8

The petition for deliverance is that God will go into action. God's mercy and intervention is the petitioner's only hope (v. 7; 7:1, 6; 10:12; 22:19). In contrast to the ridicule of foes who claim there is *no help* (v. 2), the psalm ends on a confident note; the psalmist declares that with the LORD, deliverance is sure! Those who "shoot off the mouth" will also get it in the mouth! The enemies have spoken against the psalmist; by the law of equivalent retribution (Exod 21:23-

Psalm 3

25; Deut 19:21), their organs of speech are destroyed. The imprecatory tone sounds harsh, but the psalmist gives voice to his belief that God's right must prevail. Deliverance (and vengeance) is the LORD's (Deut 32:35; Rom 12:19) *[Enemies; Imprecation; Vengeance]*.

The psalm ends with a prayer for *blessing* on the people. The cultic community expects and prays for blessing from the LORD (v. 8; Pss 29:11; 129:8). Here is reminder of the communal nature even of the individual laments, and of how the people came to use them in their worship.

THE TEXT IN THE BIBLICAL CONTEXT AND LIFE OF THE CHURCH

Facing Hostility in Prayer

Psalm 3, following the introductory Psalms 1 and 2, is the first in a series of five prayers for times of trouble. These prayers, and others that follow in the Psalter, seem to be the response that faith makes to the reality of hostile forces and the beatitude *Happy are all who take refuge in him* (2:12).

Prayers of lament are for times when trouble comes in waves. Drawing on remembrance of God's help in the past, these laments provide language that gives voice to human feelings, including abhorrence for assault on God. Psalm 3 recites the conviction *Salvation belongs to the LORD* (v. 8 NKJV) to remind persons in distress that no trouble is beyond help and no human hostility can limit God's help (Mays, 1994b:53).

Lament and the Martyrs

The lives of the martyrs give testimony to unshakable trust. At Ghent, in Flanders, two Anabaptist sisters were imprisoned for their faith. While confined, they were tortured and finally sentenced to death as heretics, and burned on November 21, 1570.

Part of a letter Barbelken Goethals wrote from prison to a fellow believer reads:

> O Jasper, . . . what courage I have to fight against the princes and rulers of darkness; I think that I could say with David: "I will not be afraid of ten thousands of people, that have set themselves against me round about." Ps 3:6. Oh, what joy I have; praise, glory and honor be to God forever for the great joy that He gives me. . . . Keep this letter in remembrance of me; I hope to seal it with my blood. Always fear God, but not men. (Braght: 870-71)

Lament for Leaders and Followers

What enemies do leaders generally encounter? Is not one that of being talked about by others? Especially leaders frequently face that situation. In the dedication of *Idylls of the King*, Tennyson wrote of "that fierce light which beats upon a throne." Every king, prime minister, president, or other political leader experiences the relentless barrage of abuse. Being in a prominent position means to be talked about, whether in a friendly or hostile way.

However, those feelings are not confined to leaders. When tongues wag, can persons of faith take courage in the fact that they are not alone? Can they go to sleep or wake up in the confidence that the Lord is their deliverer? Psalm 3 is an appropriate morning prayer, a "cry for survival that develops into the shout of the saved" (Peterson, 1989:42). No wonder that the ancient liturgical traditions of the church invited believers to start their daily round of prayer with Psalm 3.

Psalm 4

Evening Prayer to the Giver of Peaceful Sleep

PREVIEW

This evening prayer, in its interest in peaceful sleep (vv. 4, 8), follows the morning prayer of Psalm 3. Note the related language of 4:6 and 3:2: *There are many who say;* and 3:5 and 4:8: *I lie down and sleep.*

Here is a lament in form and language, but in content also a song of confidence. The psalmist is concerned about false accusations on the part of those who have lost faith in God. Their lies have damaged the writer's honor. He cries out in prayer to God, who has been gracious in the past, and who alone can bring gladness of heart and peaceful sleep.

The reference to sacrifices (v. 5) and use of the marginal note *Selah* (vv. 2, 4) indicate that the psalm was used in temple worship *[Selah].* This psalm introduces the heading *To the leader,* a term referring to the director of the temple music found in the titles of fifty-five psalms. This psalm is to be accompanied by *stringed instruments [Superscriptions].*

OUTLINE

Plea to God, Who Hears the Cry of the Faithful, 4:1-3
Exhortation to Honor the LORD, 4:4-6
Statement of Trust, 4:7-8

Alternate ways of outlining the Psalm follow the lament form, regard it as a psalm of confidence (A. Anderson, 1:76-80), or see it as a dialogue with God (Knight, 1:28-29).

Verses	Lament form	Psalm of confidence	Dialogue with God
1	cry to God	cry for help	psalmist
2	complaint	description of plight (vv. 2-6)	God replies
3	confession of trust		psalmist
4-5	reflection		God replies
6	petition		psalmist
7-8	words of assurance	joy and peace from God	so God acts

EXPLANATORY NOTES

Plea to God, Who Hears the Cry of the Faithful   4:1-3

The psalm opens with a fervent cry for help to *God of my right!* (v. 1). This God has stood by him and vindicated him in the past. "Right" has a legal connotation and can mean acquittal or a declaration of innocence. Confidence underlies this cry to God, who provided room to the petitioner when he was previously in a tight place. The prayer seeks grace (mercy) yet again.

The complaint focuses on the accusers, those who live by deception and lies (v. 2). The psalmist's *honor* (kābôd), his standing in the community, is under threat. *But know* that the LORD will be attentive to the *faithful* (ḥāsîd, v. 3). Here the psalmist identifies himself among those who remain faithful to God, those who have experienced ḥesed, God's steadfast love. Steadfast love is God's tenacious commitment to his people, God's constant love in the midst of all human frailty and fickleness *[Steadfast]*.

Exhortation to Honor the LORD   4:4-6

Most commentators view verses 4-5 as addressed to the opponents of the psalmist. Several translations and interpretations are possible. These may be words of pastoral advice to the accusers as people who have lost faith. They may be the words of a temple priest calling for appropriate sacrifice for sin (Weiser: 120-21).

The word translated *angry* (v. 4 NIV, NRSV n) literally means "tremble." *Do not sin* can also mean "and stop sinning." The enemies who are slandering the worshipper are exhorted to present *right sacrifices*. This can mean according to the proper ritual and/or in the correct frame of mind. The sacrifices demanded may help overcome the injustice done and restore the reputation of the one unjustly accused. The exhortation invites *trust in the LORD* (v. 5).

The interpreter is confronted with the question of where the quotation in verse 6 ends. Is the first half or the whole verse the expression of those who have lost faith? "Who can show . . . ?" (NIV, NASB) correctly catches the Hebrew emphasis on "who?" Dahood translates and exegetes Psalm 4 as a prayer for rain (I:22-27). That is based on comparison of the meaning of the Hebrew word *tôb*, translated *good* (v. 6), with other prayers for rain (65:9-13; 67:6-7; 85:12; Jer 5:24). The *good* par excellence in Palestine is the rain! On the other hand, *tôb* also has other meanings, such as "closeness to God" (Ps 73:28).

Let the light of your face shine upon us (v. 6b) appears to be a quote of Aaron's blessing (Num 6:25). The shining face of God is that visible expression of divine benevolence. The verse may imply that the benefits the *many* seek will only be given to those faithful to the LORD.

Statement of Trust 4:7-8

The psalm ends on the twin notes of joy and peace as the psalmist shares his experience of God. The joy of trust in the LORD supersedes that of a farmer beholding a good harvest (v. 7)! *Peace, shalom* (šālôm), often referring to a time of no warfare (1 Sam 7:14; Ps 72:7) or a prosperous harvest (72:3), is used here for the peace when people can lie down and go to sleep unafraid because their security rests in the LORD (v. 8).

THE TEXT IN THE BIBLICAL CONTEXT AND LIFE OF THE CHURCH

Martin Luther on Psalm 4

Martin Luther's lecture on Psalm 4 (1513) reveals interest in exposition of key biblical words and terms. Nine pages of the lecture are devoted to Psalm 4:1, with major attention to the phrase "God of my righteousness" (NASB, KJV), which Luther expounds in a passage on justification (1974:46):

But see how true and godly is this confession, in which the psalmist arrogates nothing of merit to himself. He does not say, "Since I did much or earned much in deed or with the mouth or some other member of mine." Therefore you are to understand that he lays claim to no righteousness, he boasts of no merit, he displays no worth, but that he praises the pure and exclusive grace and free kindness of God. He finds nothing within himself on the basis of which God should answer him.

End-of-Day Reflections

In the sixth century, when the Rule of Benedict prescribed the Hour of Compline as the day's final prayer, it established Psalm 4 as the first of the psalms to be prayed at that time. Through the centuries believers have used the psalm as an evening prayer. Evening marks the transition from the daylight world to the night world. One relinquishes control over jobs, people, and thoughts. Bedtime, when the clamor of the day ceases, can be a good time to get in touch with one's soul.

The series of paired contrasting verbs (vv. 4-5) provide sound counsel. Ephesians 4:26 quotes verse 4, "Be angry, but do not sin," with the further admonition, "Do not let the sun go down on your anger." We need to recognize the emotion of anger and deal with it rather than suppressing it. People who carry their anger to bed do not sleep well. *Ponder it on your beds, and be silent* (v. 4b). The psalm suggests, Ease off and reflect. In the silence, speak to yourself and listen to yourself. *Offer right sacrifices* and *trust in the LORD* (v. 5). What are right sacrifices before the God who gives all of life? Do people sometimes experience insomnia because they cannot let go, cannot give up control? *Put your trust in the LORD* need not be a glib statement. Can we not entrust the issues of tomorrow to the keeping of the Lord? So Jesus invites: "Therefore I tell you, do not worry about your life" (Matt 6:25-34).

Psalm 4 offers this simple prayer for use each evening:

> *I will lie down and sleep in peace,*
>   *for you alone, O LORD,*
>   *make me dwell in safety.* (v. 8 NIV)

Psalm 5

Morning Prayer to the God of Righteousness

PREVIEW

The setting is the time for morning prayer, the time for sacrifice in the temple service. The psalm is directed toward God and identifies the psalmist with God's cause and righteousness (vv. 1-3, 7-8, 11-12). The activity and fate of the enemies is described (vv. 4-6, 9-10). Like Psalms 3 and 4, this plea for help illustrates that righteousness does not go unopposed (v. 8).

Psalm 5, an individual lament and prayer song, sounds like a declaration of innocence in its use of the language of accusation, *I plead my case* (v. 3) and *The boastful will not stand before your eyes* (v. 5). The accusers speak falsehood. The power of the lie threatens the life of the faithful. With deep emotion the psalmist calls on God to pronounce a verdict of "guilty" upon his foes. The psalm ends in confidence that the LORD is protector of the righteous seeker.

As a lament, Psalm 5 contains the usual elements of petition, complaint, reference to enemies, and statement of hope. The heading associates this psalm with David and suggests a musical setting *for the flutes* (see Ps 4) *[Superscriptions]*.

OUTLINE

Appeal to God to Hear the Petition, 5:1-3
Praise for God's Judgment of the Wicked, 5:4-6
Statement of Intention to Enter the Sanctuary, 5:7-8
Description and Fate of the Accusers, 5:9-10
Celebration of the Divine Presence, 5:11-12

EXPLANATORY NOTES

Appeal to God to Hear the Petition   5:1-3

Note the intensity and repetition of the opening verbs: *Give ear, heed, listen, to you I pray*. With heavy sighing, the psalmist appeals to *my King and my God* (v. 2; 44:4; 84:3) in the expectation of a fair hearing from the God of justice and power.

The devout saw the morning as a time for prayer and divine assistance after the perils of the night (v. 3; 90:14; 143:8). In the situation of a defendant taking refuge in the sanctuary, after petitions, sacrifices, and rites of purification (7:3-5), the divine verdict would be pronounced in the morning (Kraus, 1986:132).

Praise for God's Judgment of the Wicked   5:4-6

Stanza 2 focuses on the accusers, but in the form of praise for God's judgment of the wicked. The foes are described (vv. 4-6, 9-10) *[Enemies]*. With mouth and tongue they destroy. They are *boastful* and *speak lies;* they are *bloodthirsty and deceitful* (vv. 5-6). Such persons cannot stand in God's sight; for God, such behavior must be abhorrent (v. 6). The implication is that the LORD will never permit the wicked access to the sanctuary, to which the psalmist now seeks entry.

Statement of Intention to Enter the Sanctuary   5:7-8

The place where God dwells, *your house* (v. 7), is the opposite of the wickedness just described. Anyone unjustly accused and wanting to appeal for justice in the temple had to undergo a preliminary examination at the gate (see entrance liturgies of 15; 24:3-6). The words of verse 7 may have been such an appeal, seeking admission. Entrance to the sanctuary is sought on the basis of the LORD's *steadfast love* (ḥesed, v. 7) *[Steadfast]*. In the abundance of the constant love of God, the psalmist can enter the sanctuary in total assurance of welcome there, yet with a sense of awe and reverence. The prayer (v. 8), the focal point of Psalm 5, petitions for leading by God's *righteousness*, by what God has already done. So he desires to follow God's way.

Description and Fate of the Accusers 5:9-10

Referring to the enemies and their devious conduct, the psalmist now beseeches God to pronounce a "guilty" verdict on them. The enemies are *bloodthirsty* deceivers (v. 6). The weapon for carrying out their deceitful murderous intention is slander (v. 9; 27:12; 52:2-4; 59:6-7). The psalmist's prayer conveys deep feelings that the foes should *bear their guilt* and *fall by their own counsels* and be *cast . . . out* (v. 10). We must see this imprecatory prayer in light of the psalmist's identification with God's righteousness. He seeks not private vindication, but fundamental justice, in the hope that God will vindicate his moral order. Nevertheless, questions remain concerning the language used. What place is there for righteous indignation? What are the dangers? Note also some other biblical responses (Luke 23:34) [Imprecation].

Celebration of the Divine Presence 5:11-12

In the final stanza, the psalmist identifies himself with God's cause in the confident assurance that God will bless not only him, but also the community of the righteous, who will sing for joy (v. 11), in contrast to those who are cast out (v. 10). The LORD's people turn to him in love (v. 11; Pss 18:1; 31:23) and know his *name* (69:36; 119:132). The name signifies a person's character or destiny. Such people can be certain of God's protection and blessing.

Thus, we can read Psalm 5 as the actual protection the temple offers one in danger. The poem also uses the security of the sanctuary as a metaphor. God is just and provides a place of sanctuary, protection, and favor for his people (Clifford, 2002:59).

THE TEXT IN THE BIBLICAL CONTEXT AND LIFE OF THE CHURCH

Morning Prayers and Songs

The faithful have often considered morning as the best time for prayer: "O LORD, . . . be our strength every morning" (Isa 33:2 NIV). They expect the kindness of the LORD in the morning (Pss 59:16; 90:14). Lamentations 3:23 declares that the LORD's mercies "are new every morning." The sixth-century Rule of Benedict prescribed Psalm 5 for Monday morning. Prayer as the day's first task helps people enter "the house of God." Morning prayer prepares people for action. So Psalm 5 "bridges the passivities of grace into the activities of obedience" (Peterson, 1989:65).

Morning hymns abound as well in Christian worship. From the *Katholisches Gesangbuch* (1828) comes "When morning gilds the skies." Others are Reginald Heber's (1826) "Holy, holy, holy," Amos Herr's (1890) "I owe the Lord a morning song," Thomas Chisholm's gospel hymn (1923) "Great is Thy faithfulness," and Eleanor Farjeon's (1957) "Morning has broken." Mary B. Valencia's contemporary translation (1978, 1990) of the Spanish hymn "Por la mañana" begins "At break of day I raise my voice in adoration / to God who is my only hope and salvation." These hymns affirm the renewing gift of God's mercies for each new day.

Speech That Hurts

Psalm 5 points to the lie as a dangerous form that evil takes. It is one of the most common and inhumane means of undercutting others. "Speech that is empty of truth about another is to practice the opposite of God's will" (Mays, 1994b:58). Truth-telling was identified as one of the basic commandments: "You shall not bear false witness" (Exod 20:16). Jeremiah scathingly criticized lying and deceit (9:3-6). Jesus called for integrity of speech by urging: "Let your word be 'Yes, Yes' or 'No, No'" (Matt 5:37).

Ernesto Cardenal, a poet of twentieth-century suffering, articulates how smooth talk still kills (39-40):

> Their speeches are honeyed with peace;
> they drip love and kindness
> and their stock-piles grow the faster. . . .
>
> Their wavelengths dance with lies,
> evil songs in the darkness.
> Their desks are heavy with plots.
> Lord, preserve me from their scheming.

We live by words. What will those words be? Human speech can destroy, or it can build up (James 3:5-10). Psalm 5 invites us to morning prayer, through which we offer ourselves to God, and then we wait to see what God will do.

Psalm 6

The LORD Has Heard My Weeping

PREVIEW

Like Psalms 3–5, Psalm 6 is another prayer for help. In this lament of an individual we hear the prayer of a sick person. The illness has both physical and emotional dimensions. Fear of death and fear of being cut off from God dominate. Perhaps there are even enemies beyond the illness. The final lines represent a shift in mood, the strong assurance of victory because *the LORD has heard*! A leader could have spoken them in the temple after the worshipper received assurance of answered prayer.

The poet carefully constructed this psalm (as recognized in the NIV and NRSV paragraph divisions). In the Hebrew, the four stanzas respectively have 24 words (vv. 1-3), 15 words (vv. 4-5), 15 words (vv. 6-7), and 24 words (vv. 8-10). The poetic skill of the writer is also evident in the repetition of words and ideas; the parallelism within each verse underscores or carries the idea forward, as in verse 1: *Do not rebuke me in your anger, / or discipline me in your wrath* [Hebrew Poetry].

The title includes reference to *The Sheminith*, "the eighth," a musical notation that possibly referred to a tone or mode, but not to an octave, which was unknown to Israelite musicians. It occurs also in Psalm 12:1 and 1 Chronicles 15:21 *[Musical; Superscriptions]*.

OUTLINE

Complaint and Petition for Healing, 6:1-5
Description of the Psalmist's Plight, 6:6-7
Declaration That the LORD Has Heard, 6:8-10

EXPLANATORY NOTES

Complaint and Petition for Healing   6:1-5

Psalm 6 identifies God as the psalmist's problem, but also as the solution. Struggling with a life-threatening illness, his affliction is interpreted as God's wrath in action. Though God can *rebuke* and *discipline* for positive educational purposes (Deut 8:5; Prov 3:12), the supplicant reads his situation as punishment (v. 1). The psalmist accepts the common understanding of that day, that illness is the result of divine punishment. He declares no objection, nor claims innocence, as in the book of Job, but rather makes implicit confession. However, the psalmist also believes God is moved by human anguish and so prays for mercy (*ḥānan*, v. 2). Let grace be God's way of dealing with the wrath and punishment deserved!

The plaintive question *How long?* (v. 3) is a common cry of the laments (Pss 35:17; 62:3; 74:10; 80:4; 90:13; 94:3). When suffering continues endlessly, it is the cry of exasperation: "How long are you going to let this go on?"

Feeling the vitality of his life slipping away, the worshipper prays that God may *turn* again as an expression of his *steadfast love* (*ḥesed*, v. 4). Those crying out to the LORD appeal to his covenant love (44:26) *[Steadfast]*. An additional motivation lies in the psalmist's fear of death. People saw *Sheol,* the abode of the dead, as a place cut off, a place from where one could no longer praise God (v. 5). In Sheol, located in the mysterious regions beneath the earth (Num 16:30-33), a place of darkness and gloom (Job 10:20-22), there is no remembrance of God (Pss 30:9; 88:10-12; 115:17). *Remembrance* means reliving and celebrating God's presence with his people. Death ends that possibility, though 22:29 offers another view *[Sheol]*.

Out of his anguish (vv. 1-3), the psalmist in these verses has appealed to the LORD's steadfast love (v. 4) and to the need to keep on praising God until death, which ends the praising (v. 5). The name *LORD* has been used five times (eight times in the entire psalm), underlining an intimacy, but also adding an urgency to the petition.

Description of the Psalmist's Plight   6:6-7

With poetic exaggeration, *flood my bed* and *drench my couch,* the poet describes his plight, which receives no respite in sleep (v. 6). Verse 7 suggests premature aging because of the afflictions. Though we cannot identify the specific illness, here is a person severely depressed, consumed by fear and massive grief. Some readers think that the mentioned *foes* (v. 7) have placed a curse on the psalmist. Or they might have been more like Job's friends, exploiting or shunning the afflicted one.

Declaration That the LORD Has Heard   6:8-10

An abrupt change in mood marks the final stanza: *The LORD has heard* (v. 9)! The *enemies* (vv. 8, 10), whether physical or spiritual, will be routed *[Enemies].* In verse 10 *turn back* may be a reference to "returning to Sheol." The last word in Hebrew, translated *moment,* is also a name for "underworld." Does that imply that the enemy here, death itself, is put to flight once more because *the LORD has heard*?

The confident declaration of these verses may come after an oracle of salvation spoken by an officiant in the temple (Ps 91:14-16) *[Oracle].* The psalmist's prayer is also a witness, that in frustrating the enemy and in returning the psalmist to health, the LORD hears and answers prayer.

THE TEXT IN THE BIBLICAL CONTEXT AND LIFE OF THE CHURCH
Psalm 6 as a Penitential Psalm

The ancient church considered Psalm 6 as the first of the seven penitential psalms (Pss 6; 32; 38; 51; 102; 130; 143) *[Penitential].* The psalm does not express confession, except that implicit in identifying the affliction of personal suffering with the punishment of God (v. 1). Thus, from a more general prayer for the restoration of the community, the focus shifts to that of penitence. As a penitential psalm, used especially during Lent, it becomes a prayer for all who confess the "sickness" of sin.

The penitential psalms take sin seriously. They accept the view of a causal link between sin and suffering, a view widely held in the OT (32:1-4; 38:1-4; 51:1-9), though challenged as well (Job 1:22; 2:10; John 9:1-3). Yet, sin in the human experience leaves persons weakened. The prayer, *Be gracious to me, O LORD. . . . O LORD, heal me. . . . O LORD, save my life; deliver me for the sake of your steadfast love* (Ps 6:2-4), is appropriate for times of penitence and confession of sin.

When Confronted by Death

We need not and should not view all illness as punishment for sin. However, serious illness still prompts a "cry to God." Looking death in the face mirrors human finitude and fallibility. Facing personal mortality becomes an occasion for reflection and repentance. Death confronts people with "the alternatives of final alienation from God or final acceptance by God" (Mays, 1994b:62).

While the Christian perspective provides belief in life beyond death, it is helpful to identify our fears. What things are no longer possible after death? Can we then also face death through faith's certainty: "If God is for us, who is against us" (Rom 8:31)? In illness people often ask "Why?" Bargaining with God becomes part of the response. Even when life seems out of control, can we have a sense that God hears the sound of our weeping? Can there be healing even if there is not cure?

Psalm 6 presents a pessimistic view regarding the praise of God in death (v. 5), though there are other biblical witnesses. Revelation 7 presents a vision of the martyrs, including the sevenfold ascription of praise to God (7:12). Braght's classic *Martyrs Mirror* tells the stories of Christian martyrs across sixteen centuries, who shared the faith with passionate and irrepressible joy even as they faced death.

The last part of Psalm 6:8, *The LORD has heard the sound of my weeping*, suggests the biblical theme of how God hears the groaning and weeping of the people (Exod 2:23-24). Psalm 6 has been compared with Hannah's lament in 1 Samuel 1 (Miller, 1986:56). Jesus wept with people in their sorrow (John 11:31-36). Jesus' word in the Sermon on the Mount was "Blessed are those who mourn, for they will be comforted" (Matt 5:4).

Psalm 7

Prayer to God, the Righteous Judge

PREVIEW

This lament of the individual declares innocence. The prayer song begins with the plea of one betrayed and hounded, moves to the confident conviction that God is judge of all the earth, asserts the self-defeat of wickedness, and ends in an expression of praise.

The meaning of the technical term *Shiggaion* (*šiggāyôn*) in the title is not known *[Musical; Superscriptions]*. The reference to *Cush* may be to an unknown tradition about David's life. Some have seen a possible setting in the stories about David and Saul (1 Sam 24–26). The psalm's later use suggests a situation as described in 1 Kings 8:31-34, where a person who has been accused, though innocent, cries out in the temple for God's verdict. *Selah* (v. 5) suggests the psalm's use in later temple worship *[Selah]*.

OUTLINE

Cry for Refuge and Declaration of Innocence, 7:1-5
Petition for Personal Vindication, 7:6-8
Petition for Public Vindication, 7:9-16
Vow of Praise, 7:17

EXPLANATORY NOTES

Cry for Refuge and Declaration of Innocence 7:1-5

The psalmist's cry to God expresses the plight of one pursued and helpless, of one being torn to pieces (vv. 1-2). The enemy behaves like a lion that goes for the throat (Pss 10:9; 17:12; 22:21). Yet trust characterizes the vocabulary of the opening verses. A hiding place and *refuge* (v. 1; 11:1; 16:1; 31:1; 91:1-2, 9) will be found in the LORD *my God* (vv. 1, 3).

The declaration of innocence contains a solemn oath (vv. 3-5). The psalmist, convinced that he is unjustly accused by enemies, seeks the protection of the sanctuary. With petitions, sacrifices, and rites of purification, he states the solemn vow (vv. 3-5; 18:20-24; 139:19-22). This "self-imprecation" suggests that sin contains in itself its own judgment, to show God's righteousness. Verse 5 is the "cross my heart and hope to die" statement—except that it is for real! *Ground* and *dust* (v. 5) are synonyms for Sheol, the abode of the dead *[Sheol]*.

Petition for Personal Vindication 7:6-8

The cry to God the judge, *Rise up, . . . awake* (v. 6) is synonymous with the petition "save me," "help me" (44:23; 59:4-5). The scene suggests the gathering of the nations. The psalmist calls for God to hold court over all the people. Yet God will hear the case of individuals and try them on the basis of their own righteousness and integrity (v. 8). This is not so much a declaration of self-righteousness before God, since trust in the righteousness of God has called forth the integrity of the psalmist (note vv. 10-11, 17).

Petition for Public Vindication 7:9-16

The psalmist pleads for more than personal vindication. There is a larger question: "Is this a world in which evil prevails, or do the destructive forces of evil have the last word?" (Davidson, 1998:35). The psalmist has no doubt that God will expose evil and that right will prevail, for *God is a righteous judge*. God does *test the minds and hearts* (17:3; 26:2) and God's judgment goes on *every day* (vv. 9-11). In these verses, prayer is directed not against individuals, but the wickedness in them (v. 9). Is that a possible way of understanding the other prayers of imprecation? *[Imprecation]*.

The next section suggests the workings of God's judgment on the wicked (vv. 12-16). The major questions in translation and interpretation focus on who is the subject of the verbs in verses 12-13. The

Hebrew reads: "If he will not turn, he will whet his sword." To whom does "he" refer?

The NRSV presumes the wicked as the subject of the first verb, and God as the subject of the remaining verbs. NIV understands God as the subject of all the verbs. Both suggest that God stands ready to mete out judgment on the unrepentant. However, it also makes sense to read the entire section (vv. 12-16) as about the wicked (NJPS, REB). In a series of powerful images, these verses speak of the increasing violence of the wicked (vv. 12-13), the giving birth to all forms of evil (v. 14), but how finally the oppressive power and cunning of the wicked are turned back on their own heads. They are snared in their own trap. So the psalmist declares, "Crime does not pay," since the mysterious working of God's righteousness causes sin to bring judgment upon itself. This is the law of the talion, or equivalent retribution (3:7; 9:15-16; 35:7-8).

Vow of Praise 7:17

The final verse expresses praise for God's righteousness, for God's vindication of the right. This statement of trust extols the divine name, the theme of the psalm that follows. The *name of the LORD* expresses all the mystery and wonder of the power of God over all other forces; it is the object of all prayer, praise, and reflection (20:7; 103:1; 135:1; 148:5, 13). Note the unusual accumulation of divine titles in this psalm. Dahood (I:40-41) translates these: "O Yahweh," "O my God," "O Exalted One," "O Most High," "God the Just," with v. 11 reading, "My Suzerain is the Most High God, the Savior of the upright of heart." Others are "El" (v. 11), "Victor" (v. 12), and "Yahweh Most High" (v. 17) *[Names of God]*.

THE TEXT IN THE BIBLICAL CONTEXT AND LIFE OF THE CHURCH

Proclaiming Innocence

Many who read Psalm 7 are uncomfortable with the poet's claim of innocence (vv. 3-5). Who can with honesty assert such purity? Recognize that such prayers were composed for a person in the right when compared with an antagonist. Such prayers profess faithfulness to the LORD and appeal to the righteousness of God (vv. 9-11, 17).

Another way is to see this as a psalm of the Lord's redemptive suffering at the hands of injustice. Thus, we can pray the psalm as Jesus might have prayed it in the context of his redemptive passion. To pray the psalm not as an expression of one's own personal feelings, but to discover something of Jesus' passion in Holy Week, is "to taste, in some measure, the bitterness and the gall" (Reardon: 14).

Thinking About Judgment

How do we think of judgment? As positive or negative? Psalm 7 appeals for God's anger to be activated (v. 6), petitions for the wicked to get their deserts (v. 9), and states the stark one-to-one ratio of action and consequence (vv. 12-16). Yet the biblical concept is positive, as in God working to establish justice.

Understandings of judgment may also be colored by images from the church of the Middle Ages. A popular woodcut, which illustrated many books of that time, portrays Christ the judge sitting upon the rainbow. A lily, which extends from his right ear, signifies the redeemed being ushered by angels into paradise. From the left ear protrudes a sword, symbolizing the doom of the damned. The devils drag the damned by their hair from the tombs and cast them into the flames of hell (Bainton: 22-23).

While judgment, as understood in the Bible, has a sharp side, it is ultimately a message of hope for God's people. Judgment will take place not only at the end of human life or the end of earthly history. In the parable about the separation of the sheep and the goats (Matt 25:31-46), Jesus declares that every day "the king" comes in judgment and mercy. Everyone will ask, "When was it that we saw you hungry or thirsty or a stranger . . . or in prison?" Christ will answer: "As you did it [or, did not do it] to one of the least of these . . ."

How does God's judgment come? Is it not often by the working out of what people themselves have set in motion? We cannot abuse the body by overwork, neglect, or by what we eat, drink, or smoke without serious consequences. People cannot waste or pollute the air, water, and the soil without paying for it, or robbing future generations. Neither can the nations of the world commit massive portions of their human energies and natural resources to armaments without reaping the whirlwind of destruction. We can read Jesus' words in the garden of Gethsemane as commentary on Psalm 7:12-16, and on the arms race of modern times: "All who take the sword will perish by the sword" (Matt 26:52).

Psalm 8

The Wonder of Creation: Creature and Creator

PREVIEW

Readers often call this hymn a song of creation. Following five laments in the Psalter, it rings in praise of the Creator. A theme of wonder dominates, wonder at the expanse and intricacy of the universe, the apparent insignificance of humanity, and yet how God has given humankind governance over the earth! Rather than being insignificant, persons are of high worth because of their relationship to the Creator God. A burst of praise to the sovereign LORD frames the Psalm (vv. 1, 9).

The usual hymn form begins with a summons to praise, followed by the announcement of the motive for praise introduced by the word "for" (*kî*, as in 30:1), and ending with a renewed summons to praise. Psalm 8 is somewhat different in that the poet has composed it completely as direct address to God. The psalm expresses praise to God, developed as a meditation on the created human being, with the structure determined by the content *[Psalm Genres]*.

The meaning of the term *Gittith* (*gittît*) in the heading, which appears also for Psalms 81 and 84, is unknown; it could refer to an instrument or melody from Gath, a Philistine city *[Musical; Superscriptions]*.

OUTLINE

An Ascription of Praise, 8:1-2
Reflection on the Dignity of Humanity, 8:3-8
An Ascription of Praise, 8:9

EXPLANATORY NOTES

An Ascription of Praise   8:1-2

Wonder at the divine name opens the hymn. *O LORD (Yahweh)* is the personal name for God revealed to Moses (Exod 3:13-15). *Our Sovereign ('ădonênû, our Lord,* NIV) has the meaning of "king." The reference is to God as king of all the earth. Since the LORD is the Creator, his name is revealed in all the earth (v. 1a).

The Hebrew text of verses 1b-2 lends itself to several readings and interpretations. Does *Out of the mouth of babes and infants* go with what precedes (NRSV, AB, JB), or with what follows (KJV, NIV, NASB, NEB)? Is there a suggestion here that the power of enemies is broken by the voice of weak children (Kraus, 1988:182)? Jesus appeared thus to quote this verse on the occasion of cleansing the temple (Matt 21:16). Note the paradox in how a tiny helpless baby has power to defeat strong enemies. The *foes, enemy* and *avenger* (v. 2), hostile powers in opposition to the creation and Lord of the peoples, might also be seen as the chaos that has been subdued in creation (Ps 89:9-12) *[Enemies]*.

Reflection on the Dignity of Humanity   8:3-8

The main body of the praise hymn is awed meditation on the created human being. The night sky, with the moon and expanse of stars, speaks to the psalmist of the handiwork of God's fingers (v. 3). However, so also speaks human life, insignificant in comparison to God's immense universe. Yet God remembers human beings to *care for them* (v. 4)! *What are human beings* might well be followed by an exclamation point, for the query about the worth of human beings expresses the wonder that God remembers and visits the frail, insignificant human race! Note that the words often translated *man ('ĕnôš* and *ben-'ādām)* are not restricted to the male sex but refer to both man and woman.

The psalmist's wonder at the worth of persons continues. Basic to *human ('ĕnôš)* is the concept of a weak, vulnerable humanity (Job 7:11-21; Ps 144:3-4). The human family has been given a position in God's creation only a *little lower than God.* Here variant readings come from the Hebrew word being plural, so also *gods*, or *angels* (KJV following LXX). The human family has been given *dominion* over the created world, including all the other creatures! The list of created beings (land animals, birds, sea creatures) is in reverse sequence to the order of creation found in Genesis 1 (sea creatures, birds, land animals). Note the royal language here. *Crowned them with glory and honor* (v. 5), *dominion,* and *under their feet* (v. 6) are added to the royal terms *Our Sovereign* and *majestic* (vv. 1, 9). God has made the human being "king" or "vice-regent" over creation (vv. 6-8)!

Throughout these verses, however, God remains the subject. The four verbs—*You have made, crowned, given them dominion, put all things*—speak of a delegated authority. Humanity's sovereign role is not by glorious self-achievement. God gives dominion. Dominion involves a pattern of responsibility with humans granted a caretaker task. Psalm 8 relates to Genesis 1:1–2:3 not only by language (the specific groups named in vv. 7-8), but also by the creation accounts, reflecting something of a co-regency on earth as well as recognizing humanity's limits (Gen 1–3).

An Ascription of Praise   8:9

The psalm ends as it began, with the call to praise, not of human glory, but of the LORD whose name is over all! All the nations will come to glorify his name.

THE TEXT IN THE BIBLICAL CONTEXT AND LIFE OF THE CHURCH

What Then Are Human Beings?

The Bible often focuses on the limits of life and the evil brought about by human beings (Gen 3:22-24; 6:5-7; Ps 104:35). The question *What are human beings?* is asked also in Psalm 144:3 and Job 7:17-18; 25:6. The answers given describe the mortal *like a breath, a passing shadow*, one tested *every moment*, a *maggot*, a *worm*! In contrast, Psalm 8 presents a high view of humanity. The psalmist's amazement focuses on the high status granted human beings, *a little lower than God* and *crowned . . . with glory and honor* (v. 5), language reminiscent of "Let us make humankind in our image" (Gen 1:26). It is God, and not animals, who is humankind's closest relative. Humans are persons of dignity because of their affinity with God. Despite fallen humanity, human beings are prime exhibits of God's majesty (Martens, 1998:203). That truth is the basis for the psalmist's awed wonder. While people do not have equality with God, but are often tempted to act like God (Gen 3:1-7), the positive self-image portrayed in Psalm 8 can be helpful in accepting the God-given role for responsible living.

Psalm 8 and the New Testament

Jesus quotes Psalm 8:2 on the occasion of cleansing the temple. The chief priests and scribes were indignant at the healing of the blind and lame, and the children crying out, "Hosanna to the Son of David!" Jesus responds with "Out of the mouth of infants and nursing babies you have prepared praise" (Matt 21:16).

The writer of Hebrews quotes the question, "What are human beings?" (Heb 2:6-7). There the focus on "subjecting all things to them" (2:8) connects with Jesus, who by the suffering of death opens the way for a new humanity. The NIV expresses this connection more clearly, using "the son of man" in translating Psalm 8:4 and Hebrews 2:6. So also the other NT quotation, "put all things under his feet" (Eph 1:22), is applied to Jesus as head of the church and Lord over all. The NT interpreters took for granted that OT ideas may prefigure Christian realities. Thus, Psalm 8, which contains the terms "Adam" (man) and "son of man," was directly applied to Jesus Christ as a way of building on the messianic theme (1 Cor 15:27; Heb 2:6-9). However, the "not yet" of Hebrews 2:8 not only leaves open the possibility but also points to the reality of humans reigning together with Christ (Luke 22:30; 2 Tim 2:12; Rev 2:26-27; 5:10; 20:6)

Dominion with Limits

An idea underlying Psalm 8 may have been that human civilization only became possible because of the domestication of animals (vv. 7-8). "Animals are dependent upon a habitat; humans depend upon their capacity to craft one" (Mays 1994b:69). Considering the contemporary rape of the earth and its resources, what does *dominion* mean for the present day? The creation story deals also with limits. What is said about human governance in Psalm 8 is framed by praise of God (vv. 1, 9). Is that not the element too often forgotten? "Human power without the context of praise of God is to profane human regency over creation" (Brueggemann, 1984:38).

Who was realistic in understanding humanity? Was it the Greeks in elevating human culture as the object of praise, or the biblical writers in asserting that humankind has no value of its own, but has value because it is the gift of God (Weiser: 144)? Copernican astronomy should have taught humans something about humility! The earth is not the center of the universe. People are not the measure of all things.

We need a sense of humility before the wonder of God as Creator lest we bring upon ourselves the judgment that Psalms 7; 9; and 10 declare. We do well to ponder the placement of Psalm 8 between Psalms 7 and 9–10, which focus on the judgment upon rebellion and wickedness. Do we want "dominion" without limits? What role does praise of God play in the realistic appraisal of human dignity? What insights are gained from Jesus, whose power and dominion took the form of a servant and whose governance took the form of obedience (Mark 10:43-45; Phil 2:5-8)?

Psalms 9–10

Thanksgiving and Prayer for God's Justice

PREVIEW

The themes for these two psalms include thanksgiving for God's justice and righteous rule, and lament over how the wicked appear to get away with thinking that God does not care. The focus on the plight of the poor and oppressed ends with confidence that God will judge rightly, punishing the wicked and remembering the afflicted.

Psalms 9 and 10 may be considered a unit. In the LXX, Psalms 9–10 appear as Psalm 9. This numbering was then followed by the Greek and Latin churches in their division of the psalms, generally one behind the Hebrew text of Psalms from this point onward. Most English translations follow the Hebrew numbering.

Both psalms employ the acrostic device, in which every two verses begin with the next letter of the Hebrew alphabet, though with modification. Psalm 9 has most of the first 11 letters of the 22-letter Hebrew alphabet as the initials of alternate verses; but Psalm 10, after beginning with the 12th letter, drops the alphabetic scheme until verses 12-18, where the last four letters appear. Psalm 10 has no title, unusual for the first book of Psalms. *Selah* appears after Psalm 9:20, but nowhere else at the end of a psalm [Selah]. The psalms are similar in language and themes, though the mood shifts between jubilation and anguish. Observe a significant mood change in Psalm 10:1. Whereas Psalm 9 reflects thanksgiving and faith in God's total rule,

Psalm 10 appears more a prayer of lament. Repetition of ideas occurs.

The meaning of the term *Muth-labben* in the heading is unknown, but might refer to a melody. *Higgaion* (after 9:16) may mean "meditation" and may be a musical notation *[Musical; Superscriptions]*. These terms suggest use of the psalm in worship. The acrostic feature, often used as a device to help in memorization, suggests that this song of praise and thanksgiving had a teaching purpose, drawing on past experiences of the Hebrew nation as a way of remembering that God judges the nations.

If outlined according to literary form (acrostic), every two verses form a stanza, as in NRSV; but NIV reflects paragraphing more according to content. The proposed outline follows content.

OUTLINE

Thanksgiving for God's Judgment on the Enemy, 9:1-6
Thanksgiving That God Does Not Forget the Oppressed, 9:7-12
Petition for Deliverance and the Cry for Justice, 9:13-20
Lament over the Prosperity of the Wicked, 10:1-11
Petition That God Remember the Afflicted and Punish the Wicked, 10:12-15
Praise That the LORD Is Judge of the Nations and Savior of the Poor, 10:16-18

EXPLANATORY NOTES

Thanksgiving for God's Judgment on the Enemy 9:1-6

The psalm begins with confident thanksgiving to the LORD on the basis of his mighty deeds in the past (vv. 1-2). As in Psalm 8, there is praise of the divine name, here identified as *Most High* (9:2; 7:17).

The *wonderful deeds* include the LORD's victory over *enemies*, in which they have met their fate (vv. 3-6). The psalm presents God not only as personal advocate (v. 4), but also as God of the nations, whose past judgments include cities and civilizations no longer even remembered (v. 5-6) *[Judge]*. In addition to the note of thanksgiving for God's just rule, a theme throughout Psalms 9–10, will be the *enemies* (9:3, 6; 10:2-11). Other terms used include *wicked* (9:16, 17; 10:2, 3, 4, 13, 15), *nations* (9:5, 15, 19, 20; 10:16), *peoples* (9:8, 11), and *evildoers* (10:15). These psalms identify the nations as the wicked *[Enemies; Wicked]*.

Thanksgiving That God Does Not Forget the Oppressed 9:7-12

The LORD as righteous judge (vv. 7-8; 7:8; 58:11; 82:8; 96:10, 13) can rebuke the nations (vv. 5-6), but is defender of the oppressed (vv. 9-10; 98:9). The central teaching of the psalm confidently asserts God as *a stronghold for the oppressed* (v. 9). God as "fortress" suggests stability and security (46:1-2, 7, 11; 59:9, 16-17). The psalmist identifies with *those who know your name* (v. 10), implying a relationship with the faithful God.

The LORD, viewed as seated on a heavenly throne (vv. 7-8), dwells as well in the sanctuary in Jerusalem (v. 11; 132:13-14). Israel has the task of telling the LORD's mighty deeds among the peoples (96:3; 105:1). This includes the message that God, who *avenges blood* (v. 12a) and holds people responsible for what they do to others (Gen 4:10; 9:5), does not forget the afflicted (v. 12b).

A cluster of Hebrew words describes *the oppressed* (9:9; 10:18), *dāk*; *the afflicted* (9:12) or *the poor* (10:2, 9) or *the oppressed* (10:12), *'ănāyîm*; *the needy* (9:18), *'ebyôn*; and *the poor* (9:18) or *the meek* (10:17), *'ănāwîm*.

We find an example of wordplay in the use of the term *forget*. Psalms 9:12, 18; and 10:12 refer to God not forgetting the oppressed. The wicked forget God (9:17). Some suspect or accuse God of forgetting justice (10:11).

Petition for Deliverance and the Cry for Justice 9:13-20

In the midst of suffering, the psalmist appeals to God to be *gracious* (v. 13). Lifted *from the gates of death* (Sheol, as abode of the dead, vv. 13, 17), the psalmist will offer joyous praise *in the gates of* the sanctuary (wordplay with *gates*) *[Sheol]*. The summary, *The nations . . . forget God* and *The needy shall not . . . be forgotten* (vv. 17-20), asserts that God's justice will prevail! God's justice includes the wicked being ensnared in their own net (9:15-16; 10:2; also the theme of 7:12-16).

Rise up (9:19) is the cry for the LORD's intervention. In God's justice, the adversaries are weak, vulnerable beings. The term *man* or *mortal* (*'ĕnôš*, vv. 19-20) is the same word used in 8:4 of God's creature, a general term for the frail world of humanity. Rebellious humans (and the nations) are but of the earth, while the LORD is king and judge and savior.

Lament over the Prosperity of the Wicked   10:1-11

The lament opens with the "Why?" question, giving vent to the psalmist's sense of abandonment in the silence of God (v. 1; 13:1; 22:1; 44:23-24; 74:1, 11; 83:1). When God's face appears hidden, there is a sense of forsakenness and terror (vv. 1, 11; 27:9; 30:7; 88:14; 102:2).

Distraught by the apparent prosperity of the wicked, the psalmist presents a lurid portrait of wickedness (vv. 2-11). This section touches on almost every aspect of the evil impulse in humanity. Note the similarity to Psalm 73:3-12. Besides the description of the wicked plotting and carrying out their oppressive acts, the psalm gives insight to the thought process (vv. 4, 6, 11). The psalmist emphasizes how they ambush and assault the helpless. They even make use of the curse to destroy persons (vv. 7-9; Isa 59:13). Above all, they charge that God has forgotten and has hidden his face (v. 11). In light of the everlasting reign of the LORD, the wicked conduct of the nations presents the perplexing issue.

Petition That God Remember the Afflicted and Punish the Wicked   10:12-15

Repeating the plea for the LORD to *rise up* (v. 12; Ps 9:19), the psalmist summarizes the folly of the wicked. The one who has forgotten God assumes that God has forgotten him and will not call him *to account* (v. 13). Such practical atheism is the height of "foolishness" (14:1).

But you do see! (v. 14). The LORD is a living God who sees and hears and remembers the plight of the oppressed (11:4; 14:2; 33:13-15). In Psalm 10 six different words are used (*helpless*, 3 times; *poor,* 3; *oppressed*, 2; *orphan*, 2; *innocent; meek*) to describe the social distress. The worshipper who prays identifies with the community of the "godly," the poor, the meek. Instead of *meek* (10:17), a better translation is "afflicted" or "oppressed," describing those who suffer at the hands of the rich and powerful. The petition climaxes in a passionate cry that the strength of the wicked might be destroyed (v. 15).

Praise That the LORD Is Judge of the Nations and Savior of the Poor   10:16-18

The LORD's kingdom is invincible and eternal and cannot be overthrown (v. 16; 29:10; 74:12; 93:1-2; 145:13). The acclamation *The LORD is king forever* affirms divine sovereignty and urges the LORD to do justice, in this case, by eliminating the nations (the wicked) *from his land* (v. 16). God upholds the rights of those most at risk—orphans, widows, and aliens (vv. 17-18; 68:5; Deut 10:18; 26:12-13).

THE TEXT IN THE BIBLICAL CONTEXT AND LIFE OF THE CHURCH

The Cry of an Afflicted People

A possible setting for this prayer song of God's people in affliction might be found in the time of the Persian occupation, after the Babylonian exile, when Israel was no longer an independent country. The congregation of the faithful is beset and threatened by conditions caused by the succession of peoples who held power over them. The nations are the wicked oppressors (Pss 9:5, 15, 17, 19, 20; 10:16). The writer personifies the congregation as an individual, giving it the role of the "lowly" (*'anî, the poor, afflicted*). The poem moves back and forth between feelings of abandonment and triumph as the Lord's people experience themselves as a neglected province in a vast empire (Mays, 1994b:71; Clifford, 2002:72).

The psalm was designed to be read or sung in the context of the gathered congregation so others could hear the recital of the wonderful deeds of the LORD (9:1-2) and take courage in the assertion that the LORD indeed is sovereign over all peoples.

Concern for the Poor and Oppressed

One of the striking themes of Psalms 9–10 is God's special concern for the poor and oppressed. This message of "doing justice" by taking up the cause of the powerless in society is at the heart of the prophets' words to the leaders of their day (Isa 1:17; 10:1-2; Amos 5:21-24; Mic 6:6-8).

The same theme is prominent in the NT. In his own life, Jesus embodied the biblical ideal of "the poor man" who trusts only in God. That faith commitment has social implications, as noted in the Song of Mary, about lifting up the lowly and filling the hungry with good things (Luke 1:51-54). Jesus' reading and application of the words from Isaiah 61:1-2 in the synagogue at Nazareth to announce his ministry has been seen as no less than declaring the Jubilee (Luke 4:16-21)!

Unfortunately, throughout history the church has often sided with those in power and become oppressor in its own way. In Romans 3:14, in a description of how all sin and that "no one" is righteous, Paul quotes Psalm 10:7, "Their mouth is full of curses and bitterness."

The description of the wicked (10:2-11) can also describe contemporary life. How easily the oppressed can become oppressor.

The Protestant Reformation of the sixteenth century called for a return to biblical faith. It was also largely a people's movement, calling for freedom from ruthless political and church leaders who suppressed the people. The Anabaptists, spiritual forebears of Mennonites, Baptists, Brethren, and other separatist groups, challenged the linking of church and state. They objected to wielding the sword and waging war as a means of bringing God's justice.

What is the justice of God for the landless, those who live in poverty, whose children are doomed to the same fate? How can this ancient worship song, out of the experience of an oppressed congregation, mobilize people to challenge oppression in the present? When the church identifies with suffering people and helps guide movements for liberation, what are the pitfalls?

A Model for Prayer

The tension sounded in Psalms 9–10 can provide a model for prayer. The psalm moves from confidence (9:1-2) to perplexity (10:1), and then from perplexity to confidence (Davidson, 1998:46).

For people who firmly believe that God is the sovereign Lord, continuing oppression of the powerless raises the question "Where is God?" This cry of lament voices the human plea for God's intervention. For people of faith living with the real events of the world, confidence and perplexity go hand in hand. The polarities of faith and doubt, confidence and questioning—all these are part of fervent prayer. When one sees vulnerable groups suffering horribly at the hands of exploiters, the result is turmoil reflected in the thanksgiving and laments that spill over each other (Clifford, 2002:76).

Psalms 9–10 invite people of faith to pray with an understanding of God as the righteous judge of the nations, who hears the cry of the lowly. Such prayer is offered with thanksgiving and hopeful trust.

Psalm 11

In the LORD I Take Refuge

PREVIEW

This song of trust expresses confidence *in the LORD* in face of counsel to *flee . . . to the mountains*. The psalmist's assurance rests in the righteous God. While we cannot reconstruct the specific setting, the psalm reflects the experience of one seeking refuge in the temple.

In contrast to prayers of lament, this psalm does not directly address God, but refers to him in the third person. Striking metaphors describe the actions and the destiny of the wicked. After an opening declaration of trust, complaint marks the first half of the psalm, and confidence the second.

Seventy-four of the psalms carry the attribution to David in the title, including Psalms 11–32 *[Superscriptions]*.

OUTLINE

Declaration of Refuge in the LORD, 11:1-3
Confidence in the LORD's Judgment Throne, 11:4-7

EXPLANATORY NOTES

Declaration of Refuge in the LORD   11:1-3

In the LORD (v. 1) identifies the psalmist's motto for his life. Other psalms (7:1; 16:1; 31:1; 71:1) open with that declaration of trust. To *take refuge* (*ḥāsāh, trust* in KJV), a key word in the OT, occurs 22 times in the Psalms (e.g., 5:11; 91:4; 144:2).

In the quotation (vv. 1b-3), the psalmist restates the advice of friends to flee, for the cause will fail. In distress, the mountains were the usual sanctuary. The graphic metaphor of the wicked shooting arrows in the dark suggests the deadly carnage and terror that concealed snipers can cause. *Foundations* (v. 3) represent the principles of law and justice as well as the established institutions that order the life of a community. In the assault on the upright and collapse of the moral order, violence and injustice prevail. One response is flight, like that of a panic-stricken bird (v. 1; Isa 16:2). The language echoes the experience of Lot fleeing Sodom and Gomorrah (vv. 2, 6; Gen 19:17, 24).

Confidence in the LORD's Judgment Throne   11:4-7

Flight, however, is not the psalmist's choice. Even in this situation of harassment, the psalmist expresses reason for confidence: *The LORD* (repeated four times, vv. 4-7)! The LORD rules, not only in the *temple*, but also from *heaven* (Pss 2:4; 103:19). God's searching eyes behold all (10:14; 14:2; 33:13-14; Jer 7:11). Because God is righteous, reckoning will come (Jer 5:1). The judge of all the earth will do right (Gen 18:25). His passion is for justice (Isa 61:8), and his throne is built on justice and righteousness (Ps 89:14). The psalmist has confidence that God *hates the lover of violence* (v. 5), whose recompense will be sure (v. 6). The *cup* (*lot*, v. 6 NIV; 75:8; Isa 51:17; Jer 25:15), or destiny, of the wicked burns like the fire of an erupting volcano, or the scorching and deadly wind off the desert *[Wicked; Wrath]*.

Much more comforting are the prospects for the upright (v. 7). They will behold the face of God (Pss 27:8-9; 42:2)! The usual belief was that to see God's face was to die (Exod 33:20; 34:29-35; 2 Cor 3:7-18). But God's countenance is made bearable to the creature, and the NT proclaims Jesus Christ as the "place" of God's presence. So Paul could write how "all of us, with unveiled faces, seeing the glory of the Lord, . . . are being transformed." Or again, "God . . . has shone in our hearts to give the light of the knowledge of the glory of God in the face of Jesus Christ" (2 Cor 3:18; 4:6).

THE TEXT IN THE BIBLICAL CONTEXT AND LIFE OF THE CHURCH

Deism, Theism, and Flight

Deism, from the Latin word for God, was an understanding about God that developed in the church. Deism spoke of God as Creator, but viewed the universe as operating without a further personal relationship with God. Psalm 11 reflects a theistic rather than deistic understanding of God, who has all-seeing eyes, a deeply personal interest in the life of creation, and an ongoing relationship with the created beings (Knight, 1:59-60).

Wherein lies our confidence? In the shaking of the foundations, when the support and institutions of society crumble, where is our refuge? The temptation of flight always beckons when difficult times come or difficult decisions loom. Refusal to face the facts, procrastination, frenzied activity, "getting religion," or "cursing God" may be ways of fleeing.

The desire to escape is a common temptation. But is there not another way? What do you do when you don't know what to do? Does the psalm not suggest that sometimes it may be best not to do anything? That is, don't flee from the spot or from the experience in which God has placed you. Placing trust in God may be the most significant action! Dare we believe that the foundations of life are safe in God's hands? How does that relate to facing a foe or to the loss of a job? How does it relate to any experience of loss or grief? All people need "a shelter in the time of storm" (Vernon J. Charlesworth, ca. 1880).

A Stance on Violence

The psalm portrays the LORD as hating *the lover of violence* (v. 5b; Hab 2:12, 17). On the contrary, the LORD loves righteous deeds (v. 7). At the beginning of the twenty-first century, the world is experiencing incredible acts of violence. We know about genocide, in which tyrant rulers seek to exterminate a whole population over such issues as land, religion, or race. Lawless bands terrorize innocent people by turning planes into missiles of death and cars into lethal weapons; they take hostages with the threat of beheading. Nations and governments retaliate with tons of bombs, tanks, and assault rifles. How God, who hates violence, must grieve!

Rather than retaliate, pitting violence against violence, this psalm suggests a different solution. It calls for neither flight nor fight. Rather than responding out of fear to violence, the psalmist trusts in God's judgment and vindication (v. 6; Rom 12:17-21). That sense of trust may offer the greatest hope for people living in violent times. Such trust does not necessarily shield people from loss, nor even from death. Yet faith can bloom in dispossession. Lawrence Wood states: "When you don't have anything else to hold on to, when you can no longer clutch lesser things, you hold on to your God, and your God holds on to you" (Wood, 2004:21). Such a stance of trust allows for deeds of justice and righteousness rather than perpetuating violence.

Psalm 12

Destructive Words and the Saving Word

PREVIEW

A piercing cry of *Help!* opens this community lament in face of the abuse of language that undermines community. The LORD's response comes in an oracle uttered by prophet or priest in the temple worship. The worshipping community responds that the LORD's promises (words) are true. Whatever the circumstance, God will protect the needy. Kraus suggests that the cultic prophet, as representative of the afflicted, may be the speaker for the whole psalm (Kraus, 1988:208).

Composition of this psalm may be preexilic, somewhat on the order of Isaiah 33:7-12 and other prophetic books (Hos 4:1-3; Mic 7:2-4; Hab 1:2-4). The title includes reference to *The Sheminith*, likely a musical notation (see Ps 6) *[Musical; Superscriptions]*.

OUTLINE

Cry for Help and Complaint About Destructive Speech, 12:1-4
Oracle of Salvation and Statement of Trust, 12:5-6
Petition for Protection from the Wicked, 12:7-8

Psalm 12

EXPLANATORY NOTES

Cry for Help and Complaint About Destructive Speech 12:1-4

Like a drowning man calling out to be saved, the psalmist introduces the problem (v. 1). He expresses despair over widespread spiritual and moral decay. In words reminiscent of Elijah's "I alone am left" when he fled to Horeb (1 Kings 19:10), the psalmist bemoans vanishing of the *godly* (*ḥāsîd*), those loyal to God (Ps 4:3).

The complaint focuses on the use of words (vv. 2-4). Language, a means of building community and sharing, here becomes a weapon. With striking description—*a lip of slipperiness/smoothnesses* (lit.) and *a double heart*—these verses speak of lying, flattery, hypocrisy, insincerity, boasting, and pretentiousness. They stress the poisonous effects of slander upon a community, climaxing with the arrogant abuse of the power of words (v. 4). The reference to the *poor* and *needy* (v. 5) suggests the temptation of those who wield power to think too highly of their mastery of language. Their propaganda is no less than blasphemy! Flattering, arrogant tongues are anathema to God (Prov 6:16-19; 10:31-32). The harsh prayer that God destroy the organs responsible for destructive acts (v. 3) appeals to the law of talion, of equivalent retribution (Ps 3:7) *[Imprecation]*.

Oracle of Salvation and Statement of Trust 12:5-6

The oracle spoken by prophet or priest in the temple, in response to the complaint, becomes the focal point of the psalm. The LORD hears the sighs and groans of the poor and the needy (Exod 2:23-25; 22:21-24; Isa 3:13-15). The LORD will arise! *"I will place them in the safety for which they long"* (v. 5). While there are other readings, *safety* (from Heb. *yāša'*, meaning "salvation") relates back to the cry *help* or "save" (also from *yāša'*, v. 1). Other examples of a prophetic oracle may be found in Psalms 60; 81; and 95 *[Oracle]*.

If the oracle has been offered as the word of the LORD in the temple, the following verses might be seen as the worshipping community's response to the saving word. God's *promises* (sayings, words) are *pure* (refined, sure, true; Isa 1:25). *Silver* was considered the purest of metals. *Seven times* suggests perfection. In contrast to the words of the arrogant, God's promises are precious and reliable.

Petition for Protection from the Wicked   12:7-8

The psalm ends with a petition for protection amid a generation of falsehood. Some translations of verse 7 read "protect them," "preserve them" (NASB, KJV), as referring to the *promises* of verse 6. NRSV and NIV reflect the view "You, O LORD, will protect us." It could also be translated as a prayer, "May you protect us," for the psalm ends with recognition that the danger still exists (v. 8).

With the ending reference to *humankind* (v. 8), the psalmist refers back to the complaint identified at the beginning (v. 1). However, the psalm by contrast also declares the power of the saving word over the destructive words.

THE TEXT IN THE BIBLICAL CONTEXT AND LIFE OF THE CHURCH

The Power of Words

The third and ninth commandments, "You shall not make wrongful use of the name of the LORD your God" and "You shall not bear false witness against your neighbor" (Exod 20:7, 16), testify to the sacred character of language. Swearing falsely by God's name or using language to deceive undercuts trust, and so also community. In some sense all crime denotes a deception.

Jesus' Sermon on the Mount reaffirms abhorrence of falsehood. Citing the old saying "You shall not swear falsely," Jesus said, "Do not swear at all. . . . Let your word be 'Yes, Yes' or 'No, No'" (Matt 5:33-37; James 5:12). Be a person of integrity, whose word bears truth at all times. God is always witness.

Origen, Tertullian, Chrysostom, and other early Christian writers rejected the oath. Only after Christianity became a state religion did the oath return to use among Christians. Of the Protestant reformers, the Anabaptists rejected the oath and opposed its use on the ground of obedience to Jesus. This led to the principle of affirming rather than swearing in court and legal documents.

However, speech is more than the sharing of ideas, impressions, and feelings. Words are not just symbols; they can set events into motion. Words have power to evoke feelings and actions. Language, necessary for communication and building community, can also become destructive and abuse power. Images of a Herod or a Hitler speaking come to mind. So also do images of contemporary politicians and preachers with a slippery tongue and double heart, who use words to manipulate rather than serve.

Over against such smooth and double talk, what words will stand? What words build community and enhance life? What is the saving word? What are the promises that are true? Psalm 12 proclaims the reliability of God's truth in grand antithesis to "the generation of the lie" (Buber: 12).

Psalm 13

How Long, O LORD?

PREVIEW

Following the general lament of Psalm 12, this individual lament voices the deeply personal cry of one on the verge of death. From the opening complaint growing out of despair, the psalm moves through intimate prayer (*my God*, v. 3) to a song of thanksgiving rooted in God's covenant love and salvation. Psalm 13 represents the classic lament form of complaint, petition, statement of confidence, and vow to praise.

The mood shifts from despair to trust and praise. The description of distress deals with the relationship to God, to the psalmist's own life, and to the enemy. The actors are you (God), I (the psalmist), and they (the enemy).

OUTLINE

Invocation and Complaint, 13:1-2
Petition and Motivation, 13:3-4
Statement of Trust and Vow of Praise, 13:5-6

EXPLANATORY NOTES

Invocation and Complaint   13:1-2

The complaint begins with the fourfold cry *How long, O LORD?* Distress is rooted in God's apparent absence (v. 1), the psalmist's own struggle with *pain* and *sorrow* (v. 2), and the reality of the *enemy*

(v. 2b). The question *"How long?"* is typical lament language expressing the human cry of impatience at divine delay (Pss 4:2; 6:3; 62:3; 90:13). Has the LORD forgotten the sufferer (9:12; 10:12; 42:9)? *Hide your face* is an idiom for God's withdrawal of favor (v. 1; 44:24; 88:14; Deut 32:20; Job 13:24). The fourfold repetition of *How long?* conveys exasperation and fear *["Lament"* in *Psalm Genres].*

Petition and Motivation   13:3-4

The petition repeats the sequence found in the complaint: the cry to God (v. 3a), the psalmist's experience of facing death (v. 3b), and a gloating enemy (v. 4). Motivation for God's action and intervention is found in the verbs *consider, answer,* and *give light* (v. 3), as well as the plea not to give the *enemy* reason for gloating (v. 4).

Who is the enemy? Is it death, as the specific reference to the *sleep of death* suggests (v. 3)? The words *enemy* and *foes* (vv. 2, 4) may be a personification of death as the Enemy. So also *Give light to my eyes* (v. 3), a metaphor for vitality and joy, may be more than a prayer for the renewal of faith. Since illness is often accompanied by dullness of eyes, the expression can also mean "Restore my health" or "Grant me immortality." The Hebrew term translated *shaken (fall,* NIV) is a strong word, used elsewhere of trembling, tumbling mountains (Ps 46:3; Isa 54:10). This word *'emmôṭ,* describing tottering foundations, may here be another expression for death.

It is also possible that *my enemy* and *my foes* (vv. 2, 4) may be unidentified people who mockingly see in the psalmist's pain and suffering the sign that he has been abandoned by God (Job 30:9-23) *[Enemies].* The desperate cry is for healing and hope so that gladness may once more be experienced. Note how in Psalm 13 there is no call for God to pour out his anger upon these enemies, as in Psalms 7:9 and 10:15.

Statement of Trust and Vow of Praise   13:5-6

A major mood shift occurs as the psalm moves from anguished complaint (vv. 1-2) and anxious prayer (vv. 3-4) to calm trust (vv. 5-6). What happened between verses 4 and 5? Did someone with authority speak the salvation oracle, the "Fear not" (Isa 43:1)? *[Oracle].* Or does the process of complaint and petition lead the psalmist to a deeper faith and hope? Or might the psalm be composed in retrospect after the trouble passed? *But I* (v. 5) is an emphatic expression. The psalmist trusts in God's *steadfast love* (ḥesed), and will rejoice in God's *salvation* (yāšaʻ). This word, which expresses "deliverance," is translated "help" and "safety" (Ps 12:1, 5) and is also represented in the names Joshua and Jesus (Matt 1:21).

The psalm ends with the promise of praise because of God's beneficence (v. 6). Even in distress and in the face of death, the psalmist can declare *the LORD . . . has been good to me* (NIV). Possibly the situation has not changed, but the petitioner has. Through a glimpse of the God of compassion and justice, trust awakens new hope and a future.

THE TEXT IN THE BIBLICAL CONTEXT AND LIFE OF THE CHURCH

Lament and the Church's Prayer Language

Psalm 13 is often used to illustrate the classic lament form of complaint, petition, statement of confidence, and praise. This form is reiterated in Psalm 22, which begins with the desperate cry, *My God, my God, why have you forsaken me?* but ends in resounding praise (22:21b-31). It is also found in Jeremiah 20:7-13, one of the most piercing laments; despite its shrillness, it also ends with a reference to praise. More than one-third of the psalms are laments, and of these, all but one (Ps 88) include a note about praise.

Brueggemann refers to the lament as "Israel's characteristic way of opening a new way of daring protest" (1989:52-53). Lament is speech about God's failure and neglect in the relationship. The speech erupts in indignation and urgency. It is an act of insistence and of hope. The lament is uttered in trust that God is still listening and can reshape the relationship and the community.

This brief psalm has enriched the church's prayer language through the centuries. Christians of the East and of the West have used Psalm 13 at the hour of Compline, just before retiring for the night. As one is about to fall asleep, this psalm beseeches God that it will not be a sleep unto death (Reardon: 23). Martin Luther wrote of Psalm 13: "Hope itself despairs and despair never the less begins to hope." John Calvin selected it among the eighteen psalms set to music, published in 1539 for use in public worship. Charles Wesley's hymn, "Father, I stretch my hands to thee" (1741), expresses the psalm's desperation and confident trust. George Matheson's hymn, written as he faced a personal crisis, described the tension: "O Joy that seekest me through pain. . . . I trace the rainbow through the rain" (1882). In the midst of storm, Psalm 13 voices a reassuring presence.

Living with Psalm 13

This psalm utters the eternal human cry. People cry out in the face of extreme trouble, sickness, and death. Death need not be the only interpretation of the psalmist's situation. Verse 3 can also be read metaphorically, in the sense of "lest I be wiped out," in a situation such as bankruptcy or failure. People cry out from the depths of depression. How helpless those feel who go over thoughts again and again, only to see no good resolution of a bad situation. What can one learn from this brief prayer?

1. Intimacy with God is possible even when God appears silent and life's experiences suggest God's absence. Does God ever really forget? "My God" expresses the fullest possibilities for life.

2. In prayer, the faithful dare to speak to God in complaint and praise, of the experience of forsakenness and of grace, of abandonment and salvation (Mays, 1980:281). The agony and the ecstasy belong together. We are dying persons who cannot find God, but persons also with a salvation history and life with God in Christ (2 Cor 4:11-12).

3. Psalm prayer always has a communal aspect. One is never alone with God; others are there too. Living with God cannot be separated from living with others. The two belong together.

4. Grace is greater than "the enemy." Even though life may be filled with pain and sorrow, and death draws near, can we sense the bounty of the given and say, "God has been good to me!"?

Psalm 14

Prayer for Deliverance in a Corrupt Age

PREVIEW

A lament, Psalm 14 contains strong prophetic and wisdom themes. It opens with despair over the depravity of a generation that acts as though God is not around. The psalm moves to the reckoning that will come because God is on the side of the righteous and the poor. It ends in trust, with hope of deliverance and restoration.

The psalm reveals a powerful prophetic message against the ruling class in a land that has become divided, where the high lifestyle of oppressors is attained at the expense of the oppressed. Similar emphasis on God as judge may be observed in Psalms 10; 12; 75; and Habakkuk 1.

This psalm appears also as Psalm 53, where the name of God is consistently the broader term *God* (*'ĕlōhîm*), while here the special Israelite name *LORD* (*Yahweh*) is used four times *[Names of God]*. The major variant reading is Psalm 14:5, 6 and Psalm 53:5. These modifications may reflect Northern (Ps 53) and Southern (Ps 14) traditions (Holladay: 70).

OUTLINE

Lament About the Depravity of the Wicked, 14:1-3
Rebuke of the Wicked, 14:4-6
Prayer for Deliverance of God's People, 14:7

EXPLANATORY NOTES

Lament About the Depravity of the Wicked 14:1-3

This Psalm reflects on *the fool* (*nābāl*) by describing those who think and act as though *"There is no God"* (v. 1; Ps 10:4, 11). In Proverbs, the fool is often contrasted with the wise person (3:35; 10:1; 13:20). Here the concern is not so much the person who claims God does not exist, as the one who lives as though God is not here and that God does not matter. *Fool* designates a person who decides and acts on the basis of wrong assumptions, as in the story of Nabal in 1 Samuel 25. How mistaken the assumption that life is without norms (v. 2)! The LORD does see (Pss 33:13; 53:2; 80:14; 102:19). The rampant disregard for God leads the psalmist to throw up his hands in despair: *There is no one who does good, no, not one!* Note the repetition of the sharp phrase, *There is no one* (vv. 1, 3). NEB graphically translates, "All are rotten to the core" (v. 3).

Rebuke of the Wicked 14:4-6

Who are the *evildoers who eat up my people,* exploit others, and fail to acknowledge God (v. 4)? The reference may be to Jewish priests who took the sacrificial offerings but were not godly persons, an example of which would be Eli's sons (1 Sam 2:12-17). Or they may have been Jewish nobles who exploited people, or even foreign oppressors. "People-eating people" describes them! *[Wicked]*. It is also possible that the *evildoers* (*pō'ălê 'āwen*) made use of magic acts, the enemy swallowing a piece of bread on which was written the name of the one to be harassed (Ps 10:7-9; Kraus, 1986:135).

However, as the transitional *There* (v. 5) implies, the reckoning will come. On whose side is God? On the side of the *righteous* and the *poor,* of course! God is not a disinterested spectator. That provides reason for great terror (lit., "fearful fear") as human sin is revealed and confounded by God. Such fools, lacking a social conscience, will be terror-stricken, while God's presence will be with the righteous as their refuge (v. 6; 11:1; 46:1; 61:3).

Prayer for Deliverance of God's People 14:7

Yet God's judgment is not the last word. God's grace will be seen as the fortunes of his people are restored (v. 7). After the captivity of the exile, a remnant experienced new freedom in their return home. The expression *restored the fortunes* (*šûb šĕbût,* v. 7; 126:1) has been translated *bring back the captivity* (KJV), as though the nominal is derived from šābāh and means "captivity." Today the expression is regarded as cognate, literally, "turn the turning," with the nominal deriving from šûb (turn). The expression was used to describe restoration to an earlier condition, as in rebuilding a home following a fire. With its meaning "bring about a restoration," it became important in the prophetic promises for a reversal of fortunes, not only for Israel, but also for other nations (e.g., Elam, Jer 49:39). In Jeremiah's "book of comfort," the expression signifies a spiritual return of a people to God, a subtheme of which is the return from captivity (30:3). The phrase can also refer to any reversal of fortune, any rehabilitation of the people from oppressive circumstances (Davidson, 1998:55). Both names *Jacob* and *Israel* are probably used here to indicate the whole people of God.

This psalm, which begins with reflection on *the fool*, provides a portrait of *the righteous*. The righteous person will *seek after God* (v. 2), *do good* (vv. 1, 3), *have knowledge* (v. 4), and *call upon the LORD* (v. 4). The ancient biblical wisdom summed it up: "The fear of the LORD is the beginning of wisdom, and the knowledge of the Holy One is insight" (Prov 9:10).

THE TEXT IN THE BIBLICAL CONTEXT AND LIFE OF THE CHURCH

A Psalm with a Prophetic Nuance

As a prophetic psalm, it can be read alongside OT prophecies of Isaiah 59:4; Jeremiah 5:1-13; and Micah 7:2-3. In prophetic literature, the "fool" is described as someone who is godless, who ignores or oppresses the poor and needy, and who amasses wealth unjustly (Isa 32:6; Jer 17:11). Denial of God's authority and exploitation of the defenseless go hand in hand. Jesus also declares God to be judge in human life and to have special interest for the weak and the helpless, as does his son of man/king in the parable of Matthew 25:31-46.

Paul takes up the theme of this psalm in writing to the Roman world of the first century. In the letter to the Romans, he describes how "claiming to be wise, they became fools" when they "exchanged the truth about God for a lie and worshiped the creature rather than the Creator" (Rom 1:22, 25). In his argument demonstrating that all people are under the power of sin, Paul quotes Psalm 14:1-3 in Romans 3:10-13 along with a series of passages from other psalms (5:9; 10:7; 36:1; 140:3). All of these citations are descriptions of the wicked in psalms of lament, though Paul uses the phrases to describe all people under the power of sin.

Psalm 14

Practical Atheism

Few people openly declare themselves atheists. "Practical atheism," in the sense of people living as though God does not exist, is another matter. People live as though God does not exist or care—cheating and exploiting others, violating the rights and personality of others. Can people really have whatever they want if they can get it, and get away with it?

Menno Simons, writing on "True Christian Faith" (ca. AD 1541), described the practical denial of God by religious and political leaders of his day:

> Open idolatry, human commandments, superstitions, and ugly lies are their greatest comfort and truest worship. Their belly is their God; they love the world more than they do heaven. All their delight is in raking and scraping, in pride and pomp, gold and silver, money and goods. Their buying and selling take place in cheating and tricking. Drinking, gambling, cursing, swearing, hatred, strife, and fighting are the order of the day. They follow the flesh and its lusts. They defame and seek their neighbor's hurt, dishonor, disgrace, and shame. In short, with the fool they say in their hearts, "There is no God." Ps 14:1. (Menno: 340)

Wherein lies the wisdom that will help people from falling into the trap of practical atheism? Psalm 14 was written to encourage the lowly righteous to take refuge in God (vv. 5-6). The psalm invites people of faith to seek God, call on God's name, and act in ways that will be helpful. It encourages people to trust in the God who is with the *company of the righteous* (v. 5) and so work toward healing the rift between "those who do violence and those to whom violence is done" (Buber: 19).

Psalm 15

Admission to the Temple

PREVIEW

This liturgy for admission to the temple worship had a teaching purpose. As the worshippers approached the temple gate, they asked the requirements for admission. The priests would then respond with the basics of faith, which the people might repeat. Note the similarity to Psalm 24.

The answer of Psalm 15 lists ten qualifications of the righteous person. However, instead of stressing religious rituals, the answer emphasizes social and moral terms. To be acceptable, ceremonies of worship must come from lives that are ethically akin to God. This kinship to God is demonstrated in one's treatment of others.

OUTLINE

The Question About Admission to Worship, 15:1
The Answer, 15:2-5b
The Declaration, 15:5c

EXPLANATORY NOTES

The Question About Admission to Worship   15:1

In the words *abide* and *dwell,* the opening question presents the worshipper as eager guest and as one "coming home." *Tent* is an important symbol of God's immanent presence. When worship was localized at the temple in Jerusalem, the *tent* language reminded the people how God had been with them in the days of their early wanderings, as well as their later scattering (2 Sam 7:6; Pss 27:5; 61:4; 78:60). Zion is the LORD's holy mountain, the place of the presence (2:6; 3:4; 43:3; 48:1; 87:1; 99:9). The privilege to enter must be granted. More than worship is implied here. Who really belongs to the *company of the righteous* (14:5)? Who are God's people?

The Answer   15:2-5b

The answer is given in a series of positive and negative statements. The righteous person is described positively as one who walks blamelessly, does right, speaks truth, despises the wicked, honors the God-fearing, and keeps his oath (vv. 2, 4). The negative statements include refraining from slander, evil, reproach, exacting interest, and bribery (vv. 3, 5). In the context of worshippers entering the temple, this focus on moral requirements rather than religious ritual is highly significant; it echoes the call "You shall be holy" (Lev 19:2). The basis for integrity before God lies in relationship to others. Obedience matters more than sacrifices. Community life rests on truth and justice in relationship to others.

The center of human life is the *heart* (v. 2). The Hebrew word translated *slander* means "to foot it," the idea of "tripping up" with the tongue (v. 3). Since an evil person cannot be a guest in God's tent, so the hospitality of the godly person does not extend to the *wicked* (v. 4). *Stand by their oath* describes those who do not misuse the name of God, but keep their oath even if it hurts them (v. 4). The prohibition of *interest* (usury, NIV, KJV) refers to charitable loans made for relief of distress rather than business-type loans of a later commercial age (v. 5; Exod 22:25; Lev 25:35-37; Deut 23:20; Ezek 18:8). The Hebrew word for "taking interest" is the word for "biting." Interest rates may have been as high as $33^1/_3$ to 50 percent (Barrois, *IDB*, 1:809). In the family, one carried the poor along rather than plunging them further into debt.

The Declaration   15:5c

Righteous worshippers are rewarded by security in God (v. 5c). *Moved* (shaken, NIV) is a figure for misfortune. Even when the cosmos totters, Zion remains unshaken and the righteous can find sanctuary from the collapsing world (Pss 16:8; 46:5; 62:2, 6). Does the psalm suggest that people can earn their way into God's good grace and everything will be all right? Or are the qualities described those that God creates rather than finds in people? Trust that security is God-given underlies the final declaration. Romans 8 declares: "If God is for us, who is against us? . . . [Nothing] will be able to separate us from the love of God in Christ" (8:31-39).

THE TEXT IN THE BIBLICAL CONTEXT AND LIFE OF THE CHURCH

Worship and Morality

Psalm 15 defines genuine religion in terms of moral behavior rather than ritual action. Thus, the liturgy relates to the prophetic demands as well (Isa 1:12-17; 33:13-16; Jer 7:1-15; Amos 5:21-24; Mic 6:6-8). The worship of God is unacceptable unless it goes hand in hand with moral integrity and responsible living.

The NT follows up this psalm in its focus on moral integrity. In the Sermon on the Mount, Jesus speaks of how conduct toward others and worship of God are integrally related (Matt 5–7). If people come to worship but a barrier exists, "leave your gift there before the altar and go; first be reconciled to your brother or sister, and then come and offer your gift" (Matt 5:24). Was Jesus saying that one cannot really come to God unless one comes together with one's brother or sister? Jesus again affirms the linkage of God and neighbor when Jesus sums up all the commandments: "You shall love the Lord your God. . . . You shall love your neighbor as yourself" (22:34-40).

The one injunction that seems contradictory in this psalm is that of despising *the wicked* (v. 4). How does love for God and love for neighbor include rather than exclude? The church, in its use of the ban, or excommunication, desired to take church discipline seriously (Matt 18:15-17). While the use of the ban sought to (1) preserve the purity of the church, and (2) cause the sinner to examine oneself and reform, it often did not work that way. How God's people best express love that confronts, a tough love that redeems, needs to be worked out in each generation. Jesus did not exclude Judas.

Preparation for Worship

How is God to be approached? What can people do to prepare for worship of the holy God? When we understand worship as primarily offering praise to God, the concern about sin or the character of the worshipper is often muted. Psalm 15 suggests that worship should lead people to self-examination.

What kind of preparation will be most helpful? Some churches give opportunity to make confession before a representative of God, and to hear the word of forgiveness spoken, to open the way for the believer to receive God's blessings. Some include (or once did) a time of preparation as part of the communion service, during which participants are invited to examine themselves, and then and there, right wrongs against others (1 Cor 11:27-32). In preparation for worship, worshippers would do well to take inventory: what might we need to clear up regarding words spoken, lifestyle, relationship to others, or misuse of money as citizens of the kingdom?

Psalm 16

The LORD, a Goodly Heritage

PREVIEW

This song of trust begins with a prayer for safety, as in the laments. However, a mood of settled calm prevails, as joyous confidence in God becomes the source of life's highest joys. The psalm affirms acceptance of being chosen. It concludes with an enumeration of the blessings of faith in God, such as guidance, stability, and facing life and death in hope.

At numerous points an uncertain Hebrew text does not obscure the main thrust of the psalm: "The LORD is my life!" The psalmist may have been facing death, though the calm tone does not give indication of immediate crisis. Most commentators assign the psalm to the early postexilic period (500-450 BC) on the basis of language and the wisdom style and point of view, but we cannot rule out a preexilic time (Kraus, 1988:235). At issue, in part, is whether the attribution to David might have been added at a later time.

Mitkam in the title appears also in headings to Psalms 56–60, which are characterized by pithy sayings. It could also refer to an inscription on a stone slab; the meaning is unclear *[Musical; Superscriptions]*.

Psalm 16

OUTLINE

Confession of Faith: The Chosen Loyalty, 16:1-6
Thanksgiving: Blessings of the Goodly Heritage, 16:7-11

EXPLANATORY NOTES

Confession of Faith: The Chosen Loyalty 16:1-6

The prayer begins with petition for the protection of God, using the *In you I take refuge* formula (v. 1; Pss 7:1; 31:1; 71:1). In words of quiet confidence, the psalm states trust in the LORD as the totality of life. We can view this psalm as a powerful witness to faith in God. Noting uncertainty about the meaning of the Hebrew text, NRSV and NIV reflect the major interpretation that the *holy ones* (*saints*) and *the noble* (*glorious ones*) refer to orthodox believers with whom the one praying wishes to be associated (v. 3). The psalmist is choosing the LORD and rejecting other gods.

The references to *chosen portion, cup, lot,* and *boundary lines* (vv. 5-6) use phrases that echo those about Levitical priests (Deut 10:8-9), who possessed no property (Josh 13:14-33; 18:2-7). The LORD challenged the Israelites to consider property as loaned to them from God in order that all might share in the produce and security (Lev 25). This psalm's focus on acceptance of that heritage may suggest more than property for a livelihood. A *goodly heritage* moves beyond land, place, and temple to grace and the presence of God. The foundation of faithful optimism is a life lived in communion with God.

Thanksgiving: Blessings of the Goodly Heritage 16:7-11

The second part of the psalm begins with a vow to *bless the LORD*, to acknowledge publicly the blessings of the goodly heritage (v. 7; Ps 103:1-2). What are the blessings of faith in God? They include counsel and instruction (v. 7) and stability of life, prompting the psalmist to a single-minded loyalty (v. 8). To *keep the LORD always before me* may refer to keeping the first commandment: "You shall have no other gods before me" (Exod 20:3; Deut 5:7). The psalmist links *heart, soul* (*tongue*, NIV; *glory*, NASB, KJV), and *body* as the response of his whole being to God, the source of joy and security (v. 9).

The two lines in verse 10 should be read as parallels, *Pit* as synonym for *Sheol*, meaning death *[Sheol]*. The KJV reading of *soul in hell, . . . Holy One to see corruption* is clearly influenced by the

LXX, which translated *Pit* as *decay*. The psalmist expresses hope of preservation from a premature death, and a hope beyond (vv. 10-11). Yet Anderson aptly observes that the significant factor for the psalmist "may not be the contrast between life and death, but rather between life *with* God and life *without* him" (A. Anderson, 1:146). The psalmist contrasts *Sheol,* the place of the nonliving, with *the path of life,* where the psalmist could experience the divine presence. This reference to temple (*path of life, in your presence,* v. 11) links Psalm 16 with the previous and following psalms.

THE TEXT IN THE BIBLICAL CONTEXT AND LIFE OF THE CHURCH

Life After Death

Psalm 16 offers the view that God does not abandon human life at the grave (vv. 9-11). Here, as in a few other places in the OT, there is the prospect of communion with God beyond death (Job 19:25-26; Pss 17:15; 49:15; 139:8; Isa 26:19; Dan 12:2).

Peter quoted Psalm 16:8-11 from the LXX at Pentecost (Acts 2:25-33), and Paul cited Psalm 16:10 in his sermon at Antioch of Pisidia (13:33-35). In each case they apply the passage to Jesus and speak of the resurrection of Jesus as conquering death. In their use of these verses to demonstrate that David prophesied the resurrection of Jesus from the dead, the meaning of the psalm has been transformed. The power of the resurrection event provides God's people with a clearer hope.

How shall we view death? Even the psalmist could point toward God's liberating power beyond death. In light of the resurrection of Jesus, people of faith can live and die in the confidence that death has been overcome by God and is no longer the enemy to be feared (Rom 8:35-39; 1 Cor 15:54-55).

Walking the Path of Life in the Presence of God

The path of life (v. 11) occurs elsewhere only in Proverbs (2:19; 5:6; 10:17; 12:28; 15:24) as the opposite of the path to Sheol. In the early Christian movement, believers were identified as people of "the Way" (Acts 9:2; 19:9, 23; 22:4; 24:22). They were invited to be baptized into Christ (and into his death) so they might be raised up to "walk in newness of life" (Rom 6:4).

In the sixteenth-century Reformation, the defining word of the Anabaptists was not "faith," as with the other reformers, but "following Christ" (*Nachfolge Christi*). Baptism was to be the covenant "of a good conscience toward God" (1 Pet 3:21 NIV), the "pledge" of a complete commitment to obey Christ. The Anabaptists had faith, indeed, but they emphasized that faith must produce a certain kind of life.

This psalm rings with the joy of loyalty to the LORD as over against lesser loyalties. Every believer can pray the psalm, for one's relationship to God consists of ongoing conversation. In its function, Gerstenberger (92) compares the psalm with the Apostles' Creed in Christian worship. Charles Wesley's hymn "Forth in thy name" (1749) draws on the psalm's focus on single-minded loyalty in response to the given, and the joy of walking in communion with God:

> Thee may I set at my right hand,
> Whose eyes my inmost substance see,
> And labor on at thy command,
> And offer all my works to thee.

Finally, the psalm touches life as reminder of the *goodly heritage* (v. 6). Anniversaries (birthday, wedding, founding of an institution) become occasions to reflect from where people have come and how gift surrounds their lives. In retrospect, the given often looms larger than what is seen in the present moment. Acknowledging that life is by God's grace can aid people to move into the future. What are the *pleasant places* of heritage in terms of family, church, community, faith, and the other gifts of God?

Psalm 17

Plea of the Innocent to the Savior of Fugitives

PREVIEW

This individual lament is linked to Psalm 16 by identical Hebrew words, use of the divine name *'ēl* (16:1; 17:6), the plea *protect me, guard me* (16:1; 17:8), and similar religious ideas and actions. In Psalm 17 the petitioner looks for protection (asylum) and hopes to *behold your face* and *be satisfied, beholding your likeness* (v. 15), expressions that elsewhere mean visiting the temple (11:7; 27:4). The psalm opens as a declaration of innocence, moves to a desperate plea for protection that explodes into a prayer for vengeance, and ends with assurance of vindication.

The setting may have been the temple. The Pentateuch describes the kind of legal cases taken to the sanctuary for the verdict of God (Deut 17:8-11). The accused might spend the night in the temple (vv. 3, 15) and receive the answer communicated to him by an oracle. Or the psalmist may be asking for rescue, rather than a legal decision.

The title, *A Prayer (of David)*, appears also as title for Psalms 86, 90 (of Moses), 102 (of one afflicted), and 142. Traditionally, the psalm has been associated with the period in the life of David when he was fleeing from Saul (1 Sam 23) *[Superscriptions]*.

Psalm 17

OUTLINE

Petition for a Fair Hearing and Declaration of Innocence, 17:1-5
Petition for Refuge from the Wicked, 17:6-12
Imprecatory Prayer for God's Judgment upon the Enemies, 17:13-14
Expression of Confident Hope, 17:15

EXPLANATORY NOTES

Petition for a Fair Hearing and Declaration of Innocence   17:1-5

The Hebrew word *ṣedeq,* translated *just cause* (*righteous plea,* NIV) and *righteousness* (vv. 1, 15), binds the psalm together [*Righteous*]. The appeal (v. 2), the declaration of innocence (vv. 3-5), and the subsequent prayer of imprecation also assert God's cause at stake. The focus on lips, mouth, and words (vv. 1, 3, 6, 10) indicate that the accusation has to do with integrity of speech. The psalmist appeals on the grounds of uprightness of heart, speech, and actions.

In the protestation of innocence, a formulaic self-defense of one who has been falsely accused (vv. 3-5; Pss 26:4-5; 101:3-4), the psalmist acknowledges that the LORD alone knows and probes the depth of the heart (7:9; 26:2). He declares his integrity in that he has walked firmly in the way of the LORD (v. 5; 1:6; Prov 4:11, 26; 5:21).

Petition for Refuge from the Wicked   17:6-12

After declaring his innocence, the psalmist appeals in confidence to the God who does wonders (vv. 6-7; Ps 9:1) and whose nature is *steadfast love* (*ḥesed*) [*Steadfast*]. The psalmist has been loyal and now expects God, who is savior of those who seek refuge, to act loyally in return. This is the God whose *right hand* is ready to go into action against those who oppose his purposes (v. 7).

The striking metaphors at the center of the psalm, *the apple of the eye* and *the shadow of your wings* (v. 8), are reminiscent of Deuteronomy 32:10-11. There these terms describe God's people in the exodus, protected by the tender care of God. The reference is to the pupil, the most precious part of the eye (Prov 7:2), and to wings as a mother bird's care and protection, often used to describe safety in the temple (Pss 36:7; 57:1; 61:4; 63:7; 91:4).

The appeal for help identifies the psalmist as a fugitive (vv. 6-7, 10-12). The adversary is described as a wild, ravenous lion, ready to pounce upon its prey (vv. 9-12; 7:2; 10:8-9; 22:13, 21). The enemies are arrogant and without pity. Their feet march in violence, unlike the psalmist's feet that hold fast to God's path (v. 5) *[Enemies]*.

Imprecatory Prayer for God's Judgment upon the Enemies 17:13-14

Faced with such encircling hatred, the psalmist pleads with the LORD as divine warrior to redress the situation. *Rise up, confront, overthrow, deliver* are words of battle and rescue (v. 13; 3:7; 9:19-20). Thus, the psalm bursts forth into imprecation with the prayer that the LORD halt the wicked in their tracks (v. 13) and heap on them the very things they love (v. 14)! They are *mortals* of *this world*; give them their fill of it (Kidner, 1973:89)! The NRSV, RSV, JB, NEB, and others translate this verse as a blessing formula employed as a curse, suggesting that the enemies and their progeny will get their punishment (2 Kings 9:26; Ps 37:38). However, the text is uncertain and more positive translations are also possible. In NRSV, *what you have stored up for them* (v. 14b) could also refer to the people of God and God's abundant provision for those who truly acknowledge God (Davidson, 1998:63; Clifford, 2002:103). So NIV translates: *You still the hunger of those you cherish, . . . and they store up wealth for their children*. In either case the psalmist desires God's universe to be set free from the ravages of sinners and entrusts the vengeance he desires completely into the hands of God *[Imprecation]*.

Expression of Confident Hope 17:15

The psalm ends on triumphant confidence that the psalmist's *just cause* will be vindicated (v. 1). The emphatic opening, *As for me* (*But I*, v. 15, cf. NEB), indicates contrast (Mic 3:8). The enemy may have everything— but God! In contrast, the psalmist will stake hope and confidence in beholding God's *face* and *likeness*! There is safety from the enemy in the presence (face) of God, a reference to the temple. To *behold your face* is the epitome of the joy of worship. Seeing God is the anticipated outcome of seeking God's face (2 Chron 7:14; Pss 24:6; 27:8; Hos 5:15).

What does *awake* (v. 15) mean? Is this simply a prayer for the preservation of life? Is it an allusion to the encounter with God in the morning temple worship (Weiser: 182)? Or is this a reference to the final judgment and life after death? Although the psalm may end with a primary focus on vindication of the accused one and how dawn brings a new vision of God's presence, these psalms also point (at least from the post-Easter perspective) to the dawn of resurrection (Pss 11:7; 16:10; 49:14-15).

THE TEXT IN THE BIBLICAL CONTEXT AND LIFE OF THE CHURCH

The Cry for Vindication

This prayer shows how readily the cry of the innocent moves toward imprecation. The cry for vengeance is born of suffering. To suffer unjustly seems not only unfair, but also an affront to God's justice. Persons who are cornered may cry out in rage. They appeal to the God of justice to act justly *[Imprecation]*.

However, the Bible also provides an alternative to vengeance: Jesus, the innocent one, in the suffering of the cross could pray, "Father, forgive them; for they do not know what they are doing" (Luke 23:34). Stephen, the first Christian martyr, prayed on behalf of his tormentors: "Lord, do not hold this sin against them" (Acts 7:60).

Martyrs Mirror tells the story of Dirk Willems, an Anabaptist believer apprehended at Asperen, Holland, in 1569 by the papal authorities. As he fled on foot across the ice, his captor broke through and was in danger of drowning. Willems, who had already crossed safely, turned back and pulled his captor to safety. Then he was seized by the one whom he had saved and condemned to death by fire (Braght: 741).

Jesus said: "Love your enemies and pray for those who persecute you" (Matt 5:44). Must not the prayer for vindication also convey the understanding that vengeance is God's alone to carry out (Rom 12:19-21)?

Living in Confident Hope

Psalm 17 moves from a cry of distress to confident hope. What does it mean to live in confident hope? How does the place of worship provide security? What difference does the hope of resurrection make for understanding God and for how we live? How does the dawn of a new day provide new vision of God's presence?

Building on covenantal friendship, the psalmist does not hesitate to bring the most urgent need to God's attention (Ps 17:7). The psalm's central verse affirms that God's people are as precious to the LORD as the pupil of one's eye, and God cares for his people as a mother bird cares for her young (v. 8; Limburg, 2000:52-53). These texts hint at God's marvelous grace and power to deliver in the end time. The redeemed servants of God will finally see the face of God in a fulfillment that goes beyond all promises (Rev 22:4, quoting Ps 17:15). In the meantime, persons of faith can arise each day singing with Thomas O. Chisholm 1923):

Morning by morning new mercies I see.
All I have needed thy hand hath provided.
Great is thy faithfulness! Lord unto me!

Psalm 18

A King's Thanksgiving Hymn for Deliverance and Victory

PREVIEW

Psalm 18 is a testimony by the anointed king that the LORD has kept his promise in a time of direct need. The themes include deliverance from death by the LORD, who is mighty in power yet tender in personal concern. Righteousness and loyalty are at the heart of God's covenant. God is the source of the king's victory and dominion that extends beyond human expectation. The psalm ends with a hymn of thanksgiving for the saving intervention of the living LORD.

This royal psalm of thanksgiving appears also in 2 Samuel 22, where with only slight changes it is inserted into the prose account following David's victories over the Philistines. In its original form, the psalm may be from David, as the lengthy heading suggests [Superscriptions]. Features of early Israelite poetry—such as use of the imperfect form of the verb, the association with Canaanite language (vv. 7-15), and description of warfare before the chariot was common in that area—indicate an early date.

Later Davidic kings probably used it in public worship to celebrate their victories. The reign of Hezekiah (715–687 BC) may have been such a time. Not only is there similarity in language and ideas with Deuteronomy (vv. 20-30); the poem could also be an appropriate expression at the time of the miraculous defeat of the Assyrians outside Jerusalem (2 Kings 18–20; Isa 36–39). Probably a series of providential saving deeds lies behind this praise hymn, not just a single victory.

The language shifts from song to narrative to song. However, it is still the language of poetry. The psalm may be not so much an account of certain historical events or a description of a natural phenomenon as a collage depicting the way people experience God on the battlefield or in the temple of worship *[Hebrew Poetry]*. While the king might sing such a song of thanksgiving, the final section (vv. 46-50) could be the congregation's response. Later, the entire congregation would use the psalm.

OUTLINE

Introductory Hymn of Praise, 18:1-3
Account of Peril and Salvation, 18:4-19
    18:4-6   Metaphors of Deliverance
    18:7-15   Theophany
    18:16-19   Report of Salvation
Confession of Praise, 18:20-30
    18:20-24   Righteousness Rewarded
    18:25-30   God's Covenant Love
Thanksgiving to God as Source of the King's Victory, 18:31-45
Doxology, 18:46-50

EXPLANATORY NOTES

Introductory Hymn of Praise   18:1-3

An intimate word, *I love you*, opens the hymn (though this v. 1 is missing in 2 Sam 22). The word translated *love* (*rāḥam*) is related to a Hebrew word for "womb" (Isa 46:3) and suggests warmth and compassion. A series of descriptive names for God follows: *strength, rock, fortress, deliverer, refuge, shield, horn of salvation* (1 Kings 1:50), and *stronghold* (vv. 1-2). All these titles portray God's protective power. Each is used with the pronoun *my*, signaling the close relationship between the psalmist and the LORD. The cry to the LORD introduces the psalm's main theme, praise of God who saves the king from his enemies (v. 3).

Account of Peril and Salvation   18:4-19

The psalm portrays enemies in cosmic terms (vv. 4-5). It describes the peril, death, with images of terror, as ropes that drag one down to the underworld, and deep currents at the bottom of the sea flowing into the ocean of chaos below the pit of Sheol. We could also read the introduction as rescue from his enemies, meaning "the Foe," death personified, as do also references to *mighty waters* and *day of my calamity* (vv. 16, 18) *[Sheol]*.

God's answer to the cry of distress (v. 6), in language similar to Canaanite accounts of the storm god, portrays power as of a mighty thunderstorm (see also Ps 29). The theophany, portraying God's coming down from heaven (v. 9) to assert sovereignty in the world, opens and closes by describing the cosmic effects of God's coming (vv. 7, 15). *Cherub* refers to one of the bearers of God's throne (v. 10; Exod 25:18-20) and envisioned creatures who assisted divine mobility (Ezek 10:1-5). God is angry because the assault on his anointed is a revolt against his rule (vv. 7, 15). To the human mind, this poetic picture of God may also allude to God's deliverance of the people crossing the sea in the exodus (v. 15).

A theophany seeks to witness to, yet keep wrapped in mystery, the awesome glory and power of God (Judg 5:4-5; Pss 68:7-8, 33; 97:2-5; 114; Isa 63:1-6; Hab 3:3-15). In the sanctuary a theophany assures the praying individual that the LORD is present and has the power to save *[Theophany]*.

However, the God who rides the storm stretches out the hand to raise the sinking one. So deliverance is described as *He reached down, . . . took me, . . . drew me, . . . delivered me*, and *brought me* to a place of safety (vv. 16-19)! From a tight spot, the petitioner has now, by God's help, been given a *broad place* (Pss 4:1; 31:8; 118:5). The reason? *Because he delighted in me* (v. 19). Can we read this as an expression of the LORD's interest in the person, in contrast to the impersonal Baal gods?

Confession of Praise   18:20-30

The psalmist speaks of his obedience to the divine will in terms of *righteousness . . . rewarded* (vv. 20, 24). He speaks of his relationship with God in terms of loyalty (v. 21), obedience to God's laws (v. 22), and singleness of purpose as he declares his innocence (v. 23; 7:3-5; 101; 139:19-22). While this section may sound boastful, it asserts trust in God's faithfulness as expressed in the torah liturgy of Psalm 15.

This assertion is followed with the word ḥesed (v. 25), here translated *show yourself loyal,* to describe a fair and powerful God who assists the faithful (vv. 25-30). The *humble* (poor) are those who appeal to the LORD for mercy and for help in obtaining justice (v. 27;

9:18; 10:2, 8-11; 35:10; 74:19). There may also be a word here to the king about limits to power and the need to identify with the righteous and humble in Israel. Persons who humbly submit will find God to be their helper; those who arrogantly exalt themselves will be brought low (Weiser: 194).

The loyal God lights *my lamp* (v. 28). In that God-given vitality, the king can *crush a troop* or scale the wall of a hostile city (v. 29). With God as enabler, he can do the unthinkable. The concluding assertion states the theme of the whole psalm: *This God . . . is perfect* (v. 30, *tāmîm*, "whole, integral"). God is totally reliable.

Thanksgiving to God as Source of the King's Victory 18:31-45

There follows the description of how God has equipped the king for battle and brings triumph over the foes. *God* is the subject of the whole section. God as the king's *help* (or *gentleness*, v. 35 NASB, NRSV n) is emphasized. Unlike the psalmist's successful appeal to God, the enemies' cries for help go unanswered (v. 41). The description of the king's victory appears to be written in the style of court records (vv. 31-42). Most of the tenses are imperfect, which in Hebrew signifies either future or continuous action. The NRSV translates these as past; they might also be read as looking ahead, as reckoning that the victories already won are a promise of greater things (Kidner, 1973:94-96).

The account ends with the king's acknowledgement of his God-given universal dominion as *head of the nations* (v. 43). The royal psalms speak of the worldwide authority of the king in Jerusalem in extravagant language and surprising boldness (vv. 43-45; Pss 2; 72:8-11; 89:25; cf. Mic 7:16-17).

Doxology 18:46-50

At the psalm's close the hymn of thanksgiving reasserts the encounter with God. *The LORD lives!* (v. 46) is the theological climax. God's saving activity continues. In a series of descriptive words, the psalmist praises God, who *gave me vengeance, . . . subdued peoples, . . . delivered me, . . . exalted me* (vv. 47-48). Although the motive for vengeance is that the guilty might know the true God (v. 49), God's actions are governed by his justice, not vindictiveness (A. Anderson, 1:166). With the reference to the nations and God's promise to *his anointed* (*māšîaḥ*), what must have been seen as a promise to the Davidic dynasty took on messianic meanings for later generations (v. 50).

THE TEXT IN THE BIBLICAL CONTEXT AND LIFE OF THE CHURCH

Nuancing War

What adjustments in Israel's theology were called for by David's kingship and development of a standing army? The royal psalms may reflect this adjustment. Lind (1980:118ff.) suggests Psalm 18 may have been incorporated into the Deuteronomic history (2 Sam 22) to set forth a new theology of the Davidic kingship. While accounts of early battles (Exod 15; Judg 5) focus on the LORD's miracle, the emphasis in Psalm 18 is on arming the king for conquest of the enemy (vv. 32-42).

Yet limits to kingly power are suggested (vv. 27, 35). While David was accepted in Israel as the ideal king, kingship came under criticism as in Nathan's oracle (2 Sam 7:4-17), and at many points in what scholars refer to as the Succession Document (2 Sam 9 to 1 Kings 2, less 2 Sam 21-24).

Many modern readers will understandably be uncomfortable with the emphasis placed on military achievement (v. 38). Divine justice, of which the king was an instrument, was concrete and earthly. It meant upholding the righteous and putting down the wicked. Kings often failed in the promotion of faith and justice, as is evident from the vigorous criticism by the prophets and within the Psalter itself (Pss 2:1-4, 10-11; 20:7-8; 33:13-17; 147:10-11) *[War]*.

The Reuse of Scripture

Psalm 18 provides a good example of Scripture used and adapted to speak to later needs. Employment of the psalm can be traced from David to the history writing of Samuels–Kings, and in later years of the monarchy the temple worship to celebrate the king's victories. When there was no longer any king in Judah, the devout would read the psalm as a prophecy of a victory to come. Thus God's commitments to David were announced as given to the community of the faithful (v. 43; Isa 55:3-5; Mays, 1994b:95). The psalm would then serve to keep hope alive by proclaiming God's sovereignty over the nations. Psalm 18 was and is a profession of faith in God's will and ability to reverse the fortunes of the humble and the oppressed (v. 27; McCann, 1996:749).

Paul saw the praise of the peoples (Pss 18:49; 117:1) as the promise fulfilled in God's purpose of salvation for the Gentiles (Rom 15:9). So the psalm took on a missionary use. Martyrs also found encouragement in it. In *Martyrs Mirror*, prisoners facing death quote the expression *by my God I can leap over a wall* (v. 29). Rather than stating a wish to escape, they affirm trust in God as they quote the verse together with Philippians 4:13, "I can do all things through him who strengthens me" (Braght: 566, 772, 951, 968).

Traditional Christian interpretation understands David as a type of Christ. Thus, the psalm is the voice of a person oppressed by the power of death and crying out to God, who delivers him. In liturgical customs of the church, the psalm has been used as a morning prayer reminiscent of Jesus' trial before Pontius Pilate (Matt 27:1) and prayed in the context of that trial (Reardon: 33).

Telling One's Story

Psalm 18 represents the testimony of a king who experienced God's deliverance. The story is told as a personal witness with generous use of the first-person pronouns "I" and "my." On first reading such language may suggest personal boasting (vv. 20-24). However, the theophany (vv. 7-15) and the victory recital (vv. 31-45) place emphasis on God as the subject of the miraculous deliverance and the one who strengthens and guides God's servant. The important truth is that others have come to acknowledge the sovereignty of God (vv. 43-45). So the psalm ends with a doxology of praise, sharing the good news with others (v. 49).

As Psalm 18 is reread, how does it speak to sharing stories of deliverance? What message can be heard about deliverance from death, encounter with God, righteousness and rewards, preparing for war, victories to celebrate, hope on the basis of God's saving acts in the past, and the telling of one's story?

Psalm 19

In Praise of God's Creating and Redeeming Word

PREVIEW

This hymn combines praise of God's creation and torah (law) in a way that makes it a wisdom or teaching psalm. In lyric fashion the psalmist proclaims God's glory as revealed in nature, particularly in the majestic rising and setting of the sun each day. However, greater still is the torah, God's will through the law, with special instruction to those with whom the LORD has formed a covenant relationship. The psalm ends with a prayer for God's help to guard the petitioner from rebellious ways. It offers the words of meditation in an act of reconsecration.

    The two distinctive parts of this psalm might suggest, as some scholars have conjectured, the combining of two poems. After the time of Ezra (ca. 400 BC) a psalmist may have taken over and expanded an early poem (vv. 1-6, ca. tenth century BC) to extol the law, which was seen not as a yoke for the people, but as a joy. Most commentators today focus on the unity of the psalm. In theme and style it is linked to Psalms 1 and 119.

OUTLINE

Hymn to Creation: God's Glory Through Nature, 19:1-6
Hymn to the Torah: God's Will Through Law, 19:7-10
Petition for Pardon and Reconsecration, 19:11-14

EXPLANATORY NOTES

Hymn to Creation: God's Glory Through Nature 19:1-6

The hymn begins abruptly, without the usual call to praise. The song is in process: the heavens keep on telling, keep on proclaiming the *glory*, the wonder of God's presence in the world. The heavens are the work of God's hands (Pss 8:3; 102:25). *Glory* is the manifestation of God's holiness. The whole creation testifies to God's greatness and declares the divine handiwork in order that people may hear, praise, and worship (vv. 1-2; 97:6; 145:10-11). Yet the voice of the heavens being uttered continually is neither fully heard by human ears nor comprehended. Nature, as God's book to the world, is not read (vv. 3-4a).

The poet's ode to the sun suggests acquaintance with Babylonian and Egyptian hymns to the sun (vv. 4b-6). In Mesopotamia, the sun god, Shamash, was considered to be the upholder of justice and righteousness and a symbol for wisdom (A. Anderson, 2:169).

> The receiver of a bribe who perverts (justice)
> thou dost make to bear punishment.
> He who does not accept a bribe
> (but) intercedes for the weak,
> Is well pleasing to Shamash
> (and) enriches (his) life.

("Hymn to Shamash," *ANET* 388; http://ccat.sas.upenn.edu/humm/Resources/Ane/hym$m$.html)

Psalm 8 dwells on the relationship between Creator and creature, and 19:1-6 focuses on the peculiar character of God in nature. The sun as *bridegroom* (youth, strength) and *strong man* (athlete, hero, warrior) speaks of exuberant joy, order, discipline, and encompassing power. Yet clearly, the subject here is God as Creator, and not the sun as deity: *he* (God) *has set a tent for the sun* (v. 4c).

Hymn to the Torah, God's Will Through Law   19:7-10

To the psalmist, the testimony of the created world is not enough. There is also torah, usually translated "law," though more accurately meaning "instruction" *[Torah]*. The law or instruction of the LORD, as wisdom itself, gives more complete light than the sun! The torah inspires the psalmist more than does the sun!

The poetic passage extolling the virtues and benefits of the *law of the LORD* (vv. 7-14) is akin to the lengthy meditation on torah in Psalm 119. We may see the six names for the law as synonyms building up a powerful praise statement. The descriptive adjectives are *perfect, sure, right, clear, pure,* and *true,* in sharp contrast to the compromise of human communication (vv. 7-9). Light shines from the torah to enlighten the eyes, revive life, and make one's heart rejoice (vv. 7-8; 119:105, 130). For the godly person, the effects of the law climax in the reminder that the torah comprises the most precious good that one can know: righteousness, because they *are righteous* (ṣadaq, v. 9). The words of the LORD are dependable and true. One should desire the LORD's way for life revealed in the written word of torah as better than anything money can buy (v. 10).

Petition for Pardon and Reconsecration   19:11-14

The psalm's focus, having moved from the witness of the heavens (vv. 1-6) to divine instruction through the torah (vv. 7-10), now shifts to the psalmist (vv. 11-14). The writer identifies himself as *your servant* (v. 11), as among those belonging to the LORD (27:9; 31:16; 116:16). In light of torah, the psalmist sees his own weakness and longs for integrity to keep him innocent of rebellion against God (vv. 11-13). *Warned* (v. 11) may also be translated *enlightened* (AB) or *formed* (JB). The sin of idolatry is always a danger.

The dedicatory formula (v. 14; 104:34; 119:108) suggests this psalm's use at the offering of the sacrifice. The hymn ends with reconsecration by use of the threefold name, *O LORD, my rock and my redeemer* (gō'ēl). This final name draws on a term usually applied to the nearest kinsman, whose duty it was to look after the interests of less fortunate relatives. Note that in verses 1-6 the divine name is used once as God ('ēl), implying a relationship of power to the world. In verses 7-14 God's covenant name, *LORD* (Yahweh), appears seven times *[Names of God]*.

THE TEXT IN THE BIBLICAL CONTEXT AND LIFE OF THE CHURCH

How God Speaks

Many people of faith have viewed the world of nature as a sort of book through which God is revealed. Paul may have had the first part of Psalm 19 in mind in writing to the Romans (1:19-20): "For what can be known about God is plain to them. . . . Ever since the creation . . . his eternal power and divine nature . . . have been understood and seen through the things he has made." This refers to what has often been called "general revelation," how God speaks to all persons everywhere.

The sun's rising rays are a daily exhortation to hope. The sun raises human spirits after days of clouds, fog, or rain. The sun means light, warmth, and energy for production of food. If the sun were farther away, it would be too cold to sustain life. If it were closer, the earth would be too hot. Do human beings fully comprehend the mystery and order and life represented by the sun?

Though Psalm 19 begins with God's voice coming through the created world, it moves to the creating word (vv. 7-14; 119:89-96; 147:15-20). Israel as God's covenant people received a special word, the torah, the law of Moses. This was a word of authoritative teaching to instruct them in their community life. Reardon (35) summarizes the reciprocity between the creation account in Genesis and the Sinai event in Exodus: "What God reveals in nature, he also reveals in his law." Christian faith views the coming of Jesus as *the Word* becoming flesh and dwelling among human beings as the culmination of God's special revelation, adding yet the fuller understanding of light and grace to which Psalm 19 points. John 1:1-18 has themes similar to this psalm.

Paul quotes Psalm 19:4 in Romans 10 to climax a series of biblical texts on preaching. As the sun moves around the earth, so the apostles' preaching has spread God's word "to the ends of the world" (10:18). Psalm 19:9 is echoed in the last book of the NT, praising God's true and just judgments and his grace and power to deliver in the end time (Rev 16:7; 19:2).

Psalm 19 in Hymnody

Psalm 19 in hymnody brings to mind Joseph Haydn's majestic chorus, "The heavens are telling," the climax to part I of his oratorio *The Creation*. Also familiar is Isaac Watts' paraphrase: "The heavens declare thy glory" (1719). Joseph Addison's hymn "The spacious firmament on high" (1712), set to an arrangement adapted from Haydn, declares about creation's works:

> In reason's ear they all rejoice,
> And utter forth a glorious voice;
> Forever singing as they shine,
> "The hand that made us is divine."

However, the psalmist is not articulating a faith that moves from the world to God. He is looking at the world through the eyes of faith, as the writer of Hebrews states: "By faith we understand that the worlds were prepared by the word of God" (11:3). The same is expressed by hymn writer Jeffrey W. Rowthorn (1974):

> Creating God, your fingers trace the bold design of farthest space.
> Let sun and moon and stars and light and what lies hidden praise your might.

Questions Raised by Psalm 19

As noted above, hymn writers focus on the creation theme of Psalm 19. Is the danger that of misunderstanding the poet and viewing the world as divine? Yet we recognize that the writer keeps Creator and creation separate.

What is the role of "nature" as revelation of God? How definitive is it? How far-reaching is it? Twentieth-century theologians Karl Barth and Emil Brunner disagreed on whether nature could be an *independent* source of revelation. Brunner held that nature can independently shed light on revelatory truths; Barth disagreed.

Perhaps even more, we need to ask about the role of word (instruction) as basis for moral behavior and community life. Do the sun and the other wonders of creation provide enough understanding of the will of God for life in community? Or will human madness one day also blot out the sun? Knowledge of the workings of the universe has greatly expanded. However, is there not greater need to learn to live together on earth? What does the special revelation of the word of torah or the "Word made flesh" say to us in our day?

Psalm 20

Prayer for the King

PREVIEW

This royal psalm, connected in type with Psalm 21 and in content with Psalm 18, appears to be an urgent prayer for the king before going to battle. In response to the people's prayer in the temple, an oracle provides confidence of victory. Trust is placed in the name of the LORD as the one who determines the outcome (vv. 1, 5, 7).

This psalm may come from a time before Israel had a standing army (before Solomon, v. 7), though other verses suggest that the temple was already in existence (vv. 2-3). Though Weiser (206) sees the setting in the ritual of the New Year's festival as petition for the "grace of kingship," the psalm was likely used in the preexilic period as the king offered sacrifice before beginning battle (1 Sam 7:9; 13:9-12). Gerstenberger questions the royal designation and sees this as the prayer liturgy of a local congregation (105). As a liturgy, the psalm may have been spoken by a priest or temple prophet (vv. 1-4, 6-8), with chorus or congregation responding (vv. 5, 9).

OUTLINE

Prayer for the King, 20:1-5
Assurance of Victory, 20:6-9

Psalm 20

EXPLANATORY NOTES

Prayer for the King   20:1-5

In the day of distress, likely a military crisis, the worshippers appeal to *the name* of God to call forth God's presence (vv. 1, 5, 7). The *God of Jacob* was the God of the whole community (Gen 32:24-30; 35:9-15). The prayer reflected the meaning of the name LORD (Yahweh) as present to act in salvation (Exod 6:1-8). That God would *send you help from the sanctuary* was based on the belief that from Zion, God shines forth to help and care for the oppressed (v. 2; Pss 14:7; 53:6) *[Zion]*. Selah suggests a pause, perhaps after the sacrifices *[Selah]*.

The *heart* was seen as the locus of all thought, planning, and ambition (v. 4; 10:6; 15:2; 33:11, 21). *Plans* and *petitions* (vv. 4-5) may have reference to the counsels of war. The shout celebrating *your victory* may have been a response of the people, with banners referring to the victory celebration dramatized in the temple (v. 5). The keyword *victory* (*yĕšû'â*) can also be translated "salvation" or "help." From it derive the names Joshua and Jesus.

Assurance of Victory   20:6-9

The major shift comes with the word *now* (*'attâ*, v. 6). *Now I know* suggests confidence in God's work (Job 19:25; Pss 41:11; 56:9). Something may have occurred (between vv. 5 and 6), such as a royal oracle, a divine word announcing victory addressed to the king in the course of worship (2:6-9; 110) *[Oracle]. Anointed* (*māšîaḥ*) was a designation for the king, here identified as one of the poor who must be helped (Num 12:3; Ps 33:16; Isa 53:4) *[Anointed]*.

Following assurance of victory by God's *right hand* (v. 6), the psalm warns against depending on military might (vv. 7-8). This reference to the Yahweh war tradition is a reminder that Israel's greatest weapon was trust in the LORD (Exod 3:15). Israel was forbidden to have a standing army, according to the Torah, and was warned against keeping many horses (Deut 17:16). That changed with Solomon (1 Kings 10:26-29). However, Israel was often reminded of the Yahweh war tradition, with God as the deliverer, through the stories of Gideon (Judg 7:2-25) and David and Goliath (1 Sam 17:45), as well as later prophets (Isa 30:15-17; 31:1-3; 37:23-36). The outcome of a battle rests with God, not in the size and quality of the military equipment (Ps 33:16-17) *[War]*.

The petition for the LORD to *answer* repeats the opening prayer (vv. 1, 9), indicating that victory still lies in the future. Variant readings are possible. One can read the Hebrew text to imply that the LORD is king: *May the King answer us when we call* (NJPS). The RSV and NIV, following the LXX, translate the verse as the people's prayer to God for the king's victory in battle: *Answer us when we call*.

THE TEXT IN THE BIBLICAL CONTEXT AND LIFE OF THE CHURCH

Israel's Prayers in National Emergencies

Prayers of the people for the king or for the LORD's deliverance in national emergencies have a long history. The report of a worship service, before King Jehoshaphat led Judah's army into battle against the Moabites and Ammonites, illustrates how people prayed in times of distress (2 Chron 20:1-19). After Jehoshaphat's prayer (vv. 6-12), Jahaziel, a Levite, reminded the people assembled: "This battle is not for you to fight; take your position, stand still, and see the victory of the LORD on your behalf" (v. 17). Then a choir of Levites sang praises to the LORD: "Give thanks to the LORD, for his steadfast love endures forever" (v. 21).

We can also find such prayers in community or royal laments (Pss 89:38-51; 144:1-11). However, taking pride in the name of the LORD as the one who leads into battle or does the fighting for the people can also lead to a dangerous religious nationalism. The prophet Amos thus warned, "You only have I known of all the families on earth; therefore I will punish you for all your iniquities" (3:2).

Dealing with Current National Crises

The cry *O LORD, save the king!* (v. 9 NIV), has served as inspiration for Britain's national anthem, "God save the king." The psalm has also been used as a blessing for young men called to war and, in modern times, as a farewell to missionaries setting forth to "fight the battle of the Lord."

How do people of faith appropriately pray for their leaders (1 Tim 2:2)? What shall be the prayer when warfare threatens? What does praying in the name of the LORD for victory mean? Can followers of the Prince of Peace (Isa 9:6) honestly proclaim, "Off to war! Kill in your country's name!" and pray for God to "bless our troops!"?

A prayer that takes into account the many victims of war must reflect broader understandings, as this adaptation of a Prayer for World Peace (Appleton: 78-79):

> Lord, we pray for the power to be gentle; the strength to be forgiving; the patience to be understanding; and the endurance to accept the consequences of holding to what we believe to be right.

May we put our trust in the power of good to overcome evil and the power of love to overcome hatred. We pray for the vision to see and the faith to believe in a world emancipated from violence, a new world where fear shall no longer lead people to commit injustice, nor selfishness make them bring suffering on others. . . .

What meaning has Psalm 20 in the community of the covenant? How shall we pray it in behalf of current national governments? Where is our help? In chariots and horses—or tanks and missiles? Or elsewhere? What about "the name"? What power does the name of God have for our day?

Psalm 21

Thanksgiving Prayer for a King

PREVIEW

This royal thanksgiving prayer hymn for victory shares vocabulary and theme with Psalm 20 (compare 20:4 and 21:2; 20:6-7 and 21:9, 13). Following in the series of psalms celebrating the dependence of the king upon the strength of the LORD (18; 20), Psalm 21 proclaims thanksgiving for the LORD's strength in the king's victory and well-being. The psalm focuses on the relationship between God and the king, which depends on the king's trust in God's steadfast love (v. 7).

If Psalm 20 accompanies the sacrifice of the king before battle, Psalm 21 may be the thank offering after the victory. Another possible setting is the coronation of the king (v. 3). The first half of the psalm, addressed by the priest to the LORD, enumerates the blessings to the king (vv. 1-7). The second part (vv. 8-13) may be addressed to the king, though the interpretation of these verses is more difficult. They may describe the victory as the LORD's work, be an oracle promising success in future ventures, or express a curse on those who work against the covenant. Praise for the LORD's strength ends the psalm, with verses 1 and 13 forming an *inclusio*, or envelope *[Hebrew Poetry]*.

The psalm is in the form of a prayer in liturgy (note *Selah* after v. 2) *[Selah]*. Responses of the congregation may be found in the verses that frame the psalm by focusing on *strength* (v.1), *steadfast love* (v. 7), and *strength* (v. 13).

Psalm 21

OUTLINE

Prayer of Thanksgiving for Blessings to the King, 21:1-7
Commission of the King and Concluding Prayer, 21:8-13

EXPLANATORY NOTES

Prayer of Thanksgiving for Blessings to the King 21:1-7

While some see this as a coronation psalm, *in your help* (v. 1) may well mean *your victory* (AB), a victory achieved by divine intervention, and so the LORD's victory (cf. 20:5)! The psalm testifies to the fulfillment of the divine promise and the granting of the petition (v. 2). Now the LORD's blessings to the king are enumerated: *crown, length of days, help,* and *joy* (vv. 3-6). *Crown* represents authority for the gift of governance. In court language, the gift of life *forever and ever* (v. 4; 1 Kings 3:14; Ps 61:6) may have reference to a long life rather than immortality, an unknown concept among the Hebrews, unless borrowed from other peoples (though note Gen 3:22). The inviolable sanctity of the king's life was apparently a common idea (1 Sam 24:11; 26:23-24). The cloud of light, the *glory, . . . splendor and majesty* surrounding gods and kings (v. 5; Ps 8:5), is granted through the LORD's *help* (*yĕšû'â,* "salvation," "deliverance"). When the light of the LORD's face shines on his own (4:6), then gladness and joy reign (v. 6).

The psalm's central verse (v. 7) uses covenant language, *trusts in the LORD* and *steadfast love* (*ḥesed*), as reminder of the relationship of the LORD and the king, and so also of the LORD and the people. The king's relationship to the Most High (7:17) is based on trust in the divine steadfast love *[Steadfast].* This verse describes the king as representative of the people, trusting *in the LORD.* The kind of situation in which such consultation took place may be illustrated in 1 Kings 22:5-28. Also, in Isaiah's confrontation with King Ahaz, Ahaz had to trust himself to the God who elected and installed him (Isa 7:1-17).

Commission of the King and Concluding Prayer 21:8-13

In the second part of the psalm, the priest or prophet appears to address the king, describing the wonderful victories over all his enemies. The LORD may be addressed in verse 9, which may be a later insertion (Gerstenberger: 106). While some see verses 8-12 as pointing toward future victory for the king, or even messianic future triumph over evil, God is the subject of this section, expressing confidence that the LORD's wrath will be joined to the king's struggle with his enemies so he can overcome them.

The allusions of this Yahweh war language demonstrate the immense power of God (Ps 20:6-8) *[War]*. The idiom, *your hand will find out* (v. 8), elsewhere means "to do as one judges best" (Judg 9:33; 1 Sam 10:7; Eccles 9:10). Here it suggests that the king's sword will reach its target (Clifford, 2002:121). The fiery wrath of God stands by the king to make him invincible (v. 9; Isa 29:5-6; 66:15-16) *[Wrath]*. The success of the king in upholding the righteous poor and putting down the wicked depends upon the LORD's favor (vv. 9-12). The wholesale slaughter would guard against the ability of the enemy to retaliate (v. 10; Ps 37:38). In Hebrew, verse 12 reads, *You will make them set the shoulder*. Rather than *flight*, it could also mean that soldiers brought the captives to the king, who put his feet on their neck to illustrate their completely submissive position (cf. 2:11-12; 36:11; Gen 49:8; Josh 10:24).

The final exclamatory prayer, *Be exalted, O LORD*, celebrates once more the divine strength and power (v. 13). Thus, the congregation praises the LORD for his mighty deeds (59:16-17).

THE TEXT IN THE BIBLICAL CONTEXT AND LIFE OF THE CHURCH

National Holidays

Regular ceremonies to enhance the welfare and prosperity of a monarch are well-known. This psalm suggests an ordering of society by celebrations that wed religious and political institutions. Such elements are present in the United States in Presidents' Day, Memorial Day, Independence Day, and Thanksgiving Day celebrations.

The pitfalls of passionate patriotism persist. Particularly in times of war, high priority is given to supporting our troops, and criticism of the monarch (president or king) is deemed disloyal, even subversive. How do people appropriately pray for the welfare of those who govern without falling into the temptation of reducing God to a tribal or national god? How does one avoid the temptation of too easily branding one's own enemies, or the nation's enemies, as God's enemies?

Model for Prayer and Spiritual Warfare

In the OT, the king became the model for the indispensable place of prayer in the human relation to God (1 Kings 8:22-53; 2 Kings 19:14-19). After the monarchy ended, faithful Israelites would have read Psalm 21 as instruction that blessing and salvation come through the prayers of those who trust in the loving-kindness of the LORD (Mays, 1994b:104). The king's prayers may have served as a basis for petitions in the Lord's Prayer (Pss 2:7-8; 18:6; 20:4-5; Mark 11:23-26; Luke 11:1-13).

Christian readers, seeing in the king a model and type fulfilled in Christ, have read Psalm 21 in light of the Son, whom God has equipped to battle evil and form the community. In Christian tradition, worshippers have often prayed Psalm 21 during the earliest hours of Sunday morning, glorifying God for the victory over sin and death through Christ's resurrection.

The psalm has also been taken out of its ancient nationalistic setting and applied to spiritual warfare, the battle of good against evil. What might we say here about God's role in spiritual warfare? What about the human role? In worship, amid the skirmishes of life, the psalm invites celebration of God's *strength* (vv. 1, 13), even as people of faith live in the *steadfast love* (v. 7) from which nothing can shake them (Rom 8:31-39).

Psalm 22

My God, My God, Why Have You Forsaken Me?

PREVIEW

This psalm, best known to us from the opening words on the lips of Jesus, is an individual lament, with the final section (vv. 22-31) a hymn of thanksgiving. The themes are anguish and trust, seeking God and finding God. The theological significance of Psalm 22 for understanding the passion of Jesus has long been recognized.

The opening cry, in the face of God's absence, is followed by expressions of trust on the basis of God's acts of deliverance in the past (vv. 3-5, 9-10). Vivid animal imagery describes the distress (vv. 12-21). The fervent petitions (vv. 11, 19) repeat the opening cry. The shift comes in verse 22: God has heard! The subsequent hymn suggests a temple setting, perhaps a thank offering and meal, ending with the declaration of God's universal dominion. The psalm reflects an intensity and comprehensiveness, moving from the depths of personal anguish to exuberant praise of God, which knows no bounds. The psalm is carefully structured, with the use of doubling as seen in the two major parts (vv. 1-21, 22-33), but also within the parts (complaint, vv. 1-2, 6-8; affirmations, vv. 3-5, 9-10; petitions, vv. 11, 19).

The title, *according to the Deer of the Dawn*, may have reference to a popular tune, or might be read as in the LXX, "concerning the help (given) early in the morning" *[Musical; Superscriptions]*.

OUTLINE

The Cry of Anguish When God Is Absent, 22:1-21
    22:1-11   Address, Complaint, Affirmations, and Petition
    22:12-21   Description of the Psalmist's Plight and Petition
The Response of Thanksgiving and Praise, 22:22-31
    22:22-26   Praise in the Congregation
    22:27-31   Proclamation of the Worldwide Sovereignty of the
                    LORD

We can chart some of the dynamics in Psalm 22 by following the lament form:

Verses	Form	Pronouns	Descriptive word
1-2	address/complaint	I/me	God-forsaken
3-5	affirmation	you	trustworthy
6-8	complaint	I/me	mocked
9-10	affirmation	you	safety
11	petition	you/me	help!
12-18	complaint	I/me	death/distress
19-21	petition	you/me	save me
22-31	vow to praise	I/you	praise/dominion

EXPLANATORY NOTES

Address, Complaint, Affirmations, and Petition 22:1-11

In the opening cry of being forsaken, God seems far away (vv. 1, 11, 19). Divine abandonment, along with the silence of God, prompts the question "Why?" a major theme in psalms of lament (10:1; 43:2; 44:24; 74:1, 11; 88:14). Yet the bond of love is not broken. So the psalmist dares to call on *my God*, a term indicating a personal God (Gerstenberger: 109).

A statement of affirmation follows the complaint. God is *holy*, and the praises of Israel declare God's nature and action (v. 3). The one who feels forsaken by God finds it helpful to remember the stories of God's deliverance of the ancestors (vv. 4-5). Note the repeated affirmation of *trust* as the psalmist recalls God's mercies and help to past generations (*trusted / trusted / cried / trusted*).

The complaint resumes as the psalmist adds to divine rejection (vv. 1-2) the sense of self-rejection (vv. 6-8). He feels utterly crushed, like a *worm* (v. 6; Job 25:6). The situation appears overwhelming and hopeless. The psalmist experiences the mocking and taunts of others as slander of the LORD. Yet God does not answer.

However, the psalmist recalls how from birth God has been *my God* (vv. 9-10), and so once more he pleads that God should respond, since there is no other help (v. 11). Out of this new statement of trust in God's nearness from birth arises the petition: *Do not be far from me* (v. 11; repeated in v. 19).

Description of the Psalmist's Plight and Petition 22:12-21

The psalmist's description of distress draws on images of ravenous beasts and the physical agony of sickness. With an array of figurative animal images, the enemies are described like the *strong bulls of Bashan* (v. 12), *a ravening and roaring lion* (vv. 13, 21), and predator *dogs* (vv. 16, 20)! His life is like *water* poured out, his *bones out of joint*, his *heart* like melting *wax* (v. 14); his *strength* (Heb) is like a *potsherd* (a piece of broken clay pottery), his mouth *dried up*, and his prospect *the dust of death* (v. 15)! Animal metaphors were often used to represent demonic powers that separate from God (Keel: 85-88). The meaning of the Hebrew text for the last clause of verse 16 is uncertain. The NIV follows the LXX, translating, "They have pierced my hands and feet," a reading early Christian interpreters connected with the crucifixion of Jesus.

What was the psalmist's plight? The images suggest illness near death (vv. 15, 18), mental anguish, mockers who in the understanding of that day may have been pressing the issue of illness as punishment for sin, and the spiritual crisis of "Why, God?" and "Where are you, God?"

In hopelessness, God alone is hope. So the petition for deliverance is renewed (vv. 19-21; Pss 7:1; 10:12). The phrase *O my help* (v. 19) is unique to the psalms, appearing sixteen times (Lind, 1980:191). In the Hebrew text, the lament ends with a verb that expresses the deliverance: *From the horns of the wild oxen You answer me* (v. 21 NASB). Note also the NRSV footnote, though NRSV mistakenly divides verse 21, assigning the first colon to part 1 and the second colon to part 2. Verse 21b can also be interpreted as "Rescue me!"

rather than as a statement of past action (Clifford, 2002:127). The lack of imprecation in this psalm is significant.

Praise in the Congregation   22:22-26

God hears the cry of abandonment! What happened between verses 21 and 22? The shift in mood is obvious, possibly the result of an oracle of salvation from a temple official, giving assurance that deliverance is on the way *[Oracle]*. Or, the psalm may have been composed in retrospect of an experience. The psalmist announces the *name* of the LORD as theme for the thanksgiving song. To *tell of your name* is to declare to others what God has done (Exod 19:6; Ps 102:21). The setting now is the temple and the thank offering. A sacrifice would be made, followed by a feast to which would be invited servants and other needy (v. 26), as well as the Levites (Deut 12:17-19). The experience of deliverance and thanksgiving was to be shared with the congregation (vv. 22, 25). Those *who fear the LORD* is a frequent expression describing those who have a special trusting relationship and live in obedience to God's will (v. 23; Pss 25:12, 14; 31:19; 34:7, 9; 85:9; 103:11, 13; 112:1; 147:11). The *great congregation* refers to Israel assembled in Jerusalem for one of the great annual festivals (v. 25; 35:18; 40:9-10; 107:32).

Proclamation of the Worldwide Sovereignty of the LORD   22:27-31

The fourth part of the psalm connects the fate of the afflicted one with the future kingdom of the LORD. Was the song of thanksgiving with the powerful universal thrust (v. 27-31) added for later use in the temple? The scope has been expanded from the psalmist to the congregation, and now to worldwide *dominion* of the LORD (86:9; 117:1). God's work of *deliverance* (*ṣedāqâ*, *righteousness*, NIV) encompasses also the dying (v. 29; but contrast 6:5; 30:9; 88:10-12; 115:17) and generations yet unborn (vv. 30-31)! The advance of the praise of God knows no bounds either in time or space. The vow of praise proclaims that the LORD's dealings with the community reflect what God does for the individual (vv. 22-31; Miller, 1986:143).

From the perspective of Christian faith and the use of this psalm by the NT writers to tell the story of the passion of Christ, the psalm's last word, a verb, declares even more pointedly how God *has done it!*

THE TEXT IN THE BIBLICAL CONTEXT AND LIFE OF THE CHURCH

Lament and Praise in Israel

Psalm 22 had its beginning in the cry of one in direct distress. The cry, "My God, why . . . ?" did not originate in worship, but was brought into it from the situation of anguish. There it was transformed into a psalm for the worshipping congregation, and from generation to generation it has become part of the experience of others (Westermann, 1989:14).

This psalm illustrates how the suffering and deliverance experienced becomes praise of the LORD when spoken of in the gathered congregation (vv. 22, 25). Such individual laments were closely tied to the cult, became part of the liturgy of the temple, and were used in recurring acts of worship. The language and phrasing was often reused, as were phrases from Psalm 22:1, 7-10, 14 in Jeremiah 20:7-18. Psalms that began as individual laments could later become the community's praise. For example, after the exile Psalm 22 could speak as lament out of the depths of community despair, yet offer hope to a small minority of the faithful in a remote corner of the vast Persian Empire.

A Messianic Psalm

The NT church saw Psalm 22 as messianic and quoted it thirteen times, nine times in the passion accounts. In addition to Jesus' cry from the cross (v. 1 in Matt 27:46//Mark 15:34), references abound (v. 7 in Matt 27:39//Mark 15:29; v. 8 in Matt 27:43; v. 18 in John 19:24//Matt 27:35//Mark 15:24; v. 22 in Heb 2:12).

Jesus' cry from the cross, "My God, my God . . . ," has been heard as the cry of aloneness in that awful moment, Jesus' identity with God-forsakenness in human suffering, and an expression of trust in drawing on Psalm 22 as a resource for consolation. That Jesus uttered words from Psalm 22, a psalm that ends in trust and praise, should not detract from the way he identified with human suffering. On the cross, Jesus wrestled with the tension between the close relationship to God and the grim doom of evil, suffering, and alienation. In so doing, Jesus suffered and shared in the lament and the language of suffering. Yet he did not convey a spirit of vengeance, leaving it for God to judge. Many Christians have understood the meaning of the passion and death of Jesus as dealing with the problem of human sin. Jesus' cry of forsakenness on the cross also invites believers to see

Jesus as one who cries out in identifying with suffering humanity. The letter to the Hebrews quoted Psalm 22:22 to show that the suffering Jesus underwent in his death was suffering for his people (Heb 2:10, 17). Scholars have done some excellent work on the relationship of Psalm 22 and the passion narratives (e.g., Kraus, 1986:188-91; Mays, 1985a:322-31; Miller, 1986:100-111; Reumann: 39-58).

Jesus' use of Psalm 22 and the NT's subsequent claim on this psalm may also be linked by a theme as the "lament of the mediator" (Westermann, 1970:63-64). Biblical literature includes laments of those who mediated between God and people over the burden of responsibilities and suffering: Moses (Exod 5:22); Joshua (Josh 7:7-9); Elijah (1 Kings 19); Jeremiah (Jer 11:1-13); and Isaiah (Isa 49:1-6; 50:4-9).

Psalm 22 and the Christian

The ancient church regarded Christ, not David, as the speaker in this psalm. *First Clement* (16.15-16), written from Rome to Corinth around AD 96, cites Psalm 22:6-8 as words attributed to Jesus. For Justin Martyr (ca. 150), David predicts the story of Christ. He takes Psalm 22:22ff., *I will tell of your name to my brothers . . .* , as a prediction of the resurrection. The church condemned Theodore of Mopsuestia (ca. 350-428), who expounded the psalm as referring to a historical figure. The christological approach represented the church's view of this psalm through and beyond the Reformation. Luther, recalling how Jesus was taken at night and brought before the Sanhedrin, translated part of the title as "of the hind that is early chased." Many quotations of verses 6, 7, 16, and 18 are found in the writings of the martyrs, usually in reference to Christ's self-humiliation, suffering, and death *[Ways of Reading]*.

Beyond serving as the primary interpretive clue to the passion of Jesus in the synoptic Gospels, Psalm 22 enjoys wide use in the church today. The *Revised Common Lectionary* includes the psalm in readings for Good Friday (vv. 1-31) and for the Fifth Sunday of Easter (Year B, vv. 25-31).

The significance of this psalm for Christian faith cannot be overestimated. It is unfortunate that a phrase like "God-forsaken" has become almost like slang when people talk about a godforsaken place. Thomas Hardy's poem "God-forgotten" refers to a whole world that God seems to have forgotten! It is one of the most terrible phrases one can imagine. But the winter of the soul, in which darkness and absence dominates, also describes the human experience. Psalm 22 is a prayer of anguish and of trust. In Jesus' use of this psalm, see how near to the cry of abandonment is also the prayer of trust.

An example of contemporary use of the psalm can be found in Reuter's "Rite of Healing for Wife Battering," an antiphonal reading incorporating the psalm into a letter from an abused wife (Reuter: 153-59; Holladay: 298). Another example can be found in the Nicaraguan poet Ernesto Cardenal's paraphrase of the psalm into the language of current politics: "Why have you left me?" Part of it reads:

> I am encircled;
>> here are tanks all round me.
> Machine-gunners have me in their sights;
>> there is barbed wire about me,
>> electrified wire.
> I am on a list;
> I am called all day;
> They have tattooed me
>> and marked me with a number. (Cardenal: 25)

Thanksgiving is a corporate act for the people of God. Deliverance, rather than a private matter, becomes good news for one to share with the whole congregation. God has acted as agent of salvation. How Jesus identified with all human suffering in the experience of the cross is a part of that work of deliverance. The believer's task involves declaring it to the coming generation and to the whole world. Note the tremendous scope of this psalm, "from the depths of abandonment by God, the song of the rescued person rises to a worldwide hymn" that draws also the past and future generations into worship of God (Kraus, 1988:300).

Psalm 23

The LORD as Shepherd and Host

PREVIEW

Two intimate metaphors for God are used in this psalm of trust—the caring shepherd and the gracious host. The mood is one of serenity, as the psalmist confesses faith in the provision a shepherd makes for the flock and the divine provision made for the one whose trust is in God. Yet behind the psalm lies danger and distress (vv. 3-5). All six verses appear to express the avowal of trust, which is a motif of the individual lament (Westermann, 1989:128).

Although the OT usually thinks first of the group, and only secondarily of the individual, this psalm speaks of God as *my shepherd*. What makes this psalm a favorite is this witness to the intimate caring relationship of the believer with a God who walks with us in life and death. Psalm 23 is the most familiar psalm.

The setting has traditionally been identified as "a psalm of David," drawing on the shepherd imagery (1 Sam 16:19) as well as the deliverance from situations of distress (22:1; 23:19-29). In its reference to the temple (*house of the LORD*, v. 6) and the concern for the individual, many view the setting as postexilic. The psalm may have been used with the sacrificial meal in the temple worship as part of a thank offering as described in Psalms 22:22-26 and 116:17-19. Thus, a psalm about an individual takes on strong communal dimensions. With allusions to the exodus traditions (Exod 15:13; Ps 78:19), and drawing on the royal imagery of the king as shepherd (Ezek 34), God is portrayed as *my shepherd* and the shepherd of God's people Israel (Pss 28:9; 80:1; Jer 23:3; Ezek 34:15).

OUTLINE

The LORD Is My Shepherd, 23:1-4
The LORD Is My Gracious Host, 23:5-6

EXPLANATORY NOTES

The LORD Is My Shepherd   23:1-4

The power of this psalm lies in its simplicity. Yet a wealth of oriental imagery gives rise to a variety of interpretations. Hebrew thought was intuitive and immediate rather than philosophical. Metaphors drew on varied experiences from life and evoked the imagination. Therein lies the power of this metaphor of the shepherd (v. 1) *[Hebrew Poetry]*.

The ways of sheep and their shepherd were familiar to all. The shepherd offered provision and protection for the flock. However, the ancient Near Eastern people also used the title "shepherd" for leaders, to designate their relationship to the people in their charge. The comparison of kings or gods with the shepherd was already common in early Mesopotamia and Egypt. The traditions of Israel's life in the desert gave rise to the thought of God as their shepherd and protector (Gen 48:15; 49:24). The symbol was a favorite to depict the exodus, God as a shepherd leading the people to safe pastures (Exod 15:13, 17). Later, OT texts show God as a powerful leader, driving out other nations and making room for his own flock (Ps 78:52-55, 70-72). The prophets also use the shepherd figure to compare the return from Babylonian exile with the exodus (Isa 40:11; 49:9-13; Jer 23:1-8; 31:8-14).

The psalm thus begins with the claim of the LORD as the trustworthy center of life, in whom nothing will be lacking. The scene is pastoral, with the picture of an oasis in the desert (vv. 2-3). Yet in the background is life's uncertainty and danger. *Soul* (v. 3) here means life, or vitality, and *righteousness* (NIV) refers to *right paths*. The plea that God help and protect *for his name's sake* (v. 3) is uttered in the assurance that the LORD will keep his promises and be present to save (Pss 25:11; 31:3; 106:8; 109:21; 148:5, 13).

As the shepherd needs to lead sheep through ravines as well as on grassy hillsides, so life also has dark valleys. The *valley of the shadow of death* (NIV) can also read *valley of deep darkness* (RSV n), or *the darkest valley* (NRSV). A fearful experience, or death itself, fills people with terror. However, the Great Shepherd is *with me!* As the shepherd leads the flock through dangerous terrain with *rod* and *staff* (Lev 27:32), so also God travels with the pilgrim on the journey of life. At this point, the psalmist shifts to the use of second-person language (*you*) in speaking of God (v. 4). *For you are with me* (v. 4c), the center and very heart of the psalm, sounds like God's promise to be with the patriarch Isaac (Gen 26:3), or like the *Do not fear; . . . I will be with you* of the salvation oracle (Isa 43:1-3). The divine name, LORD (vv. 1, 6), frames this psalm, suggesting shelter under the protective power of the name.

The LORD Is My Gracious Host   23:5-6

The metaphor shifts in verse 5. God is now the gracious host. The images are still from desert life, reminiscent of the exodus and wilderness wanderings, where the sacred duty of hospitality is experienced. The shepherd treats the guest in his tent with the utmost respect, even though enemies may wait outside. Now the psalmist is thinking of the divine hospitality, which knows no limit but abides forever (Paterson: 114). Indeed, the one formerly chased by enemies is pursued and protected by God's *goodness* (*tôb*) and merciful steadfast love (*ḥesed*).

The protection offered by the sanctuary becomes the epitome of all divine protection. One can read these verses with the rites of worship in the temple as setting. As the worshipper reflects on how often God has prepared a table before him, he sees himself as the guest of God. God hosts the banquet as the psalmist hopes for the full blessing of the covenant. The Christian worshipper tends to read the meaning of life after death into *forever* (v. 6 KJV, RSV, NIV), but for the psalmist it meant "as long as I live" (Heb.: *length of days*).

We can give other interpretations for *the house of the LORD*. Might it signify the desert tabernacle where the "holy place," with its bread and wine, was akin to a royal hospitality room? Or should one think of the postexilic period, and thus of an Israel led back to *the house of the LORD*, meaning "the land of Israel"? In any case, the psalm closes on the note of certainty. The fellowship with God that the speaker's trust has won will remain as long as he lives (Westermann, 1989:131).

THE TEXT IN THE BIBLICAL CONTEXT AND LIFE OF THE CHURCH

The Pervasive Shepherd Metaphor

In the OT, the shepherd motif describes God's relationship to the people (see Explanatory Notes). However, the OT also used the image for human leaders (Isa 11:1-9; 44:28–45:1). God is said to have led the flock Israel through the wilderness by the hand of Moses and Aaron (Ps 77:20; Isa 63:11). Ezekiel 34 treats the metaphor extensively; the prophet uses the evil-shepherd theme to illustrate selfish and irresponsible leadership (vv. 2-3) and to rebuke kingship based on domination and oppression (Vancil, *ABD,* 5:1190).

The OT concepts about the shepherd as a responsible leader were continued by the disciples of Jesus, who used the motif to characterize his role and mission. The description of Jesus as the second David, and as Israel's shepherd, begins when shepherds in the fields near Bethlehem hear of the birth and the angels announce peace to humankind (Ezek 34:23-25; Luke 2:8-20). Jesus is presented as going out to "sheep without a shepherd" (Matt 9:35-36; Mark 6:34).

The Gospel of John portrays Jesus as the Good Shepherd, who lays down his life for the sheep (John 10:1-30); in Jesus Christ the shepherd-God has become incarnate. At the end time the nations are to be gathered before the Son of Man (the king) like a great flock of sheep and goats (Matt 25:31-33, 40). The book of Revelation calls the Good Shepherd the Lamb of God (7:17).

Based on the view that Jesus was the great Shepherd and Guardian of souls (1 Pet 2:25; 5:4), the early church used the symbol to describe the work of its leaders (Heb 13:17, 20-21). Church leaders were instructed to "tend the flock of God" (1 Pet 5:2). A second-century Christian named Hermas made "shepherd" the major image of Jesus in a lengthy work named *The Shepherd.* Polycarp, second-century bishop of Smyrna, referred to the Lord as "the Shepherd of the Church" (*Martyrdom of Polycarp* 19.2).

A Psalm for All Seasons

In the early church, Psalm 23 was used at the Easter vigil as the newly baptized were anointed with oil, clothed with fresh white garments, and led to the table of the eucharist (communion) for the first time (Stuhlmueller, 1983, 1:153). In Mark's Gospel, the multiplication of the loaves describes how Jesus, the Good Shepherd, "took" the bread, "blessed," "broke," and "gave" it to the believers (Mark 6:41). To eat and drink at someone's table creates a bond of mutual loyalty and is the culminating token of a covenant (Kidner, 1973:112). Eating and drinking together confirms the saying "We don't really know another until we've put our feet together under the same table." At the Lord's Supper, the participants are guests of God (1 Cor 11:23-26). Yet God invites for more than a day. Around the Lord's table, believers are welcomed into the presence for life now and forever.

The psalm's intimate nature and focus on the personal interest and care of God makes it appropriate at weddings and funerals. Psalm 23 sublimely expresses God's abiding presence through life as well as in the experience of dying.

A serene confidence characterizes the psalm's mood. Many believers pray it daily and testify to its power to "restore the soul." Is serenity possible without faith that something of an immense or (better) an eternal Someone exists to calm the soul? Thus, many have drawn on this psalm in trust as a resource for calming faith and new orientation. Through the centuries Psalm 23 has served as a model for prayer and for comfort and trust through the hymnody of the church.

Read the cry of the forlorn in Psalm 22 as a preface to the confident faith of Psalm 23. God is the sure protector and provider of security. The promise of the comforting presence resounds in Jesus' later words, "I am with you always" (Matt 28:20).

Psalm 24

The King of Glory

PREVIEW

The kingship of the LORD and the LORD's sovereign rule is the subject of Psalm 24. We understand this song best in the setting of a festal procession. Dramatic antiphonal dialogue combines early Hebrew concepts with later worship forms to illustrate the living, dynamic character of God. Linked are the themes of God as creator (vv. 1-2) and God as savior (vv. 7-10) by a torah-liturgy that focuses on the moral qualifications of the worshipper (vv. 3-6).

Interpreters have identified Psalm 24 with David's bringing the ark to Jerusalem (2 Sam 6:12-19), the preexilic Feast of Tabernacles, and the postexilic New Year Festival. References to the *gates* and *ancient doors* suggest the existence of the temple, and the nature of the entrance qualifications (v. 4) suggests a late date for the present form of the psalm. Focus on the *LORD of hosts* reminds the worshipper of the victorious God.

As entrance liturgy it relates to Psalm 15. Other songs for festal procession are Psalms 68; 118; and 132.

OUTLINE

Hymn Celebrating God the Creator, 24:1-2
An Entrance Liturgy, 24:3-6
Ceremony Welcoming the King of Glory, 24:7-10

Although we can imagine a variety of settings, the following outline of how the psalm might have been used is adapted from L. Jacquet (Stuhlmueller, 1983, 1:155). In procession, the psalm celebrates:

1-2	The grandeur of the LORD	choir 1
3-4	The demands of the LORD	choir 2
5-6	The favors of the LORD	all together

Before entering the temple, the LORD is acclaimed King.

7, 9	Appeal to the gates	temple choirs
8a, 10a	Question: Who is the King of glory?	solo voice
8bc, 10bc	Answer: The LORD of hosts!	choir

EXPLANATORY NOTES

Hymn Celebrating God the Creator   24:1-2

In Hebrew, the psalm begins with an emphatic first word: *the LORD's*. To the LORD belongs the earth and all! Using creation language, with *seas* and *rivers* as names for unstable chaos, the psalm celebrates the sovereignty of Israel's God, the LORD, over all that exists (v. 2). To tame the sea was a central act of creation (Pss 89:11; 93; 95; 102:25; Isa 48:13). These opening verses may draw imagery from a Ugaritic/Canaanite combat myth: a warrior god (Baal) battles a monster (Yam, god of the sea) threatening the world, wins the battle, and returns to the assembly to be crowned a superior deity (vv. 7-10; Clifford, 2002:134; "Ugaritic Myths, Poems About Baal," *ANET* 130-35). Here the psalm proclaims God's creation, inviting the worshipper to communion with such a powerful God.

An Entrance Liturgy   24:3-6

Zion is the LORD's holy mountain, the holy place where the LORD causes his name to dwell (v. 3). The Torah liturgy opens with the question: Who can enter the temple? The answer, like Psalm 15, focuses on moral rather than ritual qualifications. The demand calls for loyalty of the kind represented by the Ten Commandments (Exod 20:3, 7). The answer has to do with a person's will. Not perfection of life but sincerity of purpose and integrity is required (v. 4). The ancient Israelites considered the *heart* to be the seat of thought. The *soul* (*nepeš*) is the essential integrated being, sustained in life by the animating spirit that God gives (Wilson, 2002:451). Thus, the qualifications are concerned with the worshipper's inner disposition and behavior toward others, and the trust that turns toward God and the readiness to do his will.

Three strong words express the LORD's favor (v. 5): *blessing* (*berākâ*), *vindication* (*ṣedāqâ*, or "righteousness"), and *salvation* (*yēšaʻ*). These are divine gifts of provision, acceptance, and protection. If indeed the psalm reflects the LORD's enthronement after defeating the forces of chaos, such gifts are the fruit of an orderly world available to the company of those who seek God. *Seek* (v. 6), another far-reaching word frequently used in the psalms (Pss 27:8; 105:4), here means to enter the temple for the purpose of worshipping God. The marginal note *Selah* (vv. 6, 10) attests to the psalm's liturgical use *[Selah]*.

Ceremony Welcoming the King of Glory   24:7-10

In the final gate-liturgy, as the worshipper stands before the doors of the temple, a ritual is enacted. Following question and response, the worshipper speaks the proper word, *the LORD of hosts,* thus identifying the deity in whose name he has come. The gates open, symbolizing the worshipper's entry into the presence of the holy. In days of fortress cities, people often identified the gates with the king and the king's power. Here the language is metaphorical, personifying the gates. Their being *lifted up* represents openness, welcome, and hope.

The ritual may also serve as a celebration of the "warrior God" coming in triumph to the temple. Thus, *heads* as lintels or beams above a door may suggest that this king is so great that the gates are not large enough. The *King of glory* is described as *strong and mighty* (vv. 8-9; Isa 40:28-31), *mighty in battle* (Exod 15:3), and *LORD of hosts*. The title *LORD of hosts* (*Yahweh šebā'ôt*), may mean "Yahweh of armies," a title having royal and military overtones (Pss 46:7, 11; 48:8; 84:1, 3, 12). It underlines the LORD's power and combativeness (Jer 31:35; 32:18; 48:15; 50:34; 51:19, 57). The psalm drew this military language from Israel's early Yahweh war tradition of God as warrior *[War]*. It links God the deliverer (vv. 7-10) with God the creator (vv. 1-2). Into the presence of God, the creator and deliverer (redeemer), the worshipper enters (vv. 3-6). In this sovereign God there is full provision, acceptance, and protection (v. 6).

THE TEXT IN THE BIBLICAL CONTEXT AND LIFE OF THE CHURCH

Psalm 24 as Invitation to Worship

This psalm points people to the absolute priority of the worship of God. In asserting that the world belongs to God, the psalm is also saying that it belongs to no one else (Ps 50:10-12). The devout have long recognized Psalm 24 as useful for drawing people into worship of the *King of glory.*

The LXX added to the title "for the first day of the week" as a reminder of God's creative activity, and so the psalm was recited as the week began. In Israel's hymnbook it became an "advent" hymn (Mal 3:1). In modern synagogue usage, it is sung as the Torah scroll is being returned to the ark.

In Christian churches, the psalm has been widely used as a call to worship. Christians have used it in services of Advent and for celebration of Jesus' entry into Jerusalem. In reflecting on the majestic God, king of the world, as proclaimed by this psalm, Christian believers also recognize the striking contrast of the Palm Sunday procession in the Gospels. There the king is suffering servant, the humiliated one. He rides on a donkey, and the ancient doors are shut in his face (Parkander: 127). Only after Good Friday's cross does the church proclaim Christ as the victorious and exalted sovereign of the world (Phil 2:6-11). Thus, believers also use the psalm for Easter and Ascension Day, pointing to the victory of Jesus' death and resurrection and his ultimate triumph. Some traditions, such as the Reformed Church, have used the psalm before holy communion, as the elements of bread and wine, signs of God's presence in Christ, are brought to the table.

A fine example of the psalm's use in hymnody is Georg Weissel's (1642) majestic hymn, "Lift up your heads, ye mighty gates." G. F. Handel's oratorio *Messiah* contains a memorable chorus by the same name from Psalm 24:7-10. In the Liturgy of the Hours (official morning and evening prayers in many Christian churches), Psalm 24 serves as a psalm of invitation. Acknowledging the Lord as Creator of the world, it invites humans to acknowledge the Lord as they live in this world (Clifford, 2002:137).

Living in God's World

In a time of environmental crisis, Psalm 24 provides a pointed reminder that the earth does not belong to humans. It is not ours to do with as we please. The earth, all that is in it and on it, belongs to the Lord who made it.

The Bible speaks clearly about enjoying the earth, but also about the need to act responsibly in caring for this beautiful and fragile planet (Gen 1:26-28; Pss 8; 104). Israel understood this with the Jubilee legislation in which, every fifty years, debts were to be cancelled and the land was to revert to its original tribal allotment (Lev 25).

Furthermore, agricultural land was to be allowed to rest, to lie fallow every seventh year, indicating it was under the ownership of God and not to be abused.

These are understandings at odds with a capitalistic insistence on private property. A profit-driven human ownership can lead to the monopolizing of commodities and products to create scarcity and drive up prices and windfall profits for a few at the expense of many. Or it promotes a rape of the land for immediate wealth, at the expense of the environment, to the detriment of future generations. The psalm also calls into question the reliance on mere national interest as the determining motive for decisions that affect the earth and its resources. If the world is God's, it is not ours to control, exploit, and use primarily to protect and benefit ourselves. In the Sermon on the Mount, Jesus calls his followers to give up the attitude of anxious striving and to depend on the care of God (Matt 6:25-34). Unless there is recognition of divine sovereignty, will this earth survive human exploitation? "The earth is the LORD's, and everything in it, the world, and all who live in it" (Ps 24:1 NIV).

Psalm 25

To You, O LORD, I Lift Up My Soul

PREVIEW

Instruction and guidance in the way of the LORD provide the subject of this individual lament. Major themes are trust, guidance, covenant, and forgiveness. Delitzsch describes Psalm 25 as a "calmly confident prayer for help against one's foes, and for God's instructing, pardoning, and leading grace" (1976:340).

By looking at the structure, we can observe careful crafting of the poem. Two groups of petitions (vv. 1-7, 16-22) frame the center section of wisdom sayings, which declare the covenant love and way of the LORD (vv. 8-15).

As an acrostic, like Psalms 9–10, this psalm corresponds most directly in style and theme to Psalm 34. The acrostic arrangement, in which each verse begins with the next letter of the Hebrew alphabet, has only slight irregularity (no verses begin with letters *w* and *k*, but two verses begin with *r*). An additional verse at the end begins with *p*. Thus, the psalm opens with ' (א), the middle verse is *l* (ל), and the final verse *p* (פ). When joined together, these three letters form the Hebrew verb *'ālap* (אלף), "to learn" or "to teach." The same pattern is used in Psalm 34 (Stuhlmueller, 1983, 1:159) *[Hebrew Poetry]*.

In tone, the lament does not reflect an immediate distress; it may have been composed for use by any person in need. The individual lament may have been taken over for use as a congregational complaint, as indicated by the reference to *Israel* in the last verse (v. 22).

OUTLINE

Prayer of Trust and Petition, 25:1-7
Celebration of the LORD's Dependable Friendship, 25:8-15
Petition for Deliverance and Redemption, 25:16-22

EXPLANATORY NOTES

Prayer of Trust and Petition   25:1-7

The prayer opens with lifting of the *soul* to God (v. 1). Lifting one's hands in a stretched-out position was a gesture of entreaty in prayer. Here the *soul* (*nepeš*), as one's center, is offered in the midst of all life's troubles (Pss 86:4; 143:8). Trust takes seriously the covenant promises of God (v. 10), and the petitioner expects to be vindicated rather than be put to shame (vv. 2-3). Shaming of one's enemies is frequent in laments (6:10; 35:4, 26; 40:14-15) *[Enemies]*.

The petition for deliverance from shame moves to the plea for divine guidance (vv. 4-5). The theme "Teach me" will be repeated (vv. 8-10, 12-15). Underlying these verses is an understanding of torah as instruction, the gracious expression of the will of the LORD to define a right path for the individual (Prov 2:20; 3:6; 11:20). Those who rely on the word of the LORD walk in God's truth (Ps 86:11). The one who waits and hopes for God to act walks in the faithfulness of the God of his salvation (v. 5; 27:14; 31:24; 38:15; 40:1).

With an appeal for the LORD to *remember* on the basis of his *steadfast love*, the prayer continues for divine mercy and forgiveness of sins (vv. 6-7) *[Steadfast]*. Here the psalmist uses the first of three biblical words for *sin*. The verb behind the terms *sins* and *sinners* (*ḥāṭā'*, vv. 7-8) conveys the sense of missing the mark. *Transgressions* (root: *pāšaʿ*, v. 7) means to rebel. The third word, *guilt* (*ʿāwôn*, v. 11), suggests the idea of being twisted *[Sin]*. The LORD's *steadfast love* can cover sin so that it is remembered no more (v. 7; 79:8; 130:3-4).

Celebration of the LORD's Dependable Friendship 25:8-15

The second part of the psalm, shifting from second to third-person address, offers a hymnlike description of the reliable, saving God. As the good teacher, God will guide people along the right way. Focus is on the teacher (vv. 8-10) and on the ones who fear the LORD as those being instructed (vv. 12-15).

The nature of the relationship with the LORD rests upon his *steadfast love* and *faithfulness* (v. 10). These covenant terms involve a community relationship (40:11; 61:7; 89:14; 138:2). *Covenant* (*bĕrît*) is used to describe the caring relationship of God toward his people, a relationship initiated and sustained by God (v. 10; Exod 19:5; Lev 26:9, 12-13). Along with this covenant relationship, the psalmist places *the friendship of the LORD* (v. 14).

So God has acted in the past (v. 6), and the psalmist can now pray that his own past may be swallowed up in the *ḥesed* of God (v. 10). The appeal in this pivotal prayer for pardon of guilt is *for your name's sake*. The LORD's name, his essence, gives assurance of the promise to be present and to save (Pss 23:3; 31:3; 106:8; 109:21; 148:5, 13). Those who fear the LORD and are prepared to receive instruction shall be blessed (vv. 12-15). Reference to paths and ways evokes the exodus journey through the wilderness to the conquest of the land (37:28-29). The psalmist identifies with the ones who fear the LORD, who live in obedience to God's will, in permanent attentiveness and submission (vv. 12, 15; 22:23; 31:19; 34:7, 9; 61:5).

Petition for Deliverance and Redemption   25:16-22

The final plea shifts back to second-person address. It begins with the lonely petitioner giving vent to inner turmoil, seeking relief and imploring forgiveness (vv. 16-18). The Israelites saw the *heart* as the center of all thought, planning, reflection, and ambition (10:6; 15:2; 20:4; 33:11, 21). Even those whom God frees from affliction and pardons of their sin need guidance for life.

Once more the psalmist pleads for deliverance from enemies (vv. 2-3, 18-21). The LORD keeping watch is a theme throughout the psalms (v. 20; 86:2; 97:10; 116:6; 121:5-8). We may see *integrity* and *uprightness* as personified guardians to protect the psalmist (v. 21; 43:3). Having contritely confessed sin, the psalmist now relies completely on God's gracious mercy.

The closing plea for redemption (v. 22) may have been a conclusion for use in the temple worship, applying the prayer of the individual lament to the nation. The final verse could be a later addition, since it does not fit the acrostic pattern.

THE TEXT IN THE BIBLICAL CONTEXT AND LIFE OF THE CHURCH

Instruction in the Way

Jews and Christians are people with a long history of teaching and learning. In Jewish tradition, "Hear, O Israel . . . " begins the important prayer known as the Shema (šěma', Deut 6:4-9). This commandment provided the basis for the Jewish convention of binding phylacteries, containing an abstract of biblical law, upon the arm and forehead. It also was the basis for placing a mezuzah, a small box containing this and related texts, on the right doorpost so that the "instruction" might be touched upon entering and leaving the house.

In the NT, Jesus is called "Teacher" (Matt 8:19; Mark 10:17; Luke 3:12; John 13:13-14), who spoke about being "the way, and the truth, and the life" (John 14:6). Paul wrote about the gift of teaching (Rom 12:6-8; 1 Cor 12:28-29). The first Christian believers were called followers of the Way (Acts 9:2; 18:25; 19:9; 22:4; 24:14, 22).

Guidance on the Way

The central theme of Psalm 24 focuses on guidance for the way. God's purpose is to bring sinners into the covenant (v. 8). Hope and trust link the humble sinner to the covenant with God, not sinless obedience. Those who enter the kingdom of God's grace are those who acknowledge their sin, self-power, and pride, and surrender themselves to the mercy of God (Wilson, 2002:467-69).

As a prayer, the psalm has served the church in its worship. The ancient church borrowed two words from this psalm to name the second and third Sundays of Lent *Reminiscere*, "remember" (v. 6) and *Oculi*, "eyes" (v. 15). The Eastern Orthodox Church uses it for evening prayers during Lent. In the Catholic Church mass, the introit for the third Sunday of Lent consists of Psalm 25:15-16, and the response is 25:1-2. Divine liturgies continue to use the opening words, "Let us lift up our hearts," as invitation to worship or to the service of communion.

The psalm is an appropriate prayer guide for the person who has set out on God's road and wants to do God's will. One can use it in the morning to raise hearts and minds to God as the day's labor begins (vv. 1-3). It voices prayer for the Lord's guidance and deliverance throughout the rest of the day (vv. 4-5, 15). Psalm 25 invokes God's protection against the enemies of the soul (vv. 19-21). One can also use it appropriately at the close of day (vv. 6-7). Finally, the psalm reminds believers to pray for others and for the redemption of the whole world (v. 22).

Gripped by Psalm 25

Menno Simons, who served in the Catholic priesthood in Friesland from 1524-1536, struggled for several years with doubts regarding the mass. His diligent search of the Scriptures finally led him to break with the Catholic Church. In the years that followed, he became the guiding spirit of the Dutch Anabaptists. The peaceful Anabaptists came to be known as followers of Menno, and finally as Mennonites.

Menno Simons wrote a "Meditation on the Twenty-Fifth Psalm" in 1537, soon after he left the Catholic Church. In the preface he defends his honesty and declares his desire only to follow the Word of God. Written in the form of a prayer of confession, Menno admits to a sinful heart and that abstention from shameful lusts was only because he wanted a good name. He reminds the readers that only the way of the cross leads to eternal life. Meditation on the last verse is an eloquent prayer for the true church of Christ:

> O God of Israel, create in us a pure heart that longeth for Thy blessed Word and will. Send forth faithful laborers into Thy harvest, . . . wise builders who lay for us a good foundation, that in the last days Thy house may be glorious and appear above all the hills, that many people may go thither and say, Come, ye, and let us go up to the mountain of the Lord, to the house of the God of Jacob; and He will teach us of His ways, and we will walk in His paths, that we may walk before Thee in peace and liberty of conscience all the days of our lives, . . . that Thou mayest be eternally honored and praised in us as in Thy beloved children through Thy dear Son, Jesus Christ our Lord. (Menno 85).

Psalm 26

To Walk in Integrity and God's Faithfulness

PREVIEW

The theme of Psalm 26 is the integrity of walking in God's faithfulness, with an expression of love for the temple as God's dwelling. This lament of an accused person asserts innocence on the basis of the psalmist's claim of a blameless life and the LORD's steadfast love and faithfulness.

Readers have proposed a variety of settings for Psalm 26. The original context appears to be that of an individual seeking asylum in the temple. The temple was a place for dealing with false accusations and taking an oath of innocence (Exod 23:6-8; 1 Kings 8:31-32; Ps 7:1-4). Clifford, focusing on the psalm's central section (vv. 6-7), suggests that the psalm originated as a prayer in priestly circles, later used for any visitor to the temple who felt awed by the demands of the holy God dwelling within (2002:142-43). Kraus sees this psalm not as a lament but as a prayer song, filled with confidence and moving toward a song of thanksgiving (vv. 7, 12; 1988:325-29). E. Vogt views the psalm as an entrance liturgy similar to Psalms 15 and 24. Then the lament would not be the priest's declaration of innocence of idolatry, but the pilgrim's claim that he has fulfilled the conditions for admittance to the sanctuary (via Sabourin: 232).

The psalm is enclosed by repetition of key words in the opening and closing lines: *I walk in my integrity* (vv. 1, 11). Protests of innocence (vv. 4-5, 8-10) frame the Psalm's center (vv. 6-7). Similarities to Psalm 25 are found in testimonies to the singer's trust in God (25:2; 26:1) and use of the imperative verbs *redeem* (25:22; 26:11) and *be gracious* (25:16; 26:11).

OUTLINE

Prayer for Vindication, 26:1-3
Protestation of Innocence, 26:4-7
Standing in the Temple and Petition Not to Be Swept Away, 26:8-10
Reaffirmation of Innocence, 26:11-12

EXPLANATORY NOTES

Prayer for Vindication   26:1-3

An appeal to justice opens this protestation of innocence. The accused prepares himself with petitions, sacrifices, and rites of purification through a night in the temple (7:3-5). In the morning, the divine verdict was to be announced. The petition is offered: "Judge me, O LORD" (7:8; 35:22-24). The unjustly accused submits to the verdict rendered by God through the priest. The psalmist bases his plea on the uprightness of his life, but even more, on unwavering trust in God's faithfulness (v. 3 NRSV n)! *Steadfast love* (ḥesed) and *faithfulness* ('emet) are covenant words. The ground for the plea is God's covenant love *[Steadfast]*.

Protestation of Innocence   26:4-7

The psalmist declares that he has nothing in common with *the worthless* (lit., "idol worshippers"), *hypocrites*, and the *wicked* (vv. 4-5; 1:1, 4-5). If the speaker is a priest, this is a protest that he has not given in to idol worship. Verses 6-7 describe the ritual and oath of purification and the altar procession. Washing of hands symbolizes integrity (24:4) or innocence (Deut 21:6-7; Ps 73:13; Matt 27:24-26).

Standing in the Temple and Petition Not to Be Swept Away   26:8-10

The love of the psalmist's life is the temple (v. 8; Ps 23:6). Here dwells God's *glory*, the light streaming from the deity (36:9; 63:2), and here the people meet God (27:4; 84:1-2).

The petition assumes that evildoers will be denied access to the temple (15:1-5; 24:3-4) and acknowledges the fear of being "swept away" from the community of God's people (vv. 9-10). If the psalmist is a Levite, he runs the risk of being banned from the temple (Deut 27:11-26) or even put to death (17:2-7).

Reaffirmation of Innocence   26:11-12

The transitional *But as for me* brings the psalmist back to the "walking in integrity" theme (vv. 1, 11). The godly one professes integrity, deep humility (*redeem* and *be gracious*), and the confident expectation that God will act on his behalf (v. 12). Again he declares love for the temple as God's dwelling and place of the *great congregation* (Pss 22:25; 35:18; 40:9). Many of the lament psalms allude to or anticipate the praise of God, by the one or ones who have been delivered, with a vow to praise God (5:11-12; 7:17; 13:5-6; 22:22-25; 31:7-8). Psalm 26 ends with such a declaration of praise.

THE TEXT IN THE BIBLICAL CONTEXT AND LIFE OF THE CHURCH

Walking in Integrity

The theme of integrity, to "walk the talk," can be found throughout the Bible. Integrity was an issue in the encounter of Abraham with King Abimelech (Gen 20:4-7), with Jacob's deception of his father Isaac and brother Esau (27:1-41), and Joseph's refusal to be seduced by Potiphar's wife (39:1-12).

Job appeals to his integrity despite the accusations of Satan and others (Job 2:3, 9; 27:5; 31:6). The book of Proverbs speaks of the righteous as walking in integrity (11:3; 14:32; 20:7), and asserts that it is "better to be poor and walk in integrity than to be crooked in one's ways even though rich" (28:6). The prophets appealed to integrity regarding worship (Amos 5:21-24) and spoke of the courage it takes to *walk in the name of the LORD* (Mic 4:5).

Integrity, a devotion to God that governs all of life, was affirmed in the teaching of Jesus when he criticized the scribes and Pharisees who "do not practice what they teach" (Matt 23:1-12). Integrity involves honesty in speech (2 Cor 2:17). But more than simply keeping one's word, integrity also involves knowing the truth and speaking truth (John 8:32, 43-47; 14:6). The letter to the Ephesians appeals to readers to "lead a life worthy of the calling to which you have been called" (4:1) and to "be careful . . . how you live" (5:15). The writer describes the Christian's walk (Eph 4–6). Is the Christian's daily walk a life of integrity? Is it motivated and based on God's faithfulness, or a sense of duty and desire for a good name?

The claim of integrity need not be an expression of self-righteousness or legalism, but the offer to God of the wholeness of life. Paul, suspected and challenged in his mission and faith, claimed a good conscience before God (Acts 23:1; 24:16; 2 Cor 1:12; 4:2). Luther interpreted this psalm personally when he was accused of disloyalty to the church and perversion of doctrine (Mays, 1994b:130). The sixteenth-century Anabaptists, forebears of the believers church, focused not only on "faith," but also on "following." To follow Christ included living in a fellowship of love with all persons and expressing the fullness of the Christian life in daily life.

Walking in *integrity* or leading *a blameless life* (NIV) does not mean being sinless, but rather, having one's life grounded in the "fear of the LORD" and acknowledging one's absolute dependence on the gracious mercy of God. Saying *I live my life in innocence* (Ps 26:11 JB) needs the added *Redeem me, and be gracious to me* (v. 11). We are not to claim innocence except through repentance (1 John 1:9-10). Psalm 26 points people to the source and power that enables them to live in love and loyalty to both God and humanity.

Sacred Places

The sacred place of worship is another theme in Psalm 26. The temple stood on holy ground where, according to ritual law, one needed to tread carefully. The psalmist is conscious of walking in a sacred space charged with the grandeur and energy of God (26:6-8).

Yet worship owes its vitality to the corporate experience, sharing with others in drawing on a common tradition (26:12). Encounter with God in the places where God's glory abides is possible (26:7-8) and is echoed by Jesus' words, "For where two or three are gathered together in my name, I am there among them" (Matt 18:20; Davidson, 1998:94-95).

The contemporary hymn by Huub Oosterhuis (1968; trans D. Smith, ca. 1970) asks and answers:

> What is this place where we are meeting?
> Only a house, the earth its floor,
> walls and a roof sheltering people,
> windows for light, an open door.
> Yet it becomes a body that lives
> when we are gathered here,
> and know our God is near.

Psalm 27

The LORD Is My Light and My Salvation

PREVIEW

This powerful song expresses unshakable trust in God. The psalm's opening verses convey confidence that with the LORD one need not be afraid (vv. 1-6). It declares the joy and shelter of the sanctuary with gratitude. The petition of the second section begs for guidance and protection from God, the only helper, and ends with the appeal to trust and wait (vv. 7-14).

The differences in mood of the two sections (confidence and lament), the way in which God is spoken of or addressed (third person, then second person), and the sequence of the two sections—all have led some to suggest that these were originally two separate psalms. However, many reasons point to the unity of the psalm. This may be the situation of an accused man (vv. 1-6) who came to the temple to make supplication (vv. 7-13) and obtained an answer (v. 14). Or it may be a lament emphasizing the element of trust (Sabourin: 273). Several key words bind the psalm together: *my salvation* (vv. 1, 9), *adversaries* (vv. 2, 12), *heart* (vv. 3, 8, 14), *seek* (vv. 4, 8), and *life/living* (vv. 4, 13). The desire to see God's face in the temple is also repeated (vv. 4-5, 7-9, 13). Finally, confidence and perplexity, faith and questioning, may live side by side as suggested in this psalm (Davidson, 1998:95).

Psalm 27 is linked to Psalm 26 by the theme of desiring to live in the house of the LORD (26:8 and 27:4), a theme characteristic of the whole group of Psalms 23–30. The psalm's central search for the divine presence and protection (vv. 4-6, 7-12) is framed by declarations of confident trust (vv. 1-3, 13-14).

OUTLINE

The Confidence of Faith, 27:1-6
    27:1-3   Trust in the LORD as Refuge
    27:4-6   Desire to Live in the House of the LORD
The Cry for Help, 27:7-14
    27:7-12   Plea for Deliverance from Enemies
    27:13-14   Expression of Confidence and Exhortation

EXPLANATORY NOTES

The Confidence of Faith   27:1-6

In form and content, verses 1-6 are similar to Psalm 23. With strong metaphors, the psalmist declares confidence born of acquaintance with God. *My light* (Mic 7:8), *my salvation* (*yēša'*), and *stronghold of my life* (Heb.: *refuge*) point to God as the one and only power to conquer fear (vv. 1, 3). The writer pictures the viciousness of the enemy as wild, ravening beasts (v. 2; Pss 7:2; 22:12-13, 16) and as a hostile army (v. 3). The psalmist views the *heart* as the center of human life, including the emotions of sorrow, anxiety, and fear (v. 3; 25:17; 55:4; 61:2). Yet in the face of attack, the LORD is the refuge. There is One stronger than the enemy.

Now again with strong metaphors, the psalmist expresses singleness of purpose (vv. 4-5). He desires to be a member of God's household, to live in perpetual communion with God (*live in the house, . . . behold the beauty, . . . inquire in his temple,* v. 4). *Inquire* suggests asking for divine guidance in the sanctuary (2 Chron 7:14; Ps 24:6; Hos 5:15), seeking for answers to the difficulty facing him. The temple was loved as the place where people could meet God (Pss 26:8; 84:4). Then follow three pictures to describe the feeling of security in the temple. *Shelter, tent,* and *rock* (v. 5) describe the sanctuary as a place of refuge, where no foe can touch the desperate one. The raised head (v. 6) represents a sign of triumph. The response is praise. The psalmist will now offer sacrifices out of gratitude and tell others what the LORD has done.

The Cry for Help   27:7-14

A shift to second-person direct address signals the beginning of the psalm's second part. In the prayer to God who alone is helper (vv. 7-14), the psalmist recalls a word of God that is both a command and a promise (v. 8). Israel was exhorted to seek God's face continually (34:4; 105:4), and the temple was seen as the place to experience the divine presence, in contrast to earlier understandings that God's face was not to be seen (Deut 4:12). However, the LORD can also hide his face, a prospect that arouses fear and terror (Pss 13:1-2; 30:7; 104:29). With quadruple repetition of the negative verb *Do not* (v. 9), the singer begs not to be abandoned (v. 10).

Finally, however, the *God of my salvation* (18:46; 24:5) alone is helper, since even those whom one would expect to be helpful and understanding have deserted (vv. 9-10). Two requests are voiced: *Teach me . . . and lead me* (v. 11). The *way* and *level path* are words associated with the temple. Once again, the enemies are described as predators. *The will* (lit., *throat*) *of my adversaries* reaffirms the slander of false witnesses *[Enemies]*. The ten imperatives in the petition are striking: *Hear, be gracious, answer, do not hide, do not turn, do not cast me off, do not forsake me, teach, lead, do not give me up* (vv. 7-12).

Yet there is humility. Only now, after putting his relationship with God in order, does the psalmist ask God for protection. The linking of verse 13 with what precedes is well expressed by *I believe, I had fainted, unless* (KJV), *I would have despaired unless* (NASB), or *I am still confident of this* (NIV). *Land of the living* (v. 13; 52:5; 116:9; 142:5), an expression of confidence in the LORD's protection in this life, points also toward the hope of looking on the loveliness of the LORD in the next. An exhortation to wait ends the psalm, the invitation to trust through courageous hope in God. Kraus suggests that verse 14 may be an oracle of salvation, the answer of God, the "yes" to the petitions in the sanctuary (1988:332, 337). Or it could be a concluding commendation of the stance of trust addressed to the congregation.

THE TEXT IN THE BIBLICAL CONTEXT AND LIFE OF THE CHURCH

Dealing with Fears

Psalm 27 ends with words of encouragement that sound much like Moses' words to Joshua, "Be strong and bold. . . . It is the LORD who goes before you. He will be with you" (Deut 31:7-8; Josh 1:6-9).

The comforting word "Fear not" is heard throughout the OT (Gen 50:21; Pss 23:4; 46:2; 91:5; 118:6; Isa 41:10, 13; 43:1, 5; Jer 46:27-28; Hag 2:5).

This theme resounds as well in the NT (Luke 2:9-11; 1 John 4:18). The psalm's opening question, *Whom shall I fear?* draws us to Paul's question in Romans 8:31, "If God is for us, who is against us?" Paul's answer declares that no one, nothing in all creation "will be able to separate us from the love of God in Christ Jesus our Lord!" Likewise, the Lord as light (Pss 27:1; 43:3; Mic 7:8) is followed up in the NT's identification of Jesus with the light (John 12:35-36, 46; 2 Cor 4:6; Heb 1:3).

Psalm 27, as a psalm of trust, is designed for tough times. Its allusions to the exodus (vv. 5, 11, 13-14) would have given Hebrews living in the exile and postexilic period hope for living. Verbal assaults and malicious reports have marked the history of God's people. Joseph, Moses, David, Jeremiah, the exiles, Nehemiah, Jesus, Paul, the early church, and the martyrs are the kind of people to find refuge in such words of encouragement.

Yet, there are mysteries beyond human understanding. When massive tragedy struck in the form of earthquake and tsunami in the Indian Ocean on December 26, 2004, people could do little but cry out to their God. So they did—to whatever deity they could name. People of all faiths asked: Why us? Why here? Why now?

Psalm 27 acknowledges the terrible prospect that God may hide his face and presence (v. 9). However, the psalm moves on in confidence, encouraging believers to take heart and *wait for the LORD.*

The One Thing Sought

Psalm 27 celebrates the human hunger for God amid dangers and delays. The psalm moves from *Whom shall I fear?* to *Wait for the LORD!* However, life does not move in a straight line from desire to fulfillment; neither does this psalm. The psalm teaches people to honor and nurture their desire for God (Clifford, 2002:149).

When assailed by calamity, the psalmist asks for *one thing* (v. 4), to dwell in the house of the LORD and to seek him in his temple. Here the psalm confirms the importance of worship and the foundation on which the believer builds his life. The verse touches on the deeper longing of prayer, the desire to live in intimacy with God, to find joy in worship, and "to abide in the consolation and light of His sanctuary" (Reardon: 51).

Use of this psalm can help us identify our fears, the source of our strength, and to take courage in the one who is our helper (v. 9). Faith stands in bold contrast to fear. The frightened heart need not have the last word.

Hymns Addressing Fears

Hymns of comfort and hope are an important resource for God's people. Henry F. Lyte (1847) expressed the sentiment of Psalm 27 in these words:

> When other helpers fail and comforts flee,
> Help of the helpless, oh, abide with me.

So also does the refrain of Robert Lowry's "My life flows on" (1869):

> No storm can shake my inmost calm
> while to that Rock I'm clinging.
> Since love is Lord of heav'n and earth,
> how can I keep from singing?

Hymns based directly on this psalm include Paul Gerhardt's "Give to the winds thy fears" and "If God be on my side," James Montgomery's "God is my strong salvation," and Johann Hengstenberg's "God is my light."

Psalm 28

Petition and Thanksgiving

PREVIEW

This prayer song of the individual is a plea for deliverance by one suffering the malice of enemies (vv. 1-5). A contrasting mood is found in the song of thanksgiving (vv. 6-9). Echoes of preceding psalms are sounded here in the linking again of prayer and praise (Pss 26:7, 9; 27:6, 9). The complaint, petitionary elements, thanksgivings, and intercession make this "a good representative of the individual complaint psalms" (Gerstenberger: 128).

The cause for lament may be the deep despair of illness or false accusation. The psalmist fears death with disgrace. The setting may be the lament of an individual, with the psalm later expanded to include the king and the people (vv. 8-9). Clifford proposes an alternative to the usual interpretation, suggesting that the initial setting may have been a thanksgiving for a declaration of innocence in an ordeal (Clifford, 2002:150). Having undergone a legal ordeal asking for divine judgment as to innocence or guilt, the original petition was then incorporated into the thanksgiving (41:4-10). In any case, the present form of the psalm combines prayer and thanksgiving and is broadened to include the community (vv. 8-9).

OUTLINE

Petition for Deliverance and Retribution, 28:1-5
Thanksgiving and Intercession, 28:6-9

EXPLANATORY NOTES

Petition for Deliverance and Retribution   28:1-5

Urgently the psalmist addresses the LORD as *my rock* (18:2; 31:2-3; 42:9; 62:2). But what if the LORD is silent? The psalmist fears *the Pit*, that deep cistern-like abyss regarded as the place of the dead [*Sheol*]. He fears being reckoned with and swept away with the wicked to the place where neither God's word nor human praise is heard. So he pleadingly lifts up his hands toward the innermost part of the temple. Lifting up hands, often an expression of praise or joyful thanksgiving (63:4; 134:2), was also a way of reaching out to God in an urgent plea for help (1 Kings 8:22; Lam 2:19).

The petition and imprecation spell out the crisis, the plea that the LORD would preserve him from the fate of the wicked and punish them by treating them as they treat others (vv. 3-5) [*Wicked*]. The call for retribution is based on concern for the moral foundation of society (Ps 94:2). A conscientious person protests injustice in the conviction that a day of judgment is a moral necessity. Wickedness invokes its own destruction. The psalm places the work and deeds of the wicked people's hands in opposition to the work and deeds of the LORD's hands (vv. 4-5).

Thanksgiving and Intercession   28:6-9

With the exclamation *Blessed be the LORD* the mood shifts (v. 6). God has heard *my supplication* and *my pleadings* (vv. 2, 6). God has had pity on the one afflicted! Was the sick man healed? Did deliverance become reality through faith? Was an oracle of God's promised salvation spoken by the temple priest? *So I am helped* (v. 7) can more descriptively be translated *my flesh has revived* (LXX) or *I have been rejuvenated* (AB). Recovery gives rise to a song of thanksgiving! The psalmist's *heart* trusts and exults in the LORD as strength and shield (v. 7), in contrast to the malicious evil in the *hearts* of the wicked (v. 3).

The descriptive names for the LORD—*strength, shield, refuge, shepherd* (vv. 7-9)—are in keeping with the opening address to *my rock* (v. 1). The psalmist could reach out to the One in whom is power, strength, reliability, and tender care.

The closing prayer asks God to save and bless the people, and the *anointed*, the king (vv. 8-9) [*Anointed*]. It becomes an intercession for the people as a whole: *Shepherd* them and *carry* them. Were these final verses spoken by the priest or by someone sharing his experience with the rest of the congregation? In the military language (vv. 7-8) and reference to the *anointed*, some have seen the king's prayer for

Psalm 28

the people addressed to the divine shepherd king. Whoever the speaker, the prayer asks the LORD to act as the good shepherd not only for the individual, but also for the entire people. The picture of the divine shepherd (Pss 23:1; 28:9) links Psalms 23-28 as a collection of psalms drawn together by many common themes (Wilson, 2002:498).

THE TEXT IN THE BIBLICAL CONTEXT AND LIFE OF THE CHURCH

Carried by the Divine Shepherd

The closing image of the shepherd gathering the lambs in his arms and carrying them in his bosom is also used by Isaiah (40:11; 63:9). In Deuteronomy, in reference to God's protection through the desert wanderings, God carries the people as an eagle *bears them aloft on its pinions* (32:11). These images of God carrying his people would have become words of hope to Israelites scattered by the exile.

The psalms speak of leading us in the way and of the LORD as shepherd (23:1-3; 28:9; 74:1; 80:1). The images continue in the NT in Jesus' self-declaration, "I am the good shepherd" who gives life and gives it abundantly (John 10:10-16). Jesus tells Peter, "Feed my lambs. . . . Tend my sheep," words later understood as referring to the church (21:15-17). The book of Hebrews ends with reference to "our Lord Jesus, the great shepherd of the sheep" (13:20). God's people are familiar with the image from the many paintings, church bulletins, and Sunday school books that visually convey the divine shepherd carrying his sheep.

Retribution Revisited

The psalmist calls on God to judge the evildoers according to their deeds (Ps 28:4-5). The idea of retribution, that God responds on the basis of our actions, is based on a sense of orderliness by which God judges the wicked and upholds the righteous. This understanding is expressed in the wisdom literature of the Psalms and Proverbs.

The cry for retribution in the psalm is directed at persons who are two-faced in their relationship with others, who *speak peace* but *mischief is in their hearts*. Such lack of integrity in inner thought and outward expression undermines trust and community. According to understandings of divine retribution, God should do to them as they have done to others (Ps 28:4-5; Prov 11:5).

However, does the brutal imprecation to *break them down and build them up no more* also reflect a sinful human cry of revenge (vv. 4-5)? Is God's usual method of dealing with the human situation not that of breaking down *and* building up? Is the psalmist here urging God to stop at the *breaking down* point and not go forward to the *building up* that would ordinarily follow (Knight, 1:139)? *[Imprecation]*.

Words of caution regarding the cry of revenge are offered in Deuteronomy 32:35 and Romans 12:17-21. We do best in leaving vengeance up to God *[Wrath]*. Unease with the wish for commensurate hurt on enemies no doubt lies behind the omission of Psalm 28:4-5 in the Liturgy of the Hours, a Roman Catholic four-week recitation guide for the psalms (Holladay: 305).

Expressing Thanks

While malice may be in the *hearts* of the wicked (Ps 28:3), the psalmist moves on to declare the trust and exultation of his *heart* (28:7). Thanks for deliverance now breaks out in song. The poet conveys to others the sentiment of gratitude and praise through music. Numerous psalms of praise allude to God's response to the situation of distress in the past (18:4-19; 34:4-6; 40:1-2; 65:1-4), or offer a vow of praise (5:11-12; 13:5-6; 22:22-25).

The praise hymns of the church do the same. The final verse of this psalm is a prayer that has become part of the "Te Deum," an ancient and celebrated song of praise, rejoicing, and thanksgiving:

> We praise thee, O God: we acknowledge thee to be the Lord. . . .
> O Lord, save thy people, and bless thine heritage. . . .
> O Lord, let thy mercy lighten upon us, as our trust is in thee.

Psalm 29

The Voice of the LORD in the Storm

PREVIEW

Psalm 29 is an OT doxology in praise of the LORD as sovereign of the universe.

This powerful, moving hymn, emphasizing the majesty of God in the storm, may be one of the earliest psalms. The discovery of the tablets at Ras Shamra appears to substantiate that an old Canaanite hymn to Baal is borrowed, adapted, and used to praise the LORD. Thunder, lightning, and storm are precisely the manifestation of the Canaanite god Baal in the Ugaritic texts. By substituting the name *Yahweh* (*LORD*) for Baal, the earlier hymn could be adapted for worship of the LORD (Kraus, 1988:346). Eighteen times *the LORD* is proclaimed! Seven times, as the reverberating thunder, *the voice* (*qôl*) *of the LORD* is repeated (vv. 3-9).

This psalm moves from heaven (appeal to the heavenly council to ascribe glory to the LORD) to earth, where the thunderstorm moves with frightening fury from the sea, across the mountains, and on into the desert. The psalm ends with reference to the people of God and seeks strength and peace for them. Throughout, it proclaims the majesty of the LORD. The dominant image is God as king, whose rule is manifest on earth, but also over the gods of heaven (vv. 1-2, 10-11).

OUTLINE

Introduction: Summons to Praise, 29:1-2
Reason for Praise: The Voice of the LORD in the Thunderstorm, 29:3-9
Conclusion: The LORD's Enthronement as King, 29:10-11

EXPLANATORY NOTES

Introduction: Summons to Praise   29:1-2

The opening summons is addressed to divine rather than human beings. The picture is that of a heavenly court where homage is paid to the divine king by subordinate deities (Ps 82:1). The Canaanites and other Near Eastern cults had many deities. In the OT such deities were relegated to being the LORD's attendants. These are variously called *gods* (Ps 82:1), *angels* (148:1-2), or *seraphs* (Isa 6:1-2). Those addressed in Psalm 29 are *sons of gods* (v. 1 NRSV n). The translations, *O heavenly beings* (NRSV) and *O mighty ones* (NIV), may reflect unease of the translators with these traces of polytheism found in the psalms. The psalm may call the divine beings to praise because human language is inadequate to describe the glory of God (A. Anderson, 1:234).

The threefold summons calls for the ascription of *glory* (*kābôd*) to the LORD (vv. 1-2). *Glory*, literally meaning "heavy, weight," can refer to significance and importance, such as a person's standing in the community. When applied to God, it points to his standing at the center of life, his supreme power, majesty, and holy splendor, awesome and incomparable (Davidson, 1998:20). Here, *glory* is also a term for the manifestation, the dignity of the LORD's divine royalty in the world (v. 9).

Reason for Praise: The Voice of the LORD in the Thunderstorm   29:3-9

The awesome arrival of God in the storm is portrayed by repetition of *the voice of the LORD* (*qôl Yahweh*, or *qôl Adonai* when spoken), conveying the impression of a repeated roll of thunder. Thunderstorms are infrequent in Palestine, but they do develop in the spring and fall. Moving from west to east, they begin over *the waters*, the Mediterranean Sea, and come inland (v. 3). With vicious ferocity a storm may move across the mountains of Lebanon, breaking the *cedars*, well-known for their strength and grandeur (v. 5). Could the skipping of the mountains, *Lebanon* and *Sirion,* a name for Mt. Hermon, refer to quakes (v. 6)? Is the lightning descriptive of the fiery breath of God (v. 7)?

Finally the storm crashes into the desert, an awesome and fearful place. Some OT maps show a city of Kadesh on the Orontes River in Syria, north of Mt. Hermon, and a Kadesh-barnea far to the south, as an oasis in the Wilderness of Zin. While *oaks to whirl* is consistent with the storm's fury over the forests, an NRSV footnote (v. 9) suggests an alternative reading, *causes the deer to calve*, implying the storm's fury is felt also by the animals. Yet the poet describes not primarily a violent thunderstorm, but the greatness of God. This theophany proclaims the display of divine omnipotence in and through the storm. Nature itself proclaims the LORD as supreme God *[Theophany]*.

The psalm's climax comes in verse 9. To God's majestic display of power, the worshippers cry "Glory!" The scene has shifted from heaven to earth as the heavenly choir is replaced by the temple singers, whose exclamation of "Wow!" to the theophany fulfills the call to *ascribe to the LORD glory* (vv. 1-2). Heaven and earth thus proclaim the God above all deities.

Conclusion: The LORD's Enthronement as King 29:10-11

God *sits enthroned over the flood* (cf. Gen 6–9). God subdues the chaos and is more powerful than all that resists (v. 10; Ps 93:3-4). Again and again the psalms stress that the LORD's kingdom is invincible and eternal (10:16; 74:12; 93:1-2).

The final verse, an intercession, also affirms God as the source of comfort and assurance. In a dry land, the sound of thunder was the welcome voice of life-giving rains to begin a new season. In prayers of the Psalter, blessing is not primarily something given to an individual, but to the entire people (3:8; 28:2, 8-9). A psalm that begins with an appeal to the heavenly host to proclaim the glory of God ends with a prayer for *peace* on earth (shalom, *šālôm*). Only a deity with great strength, as described above, has the power to bestow peace. Having assumed his rightful place as eternal king, the LORD becomes the source of comfort and hope to his people.

THE TEXT IN THE BIBLICAL CONTEXT AND LIFE OF THE CHURCH

Theophany and Doxology

As a theophany describing God's appearance, this psalm is similar to other descriptions in seeing God as present in the storm (18:7-19; 68:7-10; 77:16-18; 97:1-5; 144:1-11). The psalm may have been used on the last day of the Feast of Tabernacles, on Pentecost, or the Feast of Weeks (Talmud and early Christian literature).

If indeed based on an earlier Canaanite hymn, the psalm is a good example of putting new content into older literary forms. In a somewhat similar way, Christians have adapted lyrics and secular tunes for Christian use. Martin Luther took the song "Innsbruck, ich muss dich lassen [Innsbruck, I must leave you]" and gave it fresh words: "Welt, ich muss dich lassen [World, I must leave you]." He commented, it is said, that it wasn't his fault that the devil had the tune first. The melody for the hymn, "Joyful, Joyful We Adore Thee," is taken from Beethoven's Ninth Symphony.

The Christian church year has connected Psalm 29 with Epiphany and the baptism of Jesus, "the mighty theophany with the quiet epiphany in the water of the Jordan," the voice "in the thunderstorm . . . with the voice from heaven. . . . The storm says, 'This is my cosmos,' the baptism, 'This is my Christ'" (Mays, 1985b:64).

As a hymn of doxology, Psalm 29 illustrates the marvelous possibility of worship to reorder life. This hymn, in its "vote for the LORD," as sung by faithful congregations, offers opportunity to declare and experience again that "glory," the majestic splendor and power of the sovereign Lord. That's what the church is doing when it sings doxology. In worship, people of faith act out who shall be God in the pantheon of loyalties (Brueggemann, 1984:142-43). Easter Sunday worship provides an example. As the congregation sings victorious resurrection hymns, the external circumstances of life may not be significantly changed, but the life of the believer is being transformed anew to live in God's resurrection power.

Demonstrations of God in Nature

God still reveals himself in the majesty of the storm. The great naturalist, John Muir, used to climb into the swaying pines during a thunderstorm to hear the needles striking against each other and to delight in the trees swaying to the storm's music and drama. Can this psalm call people to see the world anew as creation?

Psalm 29 declares that the very world is God's voice! In modern times people have found out many more wonderful things about the world. Moderns know about the atom and subatomic particles. People know about marvels in biology, genetics, mathematics, medicine, chemistry, physics, and an expanding technology. But do people today have a comparable literature of astonishment? Or is today's problem that of praising the scientist, while failing to praise the God who made both the world and the scientist?

God still reveals himself, and human beings are still dependent upon God. When the storms come—the hurricanes, fires, quakes, floods, or whatever life brings—can God be seen in these *and* beyond these? Does not God rule over all the processes of nature? "God's kingdom is what God creates *out* of pain, *out* of sorrow, *out* of floods and avalanches, and even—not strangely—*out* of sins forgiven" (Knight, 1:143).

We can mediate a sense of awe before God through use of Psalm 29 today. The poem prays that people would acknowledge the Lord's sovereignty in heaven and on earth. The opening lines of the Lord's Prayer express the same: "Hallowed be your name, . . . on earth as it is in heaven" (Matt 6:9-10). The psalm invites the whole earth to join in praise of the one God who is creator of all.

Psalm 30

You Have Turned My Mourning into Dancing

PREVIEW

This song of thanksgiving of an individual who came face to face with death, but who has now been restored to health, expresses and invites praise! The themes are faith in God and joyful thanksgiving by a person whose prayer for help has been answered, and who now brings an offering of praise and proclamation. Confessing a false confidence, and the new perspective that facing death has brought, the psalmist ends with a vow of praise and *thanks to you forever* (vv. 6-12). Note the eight uses of the direct address O LORD.

The psalm has an interesting title. Though listed as a psalm *of David*, it is also identified as *A song at the dedication of the temple* [Superscriptions]. Dedication of the temple took place under Solomon (1 Kings 8; 2 Chron 5–7), though later temple dedications included the second temple after the exile (Ezra 3:7-13), and a rededication in 164 BC by Judas Maccabaeus after the desecration by Antiochus Epiphanes (1 Macc 4:52-59).

Though the psalm is much older than the second century BC and the superscription is secondary, the devout have used the psalm at the Feast of Dedication (Hanukkah, *ḥănukkâ*), which celebrates the cleansing of the temple by Judas Maccabaeus (1 Macc 4:52-59; John 10:22). The title's association of the psalm with David and the temple may also illustrate how the faithful can take prayer song springing from the experience of an individual and appropriate it for a great communal occasion.

OUTLINE

Song of Praise for Deliverance, 30:1-3
Invitation to the Congregation to Join in Praise, 30:4-5
Narrative of the Crisis and Restoration, 30:6-12

EXPLANATORY NOTES

Song of Praise for Deliverance   30:1-3

The opening declaration, *I will extol you, O LORD*, identifies the purpose of the song. The psalmist will exalt the LORD by making known his saving acts of deliverance. Praise is proclaimed to the LORD, who has *drawn me up, . . . healed me, . . . brought up my soul,* and *restored me to life. My foes* (v. 1) may be those who, like Job's friends, confronted the stricken one as though a sinner, or may refer to the Foe, death *[Enemies]. Sheol* and the *Pit* (vv. 3, 9) are poetic names for the abode of the dead, where praise is no longer possible (Pss 6:5; 88:11-12) *[Sheol]*.

The psalmist faced a life-threatening crisis, perhaps serious illness so that he was near death, as expressed in King Hezekiah's prayer (Isa 38:10-20). Though *heal* can refer to restoration from any situation of crisis (Ps 147:3), God snatched the psalmist from premature death.

Invitation of the Congregation to Join in Praise 30:4-5

After calling himself to praise, the psalmist calls the congregation, *you his faithful ones* (ḥāsîd, "godly" or "pious"), to thanksgiving (v. 4). The psalmist has experienced rescue and must share the joy in what may have been a ritual of thanksgiving in the temple. In the testimony to the congregation, teaching about the LORD is a way of giving thanks (v. 5; 32:8; 34:11). God's *anger*, not sent to destroy, points toward grace. The psalm attributes both wrath and favor to God, but they are not equal (*a moment/a lifetime*) *[Wrath]*. The contrasts of *night/morning* and *weeping/joy* are suggestive of death/life (resurrection). The psalmist is pointing to how crisis, and reflection on God's wrath, is part of a process leading to life.

Narrative of the Crisis and Restoration   30:6-12

As for me signals a shift back to the psalmist's crisis, including his original prayer (vv. 6-10). He confesses the sin of overconfidence in his prosperity. But when the LORD's *face* turned away (10:1; 27:9; 55:1; 104:29), when God was gone, the psalmist's world fell apart. Coming near the point of death provided the jolt. In the awareness that there is no praise of God from Sheol (6:5), the cocky self-assurance was broken down so that a more proper regard for the gift of grace could develop. Recognizing that the true key to the psalmist's security lies in the LORD, he prays: *Hear, . . . be gracious, . . . be my helper!* (v. 10).

The psalm ends with the joyous proclamation that the LORD has answered. The cry and *sackcloth,* the garment of mourning, have given way to dancing, gladness, and thanksgiving (v. 11)! Because of the LORD's gracious deliverance, the psalmist has been able to replace the soiled, torn garment of sorrow and penitence with a festal robe (Gen 37:34; 41:42; Ps 35:13). One of the signs of rejoicing in the Bible is dancing (Exod 15:20; 1 Sam 18:6; Pss 149:3; 150:4). The psalmist breaks into song because God's grace has proved sufficient for all his needs (v. 12). His *soul* or *heart* (NIV; Heb.: *glory*) sounds a doxology. Thus, the psalm ends as it began, giving expression to the purpose of life as praise to God (vv. 9, 12).

THE TEXT IN THE BIBLICAL CONTEXT AND LIFE OF THE CHURCH

Thanksgiving and Praise

Psalm 30 provides a good example of how a thanksgiving psalm is a lament resolved. A deliverance, the new life given by God, makes silence impossible. By retelling the story in the context of the faith community, the memory is kept alive as it stays close to pain and rescue (Brueggemann, 1988:148). Praise completes and consummates what has begun in supplication, but moves beyond thanksgiving as mandatory reciprocation.

The verb for praise is *hôdāh* (*hiph'îl* form of *yādāh*), usually translated *give thanks* (vv. 4, 11); it has as its object a specific action in God's past and is therefore thanksgiving in the form of acknowledgement (Mays, 1994b:140). However, the OT never uses *hôdāh* when human beings are described as thanking one another. *Hôdāh* is the praise that is spontaneous. It moves beyond the one giving thanks and being the subject, to having God as subject: *You have . . . , you are*

(Ps 30:1-3, 11). Thanksgiving can be a private act by which one expresses one's gratitude; however, it is characteristic of praise that one gives it voice before other people (Ps 30:4, 11; Westermann, 1989:168).

Psalm 30 provides a good illustration of how thanksgiving moves to praise, and the expression of praise in joyful song (vv. 4, 11-12).

True Contentment

The open language of Psalm 30 invites its use to speak of the God-given changes that come in life. The psalm shows how prayer and praise can become a means of holding the experiences of life together in relation to God. Peril and exaltation, rescue and restoration, these are part of the human experience. How many have in their prosperity and self-sufficiency asserted, "I shall never be moved!" only to be brought low by illness or some other misfortune. Often the person who has looked death in the face, been compelled to search his soul, and has been brought to his senses gains a new perspective of God's grace. The guidance of the hidden God comes in many ways.

Psalm 30 cautions people not to look for security in any circumstance, feeling, or human source that seems to offer control of life. Instead, true contentment comes only from God. The testimony of a person restored through God's deliverance can be shared so that the experience of one is helpful also to others.

Psalm 30 and Resurrection

While the psalm's image of being brought up from death (v. 3) reflects recovery from serious illness, and not resurrection from death, the church has nevertheless seen a prefiguring of the resurrection in the raising to life of the person described here. Furthermore, the psalm's exuberant joy suggests what the resurrection was about (vv. 5, 11). The dawn of Easter Day broke with the news, "The Lord is risen!" Death's hold was broken, and victory over death as the final enemy was declared.

In readings of the church year, Psalm 30 is assigned to the Third Sunday after Easter, linking it with John 21. One lectionary also ties this psalm to two stories from Jesus' ministry, restoring life to a widow's only child (Luke 7:11-17) and to the little daughter of Jairus (Mark 5:21-43; Limburg, 2000:46).

Psalm 31

My Times Are in Your Hand

PREVIEW

Psalm 31 is the prayer of an individual facing a variety of ordeals. The psalmist cries to God for deliverance and trusts: *My times are in your hand* (v. 15). The original distress suggests that the person was ill (vv. 9-10, 12), persecuted (vv. 8, 11, 13, 15), and the object of a slanderous whispering campaign (vv. 11, 13, 18, 20). Recording the ups and downs of a relationship with God, the poem becomes a model of prayer, expressing confidence of being heard by the God on whom the petitioner can rely.

The literary difficulties of this psalm, a variety of moods, drawing on the language of other psalms and Jeremiah, the mixture of lament and thanksgiving and teaching—these have usually led commentators to consider it a composite psalm. William Taylor (162) suggests three laments combined (vv. 1-8, 9-12, and 13-18), with 19-24 as thanksgiving for the LORD's gracious response. Others (Schmidt, Rhodes, Leslie) suggest two laments have been combined (vv. 1-8 and 9-24). Still others, as in the approach employed here, is to view this as the prayer of one person, but a psalm used in worship expressing thanksgiving following deliverance.

The psalm can serve as a study in intertextuality. Verses 1-3 are identical to Psalm 71:1-3, and verses 23-24 echo a wisdom note from Deuteronomy 6:5. For prophetic allusions, see below.

Psalm 31

OUTLINE

Prayer for Refuge and Confession of Confidence, 31:1-8
Petition for God's Grace in Distress and Statement of Trust, 31:9-18
Hymn of Thanksgiving for Deliverance, 31:19-24

EXPLANATORY NOTES

Prayer for Refuge and Confession of Confidence 31:1-8

The opening confession of trust expresses the psalm's theme: *In you, O LORD, I seek refuge* (v. 1). The psalmist trusts himself for safekeeping into the hands of the LORD. The LORD as source of stability and protection is often called *my rock* or *Rock* (vv. 2-3; Deut 32:4, 18, 31; Pss 18:2; 28:1; 42:9; 62:2, 6-7).

In distress, the psalmist appeals to God on the basis of God's *righteousness* (*ṣedeq*, v. 1) and *steadfast love* (*ḥesed*, vv. 7, 16, 21) to keep promises of deliverance *[Righteous; Steadfast]*. The cry is *Save me* (*hôšî'ēnî*, vv. 2, 16; cf. *hôšî'â nā'*, *Save us*, 118:25; "Hosanna," Matt 21:9). *Your name's sake* means your name gives assurance that you will keep your promises and be present to save (v. 3; Pss 23:3; 25:11; 106:8; 109:21; Kraus, 1986:21). Like an animal caught in the hunter's net, the psalmist desires refuge from affliction (v. 4). Note the verbs of desperation in verses 1-4: *Deliver, rescue, save, lead, guide, free me* (NIV). The opening petition for deliverance ends with a statement of resignation, committing life into the hand of the God of faithfulness (*'ĕmet*) who redeems (*pādāh*, v. 5).

The commitment of trust describes a relationship (vv. 6-8). *You hate* (v. 6; Heb.: *I hate*) is a declaration of innocence. Worship of or keeping idols in one's possession was considered a chief cause of sickness or other misfortune. The psalmist's life is in the care of God, not entrapped in an enemy's net (v. 4; 9:15; 10:9; 25:15). References to *the hand of the enemy* may refer to death itself as a force hostile to life (vv. 7-8) *[Enemies]*. Yet the psalmist can rejoice, for the God of *steadfast love* has seen his affliction, and he has now been set free (*set my feet in a broad place*, v. 8).

Petition for God's Grace in Distress and Statement of Trust 31:9-18

The petition opens with the formulaic *Be gracious to me, O LORD* (v. 9; Pss 4:1; 6:2; 9:13). A vivid description of the acute situation follows. Note what mental distress and grief can do to bodily functions

(v. 9). My *soul* and my *body*, literally, *my throat and my belly*, suggests loss of speech, upset stomach, and loss of strength. *Misery* (NRSV n, Heb.: *iniquity*) may refer to the effect of sin and guilt (v. 10). Gerstenberger (140) calls attention to the intrusion of a guilt-oriented theology as in Psalms 14; 19:13; and Nehemiah 9. The misery is further compounded by social ostracism, by scorning and withdrawal of accusers, neighbors, and friends alike, until there is utter isolation (vv. 11-13). Considering the isolation, might the illness have been leprosy?

With *but I trust in you, O LORD,* the mood changes (v. 14). The psalmist asserts: *"You are my God." My times are in your hand* (vv. 14-15). The nonroutine experiences of life may be God's special moments. God guides the events of life and each one's destiny. So the anguish of abandonment has led the psalmist to acknowledge utter dependence upon God's mercy (*ḥānan*, v. 9) and unfailing love (*ḥesed*, vv. 16, 21). Twice the psalmist uses the striking contrast of God's *hand* and the *hand of the enemy* (vv. 5, 8, 15).

As one who belongs to the LORD (*your servant*), he appeals that God's *face shine* upon him to save him (v. 16; 67:1; 80:3, 7, 19; 119:135). Praying that he may not be disgraced publicly, he voices an imprecation upon his accusers, praying that his defamers may be frustrated and experience the contempt of Sheol, the abode of silence (vv. 17-18) *[Imprecation; Sheol]*.

Hymn of Thanksgiving for Deliverance   31:19-24

Once again, the mood shifts in the exclamation of wonder: *O how abundant is your goodness!* (v. 19). In amazement at God's rescue of the imperiled, the psalmist moves from complaint to thanksgiving. *Shelter* (*sukkâ*) can designate a tent dwelling for God (v. 20; Pss 18:11; 27:5; Amos 9:11). Shouts of praise are the immediate response of those who have been wonderfully helped because of God's steadfast love (vv. 21-22; Exod 18:10).

While the psalmist understands retribution as the LORD's repayment of those who act haughtily (v. 23b), the psalm ends with the exhortation *Love the LORD!* Though not found elsewhere in the psalms, the command recalls Deuteronomy 6:5; 10:12; and Jesus' later instruction (Matt 22:37; Mark 12:30). The praise of God has broadened out to awaken a corresponding joy in others. The final word is an invitation to take courage and to wait for the LORD (v. 24; Pss 25:5, 21; 27:14; 38:15; 40:1).

THE TEXT IN THE BIBLICAL CONTEXT AND LIFE OF THE CHURCH

The Language of Prayer

Psalm 31 includes prayer language drawn from other psalms. Verses 1-3 are identical to Psalm 71:1-3, confirming the psalmist's practice of drawing on a treasury of resources to serve in new contexts. The psalm borrows prayer language from Jeremiah, or Jeremiah may have drawn from the psalm. For example, the expression *terror all around* (*terror on every side*, NIV, 31:13) is used elsewhere only in Jeremiah 6:25; 20:3, 10; 46:5; 49:29; and Lamentations 2:22. The final two verses may reflect later use of the psalm in temple worship, certainly its deep roots in the worshipping community.

Jesus was familiar with the psalm, quoting verse 5 on the cross (Luke 23:46). Stephen's dying prayer, "Receive my spirit" (Acts 7:59), echoes the same words. Athanasius (ca. 295-373), bishop of Alexandria, encouraged Christians, who found themselves despised and persecuted for the truth's sake, to turn their mind to the future and sing Psalm 31 (Holladay: 165). Martyrs, as in the story of the torture of Tjaent Reynerts (Braght: 455), have quoted verses 5 and 15 as an expression of confident trust. But not only martyrs. "Into thy hand I commit my spirit" has been a part of the evening prayer of the Catholic Church for centuries.

Psalm 31 and the Passion of Christ

Psalm 31 gained a special place in Christian devotion and liturgy through Jesus' use of verse 5 as the final prayer of his life: "Into your hand I commit my spirit" (Luke 23:46). In the psalm's description of affliction, Christians see a witness to the suffering Jesus endured. The Gospels tell of the plot to take his life (Mark 3:6; 14:1). There are false witnesses (14:55-59). His disciples deserted him, and his enemies mocked him (14:50; 15:29-32). Reardon (59) suggests that reading Psalm 31 allows believers to see the Passion "from the inside."

Psalm 31 has become prominent in the celebration of Holy Week. In all three years of the cycle in the *Revised Common Lectionary*, the psalm selection for Passion Sunday is Psalm 31:9-16. The reading for Holy Saturday is Psalm 31:1-4, 15-16.

Committing Life into the Hand of God

The overarching theme of this poem focuses on the trust of commitment. At the heart of Psalm 31 is the resignation of life into the hand of God (vv. 5, 15). To be able to say, *My times are in your hand* (v. 15), is to view "time" as more than money and a commodity, but rather as the gift of God. It is to acknowledge that one's destiny is in the hand of God, whether in life or in death. To be able to say, *Into your hand I commit my spirit* (v. 5), is to trust that there will be safekeeping for the outcome of life through the redemptive love of God. This does not necessarily mean deliverance from suffering and death, but it does place one's trust in the refuge of God.

Consequently, these two sentences of Psalm 31 (vv. 5, 15) have often informed a personal liturgy of the dying, speaking of the spirit returning to God who gave it (as in Eccl 12:7 NIV), and have also provided hope for the process of living. Even through failure and death, the providence of the faithful God determines the "times" of his servants (Mays, 1994b:145). In such hope, God's people can take courage and *wait for the LORD* (v. 24).

Psalm 32

The Blessing of Confession and Forgiveness

PREVIEW

This second of the seven Penitential Psalms has the characteristics of a song of thanksgiving in its portrayal of distress, the appeal to God and experience of deliverance, and thanksgiving and testimony in the presence of the congregation *[Penitential]*. It is also a wisdom psalm, opening with the *Happy* (*Blessed*, NIV) of the forgiven (vv. 1-2) and ending with the teaching about confession (vv. 8-10) and witness to the congregation (v. 11), thus enclosing, as within brackets, the thanksgiving testimony (vv. 3-7).

The situation may have been healing from an illness at a time when sickness was seen as the direct consequence of sin. The individual's experience came to be shared in the temple with the congregation, as indicated by the threefold *Selah* (vv. 4, 5, 7) and the congregation's song of praise (v. 11) *[Selah]*.

The psalm stresses the crucial importance of confession of sin as leading to divine forgiveness and restoration. Major themes are the burden of the guilty conscience, the freedom and joy of forgiveness when confession is made, and instruction on being receptive to teaching. The heading associates the psalm with David and then identifies it as *A Maskil* (*maśkîl*), which may mean "instruct" or "teach," since the verb *instruct* (v. 8) comes from the same root. Other psalms identified as *Maskil* are 42; 44; 45; 52–55; 74; 78; 88; 89; and 142 *[Superscriptions]*.

OUTLINE

The Blessedness of Forgiveness Through Confession, 32:1-5
The Forgiven Sinner Teaches About Deliverance, 32:6-11

EXPLANATORY NOTES

The Blessedness of Forgiveness Through Confession 32:1-5

The psalm begins with two *Happy are those* sayings by people who have received forgiveness as the gift of God (vv. 1-2). Often translated *Blessed* (NIV), a better translation of *'ašrê* might be "fortunate" (1:1-3; 41:1-3; 112:1; 119:1-2; 127:5; 128:1).

The opening beatitude for the blessedness of forgiveness uses three different words for sin: *transgression* (*peša'*, willful disobedience breaching a relationship), *sin* (*ḥăṭā'â*, missing the mark) and *iniquity* (*'āwôn*, distortion or crookedness of character). For the same triad see the vocabulary in Leviticus 16:21 *[Sin]*. Set over against these are three expressions of forgiveness: the lifting away (*nāśā'*), the covering over (*kāsāh*), and the canceling of a debt (*ḥāšab*). Relationship with God is possible only on the basis of complete truthfulness (v. 2b).

The struggle in the psalmist's life is attributed to being silent, to bottling up things inside (vv. 3-5). With vivid imagery, the psalmist describes the prior condition of a stricken conscience as the heavy hand of God, though note also other understandings of God's hand (31:5, 15). The human body often reveals what is going on in the soul (31:9-10). While not all sickness is the result of sin, as the ancients thought, aches of the stomach, back, or head may be clues to unconfessed sin, repressed emotions, and psychosomatic illness.

The turning point comes in confession (v. 5), confirming the principle that the one who conceals sins will not prosper, but "one who confesses and forsakes them will obtain mercy" (Prov 28:13). The same three words for sin (vv. 1-2) are repeated. Deliverance comes when the afflicted sinner resolves to end the cover-up, allowing God to "cover" and no longer regard the sin (Clifford, 2002:166).

Psalm 32

The Forgiven Sinner Teaches About Deliverance
32:6-11

The appeal broadens with *Therefore* (v. 6) as the psalmist addresses onlookers, inviting them to apply this insight to their living. Let the psalmist's experience be that of others too! The nature of true confession is to share with others the source of life and hope (vv. 6-7). The NRSV footnote to verse 6, "at a time of finding," suggests turning to God from sin while the opportunity remains (Isa 55:6). The *rush of mighty waters* (v. 6) might refer to chaos (Ps 29:3) or picture the distress caused by a flash flood. In such turbulent times, the LORD is a *hiding place*, a "shelter" or "tent" (v. 7; 31:20; 61:4; 91:1; 119:114).

It is not clear who speaks the wisdom teaching (vv. 8-10). Is God speaking to the psalmist? Is this an oracle spoken by the priest? Is the psalmist speaking to himself or to others? These appear to be words from the experience of one who witnesses to the joy of forgiveness for the benefit of others. The appeal is not to be stubborn, but to be teachable (v. 9; Prov 26:3). Those who *trust in the LORD* know a different control, *steadfast love*, which keeps them close to God (v. 10; Ps 5:7). The focus on the way (v. 8) and the contrast of the two ways, *the torments of the wicked* or the *steadfast love (ḥesed)* of the LORD (v. 10), recalls Psalm 1:6. God's unavoidability presents us with a choice—resistance or yielding. Out of that choice, life will be shaped—trouble and pain, or freedom and song (Brueggemann, 1984:98). The psalm ends with a resounding call for the congregation of God's people to rejoice *in the LORD* (v. 11).

THE TEXT IN THE BIBLICAL CONTEXT AND LIFE OF THE CHURCH

Penitential Prayer and Instruction

Psalm 32 combines the prayer of penitence with public instruction about obedience. This speaker not only relates his experiences; in addition, he wishes to help the sinner get back on the right road (34:4-5, 8-9, 11-14; 51:13).

The heading associates Psalm 32 with David. However, in the psalm many commentators have seen elements of the teaching role of worship characteristic in the postexilic period, as noted in other penitential prayers from that time (Ezra 9; Neh 9; Dan 9). These prayers express more than the penitence of an individual; they also incorporate Israel's experience of God's way through judgment and restoration (Mays, 1994b:145-46). Such prayers emphasize that the pardon of God is the first and principal basis of the life of the people of God (Isa 40:2; 55:6-7).

The psalm is reenacted in the healing stories of the Gospels (Mark 2:1-12; Luke 5:20-26) and as Jesus teaches about prayer for forgiveness (Matt 6:12-15). Paul quotes Psalm 32:1-2 in Romans 4:7-8 to describe the happiness of the person who, by faith, accepts God's gift of forgiveness. Paul draws on Abraham (Rom 4:3; Gen 15:6) and David (Ps 32:1-2) to establish the principle that God graciously gives his righteousness to the circumcised Jew and the uncircumcised Gentile, apart from works. Augustine, Luther, and Calvin all take their cue from Paul and this passage in their interpretation and instruction about repentance, and how righteousness comes by faith in the grace of God (Mays 1994b:148).

Confession in Dealing with Sin

Psalm 32 urges people to stop covering up and make confession, and then to celebrate the steadfast love of God. Confession of sin must be said to God. That happens only as it is brought to speech. Secret remorse or feelings of guilt are not confession. The synagogue and the church provide settings for confession in worship. These have included the confessional booth, meeting with a confessor-pastor, or brief confessional statements in worship. Where and how does confession happen for today's worshipper? How do people of faith help each other acknowledge and voice the guilt that blocks them from God?

The twelve-step program of Alcoholics Anonymous invites the fellow struggler to come forward within a caring community and "admit to God, to ourselves, and to another human being the exact nature of our wrongs." That is confession, to admit needing help from God's power, which offers freedom from a lifetime of compulsive behavior (Wilson, 2002:552). The NT invitation appeals to the cleansing of forgiveness through Christ: "If we confess our sins, he who is faithful and just will forgive us our sins and cleanse us" (1 John 1:9).

While sin may result in sickness and illness, sickness is not inevitably caused by sin: there also are other causes of illness. Moreover, it is not acceptable to hold, as some do, that specific sins result in specific illnesses. Nor is healing necessarily assured when the sin has been identified.

Psalm 32 has been one of the more popular psalms in the Christian tradition. Its focus on freedom in forgiveness through God's grace made it Augustine's favorite. The Greek Church uses it in the baptism ritual. The priest says three times with the believer: "Happy is he whose fault is taken away, whose sin covered." The psalm declares, *I confess, . . . you forgave* (v. 5). In this new freedom, it invites God's people to "rejoice in the Lord" (Ps 32:11; Phil 4:4).

Psalm 33

Hymn to the LORD, Whose Steadfast Love Fills the Earth

PREVIEW

This hymn, in praise and description of the LORD, celebrates God as praiseworthy for his word and work in creation and history. The eye of the LORD is on all to judge the conduct of human beings and to deliver those who fear him. The hymn concludes with an affirmation of trust and hope in the reliable and steadfast love of the LORD.

The hymn appears to have been composed for use as praise and for teaching about the God who is praised. Wisdom ideas are present (vv. 13, 15b, 18a, 19) as the hymn invites the righteous to accept and trust in the God who has chosen them as his people (vv. 12, 20-22).

Though not an acrostic, the twenty-two verses correspond to the number of letters in the Hebrew alphabet (as in Psalms 38 and 103), suggesting a completeness and comprehensiveness to this hymn. The spirit of the psalm is akin to Psalms 146 and 147.

Psalm 33

OUTLINE

Call to Worship: Praise with Instruments and Voices, 33:1-3
The LORD's Praiseworthiness: His Word and Work, 33:4-19
    33:4-9   The Word of the LORD in Creation
    33:10-12   The Counsel of the LORD and the Nations
    33:13-19   The Eye of the LORD on All Humankind
Concluding Affirmation of Trust, 33:20-22

EXPLANATORY NOTES

Call to Worship: Praise with Instruments and Voices 33:1-3

Psalm 33 begins where the last verse of Psalm 32 left off, with a summons to the righteous to sing with joy the praises of God (32:11). Since no separate heading is given Psalm 33, it has at times been combined with the preceding psalm in ancient Hebrew manuscripts (Wilson, 2002:555-56). Yet Psalm 33 stands on its own as a complete hymn of praise and will be so considered here.

The praise of joyful music is noisy! Instruments, singing, and loud shouts! The Hebrew word *tĕrû'â*, to describe the loud shout of a battle cry by a military leader and his attacking army (Josh 6:5), later came to be used as a liturgical exclamation about God as king and savior: *loud shouts* (Ps 33:3). For the psalmist and his world, praise gave rise to music and formed and controlled it (vv. 1-3; 81:1-3; 92:1-3; 150:3-5). In this psalm, accompanying instruments have become part of the procedure for praising God, amplifying the sound, and extending the range of the praise sung by human voices (Westermann, 1989:211).

A *new song* responds to a new experience, a new act of deliverance enacted by the LORD (v. 3; 40:3; 96:1; 98:1; 149:1). The congregation expresses in song the sense of being gripped anew by the majesty and wonder of God.

The LORD's Praiseworthiness: His Word and Work 33:4-19

The basis for praise begins with a series of five words proclaiming the LORD's praiseworthiness: *upright, faithfulness, righteousness, justice,* and *steadfast love* (vv. 4-5) *[Steadfast]*. The terms describe a dependable and gracious God. The LORD's word has shown itself to be reliable, beginning with the creation of the heavens, the sea, and the earth (vv. 6-9). The theme of the LORD making all things by his word (vv. 4, 6, 9) points to the creation account (Gen 1:6-10). The earth is full of his *steadfast love* (v. 5), and the world's inhabitants are summoned to respond in fear and awe (v. 8; Ps 19:9; 22:23). Awe must be the keynote of praise.

The reference to nature's obedient glory (v. 9) contrasts with human defiance (v. 10). So begins this section on the counsel of the LORD and the nations (vv. 10-12). Only one plan endures forever: God's plan. The LORD is in control. He thwarts the purposes of his opponents. The *heart* was viewed as the site of all thought and planning, the place where the whole person experienced joy, sorrow, or hope (v. 11; 10:6; 15:2; 20:4; 25:17; 28:7; 55:4; 112:7). This reference to God's heart is followed by references to the human heart (vv. 15, 21). Election is recognized as a gift of God's grace in the proclaiming of *Happy* (*Blessed*, NIV) those people chosen to receive the LORD's counsel. However, people choose whether they will hear and obey (v. 12).

The psalm continues about the *eye of the LORD* being on all humankind (vv. 13-19). The LORD's discerning gaze on *all . . . all . . . all . . . all* outdoes the king's reliance on *great . . . great . . . great*, thus building up to the contrast between the LORD's reliability and everything purely human (vv. 18-19). The repetitive *not . . . not . . . cannot* underscores the truth that force does not have the last word! The psalm contends that all human power, however great, does not determine history. Even the most formidable weapons are nothing more than a lie in terms of security (20:7-8; 44:3) *[War]*. The *eye of the LORD* (v. 18) contrasts with the *heavy hand* (32:4). Here it is akin to the watchful care of the LORD, as in Psalm 32:8. Security and hope comes from God.

Concluding Affirmation of Trust   33:20-22

In contrast to the *vain hope* (v. 17), the final verses invite reaching out to the LORD's *steadfast love* (ḥesed, vv. 5, 18, 22) as the foundation for hope. For such a God one can patiently wait (v. 20; 40:1). The word *soul* (*nepeš*, v. 20) may more appropriately be translated "we," as in NIV. The noun *nepeš* refers to the total human being in both physical and psychological manifestations, whereas "soul" in English carries Hellenistic overtones as something ethereal in contrast to body (Holladay: 320). *Holy* is a statement about the LORD himself, about his name (v. 21; 99:3; 103:1; 111:9; 145:21). In liturgical use, these closing verses avowing confidence may have been the congregation's response to the praise and teaching of a speaker or singer (vv. 4-19).

THE TEXT IN THE BIBLICAL CONTEXT AND LIFE OF THE CHURCH

Majesty and Mercy

In descriptive psalms of praise such as Psalms 33 and 113, the concepts of power and grace, majesty and mercy denote two poles of God's being. In this psalm, the basis for praise is summarized in the pivot verse describing God as a lover of *righteousness* and *justice* (v. 5). Then the hymn proceeds to declare the LORD's majesty in creation (vv. 6-9) and sovereignty in history (vv. 10-12). Only in the third section (vv. 13-19) does the hymn focus on the earth and the LORD's care for humankind (v. 19). May the psalmist intentionally be asserting the LORD's love of righteousness and justice as a needed characteristic precisely also for creation and history? The psalm proclaims that the LORD's *steadfast love* permeates creation, history, and the life of all humankind.

The theme of the majestic God as lover of righteousness and justice condescending to care for the needs of the people is prominent in the psalms and the prophets (37:28; 89:14; 146:5-9; 147:1-6; Isa 53:1-9; 61:8). It is also the message of the incarnation (Luke 1:46-55; John 1:14; Phil 2:6-11).

Peace with or without Weapons

God's people are inheritors of God's mighty plan. But the majority of humankind has refused to believe that the source of security resides in God's unfailing love, rather than in weapons of war. This psalm, pointedly debunking the myth that military might can guarantee security, declares that the *earth is full of the steadfast love of the LORD* (v. 5). Perhaps only those who read creation and history from this perspective, from obedience to covenant, can live hope-filled lives (Brueggemann, 1984:36).

What do verses 13-19 say to contemporary debates about peace with weapons or peace without weapons? Can use of weapons of violence ever bring an end to violence? The biblical witness warns against the folly of such thinking (Isa 31:1-3; Zech 4:6; Matt 26:52). In God, word and deed appear to be one, the model also for God's people.

A New Song

The Psalter is the source from which the language of the spirit-inspired hymns and prayer songs of the early church developed (Col 3:16). The NT raises the "new song" (Rev 5:9-10; 14:1-3), which has its prototype in the OT psalms (33:3; 40:3; 95:1; 96:1; 98:1; 149:1).

The song of the Christian is a new song because it springs from an inner transformation into "a new creation" through the divine act of God in Christ (2 Cor 5:17-21). Transformation gives expression to walking in newness of life (Rom 6:4) and to serving in the newness of the Spirit (7:6). Thus, Christians can "sing a new song to the One who has said, 'Behold, I make all things new'" (Rev 21:5; hymn by Harris J. Loewen, "New earth, heavens new," 1981).

Psalm 34

O Taste and See That the LORD Is Good

PREVIEW

Psalm 34 is a thanksgiving psalm instructing others about how to live in *the fear of the LORD*. The psalm focuses on the LORD, the deliverer of the afflicted. Reciting what the LORD has done, the psalm tells of the nearness, tenderness, ready help, and mighty power of the LORD on behalf of all who trust. It contrasts good and evil and acknowledges retribution.

The psalm's form is that of a sage's address to students (v. 11). Gerstenberger (148-49) identifies the plural address, *O children*, for group teaching and explains how worshippers in the early synagogue may have used the psalm as a liturgical composition. In form, this wisdom psalm stands alongside Psalm 25. Both are acrostics, with each verse beginning with the next letter of the alphabet. Like Psalm 25, the letters beginning the first, middle, and final verses form the Hebrew word "to learn," or "to teach" (*'ālap*, אלף). Verses 12, 15, 16, 20, and 22 begin with the same word in both psalms. The question in verse 12 corresponds to the question in Psalm 25:12.

The title alludes to an episode of David described in 1 Samuel 21:11-15. There the king is called Achish, while in the psalm, Abimelech. The writer may have been using the name *Abimelech* as a generic title for all Philistine kings, or perhaps has confused Achish of Gath (21:10-15) with Ahimelech (1 Sam 21:2; Matthews, *ABD*, 1:21) *[Superscriptions]*.

OUTLINE

Invitation to Praise, 34:1-3
Testimony to the Goodness of the LORD, 34:4-10
    34:4-6   Narrative of the Psalmist's Experience
    34:7-10   The LORD's Care for Those Who Seek Him
Instruction on How to Live a Long and Happy Life, 34:11-21
    34:11-14   Invitation to Learn About Life
    34:15-21   The LORD's Face Toward the Righteous
Liturgical Conclusion: The LORD Redeems, 34:22

EXPLANATORY NOTES

Invitation to Praise   34:1-3

The invitation to praise at all times opens the psalm. *Bless* is used in the sense of "to praise," for whoever "blesses" the LORD praises and honors his sovereign might. Whoever praises the LORD lives as one dependent upon the source of life.

The plight of the "afflicted" (NIV, RSV) is introduced, with a variety of words repeated later. *Humble, holy ones, brokenhearted, crushed in spirit, righteous,* and *his servants* describe those who cry out for help. *Humble* describes those completely dependent upon the LORD, the afflicted delivered from oppression. In the call to worship, the psalmist proclaims that all is of God and invites the hearers to share his newfound joy.

Testimony to the Goodness of the LORD   34:4-10

The personal testimony tells of a time of trouble and fear, and of the psalmist's deliverance as springboard for teaching about life (vv. 4-6). In reciting his own story, he invites hearers to *look* to the LORD and experience the radiance that comes from the goodness of the LORD (v. 5; Jer 31:12), specifically to see the LORD's care for those who seek him (vv. 7-10). The *angel of the LORD* is a way of speaking about God's presence with his people to bring divine help and protection (v. 7; Gen 16:7; Exod 3:2; Num 22:22; Pss 35:5-6; 91:11). The psalm implies that *those who fear the LORD* (vv. 7, 9, 11) have a relationship of trust and live in obedience, attentiveness, and submission to God's will (Pss 22:23; 25:12, 14; 31:19).

With three verbs, *taste, see, fear*, the psalmist invites the worshipper to try God, to drink deeply, and to trust (v. 8). *Taste* becomes a metaphor for the invitation "to experience." *His holy ones* (v. 9) refers to those who are separated unto God, and who by their lives are calling out for the nation to be holy (Exod 19:6). The *young lions* (v. 10) may be a metaphorical term for young men (compare the expression "the young bucks") who think they know it all. But the wisdom of life holds so much more than feeble human strength and arrogance (vv. 8b and 10b)! The motif of the rich coming to naught and the hungry satisfied with good things (v. 10; Ps 107:9) is amplified in Luke 1:53.

Instruction on How to Live a Long and Happy Life
34:11-21

The teacher now exhorts the students to learn the secret to a long and prosperous life (vv. 11-14). It begins with *the fear of the LORD* (v. 11; Prov 1:7) and leads to enjoyment of the LORD's protection and provision (Ps 34:7, 9). Wherein lies the happiness of life, length of days, and enjoyment of good (v. 12)? It is an old question, found almost in identical form at El-Amarna, in an inscription in the tomb of Pharaoh Ai (or Ay, fourteenth century BC). What better answer than the appeal to the practical aspects of godly living (vv. 13-14)? Avoid the sins of the tongue, do good rather than evil, and *seek peace* (*shalom, šālôm*), the relationship of harmony and well-being pleasing to the loving God. Here the psalm links ethical concern with liturgical practice. Seeking the LORD in supplication is not to be separated from loving good, hating evil, and seeking peace (v. 14; Amos 5:15; Mays, 1994b:153).

From experience, the psalmist is convinced of the LORD's benevolent gaze on the *righteous* (vv. 15-18). The *eyes of the LORD* (Ps 33:18) and the *ears* are reminders that God sees the plight of the oppressed and hears the prayers of those who cry out. Four times the *righteous* (*ṣaddîq*) are mentioned as the special object of God's intervention (vv. 15-22) *[Righteous].* The righteous are identified with the *humble* (v. 2), the *poor* (v. 6), the *brokenhearted* (v. 18), and those who take refuge in the LORD (vv. 8, 22). They know themselves to be recipients with responsibility for reshaping life (Brueggemann, 1984:134).

These verses also articulate the contrast between the righteous and the wicked and their respective fates, a theme central in wisdom teaching (Prov 4:18-19; 10:11, 29-31; 11:30-31). The LORD cares for the righteous, but the evil people will be destroyed by their own evil deeds (vv. 19-21). Confidence in the LORD's caring concern for his people shines through these verses as the LORD intervenes on the side of the righteous and poor against their oppressors.

Liturgical Conclusion: The LORD Redeems 34:22

As in Psalm 25, the final verse appears added for the psalm's use in worship, to give a note of assurance to the righteous. Those who take refuge in the LORD need not fear condemnation nor being cut off prematurely, which is the fate of the wicked. Instead, the LORD is the one who *redeems his people* (v. 22; Ps 25:22)

THE TEXT IN THE BIBLICAL CONTEXT AND LIFE OF THE CHURCH

Wisdom for Living

A common feature of wisdom literature is the appeal to personal experience as a preface to an invitation for others to share the same attitude toward life (Job 22:15-22; Prov 4:1-9). In Psalm 34, the psalmist appeals out of his experience of deliverance: *O taste and see that the LORD is good* (v. 8). In the context of worship, this is an invitation for others also to seek God and trust in his protective care.

The movement from praising God to giving instruction is common (Pss 32:5-8, 11; 51:13-17). The goal in Psalm 34 is to teach others how to gain life (vv. 12-14; Prov 9:1-11). The instructions are clear: Tend to your tongue, hate evil, love good, and seek peace (v. 14).

In the Beatitudes of Jesus some have seen similar teaching about the wisdom of life (Matt 5:3-12). Jesus offers words of wisdom to those who acknowledge their spiritual poverty and are willing to seek the kingdom of God. "Blessing from God comes to those who eschew the power tactics of the world and rely wholly on God as refuge" (Wilson, 2002:573).

Two direct quotations from Psalm 34 are found in 1 Peter, where rules for life from the wisdom tradition are used. In 1 Peter 2:3, the writer refers to Psalm 34:8, *O taste and see that the LORD is good*, as he pleads for fellow believers to work out the implications of their personal commitment. First Peter 3:10-12 draws on the LXX translation of Psalm 34:12-16 to illustrate Christian response to suffering. The writer counsels that if there is suffering for doing good, "you are blessed. Do not fear, and . . . do not be intimidated, but in your hearts sanctify Christ as Lord" (1 Pet 3:14-15).

A Reality Check

In what does life's happiness lie? Psalm 34 provides practical advice far different from the portrayals of life in novels of the day or in what flashes across TV and movie screens. How much attention do people of faith give to the words spoken, to the warning against evil, and to striving after what is good and true and makes for peace among people?

In reality, doing good and avoiding evil will not keep people of faith from all affliction and suffering. In the experiences of life, it does not seem that the righteous *lack no good thing* (v. 10), or that God rescues them from *all* their troubles (vv. 17, 20). The psalmist was not naive, acknowledging out of his own experience that fear, oppression, and brokenness in heart, spirit, and body is also the reality of life (v. 19). However, the LORD's goodness lies in the fact that he is *near* (v. 18), present with his people, whatever life may bring (Ps 73).

As testimony to the caring presence of God in times of trouble, the *Martyrs Mirror* (Braght) has sixteen quotations from Psalm 34. Most of these are in letters written from prison to family members. They cite verses 7-9, 15, and 19 about the many afflictions of the righteous, but how the Lord delivers. Especially precious to the martyrs was the passage about how the *eyes of the LORD* are toward the righteous, and *his ears* toward their cry (v. 15). They felt that God was hearing their prayers!

When everything seems lost and we feel at the end of our endurance, let us hear this psalm's confident thanksgiving and trust in the Lord's deliverance.

Liturgical Use of Psalm 34

The daily prayers of the Jews include these words from Psalm 34:13: *Keep your tongue from evil, and your lips from speaking deceit.* Psalm 34 is appropriately used for holy communion, as well as during Passion Week, as practiced by Eastern Orthodox, Roman Catholic, Lutheran, and other churches.

In hymnody, the psalm provides the basis for the anthem "O taste and see that the Lord is good." Tate and Brady's hymn (1696) "Through all the changing scenes of life" invites the worshipper to trust and experience God's redeeming love:

> O make but trial of his love;
> Experience will decide
> How blest are they, and only they,
> Who in his truth confide.

Psalm 35

Plea from One of the Quiet in the Land

PREVIEW

From the first word, *Contend*, strident language characterizes this individual lament. The staccato of *Let them . . . , let them . . . , let them . . .* (vv. 4-6, 24-26) calls out imprecations on the adversary. This complex prayer is voiced by a person who seeks vindication because of the damaging hostility of others, perhaps even adversaries who used to be friends (vv. 13-15).

So the psalmist cries for God to do battle on his behalf, praying vehemently against his foes to the God who acts to defend the poor and defenseless against the slanders, accusations, and ensnaring of their adversaries. The desperate nature of the psalmist's situation is evident in the requests or complaints expressed in twenty-four of the twenty-eight verses. Each of the three laments (vv. 1-8, 11-17, and 19-26) ends either with a vow of joy (vv. 9-10), thanksgiving (v. 18), or praise (vv. 27-28).

Psalm 35 begins a series of individual lament psalms (Pss 35–43, except for 37). All, except 41–42, are given the ascription *Of David* [Superscriptions].

OUTLINE

Cry for Deliverance, Imprecation, and Promise, 35:1-10
Cry of Innocence, Plea, and Vow of Thanksgiving, 35:11-18
Complaint, Plea for Vindication, Imprecation, and Praise, 35:19-28

EXPLANATORY NOTES

Cry for Deliverance, Imprecation, and Promise
35:1-10

The psalmist addresses the LORD, the divine judge, with an urgent plea for divine action and deliverance. *Contend* (*rîb*), a legal term, is later translated *my cause* (v. 23). Striking phrases describe the adversaries as opponents-at-law (v. 1), foes on a battlefield (vv. 1-3), hunters spreading a net or digging a trench (vv. 7-8), robbers stripping the weak (v. 10), or wild beasts moving in to attack (vv. 15-16). The picture is of persons scheming, mobbing, and gloating. Against such foes, the sufferer, out of the depths of his troubles, longs for the LORD to speak to him and say, *"I am your salvation"* (v. 3). The military language draws on the metaphor of the divine warrior and articulates a situation out of control (Exod 15:1-18; Ps 18:6-19; Isa 63:1-3; Jer 20:11).

A repetitive *Let them . . .* introduces the prayer of imprecation (vv. 4-8, 24-26) in the conviction that God's *righteousness* (*ṣedeq*, vv. 24, 28) will prevail. Fear of those who *seek* to take one's *life* (v. 4) is common in the laments (Pss 38:12; 40:14; 54:3; 63:9; 70:2; 86:14). Thus, the plea is, "Help me and put down my enemies!" The psalmist wants to shame those committing abominable acts (v. 4): *Let their way be dark, . . . with the angel of the LORD pursuing them* (v. 6) so that they experience equivalent retribution (vv. 7-8; 7:12-16; 9:15-16; 141:10) *[Imprecation]*.

The vows after each lament are introduced with *Then* (vv. 9, 18, 28). In desperation, hope is present, as well as trust that the LORD will prevail. What is at stake is not the personal vindictiveness of the psalmist, but the character of the divine judge. To the rhetorical question, *"O LORD, who is like you?"* the obvious answer is "No one" (v. 10). The foes are the strong who trample the weak and poor, who in turn appeal to the LORD for mercy and help in obtaining justice (9:18; 10:2, 8-11; 18:27; 74:19). The greatness of the LORD lies in his bias toward the helpless.

Cry of Innocence, Plea, and Vow of Thanksgiving
35:11-18

The main complaint is about *malicious witnesses* (lit., *witnesses of violence*, vv. 11-16). The opposition he has experienced is undeserved and particularly painful since it comes from former friends (vv. 13-14). He is astonished and hurt because persons he had helped now turn against him (vv. 15-16). Appeals of persons declaring their innocence can be found in other psalms (7:3-8; 37:34-40; 69:4-21). The question, *How long, O LORD?* is at the heart of the writer's exasperation with the LORD's inaction (v. 17; 6:3; 62:3; 74:10; 119:84).

As with the acclamation of joy ending the psalm's first section (vv. 1-10), this lament concludes with a vow to give thanks in the presence of *the great congregation* (v. 18; 22:22, 25; 66:16; 109:30). The singer, who stands in the midst of the congregation, tells of the LORD's power and goodness so that the people will themselves praise and glorify God (40:9-10).

Complaint, Plea for Vindication, Imprecation, and Praise 35:19-28

In the final section, the psalmist resumes the complaint against the gloating enemies (vv. 19-22). The psalmist identifies with the *quiet in the land* (v. 20). This poetic term for the congregation as the people of God is appropriately rendered "peaceable folk" (NEB). The psalm reflects the biblical understanding that God is God of the oppressed, and that many simple folk are squeezed daily by people in power. God must not allow such malice to proceed *[Judge]*.

In a positive plea, he calls for the LORD to wake up, come to his cause, and intervene (vv. 22-25). The psalmist is sure that God has *seen* (v. 22) and will have something to say about the situation. He is confident that he will be pronounced righteous or innocent, and the gloating enemies dishonored (vv. 24-26). The final vindication is left in God's hands, but the plea is for God's justice to prevail. In contrast to the damaging speech by his adversaries (vv. 11-12, 20-22), the psalmist's testimony will tell of the LORD's victory (vv. 27-28). The final verse provides an appropriate transition to Psalm 36, which declares the LORD's righteousness in providing refuge to the righteous and presiding over the downfall of the wicked *[Righteous]*.

THE TEXT IN THE BIBLICAL CONTEXT AND LIFE OF THE CHURCH

Who Is Like God?

In the midst of an oppressive situation, the psalmist dares to ask the question *O LORD, who is like you?* The uniqueness of God was always evident when his people remembered his deeds and wonders of old (77:11-15). Such remembrance gave them courage to cry out for help, for the LORD was set apart from other gods by his wonderful works (86:8). God was also set apart by his essential character of righteousness (71:19), holiness (Exod 15:11; Ps 99:3, 5), glory (Ps 113:4-5), majesty (Exod 15:11; Deut 33:26; Ps 93:1) and faithfulness (Ps 89:8).

Above all, however, God was the One who rescued the lowly and needy from the stronger members of society who robbed the poor of the justice due them (Ps 35:10). God's trustworthiness is the result of the incomparable power used for the benefit of the powerless (Wilson, 2002:587). Such an understanding of God, who delivers the lonely and the poor, is echoed in the song of Mary (Luke 1:46-55).

Finding Ourselves in the Psalm

The biting language of imprecation always jolts. Daily life for the oppressed is anything but a calm, peaceful settledness. When people cry out in anger, it is often the cry for justice. The psalm voices rage and urges God to take action and intervene on behalf of the helpless. Thus, the psalmist will find shelter in the LORD's promise *I am your salvation* (v. 3)! But the psalm also describes a *peaceable folk* (v. 20), a people whose will is to live in peace with neighbors and oppressors.

Can we find ourselves in this psalm? Where might it touch us? Nothing cuts so deeply as false accusations and malicious gossip. We care what people think and say about us. The psalm gives testimony to the reality that in desperate situations, others have found God a refuge and saving presence. Certainly the psalm is for anyone who has to do battle alone for a just cause.

In the church's use of Psalm 35, some have seen the voice speaking as that of Jesus Christ in the drama of his passion and death. So Jesus' words "they hated me without a cause" (John 15:25) have been linked to Psalm 35:19 (cf. 69:4; 109:3). Thus, when the church prays this psalm as Jesus speaking, it shares in the suffering of Christ and in the spiritual struggle that hatred toward God shall not ultimately prevail (Reardon: 67-68). The church's worship has most often used Psalm 35 during Lent.

Not only did Jesus suffer unjustly, but also, his teachings recognize that his followers may be "persecuted for righteousness' sake" and suffer "falsely on my account" (Matt 5:10-11). Jesus taught his followers to love their enemies and pray for those who persecute them (5:44), a way of life that has not been understood, but is often ridiculed, maligned, and sometimes paid for by life itself.

Psalm 36

With You Is the Fountain of Life

PREVIEW

Against the dark background of a scathing description of the rebellious (vv. 1-4), the psalmist portrays a radiant picture of the divine lovingkindness (vv. 5-9). Standing between human wickedness and divine grace, the psalmist turns to prayer (vv. 10-12), with the final verse expressing certainty.

This reflective psalm contains elements of lament, wisdom, and hymn. As a complaint of the individual, its design for worship shapes diverse elements into a unity. The psalm describes the arrogant wicked in their self-centered depravity, and then contrasts them with the all-encompassing love of the LORD, which embraces and gives life to all creation. The psalm offers confidence to those who know the LORD and take refuge in the temple. The psalmist (and the community) asks that the LORD's steadfast love, rather than the power of the wicked, determine their present and their future. The psalm may have been used in early Jewish worship to affirm the protective care of God over the weak and needy (Gerstenberger: 157).

The title includes the descriptive phrase regarding David, *the servant of the LORD*, found also in the title of Psalm 18 [Superscriptions].

Psalm 36

OUTLINE

Complaint: Description of the Arrogant Wicked, 36:1-4
Hymn: Praise of the Gracious Love of the LORD, 36:5-9
Petition: Prayers for the LORD's Continuing Care and Protection, 36:10-12

EXPLANATORY NOTES

Complaint: Description of the Arrogant Wicked 36:1-4

The psalm begins with the technical Hebrew word *nĕ'um*, translated *speaks* or *oracle* (NIV). An oracle is commonly followed by the divine name and refers to a message received by a prophet from God. Its use here may be in a caustic sense, as if the only source of inspiration that the wicked have is their own rebellious nature (Davidson, 1998:122). *Transgression* is rebellion against lawful authority, here rebellion against the rule of God *[Wicked]*.

The awful state of the person who claims *no fear of God* is then laid out (vv. 1-4). While planning evil, the rebellious move on a downward path, oblivious to the deeper reality that human acts lie open to divine scrutiny. Destructive speech erupts as accusations and denunciations. They cease *to act wisely and do good* (v. 3). Plotting mischief around the clock, they have turned a blind eye to the destruction caused by evil deeds (v. 4). Such an intense portrayal of the arrogant wicked is as severe as any found in the psalms (Prov 6:12-15).

Hymn: Praise of the Gracious Love of the LORD 36:5-9

In sharp contrast, the hymn, adorned with covenant language, proclaims the wonder of God's protective care (vv. 5-6). In opposition to the wicked, the psalm proclaims the greatness of the LORD as it describes the character of his goodness. God's *steadfast love* overarches like the blue Mediterranean sky. God's *faithfulness* fills the vault of heaven like the massed clouds. God's *righteousness* rises like a mountain range. God's *judgments* abide like the fathomless sea (White: 65). Humans and animals alike can depend on God's saving and providential activity.

The joyous security in God's *steadfast love* (*ḥesed*) is described with images reminiscent of Psalms 23; 46; 84; and 122 (vv. 7-9; cf. 63:7, *in shadow of your wings*) *[Steadfast]*. The focus of these verses is the LORD's *steadfast love*, but the setting is the temple. The protection offered in the sanctuary became the epitome of all divine protection (v. 7;

27:1, 5; 91:1-4). Also implied here is the joy of the sacrificial meal in the sanctuary (v. 8). The word *delights* is also used for the paradise of Eden (*'ēden*, Gen 2:8, etc.), and it may be background for the messianic banquet frequently mentioned in the Qumran literature and the NT (A. Anderson, 1:291). The theme of continually abiding in God's love is a constant note in the psalms, expressing the hope of remaining always in the sphere of God's presence and deliverance (vv. 7-9; Pss 52:8-9; 61:4).

The LORD's steadfast love promises "abundance," but also access to the life-giving source (v. 9). Note the shift from third person (*they*, v. 8) to first person (*we*, v. 9). The congregation's confessional statement, *For with you is the fountain of life; in your light we see light,* is one of the finest in the Bible. *Your light* probably refers to the light of God's face (4:6; 44:3; 89:15). In this beautiful conception of life, humans originate in God and are sustained by God. Without God, they would be what the earth would be without the sun. "Just as everything subsists on the sun's life and heat, . . . so it is the 'light' of God, . . . which gives . . . (life) meaning and transparency, strength and stability" (Weiser: 311).

Petition: Prayers for the LORD's Continuing Care and Protection   36:10-12

The prayer rises out of the tension between the two attitudes toward life described, self-sufficiency in rebellion (vv. 1-4), or life illumined by God's steadfast love (vv. 5-9). The petitioners, identifying themselves with God's people (v. 10; 7:10), ask for continuance of God's *steadfast love* and *salvation* and pray that the wicked may be reduced to impotence. Describing the situation as that of a person in distress who fears the foot of the victor on the neck of the defeated, the psalmist prays that God would not allow the wicked to drive him away from the temple (v. 11). The imprecation of the final verse claims victory over the evildoers (5:5; 6:8; 59:2). *There* (v. 12) likely refers to Mt. Zion (76:3; 87:6; 122:5), though some see it as a euphemism for the underworld (Job 1:21; 3:17; Clifford, 2002:186) *[Imprecation]*.

THE TEXT IN THE BIBLICAL CONTEXT AND LIFE OF THE CHURCH

Recipe for Disaster

Psalm 36 begins with a grim portrayal of people who accept no higher authority than their own desires and plans (Gen 2–3). Devoid of any *fear of God*, they have dismissed God as irrelevant and talk themselves into believing that they will never be called into account (Pss 14:1-4; 53:1-4).

Paul wrote about the rebellious who live with no fear of God. In Romans 1:28-32 his description of those whom God "gave up to a debased mind" parallels that of Psalm 36:1-4. Paul underscores the universality and power of human sinfulness in Romans 3:10-18, using a series of citations from the psalms, including Psalm 36:1 (Rom 3:18). Paul contends that this rebellion is part of each person. No one is exempt (Rom 3:22-23). The only cure for this rebellion in human hearts is the divine gift of mercy.

The biblical period had no corner on evil. Pornographers who exploit women and children for money, drug runners who pander to the needs of addicts, and abusers who dominate innocent victims continue to reflect this delusion. Unfortunately, apart from God, the rebellious one often is not even aware of needing help (Wyrtzen: 99).

Psalm 36 points to a specific area in which humans beings do not do very well, that of care for the earth and all living creatures (v. 6). Does not focus on self and our little world too often mean destruction of God's creation, other people, the animals, and the life-giving nature of the earth itself? All living things are interrelated. Human greed diminishes the vitality of the soil, water, and air, which ultimately affects the welfare of all living things.

Life-Giving Images

This psalm, which begins with an intense portrayal of the wicked, at its center extols the cosmic reigning God. Life-giving images abound. God's love is boundless, from the heights into the depths, and inclusive of all living things (vv. 5-6). God's protective *wings* provide refuge (v. 7; Pss 17:8; 36:7; 57:1; 61:4; 63:7; 91:4). God's *feast* offers abundance (v. 8; 23:5-6; 63:5; Isa 25:6; Matt 22:1-10; John 6:25-35). Living water is offered freely (v. 8; Jer 2:13; 17:13; John 4:10; 7:38; Rev 7:17; 21:6). In the gaze of God's face, people of faith see *light* (v. 9; Pss 27:1; 118:27). A Christian reading this psalm is directed to the life-light of the incarnation of Jesus Christ: "In him was life and the life was the light of all people. The light shines in the darkness" (John 1:4).

At its best worship is life-giving, pointing to God as the source of life and light. Psalm 36 is another psalm often read during Holy Week. In hymnody, Isaac Watts' paraphrase, "High in the heavens, Eternal God" (1719), proclaims:

> Life, like a fountain, rich and free,
> Springs from the presence of the Lord;
> And in thy light our souls shall see
> The glories promised in thy Word.

Psalm 37

Commit Your Way to the LORD

PREVIEW

This pastoral psalm addresses the problem of the apparent prosperity of the wicked. Like Psalm 73, it wrestles with the topic of theodicy, God's justice in an unjust world. An aged, experienced teacher (v. 25) commends these wisdom sayings of admonition and promise to build greater trust and confidence in God in a situation when keeping faith is difficult. The psalmist projects a long view of history. God will be victorious. Therefore, the righteous need not fret in envy or fear of the wicked.

Acrostic in form, in which every two verses begin with the next letter of the Hebrew alphabet, this wisdom psalm represents a collection of proverbs. Perhaps the psalmist has altered a lament to become wisdom instruction, thus exhorting the pious to trust in God, who will eventually punish the wicked and vindicate the pious (Westermann, 1989:292). The theme of retribution is accepted (cf. Job; Pss 49; 73; Prov 10:24-25). Any evidence to the contrary is but temporary. Used in the synagogue worship, this teaching poem supported the poor and oppressed to sustain hope for fundamental social change (Gerstenberger: 160).

Powerful word images contrast the fate of the wicked (*rāšā'*) and the righteous (*ṣaddîq*). The former will *fade* (v. 2), be *cut off* (v. 9), have their arms *broken* (v. 17), and *vanish* (v. 20), but the righteous

Psalm 37

will *inherit the land* (vv. 3, 9, 11, 22, 29, 34). The two ways are clearly delineated (Deut 30:15-20; Ps 1) *[Wicked; Righteous]*.

The psalm expresses a mood of calm. Life with God is full of hope and strength. Without God, it is doomed to destruction.

OUTLINE

Fret Not Because of the Wicked, but Trust in the LORD, 37:1-11
The End of the Wicked and the Righteous Contrasted, 37:12-22
The Blessings of the Faithful, 37:23-29
The LORD Is the Helper of the Righteous, 37:30-40

EXPLANATORY NOTES

Fret Not Because of the Wicked, but Trust in the LORD 37:1-11

One can sum up the theme of Psalm 37 in a question: What does faith in God mean in a world where wickedness sometimes seems to pay handsome dividends? The central teaching is stated at the beginning (vv. 1-4), with the rest of the psalm providing variations on the theme. The acrostic form does not usually allow for neat progression of thought, but tends to accentuate repetition. The imperative mood (vv. 1-9) shifts to indicative for most of the rest of the psalm.

The poem begins with exhortation about the wrong way and the right way to respond to the success of the wicked (vv. 1-9). The psalmist offers a command to calm faith: *Do not fret* (vv. 1, 7, 8; lit., "be not heated"). Do not become overly anxious that the wicked appear to prosper, for the wicked will soon be off the scene (vv. 2, 7, 9-10; Prov 23:17-18; 24:1, 19-20). Instead, give positive attention to the LORD: *trust* (v. 3), *take delight in* (v. 4), *commit your way to* (v. 5; lit., "roll over your life"), *be still before,* and *wait patiently for him* (vv. 7, 34). The admonition, *do good* (vv. 3, 27), appeals to justice and ethical uprightness. The alternative to *anger* is to surrender and trust in what the LORD has in store (vv. 8-11).

The promise is, *The meek shall inherit the land* (vv. 9, 11). The context defines the meek as those who choose the way of patient faith instead of self-assertion (vv. 3, 9, 11, 22, 29, 34). The greedy and grasping people will not ultimately be the prosperous (vv. 16, 21, 25-26). This psalm could reflect "haves" giving counsel to the landless. But it may well reflect a hope for social reform in a situation as described in Nehemiah 5. Brueggemann's extended essay "Psalm 37: Conflict of Interpretations" identifies ideological (affirming the status quo) and utopian (anticipated promised possession of the land) readings of this psalm (1995:235-57). The poor become witnesses to God's gracious presence, to his transformation of their destiny, and to his effective provision of justice (9:18; 10:17-18; 18:27; 22:26; 69:33; 147:6; 149:4).

The End of the Wicked and the Righteous Contrasted 37:12-22

This section describes the futility of the wicked people's plotting schemes and affirms the LORD's derisive laughter at the pretense of the wicked (vv. 12-14; 2:4; 59:8). The weapons of the wicked backfire and are broken, as are their arms or "power" (vv. 14-15, 17). Resort to force is the way of the wicked, but violent aggression is a sure way to self-destruction.

Better is a little that the righteous person has than . . . are characteristic words of wisdom (v. 16; Prov 15:16-17). The LORD, who knows and probes the depths of the heart, establishes the righteous again and upholds them (v. 17; Ps 7:9). In contrast to the tentative existence of the wicked (v. 20), the ways of the righteous are known to the LORD, and their heritage is *forever* (vv. 18-19). The generosity of the righteous keeps them prosperous (vv. 21-22).

The Blessings of the Faithful   37:23-29

The theme of these verses is the overarching security of those who trust in the LORD. The autobiographical comment about not having *seen the righteous forsaken* (v. 25) does not mean that the righteous never hurt or suffer want, but points to a vision of the true reality that accords with the LORD's character and purpose. It is the psalmist's way of saying that underneath is always the LORD's steadying hand (v. 24). The admonition *Depart from evil, and do good* (v. 27) is based on belief in the LORD's justice (vv. 26-27; Job 28:28; Ps 34:14; Prov 13:19).

The LORD Is the Helper of the Righteous   37:30-40

In the end, the long view will prevail (vv. 27-28, *forever*; the graphic sketch of vv. 35-36; and the focus on *posterity,* vv. 37-38). The godly will not be permanently forsaken. Their hope and help is in the LORD (vv. 39-40). The LORD can incline the human heart to do good so that the Torah may dwell in the heart (v. 31; Pss 37:31; 40:8; 119:36, 112; 141:4). Hope means to *keep to his way* and not be distracted (v. 34). Another autobiographical comment tells of the uncertainty of the well-off (vv. 35-36; Isa 40:23-24). To those who experience suffering, these final verses offer confidence in the LORD. Salvation and rescue are from the LORD (vv. 39-40).

THE TEXT IN THE BIBLICAL CONTEXT AND LIFE OF THE CHURCH

Where Is the Justice?

People of faith find it perplexing that the wicked appear to prosper even though biblical teaching indicates that should not be so (Job 4:7-8; 8:1-7, 20; Pss 5:4-6; 7:14-16; 34:6-7, 15-16; Prov 10:16, 22; 11:19, 21, 28). At the same time, bad things do happen to good people, in spite of what is said in Psalm 37:25-26.

What can one say about the massive suffering in the world, the Holocaust, the nuclear bombs on Hiroshima and Nagasaki, and the more recent wars in Vietnam, Bosnia, and Iraq, killing and maiming countless innocent victims? The question of innocent suffering is partially addressed by the book of Job and Psalm 73. To the need for a God of retribution, the psalmist finally acknowledges, as does Job, inability to humanly understand God's mysteries. However, he asserts, "Nevertheless I am continually with you; you hold my right hand" (Ps 73:23; Job 42:1-6).

Psalm 37 proposes an alternative to fretting over the apparent lack of justice in the world, and that is to trust in God, for the way of the wicked will perish (Ps 1:1, 6). Ernesto Cardenal (63) paraphrases Psalm 37 in a prophetic mode:

> Well it is great to make a million
>   on the stock exchange,
>   but what do you get for your shares?
> They've only lasted in the end like grass
>   in a summer drought.

Why should people anxiously envy those who prosper? Even the famous and the rich will vanish. "Mortals cannot abide in their pomp; they are like the animals that perish" (Ps 49:12, 20).

In the Sermon on the Mount Jesus speaks about a sensible lifestyle based on trust in God, and a meek and humble approach toward others; this may be the best commentary on this psalm and its implication for contemporary life. The psalmist commands calm faith, as does Jesus (Ps 37:3, 5; Matt 5:5; 6:25-34).

Uses of Psalm 37

A commentary on Psalm 37 was found among the documents of the Qumran community. This work applied the psalm directly to the experiences of the community. It related Psalm 37:32-33 to "the Wicked Priest who tried to kill the Teacher of Righteousness." The Qumran community believed it was living at the climax of history and that its members were God's righteous remnant. The final separation of the wicked and the righteous would soon take place. Those at Qumran, as well as early Jewish Christians, believed that the Messiah was to restore the land to its rightful owners, to those who waited for the Lord for justice (Clifford, 2002:192; Holladay: 104, 109). The *Didache* (3.7), a short church manual from the second century, cites Psalm 37:11, "The humble shall inherit the earth," a phrase reinforced by Matthew 5:5.

In 1568, William of Orange published his "Justification" of his resistance to Philip of Spain, the beginning of the Eighty Years' War of liberation for the Netherlands. He quoted, "The wicked watch for the righteous, and seek to kill them" (Ps 37:32). Those loyal to the House of Orange reportedly sang psalms in their resistance (Holladay: 209).

German hymn writer Paul Gerhardt's twelve-stanza hymn "Befiel du deine Wege" (1656) draws on Psalm 37:5. John Wesley later translated it into two hymns, "Commit thou all thy griefs" (1739) and "Give to the winds thy fears" (1739). Gerhardt suffered deep sorrows during the disruption of the Thirty Years' War, especially the deaths of his wife and four children. The hymn speaks of comfort and hope in the midst of fear.

Psalm 37:5 also served as a motto for daily repetition by missionary David Livingstone. The psalm is useful for personal contemplation. How might one pray such a psalm that speaks about God rather than to God? Reardon (71-72) suggests that believers pray by respecting its tone of admonition, warning, and promise. "This is a psalm in which one will do more listening than talking. . . . The psalm is a meditative lesson on not being deceived by appearances, and a summons to wait patiently for God's deliverance."

Psalm 38

Do Not Forsake Me, O LORD!

PREVIEW

In the desperate personal cry of this lament, we see one like Job, sick and abandoned. But unlike Job, who claimed innocence, the psalmist admits sin, makes confession, and waits in silence. Psalm 38 connects sin and sickness and interprets sickness as the effect of God's wrath. Yet the psalm ends with a plea not to be forsaken by the God in whom alone is hope and help.

The graphic description of the illness and ostracism by family, friends, and others suggests leprosy (Lev 14), but that is not certain. In the title, *for the memorial offering* (also in Ps 70) brings to mind the thank offering burned on the altar (Lev 2:1-10). Literally, the title means "to bring to remembrance" *[Superscriptions]*. This psalm is the third in a list of Penitential Psalms (Pss 6; 32; 38; 51; 102; 130; 143) *[Penitential]*.

Though not an acrostic, this "alphabet" psalm of 22 verses (corresponding to 22 letters in the Hebrew alphabet) is in the lament form found in Lamentations (1; 2; 4; 5). Expressions of pain alternate with pleading. The theme of sin and sickness is shared in the final group of Psalms (38–41) to close book I of the Psalter.

OUTLINE

Opening Plea for Help, 38:1-2
Description of the Psalmist's Illness, 38:3-10
Abandoned by All, 38:11-20
Final Plea for Deliverance, 38:21-22

Another way to outline this psalm is to look at the names used to address God in the cry for help: *the LORD* (*Yahweh,* vv. 1-8); *Lord* (*'ădonay,* vv. 9-14); *the LORD* (*Yahweh*), *my God* (*'elohîm*), and *O Lord* (*'ădonay,* vv. 15-22). The use of all three forms may suggest increasing desperation to take hold of God in all facets of the divine being *[Names of God]*.

EXPLANATORY NOTES

Opening Plea for Help   38:1-2

This prayer of a person hurting intensely is framed by requests for help (vv. 1-2, 21-22).

The opening cry is the same as in Psalm 6:1. God's *anger* and *wrath* are pictured like *arrows* (Deut 32:23; Job 6:4; 16:12-13; Lam 3:12-13), and as a heavy *hand* (Pss 32:4; 39:10). We should not interpret divine wrath as a metaphor for the withdrawal of God's presence and power from sinful human beings, as a literal description of a volatile and fierce deity *[Wrath]*.

Description of the Psalmist's Illness   38:3-10

The picture is that of a man in the grip of a life-threatening illness. *No soundness in my flesh* describes his plight (vv. 3, 7). Festering, foul-smelling wounds (v. 5) and loins *filled with burning* (v. 7) cause the psalmist to declare, *I am utterly spent* (v. 8). The word for a corpse (*flesh,* vv. 3, 7) is used, suggesting the chill of death.

Beyond the awful physical expressions of the illness, the psalmist experiences another torment: *a burden too heavy* (v. 4), a fitting description of guilt. *My foolishness* (v. 5), a word often used in Proverbs, refers to sin that comes through stupid indifference to discipline. That sense of moral failure adds to the weight of a crushing illness: *the light of my eyes,* not only actual sight but also vitality, *has gone* (v. 10)!

The psalmist links his hurt to *your* (the LORD's) *indignation* (v. 3) and *my sin* (v. 3) and *my foolishness* (v. 5). These psalms articulate a causal connection between guilt and sickness (32:1-4; 39:8, 11). The effects of the illness and the guilt are all-consuming and compared to waves breaking over his head and threatening to drown him (v. 4). The *groan* (v. 8) and *sighing* (v. 9) is understated in translation, for the word šaʾag (*groan,* v. 8; *roared,* KJV) often describes the "roaring" of a lion (22:13; Isa 5:29). The description of the plight (vv. 3-8) is summarized in the confession that the life force has been extinguished (v. 10; Ps 13:3).

Abandoned by All 38:11-20

The psalmist now reinforces the terrible plight: even friends and family stand far off (v. 11). Aloneness carries a terrifying silence. With no defense to make, the psalmist confesses and waits for God. The fear of those who seek to take one's life is a common element in the laments (v. 12; 35:4; 40:14; 54:3; 63:9; 70:2; 86:14). What *foes* and *adversaries* are seeking to ruin the psalmist's life (vv. 12, 16, 19-20)? They may be former friends, companions, or neighbors who see his illness as punishment for sin and the psalmist as a person to be rejected and shunned. Other candidates fall in this category of enemies *[Enemies].* In depression and grief, the psalmist is no longer able to respond (vv. 13-14). Addressing God by three different names and twice using the second-person pronoun *you,* the psalmist appeals to and waits for the LORD to act as defender and vindicator (v. 15).

Following a summary of the mental and physical distress (vv. 16-17), the psalmist confesses his sin (v. 18) and once more summarizes the malice of his adversaries (vv. 19-20; 35:19; 41:7; 69:4). The confession opens with the Hebrew interjection kî, its seventh use in this psalm (opening Hebrew word for vv. 2, 4, 7, 15, 16, 17, 18). Often translated "for" or *but* (as in v. 15), its meanings include "indeed," "look," "surely," or "therefore." Sin acknowledged and unloaded can open the way to freedom and healing of forgiveness (32:3-5).

Gerstenberger (164-65), drawing on the work of K. Seybold, outlines the healing ritual, which may be background for such a psalm. Healing ceremonies may have included dressing in sackcloth, silence, weeping, and prayers, as well as acts of humiliation, purification, and offering. The goal was "to restore the guilty and remorseful patient to health and good standing by imploring the mercy of the personal God."

Final Plea for Deliverance 38:21-22

The psalmist's closing prayer pleads for God to be present with him in the midst of his pain and agony, giving him the help needed (22:11, 19; 40:13). To the psalmist, the Lord is synonymous with *salvation, my Savior* (NIV).

THE TEXT IN THE BIBLICAL CONTEXT AND LIFE OF THE CHURCH

Sin and Sickness

This psalm invites exploration of the relationship between sin and sickness. Many generations viewed sickness as God's punishment for sin. Sickness and suffering may indeed be the consequence of sin (39:11a). We see the covenant curses of the Old Testament (Lev 26:17, 21, 24; Deut 28:20-22, 60), though there was also the invitation to confession (Lev 26:40-42). The weight of guilt may affect the functions of the body. Sin also isolates and alienates, separating persons not only from God, but also from one another (Gen 3:11-13; 4:12-14). Sin may bring on sickness as smoking can bring on cancer. However, just as not all cancer is traceable to smoking, so not all sickness and suffering is traceable to sin.

The traditional view represented in this psalm, that certain specifics sins bring each instance of suffering, is not the view of Psalm 6. The book of Job certainly questions it, and Jesus refutes it (John 9:1-3). As Elihu's speech makes clear, God may allow sickness to strengthen character, or as a test of faith (Job 33:14-30; 1 Pet 1:6-7). Suffering can serve to bring glory to God or be a means of entering into closer intimacy with God (Job 42:1-6; Phil 3:10).

However, regarding a causal connection between sin and sickness, it would be just as wrong to think that this is never so, as that it is always so. Diseases of lust and excess may well be the resultant wounds that foul and fester *because of my foolishness* (v. 5). Some see in this psalm's description not leprosy, but the effect of sexual sin. In the days before sulfa drugs and penicillin, horrible debilitating effects of syphilis and gonorrhea were common. Can there be heard in this psalm "the cry of the unwilling homosexual, the pederast, . . . the drug addict, the cry in fact of all those who have made their own hell in this life?" (Knight, 1:185).

While the effect of modern medicine has been helpful in objectifying disease, viewing illness exclusively in terms of germs and medicine may reduce sickness to bodily malfunction. We must also address the emotional, spiritual, and social aspects of sickness. This graphic description of physical illness may help us to think of sin as an abscess, a malignancy that we need to arrest and remove. The Penitential Psalms are reminders that only through the surgery and treatment of confession can we receive healing from the burden of guilt [Sin]. Jesus' acts of healing the sick are signs of the kingdom of God. Jesus differentiated forgiveness and healing but held them together as part of being made whole (Mark 2:1-12).

When Distancing Is Wrong

This psalm is a reminder of the temptation, often inadvertent, to abandon persons when illness comes. When AIDS first became known, phobic fears led families, churches, and even hospitals to abandon the AIDS victim. A glib interpretation of AIDS as the judgment of God on homosexuality led to such ostracism. A friend or counselor dealing with one who is suffering will want to avoid making hasty assessments or interpreting anyone's illness as divine judgment. Many do not know how to approach one who is ill and to acknowledge that illness, whether physical, mental, or spiritual. Yet that is precisely when friends are most needed to listen and to care. The psalm ends with the final cry that God not abandon, but come quickly as the Friend in whom is saving help (yāšaʻ).

Psalm 39

I Am Your Passing Guest

PREVIEW

This individual lament expresses the prayer of a dying man for healing, or at least a brief respite before the end comes. The frailty of human life is described in metaphors of smallness: handbreadths, vapor, shadows, breath.

Submitting to God in faith and hope, the psalmist asks for forgiveness, to be spared the scorn of fools, and prays that God's hand of punishment may be lifted. The psalm ends with a plea for God's sympathy and protection. The psalmist's reflection on his experience and life's meaning (or meaninglessness) invokes a wide range of moods: faith, rebellion, despair, penitence, resignation, and trust.

While the specific date is unknown, the psalm wrestles with the issues of suffering and the transience of life, themes common in literature after the exile, when people were examining the relationship of their traditional faith to the suffering and sorrow that met them in daily life. We can visualize the Jewish community struggling with the futility of existence under foreign rule. Job, Ecclesiastes, and Psalms 73 and 90 offer similar reflection and expression.

Psalm 39 resembles the preceding psalm in phraseology and themes. The Hebrew words *rebuke* and *discipline* (Ps 38:1) recur as *chastise* and *punishment* (39:11); *affliction* (38:11) is the same Hebrew word as *stroke* (39:10). *Waiting for the LORD* occurs in both (38:15; 39:7), as does the tenuous nature of human life (38:10, 17; 39:4-5, 11). The silent waiting for God (39:1-2) is found in the

Psalm 39

opening verse of Psalm 40. Confession of sin also figures prominently in 40:12 and 41:4, suggesting that Psalms 38–41 may have been linked to form the conclusion to book I of the Psalter (Wilson, 2002:625).

The title, referring to *Jeduthun*, an ancestor of temple cantors (1 Chron 16:42; 25:1), and the use of *Selah* (vv. 5, 11) suggest a personal prayer adapted to liturgical use. *Jeduthun* is also mentioned in titles for Psalms 62 and 77 *[Musical; Superscriptions]*.

OUTLINE

Confession of Self-imposed Silence, 39:1-3
Meditation on the Frailty of Human Life, 39:4-6
Petition for Deliverance from Sin, 39:7-11
Plea for God's Pity and Protection, 39:12-13

EXPLANATORY NOTES

Confession of Self-imposed Silence 39:1-3

Initially, the psalmist vowed silence about the apparent injustice of God (vv. 1-2). But repressed pain seeks to be expressed. The *fire* within finally must be spoken (v. 3)! Pent-up protest needs to break out in speech toward God in hope, as Jeremiah's experience shows (Jer 20:9).

Meditation on the Frailty of Human Life 39:4-6

The psalmist wants to know how long his affliction will continue. A big question confronts the suffering and dying person: What is the meaning of life? Job asked, "Why should God so discipline a creature as frail and fleeting as man?" (cf. Job 7:17-18). Human life is so brief: a few *handbreadths* (the width of four fingers, about three inches), as *nothing*, as a mere *breath*, as a *shadow*. With the triple use of the Hebrew particle *'ak, surely* (vv. 5-6), the impermanence of human existence is accentuated! The empty accomplishment of human endeavor is illustrated in how people pursue money and what money can buy. They cannot take it with them or know who will control it after they are gone (v. 6; Ps 49:16-17; Luke 12:13-21; James 4:13-14).

Petition for Deliverance from Sin 39:7-11

The psalm has a distinct turning point: *And now* (v. 7). In connection with this nothingness, this "in-vain-ness" of a life so full of suffering and unrest, "What am I to hope for?" The psalmist gives answer: "The

LORD is the goal of this waiting and hoping." Only the one "who has grasped the transient character, the futility of all human nature in the sight of God," can come to understand the true nature of God and realize that "it is in God alone that he is able to find comfort and support when every human support has proved unreliable" (Weiser: 329).

The psalmist prays for forgiveness (v. 8), and that the *stroke* of God's punishment may be lifted (vv. 10-11). The *hand* of the LORD was seen as bringing the distress of sickness (Pss 32:4; 38:2). Was the illness leprosy (v. 10; Lev 13:2-17)? The *moth* (v. 11) illustrates the slow eating away of what is most precious to a person: beauty, soul, attractiveness, and desirableness. Dying takes that away. Once more the psalmist declares, *Surely everyone stands as a mere breath* (vv. 5, 11). *Selah*—and again the cymbals clash! Or was it a long pause of silence at this point in the liturgy? *[Selah]*. The Hebrew word *hebel* (*breath*, v. 11) is translated in Ecclesiastes 1:2, *Vanity of vanities! All is vanity.* Here the word refers not only to matters transient and nonsubstantial, but even, like bad vapors, to what is odious.

Plea for God's Pity and Protection 39:12-13

Yet the psalmist petitions for sympathy and protection. *Your passing guest* (*gĕr*) describes a resident alien who has the law's protection, even as the Israelites were aliens and sojourners in the promised land (Lev 25:23; Deut 10:19). The appeal is to God as host, to defend his guest against any avenger, and even to hold back his vengeance. Both *passing guest* and *alien* are used also to underline the transitoriness of life in this world (1 Chron 29:15).

Look away (v. 13 NIV) is unusual, for the afflicted usually ask God not to turn away his face (Ps 27:9). But here (as in Job 7:19; 10:20; 14:6) the psalmist asks for reprieve from further punishment, if only for a brief time, before death comes. The psalm ends without assurance.

THE TEXT IN THE BIBLICAL CONTEXT AND LIFE OF THE CHURCH

Petitions of the Dying

In Psalm 39 the death of the one praying appears immanent (vv. 10, 13). What might be learned from this and other petitions of the dying?

Jacob called his sons together, offered a suitable blessing upon each, and asked that he might be buried with his ancestors (Gen 49:1-33). King Hezekiah implored the LORD for extension of life, and he was healed (2 Kings 20:1-21). The thief on the cross prayed to Jesus, "Remember me when you come into your kingdom" (Luke 23:42). Jesus' own prayers on the cross included quotations from the psalms, "My God, my God, why have you forsaken me?" (Ps 22:1; Matt 27:46) and "Father, into your hands I commend my spirit" (Ps 31:5; Luke 23:46). Stephen, the first Christian martyr, prayed, "Lord Jesus, receive my spirit," and added intercession on behalf of his murderers, "Lord, do not hold this sin against them" (Acts 7:59-60).

Psalm 39 can help us understand the dying and the range of moods evoked by the specter of death. Sometimes unfinished business, the desire to see someone, to live through a family celebration or to complete a task—one of these may provide a brief respite before the end comes. For some people of faith, resignation into the hand of God comes more easily; others struggle. For such persons, this psalm can be a model for voicing the complexities. Psalm 39 is a "valley supplication," ending on a dark note. But these honest voices can also be prayer. "I believe, help my unbelief!" (Mark 9:24).

When pessimism about life as a fleeting breath brings discouragement, the psalm can help. Even to be a *passing guest* expresses hope in God as host. The speaker believes there is still One to whom speech may be addressed. Yet this psalm is not the last word. Christ's death and resurrection and believers' deliverance from the power of sin and death provide a strong word of assurance (Rom 8:28-39).

Use of Psalm 39

The Anglican Prayer Book of 1549 and The Book of Common Prayer (1928) recommended Psalm 39 along with Psalm 90 for reading at funerals. This reflected a somber view of death and pessimism about the brevity of life. Only in the twentieth century did funeral ceremonies shift more radically toward hope, drawing on Psalm 23 as a favorite reading (Holladay: 360).

Psalm 39 is the basis for Isaac Watts' hymn "Teach me the measure of my days" (1719). A major section of Johannes Brahms' *A German Requiem* (1866–68) focuses on the realism about life's brevity (Ps 39:4-7).

The NT alludes to Psalm 39:12, using the "alien" and "stranger" metaphor for Christians (Heb 11:13; 1 Pet 2:11). The hope of resurrection to eternal life transforms the prospects of those who know that they are no more than passing guests and sojourners in this world.

Psalm 40

The Lord Takes Thought for Me

PREVIEW

Psalm 40 is the thankful expression of one who survived a serious illness or other traumatic experience that took him near death's door. In a new song of deliverance in the presence of the congregation, he gladly witnesses to what God has done for him. Rather than the ritual of sacrifice, the psalmist makes a self-offering of obedience. In the face of present difficulties, the psalmist remembers how God has dealt mercifully in the past, commits his troubles to God, and takes comfort that *the Lord takes thought for me* (v. 17).

On first reading, the two parts of this psalm seem reversed, since the song of thanksgiving (vv. 1-10) comes before the lament (vv. 11-17). Many scholars suggest that two independent compositions were combined, with verse 12 serving as transition. Weiser (333-34), citing "the tension between the possessing of the assurance of faith and the striving for it," argues for the psalm's unity, in this instance praise preparing for prayer. Gerstenberger (173) also sees the psalm as a liturgical unit, a complaint of one who is suffering or an outcast from society. Brueggemann (1984:130) calls attention to the close liturgical ties between the two parts. Whatever the prior elements or sequence, the psalm does appear composite for a liturgical purpose. Verses 13-17 are nearly identical to Psalm 70, and several phrases and thoughts of verses 13-17 recur in 35:4, 21, 26-28.

Psalm 40

The prophetic theme, calling for obedience rather than ritual sacrifice, and the wisdom themes (vv. 4, 8) may suggest a date for this psalm in or after the exile (587-515 BC). For postexilic psalmists, praise and piety were the true responses to the salvation of the LORD (Mays, 1994b:170).

OUTLINE

Description of Past Deliverance, 40:1-4
The New Song, 40:5-10
Plea for a New Deliverance, 40:11-17

EXPLANATORY NOTES

Description of Past Deliverance   40:1-4

I waited; yet "expecting, I expected," or "hopefully, I hoped" (Westermann, 1989:181), may be more accurate according to the Hebrew word order (v. 1). Waiting for the LORD's deliverance conveys the idea of eager hopefulness (Pss 25:5, 21; 27:14; 31:24; 38:15). The LORD answered! From *the pit* (from near death, from Sheol, here described in terms of mud and filth), rescue came *[Sheol].* A specific experience of sinking into a miry pit and rescue becomes a parable of deliverance (v. 2; compare Joseph and Jeremiah, Gen 37:20-28; Jer 18:18-20, 22). Such deliverance brings forth a new song and motivation for faith witness (v. 3)! The new song contains an invitation to others to behold the wonderful deeds of the LORD and respond in trust and worship (Ps 34:9; Prov 16:20; Isa 42:10-12).

With an emphatic wisdom statement, *Happy are those . . . ,* the psalmist extols the blessedness of the pious (v. 4; Pss 1:1; 34:8; 41:1-2).

The New Song   40:5-10

Expressing awed astonishment, the psalmist testifies to the wonders God has done (v. 5). The usual procedure to celebrate thanksgiving for a deliverance was to make sacrifice and offering in the temple. Verse 6 uses four words from the sacrificial system: *sacrifice (zevaḥ),* a shared offering of animals, with part retained to be eaten by those bringing the offering; *offering (minḥâ),* a present of grain or animal; *burnt offering ('ôlâ),* entirely consumed on the altar; and *sin offering (ḥāṭā'â),* mostly returned to the priest.

In the prophetic tradition, however, the psalmist states God's preference for obedience over the oblation of animals and grain

(1 Sam 15:22; Ps 51:16-17; Isa 1:11-17; Jer 7:21-28; Hos 6:6; Amos 5:21-24; Mic 6:6-8). Does this psalm repudiate the sacrificial system? Or is it more likely a reinterpretation, a call to obedience as more important than sacrifice? Was this the offering of thanksgiving and praise that God desires (Ps 50:14, 23)? Some interpreters see the rejection of sacrifice presupposing the destruction of the temple and the exile, in contrast to the time when worshippers were invited to bring burnt offerings to the house of the LORD (Ps 66:13-15).

The psalmist declares a self-offering, *Here I am* (v. 7), as the basis of *an open ear* (v. 6), a willingness to hear and obey. He places himself at God's disposal (Isa 6:8). The *scroll of the book* may mean what is decreed from on high and immutable (v. 7; Ps 139:16; Isa 65:6). The psalmist testifies that the *law* (torah, tôrâ) has become for him the core of his being (v. 8). Having the *law* in the *heart* was the goal of covenant people (Deut 6:6-9; Jer 31:31-34; Ezek 36:25-28).

No private matter, the good news of deliverance must be shared with *the great congregation*, likely the worshipping congregation in Jerusalem (vv. 9-10; Pss 22:25; 35:18). That the psalmist has done so is emphasized in the repetition (vv. 9-10). Note also the catalog of great words descriptive of God: *saving help* (ṣedeq, righteousness, NIV), *faithfulness* ('ĕmûnâ), *salvation* (yĕšu'â), *steadfast love* (ḥesed), and *faithfulness* ('ĕmet, truth, NIV) *[Steadfast]*.

Plea for a New Deliverance   40:11-17

The plea for a new deliverance begins with an expression of trust in the LORD's past safekeeping (v. 11). However, now the mood changes to that of a person hemmed in (v. 12). Physical deterioration and a sense of personal fault lead to calling shame on those who shout "hurrah" amid calamity (vv. 14-15). The psalmist prays that the enemy be repulsed and that the community of God-seekers would join the psalmist in praise (v. 16). The psalmist acknowledges poverty and personal weakness as he expresses the desire to stand in the circle of the righteous, who can count on God's protection (v. 17). He expresses confidence with a comforting line: *The Lord takes thought for me*. The addition of this line is the major change from Psalm 70, which may be an independent poem adapted for use at the end of Psalm 40 (Wilson, 2002:643). For further comments on verses 13-17, see Psalm 70.

THE TEXT IN THE BIBLICAL CONTEXT AND LIFE OF THE CHURCH

Psalm 40 in the Book of Hebrews

The author of Hebrews summarizes the comparison between Christ's sacrifice and Israelite ritual (Heb 10:1-10). He quotes a variant of Psalm 40:6-8 in support of the contention that Jesus has fulfilled the purpose of the OT sacrificial tradition. In interpreting these verses, Hebrews presents the idea that it is impossible for animal sacrifices to take away sins.

The writer of Hebrews refers to the incarnation of Christ, who through his perfect obedience to God offered the one, eternal sacrifice, which supersedes all other sacrifices and makes them irrelevant. The author quotes the LXX: "Sacrifices and offerings you have not desired, but a body you have prepared for me" (Heb 10:5b). The speaker is understood to be Christ, and the "body" is Christ's body offered once and for all in sacrifice for sins. In Psalm 40:6, however, the talk is not about "body" but about an *open* (lit., "dug-out," "excavated") *ear*. Possibly the NT writer took "ear" as a figure of speech in which the part stands for the whole.

The body "prepared" for Christ in the incarnation became the instrument of his obedience to the will of God, by which people are redeemed and rendered holy (Heb 10:10, 14). Thus, the various sacrifices of the OT have found their fulfillment in the one self-offering of Jesus (Reardon: 78).

Relevant Themes

In Psalm 40 we find several appropriate themes for contemporary audiences. The first is the *desolate pit* and *miry bog* (v. 2). Like Psalms 37; 38; and 39; Psalm 40 may be a plea for deliverance from suffering as a consequence of personal sin (v. 12). Sin casts a sinner into a pit from which there is no escape apart from the help of the divine deliverer.

A second theme is the relationship of hearing and obedience (vv. 6-8). The integrity of faith and life is a common theme of reform and renewal groups. The Anabaptists of the sixteenth century are an example of such a renewal group. They questioned traditional worship practices, focused on the teaching of Scripture, and emphasized obedience to Jesus (*Nachfolge Christi,* following Christ). There are those who see the "core" of the radical movement in the Reformation era to be that of congruence: belief was to be fully matched by appropriate practice. A timely prayer may well be for an open ear so that one may know God's will and do it.

The third theme has to do with not keeping the good news to ourselves. The congregation needs to hear of the experiences of deliverance by God. Faith, instead of being a private matter, must be given community expression (vv. 9-10, 16). In modern and postmodern times, the individual has taken center stage, but Scripture consistently stresses the communal aspect of religious life. God is shaping a people in accord with his intent: "I will be their God, and they shall be my people" (cf. Jer 31:33, etc.). Individual expression of praise will flavor community life, producing an ethos of joy. Faith becomes most helpful to others, and to us, as a shared event. The recital of such concreteness—from trouble to complaint to divine intervention to thanksgiving—is the "clue to evangelism" (Brueggemann, 1988:83). So worship becomes witness.

Psalm 40 in Hymnody

The hymn "I waited for the Lord," in the Scottish Psalter of 1650, has found its way into many hymnals as a prayer for speedy relief from trouble. That is also the title of the well-known duet in Mendelssohn's cantata *Hymn of Praise*. The soloists lead out: "I waited for the Lord, He inclined unto me, He heard my complaint. . . ." The chorus then responds: "O bless'd are they that hope and trust in the Lord." Another familiar song on the theme is "They that wait upon the Lord," the chorus of Stuart Hamblen's 1953 composition, "Teach me, Lord, to wait."

Psalm 41

O LORD, Be Gracious to Me

PREVIEW

In its present form, the whole psalm becomes a thanksgiving, sung when the prayer for help has been answered. The liturgy contains an instructional section (vv. 1-3); the lament is descriptive of an illness bringing the psalmist near death, of gloating enemies and false friends (vv. 4-10); and the conclusion expresses joyful gratitude for deliverance and vindication (vv. 11-12). A doxological blessing serves as benediction to book I of the Psalms (v. 13).

At an early stage, this psalm was a lament, perhaps of the king who, in illness, was nearly overthrown by his enemies. If from David's time (the language of vv. 4-10 is archaic), then an incident such as 2 Samuel 15:30-31 might be the setting, with Ahithophel the "friend" (v. 9).

With the emphatic *Happy ('ašrê, blessed) are those who consider the poor*, Psalm 41 brings to a close book I of the Psalter. Framed by these two "blessed" Psalms (1 and 41), this book appears to be put together under the influence of the wisdom writers. Evidence of an earlier framing may also be observed: Psalms 3–41 (except for 10 and 33) carry superscriptions attributing them to David. Psalm 2, affirming the covenant made with David at his coronation, is balanced with Psalm 41 as the LORD's assurance of continued protection to David against his scheming enemies (Wilson, 1985:173-76, 204-6; Holladay: 77) *[Superscriptions; Composition]*.

OUTLINE

Didactic Introduction of Confidence in the LORD, 41:1-3
The Psalmist's Prayer: *O LORD, Be Gracious to Me*, 41:4-10
Concluding Statement of Confidence, 41:11-12
Doxology Concluding Book One of Psalms, 41:13

EXPLANATORY NOTES

Didactic Introduction of Confidence in the LORD 41:1-3

The psalm begins with a beatitude declaring *happy* (blessed, fortunate) is everyone who shows mercy to *the poor, the weak* (NIV), the "helpless," or those at low ebb. The extolling of the blessedness of the lowly who put their trust in the LORD is found in many psalms (Pss 1:1-3; 34:8; 84:12; 119:1-3). The psalmist, identifying with such persons, invites others to pay attention to his experiences both of calamity and deliverance. Apparently he has been spared from the jaws of death (v. 2). On his sickbed, he has been healed (v. 3). The point of the teaching is that those who are attentive to the needs of the weak can anticipate appropriate treatment from the LORD when weakness overtakes them.

The Psalmist's Prayer: *O LORD, Be Gracious to Me* 41:4-10

The prayer, framed by statements of confidence (vv. 1-3, 11-12), is offered in the form of an inclusio (vv. 4, 10). We can outline it as follows:

> Prayer of the psalmist: *O LORD, be gracious to me* (v. 4)
>   Taunt spoken by enemy (v. 5)
>   Narrative about the enemy (vv. 6-7)
>   Taunt spoken by enemy (v. 8)
>   Narrative about the enemy (v. 9)
> Prayer of the psalmist: *O LORD, be gracious to me* (v. 10)
> [Hebrew Poetry]

As for me, I said suggests this psalm is a thanksgiving by citing the petition used at the time of affliction (v. 4). The petition includes confession of sin (v. 4b). In ancient times, sickness was often considered a punishment for personal sins (Job 4:7-9; Pss 38:1-4; 39:7-11; 40:11-12). The psalmist tells the story of his plight by focusing on the response of other people to what was happening to him. He portrays enemies as gloating in the prospect of his death, which might let his *name perish* (v. 5) *[Enemies]*. That the family line should come to an end was the most horrible fate a man could imagine. A whispering, hating, slandering campaign is perceived as underway (vv. 6-7; Pss 35:19; 38:19; 69:4; 86:17). A *deadly thing* may suggest a curse, or simply a malignant disease in which the psalmist expects the worst (v. 8). The malice of enemies wishing for sickness and death to triumph destroys hope.

Even more distressing, his *bosom friend* (Heb.: *a man of my peace*), one with whom he has broken bread, has become his betrayer (v. 9). The psalmist's prayer for restoration to health ends with the words *that I may repay them* (v. 10). Is this the cry of vindictiveness? It is probable that the psalmist does not intend personally to inflict punishment on the enemies. Rather, being raised from the sickbed is a form of judgment, letting the enemies know that God has declared the psalmist innocent or righteous and declared them guilty or unrighteous (Clifford, 2002:212) *[Righteous]*.

Concluding Statement of Confidence 41:11-12

The report of rescue suggests the vindication of faith (vv. 11-12). Healing results, and the psalmist declares joyous gratitude in coming before God's presence rather than facing the jaws of death (*the enemy*, vv. 2, 11). Once excluded from the temple by illness (2 Chron 26:21), the psalmist is confident of healing and that his future is assured in the presence of God. *My integrity* may have a legal sense, meaning innocence of the charge leveled against the psalmist by the enemies. *Integrity* and being in God's presence are found also at the close of Psalms 23 and 26.

Doxology Concluding Book One of Psalms 41:13

The doxology to close book I of the Psalter returns to praise as keynote of the psalms. The phraseology *Blessed be the LORD, the God of Israel*, becomes part of the doxologies to end other "books" of the Psalms (72:18-19; 89:52; 106:48). As we go through the Psalter, we are led increasingly toward the praise of God as the final word. The Hebrew title for the book of Psalms, *tĕhillîm*, "hymns," indicates that the primary intention of the book as a whole is to render praise to God. In Psalm 150 the Psalter ends with a call for everything to praise God. With the declaration *Amen and Amen*, the congregation endorses that which is firm, reliable, and consistent and affirms thanksgiving for all the LORD does for his people (v. 13; Pss 72:19; 89:52; 106:48) *[Composition]*.

THE TEXT IN THE BIBLICAL CONTEXT AND LIFE OF THE CHURCH

Compassionate Ministries

This psalm appeals to compassion, God's compassion, but also human compassion. It invites people to help rather than to hurt. The appeal to social responsibility, so strong in verses 1-3, seems unusual. Rather than focus on a right attitude toward God, the truly blessed person is the one who respects and shows mercy to the lowly. Concern for the widow, the orphan, and the alien is a theme permeating the OT (Exod 22:21-24; Lev 19:33-34; Deut 14:28-29; 24:19-22; Isa 1:10-17, 21-26; 5:1-7; 10:1-4; Amos 2:6-8; 4:1-2; 5:10-12; 8:4-8; Mic 2:1-5; 6:6-8). Gerstenberger (175) calls attention to the concern to alleviate poverty, a tradition that grew quite strong in postexilic times (Deut 15:4; Neh 5:1-19; Prov 31:8-9; Isa 58:6-10).

Jesus continued the prophetic tradition in the Sermon on the Mount: "Blessed are the merciful, for they will receive mercy" (Matt 5:7). God heals those who show compassion to the poor and needy. The manner of Jesus' life and teaching consistently showed compassion as the only way to true blessedness (Matt 25:31-46; Mark 11:25; Luke 23:34). This theme of compassion for the needy is found throughout the NT (Acts 4:32-37; Rom 12:14-21; 1 Cor 16:1-3; James 1:26–2:7).

Taking seriously the injunction of the Scriptures to assist the poor, most denominations have established relief agencies. These include Catholic Charities and Church World Service, in which many Protestant denominations participate. Others are Emergency Response and Service Ministries of the Church of the Brethren, and Mennonite Central Committee. An example of a lesser known agency is MEDA. Mennonite Economic Development Associates was organized in 1953 when a group of Mennonite businessmen extended risk capital to European refugee settlers in Paraguay, to start industries such as a dairy and tannery. After a quarter century, MEDA was serving 422 projects globally. Much of MEDA's work focuses on making microloans to individuals and offering business counsel so they can care for themselves and better themselves. Thus, MEDA might extend credit for something as small as a fence to keep animals confined, or a plow or hammer mill, a fishing boat, a sewing machine, or cobbler's tools. The goal has been to help people help themselves. As an association of Christians in business and the professions, committed to applying biblical teachings in the marketplace, the organization has continued to grow. After fifty years MEDA was working with 100 organizations around the world, directly serving an estimated 335,000 clients.

However, compassionate ministries go beyond economics and are part of everyday life. Contemporary uses of Psalm 41 include prayer services for healing, or as a cry for help by battered women or others suffering abuse.

Psalm 41 and the Last Supper

In the narrative of the Last Supper, Jesus said, "Truly I tell you, one of you will betray me, one who is eating with me" (Mark 14:18). The words suggest Psalm 41:9 about a bosom friend who has *lifted the heel against me*. The quotation is repeated in John 13:18, where Jesus comments, "It is to fulfill the scripture." Jesus' familiarity with these psalms has led interpreters like John Calvin, or the daily office (Liturgy of the Hours) of the Catholic Church, to identify Jesus Christ as the speaker in Psalm 41.

Book Two
Psalms 42–72

Psalms 42–43

The Cry of the Soul for God

PREVIEW

These two psalms belong together as a three-stanza lament, with the refrain repeated (42:5, 11; 43:5). This individual lament is about exile, abandonment, and hope for deliverance amid injustice. The psalmist longs for the presence of God and for vindication from oppression by enemies. The poem has the character of an inner dialogue, voicing both the sense of abandonment by God and memories of past worship.

The likely setting is that of a temple singer exiled in northern Palestine in the region of Mt. Hermon. Unable to return to the temple because of illness or political reasons, the song reflects the dark night of the soul of one homesick for God's house. Later, the faithful may have used this sad poem with Judah's exile in mind, and adapted it for congregational use in the temple or in synagogues, to encourage people in their longings for God's presence.

This lament opens book II of the Psalter (Pss 42–72) [Composition]. It is related to the other psalms in the Korah groups (Pss 42–49; 84–85; 87–88) [Korah]. These Korah psalms delight in the praise of God ('ĕlōhîm) as the King who sits enthroned in Jerusalem, and express joy in the service of the temple. References to Korah suggest a demotion from an earlier prominent position (2 Chron 20:19) to "keepers of the entrance" and the "charge of making the flat cakes" (1 Chron 9:19, 31). An earlier narrative tells of a revolt of the Korahites against the Levites (Num 16:1-35; 26:9-11). Did they lose out in a struggle for rank and power? Does this psalm reflect pain over that loss, or the common lot of all Israelites in exile (Stuhlmueller, 1983, 2:227)?

This is the first of the Elohistic Psalms, a collection running from Psalm 42 through 83. These psalms prefer the more generic name 'ĕlōhîm for God. Psalms 42–43 mention *God* twenty-two times, each time as 'ĕlōhîm. The one exception is 42:8, which uses *Yahweh* (*the LORD*), and that in the context of the covenant (*ḥesed, steadfast love*) *[Names of God]*. Maskil (*maśkîl*) in the heading appears also in Psalms 32; 44; 45; 52–55; 74; 78; 88; 89; and 142. It may mean "an instructional piece" (32:8) *[Superscriptions]*.

OUTLINE

Homesickness in Exile, 42:1-5
Despair in Abandonment, 42:6-11
Hope for Vindication, 43:1-5

An alternate way of charting Psalms 42–43:

Psalmist's problem	images	psalmist's action	focus
42:1-4 homesickness in exile	the drought	nostalgic remembrance	past
v. 5 refrain (despair/hope)			
42:6-10 despair/	the depths abandonment	elegy over past sorrows	present
v. 11 refrain (despair/hope)			
43:1-4 hope for vindication	deliverance	prayer for the future	future
v. 5 refrain (despair/hope)			

EXPLANATORY NOTES

Homesickness in Exile 42:1-5

With the striking metaphor of a doe roaming the parched landscape in search of refreshing water, the psalmist describes the soul's search for the living God (vv. 1-2; Jer 14:1-6). The cry of the desperate soul rises up from nearly every verse: like insatiable *thirst* (vv. 1-2), the longing to be in God's presence (v. 2), daily *tears* (v. 3), the taunts (v. 4), memories of what can no longer be (v. 4), the "blues" (vv. 5, 11; Ps 43:5), like destructive *waves* (42:7), unanswered prayer (v. 9), suffering and the fear of death (vv. 9-10), feelings of injustice (43:1), abandonment (43:2), and homesickness for God's house (43:3-4).

Experiencing God in the temple is expressed as "seeing": *behold the face of God* (v. 2; 27:4). God's presence was visualized above the ark of the covenant in the temple. Inability to join in the pilgrimage and the days of festival is the reason for excessive tears (v. 3; 80:5; 102:9).

The "things remembered" are prior times of worship (v. 4). Procession songs for the festival pilgrimage include Psalms 48; 68; 84; and 120–134. The refrain displays a soul in conflict, depressed by mockery and taunts, but buoyed by hope of future participation in temple worship (vv. 5, 11; 43:5). The word *soul* (*nepeš*) occurs six times in the psalm.

Despair in Abandonment   42:6-11

It is awful to feel abandoned and forgotten. The geographic details are unclear. *Land of Jordan* and *Hermon* suggest the headwaters of the Jordan River, far north of Jerusalem (v. 6). *Mount Mizar* (*miṣār*, small), could also be an ironic reference to Mount Hermon in the spirit of Psalm 68:15-16. The great peaks are insignificant beside Mount Zion, where God dwells, and for which the worshipper longs. The psalmist, prohibited by distance (physical, emotional, spiritual), feels forsaken by God. The *deep* refers to the subterranean cosmic water that symbolizes chaos and death (v. 7). Distant from God, the psalmist uses images of drowning, as under the power of the sea.

Yet the psalmist remembers God and takes comfort in the LORD's *steadfast love* (vv. 6, 8) *[Steadfast]*. Some translations suggest that the psalmist may have been sick unto death. God as *my rock* contrasts with Sheol, seen as a vast quagmire with no firm footing (69:2) *[Sheol]*. The fear of death was the fear of being forgotten by God (v. 9; 6:5; 88:5). The question *"Where is your God?"* (vv. 3, 10) characterizes the nature of disbelief in God in biblical times. People saw illness as evidence of God's deserting the person because of sin. The psalmist's life is drained of vitality, and he is at the mercy of the *enemy*, whose taunts ridicule his faith. Again worshippers speak or sing the refrain, pointing to a future hope (v. 11).

Hope for Vindication   43:1-5

The third stanza opens with hope for God's intervention and deliverance. In legal language, the psalmist pleads for God to be both judge and defense counsel against the ungodly (vv. 1-2). The scene then changes from a courtroom with God as judge and advocate, to the temple with God as the object of praise and *my exceeding joy!* (v. 4). The prayer *Lead me by your light and your truth* (v. 3) pleads for God's divine messengers as necessary companions on the way to bring the psalmist back to joyous worship in the temple once again (43:3-4; 25:21; 57:3; 61:7; 91:11). Zion is God's holy mountain (2:6; 3:4; 15:1; 48:1; 87:1; 99:9).

The threefold refrain (42:5, 11; 43:5) asserts that the interrupted communion will once more be restored. God's people are not forsaken. While at times God seems hidden or God's ways difficult to understand, the psalmist expresses the hope that God's light and truth will lead to the place of worship, praise and sacrifice, and singing the songs of joy once again (42:4; 43:3-4). While the outward circumstance may not have changed, the inward circumstance has changed!

THE TEXT IN THE BIBLICAL CONTEXT AND LIFE OF THE CHURCH

Longings for God

In the wilderness Moses pitched "the tent of meeting" as a place where people who sought the LORD might go. Here the LORD spoke to Moses face to face, "as one speaks to a friend" (Exod 33:7, 11). Yet Moses wished for more, asking, "Show me your ways, so that I may know you and find favor in your sight" (33:13). Beyond that, Moses wanted to see God's glory—though at this point was only allowed to see God's back (33:23).

A NT example of longing for God can be found in Paul's letter to the Philippians (3:9-10). Paul, having given up everything to know Christ, still desired to "be found in him, not having a righteousness of my own, . . . but one that comes through faith in Christ." Thus, Paul declared: "I want to know Christ and the power of his resurrection and the sharing of his sufferings."

The thirst/water image of the longing for God is found in Jesus' words: "Blessed are those who hunger and thirst for righteousness, for they will be filled" (Matt 5:6). The Gospel of John speaks of the water that satisfies the thirst of the soul (John 4:15; 6:35). Echoes of this psalm can be heard in the agony of Jesus in the garden of Gethsemane (Matt 26:38; Mark 14:34).

The psalm has had broad use in the church's liturgical approach to God. Its double image of water as both life-giving and destructive speaks to two aspects of baptism. As expression of longing for God's presence, the psalm has also been used in services of communion. Two hymn versions include Tate and Bray's metrical setting (1696) "As pants the hart," and Christine Curtis' (1939) "As the hart with eager yearning," constructed to fit the Genevan tune from the sixteenth century. The latter ends with the strong affirmation:

> O, my soul, be not dismayed.
> Trust in God, who is our aid.
> Hope and joy his love provides thee;
> 'Tis his hand alone that guides thee.

Charles F. Gounod's popular choir anthem (1892) "Send out thy light and thy truth" is based on Psalm 43:3.

This roller-coaster psalm speaks for those who have "the blues." It expresses the basic longing of the hearts of people in all ages. The soul's thirsting is a longing for God's nearness. To hope is to live by the conviction that God will see us through. In hope we wait and long for God. What finally counts is the domain of the spirit, the inner drama. An appropriate sequel to this lament appears in Romans 8:31-39. The psalm reminds us that earlier experiences of God's people gathered in worship nurture such hope.

Psalm 44

Israel Cries Out for Help in a Time of National Crisis

PREVIEW

This psalm is a communal lament after a shattering military defeat and national humiliation. The psalm is structured by the contrast between a recital of God's mighty deeds on behalf of his covenant people in the past, particularly in conquest of the land (vv. 1-8), and lament of the terrible present, when God has allowed his people to be scattered among the nations (vv. 9-16). The psalm voices a protest of innocence, declaring that the nation was not disregarding the covenant (vv. 17-22). The psalm ends with a renewed desperate cry for God's deliverance with an appeal to God's *steadfast love* (*ḥesed*, vv. 23-26).

Though scholars have suggested many historical settings, the time of composition cannot be determined. Some propose a northern origin for the Korahite psalms on the basis of linguistic features (Goulder: 90; Holladay: 28). Specific situations identified include the Assyrian king Tiglath-pileser III's ravaging of Galilee and northern areas about 732 BC (2 Kings 15:29). Since at least some of the people suffered exile (v. 11b), the psalm might have been composed after the Assyrian destruction of Samaria in 721 BC or the Babylonian destruction of Jerusalem in 587 (or 586) BC. Still others date it as late as the Persian king Artaxerxes III's expedition into Judea in 345 BC.

More significant than the specific historical setting is this psalm's testimony to the struggle of the Jewish community to understand political defeat and national suffering. It addresses God with weighty questions: Will you allow the work you have begun to be destroyed? Will you fail to fulfill the terms of the covenant (v. 17)? The psalm may have been used liturgically on a day of fasting. Picture people crowding the temple to lament the army's defeat or to pray for deliverance. Such a deliverance event of old is described from Jehoshaphat's time (873-849 BC), when Judah was invaded by Moabite and Ammonite armies (2 Chron 20:1-23). The speaker of the psalm would be the king, or a military or religious leader. Other communal laments bemoaning national crises include Psalms 60; 74; 79; 80; 89; Lamentations 1–2; and 4–5 *[Psalm Genres]*.

Parallels between Psalms 44 and 85 should be recognized (even as 42–43 appear to be related to 84, and 48 to 87). Goulder proposes that Psalms 84; 85; and 87 were early joyful psalms in the sequence of the week of liturgy. Psalms 42–43; 44; and 48 may have been later replacements in the sequence, with a more anxious tone when the Northern Kingdom was facing military reverses after 750 BC (Goulder: 17-19; Holladay: 32). *Maskil* in the heading may mean "an instructional piece" *[Composition; Korah; Superscriptions]*.

OUTLINE

Hymn Reciting God's Mighty Deeds in the Past and Expressing Trust in God, 44:1-8
Lament over the Nation's Defeat and Shame, 44:9-16
Protestation of Innocence: Faith and Fact in Conflict, 44:17-22
Desperate Petition for God to Act Again, 44:23-26

EXPLANATORY NOTES

Hymn Reciting God's Mighty Deeds in the Past and Expressing Trust in God   44:1-8

The stories of the *ancestors*—family, tribal, and holy history accounts handed down from generation to generation—recount God's guiding hand in history (v. 1). Israel's faith had its roots in what God had done in settlement of the land of Canaan (vv. 2-3; Deut 26:1-11; Josh 24:6-13). The LORD *drove out the nations* but *planted* Israel (v. 2; Ps 80:8-11). Israel's understanding of Yahweh war significantly challenged human arrogance in military might, for it was God's *arm* that brought victory (vv. 3, 6-7; 1 Sam 17:47; Pss 20:7; 33:16-17) *[War]*.

The nation's trust in God alone provides basis for hope of the future (vv. 4-8). Jacob is another name for Israel (v. 4). Four times in these verses the verb *yāša'* (save) is used: *victory* (v. 3); *victories* (v. 4); *save me* (v. 6); and *saved us* (v. 7). If the psalm originally came from the time when Pekah, king of Israel, was killed and Hoshea (*hôšēa'*) took the throne (732 BC), the psalmist might have looked on the new king's name as a hopeful omen toward "saving" help against Assyria (2 Kings 15:29-30; Goulder: 90; Holladay: 29). Yet the psalmist is clear that God is the one deserving credit for any victory experienced (v. 8).

Lament over the Nation's Defeat and Shame   44:9-16

Selah (after v. 8) marks a break in thought as well as liturgy *[Selah]*. Yet (*But now*, NIV) signals a tone change and turning point as the psalm becomes a vehement accusation against God (v. 9). The present conditions do not square with God's care for the nation in the past. While the opening hymn recites the record of God's mighty deeds, the prayer of lament describes the present also as the work of God. *You have rejected us. . . . You have made us a byword among the nations* (vv. 9-14). God has abandoned the people to plunderers and made them refugees. The psalmist pictures God as a shepherd who has sold his sheep for a song (vv. 11-12). With varied vocabulary—*taunt, derision and scorn, a byword, a laughingstock*—the psalmist laments the shame and disgrace (vv. 13-16).

Protestation of Innocence: Faith and Fact in Conflict 44:17-22

The psalmist finds no explanation for the nation's plight and vigorously protests. If the covenant (*berît*) had been ignored, or if God had been forgotten, or if people had turned to other gods, then this calamity would have been deserved and understood. The psalmist cites the community's exemplary fidelity to the covenant (vv. 17-18). After all, God knows the depths of the human heart (vv. 20-21). The history recounted in Joshua through 2 Kings held that exile was divine punishment for Israel's failure to maintain loyalty to the LORD alone, as demanded by its covenant with the LORD (2 Kings 17). The crisis of faith comes when tragedy doesn't make sense, when people hold a rigidly literal view of retribution (Deut 28). This psalm searches for some other cause of national disaster than guilt and punishment.

The words *because of you* and the image of a lamb being led to slaughter point to a suffering role (v. 22; Isa 53:1-12). Suffering may be the lot of God's people, the result of their loyalty to him in a hostile world.

Desperate Petition for God to Act Again 44:23-26

The concluding petition uses traditional imperatives for invoking deity to intervene (v. 23; Pss 7:6; 35:23; 59:4-5). The theodicy question, "Why?" in the midst of suffering, is common in laments (vv. 23-24; 10:1; 42:9; 43:2; 74:1, 11; 88:14). Thus, in a desperate plea, God is charged with four defections: sleep, languor, indifference, and forgetfulness (vv. 23-24). Though God does not sleep (121:4), God's silence is so difficult to understand. Yet the community of faith will prostrate itself at the sanctuary (v. 25), crying out its appeal to the LORD's *steadfast love* (ḥesed, v. 26) *[Steadfast]*.

THE TEXT IN THE BIBLICAL CONTEXT AND LIFE OF THE CHURCH

Assumptions

As a national lament, the psalm warns against assuming that God is always "on our side." Israel needed yet to learn that lesson and to take the next step of faith, in defeat, and become a suffering servant. That biblical theme runs counter to common assumptions that power and success are the result of God's favor, or that defeat or suffering represents the disfavor of God.

The Price of Loyalty

As Israel of the old covenant had to take upon itself suffering and death for the sake of its election (Ps 44:22; Isa 53:1-12), so also the Christian community was plunged into the role of a suffering people in its devotion to Jesus, the crucified Lord. Paul drew on this psalm in describing the perilous state of the covenant people when he wrote, "For your sake we are being killed all day long; we are accounted as sheep to be slaughtered" (Rom 8:36). Paul used these words to describe the difficulties and dangers faced by Christians, and yet he provided the further perspective that even in calamity, God's love is not withdrawn (Rom 8:31-39).

For centuries, the context against which Jewish people have read Psalm 44 is the Diaspora of exile. More recently, the feelings of Jews, who as a people suffered mass slaughter in the Nazi Holocaust (or Shoah, catastrophe), were best expressed by this psalm.

The psalm can also speak to a martyr church. Covenant loyalty will bring God's people into conflict with some political and military forces. Suffering does not always make sense. Thieleman J. van Braght's *Martyrs Mirror* recounts the stories of Christian martyrs from the time of Christ to AD 1660. Martyrs continue to hold covenant faith dearer than life itself. That is also a perspective of reality.

The life of faith is not a sustained, uninterrupted series of triumphs. People of faith can make Psalm 44 their own prayer as they experience God's absence and feel *accounted as sheep for the slaughter.*

Psalm 45

Royal Wedding Song

PREVIEW

Psalm 45 is a song for a royal wedding, the only such song in the Psalter. A court poet (v. 1) addresses the king as bridegroom in oriental court style (vv. 2-9), then gives practical advice to the bride and describes the procession to the palace (vv. 10-15). A blessing and appeal for continuation of the royal line ends the psalm (vv. 16-17).

The specific wedding cannot be identified, though suggestions have included Solomon and the daughter of Pharaoh (1 Kings 11:1), Ahab and Jezebel (16:31), Jehoram and Athaliah (2 Kings 8:18, 26), or Jeroboam II and his unknown bride (14:23). Perhaps initially composed for a marriage in the Northern Kingdom, with its ivory palace (v. 8; 1 Kings 22:39) and its relations with Tyre and Sidon (v. 12; 1 Kings 16:31), the psalm may later have been adapted to southern royalty. Late words (*cassia*, an Aramaic word, v. 8) suggest additions in the psalm's use at later royal weddings. Later Jewish and Christian writers saw in the psalm a messianic message (vv. 6, 17).

The heading provides instruction for a possible melody, *according to Lilies* (Pss 69; 80) and identifies the content as *A love song*. *Maskil* may mean "an instructional piece" *[Korah; Musical; Superscriptions]*.

Psalm 45

OUTLINE

Dedication to the King, 45:1
The King as Bridegroom Addressed and Praised, 45:2-9
The Bride Addressed and the Procession Described, 45:10-15
Concluding Promise of Progeny and Reign, 45:16-17

EXPLANATORY NOTES

Dedication to the King 45:1

The writer, a professional scribe or court poet, bubbles over with a theme clamoring to be heard. The scribe served in the royal court and temple to make appropriate language available for a variety of occasions. Perhaps the king is the poet's patron and has commissioned this poem for his wedding day.

The King as Bridegroom Addressed and Praised 45:2-9

In grand oriental style, the poet addresses the king as *the most handsome* of them all (v. 2). Like David, the king is an ideal figure, possessing both physical beauty and military valor (1 Sam 16:12). While the warrior role of the king is highlighted (vv. 3-5), greater emphasis is laid on his commitment to righteousness than on his military successes (vv. 4, 6-7). The moral responsibility limits war. The king's commitment to justice and righteousness, especially for the powerless, is heavily emphasized in the psalms (72:1-4, 12-14; 101:1-8). These verses picture the prince of peace, whose charge, as representative for God's equity and justice, bars despotic arbitrariness such as represented by Ahab in 1 Kings 21.

The psalm's major interpretive issue centers on the phrase *Your throne, O God* (v. 6). The Hebrew, *Thy/Your throne, O God* (NRSV, NIV, NASB), suggests this as addressed to God. But the psalm addresses the king. Note the NRSV footnote, *Your throne is a throne of God, it endures.* Does this mean the Israelite kings were regarded as divine in the same sense as the kings of Egypt? That would seem strange for a people ruled by the commandment "no other gods" (Exod 20:3). The psalm immediately subordinates the king to *God, your God* (v. 7).

The anointing of the king was the central act of coronation [*Anointed*]. Here, however, anointing may refer not to the king's installation, but to preparation for marriage, in that the *oil of gladness* (v. 7) is associated with marriage metaphors (Isa 61:3; Jer 7:34; 16:9; 25:10;

33:11). The oil and spices establish a sensuous mood for the approaching consummation of the marriage (vv. 7-9; Clifford, 2002:225).

Palaces inlaid with ivory were known in the Northern Kingdom (v. 8; 1 Kings 22:39; Amos 3:15). *Ophir* may refer to the southwest coast of Arabia, Punt (Somalia), or India; it represented a standard for gold of quality and purity (v. 9; 1 Kings 9:28; 10:11; Job 28:16; Isa 13:12).

The Bride Addressed and the Procession Described 45:10-15

The royal bride, probably a Phoenician (*of Tyre*, v. 12), receives a charge: *Forget your people and your father's house* (v. 10). The advice given reflects the politics of the age when dynastic marriages reflected political needs. Old loyalties must not compete with the new; this perhaps reflects concern to avert repeating disastrous consequences of earlier foreign influences and religious practices, brought by the wives of Solomon and Ahab.

In a colorful picture, the poet describes the procession of the bride and her attendants to the palace to meet the king (vv. 13b-15).

Concluding Promise of Progeny and Reign 45:16-17

In an oracle, the poet speaks of the king's future. The purpose of the marriage is *sons* to keep the royal line (*name*) alive and extend the rule. Only after the succession has been assured are the permanence, stability, and prosperity of the kingdom secure (Keel: 284). The king's name is *to be celebrated in all generations*, a primary motivation for this psalmist's composition of such a joyous song (v. 17).

THE TEXT IN THE BIBLICAL CONTEXT AND LIFE OF THE CHURCH

The Royal Ideal

Kraus raises the question of why this royal psalm, without parallel in the OT, was included in the canon (1986:118-19; 1988:453, 457). He calls attention to the attributes of perfection ascribed to the king, the portrayal of an ideal figure, and the beauty and splendor of the kingdom and the anointed one, still hidden, but in the process of being revealed (Isa 60:3-7).

This secular royal wedding song has received attention because of its messianic association. In the new context of the exile, the LORD's kingship came to be seen as distinct from the human experience of kingship, which had collapsed. Hopes for a future "anointed one" affected the way the psalms of kingship were read and understood. Recent interpreters have shown that future hopes for the "Messiah" stand behind the shaping of the early collection of Psalms 2–89, framed by royal Psalms 2 and 89, but also bound together by royal Psalm 72 (Wilson, 2002:708-10). Psalm 89 is an anguished plea to the LORD for the restoration of the monarchy, which collapsed in the exile. However, now the hopes for kingly rule have shifted to the rule of the LORD. After Psalm 89, references to the king are for the LORD himself as king (Pss 93; 95–99).

The writers of the Targum, an early Aramaic translation of the Hebrew Bible, saw intimations of the Messiah's glory in Psalm 45, paraphrasing verse 2: "Thy beauty, O King Messiah, is greater than that of the children of men." Others likely found an allegory of the relation between God and the people of God. The marriage metaphor was commonly used to represent the LORD's election of, and covenant with, Israel in Hebrew prophecy (Isa 62:1-5; Jer 2:1-3, 30-32; Ezek 16:8-63; 23:1-49; Hos 1–3).

Christ and the Church

Christian writers accepted this psalm as testimony to Jesus, even with the notion of Christ's "marriage" to his "bride," the church (2 Cor 11:2; Eph 5:22-33). The messianic metaphor of marriage plays a prominent role in the NT (Matt 9:15; 22:2-14; 25:1-13; John 2:1-11; 3:29; Rev 21:2; 22:17).

The author of Hebrews understood Psalm 45:6 to be addressed to Jesus Christ as the Son of God, and he quoted the words from the LXX to illustrate the superiority of Christ over the angels (Heb 1:8). Christians have traditionally thus understood the psalm as a song of love between Christ and his church. For example, sixteenth-century reformer John Calvin understood the king in the first part of the psalm to be Solomon, but also took the king as referring to Christ and the bride as referring to the church.

Messianic interpretations of the psalm have also been applied to the final verse as anticipating the Messiah for all people in all generations. In that sense, the psalm points toward the invitation to the wedding banquet of the marriage supper of the Lamb (Luke 14:7-24; Rev 19:7-9).

Weddings

As a description of a wedding, the psalm can help people visualize and understand ancient royal celebrations. A royal wedding was a triumphant event, a grand occasion for display of kingly majesty and splendor. Weddings continue to serve an important social function, acknowledging a transition taking place and formalizing the union of husband and wife. At their best, weddings are occasions for communal joy and celebration.

What might this psalm say to contemporary weddings? The practical advice, "Leave to cleave," is sound; it finds further expression in Ruth's words to Naomi (Ruth 1:16-17) and Ephesians 5:31 (quoting Gen 2:24). The words to the bride, *Since he is your lord, bow to him* (v. 11), must be seen in the context of the royal tradition and not as a word for brides of all time.

Psalm 46

God Is Our Refuge and Strength

PREVIEW

This, the first of the Songs of Zion, confidently expresses a prophetic message of hope. In powerful word pictures, the confession of faith in God rises above the raging of nature (vv. 1-3), celebrates God's victory over raging nations in history (vv. 4-7), and declares God's final word in the kingdom of his peace (vv. 8-11). The refrain echoes the reality of God's presence with his people (vv. 7, 11).

Songs of Zion (Pss 46; 48; 76; 84; 87; 122) feature the importance and meaning of Jerusalem in the LORD's relation to his people and the world. Zion, a sacred name for Jerusalem, is celebrated as the unshakeable center of the world, for here the LORD dwells and the divine presence is known. More than place, however, the subject of these songs is God as refuge and help [Psalm Genres; Zion].

Historically, this psalm has been associated with the deliverance of Jerusalem from the Assyrian threat in the days of Isaiah, about 701 BC (2 Kings 18:35-37; Isa 37:33-38). Since neither Zion nor Jerusalem are mentioned in the psalm, some have suggested a possible northern origin before Jerusalem achieved its preeminence in the religious life of the people (Goulder: 139; Holladay: 29). Still others have looked for the origin of the psalm in the great autumnal festival in which the community celebrated the mighty acts of God, embracing creation and all human history—past, present, and future (Davidson, 1998:152).

The psalm is linked to themes in Isaiah 7:14 (vv. 7, 11); 8:5-8 (v. 4); and 14:31-32 (vv. 1, 4). The presence of *Selah* suggests later cultic use (vv. 3, 7, 11) *[Selah]*. In its application after the exile, the psalm points to a Jerusalem that emerges out of ashes and struggles to become a place known for a victory that overcomes the world. In a time of destabilization, the congregation confesses trust in *the LORD* (*Yahweh*) as God of the universe.

Alamoth in the heading, a form used only here and in 1 Chronicles 15:20, may have reference to a tune or tune pitch. Since the word means "girls," it could suggest a high-pitched tune (Ps 68:25) *[Korah; Musical; Superscriptions]*.

OUTLINE

God, Our Refuge in the Midst of Chaos (Creation), 46:1-3
God, Our Help in the Midst of the City (History), 46:4-7
God, Our Hope in the Midst of the Warring Nations (Kingdom), 46:8-11

EXPLANATORY NOTES

God, Our Refuge in the Midst of Chaos (Creation) 46:1-3

God's helpful presence is the theme sounded throughout the psalm (vv. 1, 5, 7, 10, 11). *Refuge* refers to God as a place where one can find safety and security. *We* represents the congregation assembled for worship in Jerusalem (v. 2). Pilgrims probably sang songs of Zion on the way to Jerusalem, but especially when they were standing immediately before the gates of the city of God.

The psalm begins with cataclysms of nature. Was the psalmist aware of chunks of Mt. Carmel falling off into the Mediterranean Sea (v. 2)? The word picture of world catastrophe may be borrowed from the primeval story of creation known from the discoveries at Ras Shamra. In the Ugaritic/Canaanite form of the myth of the combat against the dragon, the roaring waters of the primeval flood will once more rise and threaten to swallow up the world (Weiser: 368; "Ugaritic Myths, Poems About Baal," *ANET* 130-35). When the primeval waters of chaos rise against the created order, the LORD's supremacy is challenged (Ps 93:3-4). However, the psalmist declares, *We will not fear* (v. 2).

Did this psalm originally have the refrain (vv. 7, 11) also after verse 3, as suggested by Westermann (1989:284)? Or does verse 1 serve as the "refrain" to open the first stanza with affirmation of God's protecting, helping presence (Clifford, 2002:227)?

God, Our Help in the Midst of the City (History) 46:4-7

There is a river . . . What a magnificent line! A river, in contrast to the destructive waters; living water, *whose streams make glad* (v. 4). The psalm points to Jerusalem, a city under siege, as in the time when Sennacherib's army was routed by *the angel of the LORD* (2 Kings 19:35-36).

The river? Jerusalem has no river—only the spring of Gihon and Hezekiah's tunnel bringing water into the Pool of Siloam. Or is this symbolic language for the presence of God, and how the temple bestows security, prosperity, and peace in contrast to the pride of Assyria and Babylon that did not provide these gifts (Isa 8:6-10; Sabourin: 208)? Note the theme of the river also in Isaiah 33:21 and Ezekiel 47:1-12 (cf. the peaceful river in Eden, Gen 2:10-14). The central theme of stability amid instability sounds in the triple use of the Hebrew word *môṭ*—*shake* (v. 2), *shall not be moved* (v. 5), and *totter* (v. 6)—to accentuate the contrast between the secure city and insecure cosmos and history. Though the people cannot count on mountains and kingdoms, God is absolutely trustworthy!

The temple is the dwelling of the Most High (v. 4; Pss 26:8; 84:1; 132:5, 7). God is called the *Most High* (*'elyôn*), a liturgical title with roots in Canaanite religion, where El is the supreme god of the pantheon. The title is used in the psalms to stress the power of God over all the forces that seek to challenge his rule (v. 4; 9:2; 47:2; 83:18). God's voice (thunder) can make the earth tremble (29:6) and shatter his foes, here characterized as kingdoms that threaten the city (v. 6). The term *LORD of hosts* describes God's majesty; *God of Jacob* emphasizes the LORD's relationship to Israel (v. 7).

God, Our Hope in the Midst of the Warring Nations (Kingdom) 46:8-11

The final stanza points to judgment and how God will make an end to waging war. The mighty fist of God shall destroy the power of men and their weapons (vv. 8-9). The assembled nations are addressed. God will make wars to cease by destroying the weapons of war (v. 9). The prophetic oracle of verse 10 is not simply an invitation to become quiet and relax and meditate. It has more the force of command: "Leave off waging war, and know that I am God!" Dahood (1:282) suggests this to mean, "Do nothing; do not enter into military alliances with other nations." God controls history. Step back from looking for security in anyone other than God, who is *exalted among the nations.* Such was the military policy (Yahweh war) as advocated in Isaiah 30:15 *[War].*

So the psalmist dares to hope. Because he is wholly dependent on God and allows his thinking and his vision to be directed by God, he is able to arrive at such a bold conception. The refrain resounds with words of confidence in a crumbling world: *The LORD . . . is with us* (vv. 7, 11)! Immanuel: "God with us!" (cf. Isa 7:14; 8:8).

THE TEXT IN THE BIBLICAL CONTEXT AND LIFE OF THE CHURCH

God and Chaos

Psalm 46 wrestles with the dangers of an unstable world. Signs of instability in creation were seen in earthquakes, volcanoes, floods, and droughts. But the psalm is also concerned with the chaos that comes from nations whose "raging" results in the devastation of war.

Israel did not seem afraid to invoke imagery from the surrounding nations' mythologies and use it to declare God's sovereignty. For chaotic forces in the world of creation, the poets and prophets drew on stories from Canaanite literature, such as Leviathan, the forces of chaos represented as a marine monster; and Rahab, a name for the primeval chaos monster (Job 3:8; 26:12-13; 41:1; Pss 74:12-17; 89:9-14; Isa 27:1; 51:9-10). Yet while using such stories and imagery, they declared that the LORD is the victorious creator.

Psalm 46 asserts God's sovereignty also over the chaos of the nations in history. God can bring human national structures into disarray, and transform that chaos into a new world—a world without the weapons of war (vv. 8-9). The same certainty about the future is expressed in Isaiah 2:1-4 and Micah 4:1-4, that the weapons of war will be utterly destroyed, and peace will extend to the whole earth and embrace all humanity.

While we can read the psalm as a word to the nations to abandon attempts to destroy by force the "city of God," it can also be read as a renunciation of war altogether. Lohfink (117), in an essay on Psalm 46 as peace poetry, suggests: "YHWH appeared as a war god, but the opponent, whom he brought to silence with his war-god's voice, was war itself." War and its violent consequences are not a part of the world God intends, but grow out of human sin and disobedience. As used in worship from the time of the exile to the present, Psalm 46 witnesses that God would finally bring the chaos of war to an end.

A Mighty Fortress Is Our God

The importance of Psalm 46 in popular Christian piety can be attributed in large part to Martin Luther's hymn "A mighty fortress is our God." This truly ecumenical hymn has been translated into nearly 200 languages; there are over 100 English translations known.

Composition of the hymn has been linked to the event in 1529 when the Turkish army turned back after besieging the walls of Vienna without success. Luther, translating the psalm for a sixteenth-century audience in a situation of distress, transposed the enemy kings into the devil. This resulted in a fighting tone for his famous hymn, not in keeping with the psalm's note of quiet trust.

For many persons, Luther's hymn has become the battle song in spiritual warfare. There are many memorable lines:

> Did we in our own strength confide, our striving would be losing. . . .
> We will not fear, for God hath willed his truth to triumph through us. . . .
> Let goods and kindred go, this mortal life also;
> The body they may kill, God's truth abideth still.
> His kingdom is forever.

We Will Not Fear

Psalm 46, a psalm of radical trust in the face of overwhelming threat, invites people of faith to hold steady before nameless dangers. This was a popular psalm after the eruption of Mount St. Helens, or the October 1987 earthquake in Southern California. It was widely read after the December 2004 Indian Ocean tsunami that devastated Asian seacoasts.

It was also one of the psalms read when people flocked to churches following the September 11, 2001, terror attack on the Twin Towers of the World Trade Center and the Pentagon. Human-created terror instills fear. However, responding out of fear usually accentuates violence, as it did following the 9/11 event and the following wars in Afghanistan and Iraq.

How might this psalm of trust speak to our time about security? Wherein lies security? Certainly not in weapons of war. Is there not a need to "become still," and to "know" the sovereign Lord of all chaos and peace, and accept the truth of Immanuel? God with us! God is our refuge in all earth-shaking events, and is with his people to make the divine loving presence known (Rom 8:28). In a world being destabilized by many forces, this quiet song of confidence stands as a reminder to place trust in God as refuge and strength.

Psalm 47

Call to Joyful Praise of the God Who Reigns over All the Earth

PREVIEW

This exuberant hymn celebrates God's enthronement as king of all gods and of all nations. The psalm is a double hymn, each section beginning with a joyful summons: *Clap . . . shout* (v. 1), and *sing praises* (vv. 6-7). The psalm's theme, the LORD is king over all the earth (vv. 2, 7), moves from a national focus (vv. 1-5) to a worldwide mission perspective (vv. 6-9).

Psalm 47 begins where Psalm 46 left off; the defeated pagan nations (46:8-10) are called to submit to God's sovereignty and join in festive praise. This is the first of seven throne ascension psalms that declare God or the LORD as king (Pss 47; 93; 95-99). In the royal psalms, the king is king, but in these so-called "enthronement" psalms, the LORD is king *[Psalm Genres]*.

What lies behind the language of the kingship of God in these psalms? Mowinckel assumed the existence of an annual festival for the ascension of the LORD to the throne, similar to the Babylonian New Year's Festival. That thesis, and variations of a covenant festival, have more recently been questioned (Kraus, 1986:84-91; 1988:86-89). Kraus acknowledges that only Psalm 47 of the Yahweh-as-king hymns in the Psalter "transparently presents an act of enthronement." The ark, symbol of the LORD's presence and rule among his people, appears to have a prominent role in the celebration (2 Sam 6:15). Such an entrance festival likely took place on the first day of the Feast of Tabernacles.

For the heading see the essays on *Korah* and *Superscriptions*.

OUTLINE

Summons to Praise of God, Who Has Subdued the Nations, 47:1-5
Sing Praises, for God Is King of All the Earth, 47:6-9

EXPLANATORY NOTES

Summons to Praise of God, Who Has Subdued the Nations 47:1-5

Whatever the specific event calling forth this dramatic liturgy of the people, several features of the psalm deserve note. The names for deity include *God* (seven times), *LORD* (twice), *the Most High* (once), *God of Abraham* (once), and *king* (thrice) [*Names of God*]. The triple use of *kî* (*for*, vv. 2, 7, 9) gives reasons for this joyous exclamation: the LORD has subdued nations and chosen Israel (vv. 2-4), and all peoples belong to the sovereign God (vv. 7-9).

Clap your hands may suggest more than a summons to joyful praise (v. 1). It can also be a call to the nations to come to agreement regarding their relationship to the LORD, the God of Israel (Wilson, 2002:727). The name *Most High* (*'elyôn*), a title for the chief god in the assembly of gods, implies supremacy and echoes the verb translated *gone up* (v. 5) and *highly exalted* (v. 9). *All the earth* identifies the realm over which the God Most High exercises lordship (Pss 83:18; 97:9). This call to the nations and peoples is pervasive in the psalms (66:8; 67:2-7; 148:11-13).

The reason for praise links history and mission, beginning with remembrance of the tradition of how Israel received the land and gained dominion through the assumption of kingship (vv. 3-4). A striking claim of the enthronement psalms is that while God's sovereignty is universal, it is exercised in a particular place: Zion (Clifford, 2002:232). *God has gone up with a shout* suggests the cultic rite of enthronement as similar to a coronation ritual (v. 5; 1 Kings 1:39-40). It is possible that the ark of the covenant was carried in solemn procession into the temple (Ps 132; 2 Sam 6:12-19). The trumpet blasts are characteristic of enthronement when a new king was proclaimed

(2 Sam 15:10; 2 Kings 9:13; 11:12). *Selah* (v. 4) may mark a pause in the liturgy, though some have questioned whether stanza one does not more appropriately end after verse 5 *[Selah]*.

Sing Praises, for God Is King of All the Earth 47:6-9

The second summons, *to sing praises* (five times in vv. 5-6), includes singing praises with *a psalm,* a *Maśkîl* (v. 7 NRSV n). Elsewhere in the book of Psalms, *Maskil (maśkîl)* occurs only in the headings (from *śākal,* "teach, instruct"). This may have been a particular kind of psalm designed to teach the people about the great things God has done for them. NEB translates, *Sing psalms with all your art [Superscriptions; Musical].* The reason for such praise is found in an acclamation: *God is the king of all the earth* and *king over the nations* (vv. 7-8; Ps 99:2).

The psalm ends with the exaltation of the LORD and a wide understanding of the people of God. Not the one nation only, but also all the princes are seen as submissive to his rule, and so they become *the people of the God of Abraham.* Does this text claim too much? The NRSV and NIV translate *as the people of the God of Abraham.* NEB translates *with the families of Abraham's line. As* points to a universal hope rooted in the promise that God made to Abraham in Genesis 12:3 (Isa 2:2-4; Mic 4:1-3). *With* suggests that the princes of the peoples represent subject peoples, witnessing the kingship of God, a translation perhaps more in line with the nationalistic tone of verse 3 (Davidson, 1998:156; Brueggemann, 1984:150).

THE TEXT IN THE BIBLICAL CONTEXT AND LIFE OF THE CHURCH

The Kingdom of God

This psalm provides significant background for the NT concept of the kingdom of God. The prophets proclaimed that the Gentiles will one day join the people of God (Isa 49:22-23; 56:6-8; 60:1-3; Zech 8:22-23). In this psalm the nations themselves become *the people of the God of Abraham,* a view voiced in the NT: "So there will be one flock, one shepherd" (John 10:16; Gal 3:7-9).

Isaiah of the exile connected return of the Babylonian refugees to Zion with the announcement of the reign of the LORD (Isa 52:7-10). Jesus connected his ministry with the announcement of the reign of God (Mark 1:14-15). This enthronement psalm adds power to the NT concept of enthronement on the cross: "And I, when I am lifted up, . . .

will draw all people to myself" (John 12:32; Eph 1:20-21; 2:6). The book of Revelation illustrates the exaltation and world dominion of God through Christ (Rev 4:2, 9; 7:10, 17; 21:5).

Beyond the broad mission outlook, the psalm's final verse makes an astounding claim: *For the shields of the earth belong to God* (v. 9). *Shields* are the rulers, the guardians of the people (Pss 84:9; 89:18). Does such a claim suggest that God alone has at his disposal all the forces of war, and that no human power will arise anymore? Is this another expression of the prophetic ideal of God's everlasting kingdom of peace and how the LORD makes wars to cease in the world (Ps 46:9; Isa 2:4; 9:5; Zech 9:10; Weiser: 379)?

To speak of God as *a great king over all the earth* (v. 2) must, in the end, lead to a God who cannot be only "our God" in a narrow, exclusive sense. Thus, "national interest" and empire building can never be the highest criterion for any people, especially people of faith. Jesus admonished his followers: "Seek ye first the kingdom of God, and his righteousness" (Matt 6:33 KJV).

Worship of God

After the end of the monarchy, the praise of God as king moved into the foreground (Pss 47; 93; 95–99), and the old royal psalms were interpreted messianically and kept in worship. Jewish worshippers continue to recite Psalm 47 seven times, before sounding the trumpet to inaugurate their New Year. The early church, drawing on the psalm's last words, *He is highly exalted*, celebrated the ascension of Jesus with Psalm 47, the psalm still used in the liturgy for Ascension Day. The image of ascending to the throne also evokes the resurrection, by which Jesus begins to exercise sovereignty over the world.

Finally, this communal song of celebration demonstrates the place of exultation in worship. *Clap your hands, . . . shout to God with loud songs of joy, . . . sing praises!* In procession, accompanied by trumpet fanfare and musical instruments, the people form a great choir of highly involved worshippers. Worship of God, *king of all the earth,* is not spectator activity. Worship "should be dynamic encounters with God—challenging, convicting, and somewhat uncomfortable" (Wyrtzen: 135).

Psalm 48

Zion, City of Our God

PREVIEW

This song of Zion, a pilgrim hymn, celebrates the beauty and security of Jerusalem. God is her protector, making the city unconquerable. In the atmosphere of elation after a great deliverance, Psalm 48 resembles Psalms 46 and 76. In expressing adoration for the LORD, who loves Zion, it is similar to Psalm 87. Zion songs celebrate the glory and honor of Mount Zion as the place of God's dwelling and reign [Psalm Genres; Zion].

The origin of the psalm has been linked historically to a deliverance, as in the time of Hezekiah when Sennacherib's Assyrian army panicked and fled (2 Kings 19:32-37; Isa 37:33-37). Or the psalm may come out of Israel's cultic celebration, such as the Feast of Tabernacles, which included a procession around the city. Psalm 48 proclaims Jerusalem above all rivals. A mood of praise and confidence pervades the psalm. In Israel's worship it tells the story of a famous victory as a supreme example of divine care. This Korah psalm looks to the future, proclaiming to the next generation that this great God will remain the same protecting guide forever [Korah; Superscriptions].

OUTLINE

Call to Praise the LORD in Zion, 48:1-3
Description of a Deliverance from Enemies, 48:4-8
The Worshipping Pilgrims Ponder God's Steadfast Love, 48:9-11
The Procession and Acclamation, 48:12-14

Psalm 48

EXPLANATORY NOTES

Call to Praise the LORD in Zion   48:1-3

The cry of adoration, *Great is the LORD*, appears to be an exclamation widely used in ancient worship (Pss 86:10; 99:2-3; 135:5). The divine names appear: *God* (*'ĕlōhîm*), eight times; *LORD* and *great King* and *LORD of hosts*, once each.

The psalm's focus is on Jerusalem, for which superlative titles abound: *city of our God* (vv. 1, 8), *his holy mountain, beautiful in elevation, joy of all the earth, Mount Zion, in the far north, city of the great King, a sure defense, the city of the LORD of hosts, your temple,* and *this is God* (v. 14). These lofty titles suggest theology more than geography. Mount Zion, about 2,600 feet in elevation, is compared to *the far north* (Mt. Zaphon, NIV), where Phoenician and Canaanite texts located the residence of the gods. The psalmist suggests that Mount Zion is to the LORD what Mt. Zaphon (present-day Mt. Casius) is to Canaanite religion, the dwelling of God and the most hallowed spot of the land. Theologically, Mount Zion is Israel's equivalent to the highest of all the mountains of the world (Isa 2:2-3; Ezek 5:5; 38:12).

While Zion is celebrated, the psalm's real object of praise is the LORD. The decisive reason for the invincibility of the city of God is the fact that the LORD dwells there (v. 3; Ps 46:5). The LORD is the great saving king and defender.

Description of a Deliverance from Enemies   48:4-8

Stanza 1 proclaims the God of all the earth; in stanza 2 the scene shifts to Jerusalem, describing the gathering of hostile kings and their subsequent flight (Ezek 38–39; Zech 12; 14). Their panic appears to be caused by some revelation of God himself, as in Yahweh war where the decisive action comes from the LORD, while the human contribution is trust and faith (1 Sam 7:10; A. Anderson, 1:370) *[War]*. *The ships of Tarshish,* the large Phoenician treasure ships that could sail as far as Spain, are shattered by mighty storms and serve as metaphor for God's might over human power (Ezek 27:25-36). These verses depict the futility of any attack on the holy city. *Kings* can represent all those who have ever or will ever threaten the power of *the great King* in Jerusalem. Related to the image of the King is that of God as divine warrior. By the LORD's victory over the forces of chaos (Job 9:8; 26:12; 38:8-12; Pss 89:10; 93:1-4) and the enemies of Israel (Exod 15:1-18; Pss 47:1-4; 98:1-3; Isa 42:13), the divine rule is established (Miller, 1986:76).

A single speaker may have uttered the victory hymn (vv. 4-7). The enemy hosts look on Mount Zion, tremble, and flee to their destruction.

By contrast, the psalmist and the worshipping pilgrims look at *the city of our God* and find enduring security. *As we have heard, so have we seen* summarizes their response to this city protected by *the LORD of hosts* (v. 8). The pilgrims now see for themselves the majesty and invincibility of the city from which the LORD reigns. The musical term *Selah* may suggest a pause at the end of stanza 2, which ends with the word *forever*, the word also concluding the psalm (vv. 8, 14) *[Selah]*.

The Worshipping Pilgrims Ponder God's Steadfast Love 48:9-11

Stanza 3 can be seen as a hymnic response as pilgrims ponder God's *steadfast love, name,* and *right hand.* There is no better place to ponder God's divine love than in the temple (v. 9). Here is astonished acknowledgment of the power of the LORD on Zion and in all the world. The LORD appears before the world, his right hand filled with *righteousness* (NIV, here preferred over NRSV's *victory*). In that divine justice rooted in covenant love (*ḥesed*), *the towns of Judah rejoice* *[Steadfast].* Songs declaring the LORD's victory are scattered throughout the hymns of praise (Pss 98:1-2; 118:15; Isa 40:10; 52:10).

The Procession and Acclamation 48:12-14

The call sounds for procession around the city walls (Ps 24:7-10). The magnificent buildings symbolized God's power over every threat and God's loving commitment to dwell with the holy community. Review of the *ramparts* may have been less an inspection of the city than the cultic rite of a thanksgiving procession. The real purpose is to *tell the next generation that this is God.* Zion's God is shepherd of the flock and *our guide forever* (vv. 8, 14; Deut 4:27; Ps 78:52; Isa 49:10; 63:14). The children need to know about this city and this God! Some versions render the last Hebrew words as *unto death* (KJV), but recent translations often omit them. The translation *forever* reflects the LXX, which seems to run two Hebrew words together. Another possibility is that it was a musical directive introducing the next psalm, as in Psalm 46, *According to Alamoth.*

THE TEXT IN THE BIBLICAL CONTEXT AND LIFE OF THE CHURCH

Zion Theology

As a hymn of the early Jewish community worship, Psalm 48 reflects a Zion ideology that makes Jerusalem the absolute center of the world and sees it as invincible, since God is present there. The "theology" was later misappropriated (Jer 7:1-15, esp. v. 4). So strong and popular was the rash presumption that God's protection of the city would forever save it that Jeremiah's words fell on the deaf ears of a people not convinced of their need for conversion. Zion theology drew on the promises of God, whose ark of the covenant was taken up to Jerusalem (Ps 132). Worshippers used the psalm to pledge allegiance to God, giving thanks and praise for the possibility of living in Jerusalem and for the protection received.

The significance of the word "Zion" grew through the centuries, from a place where the temple and royal palace stood, to the city, to a poetic name for the people of Israel, and even to the whole land of Israel. Christians transferred the name to the whole people of God, calling the church "Zion" and "City of Our God," as expressed in John Newton's hymn "Glorious things of thee are spoken" (1779). In the church's liturgy, Zion is also used as a name for the heavenly city (Heb 12:22; 1 Pet 2:6; Rev 14:1). The psalm is often used at Pentecost [Zion].

Beyond the Visible

This psalm illustrates the use of language to point toward realities beyond the visible. The city is viewed "as a medium through which God can be known. . . . The visible is transparent to the invisible and focuses mind and spirit on what cannot be seen" (Mays, 1994b:190). Hence, city, temple, and cathedral become pointers to a reality that transcends everything human. For Judaism, Jerusalem as the place of meeting and of teaching became especially sacred. For Christians, God's dwelling is realized in different ways. The privileged "place" of encounter with God is Jesus Christ (Clifford, 2002:237).

In the fourth century AD, John Cassian distinguished four meanings of the name "Jerusalem" in Scripture: city of the Jews, the church of Christ, the heavenly city of God, and the soul of man (Reardon, 2000:93). So the NT community might appropriately see in the psalm's assertion *This is God* (v. 14) allusion to the incarnation and how "the Word became flesh, . . . and we have seen his glory" (John 1:14). Or the church will try to understand Psalm 48 in light of Matthew 16:18: "And I tell you, you are Peter, and on this rock I will build my church."

Psalm 49

Not Wealth, but God

PREVIEW

The theme of this wisdom psalm is centered on the transitoriness of wealth and the inevitability of death. As a teaching psalm, it offers comfort and reassurance for poor and oppressed people. With death as the great leveler, they need not fear those who have wealth and power. People cannot ransom themselves by self-reliance, but God liberates the faithful (vv. 8, 15). The psalm confirms the reality of death, but God is stronger than *the power of Sheol* (v. 15).

As the last of the Korahite psalms in this sequence (Pss 42–49), this psalm develops the theme that the LORD rules the world; the rich and powerful do not *[Korah; Superscriptions]*. Psalms 37 and 73 also deal with the problem of the powerful wicked, reassuring the righteous of their vindication while the wicked will be undone. Here the resolution lies in the reality that, like the animals, all people will one day die (note the proverbial refrain, vv. 12, 20). Wisdom reflection on human transitoriness is common (Job 7:6-10; 9:25-26; 14:1-2, 10-12; Pss 39:4-6; 62:9; Eccles 3:16-21; 5:13-17).

Textual difficulties are numerous in this psalm. The NRSV has seven footnotes, six suggesting readings that depart from the Hebrew text. The style is enigmatic, with contradictory, contrasting, and unorthodox statements. Yet the psalm provides a powerful expression of wisdom and hope.

Psalm 49

OUTLINE

The Wisdom Teacher's Introduction, 49:1-4
Reflective Teaching on the Transitoriness of Wealth and Inevitability of Death, 49:5-12
Lament for Those Trusting in Themselves; Comfort in God's Ransom, 49:13-20

EXPLANATORY NOTES

The Wisdom Teacher's Introduction 49:1-4

The introduction declares a missionary purpose: *Hear this, all you peoples* (v. 1). All people everywhere are addressed, not just Israel, and all economic and social groups are invited to listen (v. 2). This will be a meditation on the pursuit of wisdom and how to gain understanding for life (v. 3). Wisdom as skill in living through *torah* (*tôrâ*, teaching) is to be expected in the psalms (Ps 1:2).

The source of the teaching is a proverb, the unfolding of a *riddle* set to music, a teaching that is not the obvious truth of common sense (Brueggemann, 1984:106). The riddle seems to be the apparent injustice of a world in which wicked fools prosper while the righteous wise live in poverty.

Reflective Teaching on the Transitoriness of Wealth and Inevitability of Death 49:5-12

The key issue is identified in verse 5: *Why should I fear* because of powerful ones? That personal question will then be turned into the teaching of verses 16-20: *Do not be afraid when some become rich.* The problem appears to be the fear people experience when confronted with the power and violence of the strong, and the envy of the poor, who are made to feel weak and insignificant in face of the powerful wealthy.

The psalmist testifies to how we can overcome these feelings. Death is the great equalizer. In the end, all die. There is no buying one's way out of dying (vv. 7-9). Even those who in this life control huge estates will have to leave everything to others, and their grave will be the only real estate they can claim (vv. 10-11).

The problem lies not in wealth itself, but in the way people orient their lives to its acquisition and possession. Wealth disorients people in their relationship to God, and often in how they relate to their fellow human beings (Jer 9:23-24). Wealth creates a false sense of security and fosters the denial of death. However, "trust in riches as an immortality strategy doesn't work" (Mays, 1994b:192). Human beings die just as the animals do (vv. 12, 20).

Lament for Those Trusting in Themselves; Comfort in God's Ransom 49:13-20

With a vivid image, the psalmist laments the fate of those who trust only in themselves. Those *foolhardy* enough to believe their power and wealth will abide are like sheep fattened for the slaughter in a death dance (vv. 13-14). In reversal of the "Good Shepherd" image (Ps 23; John 10), death is now the shepherd of those who live for themselves, the Grim Reaper, the Great Leveler. The sheep will be swept into their true home—*Sheol* (Knight, 1:232)! Sheol, the abode of the dead, was to the Hebrews little more than a shadowy existence, where they would *never again see the light* (v. 19) *[Sheol]*. The psalm ends with repetition of the refrain, proclaiming that mortals die and perish *like the animals* (vv. 12, 20).

However, there is a word of hope in the verse that begins *But God* (v. 15): *But God will ransom my soul!* This is the most significant and interesting verse in the psalm. Here is the only mention of God in the psalm (except v. 7, with God as object). The brief line *for he will receive me* connects with the stories of Enoch and Elijah (Gen 5:24; 2 Kings 2:9-11; Pss 16:10-11; 73:23-26). Though the psalm here gives no full-blown understanding of life after death, it does envision the hope of being ushered into God's presence. People cannot ransom themselves (v. 7), but God liberates the faithful (v. 15). Religious certitude comes not in knowing what will happen when we die, but in knowing the Power that will sustain. So the psalmist invites the hearer not to be afraid, since God is at the center and end of life. The wisdom of life lies not in wealth, but in God (Ps 111:10; Prov 1:7). If *Selah* was a notation for the cymbal's clash to call attention and to reflect on what had just been said or sung, how appropriate after verses 13 and 15! *[Selah]*.

THE TEXT IN THE BIBLICAL CONTEXT AND LIFE OF THE CHURCH

The Ransom of Life

In this psalm about the transitoriness of wealth and its relationship to death, the term *ransom* plays a prominent role (vv. 7-8, 15; *ransom, redeem*, NIV). The idea of ransom was relatively common in ancient Israel. A ransom was something given that covered or cancelled an incurred claim over a person or a group, the price of deliverance from an incurred status (Exod 21:30; 1 Sam 14:45; Job 33:23-25; Isa 43:3; Jer 31:11).

Psalm 49 states clearly that the ransom for a life is costly. One cannot buy a ticket to everlasting life for oneself or for one's *brother* (v. 7 NRSV n). Only God can and will ransom *from the power of Sheol* (v. 15).

For Christian readers, this passage is suggestive of NT understandings of how Jesus "came not to be served but to serve, and to give his life a ransom for many" (Matt 20:28; Mark 10:45; 1 Tim 2:5-6; Heb 9:15; 1 Pet 1:18-19). The high cost of redemption is acknowledged in Jesus' words: "What will it profit them if they gain the whole world but forfeit their life? Or what will they give in return for their life?" (Matt 16:26).

Wealth and Death

This psalm, with its realism about death, speaks to Western materialistic society, bent on chasing money. Access to wealth can lull people into thinking they do not need God. In their affluence, Westerners especially have important sorting out to do because they find it difficult not to value the things the rich treasure (Brueggemann, 1984:110).

Economists estimate that in the United States more than $8 trillion in collective wealth will transfer from one generation to the next during the first two decades of the twenty-first century. What will people do with it—as accumulated assets are passed on to children, or received from the preceding generation? What place will there be for "Jubilee thinking" and redistribution as people prepare for the grave? Jesus' stories in Luke 12:13-21 and 16:19-31 provide sequel and commentary on this psalm. Further teaching about the impermanence of wealth can be found in 1 Timothy 6:6-10, 17.

Latin America's prophetic poet Ernesto Cardenal (41), writes on Psalm 49 in the context of bankers and heavy-chested dictators:

> So do not for the mighty care a straw;
> they teeter on the brink of nothingness
> and are life's posturing antithesis;
> their medals but bits of metal, nothing more.

The reality of death can bring perspective on wealth. A prominent and influential community leader, stricken with pancreatic cancer at the age of seventy, confided during his last months, "Life sifts down to two things: a sense that life has counted for something, and the people—my family, my church, and those persons I have been able to help in some way."

Psalm 50

The Judge Speaks

PREVIEW

"Hear ye! Hear ye!" The courtroom, with God as plaintiff and judge, provides the scene for this prophetic liturgy. It presents the LORD as a judge who holds the people accountable for their worship and conduct.

The psalm is composed on the model of a speech for trial proceedings. The introduction announces the coming of God as judge (vv. 1-6). The first judgment speech critiques the congregation's understanding of sacrifices (vv. 7-15). The second judgment speech rebukes people as wicked because of the disparity between confession and conduct (vv. 16-23). The psalm ends with an exhortation to thanksgiving and the way of obedience.

The psalm is one of three covenant renewal liturgies (Pss 50; 81; 95), which may have been used at one of the great pilgrim festivals. A likely occasion was the Feast of Weeks (Pentecost), when the law was proclaimed and the covenant renewed (Ps 81:4, 9-10). The psalm could have come from the time of prophetic reforms in the days of Hezekiah or Josiah. Or it could be a liturgical sermon, an example of Levitical preaching, used to stabilize the new community of the faithful after the exile (Gerstenberger: 211).

Similar to the preceding and following psalms, Psalm 50 serves as a bridge between the first collection of Korah psalms (Pss 42-49) and the second collection of David psalms (51-65; 68-70). This is the first of the twelve psalms of Asaph (the others, 73-83, open book III of the Psalter). This guild of temple singers participated in nearly every major celebration relating to the temple, both before and after the exile (1 Chron 25:1-2; 2 Chron 29:30). Usually psalms of Asaph use the name *'ĕlōhîm* for God *[Asaph; Names of God; Superscriptions]*.

OUTLINE

The Coming of God, the Judge, 50:1-6
Address to the Congregation: Judgment of Worship, 50:7-15
Address to the Wicked: Judgment of Conduct, 50:16-23

EXPLANATORY NOTES

The Coming of God, the Judge   50:1-6

A mighty crescendo of cymbals breaks the silence. God who spoke at Sinai is now announced as speaking from Zion. The introduction may be describing what has been happening in the temple liturgy, a theophany of God appearing to judge his people (vv. 1-3). The opening trinity of names introducing the judge, *mighty one* (*'ēl*), *God* (*'ĕlōhîm*), and *LORD* (*Yahweh*), emphasizes his deity, power, and authority. The *sun*, with its constant scrutiny of human activity from its position in the heavens, is often connected with judgment (v. 1; Pss 19:4-6; 84:11). God *shines forth* likely means "appears in a storm theophany" (v. 2; Exod 19:16-18; Deut 4:11-12; 33:2; Job 37:15; Pss 80:1; 94:1-2; Isa 29:6). The function of theophany is to portray the miraculous and overwhelming power of God's intervention *[Theophany]*.

As the court convenes, God summons heaven and earth as witnesses, characteristic of the lawsuit God is about to bring against his people (v. 4; Deut 32:1; Isa 1:2; Jer 2:12). As defendants, the LORD calls those who made a covenant *my faithful ones*. The Hebrew word *zebah*, a *sacrifice* that establishes community, occurs here in the relationship of God to his people (v. 5). That relationship is now under severe stress. The heavens present God as the one who comes, as the one to set things right (v. 6). *Selah*, the liturgical note in the margin, may call for sounding of the cymbal, or for a pause before the judgment speech. *[Selah]*

Address to the Congregation: Judgment of Worship 50:7-15

God, who identifies himself as *God, your God*, asks the people to hear what he will say (v. 7). The concern of the first judgment speech is the relationship of the people with God, as expressed through worship. The problem is not their *sacrifices,* but the misunderstanding and misuse of their offerings (v. 8). The sacrifices have been offered as though God has need of them. In reality, sacrifices may be most useful to the one making them. God does not need anything. Everything already belongs to God (vv. 10-12). *I am God, your God* (v. 7) implies "and you are my child." *Offer* a heart of *thanksgiving,* and *call on me. . . . I will deliver* (vv. 14-15).

Faithfulness to the demands of the covenant is at stake here. Thank offerings acknowledge the worshipper's absolute dependence on God's grace and mercy. The LORD is not in need of nourishment by means of a sacrifice, nor is it possible to buy his favor. It is the human worshipper who, in his need, is dependent on the LORD, and who can bring the LORD no better sacrifice than thanks for such help and deliverance (Kraus, 1986:96).

Address to the Wicked: Judgment of Conduct 50:16-23

The second judgment speech is directed to *the wicked* (v. 16) *[Wicked].* This accusation addresses the discrepancy between confession and conduct (vv. 16-17). When people mouth the statutes and claim covenant promises without any intent to observe the requirements, they disregard God's claims. Israel's worship is to result in justice and righteousness (Pss 37:28; 82:3; 98:9; 99:4; 103:6; 119:5-7; 146:7; 147:19). Yet people *hate discipline* and are unwilling to take instruction (v. 17; Prov 1:2-3, 7; 15:5, 32-33). They may recite the words of *statutes* and *covenant* (v. 16), but then disregard them (v. 17).

People say the words of the covenant but ignore the commandments (against stealing, adultery, bearing false witness) and act in ways that make community impossible. By what right do they dare to act as though God does not exist (vv. 18-20)? When God is not honored, "when the first tablet of the commandments is not taken seriously, . . . the second tablet of neighbor relations will lose its power" (Brueggemann, 1984:91). God will now break the silence (v. 21).

The psalm ends with an exhortation and invitation. The aim of the covenant mediator is to lead people back to observe the covenant in loyalty to God. First the warning: If they want destruction, God will allow it to their ruin (v. 22; Hos 5:14). Yet the final word is not threat, but the promise of divine help. Those who become conscious of their forgetfulness of God can *call . . . in the day of trouble* (v. 15) and receive *the salvation of God* (v. 23).

THE TEXT IN THE BIBLICAL CONTEXT AND LIFE OF THE CHURCH

Appropriate Worship

Psalm 50, as a prophetic judgment psalm, contends that how people worship needs to be connected with how they live. Outward performance without inward commitment is unacceptable. The psalm does not condemn the sacrificial system, but cautions against its abuse. Various psalms give additional qualifications of sacrifice (Pss 40:6-8; 51:16-19; 69:30-31).

The prophets sound the same note. Amos (5:21-24) announced the LORD's fury against a people who conducted elaborate worship ceremonies but showed no concern for the poor in their midst. Hosea (6:6) spoke for God as saying, "I desire steadfast love and not sacrifice, the knowledge of God rather than burnt offerings." Isaiah (1:10-17; 10:1-4) declared that the LORD was fed up with people who were busy with their liturgies and sacrifices, but enacted legislation biased against widows, orphans, and other poor and powerless people. Micah (6:6-8) declared that what the LORD wanted was not burnt offerings and rivers of oil, but "to do justice, and to love kindness, and to walk humbly with your God." Jeremiah (7:1-15) censured those who made the temple a fetish and whose religion never got out of the worship place into daily living.

Worship, and the accompanying sacrifices and offerings, is not about people bringing to God what belongs to them. They can only bring what is already God's. God wants to find in the hearts of his people love and compassion for the helpless, the victims of greed and oppression, the orphan and the widow (Isa 58:6-7; John 4:23-24; Rom 12:1-13; Col 3:12-17). The Bible declares the impossibility of loving God, whom we do not see, without loving the people around us, whom we do see (1 John 4:20-21). One cannot come to God without coming to him together with one's sister or brother (Matt 5:22-24).

Jesus spoke about being doers of the word and not hearers only (Matt 7:24-27). James (2:14-26) wrote of how faith without works is dead. Worship in spirit and in truth links faith and act. In the words of the sixteenth-century reformer Menno Simons, "True evangelical faith cannot lie dormant; . . . it clothes the naked; it feeds the hungry; it comforts the sorrowful; it shelters the destitute; . . . it has become all things to all" (Menno: 307).

Renewing the Covenant

Psalm 50 acknowledges both the covenant God established with his people and the reality of sin. The biblical God is ready to forgive sin and to allow new beginnings (Ps 51). The psalmist's purpose is to lead people back to faithful observance of the covenant (vv. 15, 23).

A covenant renewal service may have taken place at the annual Feast of Weeks (Pentecost), associated with the law in postbiblical times, probably as a continuation of an earlier tradition (Clifford, 2002:245; VanderKam, *ABD,* 6:896). Covenant renewal was an invitation for repentance and recommitment to follow the law given at Sinai (Exod 19:1-8; 2 Chron 15:8-15).

The Christian community has been incorporated into the people of the LORD by a covenant made through the sacrifice of Jesus (Mark 14:24). Celebration of the Lord's Supper is an occasion for the church to work at covenant renewal. While communion practices and understandings change, the Anabaptists often used an old parable from the early church to emphasize the discipline of the believers in Christ. Andreas Ehrenpreis wrote in 1652 (Friedmann, *ME,* 3:394):

> As the grain-kernels are altogether merged and each must give its content or strength into the one flour and bread, likewise also the wine, where the grapes are crushed under the press, and each grape gives away all its juice and all its strength into one wine. Whichever kernel and whichever grape, however, is not crushed and retains its strength for itself alone, such an one is unworthy and is cast out. This is what Christ wanted to bring home to his companions and guests at the Last Supper as an example of how they should be together in such a fellowship.

Traditional patterns of discipline were often negative, legalistic, harsh, and unloving. Redemptive discipline will seek to reclaim the offender and recall the whole fellowship to life and discipleship in Christ.

Psalm 50 serves notice that a permissive society dare not ignore the sovereign God. If the judgment of God is not proclaimed in the church, then heaven will proclaim it (v. 6). The warning about "tearing apart" suggests that if God will not deliver, there is no one who will (v. 22). Forget not, but give thanks!

Psalm 51

Have Mercy on Me, O God. . . . I Have Sinned

PREVIEW

This lament, a confession of sin by an individual, is the most important of the seven Penitential Psalms *[Penitential]*. Using strong personal language, the psalmist provides an amazing catalog of theological words for sin and forgiveness, God's character and action. The psalm deals with the seriousness and significance of sin. This lament not only testifies to the need for confession, but also offers a model in which sin is owned. The psalmist comes empty-handed and prays for the miracle of God's creating, renewing spirit.

Psalm 51 is the first of eighteen Davidic psalms in book II of the Psalter. Eight of these have been given historical settings in the headings, with Psalm 51 connected to the story of the prophet Nathan's rebuke of David for his affair with Bathsheba (2 Sam 11–12). Whoever added the heading saw in the psalmist's declaration *Against you, you alone, have I sinned* (v. 4) the connection with David's response to Nathan, "I have sinned against the LORD" (2 Sam 12:13). The psalm makes sense in the context of this terrible story about David *[Superscriptions]*.

Some scholars see reasons for dating the psalm after the exile and before rebuilding of the city walls by Nehemiah, between 539 and 445 BC (v. 18; Neh 2:17; Kraus, 1988:501; Stuhlmueller, 1983, 1:251). If we accept this view, there are several possibilities regarding the historical reference in the superscription. The psalm may have been an old Davidic composition modified in the course of time. A later editor may have misunderstood the phrase "of David" to imply authorship and provided what, in his opinion, was its appropriate historical setting. The psalm may have been composed with David in mind, to be used by others who were conscious of heinous sins (A. Anderson, 1:390).

Questions about authorship and date of composition should not diminish the power of this psalm. In its focus on confession and renewal of life through God's gracious forgiveness, Psalm 51 has had a profound impact on individual and corporate penance. The psalm is carefully constructed, with "sin/sinner/purge" (ḥāṭā/ḥaṭṭā'â) mentioned six times in the first part (vv. 1-9) and once in the second part (vv. 10-19). It names "God" or "Lord" once in the first part and six times in the second part. Thus, the focus moves from sin and cleansing toward the joy of new life in forgiveness.

OUTLINE

Plea for Mercy, 51:1-2
Confession of Sin, 51:3-6
Petition for Cleansing from Sin, 51:7-9
Petition for Spiritual Restoration, 51:10-12
Vow of Praise and Public Contrition, 51:13-17
Prayer for Jerusalem, 51:18-19

EXPLANATORY NOTES

Plea for Mercy 51:1-2

The penitent opens with a fourfold plea for mercy in the recognition of total dependence on God's *steadfast love* (ḥesed) *[Steadfast]*. The Hebrew term *rōb raḥămîm*, translated *abundant mercy*, or *great compassion* (NIV), literally means "great wombs" and suggests that the mercy of God is comparable to the love of a mother for her child (Ps 103:4, 13; Isa 66:13).

Three word pictures describe the psalmist's separation from God, with corresponding verbs pleading for action: *Blot out my transgressions* (pešaʿ, rebellion), *wash me from my iniquity* (ʿāwôn, crookedness, perverseness), and *cleanse me* from *my sin* (ḥaṭṭā'â, failure, missing the mark). This final word for sin, the most frequent for sin in the OT, is used seven times (vv. 2, 3, 4, 5, 7 [purge], 9, 13). In the plea for mercy, all three verbs understand sin as something that defiles a person. The petitioner, feeling dirty and stained, pleads for a thorough cleansing of his guilt (vv. 7, 9) *[Sin]*.

Confession of Sin   51:3-6

We find perhaps the most basic sentence of this confession psalm at the beginning of verse 3: *For I know my transgressions.* There is no protestation of innocence. All that matters is, "I have sinned against you." Consciousness of sin is a precondition to forgiveness (Ps 32:5; though cf. Mark 2:5; Luke 23:34; Acts 7:60). Sin can be against oneself or against the neighbor, but it is always a flaunting of God (Gen 39:9; 2 Sam 11:27). So the psalmist acknowledges that whatever punishment he has received or deserves, God has been both right and just (v. 4b).

The psalmist's confession is rooted in this self-awareness of failure, that God is utterly in the right, and finally, that he himself is powerless to rectify the situation. The psalmist cannot escape from the web of evil entangling him from birth (v. 5). This perplexing verse has nothing to do with marriage, the sexual act in conception, or (arguably) "original sin." It speaks to the psalmist's solidarity with others in the human predicament (Isa 6:5), and how all claim to righteousness is denied every human being (Gen 8:21; Job 4:17; 25:4; Pss 14:3; 130:3; 143:2; Rom 3:20; Gal 2:16). In God alone one must find any ground for mercy. The text and meaning of verse 6 is uncertain; it might have been a marginal note later incorporated into the text, as indicated by the repetition of the introductory *Indeed* (ḥēn, *Surely*, NIV) to open verses 5 and 6 (Westermann, 1989:97). As translated, it expresses the painful realization of the gap between God's demands and the sinner's state, inviting introspection to ponder one's self before God.

Petition for Cleansing from Sin   51:7-9

As the petition for forgiveness rises, the supplicant uses thirteen imperatives, from *teach me* (v. 6) to *deliver me* (v. 14), to ask God to do what the psalmist cannot do for himself. He pleads not only that the sin be removed, but also that the whole heart and life be changed. *Hyssop* (v. 7) was a wild herb associated with cleansing rites, such as for lepers (Lev 14:4; Num 19:6). *Whiter than snow* (v. 7) is reminiscent of Isaiah 1:18. The pair *joy and gladness* (v. 8), is found five times in Jeremiah (7:34; 15:16; 16:9; 25:10; 33:11). The crushed *bones* suggest serious illness or spiritual anguish (v. 8). The ancient world often regarded illness as the consequence of sin. This verse and psalm as a whole may suggest that we should give more attention to the act of sin and what it does physically to the body (Brueggemann, 1984:100). Verse 9 is similar to verse 1, expressing the sinner's painful awareness of defilement. The petitioner, open to reproof, profoundly desires cleansing and restoration of the relationship with God.

Petition for Spiritual Restoration 51:10-12

The psalm's petition comes to a climax with the plea for spiritual restoration (vv. 10-12). It now places emphasis on the positive, not only on sin's removal, but also on the miracle that God makes possible a new and changed life. *Create in me a clean heart.* The *heart* was regarded as the mainspring of a person's life, not the seat of emotions, as in Western thought. The verb *create* (*bārā'*) is used only of God, as in Genesis 1:1. Only an act of God's intervention can turn things around. The psalmist asks for a clean heart, a new beginning, a capacity for new living. Of the three references to *spirit* (*rûaḥ*, vv. 10-12; the word can mean "wind" or "breath"), the first is a request for *a new and right spirit*, a chance to begin again (v. 10; Ezek 36:26). In the OT, *holy spirit* (v. 11) is used only here and in Isaiah 63:10-11, since the predominant characteristic of God's Spirit in the OT is that of energizing force. The prayer is for *a willing spirit* (v. 12), for a life renewed and yielded to God once again. Sin can leave us powerless and without authority for living our lives (Brueggemann, 1984:100-101). Only a new heart and transformed spirit will restore the joy of salvation.

Vow of Praise and Public Contrition 51:13-17

Though the petitions are not yet ended, the psalmist proceeds to the vow (vv. 13-14). "Let me show gratitude," he is saying, "as I *teach transgressors your ways.*" The renewed life must be shared (Ps 34:11-12). Salvation is more than being sorry, repenting, and receiving pardon. It also means acting in love toward others in obedience to God. Salvation is followed by evangelism. *Bloodshed,* or *bloodguilt* (v. 14 NIV), may refer to the guilt of those who have been responsible for the violent deaths of others (as David was for the murder of Uriah). Or it may mean death as the result of some sickness or persecution (30:9). The petition is a decisive plea and hope, with the promise of praise (v. 14).

The mood changes in verses 15-17 as the grace, steadfast love, and compassion requested in verse 1 appear to have been granted. The psalmist offers humble worship, thankfulness out of a penitent heart. These verses deal with the value of sacrifice and its nature. The law did not prescribe any atoning sacrifices for such offenses as murder and adultery. The only alternative was penance (v. 17; 2 Sam 12:13-16; A. Anderson, 1:401). Cleansing depends upon the faithfulness of God. Yet God claims the whole person. Sacrifice of a person's self-will is a way of opening oneself again to the life-giving spirit of God.

The second part of the psalm is framed by verses repeating the words *heart, God,* and *spirit* (vv. 10, 17).

When the temple was destroyed, the psalmist could only offer hymns of praise and a penitent heart in place of sacrifice. The antisacrificial sentiment (vv. 16-17), though tempered in the following verses, may explain the psalm's juxtaposition to Psalm 50.

Prayer for Jerusalem   51:18-19

The psalm ends with two verses that appear as a later addition, to modify the antisacrificial tone of verse 16 and add to the psalm's liturgical use. This "people's prayer" may have been added when, or just before, the walls of Jerusalem were restored under Nehemiah (Neh 2:17; Pss 102:13, 16; 147:2; Jer 31:38). Despite criticism of sacrifice in the prophetic literature, sacrifices in the temple were restored. A message in these verses may be God's interest in *transformed intentionality* (Brueggemann, 1984:102). The restoration of the city of God is part of the renewal of the people of God. In the contrite national mood that followed the exile, this personal confession, already at hand, likely became an important vehicle for corporate repentance (White: 86). These verses function to emphasize public prayer as a complement to personal piety.

THE TEXT IN THE BIBLICAL CONTEXT AND LIFE OF THE CHURCH

Sin and Repentance

Seven Penitential Psalms have been identified as suitable for experiencing contrition and the desire for forgiveness (Pss 6; 32; 38; 51; 102; 130; 143). Other OT texts also speak to the issue of sin and the need for release from its hold on human life (Gen 4:7; Exod 34:6-9; Isa 53:4-6; 59:9-15; Dan 9:20-24; Zech 13:1). Commentators acknowledge the correspondence of theological ideas of Psalm 51, with its prayer for a clean heart of obedience (vv. 10-12), to similar prophetic statements (Jer 24:7; 31:33; 32:39; Ezek 36:25-28); but they are not agreed on who may depend on whom.

The NT invites repentance as in the prodigal son's confession, "Father, I have sinned against heaven and before you" (Luke 15:21). The promise of forgiveness is present in Jesus' words offering eternal life (John 3:16) and in the blessing on "the pure in heart" (Matt 5:8). Cleansing for sin through the blood of Jesus is promised: "If we confess our sins, he who is faithful and just will forgive us our sins and cleanse us from all unrighteousness" (1 John 1:9).

Christian doctrine about sin and repentance is based heavily on Romans, where Paul quotes Psalm 51:4b in an argument about Israel's unbelief and the faithfulness of God (Rom 3:4). Paul echoes the original context and mood of this psalm as he wrestles with the problem of sin in Romans 11:32-36. He concludes that the glory of God can deal with human sin positively, for in the midst of divine judgment on sin, the love that lifts sin away and renews human life is revealed. The words that follow in Romans 12:1, "to present your bodies as a living sacrifice, holy and acceptable to God, which is your spiritual worship," appear to build on Psalm 51:17.

Liturgical Use of Psalm 51

In Jewish usage, this is a psalm for the Day of Atonement (Lev 16:30). The Qumran community drew on Psalm 51:17 and the phrase "broken spirit" to describe the characteristics of those making up the council of the community. One of their *Thanksgiving Hymns* (1QH 9.25 = 1.25) reflects the spirit of Psalm 51 (Holladay: 110): "How shall a man tell his sin, and how plead concerning his iniquities?"

Clement, the bishop of Rome, writing about AD 96, cites Psalm 51:1-17 as words of David, who is to be emulated in confession (*1 Clem.* 18; 52.4). Francis of Assisi (1221) made a rule that for the failings and negligence of the brothers, the clergy should daily say the "Miserere mei, Deus [Have mercy on me, O God]" (Ps 51).

Psalm 51 was among the influential texts to which Martin Luther appealed for his doctrine of justification. The petitioner knows he is entirely dependent upon the merciful activity of God. Only by God's creative, renewing power can the heart be cleansed and led to a new obedience (Kraus, 1988:507). Reformer John Calvin urged that the prayer for renewal from sin direct attention to the great sacrifice by which Christ has reconciled us to God (J. Anderson, 2:297-98).

This psalm's influence on Christian worship is immense, far beyond the penitential season of Lent. It is a source for hymns, prayers of confession, liturgical sentences, promptings for spiritual renewal, and a text for reflection on Christian doctrine. Psalm 51 is prescribed to be recited in its entirety during every celebration of the Eastern Orthodox Divine liturgy, the priest offering by memory these words of confession and petition for God's mercy and forgiveness (Reardon: 99). The Liturgy of the Hours of the Roman Catholic Church introduces recitation of the psalm with a citation from Ephesians 4:23-24 and follows with this Psalm-prayer (Holladay: 332):

Father, he who knew no sin was made sin for us, to save us and restore us to your friendship. Look upon our contrite heart and afflicted spirit and heal our troubled conscience, so that in the joy and strength of the Holy Spirit we may proclaim your praise and glory before all the nations.

A Guide to Repentance

Psalm 51 provides instructive statements that can guide the process of repentance. We must confess sin. God seeks open access to the parts of life that we have chosen to keep hidden. Sin has deep roots in human nature. Contrition has more value than the offering of sacrifice. We need the grace of God for conversion and for renewal of the heart and spirit. The inner relationship of the believer to God gives value to the outward acts. A renewed fellowship with God leads to obedience and acts of love towards others.

Psalm 52

To Boast, or to Thank?

PREVIEW

Psalm 52 is an accusation directed against someone whose life is characterized by a false sense of values, deceit, and the abuse of power for self-interest. In terse and graphic language, the psalmist utters prophetic judgment upon the boasting, lying bully. From sarcasm and invective, the psalmist moves on to a warm profession of faith in God's goodness. The psalm presents a simple but stark contrast between good and evil.

Regarding form, the psalm begins as a lament of the individual (vv. 1-7) and ends as a song of thanksgiving (vv. 8-9). The mood is one of trust. Closely related in style to Psalm 58, this psalm recalls the denunciation by the prophet (Isa 22:15-19). It shares with Psalm 49 concern about the arrogance of the wicked and their reliance on wealth rather than on God.

The title provides a setting, *when Doeg the Edomite came to Saul . . .* , a story told in 1 Sam 21:7–22:23. Some commentators question whether the story of Saul's chief herdsman, an informer, fits the psalmist's invective. Others point to how Doeg caused a massacre by the cunning of his tongue. Reference to the temple (v. 8) suggests a later historical period. In any case, the psalm is identified as a *Maskil* (instruction). This group of *Maskils* (Psalms 52–55) conveys timeless teachings for every generation *[Superscriptions]*.

OUTLINE

Accusation Against the Arrogant Wicked, 52:1-4
Divine Judgment and the Response of the Righteous, 52:5-7
Confession of Trust and Praise, 52:8-9

EXPLANATORY NOTES

Accusation Against the Arrogant Wicked   52:1-4

The accusation is addressed to an enemy of the godly for planning and doing evil against God's people. *O mighty one*, the Hebrew military term *gibbôr*, is used derisively in the sense of "big shot," "tycoon," "tyrant." Its tone implies, "How stupid!" The weapon of the arrogant wicked is treacherous, deceitful speech as illustrated by a razor-sharp tongue (vv. 2-4; Ps 36:1-4) *[Wicked]*. The ultimate fate of those whose lives are rooted in falsehood and propped up by destroying others is contrasted with those who are embraced and held in the steadfast love of God (vv. 8-9). *Selah,* likely a liturgical notation, may represent a pause or point of emphasis (vv. 3, 5) *[Selah]*.

Divine Judgment and the Response of the Righteous 52:5-7

But God . . . (v. 5) signals a shift in the psalm. In the description of the divine reaction, violent verbs jostle the senses: *break down, snatch, tear, uproot* (v. 5)! *Your tent* and *land of the living* may be idiomatic expressions for the temple. As God judges and uproots the wicked, the righteous in contrast will respond in joyous celebration (vv. 6-7). God's people will see it, and in awe laugh at the folly of the one who trusted in wealth and the seeming strength that has come *by destroying others* (v. 7 NIV, Ps 49:5-7, 16-17). The fall of the deceitful wicked provides an object lesson for the righteous to take to heart. Trust in God, not in worldly wealth (v. 7) *[Judge]*.

Confession of Trust and Praise   52:8-9

But I . . . (v. 8) signals the contrast between the psalmist and the arrogant wicked. The basic premise of the psalm is that God will overrule the way of the wicked. The betrayer is like an uprooted tree. But the one who trusts in God's *steadfast love* stands firm, and is like a green-foliaged olive tree planted in the house of God, in sacred and life-producing soil (Pss 1:3; 92:12-15a; Jer 17:7-8). The theme of continually abiding in God's house is constant in the psalms (v. 8; Pss 27:4-6; 37:7-9; 65:4).

God's *steadfast love* is the object and basis of great trust (v. 8; 13:5). Here rejoicing can begin. Here is bright prospect for the future. Here is the strength of hope *[Steadfast]*. The Hebrew text of the final verse does not say, *I will proclaim,* as the NRSV translates, but *I will wait for* [or, *hope for*] *your name* (KJV, NRSV n, NIV). This is not done privately, but openly, *in the presence of the faithful*, and with deep gratitude *because of what you* [*God*] *have done.* The psalm thus ends with another contrast. Instead of boasting about self (vv. 3-4, 7), the psalmist boasts about God.

THE TEXT IN THE BIBLICAL CONTEXT AND LIFE OF THE CHURCH

Responding to Evil

Psalm 52 denounces and sharply contrasts those who *love evil* (v. 3) with those who are godly and place their trust in the *steadfast love of God* (v. 8). In doing so, the psalm names evil for what it is and portrays it in all its destructive ugliness.

No wonder an early interpreter came to identify the vicious person described in this psalm with Doeg the Edomite, thereby linking this psalm with an incident in David's life. Doeg informed Saul that David had received assistance from the priestly family of Ahimelech of Nob. Consequently, Saul condemned Ahimelech and his family to death. When Saul's soldiers refused to carry out the sentence, Doeg himself killed eighty-five priests of the LORD and slaughtered the whole town of Nob—men, women, and children (1 Sam 21:7–22:23). Doeg—evil personified!

The psalm tells of the response of the righteous to God's judgment of the wicked as fear and laughter (v. 6). God's judgment is awesome and confirms in the righteous a fear of the Lord that leads to greater trust and dependence on the holy God. Laughter (and joy) is the spontaneous relief of escaping the punishment of the wicked (Wilson, 2002:790). Yet we should avoid any attitude of gloating over the fall of one's enemies. The NT is clear that believers are not to resist evil with evil, but to overcome evil with good (Rom 12:17-21; 1 Thess 5:15; 1 Pet 3:9).

What is the strength that sustains life and overcomes evil? Psalm 52 suggests a relationship to God that draws on all the resources of worship and instruction provided in the place of worship and in the community of God's people, in contrast to the deceptive illusion of the power of the arrogant. "Isolation, alienation, and aloneness result in weakness. The fellowship of brothers and sisters in Christ lends strength" (Wyrtzen: 152).

Speaking Truth

The *tongue* is spoken of twenty times in the Psalms, and nineteen times in Proverbs, which declares, "Death and life are in the power of the tongue" (Prov 18:21). The tongue is used in these passages as symbol for speaking truth. In a nonliterary society, speaking truth was crucial because receipts, wills, and other written agreements were useless for people who could not read. A person's spoken word and integrity served as the basis of social order and justice.

Is the basis for justice any different today? In the Sermon on the Mount Jesus invites our "yes" to mean "yes" and "no" to mean "no" at all times, not only when under oath (Matt 5:37). James and Peter connect the use of the tongue with justice and blessing (James 1:26-27; 3:5-12; 1 Pet 3:10).

Psalm 53

God, the Deliverer, in a Corrupt World

EXPLANATORY NOTES

See comments on Psalm 14, of which this poem is an edition. Only major modifications will be noted here.

1. *Title: Mahalath*, a term of uncertain meaning found also in the title to Psalm 88, could suggest "according to a sad tune or melody" *[Musical]*. A *Maskil* may have to do with "instruction" *[Superscriptions]*.
2. The divine name is *God* (*'ĕlōhîm*), whereas in Psalm 14 *The LORD* (*Yahweh*) occurs four times. Use of the generic term *God* (*'ĕlōhîm*) is characteristic in the Elohistic Psalter (Ps 42–83) *[Names of God]*.
3. The major variant from Psalm 14 is found in verse 5, which in the Hebrew begins with a triple use of the word for fear: *paḥad, great terror, in terror*. The Hebrew reads *him who encamps against you* instead of *ungodly*. This may allude to an historical event when besiegers were scattered, such as the miraculous deliverance when a sudden panic routed the enemy (2 Kings 7:6-7), or the angel of the LORD slew the Assyrian army (19:35-36). The verse points to a God-wrought panic. It emphasizes the shameful judgment upon the wicked: the scattered bones show how God evaluates their lives (Ps 141:7; Jer 8:1-12; Ezek 6:5).

How verse 5c should be read is uncertain. If the reference is to God's miraculous deliverance, then *They will be put to shame* is preferable to *You put them to shame* (NIV, NASB). The issue may also be focused by asking, What does it mean for *deliverance* (*yĕšu'â*) to come out of Zion (v. 6)? Israel's Yahweh war theology emphasized God's intervention rather than human action. Might Zion be a symbol meaning "Zion of righteousness fulfilled in the land" rather than a place name or fortress (Buber: 19)? *[War].*
4. Theme and function: Like Psalm 14, this lament is also a wisdom meditation on the folly of the wicked, who deny the effective existence of God and live corrupt lives through the oppression of the poor. Psalms 52 and 53 depict the arrogance of the wicked and the futility of their hopes to escape God's scrutiny and judgment. The psalm sets forth the doom awaiting the godless in the time when God intervenes on behalf of the covenant people.
5. Placement of psalm: Like the story of Nabal (1 Sam 25), the meditation on the arrogant fool (*nābāl*) is placed in this collection, book II, between material relating to Doeg (Ps 52; 1 Sam 22) and the Ziphites (Ps 54; 1 Sam 23; 26).

Psalm 54

Confidence in God's Name

PREVIEW

In this lament of the individual, the plea for help begins and ends with the divine name (vv. 1, 6). The psalmist bases his prayer and hope on the *name* of the LORD. Insolent and ruthless persons seek his life. In time of crisis the psalmist discovers a sustaining truth: *God is my helper* (v. 4). Confident in the power of God's name, he anticipates complete vindication and promises a thank offering.

The psalm could be the lament of a king attacked by savage enemies (Clifford). There is no assertion of innocence. Others see it as the lament of an accused person who takes refuge in the temple area (Gerstenberger; Kraus). While a lament of the individual, later use of this psalm by the community is suggested in the musical notation *Selah* (v. 3) and the reference to the thank offering (v. 6) *[Selah]*. This psalm may illustrate how individual preexilic psalms were transformed for use by the community, with the "I" representing Israel at a later time (Miller, 1986:12). As a plea for deliverance, Psalm 54 shares with Psalms 52 and 53 the theme of enemies who have no regard for God.

The title, added by a later scribe, identifies this psalm with the stories told in 1 Samuel 23:19-29 and 26:1-5. Ziphites, the inhabitants of Ziph, a town three miles southeast of Hebron, had informed Saul of the fugitive David's hiding place. The psalm is identified as a

Maskil, "instruction," (as are Pss 52–55). The musical reference *with stringed instruments* is also found in headings to Psalms 4; 6; 55; 67; and 76 *[Superscriptions; Musical].*

OUTLINE

Petition for Help and Complaint, 54:1-3
Statement of Confidence and Vow of Thanksgiving, 54:4-7

EXPLANATORY NOTES

Petition for Help and Complaint   54:1-3

The psalm opens with a desperate cry for help, as verses 1 and 2 both begin, in Hebrew, with "O God." The saving name of God is the prominent feature of this lament, framing the psalm (vv. 1, 6). To the Israelites, the name *'ĕlōhîm* (God) revealed the character and nature of God as power and authority. Invoking the name called forth the presence of God. The sense of *save* and *vindicate* is to rescue. *Vindicate me*, a judicial term, is an appeal to the judge par excellence, God, to "render the justice due me." To judge does not exclusively mean "to condemn." In the first place, it signifies "to establish justice in favor of" (Pss 26:1; 35:1; 50:4-6) *[Judge].*

The psalmist's plight is described as an attack by *the insolent* (*strangers*, NIV; *foreigners*, Heb., NJPS) and *ruthless* persons (v. 3; Pss 86:14; Jer 15:21). The fear of those who seek to take one's life is a common complaint of laments (Pss 31:13; 35:4; 38:12; 40:14; 63:9; 70:2; 86:14). Without regard for God, like the "fool" (53:1), these enemies refuse to acknowledge the authority of God over their lives.

Statement of Confidence and Vow of Thanksgiving 54:4-7

The mood shift in this psalm comes with the emphatic *But surely* (*See/Look/Behold!* v. 4 NJPS). Here the center of the psalm describes God's response to the psalmist's plight. God is *helper* and *upholder* (*sustains*, NIV), words reminiscent of the trust motif in other psalms where the LORD is described as protector, guide, and shepherd (Ps 23). Those surrounded by enemies can appeal to the saving faithfulness of God and pray for the defeat of the destructive powers (v. 5). The psalm here expresses the lex talionis, the principle of equity in the ancient world of "an eye for an eye" (Exod 21:23-25), in which the foes are to be paid with what they intended to inflict on the psalmist

(Pss 7:16; 12:3-4; 37:14-15). Threatened by faithless friends, the psalmist appeals to the faithfulness (*'ĕmet*) of God to act against evil.

The psalm ends on a note of thanksgiving. The *freewill offering* is an extraspecial thanks to God for his gracious, saving love (v. 6; Lev 7:11-18; 22:18-30; Num 15:1-10). The sacrifice and praise, likely offered in the context of temple worship, expresses gratitude for unexpected and undeserved grace for deliverance (Pss 7:1; 31:1). The LORD's name *YHWH*, with its meaning of "present to act in salvation," is extolled for its goodness (v. 6). The vow is made as if the rescue had already taken place (v. 7). The final words are a statement of role reversal. The psalmist, once under threat, is now delivered; the enemies, once out to get him, have received their deserved rebuke (Davidson, 1998:175).

THE TEXT IN THE BIBLICAL CONTEXT AND LIFE OF THE CHURCH

An Attitude Toward Enemies

The psalmist's plight is caused by persons who *do not set God before them* (v. 3). The Ten Commandments begin with the prohibition of allegiance to "other gods" (Exod 20:2-6). In Israel's focus on trust in the LORD alone, it is understandable that persons who flaunted God should be viewed as enemies (Ps 54:3). The psalm ends on a note that we might interpret as gloating over the fate of the enemy (v. 7b; Ps 52:6). When the Lord delivers, can gloating over one's foes ever be appropriate?

The psalmist understood God's justice as needing to be displayed in this world, or it will not be displayed at all. For persons who survived the Nazi Holocaust (Shoah), the abuses of apartheid in South Africa, or violent revolutions anywhere, these words of intense longing for justice and retribution are quite understandable. The victimized know what it means to cry out for God to bring an end to evil, to set things right, and to establish justice.

In this sense, Christian people who are oppressed can find Psalm 54 helpful in seeking an end to their oppression and vindication among their peers and before their enemies. But gloating over the enemy? It is instructive that Jesus never asked for personal vindication. On the cross, he prayed, "Father, forgive them; for they do not know what they are doing" (Luke 23:34). Christians do well to live out the perspectives of the NT on the issue of vengeance (Matt 5:38-48; Rom 12:14-21).

In the Name of God

One of the Ten Commandments warns against making "wrongful use of the name of the LORD your God" (Exod 20:7). The name has power. It calls forth the presence of the one named. God's name is one of the ways in which God is represented on earth. Psalm 54 calls attention to how the name means God's might (v. 1) and God's goodness (v. 6). The psalm appears to play on the name of deity by using both 'ĕlōhîm (God) and Yahweh (LORD). The more generic name 'ĕlōhîm elicits the idea of power; Yahweh, as the covenant name, speaks of a deity who "is present to act in salvation." The psalm begins with the general word for God, but the psalmist concludes with recognition that it is the God known to Israel as Yahweh (LORD) who has come through for him as a saving deity *[Names of God]*.

This psalm's emphasis on power and saving help in the divine name suggests NT passages where the name of Jesus is invoked as the essence of salvation (Matt 1:21-23; John 12:13; 14:13-14; Acts 2:21, 38; 3:16; 4:10).

When the church prays, "Our Father, . . . hallowed be your name" (Matt 6:9), it is calling forth God's presence "on earth as it is in heaven." When believers end a prayer, "in Jesus' name," they are calling for the presence and power of the divine Savior and Lord. The name is a pledge of help on the way.

Psalm 55

Betrayed by a Friend

PREVIEW

This lament is the complaint of an individual praying for deliverance from enemies (vv. 3, 15, 23). The psalmist is distraught because of harassment by the wicked (v. 3), corruption in the city (vv. 9-11), and most distressing of all, betrayal by a friend (vv. 13-14, 20-21). Amid the distress he calls to the saving God (vv. 1-2, 16-19, 23). This turbulent psalm leads to a wonderful declaration of faith, ending with a magnificent line: *But I will trust in you* (v. 23).

Psalm 55 is rich in striking images: *noise of the enemy, wings like a dove, my companion, my familiar friend,* and the smooth talker whose words are daggers (v. 21). Commentators have associated this psalm with David's betrayal by his counselor Ahithophel (2 Sam 16:15-23), or with Jeremiah (Jer 9:2; 12:6; 20:2), or an Israelite resident in a heathen city. Kraus (1988:520) suggests that the psalm is a composite of two independent units, vv. 1-18 and vv. 19-23. The following outline views the psalm as a literary unit.

The heading is identical to the opening words of the heading given Psalm 54. It concludes the group of four *Maskil* (instruction) psalms that begins with Psalm 52. All are prayers for deliverance from the enemy *[Superscriptions]*.

OUTLINE

Desperate Cry for Help, 55:1-5
The Temptation to Flee, 55:6-8
Complaint: Violence in the City, 55:9-11
Complaint: Betrayal by a Friend, 55:12-15
The Psalmist Calls upon God, 55:16-19
Reprise: The Unfaithful Friend, 55:20-21
Confident Trust in God, 55:22-23

EXPLANATORY NOTES

Desperate Cry for Help   55:1-5

In his urgent appeal to God to hear his complaint, the psalmist begs God not to hide, look away, or be indifferent (vv. 1-2; Ps 54:1-2). Hounded by vociferous attacks from *the enemy, . . . the wicked*, the psalmist's circumstance is dominated by mental and emotional turmoil (vv. 2b-5). The *heart* is the place where the whole person experiences joy, sorrow, anxiety, and fear (v. 4; 25:17; 27:3; 61:2). If the body is burning with fear and anxiety, the sufferer can say, *The terrors of death have fallen upon me* (vv. 4-5). Throughout the psalm recurring lament and complaints reflect the psalmist's anguish of spirit *[Enemies; Wicked]*.

The Temptation to Flee   55:6-8

The panic-stricken psalmist, longing for safety from his enemies, is tempted to flee into the wilderness (vv. 6-7; 11:1). Flight is a common alternative for fearful and frustrated people. Jeremiah, similarly confronted with deception and lies, exclaims: "O that I had in the desert a traveler's lodging place, that I might leave my people and go away from them!" (Jer 9:2). Twice the liturgical note *Selah* appears (vv. 7, 19) *[Selah]*.

Complaint: Violence in the City   55:9-11

Safety in the wilderness is contrasted with the violent city, where the psalmist's enemies appear to be located (Jer 6:6-7; Ezek 7:23; 12:19-20). The city is described as a place of trouble, where evil has its home and lawlessness threatens life. The negative effect of the wicked upon community is described by piling up austere words: *violence, strife, iniquity, trouble, ruin, oppression,* and *fraud*. Consequently, the psalmist calls on God to confuse the enemy as at the time of Babel (v. 9; Gen 11:9).

Complaint: Betrayal by a Friend   55:12-15

The experience of God's help offers a space where the petitioner no longer needs to feel trapped (v. 12; Pss 4:1; 18:19, 36; 31:8; 118:5). But a stab in the back by an *equal companion, familiar friend,* and worship partner (vv. 13-14) is too much to take!

The psalmist calls for God's judgment (v. 15). Death seems the only appropriate punishment for the corruption in the city (vv. 9-11) or the terror of betrayal (vv. 13-14). The denunciation is that of a fiery death, as happened to the company of Korah (Num 16:3-35). Letting them go *alive to Sheol,* the abode of the dead, suggests cutting off people in the prime of life *[Sheol].*

The Psalmist Calls upon God   55:16-19

In contrast to the devious speech and behavior of the enemies, the psalmist will call upon God in the certainty that God will deliver (vv. 16-19). His confidence is based on the name and character of God. Note the change in name to the saving *LORD* (v. 16). God is described as *enthroned from of old* (v. 19), with power to redeem the faithful (v. 18). The foes of the individual are often likened to a hostile army that attacks the helpless (Pss 3:6; 27:3; 56:1; 59:1-3). Thus, rather than fleeing the enemy, the psalmist will give himself to prayer morning, noon, and evening, trusting that God will *hear* and act (vv. 17, 19).

Reprise: The Unfaithful Friend   55:20-21

The psalmist returns to the subject of the treacherous attack by a close friend (vv. 13-14). The covenant between them has been violated by sweet talk covering deceit, by soft words that are daggers in masquerade. The psalmist's reprise (vv. 20-21) expresses pent-up bitterness toward one he once trusted.

Confident Trust in God   55:22-23

The psalm ends on a positive note, with encouragement to others to trust God by casting their cares on the LORD (v. 22). *Cast your burden on the LORD* may be the words of the psalmist reflecting on his own experience, or an oracle of salvation spoken by a temple officiant *[Oracle].*

The final verse confirms the psalmist's belief in divine retribution and once more proclaims God's judgment and premature death on the wicked (vv. 15, 23). In contrast, the psalmist can say, *But I will trust in you.* This note of trust will be repeated three times in the next psalm (Ps 56:3, 4, 11).

THE TEXT IN THE BIBLICAL CONTEXT AND LIFE OF THE CHURCH

City and Wilderness

The psalm's first complaint focuses on the lawlessness of the city (vv. 9-11). The psalmist indicts the city as a place of violence and strife, oppression and fraud. The psalmist also voices the temptation to escape to the wilderness as a place of rest and shelter (vv. 6-8).

Biblical literature deals with city and wilderness throughout its accounts of God's people seeking to live in faithfulness. Cain built a city (Gen 4:17). Abraham and his nephew Lot encountered the cities of the Plain such as Sodom and Gomorrah (Gen 18:16–19:29). When the Israelites came into the land of Canaan, cities were already there (Deut 6:10; 1 Sam 6:18). Jerusalem was established as the glorious city of the great King (Pss 46:5; 48:1-3; 87:1-3). Christians proclaimed the NT Gospel in the cities of Judea, Samaria, and Galilee, but also throughout the cities of the Mediterranean world as far as Rome (Acts 1:8; 19:21). The last book of the Bible is a vision of the "holy city, the new Jerusalem" (Rev 21:2, 10), in contrast to Babylon (and Rome), the great symbol of violence (17:9, 18; 18:2-24).

The events of the Bible also take place in the rural areas of the land, the desert and the wilderness. Moses heard the voice of the LORD in the wilderness (Exod 3:1-15). David was called from tending his father's sheep (1 Sam 16:19; 2 Sam 7:8). Elijah fled from Jezebel into the wilderness, where God spoke to him (1 Kings 19:1-18). John the Baptist wandered the Judean wilderness in preparation for the coming Messiah (Matt 3:1; Luke 1:80). Jesus withdrew to the wilderness for forty days following his baptism (Matt 4:1) and returned on occasion for times of prayer and renewal (Luke 5:16).

While some have viewed the Bible as conveying an anticity bias, both city and country are venues for hearing the voice of the Lord and celebrating the divine presence. Living in a time when more and more people live in large cities, we cannot ignore the problems of high population density and lawlessness in impersonal neighborhoods. However, neither should we look upon the isolation of sparsely populated rural areas as God-forsaken places. Instead of running away, the psalmist prayed, *But I will trust in you* (v. 23).

Betrayal

The psalm's vivid description of betrayal by a friend (vv. 13-14, 20-21) is echoed in the experience of Jesus, who was betrayed by one from his inner circle. All four of the Gospels identify Judas as the one who betrayed his Master (Matt 26:14-49; Mark 14:10-21, 43-45; Luke 22:1-6, 47-53; John 13:2; 18:1-5).

The Lord's betrayal became part of the wording of the liturgy of the Lord's Supper (1 Cor 11:23). Remembering the treachery of Judas in the context of communion is a warning to "discern the body" (11:29). When a spirit of reverence is lacking, when people fail to recognize the significance of this act of worship or go through the motions while at odds with other members in Christ's church, then they partake of the Lord's Supper unworthily. Such betrayal from within undercuts community. That makes Jesus' redemptive attitude all the more remarkable.

Betrayal by a friend is the violation of covenant (Ps 55:20) and the destructive pain inflicted in abusive relationships. Persons whom a spouse has battered will find in Psalm 55 the grief, the frustration, the fury of someone who has been betrayed at the deepest level. The psalm calls for divine vengeance, but leaves the execution to God. It maintains a passion for divine justice and personal healing.

Psalm 55 in Prayer and Song

The reference to prayer *evening and morning and at noon* (v. 17) has influenced synagogue and church prayers. *Cast your burden on the LORD* is echoed in words of Jesus inviting people to turn their cares over to God (v. 22; Matt 6:25-34; Luke 12:22-31). The same verse is later quoted in the context of the suffering church (1 Pet 5:7).

Psalm 55:22 serves as the text for the wonderful chorale in Mendelssohn's oratorio *Elijah*:

> Cast thy burden upon the Lord; and he shall sustain thee.
> He never will suffer the righteous to fall. He is at thy right hand.
> Thy mercy, Lord, is great, and far above the heav'ns.
> Let none be made ashamed, that wait upon thee!

Psalm 56
In God I Trust

PREVIEW

This prayer song is of the same type as Psalms 54 and 55, a plea for deliverance from the attack of personal enemies. The trust motif dominates, with nearly half of the psalm's lines given to promises and affirmations of confidence. The sequence is lament/trust (vv. 1-4), lament/trust (vv. 5-11), and vow of thanksgiving (vv. 12-13). The refrain *in God I trust* is repeated (vv. 3-4, 10-11). Though an individual lament, the community may also sing it (Pss 116:8-9; 118:6).

The heading suggests a tune to which the psalm might have been sung: *The Dove on Far-off Terebinths.* Psalm 56 is the first of five consecutive psalms (Pss 56–60) described as *A Mitkam.* The LXX translated the term as a poem "to be inscribed on a stele," but the original meaning is uncertain. Early editors suggested that the psalm would fit a situation such as David faced when he was among the Philistines in Gath (1 Sam 21:10-15). Some words of the psalm would be appropriate on the lips of a king under threat from foreign enemies *[Superscriptions; Musical].*

OUTLINE

Petition, Complaint, and Affirmation of Trust, 56:1-4
Complaint, Petition, and Affirmation of Trust, 56:5-11
Vow of Thanksgiving, 56:12-13

EXPLANATORY NOTES

Petition, Complaint, and Affirmation of Trust   56:1-4

The psalmist's opening plea for mercy immediately turns into a complaint depicting the enemies as particularly oppressive, trampling underfoot those they would destroy [*Enemies*]. The foes are compared to a hostile army that attacks the helpless (vv. 1-2; Pss 3:6; 27:3; 55:18; 59:1-3). The opponents are slanderers who attack the psalmist from a position of advantage (*mārôm*, *pride*, v. 2b NIV). NRSV follows an ancient exegetical tradition in translating *mārôm* (elevated site, heaven) as a divine name, *Most High* (Clifford, 2002:266).

This lament vividly describes the enemy's tactics: *trample, oppress, fight, stir up strife, lurk, watch my steps*. Yet *I am not afraid*, declares the psalmist (vv. 3-4, 10-11). His faith rests in God and finds its content in his *word* (vv. 4, 10). The psalmist's plea is directed to the one in whom he believes true security can be found. A divine name (*God, LORD*) appears ten times in the psalm. In contrast, three Hebrew words are used to underscore that the enemies are but vulnerable human beings: *people*, *'ĕnôš* (v. 1); *flesh*, *bāśār* (v. 4); and *mere mortal*, *'ādām* (v. 11). The refrain asserts, *in God I trust; I am not afraid* (vv. 4, 11; Ps 55:23).

Complaint, Petition, and Affirmation of Trust   56:5-11

The psalmist's complaint resumes. The enemies twist his words, plot harm, and look for opportunity to snuff out his life (vv. 5-6; Ps 140:1-2). Fear of those seeking to take one's life is often expressed in laments (31:13; 35:4; 38:12; 40:14; 54:3; 63:9; 70:2; 86:14). The complaint becomes a petition seeking redress (v. 7). Appealing to the wrath of God, the psalmist hopes the enemies will reap what they have sowed. Let God repay them by casting them down into Sheol, the abode of the dead (55:23)! [*Wrath; Sheol*].

The picturesque description of God keeping *count of my tossings* (*wanderings*, NJPS), putting *my tears in your bottle*, and keeping *your record* emphasizes God's concern with the sorrows of the individual (v. 8; 139:16; Mal 3:16-17). God is pictured as one who knows what is going on. God knows the suffering of the faithful, and because *God is for me*, will send the enemies into retreat (v. 9). Sooner or later full justice will be done (A. Anderson, 1:428).

The refrain of trust repeats and expands verse 4. The source of the psalmist's confidence is the LORD, Yahweh, with all the associations that name implies (v. 10; Exod 3:13-16). Defiant questions come at the end of verses 4 and 11. If *God is for me* (v. 9), what can *a mere mortal do to me* (v. 11)?

Vow of Thanksgiving 56:12-13

The psalm ends with the promise of *thank offerings* in the temple. These might be literal sacrifices or songs of gratitude, or both (Lev 7:12; Pss 26:6-7; 50:14; 66:13). The thanksgiving psalm repeats the final verse (116:8-9). Thanksgiving songs of the individual mention the event of deliverance from death, expressing the conviction that the psalmist owes his life to the LORD alone (16:9-11; 49:15; 73:24; Kraus, 1986:166-67). Walking *in the light of life* is in contrast to the darkness of the dead in Sheol (Job 10:21-22).

THE TEXT IN THE BIBLICAL CONTEXT AND LIFE OF THE CHURCH

Trust to Quiet Our Fears

Psalm 56 acknowledges the reality of destructive forces in life, including people who trample on the helpless. Fear is the common reaction in the face of insecurity and whatever threatens life. However, the psalmist is not overcome by fear; instead, he overcomes his fear by trust in God. Trust in God robs fear of its quality of terror. "In God I trust" constitutes a powerful antidote to apprehension and foreboding, and also represents a basic spiritual posture. To the extent that the king in the psalm was a spokesperson for his country, the mantra of the psalm, as in coins in United States currency, might be, "In God we trust."

The reassuring word of Scripture, "Fear not, for I am with you," appears throughout the Bible. Abraham heard the word of the LORD saying, "Do not be afraid, Abram, I am your shield" (Gen 15:1). When Moses was afraid to look at God and to become leader of his people, the LORD promised his reassuring presence (Exod 4:15-17). Isaiah spoke these words of the LORD to people of a fearful heart (Isa 35:4; 40:9; 41:10, 13; 43:1-2). In the psalms, the abiding presence of God is often stated (Pss 23:4; 27:1-3; 46:1-2; 48:3-5; 91:1-6; 118:6).

In the Gospels, the reassuring words, "Fear not," are found in the stories of the birth of Jesus (Matt 1:20; Luke 1:13, 30; 2:10) and at the resurrection of the Lord (Matt 28:5, 10; Luke 24:36; John 20:19-22, 26). Reminding the disciples that suffering may come upon them, but that God knows the sparrow and even the hairs of the head, Jesus said, "Do not fear those who kill the body but cannot kill the soul"

(Matt 10:26-31; Luke 12:4-7). So Jesus affirmed God's care for the individual, even as the psalmist could envision God carrying around bottles filled with the tears of the sorrowing (Ps 56:8). Paul's bold declaration to the Romans echoes the same assurance that "nothing in all creation" will be able to separate the believer from the love of God (Rom 8:31-39 NEB).

Trust is not an independent act of human will, but the response to a deliverance already experienced. The psalmist had learned that God cares (*This I know!* Ps 56:9). In the knowledge that *God is for me*, we can trust God.

Paul Gerhardt's hymn "Befiel du deine Wege" (1656; trans. John Wesley, 1739) expresses it for the church:

> Give to the winds thy fears.
> Hope and be undismayed.
> God hears thy sighs and counts thy tears.
> God shall lift up thy head.

Psalm 57

Be Exalted, O God

PREVIEW

Like preceding Psalms 54–56, Psalm 57 is a prayer for deliverance from enemies. This individual lament ends in a song of thanksgiving. The prayer for help is voiced by one who knows that God will answer. The tone is assured and positive. The bridge from the prayer for help (vv. 1-4) to the hymn of thanksgiving (vv. 7-10) is found in verse 6, which tells of the problem and points to the solution. Both parts of the psalm proclaim God's *steadfast love* and *faithfulness* (vv. 3, 10). The refrain exalts God and declares God's *glory . . . over all the earth* (vv. 5, 11).

    The heading mentions a melody, *Do Not Destroy*, also found in titles to Psalms 58; 59; and 75, and the words appear in a vintage song (Isa 65:8) *[Superscriptions; Musical]*. This is the second of five consecutive psalms (56–60) identified as *A Mitkam*, a term of uncertain meaning. Editors proposed a possible setting for the psalm, as when David fled from Saul (1 Sam 23:19–24:7). References within the psalm, however, suggest the sanctuary as place of refuge for the accused (v. 1), where the musicians are invited to join the thanksgiving song (vv. 7-9). The use of *Selah* (vv. 3, 6) intimates that at least at a later time, the psalm was used in the community's worship *[Selah]*. The confident hymn of thanksgiving (vv. 7-11) is combined with a lament and oracle (Ps 60:5-12) to form Psalm 108.

Psalm 57

OUTLINE

Lament, Refrain, and Transition, 57:1-6
Hymn of Confidence and Refrain, 57:7-11

EXPLANATORY NOTES

Lament, Refrain, and Transition   57:1-6

The opening cry for help is similar to that in Psalm 56:1, though the psalmist appears to be in the safety of the sanctuary. The emphasis is on God as refuge in time of trouble. *In the shadow of your wings* brings to mind God's gentle, protecting love (v. 1; Pss 17:8; 36:7; 91:4). The prayer is to *God Most High* (v. 2), whose dimensions in this psalm are immense: love wide as the heavens, truth reaching the skies (v. 10). In answer to the appeal of the psalmist, God will send aid (25:21; 43:3; 61:7). From heaven God will send his divine guardians, *steadfast love* and *faithfulness*, to save the psalmist from those trampling over him (v. 3) *[Steadfast]*. The refrain proclaims a God *above the heavens* whose glory is *over all the earth* (v. 5, 11).

The enemies, perhaps leaders of some kind, are compared to bloodthirsty lions, armed with the sharp sword of their malicious tongue, who go hunting with net and pit (vv. 4, 6). The metaphors suggest the brutal power and deception of those who exploit the weak. Psalms often refer to the offensive word of false accusation as the most dangerous weapon in human conflict (12:2; 52:2; 59:7; 64:3). However, wickedness is self-destructive, as the law of the talion or equivalent retribution asserts. The enemies have fallen into their own trap (v. 6; 7:15; 141:10; Prov 1:18-19; 26:27; Eccles 10:18). The psalmist firmly believes that God's justice will be done *[Judge]*.

Hymn of Confidence and Refrain   57:7-11

The mood change is obvious: a robust confidence characterizes the second half of the psalm. *My heart is steadfast* is repeated by the psalmist in opening the hymn of praise (v. 7). If the accused had taken refuge in the sanctuary, awaiting acquittal by God in the morning (Kraus, 1988:530), the thanksgiving song now declares the supplicant safe and joyous (vv. 7-10). The musicians are part of the celebration. One can imagine also family, neighbors, and friends as participating in the joyous celebration. Morning was seen as a time to praise God for the bestowal of salvation and help (v. 8; Pss 5:3; 30:5; 46:5; 59:16; 88:13; 90:14; 143:8).

God's *steadfast love* and *faithfulness*, God's covenant loyalty and dependability, are portrayed as guardians sent to protect the psalmist (vv. 3, 10; 26:3; 36:5). The refrain *Be exalted, O God . . .* serves as a summary of the psalmist's confidence and hope. It expresses the longing for a display of God's power.

THE TEXT IN THE BIBLICAL CONTEXT AND LIFE OF THE CHURCH

Crying Out from the Depths to God Most High

The psalmist's prayer to *God Most High* (v. 2), God of the heavens and the earth (vv. 5, 6), portrays an exalted, lofty vision of God. When Christians pray the Lord's Prayer, *Your kingdom come. Your will be done, on earth as it is in heaven . . .* (Matt 6:10), they voice a similar far-reaching prayer.

This psalm's focus on morning, *I will awake the dawn* (v. 8), has led Christians to recite it on Easter morning. They have long prayed it as a morning psalm. The Book of Common Prayer assigns it for morning prayer on the eleventh day of each month. Joachim Neander's hymn "Praise to the Lord, the Almighty" (1680) draws on images from Psalm 57, the Creator God whose steadfast love is higher than the heavens, but who shelters us under his wings and gently sustains us. Joseph Haydn's oratorio *The Creation* contains a joyful chorus titled "Awake the harp." Recent worship songs frequently employ lyrics directly from Scripture; one by Brent Chambers is based on this psalm: "Be exalted, O God, above the heavens" (1977).

The setting given this psalm in the title makes reference to David *in the cave*. Such laments of persons seeking refuge from persecution bring to mind the long history of suffering by Christian believers. In the first century, some took refuge in the catacombs under Rome, where they sang their songs of faith. Sixteenth-century Anabaptists in Switzerland hid under bridges or in caves to pray and sing. In the twentieth century, worshipping believers needed to go "underground" in Ethiopia, Russia, China, and other places. So let the prayers and songs continue:

> *Be exalted, O God, above the heavens,*
> *Let your glory be over all the earth.* (v. 11)

Psalm 58

A God Who Judges on Earth

PREVIEW

Psalm 58 is a collective lament and curse against wicked judges who use their high office for their advantage against the poor and defenseless. The theme is justice and equity, in which the governance of God is contrasted with the governance of unjust rulers. The plea to God for deliverance and redress contends that justice should be done and be visible on earth.

The psalm features an inclusio (bookends) and has characteristics of a chiasmus *[Hebrew Poetry]*. The one who *judges* fairly (v. 11) is contrasted with those who do not (v. 1). *Violence* (v. 10) is the end of those who *deal out violence* (v. 2). Verses 3-9 describe the abortive destiny of the wicked, with a prayer for the justice of the LORD at the psalm's center (v. 6). The writer may have intended the psalm as instruction for the early Jewish community, like Psalms 36; 49; 52; and 73 (Gerstenberger: 235).

The heading is the same as that for Psalms 57 and 59, though without connecting the psalm to a specific historical event. The editors appear to group psalms according to similarities, placing together these three using the same tune, *Do Not Destroy [Superscriptions; Musical]*.

OUTLINE

Complaint: Judgment upon the Wicked Leaders, 58:1-5
Petition for God's Intervention: Sevenfold Curse, 58:6-9
Declaration: Vindication of the Righteous, 58:10-11

EXPLANATORY NOTES

Complaint: Judgment upon the Wicked Leaders 58:1-5

The psalmist, suffering under a corrupt world order, accuses *you gods* (v. 1), a phrase perhaps best understood as *you rulers* (NIV) or *mighty ones* (NJPS). Although the identity of these "gods" could be lesser divinities (Ps 82:1, 6), more likely they were the earthly leaders and royal counselors who abused their power (Exod 4:16; Ps 45:7; Zech 12:8). The psalm accuses them of applying wrong judgment and provoking violence (v. 2). It sounds a note of sarcasm in that people of power are, after all, mere mortals (v. 3; Pss 49:12; 56:11).

The corruption of the wicked has persisted from their birth (v. 3) *[Wicked]*. The text charges unjust rulers with *speaking lies* (v. 3). The psalms often couple wickedness with untruthfulness, which is self-deceiving (5:6; 63:11; 101:7). The ultimate lie is the belief that one can use a heritage of privilege in selfish destruction of the society without dire consequences. The phrase *venom of a serpent* portrays a vivid picture of wickedness. Like a *deaf adder* or *cobra* (NIV) unwilling to be controlled by the snake charmer, the wicked do their destructive deeds (vv. 4-5; Eccles 10:11; Jer 8:17).

Petition for God's Intervention: Sevenfold Curse 58:6-9

Although the Hebrew text is difficult and unclear at places, the passionate plea by the powerless for God's help against those who perpetuate wrong and violence appears to contain seven curses. The harsh prayer begins with the plea for God to destroy the organs of speech of liars and slanderers (v. 6); it moves to the wish that their life be as futile as that of an aborted fetus (v. 8b), swept away like twigs of a thornbush before they can heat the pot (v. 9) *[Imprecation]*. Appealing for the justice of the LORD, and invoking the law of equivalent retribution (Ps 57:6), the psalmist pleads that the wicked may lose their strength and disappear.

Psalm 58

Declaration: Vindication of the Righteous 58:10-11

The psalm ends with a focus on the righteous who have been on the receiving end of injustice *[Righteous]*. The psalmist affirms that God is judge of the nations and will punish the wicked (v. 10; 7:8; 9:8, 19; 82:1-2, 8; 94:2; 96:10, 13; 98:9; 110:6). Bathing one's *feet in the blood of the wicked* is a gesture of revenge (v. 10; 68:23; Isa 63:3-6). This gory image expresses the totality of God's victory. The psalm ends with rejoicing in divine retribution, the vindication of the righteous, and the conviction that *surely there is a God who judges on earth* (v. 11) *[Judge]*.

THE TEXT IN THE BIBLICAL CONTEXT AND LIFE OF THE CHURCH

When Justice Is Perverted

When injustice has become intolerable, the plea for God's intervention resounds (vv. 10-11). The story of the Hebrews begins with their groaning under slavery and their cry to God for relief (Exod 2:23-25). Later, in their life together as a people of God, they needed to guard against perverting justice for the poor (23:1-3, 6-8). That prophetic theme of warning against bribes and calling for integrity in the court system carries throughout the OT (Deut 10:17-18; 16:18-20; Ps 15:5; Prov 17:23; 31:5; Isa 5:23; Amos 5:12; Mic 3:9-11; 7:3).

At the end of the NT, the voices of the martyrs cry out for justice upon the earth (Rev 6:9-11). Written in a time of severe persecution, the Revelation of John, a tract of faith, invites believers to rejoice over the redeeming, embracing judgment of God as Lord and ruler of the world (18:9-10; Kraus, 1988:537).

In the biblical context, the prayer of Psalm 58 is understandable, but also difficult. This is illustrated by its omission in the Roman Catholic Liturgy of the Hours and the four-week Psalter for those who choose to recite the psalms in the course of four weeks. Psalms 58; 83; and 109 are omitted altogether, as are one or more verses from nineteen other psalms that contain harsh imprecation and curses (Holladay: 304, 311). Psalm 58 expresses the anguish of living in an evil age. As words from the depth of human pain, the psalm blazes with indignation at injustice and zeal for the coming of God's reign.

The danger is that readers may use such passages to justify gloating and cruel vindictiveness, fanning into flame an intolerant religious fanaticism. Those inclined to congratulate themselves on their own righteousness and the downfall of the wicked need to be reminded of other biblical words, such as "Vengeance is mine [the LORD's]. I will repay" and "The Lord will judge his people" (Deut 32:35; Heb 10:30).

Belief in *a reward for the righteous* (Ps 58:11) is echoed in Luke 6:23 and 35, though there Jesus' words are tempered by mercy and the reminder that God is also "kind to the ungrateful and the wicked." Jesus further enjoins: "Be merciful, just as your Father is merciful" (Luke 6:36).

Psalm 59

Deliver Me, O God of Steadfast Love

PREVIEW

Psalm 59 appears to be an individual lament about opposition, adapted to form a collective lament for ritual use during national mourning in the face of enemies. The main elements include petition (vv. 1-2, 4b-5, 11-13), description of trouble (vv. 3a, 6-7, 14-15), declaration of innocence (vv. 3b-4a), assertion of trust (vv. 8-10), and vow of thanksgiving (vv. 16-17).

The psalm interweaves two motifs. The first is that of adversaries, characterized as wild dogs (vv. 6-7, 14-15). The second is the motif of trust (vv. 8, 16), along with its corollary praise (vv. 9-10, 17). The psalm begins with petition for deliverance from enemies (vv. 1-10) and then moves to petition for judgment upon the enemies (vv. 11-17).

The title identifies David's escape by night from Saul's messengers as a possible setting (1 Sam 19:11-17). The similarity in language and style to royal laments and the military images may be reasons to think the psalmist is a king facing foreign enemies (v. 5) and domestic defamers (vv. 8, 11). Weiser (424) sees the psalm as coming from the experience of a persecuted innocent person who takes refuge in the sanctuary. The psalm is recited in the presence of the congregation, with a vow to sing praises in the morning. The reference that God *be known to the ends of the earth* (v. 13) suggests to some that this might be a late psalm, adapted to the needs of the postexilic community.

Psalm 59 continues the series of laments that began with Psalm 54. The editorial heading identifies Psalms 57–59 with the tune *Do Not Destroy*. This is the fourth consecutive psalm listed as *A Mitkam*, a term of uncertain meaning *[Superscriptions; Musical]*.

OUTLINE

Petition for Deliverance from Enemies and Refrain of Trust, 59:1-10
    59:1-2   Plea for Help
    59:3-4a   Lament and Declaration of Innocence
    59:4b-5   Appeal for the LORD's Intervention
    59:6-7   Description of the Enemies
    59:8-10   Refrain: Trust in God's Steadfast Love
Petition for Judgment upon the Enemies and Refrain of Trust, 59:11-17
    59:11-13   Plea for Judgment upon the Enemies
    59:14-15   Description of the Enemies
    59:16-17   Refrain: Trust in God's Steadfast Love

EXPLANATORY NOTES

Petition for Deliverance from Enemies and Refrain of Trust   59:1-10

The desperate fourfold cry for help—*deliver, protect, deliver, save* (vv. 1-2)—is made in the face of intense opposition described as howling wild dogs who come out at night to prowl among the city's rubbish (vv. 6-7, 14-15; Ps 22:16). With sharp *swords on their lips*, they tear and destroy (v. 7 NRSV n). This image evokes the bark of harsh speech, the threat of being hurt *[Enemies]*.

Those who find themselves in such unhappy circumstances often seek a reason for their trouble. They may begin with introspection, as does the psalmist, who concludes, rightly or wrongly, that he is innocent (vv. 3-4a; 26:1; 73:13). In declaring his innocence, the psalmist uses all three of the classic OT words for sin: *peša'*, transgression or rebellion; *ḥaṭṭā'â*, sin or missing the mark; and *'āwôn*, fault or iniquity (51:1-2).

The psalmist reacts further to the maligning threat by crying out to *rouse* God, to awaken God to act (v. 4b). The metaphor of waking deity was widely used and synonymous with "save me," "help me" (44:23; 78:65; 121:4; Isa 51:9). The conviction that God hears and sees was deeply rooted in the experience of their history as a people (Exod 2:23-25). Belief about the God who controls the forces in the universe is expressed in the appellation *You, LORD God of hosts, are God of Israel* (v. 5; Pss 24:10; 46:7, 11; 48:8; 69:6; 84:1, 3, 12).

The LORD will act in judgment against all who challenge his authority (v. 5) or think they can speak and act with impunity (v. 7).

But you (v. 8) signals a shift in tone from fear to anticipated triumph as the psalmist takes comfort in the derisive laughter of God over the nations and human folly (2:4; 37:13). The refrain expresses trust in the LORD (Yahweh) as the psalmist's *strength* and *fortress* (vv. 8-9); he asserts that triumph will come through God's *steadfast love* (vv. 10, 17; 54:7) *[Steadfast]*.

Petition for Judgment upon the Enemies and Refrain of Trust   59:11-17

The psalmist asks God to deal forcibly with those who throw their weight around (vv. 11-13). *Do not kill them* is surprising (v. 11). Why not? Is death too good for the enemies? Will God's punishment, over time, make a more striking example of them? The psalmist can hope they might become *trapped in their pride* (v. 12; Prov 16:18), but in the end he wishes for God to take away the power of the enemy to oppress. The proper perspective to the harsh words *Consume them in wrath; consume them until they are no more* (v. 13) must be found in the last line of the petition. Rather than the cruel demand for revenge, the plea is that the rule of God in Israel may not be overlooked or forgotten, but may be known in all the world! The primary concern is that the people not forget God (v. 11; Deut 8:11-20; Pss 78; 106). The liturgical notation *Selah* may invite the congregation's reflection and response to the purpose of God in Israel (vv. 5, 13) *[Selah]*.

Following repetition of the complaint (vv. 14-15; cf. vv. 6-7), the psalm moves to the refrain expressing trust (vv. 16-17). *But I* marks the transition from anxiety to hope as the *strength, fortress,* and *steadfast love* themes are reiterated in the vow of praise (vv. 9-10, 16-17). The psalm moves from petition for rescue (vv. 1-5) to petition for destruction of the enemies (vv. 11-13), but with more hope that justice will be done. After praying, *O my strength, I will watch for you* (v. 9), the prayer *O my strength* (in v. 17) has become the reason for praise; the psalmist's own strength is in *the God who shows me steadfast love* (ḥesed, v. 17).

THE TEXT IN THE BIBLICAL CONTEXT AND LIFE OF THE CHURCH

Facing Opposition

Leaders often face adversarial forces, most often persons who challenge their course of action or seek to undermine them. Examples of leaders facing opposition are readily found in the stories of Moses, Daniel, Jesus, and Paul.

After crossing the Red Sea and trekking three days into the wilderness, the people complained against Moses (Exod 15:22-25). Within weeks they charged Moses of trying to kill them by bringing them into a barren land (16:1-3). They quarreled with Moses and threatened him until he asked the LORD in exasperation, "What shall I do with this people?" (17:1-4). At Mount Sinai the people lost patience, charging that Moses had abandoned them (32:1).

One of the stories about Daniel tells how Darius the Mede was about to appoint him ruler over the whole kingdom (Dan 6). Jealous conspirators tricked the king into signing an ordinance commanding that prayer be offered only to the king, with a penalty of death in "the den of lions." That did not deter Daniel from praying three times a day to his God as he had done previously.

The life of Jesus was cut short by religious leaders who found themselves threatened by the teachings of the prophet from Galilee (Matt 26:1-5; John 5:18; 7:1). Consequently, the church has often read Psalm 59 in the context of Jesus' passion, identifying the psalm's voice as that of Christ the Lord. Many have seen in Psalm 59 a powerful description of Jesus, innocent but hounded by his enemies, blameless but pursued unto death, trusting in the righteousness of God to vindicate his innocence (Reardon: 116).

Paul, the early prominent missionary of the Christian Way, faced opposition from without and within the community of faith (Acts 9:19-30; 26:19-23). Paul did not hesitate to speak about those who opposed him, and he claimed God's empowerment (2 Cor 11:21-33). When facing opposition, some naively adopt the response of denial. It is better to be in touch with the emotions, even to express them; but the most wholesome of all is to commit one's cause to God, and from that vantage point one can gain some reorientation.

What might be gained from this psalm, with its conglomeration of lament, complaint, petition, and imprecation? The psalmist is in trouble. Yet the psalm ends with a vigorous *I will sing* (vv. 16-17)! Instructive throughout the psalm are the twelve appearances of the names *God, LORD,* and *LORD God of hosts*. God is also referred to as *my strength* (vv. 9, 17), *my fortress* (vv. 9, 17), and *our shield* (v. 11). The writer expresses an exalted view of God (v. 5), but also affirms God's concern for the individual (vv. 10, 17). Most instructive of all, the psalm ends with the word ḥesed. Because of God's *steadfast love* (vv. 10, 16, 17), the psalmist *will sing*. And so can we.

Awakening Dangerous Emotions

The church has struggled in its use of psalms like Psalm 59. In special masses, such as Mass in Time of War, the Catholic Church used Psalm 59:1 and 16, as well as Psalms 31:2a and 77:14-15. Yet in the Liturgy of the Hours, which identifies the speaker of Psalm 59 as Jesus Christ, the harsh words (vv. 5-8, 11-15) are not included (Holladay: 222, 308).

Emotions awakened by this and other psalms of imprecation may be particularly dangerous. The psalm is passionate and zealous, but it is careful to allow God to judge *[Imprecation]*.

Psalm 60

With God, . . . for Human Help Is Worthless

PREVIEW

Psalm 60 is a communal lament following a humiliating military defeat, probably at the hand of the Edomites (v. 9). It views the painful defeat as divine rejection and the punishment of God (vv. 1, 10). Between the lamentations (vv. 1-5, 9-12), a divine oracle, spoken by temple priest or prophet, reminds the people of God's earlier promises (vv. 6-8). Even though regions of Shechem, Succoth, Gilead, and Manasseh are in the hands of foreigners, they belong to God. The psalm begins on a note of despair, but ends with confidence in the victory that comes through the help of God.

The lengthy heading suggests a setting for the psalm from a time when King David was developing a reputation as a great fighter (2 Sam 8:3-8, 13-14). *Aram-zobah* was a city state in northern modern Syria, likely between the Euphrates and the Orontes; the region of *Aram-naharaim* was in eastern modern Syria, between the Euphrates and the Tigris. The narrative in this superscription describes a military victory, but the psalm presumes a significant defeat for Israel. Most commentators view the fall of Samaria (721 BC) or the fall of Jerusalem (587or 586 BC) as a more likely setting.

Psalm 60

This psalm describes a situation similar to that which gave rise to the laments of Psalms 44; 74; and 83.

Probably not all the sections of Psalm 60 date from the same period. Stuhlmueller's outline of the possible literary history is helpful: the national lament (vv. 1-4) comes from just before or at the time of exile; the transitional verse 5 and the prayer of petition (vv. 9-12) are the latest parts of this psalm. The ancient oracle (vv. 6-8), affirming the Israelite settlement of their tribal portions and the conquests of King David (1000–961 BC), is the oldest part of the psalm (Stuhlmueller, 1983, 1:277).

The psalm heading refers to a possible tune, *Lily of the Covenant* (cf. Ps 80). It is the last of the series of *Miktam* psalms (16; 56–60). The heading further identifies it as *for instruction*, though it does not exhibit particular didactic characteristics *[Superscriptions; Musical]*.

OUTLINE

Lament: National Distress, 60:1-5
    60:1-3   The People's Situation Described
    60:4-5   Prayer for Deliverance
Divine Oracle: God Lays Claim to the Hebrew Territories, 60:6-8
Lament and Prayer for Victory, 60:9-12

EXPLANATORY NOTES

Lament: National Distress   60:1-5

The lamenting community is certain that God has rejected and forsaken it. By abandoning his people during a battle, God was considered responsible for the defeat (Pss 44:9, 23-24; 74:1; 89:38). In military defeat, their world had collapsed and been devastated as by an earthquake (v. 2). *Wine to drink* symbolizes punishment, as when the master forces his underlings to drink to the bitter dregs (v. 3; Ps 75:8; Isa 51:17, 22; Zech 12:2; Rev 18:6).

Translations and interpretations of verse 4 vary. The NRSV and NIV take the verse as a positive action by God to express a prayer, such as "Please set up a banner for those loyal to you, so they rally around it out of range" (Clifford, 2002:283). Or the *banner* may have been a banner to flee (v. 9). After the collapse of the Southern Kingdom (587or 586 BC), the inhabitants of Judah fled not only to Egypt, but also to other places, including Edom (Jer 40:11-12; Obad 1:14). The term *Selah* may have suggested a pause or emphasis in the liturgical use of the psalm *[Selah]*.

The community of those *who fear you* (v. 4) are also those *whom you love* (v. 5). Thus, despite feeling abandoned, the people dare to make earnest prayer for *victory* through God's presence.

Divine Oracle: God Lays Claim to the Hebrew Territories   60:6-8

At the center of this communal lament is heard God's word. The temple and inner sanctuary are the holy place from where the divine word is communicated as help and comfort for those who are oppressed and needy (v. 6; Pss 20:2; 108:7). The oracle takes the form of a divine utterance borrowed from the sacred tradition of the land's distribution. Uttered by a priest or prophet, it gives assurance that God is still the master of nations and will intervene on Israel's behalf [Oracle].

All of the territories listed, *Shechem* (a city in central Palestine), *Succoth* (a valley east of the Jordan River), *Gilead* (a grassland plateau east of the Jordan), *Manasseh,* and *Ephraim* (tribal allotments in north-central Palestine), and *Judah* (which included Jerusalem, in the southern region), were part of the Hebrew empire under the United Monarchy. *Moab, Edom,* and *Philistia* were kingdoms east, south, and west of the Dead Sea, but were provinces or vassal states during and after the time of David (2 Sam 8:11-12).

The metaphors *washbasin* and *shoe* (v. 8) may suggest symbols of menial service and defeat. Throwing the *shoe* over a territory was a symbolic act to proclaim possession of it (Ruth 4:8-9). The point of Psalm 60 is God's claim of lordship over the whole region. God is depicted as victoriously subduing the enemy nations and subjecting them to servitude.

Lament and Prayer for Victory   60:9-12

The psalmist (*me,* v. 9), perhaps a king, reminds God of his promises, which the events of history seem to be mocking; then he returns to the realities of the disaster. The *fortified city* (v. 9) may have been Sela in Edom, where later the Nabatean city Petra was built as a rock fortress. The psalm continues with a plea for help against the foe because human strength is not enough (v. 11). The conclusion is an assertion of confidence in God (v. 12; Ps 44:5; Isa 63:6).

THE TEXT IN THE BIBLICAL CONTEXT AND LIFE OF THE CHURCH

Religious Faith and Political Reality

Psalm 60:5-12, like 57:7-11, was used by the compiler of Psalm 108. Verses 5-12 are identical to Psalm 108:6-13. There the preface is not by a lament, but a song of thanksgiving and praise. This is a good example of how a psalmist could apply existing material in a new context, to speak to different settings and times (see comments on Ps 108).

Deeply rooted in historical and geographical realities, Psalm 60 illustrates how religion does not exist separately from politics, economics, and armaments. Delitzsch calls Psalm 60 "the most martial of all the psalms." Stuhlmueller suggests that Psalm 60 is dealing not so much with military operations as with such spiritual questions as "the fidelity of God in the midst of national defeat and with the necessity of hope during the collapse of one's homeland" (Stuhlmueller, 1983, 1:279). The congregation is led through lament to listen to God's reaffirming word and then to find new hope and courage. Living between promise and fulfillment is the situation of believers in every age.

If verses 11 and 12 relate to Israel's understanding of Yahweh war, they remind readers today that *bow* and *sword* (Ps 44:6) and guns and bombs will not save. Prayers for victory in military battle are usually narrowly nationalistic and self-justifying. The great spiritual understanding of God's kingdom, which transcends military victories, is set forth in the NT *[War]*.

Psalm 61

God, a Refuge in Time of Trouble

PREVIEW

Psalm 61 is a prayer song of lament in which the suppliant seeks refuge in God's presence. The psalm then moves to thanksgiving, intercession for the king, and a promise to praise. Because of the prayer for the king (vv. 6-7), some commentators also classify it as a royal psalm.

Many possible settings have been suggested: a member of the community in a foreign land longs to return to the temple; an individual makes lament in distress (vv. 1-5, 8), with verses 6-7 added later for use in another setting; an individual in the temple for the Covenant Festival; or the supplication of a king for deliverance from death. The central theme focuses on God as refuge in time of trouble.

The heading associates Psalm 61 with David, as is true for the collection of Psalms 51–65. It was identified to be sung or chanted *with stringed instruments*, a reminder that whatever their origin, the psalms found their home in worship *[Superscriptions; Musical]*.

OUTLINE

Opening Plea for Refuge, 61:1-4
Prayer for the King and Vow of Praise, 61:5-8

EXPLANATORY NOTES

Opening Plea for Refuge   61:1-4

The plaintive cry is voiced by one whose *heart is faint* (v. 2). The heart was seen as the center of human life, from where the person experienced sorrow, anxiety, or fear (Pss 25:17; 27:3; 55:4). The psalm suggests a sense of isolation and distance from the traditional sources of hope and security (land, family, community, or nation). *From the end of the earth* (v. 2) may simply be a place far from home (Deut 28:49; Isa 5:26; 43:6), or even exile with a deep longing to return to the familiar holy place (Ps 137:1). *The enemy* (v. 3) was sometimes used as a term for death *[Enemies]*.

Whatever the distress, a cluster of strong images depict God's protective care: *rock, refuge, strong tower, tent, shelter of your wings* (vv. 2b-4). Though these may refer to the security available within the temple, they also point beyond, to the loving and protective care of God in any situation of distress. God as a high rock and strong tower provides security against the enemy (18:2, 31, 46; 94:22; 95:1). *Refuge in your tent* (15:1; 27:5-6) or *under the shelter of your wings* (17:8; 36:7; 57:1; 61:4; 63:7; 91:4) denies the power of the pit (*Sheol*) or whatever enemy threatens (v. 3). The theme of continually abiding in God's house is a constant note in the psalms (v. 4; 23:6; 52:8-9). While the surface reference is to the sanctuary, "God's house" can also be expanded to include the sphere of God's presence and deliverance beyond geographical location. The liturgical term *Selah* may signal a pause or point of emphasis to conclude stanza one (v. 4) *[Selah]*.

Prayer for the King and Vow of Praise   61:5-8

The psalmist recalls his vows and expresses certainty that God has heard and will grant his wish (v. 5). *The heritage of those who fear your name* likely refers to the gift of the land (Deut 2:5, 9, 19; Josh 1:11-15; Ps 60:6-8), but also sustains those who call out to God *from the end of the earth* (v. 2).

The prayer for the king bears witness to the key role the monarchy played in the life of the nation (vv. 6-7). On its stability depended the stability of the nation. The king represented the people. Their prosperity was bound up with his. Life as the gift of God was the highest good. The people prayed for and waited expectantly for "long life" as the most precious gift and the most marvelous blessing (Pss 21:4; 91:16; 113:2-3; Kraus, 1986:164). The petition asks for *steadfast love* (*ḥesed*) *and faithfulness* as a pair of personified guardians of the king (57:3). *Steadfast love* involves the element of loyalty to community (25:10; 40:11; 89:14; 138:2) *[Steadfast]*.

We may read the prayer as the people interceding for the king. Sometimes a psalmist would add a petition for the king to an individual lament (20; 63; 72; Westermann, 1989:58). If the speaker of the psalm is a king, he likely used the third person in referring to himself (18:8; 63:11; Holladay: 38-39).

The psalm ends with the promise to praise God's name daily as fulfillment of the vows already mentioned. Thus verses 5 and 8 frame and form an inclusio around the prayer for the king *[Hebrew Poetry]*.

THE TEXT IN THE BIBLICAL CONTEXT AND LIFE OF THE CHURCH

Insights Offered by Psalm 61

Isolation makes one an easy target for discouragement. The anguish motivating the prayer is separation from God and the holy community. Similar ardent longings are expressed in Psalms 27; 42–43; 63; and 84. Separated from his roots, the psalmist knew his sole security lay in worship. Worship provides renewed hope for the discouraged person and isolated community of faith in troubled times.

There is a place of refuge. The biblical story tells of "cities of refuge" offering protection and grace (Num 35:9-15). The sanctuary became a haven and place of safety. Forty-six references in the psalms describe God as "refuge." The prophets spoke of refuge in the name of the LORD for the poor and needy in distress (Isa 25:4; Joel 3:16; Zeph 3:12).

God hears the cry of the desperate. When the Israelites groaned under their slavery and cried out, God heard their groaning and remembered his covenant (Exod 2:23-25). In similar manner, oppressed African-Americans have cried out to God through their spiritual songs, such as "When Israel was in Egypt land, let my people go," "Wade in the water, children," and "There is a balm in Gilead."

People of faith will pray for their religious and civil leaders. The psalmist prays for the one who has political responsibility over his life, the king. Paul reminds his readers that rulers are "not a terror to good conduct, but to bad," and urges respect and prayer for them (Rom 13:1-7; cf. Titus 3:1-2), for Christ is "head of every ruler and authority" (Col 2:10). Intercession for leaders will ask for just rule, motivated by steadfast love and faithfulness (Ps 61:7).

God deserves daily vows of devotion. Some OT examples of prayer connected with vows include Jacob (Gen 28:20-22), Jephthah

(Judg 11:30-31, 34-35), and Hannah (1 Sam 1:11, 21). In Psalm 61, the movement is from "far" to "near," which is what happens in prayer (Eph 2:13; Heb 7:19; 10:21-22). "Drawing near to God in prayer is based on His drawing near to us in Christ" (Reardon: 120).

Lead Me to the Rock

In Psalm 62 we will again hear the cry for shelter and a high refuge, but there it comes as a ringing affirmation: *He alone is my rock and my salvation* (Ps 62:2, 6-7). Images in these psalms have inspired hymns such as Augustus Toplady's "Rock of Ages, cleft for me" (1776), Mary Dagworthy James' "In the rifted Rock I'm resting" (1875), and M. Gerald Derstine's "Jesus, Rock of ages" (1973).

Psalm 62

For God Alone My Soul Waits in Silence

PREVIEW

This individual prayer song of confidence is a sustained declaration of trust in God in spite of the lament of verses 3-4. One who has known the destructive power of vicious slander utters the song of trust. Finding refuge under God's protection in the sanctuary (vv. 2, 6-7), this broken and persecuted one knows safety and can celebrate God's power and love.

The psalm progresses from inner dialogue (vv. 1-2), to rebuke of enemies (vv. 3-4), refrain as exhortation to self (vv. 5-7; cf. vv. 1-2), teaching the uninstructed (vv. 8-10), and prayer to God (vv. 11-12). The two major sections of the psalm move from God as refuge of the individual (vv. 1-7) to God as refuge of the community (vv. 8-12).

Other songs of the individual's confidence include Psalms 11; 16; 23; 27; 91; 121; and 131. The heading is similar to that found in Psalms 39 and 77. *Jeduthun* is listed among the temple Levites of David's time and linked with the musical accompaniment for sacred songs (1 Chron 16:41-42). Or, the term may have come to refer to the name of a tune or musical setting *[Superscriptions; Musical]*.

Psalm 62

OUTLINE

Avowal of Trust in God, 62:1-7
    62:1-2, 5-7 Refrain-like Statement of Confidence
    62:3-4   Lament: The Psalmist's Situation
Instruction to the Community to Trust in God Alone, 62:8-12
    62:8   Summons to Trust
    62:9-10   Admonition About Human Mortality and Greed
    62:11-12   Prayer Addressed to God

EXPLANATORY NOTES

Avowal of Trust in God   62:1-7

Prominent in the Hebrew text of Psalm 62 is the emphatic assertion *'ak,* with which six verses begin (1, 2, 4, 5, 6, 9). The Hebrew word can be translated "surely," (*truly,* NEB) but does not show in many of the English translations. In the NRSV it is rendered *alone* (vv. 1, 2, 5, 6), *only* (v. 4), and *but* (v. 9). It is the declaration "Yes, but . . . " Such assertions are the language of faith, with which, in face of all assaults, established truths are confessed and affirmed. These assertions set the tone for the entire psalm: none but God will prevail!

The psalm begins with an appeal to silent waiting before God, the calm that trusting brings (vv. 1, 5). As in Psalm 61, strong words name and describe God's protective power and action: *my salvation* (vv. 1, 2, 6), *my rock* (vv. 2, 6, 7), *my fortress* (vv. 2, 6), *my hope* (v. 5), *my deliverance* (v. 7), *my honor* (v. 7), *my refuge* (vv. 7, 8). The language suggests the temple. *My rock,* as an appellation for God, is more than metaphorical (Pss 18:2; 28:1; 31:2, 3; 42:9). The temple sanctuary in Jerusalem was built on the "holy rock." These terms, including "fortress" and "refuge," bear a special relationship to the role of Jerusalem, where God functioned as the righteous judge (Kraus, 1986:31).

Consequently, the lament describing the psalmist beset by vicious slandering enemies (vv. 3-4) is framed by the refrain asserting the secure and saving power of God (vv. 1-2, 5-7). The foes of the individual are often compared with a hostile army that attacks the helpless and surrounds them with overwhelming forces (3:6; 27:3; 55:18; 56:1-2; 59:1-3). Here the hapless victim is described as a *leaning wall* or *tottering fence* (v. 3). The inclusio declaring the protecting power of God (vv. 1-2, 5-6) surrounds the description of the foes (vv. 3-4), nullifying the strength and effectiveness of the enemy (Wilson, 2002:878) *[Hebrew Poetry].* The psalmist thus restates his faith: *My refuge is in God* (v. 7).

Instruction to the Community to Trust in God Alone 62:8-12

A summons to trust, addressed to the circle to which the psalmist belongs, follows the avowal of confidence (v. 8). God, who is the psalmist's refuge (v. 7), is now exalted as *refuge for us* (v. 8). To trust is to take for granted that one can confide in God all one's deepest emotions, including lament (v. 8b; 1 Sam 1:15; Lam 2:19). The liturgical word *Selah* (v. 8) may be an invitation for the congregation to ponder the meaning of God as *refuge for us*, even as previously it invited the congregation's reflection on the devious conduct of the foes (v. 4) *[Selah]*.

Instruction is offered in a series of aphorisms about social and economic status, greed and acquisition (vv. 9-10; Prov 21:6). The admonition is that frail mortals and human devices are unreliable. Human ingenuity, national prosperity, and fascination with money-making are meaningless when weighed against the majesty and might of God (Isa 40:15). The brevity of human life is a common theme in the psalms (39:5-6; 90:3-10; 144:4). The heart can be set on riches and fall victim to them. It is more dependable to trust in God than in ill-gotten wealth (49:6, 16-17).

A numerical proverb, *Once . . . twice . . .* , common in wisdom literature, introduces the prayer addressing God directly for the first time (v. 11; Prov 6:16; 30:15-31). The point of *power . . . steadfast love . . .* (vv. 11-12) is that God will vindicate those who trust him and shatter the illusions of those who trust human strength and violence (Mays, 1994b:217). Believers can trust God because he is, at the same time, strong and loving. God's omnipotence and kindness work together to the end that every person, good or evil, receives just recompense.

THE TEXT IN THE BIBLICAL CONTEXT AND LIFE OF THE CHURCH

The Inner Stillness of Trust

Striking in Psalm 62 is the emphasis on the silence of turning toward God (vv. 1, 5). This is not so much the silence of contemplative piety as the silence "after the storm," the quietness entered in trust by the one who has escaped. There is an inner stillness, a calm that trust brings (Westermann, 1989:152). The psalm speaks to a quietness of soul, an inner stillness that comes with yielding all fear and anxieties and insecurities to God in an act of trust.

The psalms express this in the personal admonition, "When you are disturbed, do not sin; ponder it on your beds and be silent" (4:4), or again in the psalm of trust, "Be still, and know that I am God! I am exalted" (46:10). Or in complaint against enemies, the psalmist can say, "In God I trust; I am not afraid" (56:3-4, 11). This stillness is like "the peace of God, which surpasses all understanding [and] will guard your hearts and your minds in Christ Jesus" (Phil 4:7).

The Bible portrays a God both of power and of steadfast love (Ps 62:11-12). The vision of power and love come together in the self-emptying (cross and resurrection) told about in the Christ hymn (Phil 2:6-11). Out of that inner stillness of trust evolves the conviction that "true power must express itself in steadfast love, and that steadfast love is ultimately the sole powerful answer to the needs and troubles of our world" (Davidson, 1998:197).

Jesus witnessed to an inner stillness of trust. Drawing on psalms to clarify his identity and mission (cf. Ps 62:12 and Matt 16:27), Jesus did not take on a spirit of "us against them," which many of the psalms convey. In Romans 2:6, Paul quotes Psalm 62:12 about reward according to what each person has done (NIV, NEB). For Paul, this verse is set within the context of a final judgment. Other verses from Psalm 62 to which NT passages relate include verse 10, *riches* (Matt 6:19-21; 1 Tim 6:7-10); verse 11, *Power belongs to God* (Rev 19:1); and verse 12, *repay* (2 Tim 4:14; Rev 22:12).

Finding Our Strength

How do you find your strength? Catharina A. D. von Schlegel's hymn, "Be still, my soul" (1752), usually sung to the tune Finlandia, appears to come right out of the opening line of Psalm 62: *For God alone my soul waits in silence.* Sometimes by going nowhere, but remaining silently in God's presence, people grow in dignity, strength, and self-hood. Unbelievable strength is drawn in rest and waiting in silence, which implies utter trust.

Margaret Guenther's book of eight meditations on Psalm 62 offers practical suggestions to focus personal retreat time. Meditative themes follow the outline of the psalm: longing for God alone, silence, my soul waits, God is my rock, our enemies, God as our refuge, trust in God, addressing God. Guenther concludes that God promises us *shalom*, God's peace. The simple act of carving out small spaces in the midst of our busy world can lead to a new openness to God.

Psalm 63

Your Steadfast Love Is Better Than Life

PREVIEW

Psalm 63 is a lament dominated by trust, and so it becomes also a psalm of confidence and thanksgiving. The psalmist is filled with a desire for the presence of God in the temple (v. 2). The psalm pictures one battered by conflict, thirsting for God, like parched land longing for water. However, this psalm moves quickly to the central declaration, *Your steadfast love is better than life* (v. 3), and the expression of communion within God's embrace (v. 8). Connections to Psalm 61 can be found in the shelter of God's wings (v. 7), a vow to endless praise of God's name (v. 4), and a shift to third person in reference to the king (v. 11).

The text is complex and appears disconnected. Some commentators think that verses 9-11 could be a later addition. They have suggested various settings: the covenant celebration before the sacred ark in the temple, a person in exile in a desert place, or a royal psalm, since the king is mentioned (v. 11).

The following outline draws on the three-stanza arrangement of NRSV and considers the psalm a unit, the lament prayer of an accused man (vv. 1, 9-11) in the protective area of the sanctuary (vv. 2, 7). The divine verdict against the enemy may not yet have been spoken (vv. 9-11), but in the protection of God already being experienced, the words of assurance, trust, and thanksgiving are uttered

(vv. 5-8). The psalm ends with imprecation upon the enemy and a prayer for the king as lord of the people and guarantor of salvation (Ps 72).

An alternative outline offered by Clifford (2002:295) divides the psalm into two parts. Part 1 expresses the hope of "seeing" God in the sanctuary (vv. 1-5), and part 2 expresses the awareness that God is present even now (vv. 6-11).

The heading attributes the psalm to David, when he hid from Saul *in the Wilderness of Judah* (1 Sam 23:14-15; 24:1) *[Superscriptions]*.

OUTLINE

The Soul's Thirst for God, 63:1-4
Satisfied by God's Protective Help, 63:5-8
Confident of Deliverance, 63:9-11

EXPLANATORY NOTES

The Soul's Thirst for God   63:1-4

My soul thirsts is a metaphor of one's most imperative need (v. 1). The psalmist thirsts for God as an exhausted wanderer needs water in a parched desert (Pss 42:1-2; 143:6). The *sanctuary* was looked upon as place where God's glorious presence and power were revealed (v. 2; 27:4; Isa 6:1-5).

The psalmist's adoration (v. 4) is born of a deep sense of God's gracious ḥesed, translated as "love, loving-kindness, or steadfast love" (v. 3) *[Steadfast]*. God's *steadfast love is better than life* may seem an unusual hyperbole for Israelites, for whom life was considered the highest good. Yet enjoying God's love in the temple is better than survival in the wilderness, geographical or metaphorical. Communion with God, lovingly bestowed, is the highest and best gift possible (Ps 73:23-26). The covenant relation with God is better than "length of days," superior to biological existence. Living in the certainty of *steadfast love*, even in a time of spiritual drought, allows praise of God with one's lips and hands (v. 4).

Satisfied by God's Protective Help   63:5-8

The theme of trust dominates these verses. The refreshing power of the nearness of God is compared to a *rich feast* (v. 5; 23:5; 34:8; 36:8). While the hours of *night* were often regarded as a dangerous time, when demons and evil spirits were active (v. 6; A. Anderson, 1:458), night was also considered a suitable time to seek God's presence in prayer and meditation (4:4; 16:7; 77:6; 119:55, 62). Remembering and reciting God's past divine acts gave reassurance of God's present love and protection. Even during the difficult night hours, the psalmist is safe *in the shadow of your wings* (v.7; 17:8; 36:7; 57:1; 61:4; 91:4). The thanksgiving ends with the wonderful picture of being upheld in the divine embrace (v. 8).

Confident of Deliverance 63:9-11

The word *soul (nepeš)* is prominent in Psalm 63:1, 5, 8 and occurs once more in verse 9, where it is translated *life* to indicate the whole person. In these verses, the psalmist turns his attention to those who threaten to destroy him (35:4; 38:12; 40:14; 54:3; 70:2; 86:14). Not knowing the joy of God's steadfast love, his enemies have no future. In contrast, the psalmist, upheld by God, will not be consigned to Sheol. The phrase *depths of the earth* describes Sheol, the place of the dead *[Sheol]*. The psalmist also points to a fate worse than burial: becoming *prey for jackals* (v. 10).

The final verse is a prayer for the king, expressing the confidence of the community that king and people will find cause for rejoicing and praise, while those who attack the king will be silenced. Alternatively, if as seems likely some of the psalms were written by a king, the author may be switching from the first person, *I* and *my*, to the third person, *the king*, as a way of saying, "I shall rejoice in God" (Ps 61:6-7).

THE TEXT IN THE BIBLICAL CONTEXT AND LIFE OF THE CHURCH

Thirsting for God

Thirst *in a dry and weary land* is the classic metaphor for spiritual longing. It expresses a need for the presence of God, without which the soul cannot live. Thirst surfaces prominently in the journey of the Hebrews through the wilderness (Exod 15:22-27; 17:1-6; Num 20:2-11; Deut 8:15). Psalms of longing for the presence of God, especially in the temple, include Psalms 27; 42–43; 61; and 84. The prophet Isaiah promised satisfaction to those who thirst after God (55:1-2).

Biblical images of life and refreshment include rain (Deut 11:11-14; 32:2; Job 5:10; Pss 68:8-9; 147:8; Isa 30:23), springs (Deut 8:7; Pss 74:15; 84:6; 104:10; 107:33, 35; Isa 35:7; Rev 7:17), and cisterns and wells (Deut 6:10-11; Isa 12:3; Jer 2:13; John 4:6-7). Jesus assures his followers of the water that satisfies (Matt 5:6; John 4:13-

14; 7:37-38). The Bible ends with the invitation to drink deeply of the life-giving water (Rev 22:17).

According to the NT, thirst for God is prompted by the Holy Spirit, who causes us to yearn for God beyond our own ability to aspire (Rom 8:26-27). The well-known prayer of Augustine of Hippo (AD 354-450) expresses the stirring of that inner longing:

> Thou awakest us to delight in thy praises;
> for Thou madest us for Thyself,
> and our heart is restless, until it repose in Thee.
> (Appleton: 64; Augustine, *Confessions* 1.1)

The Rich Feast of Communion with God

In the life of the early church, Psalm 63 became the classic morning prayer. The reference to singing for joy after meditation during the night (vv. 6-7) made it a suitable introductory psalm for Sunday morning worship. A fourth-century Christian writing, *Apostolic Constitutions* (2.59), exhorts the faithful, "Assemble yourselves together every day, morning and evening, singing psalms and praying in the Lord's house; in the morning, saying the sixty-second psalm [= 63]" (Stuhlmueller, 1:289). The satisfying rich feast leading to praise (v. 5) made this an appropriate psalm for the eucharist.

Those who contend that the OT is law and the NT is grace may be surprised by the psalmist's insistence that all a person can have and experience in life is inferior to grace (v. 3). Paul reaffirmed it: "I do not count my life of any value to myself, if only I may . . . testify to the good news of God's grace" (Acts 20:24; cf. Gal 2:20). Yes, there is something better than this mortal life: communion with God. In patristic times and beyond, this confession was associated with martyrs, who valued God more than life and gave up their lives rather than deny their testimony (Mays, 1994b:218).

Psalm 64

Wicked Tongues and Tongues of Witness

PREVIEW

This individual lament serves as an appeal for protection from the schemes of cunning enemies. The maligned psalmist, who likely has taken asylum in the sanctuary (v. 2), describes the enemies with a series of metaphors drawn from those who stalk wild animals (vv. 3-6). He expresses outrage at the secrecy of evil and the arrogance of the schemers.

The second part of the psalm expresses confidence in God's protection and trust in God as righteous judge. The judgment of God will pursue the enemies, and their sin will produce its own punishment (vv. 7-8). Deliverance of the psalmist will cause even those outside Israel to fear God, to tell what he has wrought, and to ponder what he has done (v. 9). The righteous will rejoice and take courage (v. 10). So this vigorous complaint about malicious tongues (vv. 3-5, 8) ends with tongues of witness to the salvation of God.

The presence of many footnotes in NRSV and NEB and variant readings (vv. 3-8) reveals a text in poor condition and uncertain in places. Several wordplays using repetition (vv. 2, 4, 5, 8) mark the style of the poem *[Hebrew Poetry]*.

Psalm 64

OUTLINE

Complaint About the Cutting Tongue, 64:1-6
Confidence in God's Arrow of Recompense, 64:7-10

EXPLANATORY NOTES

Complaint About the Cutting Tongue   64:1-6

The petition for preservation from evildoers characterizes the attack as a conspiracy (vv. 1-2) *[Enemies; Wicked]*. Rather than simply saying that wicked people are scheming against the psalmist, the poet compares their tongues to sharp swords and their words to arrows (vv. 3-4). *Swords* and *arrows* are frequently used metaphors for slander and malicious gossip (Pss 52:2; 55:21; 57:4; 59:7; 120:2-4).

Like snipers, *shooting . . . without fear* (v. 4), they proceed to harass with deceit and lies, with no thought of being punished by God (v. 5). A question expresses the arrogance of the wicked: *"Who can see us?"* This calls into question God's capacity to rule the world justly (Isa 29:15). *"Who can search . . . ?"* (v. 6) uses the impersonal *Who?* as a way of describing divine activity, with the psalmist meaning, "It will be searched out" (Clifford, 2002:299). The psalmist is expressing confidence that secret schemes will be exposed.

For the human heart and mind are deep (v. 6b, *cunning*, NIV) may be an old proverb (cf. Jer 17:9, "The heart is devious above all else"). Thus, the psalmist warns the reader about the capacity for self-deception.

Confidence in God's Arrow of Recompense   64:7-10

Confidence in God's protection and divine recompense is expressed in the opening words of part 2: *But God . . .* (v. 7). In the report of God's intervention, the focus is on what God has done as judge of the wicked, and as helper and refuge of the righteous. In divine retribution, not only do the workers of mischief suffer the end they are devising (vv. 7-8; Ps 35:8), but ironically, their end becomes a blessing as people see and hear *what God . . . has done* (v. 9)!

The writer uses repetition to underscore his point. God will shoot arrows at those who have shot arrows (with their tongues) at the righteous. The boast that no one is in charge of the world (vv. 5-6) is an attack upon God's justice and commitment. God must act for the sake of justice. After the ruin of these schemers, others will fear and worship God and tell the stories of God's mighty acts (v. 9). The people who rejoice in the LORD are understood to be the righteous or innocent, among whom the psalmist reckons himself (v. 10; 68:3).

THE TEXT IN THE BIBLICAL CONTEXT AND LIFE OF THE CHURCH

Vengeance Is Mine

Psalm 64 pictures God as an archer (vv. 7-8). Vengeance, commonly understood as retaliatory punishment inflicted in return for an injury or offense, is not the issue in the psalm. When God said, "Vengeance is mine, and recompense . . ." (Deut 32:35), the implication was not vindictive action, but the justice of God. In the psalms, the cry for recompense proceeds from the fact that God is being treated with contempt and his honor is defiled (vv. 5-6; Ps 79:12) *[Vengeance]*.

To trust in God is to hold that the individual wronged need not redress the wrong, but God will bring about the right and will redress the wrong. The reason for the call to rejoice, then, is that this kind of trust has been vindicated (v. 10). That evil people are unmasked and punished is a theme shared with the wisdom literature (Ps 1).

Paul, writing to the Romans, encouraged people to live in harmony with one another and not to be haughty. He cautioned people about the temptation to avenge themselves by quoting Deuteronomy 32:35: "Vengeance is mine, I will repay, says the Lord." Finally, he commends people not to be overcome by evil, but to "overcome evil with good" (Rom 12:19-21).

Victims of Malice and the Purpose of Speech

Psalm 64 is suitable for those who are the victims of malice. It echoes the cry of countless men and women who, through the centuries, have felt the terror of being hunted by accusers, persecutors, or secret police. People who operate under a cloak of secrecy instill fear. However, the dynamic of self-deception (vv. 5-6) is often the very undoing of the cunning (vv. 7-8).

This is also a psalm about hostile talk. In a largely nonliterary society, a person's spoken word in promise, testimony, accusation, and oath was all-important. Integrity is the basis of social order and justice (White: 39). Hence, Scripture places emphasis on simple truthfulness. Jesus said, "Let your word be 'Yes, Yes' or 'No, No'; anything more than this comes from the evil one" (Matt 5:37). In similar manner, Paul wrote about integrity and truth-speaking (2 Cor 13:8; Eph 4:25).

Through the centuries, this psalm has been used in prayers of the church, likely in remembrance of Judas' betrayal of Jesus, an example of speech misused. Wednesday was the day before the Last Supper (Matt 26:2-4; John 13:21); the Rule of St. Benedict (ca. AD

530) apparently testifies to the custom of praying Psalm 64 on Wednesday mornings (Reardon: 125).

Human speech is not for cutting persons down or for poisoning human relationships. Rather, let our tongues *tell what God has brought about, and ponder what he has done* (Ps 64:9).

Psalm 65

Thanks for God-given Bounty

PREVIEW

The theme of this community song of thanksgiving is wide-ranging. While the psalm expresses exuberant thanks for a good harvest (vv. 9-13), God is also praised for *awesome deeds* of *deliverance* in history and creation (vv. 5-8). However, praise is offered first of all for God's gracious bounty in the gifts of sanctuary and the forgiveness of sins (vv. 1-4).

Various settings for this psalm are possible: the beginning of the barley harvest (Feast of Unleavened Bread), when the earliest crops had ripened (Deut 16:8-9); end of the grain harvest (Feast of Weeks; Pentecost in NT); a national song of thanksgiving offered after a threatening drought and famine had been averted (1 Kings 8:33-36); or an enthronement festival (Pss 95:6; 96:9; 99:5, 9). However, the festival that best matches the theme of the psalm is Tabernacles, or Booths (Exod 23:16; 34:22; Deut 16:13-15). Celebrated in the early fall, the festival gives thanks for the harvest of threshing floor and winepress, and also commemorates the exodus. The festival is characterized by public rejoicing, giving thanks for life-giving water, and concern for the nations (Clifford, 2002:302). We can imagine the psalm recited in the context of a pilgrimage to the temple.

The first two stanzas (vv. 1-4, 5-8) have a common form, while verses 9-13 are structured differently, suggesting the possibility that the final part may have been added later. The heading identifies the poem as *A Song*, binding it to the following three psalms. The term *A Song* (šîr) may at one time have had a technical meaning, but that meaning is lost to us. A total of fifteen psalms are given this designation in the headings *[Superscriptions; Musical]*.

OUTLINE

God of the Temple: Forgiveness and Blessing, 65:1-4
God of the World: Awesome Stabilizing Power, 65:5-8
God as Giver of Rain: The Bounty of the Land, 65:9-13

EXPLANATORY NOTES

God of the Temple: Forgiveness and Blessing 65:1-4

In Hebrew the first two lines begin with *to you*, emphasizing the centrality of God and dependence of the people on the divine bounty. Throughout, this psalm directly addresses God. A long list specifies why *praise is due* to God: *You . . . answer prayer!* (v. 2), *forgive our transgressions* (v. 3), *choose and bring [us] near to live in your courts* (v. 4), *answer us with deliverance* (v. 5), *are the hope of . . . the earth* (v. 5), *established the mountains* (v. 6), *silence . . . the seas* (v. 7), *make the gateways . . . shout for joy* (v. 8), *visit the earth and water it* (v. 9), *provide the people with grain* (v. 9), and *crown the year with your bounty* (v. 11). Almost all of these refer to divine activity, not primarily to God's essence.

The psalm gives the invitation to praise (vv. 1-4) in the literary form of an envelope, framed by Zion (v. 1) and temple (v. 4). On Zion, Israel's songs of praise ring out (Ps 147:12). In the temple, vows are fulfilled (61:8; 66:13-14). Here not only the Israelites offer worship, but also, *to you all flesh shall come* (v. 2) speaks of God's intent to reunite all humanity. God is accessible to everyone, an understanding that became more prominent after the exile (Isa 66:18-23).

The psalmist acknowledges the problem of sin (v. 3). Divine forgiveness of sin was seen as a precondition for winter rains and an abundant harvest (Deut 11:13-17). However, God can forgive sin; God can make atonement and wipe the slate clean (v. 3; Pss 78:38; 79:9). Forgiveness of sin is the prerequisite of a true relationship with God and the beginning of thanksgiving (32:1-2). Even as only God can forgive, people are in the temple by God's invitation (v. 4). *Happy are [O the blessedness of;* cf. NIV] those chosen to come into the courts of God, as expressed fully in Psalm 84.

God of the World: Awesome Stabilizing Power
65:5-8

The second stanza celebrates the mighty wonders of God, who has the world in his hands. The title *God of our salvation* implies liberating, saving, helping power (v. 5; 79:9; 85:4). The *awesome deeds* (v. 5) refer to the miracle of the exodus and conquest (Exod 34:10; Deut 10:21-22; Ps 106:21-23, 43-46). The God enthroned in Zion is the Creator of the world, with references to mountains (v. 6), seas (v. 7), and the heavens (v. 8), if we take *signs* and *gateways* as referring to the stars). Mythical conceptions of the struggle of primeval times may be behind this imagery describing God's victory over the watery forces of chaos and destruction (Pss 46:3; 89:9-11; 93:3-4). There also may be a metaphorical use of the roaring of the waves and the wild tumult of the peoples, both stilled by the God of Israel (Isa 17:12-14).

The thrust of these verses affirms the awesome stabilizing power of the God of creation and deliverance (v. 8). *Signs* may be events in the world that direct attention to the majesty and greatness of the Creator. *Gateways*, literally "outgoings," may be the poet's way of speaking of the whole wide world.

God as Giver of Rain: The Bounty of the Land
65:9-13

In the movement of the psalm, *You visit the earth* (v. 9) is the counterpart to *You who answer prayer* (v. 2) and *You answer us with deliverance* (v. 5). In verses 9-13 the focus is on water and the bounty of well-watered fertile land. In an arid area, rain was God's good gift. Most rain fell during January and February, but the early and latter rains helped prepare the soil for the growing season and mature the grain. Rain meant green pastures for the sheep, goats, and cattle. A bountiful crop signified life and prosperity. All this was seen as coming from *the river of God*, the conduit that brings rain to the earth (v. 9; Job 38:25; Ps 104:13; Isa 33:21; Joel 3:18). *Your wagon tracks* may refer to the cloud-chariot of God "who rides upon the clouds" (v. 11; Deut 33:26; Ps 68:4, 33; Hab 3:8). In the psalm's final verses, the natural world joins humankind in praise of the beneficent God (vv. 12-13). Nature awakened to new life resounds with ringing and singing (Pss 96:11-13; 98:7-8).

THE TEXT IN THE BIBLICAL CONTEXT AND LIFE OF THE CHURCH

God's Bounty for Those at Earth's Farthest Bounds

Psalm 65 is a mission psalm, pointing to how God's deeds inspire universal awe. It refers to *all flesh* (the whole of humankind, v. 2), *the ends of the earth* (the whole world, v. 5), and those *who live at earth's farthest bounds* (no national boundaries, v. 8). We also find such mission concern in other psalms (22:27-31; 47:8-9; 67:1-7; 98:2, 7-9). The covenant God is the source of forgiveness and new life for everyone. God desires nothing less than the restoration of all humanity to his original intention in creation (Isa 66:18-23).

The missionary movement of the church developed out of a desire to fulfill this calling as laid out in Jesus' great commission: "Go therefore and make disciples of all nations, baptizing them in the name of the Father and of the Son and of the Holy Spirit, and teaching them to obey everything that I have commanded you" (Matt 28:19-20).

First-century missionary Paul sought to reach people wherever they were. In the streets of Lystra he reminded a crowd that God "has not left himself without a witness in doing good—giving you rains from heaven and fruitful seasons, and filling you with food and your hearts with joy" (Acts 14:17). The NT expresses the universality of God's love and how all are children of God through faith in Christ Jesus, and thus no longer primarily "Jew or Greek, . . . slave or free, . . . male and female" (Gal 3:28).

A Harvest Thanksgiving Psalm

If indeed the Feast of Tabernacles provided an original setting for Psalm 65, it is natural that it should later be used for the Jewish autumn feast called Rosh Hashanah (lit., "the head of the year"). The Orthodox Church has traditionally associated Psalm 65 with the beginning of the church's new year on September 1 and called the date "the crown of the year" (Ps 65:11; Reardon: 127).

North Americans have often used it as a harvest thanksgiving psalm at celebrations of the Thanksgiving Day. While methods of food production have changed, agricultural communities continue to have a high sense of dependency on the God-given rain that waters the earth. Use of this psalm can transcend "our growing habit of thinking of productivity in a technological fashion and allows us to speak of the One upon whose gifts of a fertile earth all our science and economics depend" (Mays, 1994b:221). Such a doxology can prevent the reduction of life to a commodity.

Harvest thanksgiving hymnody draws liberally from Psalm 65. The two-part poem by Anna L. Barbauld, "Praise to God, immortal praise" and "Lord, should rising whirlwinds" (1772), was inspired by Psalm 65:6-13. Other hymns include "We plow the fields and scatter" (Matthias Claudius, 1782), "Sing to the Lord of harvest" (John S. B. Monsell, 1866), and "Creating God, your fingers trace" (Jeffery W. Rothhorn, 1974).

Psalm 66

Come and See. . . .
Come and Hear!

PREVIEW

This liturgy of praise and thanksgiving celebrates the deeds of God in the past (vv. 5-7) and through present trials (vv. 8-12), with a mission thrust for *all the earth* (vv. 1, 4, 16). The theme is *Come and see what God has done* (v. 5) and *Come and hear . . . what he has done for me* (v. 16).

The psalm is composed of two distinct parts, a hymn in praise of God for deliverance of the community (vv. 1-12) and the psalmist's personal testimony (vv. 13-20). Readers have given various explanations for the "we" language of the first part and the "I" language from verse 13 onward: an individual borrowed verses 1-12 as a hymnic introduction to his own prayer of thanks; an individual worshipper's thanksgiving was set within the framework of the liturgy of the annual festival of Yahweh; or the king or some other national figure is the speaker in verses 13-20 at a thanksgiving after a victory or some deliverance (A. Anderson, 1:472).

Reasons given for a postexilic date include the mixed genres (hymn of praise, communal thanksgiving, and individual thanksgiving), the influence of Isaiah 40–66, emphasis on the universality of God's dominion, and the developed ritual and sacrificial system of the temple (W. Taylor: 344). The following outline assumes the unity of the psalm. The exodus has given the people identity and continues to affect and define them in present crises. The psalm invites the nations to acknowledge God's universal rule and join in praise of God.

The liturgical notation *Selah* (vv. 4, 7, 15) marks off significant divisions *[Selah]*. The heading does not identify Psalms 66 and 67 with David, but binds 65–68 with the two labels *A Song* and *A Psalm*. *[Superscriptions]*.

OUTLINE

Summons to Praise for God's Awesome Deeds, 66:1-4
Thanksgiving for Past Deliverance, 66:5-7
Summons to Praise for Present Deliverance, 66:8-12
Vow of Thanksgiving Sacrifice, 66:13-15
Testimony to What God Has Done for the Psalmist, 66:16-20

EXPLANATORY NOTES

Summons to Praise for God's Awesome Deeds 66:1-4

The opening summons to praise is dominated by the imperatives *shout* (NIV), *sing, give glory,* and *say*. These are answered with the description of what they did: *worship, sing, sing* (v. 4). The summons is addressed to *all the earth* since the psalmist holds God to be God of the whole world and of all peoples (vv. 1, 4). This call to the nations and peoples to praise the LORD is pervasive in the psalms (33:8; 47:2; 65:5, 8; 67:4-7; 98:4; 100:1; 148:11).

Thanksgiving for Past Deliverance 66:5-7

At the heart of the recital of God's awesome deeds is the crossing of the Red Sea in the exodus (Exod 14:21-22; 15:1-19) and crossing the Jordan River in the conquest (Josh 3:14-17; 4:19-24). Psalms 114 and 136 also exhibit Israel's memory of this act of deliverance. As the psalm tells the story, the pronoun *they* shifts to *we* (v. 6). Through recital, the events of long ago become the story of the listeners as well.

This story of God's sovereign might and deliverance of his people took place in history. Exodus and conquest, and later exile and return, happened before the eyes of the nations. These great saving acts establish the authority of God over the nations (v. 7). As sentinel of the universe, God's *eyes keep watch on the nations* (v. 7; Pss 11:4; 33:13), challenging any absolutist political claims and arrogant rebellion.

Summons to Praise for Present Deliverance   66:8-12

The psalm turns from the past to a more recent time of testing, in a series of actions: You *tested us, tried us, brought us into the net, laid burdens on our backs, let people ride over our heads,* and as a result *we went through fire and water* (vv. 10-12a). The recital could describe difficult experiences from the Sinai wilderness wanderings to the exile. The trouble is surrounded by two affirmations: You *kept us in the land of the living* (v. 9 NRSV/NEB); . . . *you have brought us to a spacious place* (v. 12b). The history of God's dealing with his people is, at the same time, the history of his judgments. So the song of thanksgiving stays close to pain and rescue. "Testing," alluded to here by the figure of *fire* and *water* (v. 12), is a prominent biblical theme (Gen 22:1; Deut 8:2-3, 16; Ps 26:2). Yet the emphasis is on the release and restoration that comes through God's action (vv. 12, 20). This persevering with God through all disasters, *through fire and through water,* is characteristic of Israel's religion (Westermann, 1989:221).

Vow of Thanksgiving Sacrifice   66:13-15

Here is the shift from first-person plural (*we/us*) to first-person singular (*I/my*) for the rest of the psalm. With the crisis over, the psalmist comes to pay the vows he has promised (vv. 13-14). A vow made in time of distress is a promise to do something for God in return for his saving action. In a vow, life's depths and heights are bound together as a link is forged between the distressed person and God (Gen 28:20-22; Num 21:1-3; Judg 11:30-31; 1 Sam 1:11; 2 Sam 15:7-8).

These verses contain the standard vow of thanksgiving, though the plethora of gifts offered—*fatlings, rams, bulls,* and *goats* (v. 15)—suggests a person of wealth and position, or the psalmist's vow that everything be given to God in return for deliverance. If the psalm was intended to be recited by a variety of individuals, the list need not imply that one person would offer them on a single occasion, but enumerates a variety of animal sacrifices that could be offered. Psalm 66 thus takes a positive attitude toward such sacrifices, whereas Psalm 40 is critical (cf. Pss 50:7-15; 51:15-19).

Testimony to What God Has Done for the Psalmist   66:16-20

Ritual sacrifice of animals was not enough. The psalmist addressed the bystanders, giving testimony to the Lord's intervention (v. 16). He cried out to God (v. 17) and sought to be fully open with God (v. 18). The turning point came when God turned toward him (vv. 19-20).

This is the story of God hearing prayer and in *steadfast love* (*hesed*) coming to the aid of those in need *[Steadfast]*. The goal of the testimony is to call all the earth (v. 1) and the peoples (v. 8) to experience the blessing and join in the praise of God.

THE TEXT IN THE BIBLICAL CONTEXT AND LIFE OF THE CHURCH

Giving Testimony to Saving Deeds

At the core of Psalm 66 is its testimony to God's wondrous deeds of deliverance at the time of exodus, but also in present crises. The worshippers need to tell the story to the nations. The mission theme of acknowledging God worldwide in Psalm 66 suggests affinity with Isaiah 40–66 (e.g., 45:22; 49:6; 56:1-7; 60:1-3; 66:18-23).

The relationship of themes, as well as similar notations in the superscriptions, links Psalms 65–68, four psalms of praise that stand out in contrast to their immediate context, where pleas for deliverance dominate. Wilson (2002:920) has pointed out how the two non-Davidic Psalms 66 and 67 provide the universal perspective needed to shift the national concerns of Diaspora Israel to the universal praise of Psalm 68.

Psalm 66 tells how God deals with his people to rescue and deliver. In retelling God's awesome deeds in the past and present, the story is appropriated in the people's lives as they are made aware of the unbroken relationships through God's steadfast love. Telling the story asserts God's liberation of a people and his help to an individual person. Salvation is through God's *steadfast love* (Ps 66:20), but may also include the *testing* of suffering (vv. 10-12), through which God's people become transformed and ready to respond in joy to faith (1 Pet 1:6-7).

Paul's letter to the Romans can help interpret Psalm 66. In the first eleven chapters, Paul expounds God's salvation as coming through his free grace. In chapter 12, beginning with the word *Therefore,* he turns to God's empowering a "saved" person to take up his own cross, and so to present his body as a living sacrifice in response (Knight, 1:301).

Testimony to the saving events crowns the final book of the Bible in the singing of the song of Moses and the song of the Lamb:

> Great and amazing are your deeds,
> Lord God the Almighty! . . .
> For you alone are holy.
> All nations will come and worship before you. . . .
> (Rev 15:3-4).

Christian Use of Psalm 66

Christians have related the psalm to Jesus' resurrection through the paschal mystery of exodus (v. 6) as well as the reference to *a spacious place* (v. 12). In early Greek manuscripts, a word meaning "of the resurrection" was added to the inscription, suggesting that the psalm was sung on the Feast of the Resurrection in the second or the first century (Reardon: 129). The first four lines from Psalm 66 are still used in liturgies for Easter. Epiphany liturgies include verses 1 and 4.

Hymns alluding to verses 1-4 include "From all that dwell below the skies" (Isaac Watts, 1719) and "Praise God from whom all blessings flow" (Thomas Ken, 1695). Allusions to verses 16-20 are found in "Oh, that I had a thousand voices" (Johann Mentzer, 1704).

Psalm 67

The Blessing—for All Nations

PREVIEW

This community psalm of thanksgiving is prompted by a bountiful harvest (vv. 6-7). It is often linked with Psalm 65:11-13, where the harvest is anticipated. This psalm may have been used at the autumn Feast of Tabernacles, or Booths, which celebrated completion of the agricultural year, recalled Israel's wilderness pilgrimage, and served as a renewal of the covenant (Lev 23:34-36; Num 29:12-38; Deut 16:13-15). A likely setting for this poetic liturgy is the assembled congregation, led by priest and choir, with the congregation joining in the refrain (vv. 3, 5). The mood is celebratory and joyous. In these festivals the people look back to God's mercies, but also look to the future and pray for God's blessings to continue.

An issue for interpretation of Psalm 67 focuses on the form of the verbs in verse 6. Perhaps they describe a past event: *The earth has yielded its increase; God . . . has blessed us* (NRSV). Or perhaps it looks to the future as promise (NIV) or as prayer: *May the earth yield its produce; may God . . . bless us* (NJPS). Alternative interpretations, based on the second reading, identify the psalm as a national lament, a prayer for blessing, even a prayer for rain as in Malachi 3:10 (Dahood, 2:127).

However, more important even than the harvest (already received, anticipated, or prayed for) is the worldwide scope of the prayer for blessing. Words and phrases such as *all nations, ends of the earth,* and *the peoples* appear no less than ten times in the seven verses. The Giver, not the gifts, is central. God's blessing rests on Israel, but the psalmist understands this blessing as a witness to the saving activity of God for all people.

As in Psalm 65, the heading does not identify this psalm with David, but binds Psalms 65-68 with the two labels *A Song* and *A Psalm.* The instruction, *with stringed instruments,* suggests various types of lyres or harps and is found also in headings for Psalms 4; 6; 54; 55; and 76 *[Superscriptions; Musical].*

OUTLINE

Blessing upon an Assembled People and Petition for All Peoples, 67:1-3
Petition for the Nations to Recognize God's Just Rule, 67:4-5
The Universal Blessing and Mission of God, 67:6-7

EXPLANATORY NOTES

Blessing upon an Assembled People and Petition for All Peoples 67:1-3

The opening words recall the Aaronic blessing, the benediction that has blessed people for generations (Num 6:24-26). The worshipping community expected and prayed for blessing from God (Pss 3:8; 28:9; 29:11; 67:1, 6-7; 129:8). Blessing is the support of life in community, in its growth, prosperity, happiness, and well-being. The people expect help from God, who makes *his face to shine,* showing favor and graciousness toward his people (v. 1; 4:6; 31:16; 80:3, 7, 19; 119:135). They appeal that God's *saving power* may come to be known among all nations (v. 2).

Petition for the Nations to Recognize God's Just Rule 67:4-5

The psalm expresses the desire that the nations come to know God as savior (v. 2). God's salvation of Israel revealed his identity as judge and shepherd of the nations (v. 4; 96:10-13; 98:7-9). The Psalm's central verse (4) is framed by the refrain (vv. 3, 5), directing focus on God, who acts in history, judges the people, and guides the nations (Deut 26:5-10). The land and its fertility were the gift of God, who revealed his true character to his people in the course of their history. Through God's just rule, rebellious nations are held in check (Ps 66:7).

The psalm invites the people to acknowledge God as the most powerful God worthy of praise (vv. 4-5). The liturgical word *Selah* may indicate a pause for emphasis or reflection (vv. 1, 4) *[Selah]*.

The Universal Blessing and Mission of God   67:6-7

As an expression of thanksgiving, the people declare: *God, our God, has blessed us,* with copious rain so that there is a bountiful harvest (v. 6 NRSV; Deut 11:11-12, 17; Ezek 34:26-27). The NIV takes it as a future hope, *Then the land will yield its harvest,* and NJPS as a prayer for the future. All peoples should see God's blessing to Israel as reason to revere and praise God (vv. 6-7). Each plentiful harvest is a fulfillment of the promise (Lev 26:4-6) and a pledge that God is with his people Israel and its mission to all peoples (Jer 33:9; Isa 60:3).

The final verse reintroduces the theme that brings together the group of Psalms 56–68. Psalm 67 concludes with the expectation that *all the ends of the earth [will] revere him* (v. 7). Then the following psalm (68) celebrates the universal power and rule of God.

THE TEXT IN THE BIBLICAL CONTEXT AND LIFE OF THE CHURCH

Underlying Traditions

God's blessing for all peoples is a key theme in Psalm 67 and is rooted in the promise to Abraham (Gen 12:1-3). The narrative that follows spells out God's promise: "In you all the families of the earth shall be blessed." Abraham and his heirs were recognized as providing special blessing by foreigners like Abimelech (26:26-28), Laban (30:27), Potiphar (39:3-5), Joseph's jailer (39:21-23) and Jethro (Exod 18:10-12). The OT envisions other nations looking to Abraham's great blessing and wishing a similar one on themselves (Gen 48:20; Ps 72:17).

Similarly, the prophetic tradition proclaims that the salvation of Israel will be a revelation to the nations of the LORD's reign and lead the ends of the earth to praise God (Isa 40:1-5; 45:20-25; 49:22-26).

The Christian tradition drew on this promise of God's blessing for all people. Peter's sermon after Pentecost asserts, "You are the descendants of the prophets and of the covenant that God gave to your ancestors, saying to Abraham, 'And in your descendants all the families of the earth shall be blessed'" (Acts 3:25). Paul interpreted this as a blessing also of the Gentiles through Abraham (Gal 3:8).

Connecting Worship and Mission

This psalm connects worship and mission (Ps 67:1-2). It speaks to the relationship of the inward and the outward, gathering and scattering. In worship, people pray for God's presence in their midst and a pouring out of God's blessings, so they can carry the good news of saving love outward as they scatter.

This was true regarding Israel's praise and mission. "To praise God is the destiny of Israel, because praise includes the confession that God's people know that they are 'absolutely dependent' on Yahweh and that everything which they have received or will receive is the result of his goodness as creator. . . . God's people never celebrate their own glorification, but understand it as the consequence of divine election, destiny and mission in the world" (Kraus, 1986:69, 100).

The church has used Psalm 67 for its missionary purpose, often combining harvest thanksgiving celebrations with mission. We ought to share earthly blessings and also the proclamation of the gospel. The purpose of public worship is to help believers realize God's will to save. It also points to the final harvest at the consummation of the kingdom of God (Matt 9:37-38; John 4:35-38), when all the ends of the earth will fear God and all the nations will praise him in response to the revelation of his salvation (Weiser: 474).

Other NT allusions to Psalm 67 can be found in words about God's witness to all people (Acts 14:16-17; 17:24-28; Rom 1:20), and in the reference to God making his face to shine upon us in Jesus (Heb 1:3). Jesus' words summarize the psalm's purpose: "Let your light shine before others, so that they may see your good works and give glory to your Father in heaven" (Matt 5:16).

A Psalm for the Break of Day

For many centuries Western Christians have recited Psalm 67 at the break of dawn each morning: *May God be gracious to us and bless us and make his face shine upon us.* . . . The Eastern Orthodox Church uses Psalm 67:1-3, along with 66:1-4 and 68:1-3a, as antiphons for Easter. The anonymous hymn, "Lord, bless and pity us" (*Scottish Psalter,* 1912), is a metrical version of Psalm 67.

Psalm 68
Procession Hymn of Praise to the Ascended God

PREVIEW

Psalm 68 stretches the reader. Uncertain texts, bold language, disjointed themes, and elusive allusions confront the interpreter of this psalm. The following comments are suggestive.

In its present form, Psalm 68 appears to be a triumphal hymn, a liturgy for a festival celebration in the temple. The procession described in verses 24-27 points to such a setting. The psalm praises God for his deeds of delivering Israel from Egypt and establishing them in the land, climaxing with the enthronement of the LORD as King in Zion (vv. 17-18). Jerusalem is the new Sinai (v. 29).

Beginning with the marching song of Numbers 10:35, the psalm calls all people to extol the might, the victories, and the glorious character of the God of Israel (vv. 3-4, 32-35). The celebration closes with a call for all nations to praise the Lord.

Interpretations of Psalm 68 include the "eschatological," a hope for the future (Gunkel), or "historical," describing a historic battle, with many variations as to which battle(s). Mowinckel called Psalm 68 a cultic victory thanksgiving psalm. H. Schmidt explained the psalm as a hymnbook for the enthronement and New Year Festival. W. F. Albright saw it as a catalog of thirty first lines of songs composed or adapted from Canaanite originals. Dates suggested for initial composition include eleventh century BC (Kraus), tenth century (Albright), and somewhere in the monarchic period (Weiser; Barth: 473). Commentators acknowledge that verses 30-31 may be a later addition, referring to a current threat from Egypt. The conclusion, with its appeal to the *kingdoms of the earth* (v. 32), may also be late. The presence of the liturgical instruction *Selah* at the conclusion of verses 7, 19, and 32 further appears to set these verses apart as beginning a new section (see outline below) *[Selah]*.

In content and language, this is not a genteel psalm. Military imagery abounds. Thirteen words used here do not appear elsewhere in the psalms (Delitzsch: 244). The list of names for God is impressive: *'ĕlōhîm*, the second most frequent designation for God, is used twenty-three times; *'ădōnāy*, a general title of respect, as in *Lord*, six times; *'ēl*, the generic name for a deity, twice; and once each, *Yahweh*, translated in English Bibles as *LORD*; *Yah*, an abbreviation for the name of God; *Yahweh 'ădōnāy*; and *Yahweh 'ĕlōhîm,* which can be rendered *LORD God [Names of God]*.

OUTLINE

Exultant Call to Praise God, Who Comes to Battle Injustice, 68:1-6
    68:1-3   Let God Scatter the Enemies
    68:4-6   Praise for Protection of the Defenseless
Praise God for Past Deliverance, 68:7-18
    68:7-10   The Wilderness, Sinai, Abundant Rain
    68:11-14   The Divine Word Scatters the Enemies
    68:15-18   God's Ascension to the Holy Mountain
Praise God, Who Daily Bears His People Up, 68:19-31
    68:19-20   The God of Salvation
    68:21-23   Assurance of Deliverance from All Enemies
    68:24-27   Description of God's Entry into the Sanctuary
    68:28-31   Petition for Display of God's Power to Defeat a Present Threat
Concluding Summons for All to Praise the Awesome God, 68:32-35

EXPLANATORY NOTES

Exultant Call to Praise God, Who Comes to Battle Injustice   68:1-6

This psalm of God's manifestation as a divine warrior begins with words from Moses when the ark of the covenant was moved (Num

10:35). God is event, action, and deed, making himself known (v. 1; Pss 9:19; 21:13; 57:5; 94:2; 99:4). Hostile powers have set themselves against God, and the purpose of his intervention is to establish justice (vv. 1-2, 5-6). In God's coming, the utter defeat of the enemies is described (vv. 1-2). Metaphors of *smoke* and *wax* for the wicked denote the ephemeral and unstable.

The summons is to exult the highly exalted One, who rules in all history and takes interest in the lowly (Ps 113). God loves the righteous and restores their joy (v. 3; 32:11; 58:10-11). The coming of God is an occasion of gladness, to be heralded by song (v. 4). *To him who rides upon the clouds* (v. 4), a name given the god Baal, is here used of God (vv. 4, 33; 18:10; 65:11). The divine name LORD (*Yahweh*), its first appearance in the Elohistic Psalter since 64:10, tells us there is no doubt that the God who comes is the LORD of Israel (Wilson, 2002:936). The meaning of *Yahweh*, most fitting for this psalm, is "present to act in salvation."

The God whose power is unmistakably displayed in the storm images (vv. 2, 4; Ps 29) is also the compassionate deity, concerned for individuals who need help (vv. 5-6). God will vindicate the downtrodden, those who do not have the strength and resources to gain justice for themselves (9:9, 12, 18; 10:14). The *desolate* and *prisoners* may refer to Israel in Egypt (v. 6).

Praise God for Past Deliverance   68:7-18

O God, when you went out before your people (v. 7) looks back to the wilderness and Sinai experiences. God led the people like a flock into the Promised Land. This celebration of key events in Israel's salvation story provides only the briefest outline: the wilderness, Sinai, and God's bounty in the well-watered land. The psalm presents God's coming in the form of a theophany (vv. 8-9, 33). A theophany is a description of God's intervention to deliver his people (18:7-15; 29:3-9; 50:2-4; 97:2-5; 114). Its function is to portray the miraculous and overwhelming power of God's intervention *[Theophany]*. In this theophany, the God of Israel is manifested through abundant rain to provide goodness to the people (vv. 8-10).

The divine word scatters the enemies, an echo of Deborah's victory song at the defeat of Sisera (vv. 11-14; Judg 5:28-30). *Kings of the armies* (vv. 12, 14) are among the foes of the LORD (Ps 135:10). The silver *dove* (v. 13) may have been some emblem captured in battle, or perhaps a metaphorical reference to Israel (74:19; Hos 7:11). Zalmon was a hill overlooking Shechem (v. 14; Judg 9:48). Snow on the dark mountain may refer to sun-bleached bones of a defeated enemy. Or an unusual snowfall concurring with victory might be taken as a divine sign.

God as the divine warrior is portrayed as on a celestial march from Sinai (vv. 7-8, 17) to Zion (vv. 18, 24; Ps 132:13-14). *Bashan*, a fertile plateau east of the Jordan, was bordered on the west by what today is known as the Golan Heights. On the north border, Mt. Hermon was highest peak and associated with worship of the Baal gods (Judg 3:3). *The mount that God desired for his abode* (vv. 16-18) appears to refer to Jerusalem, where the ark of the covenant was finally brought in the trek that led from Sinai (2 Sam 7:2; 1 Kings 8:1-11). At least after Solomon's time, *the holy place* would have been so interpreted in processionals.

Praise God, Who Daily Bears His People Up   68:19-31

The second part of the psalm celebrates God's salvation in the present (vv. 19-20). *Blessed be the Lord*, originally an individual's shout of praise, becomes the acclamation of the community (v. 19-20; Pss 31:21; 72:18; 124:6; 144:1). In the word *salvation/deliverance* (NJPS), the psalm can sum up the presence of God in the sanctuary and God's essential nature (3:8). The verses affirm God's sovereign power even over the sphere of death, not only in the escape from the Egyptians (Exod 11–14), but also in God's continuing care for those who belong to him (Ps 116:15). If the liturgical word *Selah* invites a pause for emphasis or reflection, or even recital of a section of national tradition, as suggested by Goulder, the placement of *Selah* in this psalm seems particularly apropos (vv. 7, 19, 32) *[Selah]*.

The victory-poem section begins with the word *'ak*. "Yes, indeed," *God will shatter the heads of his enemies* (v. 21). In this psalm, Egypt appears to be the major enemy, not only in the past, but also perhaps threatening again in the present. *The depths of the sea* (v. 22) with the serpent of the deep may here be a metaphorical reference to Egypt. Verse 30 speaks of the *wild animals that live among the reeds*, likely another reference to Egypt. The *tongues of your dogs* (v. 23) recalls the gruesome scene of dogs lapping up the blood of persons killed, reminiscent of the fate of Ahab and Jezebel (1 Kings 21:19; 22:38; 2 Kings 9:36).

God's triumphant entrance into Zion is pictured as a victory parade, complete with singers, dancers, and instrumentalists (vv. 24-27). It combines images of the victorious king entering his capital city, defeated enemies following in his train, with the cultic procession of celebrants to the Jerusalem temple. Led by representatives from the southern tribes of Benjamin and Judah and the northern tribes of Zebulun and Naphtali, the whole land was represented.

The petition for God to *show your strength . . . as you have done for us before* (v. 28) suggests a current threat. The longing is for victory, for tribute brought to the temple, and for lasting peace (v. 30b). The psalmist calls upon two specific nations to recognize God's authority (v. 31). *Egypt* signifies the traditional oppressors of God's people, and *Cush* (NIV n: Upper Nile region), in the far south, probably stands for people at the far corners of the world. Thus, the whole world is being invited to reach out to embrace the God of Israel (Davidson, 1998:216).

Concluding Summons for All to Praise the Awesome God 68:32-35

The concluding summons to praise (vv. 32-35) is addressed beyond Israel and has a similar worldwide appeal, as does Psalm 67. The final verses about God's voice and awesome power are reminiscent of Psalm 29. There is none like God who gives power and strength to his people. When the victorious God takes up residence in the royal center of the world, other kings come with their tribute. On this confident note, these songs of praise (Pss 65–68) come to an end. This hymn of the LORD's enthronement must have been useful to validate the legitimacy of the Jerusalem king (Brueggemann, 1988:118).

THE TEXT IN THE BIBLICAL CONTEXT AND LIFE OF THE CHURCH

Liberty from Bondage and Formation of a Community

This triumphal hymn of God's march on behalf of his people is rooted in the experience of the exodus from Egypt (Exod 15:1-18). Psalm 68 identifies God as divine warrior, who subdues enemy nations. The story comes to a climax with God in his divine abode (v. 18; cf. Exod 15:17).

God marching on behalf of his people can be found in theophanies as Psalm 18:7-19, where God is graphically portrayed as on a celestial march in behalf of delivering someone in trouble (cf. Hab 3:3-15). In these presentations of God's coming to his people, the motif of water is common—water as chaos and life-destroying (Ps 68:22), but also water as life-giving in abundant rain (vv. 8-10). The psalm ends with affirmation of God's awesome power in creation and history, and the power and strength he gives from his sanctuary (vv. 34-35).

In the NT, the theme of exodus continues. Liberation from bondage and formation of a new community is rooted in the death and resurrection of Jesus (Clifford, 2002:320). Christian readers have seen Psalm 68 as pointing to the new exodus through Christ.

The quotation of Psalm 68:18 in Ephesians 4:8-10 is notable. In the psalm, the victorious LORD demanded and received gifts from the people. In Ephesians, the ascended Christ offers and gives gifts, and the gifts given refer to the various ministries of the church. The application of this text to Christ signifies the proclamation of the lordship of the exalted one throughout the world. The gifts that he distributes in his community have cosmic and universal meaning and effect (Kraus, 1986:201). This quotation of Psalm 68 has led to its use at Pentecost. The Jews have used it in celebration of Pentecost, reading verse 18 as referring to Moses ascending Mt. Sinai and returning to give the torah to Israel.

Use and Misuse of Psalm 68

How does the church read and use a psalm like this, with its triumphal language, portrayal of the divine warrior, and military images? This psalm was a favorite of those leading the Crusades and others who felt they were fighting God's battles. Psalm 68, "Let God rise up," was preferred by Charlemagne, king of the Franks (768-814), and was popular with the Huguenot armies in the sixteenth and seventeenth centuries. Though the violence portrayed has as its purpose preservation of the divine order, people can misuse such psalms if they identify their own interest with God's will.

James Mays' comments are helpful: "The military imagery of the psalm's theology reflects the conditions that were common to its time. Israel existed both as a national state and as people of the LORD. Their corporate security was a religious as well as a political issue.... But in spite of its militant character and victorious confidence, such is not its spirit" (1994b:228).

This psalm begins by declaring that the majestic God is *father of orphans* and *protector of widows* (vv. 5-6). God provides for the needs as a tender shepherd (v. 10). Finally, the awfulness of war is not glorified (vv. 11-14, 23, 30). *Trample under foot those who lust after tribute; scatter the peoples who delight in war* conveys an unmistakable longing for an end to all war. There is no glory in war. The psalm stresses a spirit of dependence upon God. "The song belongs to the lowly, who in the midst of the powers of this world remember and hope for the victory of God. Long after the ark was lost and Israel was no longer a national state, the psalm provided a liturgy of dependence on the power of God for the faithful righteous" (Mays, 1994b:229) *[War]*.

Regarding the mission theme, the church has seen, in the story of the Ethiopian eunuch (Acts 8:27-40), the response prayed for in Psalm 68:31: *Let Ethiopia hasten to stretch out its hands to God.* This same verse provided hope for African-Americans of Christian faith in the time of slavery. In their spirituals, they understood America as Egypt and themselves to be Israel in need of liberation. The KJV reads, "Princes shall come out of Egypt; Ethiopia shall soon stretch out her hands unto God" (Ps 68:31; Holladay: 238).

Psalm 69

The Desperate Cry of God's Suffering Servant

PREVIEW

Desperate petitions to God and descriptions of distress dominate this individual lament. Deathly ill, hounded by false accusations, and ostracized by family, the psalmist is "up to his neck" in deep water and mire, out of which he sees no escape. Only in the LORD's *steadfast love* will one find protection (vv. 13, 16, 29). The psalmist sees his suffering related to his loyalty to God: *For your sake . . . I have borne reproach* (v. 7). *Zeal for your house has consumed me* (v. 9).

The shift comes with verse 30, but not before the psalmist has vented his frustration with a series of curses directed at the enemies who have falsely accused him (vv. 19-29). Now the psalm turns into a vow of thanksgiving. Perhaps a priest delivered an oracle of assurance, or the psalmist's distress has already been resolved. The psalm ends in confidence, with an invitation for all creation to praise God, for God *hears the needy* (v. 33). The final verses illustrate how a lament can move from individual to communal concern.

The situation resembles the times of Jeremiah and his suffering (Jer 5:15-18; 7:1-15; 17:14-18; 18:21-23; 20:8; 23:9; 38:6; 45:3; 51:51). Lamentations 3 describes similar distress. Some interpreters suggest that the psalmist might have been a member of the Jewish community in exile in Babylon (cf. vv. 35-36), or one of the Jews anxious to have the temple rebuilt in the period of reconstruction after

537 BC, or from the time of Ezra in the fifth century BC (Ezra 4:4-5, 23-24; 5:2-3).

Doubling of words conveys the intensity of feelings expressed (vv. 1-13ab are somewhat parallel to vv. 13cd-29). Psalm 69 is similar to Psalms 22 and 102 in mood and theme. Except for Psalm 22, no other psalm is referred to as frequently in the NT as Psalm 69 in relation to the passion of Christ. *According to Lilies* in the heading may refer to a melody (Ps 45) *[Superscriptions]*.

OUTLINE

Call for Help and Initial Lament, 69:1-4
Confession, Petition, and Lament Resumed, 69:5-12
Renewed Plea for Deliverance, 69:13-18
Description of Disgrace Suffered and Petition for Punishment of the Enemies, 69:19-29
Vow of Thanksgiving and Prayer for Zion, 69:30-36

EXPLANATORY NOTES

Call for Help and Initial Lament   69:1-4

The cry *Save me* voices the urgent plea for deliverance from those seeking the psalmist's destruction. With striking metaphors of *deep waters* and *mire* (Pss 32:6; 40:2; 88:7, 17), the psalmist describes his distress (vv. 1-2, 14-15). These are also symbols of the final enemy, death, which is closing in on the writer, accounting for the desperate cries for rescue and the fervent prayers.

Waiting for my God is not silent expectation that there will be a turn for the better (v. 3). It involves calling and crying out until the throat is sore and the eyes are dim with weariness. But to wait means not to give up. The threat lies in *those who hate me without cause* (v. 4; 35:19; 38:19; 41:7). The psalmist appears to be falsely accused of theft.

Confession, Petition, and Lament Resumed   69:5-12

Confession is a part of prayer (v. 5), and while the psalmist pleads innocent to the accusation of theft, he knows of faults in his life (perhaps a temper, sharp tongue, or vindictive spirit, as seen in vv. 22-28). The connection between sin and suffering was deeply engrained in OT thinking (38:3-5), though here the confession sounds more like a protestation of innocence. The *shame* and suffering he has experienced have really been for God's sake (vv. 6-7; cf. Jer 15:15).

Alienation from the family indicates total isolation (Ps 38:11; Job 19:13-15). He claims zeal for the LORD's house (v. 9; Pss 42–43; 84). He has practiced penance (v. 10-11). Yet the insults and accusations have come. Even the elders at the city gate and the drunkards make sport of him (v. 12). Was this an "enthusiast for the sake of the house of the LORD" (Zech 7:3), written off as overly pious by others (Kraus, 1989:62)?

Renewed Plea for Deliverance   69:13-18

The psalmist renews the fervent activity of prayer in the conviction that the LORD's *steadfast love* is good (vv. 13, 16). We hear desperation in the threefold appeal, Answer me (vv. 13, 16, 17). Though one cannot rely on human help, the LORD's help is dependable (vv. 13-14). *The Pit* is the final fate of the lamenter if God does not come to rescue him (vv. 14-15; Pss 28:1; 30:3; 88:4, 6; 143:7).

Thus the psalmist prays that God not be inattentive (vv. 16-18). If God would hide his face, the psalmist would consider that as a sign of divine rejection and punishment for sin (13:1; 27:9; 30:7-8; 44:24; 88:14; 89:46; 102:2; 104:29). In these verses at the heart of the psalm, the suppliant acknowledges total dependence on an answer from God, a response out of his great and powerful love and compassion *[Steadfast]*.

Description of Disgrace Suffered and Petition for Punishment of the Enemies   69:19-29

The psalmist comes to a breaking point. Following the prayer for himself based on God's steadfast love, he utters a bitter prayer for retribution on his enemies. Instead of pity, he has been given poison for food and vinegar to drink (vv. 20-21), a possible reference to the "death meal" offered a dying person. In any case, he breaks, and what follows is the imprecation, a string of nasty wishes upon his persecutors, that God's wrath would exterminate them all (vv. 22-28)! The curses upon the enemy begin with the wish that they be entrapped (v. 22) and that they be stricken blind (v. 23). Let no one live in their tents (v. 25) implies "may they and their families perish." Finally, let there be no acquittal (v. 27). Let them be blotted out of the book of the living (v. 28). The idea of heavenly books that record the good and bad deeds, or the names of the righteous, was well known (56:8; 69:28; 109:13; 139:16; cf. Rev 3:5) [Imprecation].

The reality of enemies who hound the psalmist by trying to do him in is a familiar theme of the psalms (Pss 7:5; 71:11; 109:16; 119:86;

142:6). The psalmist, identifying himself with the lowly, is asking God to set things right by appealing to God's character as loving, faithful, and compassionate (v. 29). In the psalmist's understanding, the law of divine retribution will have God avenge the deeds of the evildoers by their own demise. How that ultimately will happen is left up to God. With verse 29, the psalmist is spent. Only God can save and protect.

Vow of Thanksgiving and Prayer for Zion   69:30-36

The vow of thanksgiving may possibly be a response to an oracle of assurance [Oracle]. The vow is a šîr (song) rather than a šôr (ox, vv. 30-31). The LORD is more pleased with a song that expresses true gratitude than with the finest and best bull! What does God need horns and hoofs for, anyway? The point of the thanksgiving is that other oppressed persons may see and their hearts be encouraged (v. 32). Personal thanksgiving leads to shared thanksgiving. The psalmist's witness points to God's way of forgiveness and deliverance; it calls the congregation to similar worship and praise (Ps 22:21-31). The hearts of those who seek God can revive, for the LORD hears the needy and will answer (v. 33). The psalm's focus is on the poor and needy, the recipients of salvation. They become witness to God's gracious presence, to his transformation of their destiny, and to his effective provision of justice (9:18; 10:17; 18:27; Kraus, 1986:153).

The concluding call to praise broadens the perspective to include the entire universe and the fortunes of Israel (vv. 34-36). The whole creation is called to praise God (v. 34; 97:6; 98:7-8; 148). The psalmist envisions God's salvation of Zion, with reconstruction and repopulation (vv. 35-36). The replacement of animal sacrifice with prayer (vv. 30-31; 51:16-17), the reference to "his captive people" (v. 33 NIV), and the wish that all nations will praise God—these suggest the exile or postexilic period, at least for verses 30-36. The strong hope expressed at the end brings balance to the bitter feelings voiced in earlier verses.

THE TEXT IN THE BIBLICAL CONTEXT AND LIFE OF THE CHURCH

A Psalm to Reflect on the Passion of Christ

Emphasis on the suffering of a devoted servant for God's sake made this psalm well suited for the Christian church in reflecting on the passion of Christ. Like Psalm 22 in its composition and in its use in the NT, Psalm 69 has traditionally been read on Good Friday. Both psalms not only end on the note of praise, but they also look beyond the immediate situation to a wider circle of people for whom God's deliverance will serve as an encouragement.

The NT cites the psalm in four different contexts of Jesus' life and ministry. Jesus quotes verse 9 about "zeal for your house" as he drives the money changers from the temple (John 2:17). When Jesus spoke of the hatred his followers would experience, he cited, "They hated me without a cause" (v. 4; John 15:25). When Jesus was near death on the cross, he said, "I am thirsty," and was offered soured wine. The Gospel writers understood this as a fulfillment of Psalm 69:21 (Matt 27:34, 48; Mark 15:36; Luke 23:36; John 19:29). Acts 1:20 gives an account of the death of Judas that is understood as the fulfillment of Psalm 69:25.

Paul draws on Psalm 69:22-23 as an explanation for the Jewish rejection of Jesus (Rom 11:9-10). Revelation 16:1 refers to the pouring out of God's wrath, expressed as a wish in the psalmist's bitter prayer (Ps 69:24). These are examples of how OT passages were used to enhance insights into the mystery of the work of Christ.

Prayer and the Language of Anger

Since people have often read this psalm as describing the exemplary suffering of an innocent person and as pointing toward Christ, what shall be done with the particularly vehement imprecation of verses 22-28? The Catholic Church's Liturgy of the Hours, a guide for daily prayer, omits these harsh verses. How can we best understand the curse language of such psalms?

First, we must see the psalmist in his times. Little distinction was made between the sinner and his sin. Justice and vindication, the Israelite believed, must come in this world. The covenant God had set before the people included both blessings and curses (Josh 8:34), and the psalmist uses the terminology of the day in depicting the fate of the godless (Deut 27:15-26; 28:15-68; Lev 26:14-39; A. Anderson, 1:506).

Prayers of imprecation have often been called prayers of frustration and include the use of hyperbolic language. The psalmist vents feelings, without suppressing them; the key is that the prayer is offered to God and so is in full compliance with "Vengeance is mine, I will repay, says the Lord" (Deut 32:35; Rom 12:19) *[Imprecation]*.

But ought God's people pray in this way and mete out feelings of vengeance? Jesus, in his passion, prayed for his enemies, "Father, forgive them . . ." (Luke 23:34). Zeal for God, as we know God through Christ, can also stir believers differently, cooling anger rather than kindling it, fostering rather than stifling compassion (Kidner, 1973:248).

This psalm can teach believers about being fervent in prayer, yet respect God's timing (v. 13). Christians need to pray, trusting in the good purpose of God's steadfast love (vv. 13, 16, 29). Finally, even the most desperate prayer can end in doxology.

Psalm 70

O LORD, Make Haste to Help Me!

PREVIEW

This brief psalm of five verses is the desperate prayer of one who needs help immediately. The psalmist petitions God to shame enemies who seek to take his life and desire his ruin. After pleas on behalf of those who seek God, he confesses his dependence upon the LORD as one of the *poor and needy*, those whose only recourse is trust in divine deliverance. The mood of this psalm is urgency.

The lament is identical to Psalm 40:13-17, with only minor variations. The psalm uses *'ĕlōhîm* as the divine name (vv. 1, 4, 5), rather than *Yahweh* (in Ps 40). Psalm 40:17b is an addition. Duplication may have come about in the compiling of separate collections of psalms and placing them for a distinct liturgical purpose. The text of Psalm 70 appears better preserved; its literary completeness suggests that it might have been used in the composition of Psalm 40. Since Psalm 70 is followed by a psalm with no heading of its own and shares common themes, some suggest that it may have been used as an introduction to Psalm 71. In some Hebrew manuscripts, the two psalms are combined and read as one psalm (Wilson, 2002:965-66).

The designation in the title, *for the memorial offering*, is found also before Psalm 38. The term may refer to the memorial portion of a sacrifice (Lev 5:12) *[Superscriptions]*.

OUTLINE

Petition for the Psalmist's Deliverance and Shaming of the Enemies, 70:1-3

Petition for God-Seekers to Rejoice and Deliverance of the Psalmist, 70:4-5

EXPLANATORY NOTES

Petition for the Psalmist's Deliverance and Shaming of the Enemies   70:1-3

The desperate plea, *God, . . . deliver, . . . make haste, . . . help*, appears at the beginning and end of the psalm, thus forming an inclusio of urgency (vv. 1, 5). Fear of those who seek to take one's life is a common element in the laments (v. 2; Pss 35:4; 38:12; 40:14; 54:3; 63:9; 86:14). The enemies in the laments speak taunting words (v. 3; 3:2; 40:15). The psalmist prays that the enemies be shamed by having their schemes exposed in public, so that the frustration will function as a judgment upon them (v. 3). The psalmist desires that God's justice be done and seen *[Imprecation]*.

Petition for God-Seekers to Rejoice and Deliverance of the Psalmist   70:4-5

The psalmist hopes those who seek God will rejoice. Joy is the response to a saving intervention of God. Note the wordplay on *seek* (vv. 2b, 4a, *seek my life* and *seek [God]*). The exclamation of those who love the LORD's salvation, *"God is great!"* (v. 4), contrasts with the *"Aha, Aha!"* of those who mock others. Let God be exulted, declares the psalmist, who then identifies himself with those who are in total dependence on God, *my help and my deliverer* (v. 5).

THE TEXT IN THE BIBLICAL CONTEXT AND LIFE OF THE CHURCH

An Appropriate Prayer

This plea for help in distress is a prayer appropriate to many circumstances in life. In the sixth century, the Rule of St. Benedict prescribed that each of the seven "day hours" should begin with the psalm's opening line: "O God, come to my assistance; O Lord, make haste to help me." This usage became common and carries over to the present time, beginning the Anglican daily Evensong. Some see this verse as a historical forerunner to the "Jesus Prayer," "Lord Jesus Christ, Son of the living God, have mercy on me a sinner" (Reardon: 137).

Believers can use Psalm 70:1 as an invocation to God in the face of any crisis. The entire psalm is bold, direct, and urgent. It exudes assurance of being heard and confidence in a protection that is always present. The Revised Common Lectionary includes Psalm 70 as a reading for Wednesday of Holy Week.

Psalm 71

Do Not Cast Me Off in Old Age

PREVIEW

This prayer song of the individual is classified as a lament, though a sense of confidence permeates the psalm. The song becomes a vow to praise God for his faithfulness (vv. 14-24). The two primary concepts are God's righteousness and praise or joyful thanks.

The writer, an old man (vv. 9, 18), is suffering some illness and is in danger of death (vv. 2, 4, 20). Enemies conspire to accuse him of guilt (vv. 4, 7, 10-11, 13), old age has sapped his energies, and he even fears the Lord may forsake him (vv. 9, 11, 18) *[Enemies]*. He appears to make his petitions from the protection of the sanctuary (vv. 1, 22-23). As musician, the writer may have been consecrated to God from birth, either as a Levite or even a nazirite (Num 6:1-21) (Stuhlmueller, 1983, 1:316).

The psalmist draws on a rich heritage of faith and finds it a safe haven. The verses carry echoes from many of the other psalms: vv. 1-3 (31:1-3a); vv. 5-6 (22:9-10); v. 12a (22:1, 11, 19); v. 12b (38:22; 40:13); v. 13 (35:4, 6); v. 18 (22:20-31); v. 19 (36:6). Psalm 71 is characterized by alternating requests, statements of confidence, trust, and vows. This familiarity with the language of worship and the mixing of psalm forms suggests a postexilic date. In its present form, such a confident lament would have spoken for the communities of faithful Israelites struggling with the oppression of exile (Tate, 1990:212).

Psalm 71

This is the first psalm since Psalm 43 without a heading. It may have been connected to Psalm 70, which served to introduce the more extensive plea of Psalm 71 [*Superscriptions*].

OUTLINE

An Elderly Person Appeals for Help, 71:1-13
    71:1-4   Petition for Deliverance (from Position of Trust)
    71:5-8   Declaration of Trust and Continuous Praise to God
    71:9-13   Petition Not to Be Cast Off (by Age, Enemies, or God)
Song of Praise for God's Mighty Deeds, 71:14-24
    71:14-18   Declaration of Trust and Hope for Continuous Praise to God
    71:19-21   Declaration of Confidence That the Prayer May Be Heard
    71:22-24   Vow of Praise to God in Song and Word

EXPLANATORY NOTES

An Elderly Person Appeals for Help   71:1-13

While the anxieties of old age (vv. 9, 18) are an important part of this psalm (diminished energies, nearness to death, feeling abandoned), the dominant themes of this psalm are confident trust, hope, and praise. The words *praise, praising,* or *praises* appear eight times. There are thirteen references to giving testimony to faith in God. While his fears are real, the psalmist meets them by hiding in God as refuge (v. 1), calling upon God for rescue (v. 4), relying on God's righteousness (v. 2), and pleading with God to draw near (v. 12; White: 109).

The petition for deliverance, for freedom and protection, begins with a formulaic expression: *In you, O LORD, I take refuge.* This is rooted in the custom of seeking asylum and protection in the sanctuary (v. 1; 1 Kings 1:49-53; 8:31-34). God is implored to turn his ear and hear the petition (v. 2b; Ps 31:2-3a). The appeal is to God's righteousness (vv. 2a, 15, 16, 19, 24), a juridical term meaning "performing or upholding right." The words *deliver, rescue, save* (v. 2) describe the hoped-for deliverance by God as a function of the divine righteousness to care for the poor and oppressed [*Righteous*]. The writer trusts that God rules the world, not the wicked (v. 4).

Speaking from the experience and vulnerability of waning years, the psalmist gives witness to divine care from birth to old age (vv. 5-8). *My hope* suggests a future with God, who is the only reliable object of trust (v. 5; Jer 29:11). God is depicted as a caring midwife (v. 6).

The words *continually* (vv. 6, 14), *all day long* (vv. 8, 15, 24), and praise *yet more and more* (v. 14) underscore a lifetime of praise.

The psalmist sees his life as an example, as *a portent to many* (v. 7). It is not clear if others have regarded the psalmist as a sign of God's favor or an example of divine punishment. The Hebrew word *môpēt* may be used for an extraordinary occurrence or a warning. In this context, perhaps the latter is meant (Deut 28:45-46). However, it could also mean that though some saw his suffering as a warning, he viewed God as his refuge and will continue to do so into the future. *Do not cast me off* is an appeal not to be excluded from fellowship with God (v. 9). The trouble is a conspiracy of verbal and false accusations (vv. 10-13). Pursuit by enemies, whose intent is the person's destruction, is a familiar theme in laments (Pss 7:5; 69:26; 109:16; 119:86; 142:6). To pray that enemies be shamed is to pray that their plans be thwarted (v. 13).

Song of Praise for God's Mighty Deeds   71:14-24

But I will hope . . . introduces the shift in the psalm and states the psalmist's perspective: continual hope and praise (v. 14). This is expectant, waiting hope (130:7). It is an active hope, so the psalmist will continue to praise God *yet more and more*. He insists on proclaiming the Lord's *righteousness,* or *saving/mighty acts* (vv. 15-16, 19, 24 REB), here referring to the deliverance of the psalmist. Reflecting on God's protective care since infancy (vv. 17-18), the psalmist is convinced that God will not abandon him even in old age.

God's *wondrous deeds* (v. 17) and *great things* (v. 19) suggest the exodus miracle (Exod 15:11). The rhetorical question, *Who is like you?* implies the answer, "No one!" (v. 19). So present *troubles* are placed in a larger context (v. 20). *Depths of the earth* refers to the subterranean waters of chaos, representing the arena of death in ancient Near Eastern thought. *Revive me, bring me up again, increase my honor, comfort me*—these are phrases of hope about deliverance from a life-threatening circumstance. We are not to lose faith when God lays suffering upon us, because God will certainly "bring us back to life" again (Deut 32:39; Knight, 1:328).

His illness healed, the psalmist performs a thanksgiving ritual in the temple (vv. 22-24; Pss 50:14; 56:12). The praise of God has been his passion. He will continue to praise the God characterized by *faithfulness* that spans life from the cradle to the grave (vv. 22, 6). The name *Holy One of Israel* (v. 22) is rarely found outside Isaiah, where it is used twenty-five times; it appears also in Psalms 78:41 and 89:18. At the end, the psalmist's faith has not been defeated. God has not abandoned the worshipper. The final verse ends in assurance of rescue: those who wanted to harm him have been put to shame and disgraced (v. 24; 70:1-3), suggesting that Psalms 70–71 may have been intended to be read together.

THE TEXT IN THE BIBLICAL CONTEXT AND LIFE OF THE CHURCH

The Incomparable God

The psalmist, in considering present trials, recalls how, over the span of a lifetime, God has been faithful (Ps 71:17-22). Even more, from the very beginning of the people of God, *the Holy One of Israel* has delivered his people (Exod 15:11). Israel's God is incomparable among the gods who compose the heavenly council (Exod 12:12; Pss 82:1; 86:8; 89:5-8).

The question *O God, who is like you?* (71:19; 77:13) must be understood against a background where polytheism was the dominant paradigm. For the Hebrew people, the LORD (Yahweh) was not only in a class by himself among the deities; he also was the great God of creation and the Lord of history. In Psalm 71, the psalmist's confidence is founded on awareness of God's righteousness (vv. 16, 19, 24). God's mighty acts include, first of all, his "putting things right." The righteousness of God is his will for order and fairness in all the realms. To this aspect and activity of God's character, the poor and oppressed dared appeal in the hope of deliverance, protection, and restoration of life.

In the life of the church, Psalm 71, along with Psalms 22 and 31, has been associated with the passion of Jesus and used during services of Holy Week. We can hear a NT echo of verse 10 in Matthew 27:1, where the chief priests and elders confer together against Jesus in order to bring about his death. Some have seen the psalm as pointing to the resurrection (vv. 19-20). The psalm ends on a clear note of God's victory over evil (v. 24).

A Favorite Psalm for the Elderly

This psalm, written by one who is old, is a favorite among the elderly. Part of the grace of old age is to look back on a wealth of experience and draw new hope from it. Self-control and faith keep this psalmist from cursing his enemies (as in Ps 69). The tone is tranquil. The years often have a mellowing effect. A person who has experienced the marvelous faithfulness of God for a lifetime is prepared for whatever the future holds.

Older persons have learned the paradox that dependence on the Lord is the secret to freedom. Those who have stored up in their memory the poetry of Scripture and hymns have a rich resource on which to draw. This psalm encourages praying the psalms as a source of consolation, hope, and inspiration.

The practice of praise produces inner beauty and strength. Praying the psalms increases the awareness that God remains faithful. Paul, after being beaten at Philippi, sang songs of praise during the night in his jail cell. In the second century AD, Polycarp, Bishop of Smyrna, was ordered to curse Christ or die. He responded, "For eighty-six years I have been serving him, and he has done me no wrong. How then can I blaspheme my King who has saved me?" (*Martyrdom of Polycarp* 9.3).

The Anabaptists of the sixteenth century chose to sacrifice their lives and property rather than violate Christ's commandment "to love one another." Thieleman J. van Braght's *Martyrs Mirror* tells these stories of men and women, who in the midst of such trials, continued to praise God.

Psalm 72

Prayer for the King: May Righteousness Flourish and Peace Abound!

PREVIEW

This royal psalm is a prayer of intercession for the king, perhaps composed for a coronation or its annual commemoration.

Psalm 72 expresses the prophetic ideal. The king's job description is to enact God's purpose, to govern with justice and righteousness (vv. 1-3, 7), resulting in *shalom* (šālōm), translated as *prosperity* (v. 3) and *peace* (v. 7). *Shalom* will be measured especially in terms of the attention given to the poor and needy (vv. 2, 4, 12-14). Using common images and terminology about ancient Near-Eastern kingship, the psalm expresses hyperbolic wishes for the longevity of the king or his dynasty (v. 5), the extent of his dominion (vv. 8-11), and the durability of his fame (v. 17). Such a broad and idealized portrait of the king has given rise to messianic interpretations of the psalm (see below).

The title, *Of Solomon* (only here and for Ps 127), was likely assigned to this psalm because of verses that can be applied to Solomon (vv. 1, 8, 10, 15) *[Superscriptions]*. For the reign of Solomon, who greatly expanded the kingdom of his father David, see 1 Kings 1–12. Solomon's reign appears to echo Psalm 72:7-8 in terms of peace and dominion, and even the name *Solomon* (*šĕlōmōh*) means "peaceable." Yet there was also oppression and exploitation, with the people finally refusing to pledge continued loyalty to the crown (1 Kings 11–12). Since the king in Psalm 72 is David's descendant, the psalmist could have composed this for a later king of Judah. Worshippers might then have repeated the liturgy at different royal occasions to commend the office and vocation of kingship.

The psalm closes with what appear to be later additions by compilers of the Psalter, since they bring closure to book II of the Psalms (vv. 18-19, 20).

OUTLINE

Introduction: Petition for a Just Reign, 72:1-4
Petition for a Long and Beneficent Reign, 72:5-7
Petition for a Worldwide Reign, 72:8-11
Statement About the King as Deliverer of the Needy, 72:12-14
Conclusion: Petition for the Fulfillment of the Patriarchal Blessing, 72:15-17
Doxology and Compiler's Notation, 72:18-20

EXPLANATORY NOTES

Introduction: Petition for a Just Reign   72:1-4

The intercession is addressed to God on behalf of the king, who is to be guarantor of justice for the helpless. The prayer moves on in a series of wishes for the king's reign, *May he . . .* (vv. 1-5, 8-11, 15-17). The NIV and NEB translate most of the petitions as statements, *He will/shall. . . .*

The ancients in the Near East considered the king to be the viceroy of God. The king became highest judge and final court of appeal (2 Sam 8:15; 1 Kings 3:16-28). The writer leaves no doubt about the king's role. The first priority, the foundation on which all else depends, is *justice* and *righteousness*. The king shows justice in caring for the poor (vv. 2, 4, 12). The psalm focuses on social responsibility of the new ruler. God is the source of right rule, and the monarchs who allow themselves to be so empowered will rule so that the defenseless are protected, the oppressor crushed, and the whole land experiences *shalom* (Wilson, 2002:986-987). The Hebrew word *shalom* (*šālôm*), here translated *prosperity* (v. 3, NRSV, NIV), means *well-being* (NJPS) in the sense of completeness and wholeness.

Petition for a Long and Beneficent Reign   72:5-7

The intercession appeals for the long life of the king or dynasty (vv. 5, 15-17; Pss 61:6; 89:36-37). A just and righteous king is as great a blessing to his people as the *rain* and *showers* are to the soil, to bring forth abundance and prosperity (vv. 6-7, 16). Ancient Near Eastern thought bound up the health, fertility, and success of a nation with the well-being of its monarch (2 Sam 23:1-7).

Petition for a Worldwide Reign   72:8-11

True *peace* (*šālôm*, v. 7) involves freedom and security from domination by foreign oppressors. In the psalms, Israel perceives herself as surrounded by nations and kings of the earth, who will come to cringe and *lick the dust* before the king (v. 9; Ps 18:44-45).

The geographical references identify wishes for the worldwide rule of the king (vv. 8-11). They represent all the world from east (*the River* = Euphrates) to west (*Tarshish* = in Spain and *the isles* in the Mediterranean), and from north (*Lebanon*, v. 16) to south (*Sheba* = south Arabia, and *Seba* = in Africa, perhaps Ethiopia). The king does not necessarily conquer the nations. Rather, "as representative of the Most High God, he receives their tribute, which is ultimately intended to honor God" (Clifford, 2002:333). The theme of the world's people coming to worship God in Jerusalem appears also in Zechariah 8:20-23 and 14:16-17.

Statement About the King as Deliverer of the Needy 72:12-14

The psalmist returns to the theme of the opening petition for a just reign (vv. 2, 4). It is the king's duty to answer the cry of the needy and to be a helper to those who have no other help. He is responsible to protect their *blood*, their life (v. 14). The righteous king will not allow those on the margins to be oppressed. These verses suggest the king's move beyond legal aid to saving intervention.

Conclusion: Petition for the Fulfillment of the Patriarchal Blessing   72:15-17

The king's establishment of justice is life-giving, so people are asked to pray for him continually. The petitions invite tribute from all over the world (1 Kings 10:2, 10), prosperity in the land, and finally, that the patriarchal blessing (Gen 12:1-3; 22:18-19) be known among all nations through the reign of the king. The king's *name* means both his fame and his progeny (v. 17). Psalm 72 views the ultimate purpose of the monarch in terms of the fulfillment of God's purpose for the whole creation (Ps 47:8-9; Isa 2:2-4; 19:23-25).

Doxology and Compiler's Notation   72:18-20

A doxology ends the psalm (vv. 18-19). *Blessed be the LORD, . . . who alone does wondrous things* may initially have been a shout of praise (Pss 66:20; 68:19; 144:1). The doxology entreats God to fill the whole earth with his glory as reminder that God alone is the giver of life, justice, and power.

Book II of the Psalter concludes with the doxology and a compiler's note about when *this* collection of Davidic psalms was completed, before the final compilation of the Psalter (v. 20). We find eighteen more psalms *of David* in Psalms 86 to 145. Royal Psalms 2 and 72 frame books I and II of the Psalter (with Psalm 1 introducing the whole Psalter). Another royal psalm (89) concludes book III. These royal psalms call attention to God's reign at strategic points in the Psalter; they lead up to the climactic proclamation of God's reign (Pss 93, 95-99) that forms the theological heart of the book of Psalms (McCann, 1996:963). Even though the monarchy may have ended by the time of the compiler's work, the royal psalms were not discarded; instead, they were reread as announcements of the future king and expressing the hopes for the messianic age (Stuhlmueller, 1983, 1:319) *[Composition].*

THE TEXT IN THE BIBLICAL CONTEXT AND LIFE OF THE CHURCH

Ruling in Justice and Righteousness

At the heart of the prayer for the king's rule is the focus on justice and righteousness. The essential nature of social justice in the service of God appears throughout the OT (Exod 2:23-25; Isa 1:12-17; Amos 5:14-15, 24). Jeremiah admonished the King of Judah: "Execute justice in the morning, and deliver from the hand of the oppressor anyone who has been robbed. . . . And do no wrong or violence to the alien, the orphan, and the widow, or shed innocent blood" (Jer 21:11; 22:3).

Justice is not simply the pursuit of fairness and punishment of offenders, but also concern for the victims of harsh and evil treatment. Justice has to do with safeguarding creation order. Doing justice involves correcting deviations, particularly when they lead to deprivation of the poor. The existence of the poor is an affront to the generous God who created a bountiful world. "Biblical justice is interventionist, in contrast to the modern Western notion of justice as disinterested decisions" (Clifford, 2002:332). Royal justice as portrayed in Psalm 72 draws on the righteousness of God and favors the poor and the weak *[Judge; Righteous]*.

We can apply this prayer for the king's just rule to government leaders in every generation. The NT urged that "supplications, prayers, intercessions, and thanksgivings be made for everyone, for kings and all who are in high positions" (1 Tim 2:1-2). Psalm 72 is appropriate for chaplains to pray in government chambers. The psalm is supportive of good government, but also nudges rulers to know their job description before God.

Messianic Interpretations

Early Jewish exegetes, as well as the early church, understood this psalm as messianic. It is often used in prayers for Christmas, Epiphany, Holy Thursday, and Christ the King Sunday.

While written as a prayer for the king, the messianic interpretations are understandable. The impossible idealized role of king depicted in Psalm 72 gave rise to belief in the "One to come" (Isa 11:1-9), for no king in history fulfilled the hopes outlined. The early Christian community had no difficulty in seeing Jesus as the anointed one, the messiah in the line of David (Matt 2:9-11; Mark 12:35-37; Luke 1:32-33; 11:31). In Jesus they saw God's deliverer, in whom the reign of God on earth, in the people of God, and among the nations finds its fulfillment (Kraus, 1989:81) *[Anointed]*.

While messianic interpretations have appeal, they should not detract from a clear message in this psalm about *shalom* as the fullest integration of life's blessings, from God and the human family. The Bible continually calls persons and nations to wholeness. Psalm 72 is a reminder that God's gifts focus on fertility and life, tenderness and justice. Prosperity of a people can be a reality only when we all share love and concern with those in need.

A key interpretive issue has to do with the incongruity between Psalm 72 and the historical realities. Brueggemann (1988:68-74) calls attention to how the royal liturgy shapes the king. The psalm is closely linked to the memory of hurt (vv. 1-4, 12-14), but also deeply informed by the grand dream of the royal vision. Unfortunately, kings tend to be more attracted to majesty than to mercy. First Kings 4:20-28 echoes Psalm 72. However, the narrative also tells about "forced labor" (1 Kings 11:28) and the "heavy yoke" placed on the people

(12:4). In the end, Solomon's kingdom (and David's dynasty) suffered division. In spite of Nathan's great prophecy about the royal house of David (2 Sam 7), more than half of the kingdom broke away after the death of David's first successor (Solomon). No Davidic king reigned again after the fall of Jerusalem in 586 BC. Solomon's vaunted wisdom as ruler (1 Kings 3–4) did not last even to the end of his lifetime. Brueggemann (1988:73) points to Ezekiel 34 as "a *responsive alternative* out of the memory of hurt to the failed monarchy." Ezekiel, prophet of the exile, calls for God to do what Jerusalem's kings were to do, but did not—to care for the weak and vulnerable and give them a place in the community, as a faithful shepherd tends the flock.

For believers, Jesus is the clearest sign that God rules the world. They profess him to be the one who proclaimed and ultimately embodied the reign of God by defending the poor and needy, by offering peace, and by inviting all nations to be blessed. So the church prays, "Your kingdom come . . ." (Matt 6:10). And so the church sings the glorious mission hymns based on Psalm 72, "Jesus shall reign" (Isaac Watts, 1719) and "Hail to the Lord's Anointed" (James Montgomery, 1821).

Book Three
Psalms 73-89

Psalm 73

Nevertheless—the Great Affirmation

PREVIEW

Psalm 73 may well be one of the most remarkable and satisfying of all the psalms. Wrestling with the topic of theodicy, God's justice in an unjust world, the writer comes to a position of trust and confidence. It is a psalm that fits the condition of many who struggle through doubt to greater understandings of God's will and way.

Often identified as a wisdom psalm because of its themes of the two ways and God's justice and retribution, in style it resembles a thanksgiving. Much of the psalm is personal narrative, including confession, thanksgiving, and witness. In the end, the psalm becomes a reflective testimony, providing others in the community with guidance and insight regarding the problem of the disparity between faith and experience.

Psalm 73 begins with the reason for the poet's grateful prayer: *Truly God is good to the upright* (v. 1). But then the psalmist wrestles with the question of faith's validity (vv. 2-12). What difference does God make? How can one reconcile the justice of God with the inequities in this world, including personal suffering? The insight of a larger perspective comes in the sanctuary (vv. 13-17). The psalmist finds himself in God's love and care, and that is sufficient—the good above all earthly goods (vv. 18-28). The real theme of the psalm "is not the suffering, toiling individual, but the gracious God who rescues those who trust him" (Kraus, 1986:169).

Psalm 73

This psalm introduces the collection of Asaph psalms (Pss 73–83 plus 50). Asaph is mentioned elsewhere as a singer and cymbal player, and chief among David's musicians (1 Chron 6:31-32, 39; 15:16-19; 16:4-7; 25:1-2; 2 Chron 5:12) *[Asaph; Superscriptions]*.

The psalm opens book III of the Psalter. In addition to the major collection of psalms associated with Asaph, book III contains four psalms associated with the sons of Korah (84–85, 87–88), one connected with David (Ps 86), and one with Ethan (Ps 89). Book III is still part of the Elohistic Psalter and contains a number of communal laments (Pss 74; 79; 80; 83; and elements of 85 and 89) *[Composition]*.

OUTLINE

The Problem, 73:1-12
Transition, 73:13-17
The Resolution, 73:18-28

EXPLANATORY NOTES

The Problem   73:1-12

This carefully crafted psalm sparkles with striking word pairs, used in contrast or as links to meaning. The *good* (v. 1) is much more clearly defined by the *good* of being *near God* (v. 28). Observe *truly* (vv. 1, 18), *as for me* (vv. 2, 28), or the *indeed* (*behold*) with which verses 12 and 27 begin (Heb., NASB). No one will want to miss the six uses of *heart* (vv. 1, 7, 13, 21, 26, 26). Significant shifts in the psalm appear in verses 2, 17, and 23.

The psalm begins with a proverb stating the ancient wisdom thesis: *God is good to the upright* (v. 1). This is the worldview of an order to life that, for those who align themselves with God's purposes, some payback in the form of reward can be expected (Ps 1; Prov 12:21; Isa 3:10). An alternative reading retains God is good *to Israel* from the Hebrew (NIV, NRSV n, NJPS). We should not reduce the psalm to personal experiences alone; it can also speak for Israel, as it did particularly during and after the exile.

If the declaration of the first verse is also the conclusion of the psalm, as suggested by some interpreters (Brueggemann, 1984:116), then the psalmist invites the hearer to hear how he came to find out that faith holds, and what God's good truly is. The confession indicates a close call (vv. 2-3). The psalmist had become envious of the success of the wicked. He was on the slippery slope of buying into common wisdom: self-interest and materialism (vv. 6-7, 12).

The psalm describes the wicked as enjoying the popularity that often comes with success. In their arrogance, they refuse to accept any authority or restraint (vv. 4-9). They deny having any responsibility toward God (vv. 10-11; Pss 10:11; 64:6; 94:7). In their lifestyle, they talk big, eat and drink freely, and worship power as the path to happiness (v. 12) *[Wicked]*.

Transition   73:13-17

The psalmist thus wrestled with feelings of envy until weariness almost overcame him (vv. 13-16). Here the Hebrew text marks the transition: the same word (*'ak*) begins verses 1, 13, and 18; the NRSV translates it as *truly/all/truly*, and NIV thrice as *surely*. The one praying has been smitten with severe sorrows and is near despair (vv. 14, 26). He has already washed his hands in a ritual act of innocence (v. 13; Ps 26:6), sure that he has *kept [his] heart clean*. In the first direct address to God (v. 15), he claims identity as a member of God's people, in *the circle of your children* (Deut 14:1).

A visit to the sanctuary saved him by providing a broader perspective (v. 17). Led to the sanctuary by solidarity with God's people, he entered the powerful presence of God. Here his efforts to understand (v. 16) were supported by worship. Now he perceived the fate of the wicked.

The Resolution   73:18-28

Though tempted to throw in his lot with the wicked, the experience in the sanctuary dissuaded him from falling into the world of the dead. Will a life of ease and pleasure, and all the things that fat bank accounts can provide, stand up in the end? In a moment health and wealth can be swept away like a dream that evaporates (vv. 18-20). The psalmist is chagrined at his own temptation to such slippery thinking (vv. 21-22).

Nevertheless! "Yet," the psalmist is saying, *I am continually with you* (v. 23). The relationship in God's love and care provides friendship, honor (*right hand*, v. 23), *counsel*, and at the end—*God* (vv. 24-26). In worship he discovers that faith depends not on his fragile grasp of God, but on God's sure grasp of him. In short, as Martin Luther translated verse 26, "as long as I have thee, I wish for nothing else in heaven or on earth."

Did the psalmist think here of life after death? Likely not in terms of resurrection, but the idea of life after death was not some unheard-of novelty (Ps 49:15) and may also be explored here (Rad, 1962:406).

In any case, the psalmist belongs to God, and nothing can destroy the communion of life given by God (Kraus, 1989:93). God guides his course of life. His future is in the care of God. Here he celebrates not an individual's faith, but what God does for him.

As in many laments, the final request is two-sided, corresponding to the blessing and the curse (vv. 27-28; 1:6). In contrast to those *far from [God]* who face destruction, the everlasting shalom is *to be near God*. In the last line the psalmist in effect vows, "I will tell!" In spite of suffering and pain and struggle and doubt, he can now say, *But for me it is good to be near God*. With *the Lord* ['ădōnāy] GOD [*Yahweh,* only here in Ps 73] as his *refuge*, the psalmist is now prepared to go out and recite all the good stories of God's grace!

THE TEXT IN THE BIBLICAL CONTEXT AND LIFE OF THE CHURCH

God and the Prosperous Wicked

What is one to do with the oft-expressed convictions of faith when these clash with everyday experience? What is one to do when old answers no longer fit present realities? We often relate Psalm 73 to the books of Job and Habakkuk and Psalms 37 and 49 because it deals with the issue of the justice of God in a world where evil exists and appears to prosper.

Abraham articulated the issue: "Shall not the Judge of all the earth do what is just?" (Gen 18:25). The book of Job offers several practical answers to the problem of theodicy: human ignorance, divine mystery, corrective discipline, delayed punishments and rewards. However, it acknowledges the problem as an insolvable enigma, before which the best response is silence in the presence of a self-revealing creator (Job 42:1-6). Habakkuk, prophesying at the end of the seventh century BC, had to deal with the question of an invading foreign power as judgment against Judah (Hab 1:6-11). He concluded that God is still sovereign and in God's own way and at the proper time will deal with the wicked (3:2-19).

Psalm 37 responds to the problem of theodicy by acrostic repetition of the certainty of retribution. Psalm 49 appeals to mystery and the transience of human life. In Psalm 73, the focus is on the deity's presence in the sanctuary and assurance of God's goodness. According to the psalmist, the affluence of evil people has no more substance than images in a dream that pass away upon awaking. The psalmist emerges from the darkness with a mighty shout: "If I have you, I want nothing else." This is a new and different attitude: "One must hold fast to God and continue to trust Him even when one no longer understands what He is doing" (Westermann, 1989:145).

"Nice guys finish last!" That dictum flashed on bumper stickers has deep roots and a long history. The "me generation" has been reared on the goals of fit bodies, sports cars, and "spend now." Even TV evangelists promote the success image as possible for everyone. But materialism is flawed. It can put food on the table, but it does not guarantee fellowship around the table. It can provide a house, but not a home. It can adorn people with fine things, but not with love. "Materialism generates the notion of loving things and using people" (Wyrtzen: 207). Psalm 73 conveys another perspective, confirmed by Jesus in the Sermon on the Mount (Matt 5:3-10; 6:24-33).

Into the Sanctuary of God

An anonymous text from a hymnal published in 1880 appears to summarize the experience of the writer of Psalm 73:

> I sought the Lord, and afterward I knew
>   he moved my soul to seek him, seeking me.
> It was not I that found, O Savior true,
>   no, I was found of thee.

What happens when worshippers go *into the sanctuary of God* (v. 17)? For some there may be a mystical experience, an encounter with the holiness of God. Many find in the liturgy help toward a new orientation, a new world. As God's people gather for praise and prayer, they often receive new understandings of God's moral requirements beyond self-sufficiency, affluence, and autonomy. For the psalmist, it was not enough to try to think it through (v. 16). Though the questions and doubts were catalyst to a more mature faith, understanding came when surrounded by the community in the presence of God. Jesus spoke of "the pure in heart" as those who "will see God" (Matt 5:8). Seeing God is the desired goal as worshippers enter into the holy mysteries, whether in public places of worship or when approaching God in solitude.

What does it mean to be *near God* (v. 28)? The psalmist's great affirmation is emphatically underscored by Paul's magnificent confession: "For I am convinced that neither death, nor life, nor angels, nor rulers, nor things present, nor things to come, nor powers, nor height, nor depth, nor anything else in all creation, will be able to separate us from the love of God in Christ Jesus our Lord" (Rom 8:38-39).

Additional Perspectives

Some scholars see Psalm 73 as standing at the center of the Psalter theologically as well as canonically. The psalm reinforces the central message already offered in Psalms 1–72: "that goodness means to live not in dependence upon oneself but in taking refuge in God" (2:12; 73:28; McCann, 1996:968).

For further study, I commend several extended essays on Psalm 73, by Leslie Allen (1982), Walter Brueggemann (1984:115-21), Martin Buber (1953:31-50), Hans-Joachim Kraus (1986:168-75), and Elmer Martens (1983).

Psalm 74

Remember Your Congregation

PREVIEW

This community prayer song of lament bewails the destruction of the temple by a foreign invader. Among the suggested historical settings for the psalm, here are two: (1) the looting (169 BC) and profaning of the temple (167 BC) by Antiochus Epiphanes (Dan 11:31; 12:11; 1 Macc 1:16-24, 54, 59; 9:27; 2 Macc 6:4-5); and (2), more probably, the destruction of city and temple by the Babylonians in 587 or 586 BC (2 Kings 25:9; Isa 64:10-11). The temple lay in ruins until rebuilt in 520–515 BC. The psalmist may have composed this prayer for services of mourning at the site of the temple ruins some years after the destruction took place (vv. 1, 3, 9).

The psalm is in three parts, beginning with the complaint to God and description of the situation (vv. 1-11). The hymn, affirming trust, proclaims God's power in creation and history (vv. 12-17). The psalm ends with a second passionate appeal for God to rise up and act (vv. 18-22). After the initial *"Why?"* about God's *anger* (v. 1), the two appeals are introduced by *remember* (vv. 2, 18). The creation hymn in the middle is a reminder of God's power over chaos. From the beginning, the psalmist expresses bewilderment over the contradiction between God's *anger* leading to this apparent rejection, and the divine love, which originally made Judah *the sheep of [God's] pasture*. But most of all, God's name and honor are at stake (vv. 7, 10, 18, 22). In the end, even with the temple in ruins, the psalmist can cry out to *God my King* (v. 12) and dare to hope that the silent, absent God will yet act (v. 22).

The heading identifies Psalm 74 as *A Maskil of Asaph.* The term *Maskil* occurs in the superscription of twelve psalms and may mean "a didactic song" or "artistic song" *[Asaph; Superscriptions].*

OUTLINE

The Complaint and Appeal to God, 74:1-11
    74:1-3   Lament of Abandonment by God
    74:4-8   Graphic Description of the Temple's Destruction
    74:9-11   Lament of Bewilderment at God's Silence and Inaction
Hymn to God's Power in History and Creation, 74:12-17
Concluding Appeal for God's Intervention, 74:18-23

EXPLANATORY NOTES

The Complaint and Appeal to God   74:1-11

The complaint questions *Why?* and *How long?* frame the first part of the psalm (vv. 1, 10-11). Why has God's *smoking* wrath been turned against the *sheep* of his pasture (Ps 79:13; Jer 23:1)? The devastation of city and temple means not only the fearsome experience of encountering the wrath of God (Ps 80:4), but also the feeling of being forsaken and rejected by God (60:1-3; 77:7-10) *[Wrath].*

The psalmist appeals to God to *remember* two great facts, the redemption of his people from Egypt and God's dwelling in their midst (v. 2). How is it possible that this sacrilegious vandalism should go unpunished? He pleads for God to come and look at the destruction (v. 3), but most of all, for God to do something now! Let God intervene once again for his defeated and scattered people!

In graphic detail the psalmist describes the beastly devastation (vv. 4-8). One can hear the gleeful shouts of the crazed marauders and the hacking axe blows upon the glorious temple (Jer 46:22-23). This symbol of God's dwelling for nearly four hundred years is quickly burned into a pile of rubble. And to eradicate the worship of God completely, the vandals even burned the local shrines in the villages of Judah. As in the opening complaint, the purpose of the description is to move God to action.

The complaint resumes: *We do not see our emblems*—the ark, the temple, the priests, and prophets (vv. 9-11). Now only the military emblems of the enemy mark the temple ruins, and God is silent. God's folded hands are the deepest wounds of all. The psalmist sees no signs through which God announces his intention. *No . . . prophet* (v. 9) may not mean the physical absence of prophets, but can be interpreted in the sense of no persons reliable to answer the dilemma presented by the invaders (1 Sam 3:1; Lam 2:9; Ezek 7:26). Everything points to an intolerable situation. *How long, O God? . . . Why? . . . Why?* is the theodicy question voiced from the midst of suffering, after giving vent to feelings of abandonment (vv. 10-11). In this sense, Psalm 74 is addressing the same problem faced by the individual in Psalm 73, the apparent triumph of the wicked.

Hymn to God's Power in History and Creation 74:12-17

Yet God my King is from of old, working salvation (v. 12). With this reminder of God's great deeds of salvation in the past, in history, and in creation, the mood changes as the psalmist takes comfort and expresses hope (vv. 12-17). Every line in this section begins by repeating the second-person pronoun: *You. You divided, you broke, you crushed, you gave. . . .* We can read these verses as references to Israel's salvation history, the crossing of the sea (Exod 14:29), the defeat of the Egyptians (Ezek 29:3; 32:2-4), the exodus miracles (Num 20:11), and the miraculous crossing of the Jordan (Josh 3:11).

Yet the language used draws on the Babylonian tradition concerning precreation conflict, in which Marduk supposedly split Tiamat in two to make earth and sky. Here the psalmist addresses God as a great warrior who defeats primitive chaos (Isa 51:9-11). He appeals to the LORD's victory over the forces of chaos and evil, for whom even the dreaded mythical sea monster, *Leviathan*, is a mere plaything (Ps 104:26). Finally, the psalmist claims for God the whole created order, with its contrasts, power, and changes (vv. 16-17). All this God has done, achieving victory in far greater battles against cosmic foes. God alone is supreme! Why should the enemy scoff at God's inactivity (vv. 18-19, 23)? On the other hand, in light of God's historic interventions, God's inactivity, at this moment of crisis, is all the more incomprehensible.

Concluding Appeal for God's Intervention 74:18-23

There is no question that the LORD is powerful, but will there be action? The proclamation of God's eternal sovereignty provides the basis for the psalmist's plea to God to keep his promise and intervene (vv. 18-23). The psalmist reminds God of the vaunting of the enemy

(vv. 18, 22), of his former love for Judah and care for his *poor* people (vv. 19, 21), and of his *covenant* and his *cause* (vv. 20, 22). In these verses *your dove* (v. 19), a metaphor for Israel used only here, indicating defenselessness, is in contrast to the *impious* (vv. 18, 22). *Impious* translates the word *nābāl*, the blasphemous and overbearing fools who say, *"There is no God"* (Ps 14:1).

Psalm 74 speaks of the destruction wrought by the enemy, but in Israel itself *an impious people* cooperates with the foe to cause God to cast aside his people (v. 18; Kraus, 1986:65). However, the psalm also charges God with ignoring the obligations of his covenant (v. 20). Law and order have broken down, and wherever one turns, the land is full of danger.

The psalm ends with the urgent appeal: *Rise up, O God, plead your cause* . . . (vv. 22-23). So God, why don't you act and restore the honor of your name now? The questions remain unanswered, but the psalmist must believe that cruelty and violence cannot have the last word.

THE TEXT IN THE BIBLICAL CONTEXT AND LIFE OF THE CHURCH

God, Where Are You?

Psalms 74 and 79 have had strong influence on the prayers and liturgy of the Jewish people when they remember the destruction and profanation of Jerusalem by the Babylonians (587 or 586 BC), Antiochus Epiphanes (167 BC), and the Romans (AD 70). For example, several bursts of poetry in 1 Maccabees draw from these communal lamentations in remembering the desecration of God's holy place (1:36-40; 2:7-13; 3:45, 50-53).

The destruction of the temple represented an immense national and religious catastrophe. In more recent times, prisoners in a Nazi concentration or death camp or a Soviet psychiatric hospital must have cried out, *O God, why do you cast us off forever?* People have voiced similar laments over the attack on Pearl Harbor, the atomic bombs dropped on Hiroshima and Nagasaki, wars in Central America and Vietnam, Desert Storm, and the terrorist attacks that brought down the World Trade Center in New York. "Where was God on September 11?"

Jerusalem represented a center for Israel's faith and life. What happens when the center gives way? Is the demise of Western hegemony a contemporary example? People long for an order that holds life together and grieve the losses when a previous order is gone (Brueggemann, 1984:69).

The community lament psalms can help in processing national catastrophes. We can use them for public prayer and ceremonies of lamentation. There is a place for grief. Sorrow has its purpose. For ancient Israel, the loss of the temple did not mean the loss of God. God is still a powerful God, and even with the loss of the temple, God remains someone we can address. Sorrow in grieving can transform a people. The exile changed Israel's self-understanding. They came to think of themselves as the lowly. Is that the transformation wrought by suffering (Jer 31:33; Ezek 36:26; Matt 5:3, 5)? Amid loss of what people hold most dear, by faith we can still affirm God's working (Rom 8:28, 31-39). Psalms enrich the church's worship not only for times of abundance, but also in periods of suffering and abasement.

Persistence and Patience and the Reign of God

Psalm 74, in focusing on the question of God's sovereignty, also deals with issues of persistence and patience. Can God ultimately enact God's purposes for the whole creation? The psalmist cannot understand how such an active God is passive in face of the enemy's desecration of God's dwelling and name. Why doesn't God strike back on behalf of his people with dramatic force and energy?

However, God's ways are not necessarily our ways. God's timetable may not be identical with ours. The reign of God is proclaimed amid circumstances that seem to deny it: the destruction of the temple and the later crucifixion of Jesus are prime examples. Psalm 74 anticipates Jesus' eschatological proclamation of the reign of God (Mark 1:14-15), not by avoidance of suffering, but by taking up a cross (Mark 8:34; McCann, 1996:974-75).

The biblical message is that *my times are in your hand* (Ps 31:15); such a faith is better than taking our times and God's prerogative into our own hands (Rom 12:19-21). Suffering calls for persistence in prayer and patience in perseverance.

Psalm 75

God Executes Judgment,
. . . Eventually

PREVIEW

Psalm 74 addresses the issue of God's silence and inactivity. The editors of the Psalter apparently placed Psalm 75 as answer to the plea in Psalm 74:22. Here God is speaking, with action promised, through the prophetic oracle (vv. 2-5) and the further commentary by priest or temple prophet (vv. 6-8). The prophetic liturgy is set within a hymnic invocation and thanksgiving (vv. 1, 9), with a concluding divine saying (v. 10). God will bring the power of the wicked to an end and vindicate the righteous.

Even though the literary forms are mixed and the psalm is difficult to classify, the point is clear. God is the one who upholds the cosmic and moral order (vv. 2-9). In God's own time he will exercise judgment with equity (vv. 2, 7). His judgments will be thorough and complete (vv. 8, 10). Surely God will punish the wicked. But when?

Although it is not possible to date this psalm, some see an allusion to an earthquake (v. 3). In any case, it is a psalm for troubled times, with a warning to the arrogant and boastful (vv. 4-5, 10).

The heading apparently identifies a tune, *Do Not Destroy* (Pss 57; 58; 59; Isa 65:8) *[Asaph; Superscriptions]*. The liturgical notation *Selah* (v. 3) suggests the song's use in the temple worship *[Selah]*. Voices for the liturgy may have been from the congregation (v. 1), the cultic prophet speaking for God (vv. 2-5), prophet or choir (vv. 6-8), singer or congregation (v. 9), and cultic prophet (v. 10).

OUTLINE

Introductory Statement of Congregational Praise, 75:1
Oracle of Assurance and Judgment, 75:2-5
Prophetic Exhortation, 75:6-8
Vow of Praise and Closing Oracle, 75:9-10

EXPLANATORY NOTES

Introductory Statement of Congregational Praise 75:1

The congregation's double acclamation of thanks calls on God's name. God's *name* is of great significance, suggesting God's character and presence (Exod 3:13-15; Jer 33:2; Amos 5:8; 9:6). Possible readings, in addition to *Your name is near*, include *We call on your name* (LXX) or *They that call upon your name* (A. Anderson, 2:548). In the psalms, giving thanks and proclamation of God's wondrous deeds often go together (Pss 9:1; 26:7).

Oracle of Assurance and Judgment 75:2-5

The prophetic oracle is directed as a warning to the boastful (vv. 2-5) [Oracle]. The NIV inserts *You say* and uses quotation marks to set off the divine speech spoken through a cultic prophet. The oracle begins with assurance of God acting in human affairs, at a time of his choosing, to guarantee the world's stability and the moral order. The *pillars of the earth* are its foundation (1 Sam 2:8; Job 9:6; 38:4-6; Ps 104:5), and in this context, the basis of human life. God *will judge with equity* is a theme elsewhere associated with the proclamation of God's reign (Pss 9:8; 96:10; 98:9; 99:4).

Readers have often recognized the connection between Psalm 75 and Habakkuk (1:4, 12-13; 2:3-5, 15-16). Habakkuk wrestled with the problem of the power of wicked Babylon. Read in that context, the wicked are the arrogant, who think of themselves as the true powers of history (Mays, 1994b:249). However, these verses can also have a more generic meaning, as the arrogance of self-importance and autonomous power always stands under the judgment of God. *Horn*, a common metaphor for power and strength, here stands for arrogance; the closing oracle will again refer to it (v. 10).

Prophetic Exhortation 75:6-8

The commentary on the oracle is a further warning. No need to look to the *east, west,* or *wilderness*: God alone is the one *who executes judgment* (vv. 6-7). Search where you will, but there is no arbiter who judges with equity but God. *Putting down one and lifting up another* (v. 7) is the prerogative of kings. This psalm portrays God as judge of all the nations. Therefore, no worldly rank is anything but provisional.

Although God appears inactive, he has appointed a time for judgment (v. 2). The metaphor of the *cup with foaming wine* (v. 8) means that this judgment will surely come, and it will be complete. The seventh- and sixth-century (BC) prophets used this symbol widely to dramatize God's wrath and judgment upon the wicked (Isa 51:17, 21-23; Jer 25:15-16; 49:12; Ezek 23:33-34; Hab 2:15-16). The wicked shall receive their due punishment to the full: they *shall drink it down to the dregs* (v. 8) *[Wrath]*.

Vow of Praise and Closing Oracle 75:9-10

In contrast to the wicked, the psalmist has a different role to play. *But I . . . will sing praises* (v. 9) identifies the singer with the *righteous* as a perpetual herald of the wondrous deeds of God (vv. 1, 10). A divine saying, with God as speaker through the cultic prophet (v. 10), reiterates the main point: judgment is God's alone; this forbids all rash impatience with God's judgments.

The final word from God tells of the divine intention to cut off the power of the wicked and give victory to the righteous. The contrasting fate of the wicked and the righteous is similar to Psalm 1. The psalm's final word, promising exaltation to ṣaddîq (*the righteous*), forms an inclusio with verse 2, where God declares, *I will judge with equity.*

THE TEXT IN THE BIBLICAL CONTEXT AND LIFE OF THE CHURCH

The Last Word

Psalm 75 addresses the question of whose directive will carry the day in the affairs of the world—the word of human arrogance or the word of God? The psalm leaves no doubt: the final word never lies with human wickedness, however powerful and triumphant it may momentarily seem.

The psalm can be useful to those who live in an environment where ruthless abuses of power seem to hold sway. Nation states, particularly those who see themselves as world powers, constantly face this temptation. Self-interest under the guise of national security leads to arrogance and domination, even by the nations who consider themselves benevolent.

Psalm 75 challenges people in every generation to live in hope; it asserts that the last word lies with the God who *will judge with equity* (Pss 75:2; 96:10-13; 98:7-9).

God's Great Reversals

Psalm 75 tells of God's great reversals. God's *putting down one and lifting up another* (v. 7) is a theme shared with the Song of Hannah (1 Sam 2:1-10) and the Magnificat (Luke 1:46-55). Hymns of praise exalt the power of God to create a new reality that is in accord with the Lord's just and loving purposes, by putting down the mighty and the powerful, and raising up the lowly and the weak (Job 5:11-16; 12:17-25; Pss 107:33-42; 113:7-9; 146:9; 147:6). In this sense, Psalm 75 points toward the coming kingdom of God, and Jesus' words that "all who exalt themselves will be humbled, and all who humble themselves will be exalted" (Matt 23:12).

As moderns, people have lost the sense of living in a world where God's judgments are around them all the time. Here is a psalm where the theme of judgment spills over into the NT and into the present time. Psalm 75 conveys the certainty that "the Judge is standing at the doors" (James 5:8-9). In the book of Revelation, images of God's judgment in troubled times include the "cup of his anger" (14:10; 16:19; 18:6).

Stuhlmueller (1983, 2:18) points out how Psalm 75 deals with blessings under the *name* of the Lord (v. 1; Deut 12:11; 21:5), and curses or punishment meted out by drinking from the *cup* (v. 8; Isa 51:17-23). These themes of *name* and *cup* continue through the NT (Mark 10:38-39; 14:36; Col 3:17). All can rejoice that Jesus did not insist that the cup (of suffering) pass from him. Consequently, Christians drink the cup of the new covenant in forgiveness and peace (1 Cor 11:25-28).

Psalm 76

The Awesome God

PREVIEW

This song of Zion in hymn style is linked with Psalms 46 and 48 in theme: the awesome power of the God who dwells in Zion. Additional songs of Zion include Psalms 84; 87; and 122 to proclaim the praiseworthiness of the majestic LORD *[Zion]*. Psalm 76 also relates to the two preceding psalms, with focus on God's divine deed of judgment on human arrogance, particularly on the weapons of war. When aroused, God's anger spells the end of earthly despotism. The object of God's justice upon earth is peace (*šālôm*), the help and salvation of *all the oppressed of the earth* (v. 9). The song ends with an invitation to worship by means of vows and gifts to God.

Scholars have offered various historical settings for Psalm 76: the achievements of David, the defeat of Sennacherib's Assyrian army in 701 BC, and the skirmishes of the Maccabees (second century BC). Most interpreters see allusions to the Assyrian defeat by God's intervention as told in 2 Kings 18:13–19:37 and Isaiah 36–37. The title in the LXX adds, "with reference to the Assyrians." However, interpretation of this psalm has moved from the historical, which focused on the memory of divine intervention defeating foes who plundered Jerusalem; and on to the psalm's use in temple worship, to tell the salvation history about God's mighty deeds and power over all kings and nations. Some see in the psalm also the eschatological defeat of the nations in the last judgment. Worshippers likely used the psalm in the Jerusalem temple to celebrate the triumphs of the LORD and the choice of Zion as his dwelling place, and to urge response to the majesty of God. Though the psalm alludes to Zion's past, it is more about the future that God will create for the people and for the earth [Ways of Reading].

The four-point outline below follows the traditional division as shown in the NRSV. An alternative three-point outline, with breaks following the liturgical notation *Selah* (after vv. 3 and 9), is also possible (Tate, 1990:264) [Selah]. The heading suggests that the song is to be accompanied *with stringed instruments* [Asaph; Superscriptions].

OUTLINE

God's Greatness Associated with Zion, 76:1-3
Address to the God of Glory and Majesty, 76:4-6
Address to the God of All Power and Saving Grace, 76:7-9
Invitation to Make Vows to the Awesome God, 76:10-12

EXPLANATORY NOTES

God's Greatness Associated with Zion   76:1-3

Psalm 76 recalls a great victory achieved by God, possibly the defeat of the Assyrians in 701 BC (2 Kings 19:32-35). God has entrusted to Israel the mystery and wonder of his *name* (*Yahweh*, present to act in salvation; v. 1). *Salem*, an archaic name for Jerusalem (v. 2; Gen 14:18), brings to mind the word *šālôm* (peace, salvation). The God who rules in Salem is the one who creates peace in the world. Zion, where God is present and has his holy habitation (Ps 68:5), refers here not just to a specific place; Zion also functions as a symbol of God's sovereignty in all times and places.

The motif of God destroying the weapons of war appears in many texts (v. 3; 46:9; 76:3-6; Jer 49:35; Hos 1:5; 2:18; Mic 5:10; Zech 9:10). *Selah* may be placed here for emphasis or as a pause for reflection.

Address to the God of Glory and Majesty   76:4-6

The psalm celebrates the greatness and power of God by use of an emphatic *you* for God and a tightly worded statement (v. 4). *Glorious*, a word suggesting light, is also translated "terrible" or "awe-inspiring." The *everlasting mountains* may denote Mount Zion, mountains in general, or a symbol of all that is lasting and mighty. The OT views God as both terrible and glorious (Exod 15:11).

In remembering a great victory achieved by the LORD, the portrayal of war describes the collapse of every human power (vv. 5-6). The people remembered historical events when God's intervention discomfited enemy forces (Exod 15:1-19; Josh 6:1-21; Judg 4:15-16; 7:19-22; 2 Kings 19:32-36). Sometimes referred to as holy war, in this Yahweh war the LORD defeated the enemy by means of divine terror, without or with only minimal help from human warriors. The language recalls the triumphant song of Miriam (v. 6; Exod 15:21). Supplementing these stories of the LORD as warrior of Israel are allusions to ancient mythical concepts of God's judgment over the powerful forces of chaos, as represented in lightning as the *flashing arrows* of God, and God's *rebuke* in the thunder (vv. 3, 6) *[War]*.

Address to the God of All Power and Saving Grace 76:7-9

The first half of the psalm looks to the past, and now the second half looks to the future. In Psalm 76, the awesome warrior judge has spoken his mighty judgment from heaven, and earth is stilled in fear and awe (vv. 7-8; Ps 46:10). The LORD is rising up *to save all the oppressed of the earth* (v. 9; 75:7, 10). The lowly may refer to the poor, meek state of Judah, or more broadly, to all those who base their life on trust in God, rather than on their own strength. God judges to save them (Mays, 1994b:251). The picture is one of peace (*shalom*) brought about through the just decisions of God. Again, *Selah* may signify emphasis or invite a pause for reflection.

Invitation to Make Vows to the Awesome God 76:10-12

This most difficult part of the psalm has given rise to many different translations and interpretations (v. 10). *Human wrath serves only to praise you* suggests that God can make even human hostility serve his purpose (Rom 8:28 n). The NIV translates, *Surely your wrath . . . brings you praise*, focusing on human response to God's wrath. Drawing on corrections to the Hebrew text, NEB translates, *Edom shall confess thee. . . . Hamath shall dance*, thus focusing on the homage of the foreign nations. Knight (2:22) calls attention to a literal reading of verse 10b: "The survivors of your wrath you will make into your belt." God's people are to be as close to God as a belt is around the body (Jer 13:10-11; Eph 6:10-17). While the sense is elusive, the verse may suggest that even human wrath or recalcitrance eventually ends up honoring the sovereign God (McCann, 1996:980).

God's awesome power implies human wrath as useless. The real ruler of the world is the LORD. The congregation is encouraged to acknowledge the kingship of the LORD with vows of service and gifts (v. 11). God's power and judgment provide hope for the coming of God's kingdom of peace. The final verse summarizes that the LORD humbles the proud rulers and instills *fear in the kings of the earth*. These find themselves under the judgment of a fearsome God (Ps 75:10; Isa 18:4-6; Rev 14:18-20).

THE TEXT IN THE BIBLICAL CONTEXT AND LIFE OF THE CHURCH

The Language of Conflict and Victory

On first reading, such a psalm celebrating a military victory seems offensive. Peoples and nations with militant tone have often identified God with the defeat of opposing forces; this has happened too many times for people of peace to be comfortable with such human assessment. At the same time, it seems that in the biblical worldview, salvation comes at the expense of warlike destruction of the enemy forces. Tate (1990:267-68) offers helpful comments about the language of conflict and victory. First, the imagery is a poetic description of the terrible evil that pervades life in this world. Second, the language, rooted in cultic worship, seeks to engender a catharsis that can transform resentment and despair into praise. Third, the language seeks to evoke commitment to a counter worldview: "There is a judgment which sets right the horrible endemic evil in human existence." The psalm emphasizes the LORD's power and his willingness to use it on behalf of his people.

Finally, in Psalm 76, as so often in the Scriptures, we may discover meaning at different levels. In the OT a permanent feature of the prophets' hope for the future is that God will make obsolete the weapons of war (Ps 46:9; Isa 2:4; 9:5; Hos 2:18). This psalm represents God as smashing all implements of war, those symbols of human arrogance (vv. 3, 5-6). God's judgment aims at peace (*shalom*). It represents help and salvation for the poor, which warfare does not. War compounds the lot of the poor and increases the number of the poor and oppressed. Often overlooked in the toll of modern warfare is the effect on the soldiers who return, many deeply scarred by traumatic stress and depression. The high rate of suicides and marital breakup among military personnel affects their families as well. At its deeper level, Psalm 76 challenges the surface meanings of a military victory psalm.

The Wrath of God and the Power of Love

A cluster of words in this psalm speaks of God as glorious or terrible (v. 4), awesome (vv. 7, 11), and displaying anger and wrath (vv. 7, 10) that instills fear (vv. 8, 12). Do people today have a sense that God is awesome? The notion of the "terror of God" does not sit comfortably in Christian minds, though even the NT warns, "It is a fearful thing to fall into the hands of the living God" (Heb 10:31), or "our God is a consuming fire" (12:29). Revelation (6:12-17) also echoes the theme of the great day of wrath.

The wrath of God is a driving force by which God exerts himself despite human resistance; it has nothing to do with moody susceptibilities that allow themselves to be overcome by anger (Weiser: 528) [Wrath]. This psalm, and all of the OT and NT, still highlights the benevolent love of God (v. 9). The chief aspect of justice in the Psalms is the concern for those who cannot or will not strike back at the ruthless (Kidner, 2:275). God's care for the oppressed and the breadth of God's care as wide as the earth (v. 9) are equally awesome.

God exercises his sovereignty not as sheer force but as the power of love (1 Cor 1:25). The children of God are inevitably peacemakers (Matt 5:9); they dare to tell the world of a power that is greater than weapons, kings, prime ministers, and presidents—the power of God's love symbolized by Zion and made known ultimately in the cross of Jesus Christ (McCann, 1996:981).

Among Mennonites of Russian heritage, many of whom fled the Ukraine as refugees from war in the twentieth century, a favorite hymn is Gerhard Tersteegen's "O Power of Love" (1757):

> O Pow'r of love, all else transcending, in Jesus present evermore,
> I worship thee, in homage bending, thy name to honor and adore.
> Yea, let my soul, in deep devotion, bathe in love's mighty boundless ocean.

Psalm 77

Questions About the God Who Works Wonders

PREVIEW

Psalm 77 is an individual lament (vv.1-10), with a hymn of praise (vv. 11-20) in place of the usual vow, serving as motive in eliciting God's saving action. The psalmist laments not for personal calamities suffered, but gives the cry of one deeply involved in a national distress. The perception that God has rejected his people overwhelms the petitioner, leading to the series of questions about the character of God (vv. 7-9). In the midst of disaster, God's voice appears to be silent, his hand stayed, and his people abandoned (v. 10).

The shift in tone comes when the psalmist recalls *the deeds of the LORD* (v. 11). In hymn form, the psalmist remembers God's self-revelation in history and in creation. God has redeemed his people in the exodus (vv. 15, 20). The psalmist takes comfort in trusting that God will spare his people again (v. 19). The psalmist may have taken the examples of God's mighty deeds of creation, thunderstorm, and exodus from an earlier hymn, or from early traditions in Israel's faith (vv. 16-19). Though the psalm may use older traditional material, many commentators consider the psalm, in its present form, to have come from the exile or postexilic period, since the calamity that

Psalm 77

prompts the questions (vv. 7-10) appears to be of a long duration. The psalm has similarities to Habakkuk 3 and the salvation prophecies of Isaiah 40–55.

The title refers to Jeduthun, a Levitical singer, mentioned also in the titles to Psalms 39 and 62 (1 Chron 16:41-42; 25:1, 3, 6; 2 Chron 5:11-12). Reference to this name and the use of *Selah* (vv. 3, 9, 15) confirm the psalm's liturgical use *[Asaph; Superscriptions; Selah]*.

OUTLINE

Individual Lament Also Representing the Community, 77:1-10
    77:1-3   The Cry of Distress
    77:4-10   Questions in the Night
Hymn About the Mighty Acts of God, 77:11-20
    77:11-15   Meditation on the Wonderful Deeds of God
    77:16-20   Description of God's Coming to Save His People

EXPLANATORY NOTES

Individual Lament Also Representing the Community 77:1-10

The urgent cry to God is one of distress and mental anguish (vv. 1-3; Ps 142:1-3). The unspecified trouble could be the calamity of the exile or personal fears of the people of God. Memory and meditation bring no consolation, only weariness, groaning, sleeplessness, and restless thoughts (v. 2). Verbs of reflection cluster here: *meditate, consider, remember, search, call to mind, muse* (vv. 3, 5-6, 11-12). The lament moves to deliberation (v. 3) and will be developed into a meditation on God's works (vv. 11-20).

Remembering *the days of old* (v. 5) must have included the exodus, the paradigmatic act of divine liberation (vv. 19-20). But sleep does not come, only inner searching (v. 6). With a string of six questions, the psalmist doubts whether God's favor and compassion will return (vv. 7-9, counting v. 7 as two questions). Is the rejection of the Lord (*'ădōnāy*) final? In his query the psalmist uses the list of attributes that have characterized the Lord's way with Israel: favor, covenant loyalty (*ḥesed*), promise, graciousness, compassion (Mays, 1994b:212). He questions God's fundamental character as expressed in the creed of Exodus 34:6 *[Steadfast]*.

The conclusion to the series of questions, *It is my grief that the right hand of the Most High has changed* (v. 10), conveys the psalmist's dismay that God's manner of action has changed. So has God also changed? The NIV connects verse 10 to the verses that follow as an appeal to God's power. The word translated *grief* could also read "infirmity" or "entreaty," and the word translated *changed* could mean "years," "renewal," or "recital" (Kidner, 1975:278).

Hymn About the Mighty Acts of God   77:11-20

Though the psalmist has not yet received answers to his questions, the psalm now moves from lament to praise. The pondering of inscrutable questions continues as the psalmist calls to mind *the deeds of the LORD* (vv. 11-12). Israel's salvation story focuses on the exodus (vv. 15, 20), but also on all of the LORD's great *wonders of old* (vv. 11, 14). The holiness of God's way suggests that God is different, mysterious, and hence incomparable (v. 13). The question *What god is so great. . . ?* is rhetorical. There is only one sovereign God! Even among the nations, the God of Israel has displayed his incomparable might (v. 14; Ps 106:8). *With your strong arm you redeemed your people* (v. 15; 111:9) refers to the exodus, implying that God can deliver his people again.

These verses at the center of the psalm (vv. 13-15) are the psalmist's way of bringing the past into the present. God remains the same as he always was. God's majesty has in no way been altered. Through active remembrance, the historical credo is a living reality (vv. 5, 11; Westermann, 1989:105).

Now the hymn describes the crossing of the sea in terms of a victory over the primordial waters by the God of thunder and lightning (Pss 29; 76:3, 6; Hab 3:14-15). The psalm blends God's majesty in creation and history into one story. In this theophany the main emphasis is on God's coming, which reveals his majesty and power. God is on the move (cf. Pss 18:12-19; 96:13). His approaching is a frequent theme of the prophets, often as here, in a cosmic setting (Isa 30:27-33; 63:1-6). God comes by way of a breakthrough to aid the individual, to deliver the nation, and then at last in Jesus, to save the world *[Theophany]*.

Due to the work of God's holiness and inscrutable ways, he leaves no recognizable *footprints* behind (v. 19). The psalmist recognizes that God's workings often leave no visible trace (Job 9:11; 23:8-9). God is at work beyond human knowing (27:5). Therefore, faith and trust are necessary. Displays of power are means, not ends. God's overriding concern is for his flock (v. 20; Pss 78:52-53; 95:7-11; 100). In the past, God led his people through Moses and Aaron. The psalm ends abruptly with the implication and hope that God's mighty wonders will continue. Comfort in these saving events now overcomes all afflictions.

THE TEXT IN THE BIBLICAL CONTEXT AND LIFE OF THE CHURCH

A Memory of God's Mighty Deeds

The perplexing faith questions raised about God in Psalm 77:7-9 remain. The psalm provides no satisfying answers. The footprints of the divine are unseen (v. 19). There is only the story of what God has done, told in this psalm and retold from generation to generation.

Read against the background of the refugee experience of God's people in exile, Psalm 77 makes sense. It can speak as well to personal experiences of "exile" and loss of faith when God seems absent from human lives. A jolting medical diagnosis, the sudden death of a loved one, or an act of terrorism may elicit similar questions about abandonment by God. Personal experiences of "exile" often push people to pray with new urgency.

Psalm 77 suggests that through earnest prayer, God will lovingly lead his people back to faith. In meditation and confession, inner contradictions may be clarified. However, we cannot transform pain into praise by focusing on the questions about God. The psalmist turns attention from self to God's mighty deeds. The revelation of God's continuing redemptive power comes in the memory of what God is like through what God has done. This psalm provides an example of the significance of the communal memory (Brueggemann, 1988:137-39). The credo, the salvation story of God's care for his people in the past, is a reminder that even one's present circumstance is not hopeless. God can work in it!

Readers may ponder the mystery of the unknown tracking of God in their distress. Since God moves on his own schedule, the faithful may need to endure the anguish of waiting. But as people of memory and hope, believers wait with trust in "God, our help in ages past, our hope for years to come" (Isaac Watts, 1719).

This psalm has found its place in the worship of the Christian church through use of verses 13-14 for the majestic hymn "Who is so great a God," the Great Prokeimenon from the Russian Orthodox liturgy.

Psalm 78

That the Next Generation Might Know

PREVIEW

At the end of Psalm 77, Israel appears as a flock led by Moses and Aaron. The last verse of Psalm 78 presents Israel as a flock led by David.

This historical review, with a teaching purpose, belongs with Psalms 105; 106; 135; and 136. These psalms are concerned with the past and its bearing on present and future generations. The psalmist is an interpreter of history, not primarily an archivist who preserves data. He retells Israel's story so that his people may learn a lesson about God's glorious deeds, the rebellion of the ancestors, and God's judgments and amazing compassion. The psalmist tells the story to inspire hope and obedience in the hearers and the generations to come.

Psalm 78 is composed as a speech that a priest or prophet may have recited at the great festivals. An elaborate introduction outlines the psalmist's purpose: to teach the people, especially the children, the things God has done in order to provide hope and confidence to future generations (vv. 1-11). Then the psalm recounts the failures of the wilderness generation (vv. 12-39) and of the ancestors in Ephraimite territory (vv. 40-72). Yet God's mercy has prevailed, offering new beginnings. Each of the two main parts, beginning with verse 12, has a pattern: recitation of the Lord's marvelous deeds for Israel, an instance of failure, the responding divine wrath, and a concluding account of how God maintained relationship with his wayward people.

The psalmist composes the introduction in the wisdom style (Ps 49:1-4; Prov 3:1, 5). He uses history as a lesson. Fidelity to God brings blessings; sinfulness invites severe punishment. Note the refrain-like comments (vv. 17, 32, 40, 56). Yet God is *compassionate* (v. 38). Even after rejecting the tribe of Ephraim, God chose the tribe of Judah, and chose David *to be the shepherd of his people* (vv. 67-72).

This psalm's bias against the northern tribes and in favor of Judah, Zion, and David may suggest composition after the divided monarchy and fall of Samaria (721 BC), perhaps during the reform of Hezekiah (2 Kings 18) or the reform of Josiah (2 Kings 22–23). In thought and teaching, it is similar to Deuteronomy 32:4-5, 7, 36. In any case, the worship leaders would have put the psalm to continuous use. In the postexilic era, Zion could have functioned symbolically, and increasingly worshippers would have understood the references to David messianically (McCann, 1996:990).

The heading identifies the psalm as *A Maskil of Asaph. Maskil* may refer to instructional or didactic writing *[Asaph; Superscriptions]*. The following outline is adapted from Richard J. Clifford (1981:127-29).

OUTLINE

Introduction, 78:1-11
    78:1-4   Listen to the Story of God's Wonders
    78:5-8   Teach the Next Generation
    78:9-11   Failure of the Ephraimites
Recital: The Wilderness Events, 78:12-32
    78:12-16   God's Gracious Acts
    78:17-20   Israel's Rebellion
    78:21-32   God's Anger
Meditative Response: God's Restraint and Compassion, 78:33-39
Recital: From Egypt to Canaan, 78:40-64
    78:40-55   God's Gracious Acts
    78:56-58   Israel's Rebellion
    78:59-64   God's Anger
Meditative Response: God Chooses Judah, Zion, David, 78:65-72

EXPLANATORY NOTES

Introduction   78:1-11

The teaching to be heeded is given in the forms of *a parable* (*māšāl*) and *dark sayings* (*ḥîdôt,* v. 2). A parable is any form of saying that the hearer could see with the mind's eye. Here it signifies a wise saying, a comparison. The *dark sayings* suggest a riddle, mystery, something that is puzzling. History's meaning is such a mystery. In the face of God's wonderful deeds, why did the people keep turning away from God? Why did God not give up on them? Why did God reject the tribe of Ephraim and the sanctuary at Shiloh? Why did God turn to the shepherd David to lead the people? Such are the stories to be told to the coming generations—God's faithfulness amid the people's unfaithfulness.

The psalmist is undaunted with the task of handing on the traditions to the clans and families of Israel (vv. 3-4; Exod 12:26-27; Deut 6:6-9). He begins by recounting the *glorious deeds* and *wonders* of the LORD (vv. 4, 11-12, 32). The purpose of these historical psalms is to recall God's formative acts in the past, including the "stories of impossibility," so that every generation may know God's sovereignty and life-saving hope.

Through the *law* (*tôrâ*) the LORD made his gracious will known to his people (v. 5). Torah is a combination of story and commandments to be passed on to the children (vv. 6-7). But an earlier generation's heart was *not steadfast.* To make the point, the psalm contrasts the ancestors' rebellion and disobedience with God's graciousness (v. 8; Deut 32:5-6).

Ephraim was the most important of the northern tribes of Israel, and often, as here, the name refers to the Northern Kingdom (v. 9). The incident referred to is uncertain. Here the Ephraimites are characterized by military power that proved ineffective, and with religious apostasy, forgetting God's goodness and wondrous works (vv. 9-11; Exod 15:11).

Recital: The Wilderness Events   78:12-32

The recital of God's wonders draws freely on stories from Exodus and Numbers. It focuses on God's deeds to the wilderness generation, beginning with deliverance from bondage in the exodus (vv. 12-16; Ps 77:11, 14). *Zoan,* in Egypt's Nile delta, was the capital city for Ramses (or Rameses) II during the time of the exodus (v. 12). God is the subject of every verb in verses 12-16, emphasizing God's grace alone as the basis of Israelite life.

The people sinned and rebelled in that they *tested* God by their demands for more (vv. 17-18) and doubted God's ability to provide for their needs (vv. 19-20). God's response to such unfaithfulness was anger (vv. 21-31; cf. vv. 7, 32, 37-39). That anger burned against his people, for they did not trust in his saving power (vv. 21-22, 38-39, 49-50, 58-64) *[Wrath]*. Even though they angered God, his bounties continued with manna and quail (vv. 22-30; Exod 16; Num 11). Ironically, in these acts of the LORD, he gives them what they want, but then strikes them down with a plague at the very moment when they are filling themselves with the food they craved (vv. 29-31; Num 11:33-34). The sad result was that *in spite of all this they still sinned* and refused to trust in the wonders of God (v. 32).

Meditative Response: God's Restraint and Compassion 78:33-39

The storyteller reviews the cycle: God's wonders, the unfaithfulness of the people, God's acts against them, repentant searching and remembering God their rock and redeemer (vv. 32-33). Yet their heart was not loyal to God (vv. 36-37). Nevertheless, God was *compassionate . . . and did not destroy them* (v. 38). Remembering their human condition, God turned back his anger to forgive (vv. 38-39). The wilderness generation was characterized by a succession of sin, punishment, repentance, and pardon. The evanescence of human life is contrasted with divine stability (vv. 33, 35; Ps 57:5, 11). The outstanding lesson in all of this is the patience and love of God (A. Anderson, 2:569).

Recital: From Egypt to Canaan 78:40-64

The second recital tells the traditional story again, this time from Egypt to settlement in the Promised Land. Again, it is a story of human failure and disobedience (vv. 40-42). God's gracious acts on behalf of the people included the *signs* and *miracles* (v. 43), the plagues that led to the exodus (vv. 40-55). The psalmist's account differs from the order in Exodus 7:1–12:51 in that no reference is made to plagues 3, 5, 6, and 9. The climax comes in God's leading his people out of bondage, and then guiding and caring for them in their wanderings (vv. 52-53; Exod 15:13; Ps 77:20). Two centuries of history are compressed into verses 54-55, telling the story of the conquest and settling of the land of Canaan. The themes are the same: the sinfulness of the people, and God's judgment and mercy (Judg 2:12-23). The LORD creates a space for his people as he drives out nations before them (v. 55; Ps 44:2). The settlement of the tribal territories may have been by conquest or by means of gradual infiltration and absorption of the indigenous population.

Once again, the storyteller returns to the theme of Israel's rebellion (vv. 56-58; cf. vv. 17-20, 41). He knows about the religious syncretism of the northern tribes, worshipping at Canaanite shrines, and not putting away amulets and household *idols* associated with the gods of Baal and Astarte (vv. 56-58); all this may have been reason for Ephraim's rejection (vv. 9-11, 67). God responds with his wrath (vv. 59-64). These verses refer to God's giving up his sanctuary at Shiloh, site of an early Israelite center, where the ark of the covenant and the tabernacle remained from the time of Joshua to Samuel (Josh 18:1; 1 Sam 3:21). With the loss of the ark and defeat at the hands of the Philistines around 1050 BC, Shiloh ceased to be an Israelite shrine (Jer 7:12; 26:6; Bright: 165). His *power* and *glory* refer to the ark of the covenant, the sign of God's presence with his people (v. 61). *Fire* refers to the fire of war (v. 63). The young men were killed, leaving the young women with no one to marry—one of the many tragedies of war. Throughout, the speaker makes clear that the destruction did not represent God's defeat at the hands of the Philistines, "but rather God's judgment upon his own faithless people" (Tate, 1990:294).

Meditative Response: God Chooses Judah, Zion, David 78:65-72

The concluding reflection opens with a daring image: *Then the LORD awoke,* like a mighty warrior stirred to great deeds by strong wine (v. 65; Pss 35:23; 44:23)! The LORD defeated the *adversary,* the Philistines. A compassionate God will not finally abandon his people.

In the final verses, Israel's waywardness receives no further mention (vv. 67-72). Instead, the focus is on God's choice of the tribe of Judah, Mount Zion, and David, and realignment with the LORD's purposes. Is this the riddle, the mystery, the puzzling thing (v. 2), that God should reject that which he brought into being, Ephraim and Shiloh and the line of Saul? God's choice was Judah, a tribe that won no glory in the days of the judges; Mt. Zion, a stronghold still in enemy hands (2 Sam 5:6-9; Ps 132:11-14); and David, a shepherd recruited from tending sheep. Human understanding is unable to fathom the power of human sin, the power of God, and the new beginnings offered.

THE TEXT IN THE BIBLICAL CONTEXT AND LIFE OF THE CHURCH

Jewish and Christian Uses of Psalm 78

According to the rabbis, Psalm 78:38 stands in the middle of the 5,896 verses of the Psalter. This verse, which speaks of God's compassion, forgiveness, and restraint of his anger, was recited with Deuteronomy 28:58-59, when a person was punished with forty lashes less one (2 Cor 11:24). The same verse plays a prominent role in Jewish morning blessings and is the designated verse to open the evening service (Holladay: 144).

In several places the NT refers to Psalm 78. The Gospel writer Matthew explained Jesus' teaching in parables by quoting Psalm 78:2 (13:35). Jesus cited Psalm 78:24 when he spoke about the bread of life (John 6:31). Psalm 78:3 is alluded to in 1 John 1:1-4, and Psalm 78:18 in 1 Corinthians 10:9. Peter quotes verse 37 (Acts 8:21), and verse 44 is evoked by Revelation 16:4-6.

Telling the Story

To tell the deeds of the Lord to the next generation has been called Israel's "eleventh commandment." So pastors and teachers have often cited the introduction to Psalm 78 and Deuteronomy 6:4-7 to remind parents to keep the story of faith alive by telling the story of their people to their children. Remembering and telling are essential to the people of God. We tell the stories to lead to the praise of God and to nurture a heart of obedience.

This telling of Israel's story instructs the people of God not only by what God has done, but also by the failures of their ancestors. It may be an ultimate distinction of the Bible that it is a record not only of the glory of the people's past, but also of the inglorious side of their history. Divine grace and divine judgment are interwoven. The Bible's frankness is marvelous!

The story is not finished; that is why we are still telling it. Beyond Psalm 78 are the stories of the fall of Judah, the exile, and the restoration, including rebuilding the temple, the synagogue, and gathering the sacred writings. Then comes the NT era, the stories of Jesus, and a new community of faith. The Christian community can now look back on nearly two thousand years of a faith heritage, including the Protestant Reformation in Europe and the sixteenth-century Anabaptist movement, whose stories have shaped the faith tradition of the believers church. Those stories of faith, failure, and redemption through God's grace continue to impact the lives of believers many generations later.

Why do we tell our faith stories? To be reminded of God's wonders, and that in spite of our failures, God's grace continues and offers new beginnings. Psalm 78 is our history, too. We tell the story because the whole history of God's people now passes through us to the next generation.

The Wagon Wheels

One of my childhood memories is that of the wagon wheels. On our farm in southeastern South Dakota, we had a Russian wagon that my great-grandfather brought from the Ukraine when the family came in 1874. The story, as I often heard my father tell it, was that when his grandfather's family came with the migration of Mennonites in search of religious freedom, they disassembled a wagon, crated it, and shipped it to America. Upon arrival at Yankton, they reassembled the wagon, bought a team of horses, and moved the family thirty miles north to the Freeman area.

Many years later, when the old wagon was retired, my father saved the wooden wheels by storing them in the machine shed. I was already an adult, but whenever we walked into that shed and saw the wheels, my father would tell me the story again of the family's migration to this country for freedom of faith. Later, the family placed the wheels in the Heritage Hall Museum at Freeman. During a recent summer I had an opportunity to tell the story to our children and grandchildren as we stood next to those old wagon wheels!

Psalm 79

Help Us, O God of Our Salvation

PREVIEW

The taunting question *Where is their God?* (v. 10) and the memory of the horrible massacre at the destruction of Jerusalem and the temple shape this prayer for God to act. This community lament repeats the themes of Psalm 74, but even more sharply. The opening wail of grief (vv. 1-5) passes into petitions for pity, deliverance, and revenge (vv. 6-12), ending with a vow of thanks and praise (v. 13). It is one of several community laments in book III of the Psalter (Pss 74; 79; 80; 83; 85), and exhibits the typical elements of community laments: complaint, petition, affirmation of trust, and vow of praise.

The situation is similar to Psalms 44 and 74, likely the destruction of the city and temple by the Babylonians in 587 (or 586) BC (2 Kings 25:8-21; Isa 63:7–64:12). As with Psalm 74, this psalm may have been written a generation or more after the devastating event. The fall of Jerusalem became a paradigm for all other invasions and oppressions. The language is similar to Psalm 89 and the books of Jeremiah and Lamentations.

The mood is gloom: the psalmist is bewildered that God would withhold his great power so long (vv. 9-11). Yet the psalm's first word is *God* as the psalmist appeals to God's anger, compassion, salvation, glory, forgiveness, and avenging power. The psalm ends with a promise of thanks and praise.

OUTLINE

Complaint and Description of Distress, 79:1-5
Petitions for God's Intervention, 79:6-12
    79:6-7   To Turn His Anger on the Nations
    79:8-9   To Deal Compassionately with the Sins of His People
    79:10   To Make the Nations Know the Vindication of His People
    79:11   To Respond to the Afflicted
    79:12   To Deal with the Taunts Against the LORD
Vow of Thanks and Praise, 79:13

EXPLANATORY NOTES

Complaint and Description of Distress   79:1-5

The complaint begins with how the ritually unclean outsiders have invaded God's inheritance—the land, holy temple, city, and people (vv. 1-3). The destruction of Jerusalem called God's sovereignty into question (Exod 15:17-18). The enemy left corpses exposed for the birds to scavenge. Blood was flowing like water around Jerusalem, and no one was left to bury the dead. Lack of a proper burial, even for one's enemies, was the final indignity (Num 19:11-16; Deut 28:26; Jer 7:33-34; 8:1-2; 9:22; 19:7; 22:18-19). These graphic pictures of corpses strewn about to rot, with bones picked clean by wild birds and animals, describe one of the many horrors of war.

Although the fighting is over, Israel's suffering continues in the mocking by her neighbors (v. 4; Ps 137:7). The taunts against the people are taunts against God's name, his reputation and character (vv. 4, 12). The community in distress, believing it is on the receiving end of God's anger and therefore abandoned by God's care, desperately cries out, *How long, O LORD?* (v. 5; 13:1-2; 44:24; 79:5; 89:46).

Petitions for God's Intervention   79:6-12

The petitions for God's intervention acknowledge the nation's calamity as God's wrath against sinfulness (vv. 6-12; Deut 4:24; Jer 25:1-14) *[Wrath]*. However, the initial plea is that God should punish the nations, the heathen who have not offered prayers to him (vv. 6-7; Jer 10:25).

Appealing to God's compassion, the people pray that God will not continue to remember the sins of their forefathers against them (v. 8; Exod 20:5; Ps 78:21-22, 30-31, 56-64; Lam 5:7). Instead, they petition the God of salvation to forgive their sins (v. 9; Pss 65:5; 85:4). Psalm 79 is the only community lament that includes confession for sin. The afflicted appeal to God's concern for his own honor (*name*) since the nations taunt, *Where is their God?* (v. 10). The word normally translated "avenge" or "vengeance" (*nĕqāmâ*) may be better translated "vindication" (v. 10) *[Vengeance]*. The appeal is for God to make known to the nations the vindication of his people. They petition God on behalf of the "prisoners of war" doomed to die.

Finally, the suffering community prays for retaliation upon Judah's taunting neighbors (likely Ammon, Moab, and Edom) *[Imprecation]*. The payback, *sevenfold into the bosom* (v. 12), is an expression derived from the folds of the outer garments, a metaphor for full, complete punishment, the most extreme example for the settling of accounts by God (Gen 4:15; Lev 26:18, 21; Prov 6:31). This prayer begs God not to leave unanswered the taunting question "Where is your God?" but to respond promptly and definitively.

Vow of Thanks and Praise   79:13

In confidence that God will answer their petitions, the psalm closes on a note of thanksgiving and praise. Israel can affirm the close relationship of God with his people as that of the shepherd with his flock (Pss 23:1-2; 80:1; 95:7; 100:3). Like Psalms 77 and 78, this psalm ends and Psalm 80 begins with the image of the divine shepherd, joining together this cluster of Asaph psalms *[Asaph; Superscriptions]*.

THE TEXT IN THE BIBLICAL CONTEXT AND LIFE OF THE CHURCH

Psalm 79 as a Penitential Liturgy

How do people of faith cope with disaster in the face of God's seeming absence? The Israelites saw the devastation of the temple and the wasting of Jerusalem as the destruction of God's dwelling on earth. Yet the people needed to hope that God had not abandoned them, but would act for their deliverance.

This prayer, probably used first in services of grief and lament in the sixth century BC, may have been recited on certain days of fasting (Zech 7:2-7; 8:18-23). The writer of 1 Maccabees 7:16-17 quotes Psalm 79:2-3 in describing the murder of a delegation of Hasidean scribes who came to the Seleucid governor Bacchides to sue for peace in 161 BC. The psalm is used as a prayer on the anniversaries of the destruction of Jerusalem in 587 (or 586) BC and again in AD 70. It is one of the prayers recited each Friday afternoon at the Western (Wailing) Wall of Jerusalem, at the site of the former temple (Stuhlmueller, 1983, 2:33).

So this cry of outrage has echoed through the years. It is heard again rising up from the Holocaust, in the eerie silence over the smoldering rubble of Hiroshima, or the Soviet Union's closing of churches for decades across the land. It is heard from Latin America, in the poet's paraphrase of Psalm 79: "Hear the groans of the prisoners and the sigh of those condemned to forced labours and those to death sentenced" (Cardenal: 43)

The vindication sought by the psalmist against the enemy is unashamedly cruel (vv. 10-12), but how can those who have never experienced such horror tell suffering people how to respond? The cry *How long?* is heard often from the lips of the psalmists (74:10; 89:46) and the prophets (Isa 6:11; Dan 8:13; 12:6; Hab 1:2; Zech 1:12). It turns up as well in the NT where the blood of the martyrs cries out (Rev 6:9-10; 16:4-6).

Psalm 79 can be useful to people of God. Is there a parallel to pagan cultural values invading the church community and worship, thus defiling it, God's temple? Positively, the psalmist clings to the hope that human brutality is not the last word. The psalm, read in the context of the NT, opens the way to a new understanding of God's sovereignty as power made perfect in weakness (2 Cor 12:9), symbolized most strikingly in the cross.

Vengeance or Vindication?

We must hear the question *How long?* not as a petition for personal vengeance, which is forbidden God's people. It is the prayer that God's own justice be validated by a decisive divine act. God does not need or desire people to become his vigilantes, to mete out retaliation. Even in the psalmist's cry for vindication, he seeks God's acts, not permission to embark on a crusade of vengeance. In God's larger plan, people of faith may need to wait "a little longer" for his judgments to be complete (Rev 6:11; cf. Lev 19:18; Deut 32:35; 1 Sam 25:26; Rom 12:19-21; Heb 10:30-31).

Like Psalm 78, Psalm 79 confronts the believer with the mystery of God's judgment and compassion. The psalm also reveals the yearning for both. The psalmist's prayer offers both the reliance on forgiveness and the hunger for vengeance to God "who will deal with both needs in his utter sovereignty" (Brueggemann, 1984:73).

Psalm 80

Restore Us, O God

PREVIEW

Psalm 80 is a prayer for deliverance from national enemies (v. 13). As a communal lament, it continues the flock/shepherd imagery (Pss 77:20; 78:70-72; 79:13), voicing complaint about God's anger toward his people (vv. 1-7). With the parable of the vine, the psalmist retells the story of the exodus and the people settling in the land. Outside marauders are now destroying what God has planted (vv. 8-16a). The psalmist prays not only that the God of Israel will come and appear to his people, but also that God will bring about a total restoration (vv. 3, 7, 19). The expanding refrain heightens the prayer's fervency: *O God . . . , O God of hosts . . . , O LORD God of hosts!*

This community prayer song may come from the last years of the Northern Kingdom (732–722 BC), or possibly from Josiah's reign (640–609 BC). The Assyrians, successors to the Hittites, who had learned the use of iron, had an army with iron weapons by 800 BC. For the next 250 years, they dominated their neighbors. The exile of God's people Israel, whether in 721, 597, or 587 (or 586) BC, is a reality so terrible that it demands an answer. Many commentators see the origin of Psalm 80 in northern worship centers before the downfall of the kingdom of Israel, but it may not have reached its present form until after the exile. Through the years people would have used it as a prayer of lamentation for national calamity (Tate, 1990:312-13; Davidson, 1998:263).

The heading dedicates the psalm to the worship leader, to be sung to a tune no longer known: *Lilies, a Covenant* (cf. Ps 60). The LXX adds *concerning the Assyrians,* an early attempt to fix the precise historical context *[Asaph; Musical; Superscriptions].*

OUTLINE

Invocation and Petition—Refrain, 80:1-3
Complaint Describing the Nation's Plight—Refrain, 80:4-7
Parable of the Vine, 80:8-16a
Petition and Vow—Refrain, 80:16b-19

EXPLANATORY NOTES

Invocation and Petition—Refrain   80:1-3

We hear the psalm's basic motif in the opening words: *Give ear.... Come to save us!* (vv. 1-2). The speaker calls on God as *Shepherd of Israel* and leader of *Joseph,* the one *enthroned upon the cherubim. Shepherd* was a title of royalty. *Cherubim* were winged creatures that decorated thrones and sacred places in Israel's world (1 Sam 4:4). They were seen as guardians of holiness and agents of judgment, functioning as symbols for divine presence and sovereignty. The invocation stresses the caring closeness of God to his people.

The petition *shine forth* (v. 1) is the language of theophany, the longing for God's appearing (Deut 33:2; Pss 50:2; 94:1) *[Theophany].* The names *Israel, Joseph, Ephraim, Benjamin,* and *Manasseh* may represent all the northern tribes. In its attitude toward the Northern Kingdom, Psalm 80 contrasts sharply with Psalm 78. The Shepherd is urged to rouse his mighty powers and come forth to save his people. The word *save* is central to the psalm (vv. 2, 3, 7, 19).

For the psalmist, the present darkness engulfing Israel is due to God's absence. The fervent prayer, *Let your face shine,* cries out for the light of divine favor (Num 6:24-26). The shining face of God expressed God's beneficence (Pss 31:16; 67:1; 119:135). The petition *Restore us* (v. 3) could also be translated "Cause us to return," suggesting that in the broken relationship, only a renewal of God's favor and goodwill can restore Israel.

Complaint Describing the Nation's Plight—Refrain 80:4-7

The lament centers on unanswered prayer. The people are not sure how much longer they can endure it (v. 4; 79:5). Vivid imagery is a strong feature of this psalm. Here the Hebrew portrays God's anger as "the smoking of God's nostrils" (v. 4). The psalm accuses God of feeding the people *with the bread of tears"* (v. 5; 42:3; 102:9). Neighbors and enemies alike have made the afflicted people of God an object of scorn (v. 6; 74:10; 79:4, 12). Yet there is certainty that the LORD *God of hosts* (Yahweh *'ĕlōhîm ṣĕbā'ôt*, vv. 4, 7), who is enthroned above the cherubim, possesses power in the highest degree. Thus, the psalm again voices the refrain: *Restore us* (v. 7).

Parable of the Vine   80:8-16a

The psalm does not utter petitions of the suffering community in a vacuum: it appeals to the LORD's great deeds and miracles. The parable of the vine reminds God of his own great acts so that he may remember his people. It depicts Israel as a vine that God transplanted from Egypt to Canaan. The nation's expanse is from the southern desert to the *cedars* of Lebanon in the north, and from the *sea* (Mediterranean) to the *River* (Euphrates), much as in David's time (vv. 10-11). Now the vine has been ravaged by the wild boar, an unclean animal and fitting designation for Israel's enemy, all because God has broken down the walls and allowed it to happen (vv. 12-13; Ezek 19:10-14).

The unanswered question "Why?" (v. 12) leads to the petition asking God to see and tend to this vine again (vv. 14-16). The word *turn* (v. 14) is used elsewhere for human repentance (Pss 22:27; 85:8). How daring to tell God to repent, or at a minimum to change direction, to make an about turn! Yet the plea is for God to turn toward his people. Restoration rests exclusively on God. The NIV includes verse 15b, *the son you have raised up for yourself*, while NRSV and some others omit it as a double of verse 17b.

Petition and Vow—Refrain   80:16b-19

The psalmist's petition is for the enemy to perish at God's rebuke (v. 16b), and that there be prosperity for the Israelite king and thus for the nation (v. 17). The NIV translates *ben-'adam* (v. 17b) as *the son of man*, whereas NRSV renders it *one whom*. Some commentators think this refers to the king; others suggest that it more likely refers to the nation Israel (McCann, 1996:1000).

At the psalm's end is another use of *turn*, the vow *never* to turn away from God, never to backslide again. The psalmist vows to obey and praise God when deliverance has come. This follows the appeal that God *see* the king and the nation, *have regard for* them, and place his restorative divine *hand* upon them once more (vv. 14, 17). As Stuhlmueller (1983, 2:36) comments, "Israel begins every prayer and discussion with firm faith in God."

THE TEXT IN THE BIBLICAL CONTEXT AND LIFE OF THE CHURCH

Daring to Cry Out for Restoration

Communal laments are born in times of national disaster, which easily lead to a crisis of faith. It is characteristic of these communal laments to remind God, and each other, how God has delivered in the past (Pss 44; 74; 79; 83; 85; 94). Drawing on the common image of "shepherd" (Ps 23; Isa 40:11; Ezek 34:11-16), God is depicted as bringing his people into his land. When they are in the land and all seems to disintegrate, they appeal to the divine Shepherd for help. To whom else will the suffering ones cry out in their hurt, their bewilderment, sense of abandonment, and anger?

A second image is that of Israel as a vine transplanted from Egypt to the land of promise. Ezekiel capitalizes on that image, mostly by recasting it (17:7-10), or even turning it on its head (15:1-8). The psalmist captures both the glory of a luxuriant vine (80:8-11) and the uninspiring sight of a mangled, even burnt vine (vv. 12-16). Here too, though now from a humbled position, Israel can do no other than cry to its God for restoration.

These images continue into the NT. God is still the gracious Shepherd (Luke 15:1-7) and Vinegrower, so that our "joy may be complete" (John 15:1-11). And Jesus is the Good Shepherd and the vine (John 10:11-18; 15:1-11; Heb 13:20; 1 Pet 2:25; 5:2, 4).

A Psalm for Advent

Psalm 80 is appropriate for Advent. Many commentators see verse 17 pointing toward a future king or messiah because of the mention of the *son of man* in the Hebrew (cf. NIV; paraphrased in NRSV). It is natural to read such language as referring to the king (Ps 110:1) and giving the "son" a royal meaning (2:7). Then it becomes possible to read this section in a future messianic sense, as later Jewish and early Christian tradition did (Davidson, 1998:266).

As a king was supposed to do, Jesus embodied both the experience of his people and the reign of God (John 15:1-11). His crowning glory appeared to be a God-forsaken exile—the cross (McCann, 1996:1001). Followers of Jesus dare to affirm that in Jesus the light of God shines, and that through Jesus there is restoration and life (cf. Ps 80:18-19). During Advent, Christians both celebrate and wait. They continue to address God out of their corporate affliction and look to God as the only source of light and life. Believers celebrate the good news that "the Lord is here," even as they wait and pray, *Come to save us!* (v. 2).

Psalm 81

If You Want to Live, Listen!

PREVIEW

The fanfare of trumpet and joyful song summons Israel to the great festival, likely Tabernacles (also called Booths). In this song for a feast day, the prophet-poet speaks for God, admonishing the people, as praise of God turns to preaching. God's voice utters again the first two commandments given on Sinai, laments the waywardness of the people of the covenant, and closes with love and longing.

The psalm's key word is *šāma'*, translated *hear* or *listen* (vv. 5, 8 twice, 11, 13). God yearns for the covenant people, who experienced the great deliverance of the exodus from slavery in Egypt. But they did not *listen* to God alone. Now they suffer the consequences of following their own plans. The psalm ends with the good news that the invitation to *listen* is still open. This prophetic liturgy connects with the other great festival psalms (50; 95). The admonition is reminiscent of the Shema (*šĕma'*, "Hear . . ."; Deut 6:4-9), recited daily by the covenant people.

The title *God of Jacob* (v. 4) and references to *Israel* (vv. 4, 8, 11, 13) and *Joseph* (v. 5) suggest origins of the psalm in northern worship centers. However, its present form and position in the Asaph collection (Pss 50; 73–83) point toward exilic and postexilic contexts. The psalm may represent the preaching of the Levitical priests who carried on the prophetic tradition (Tate, 1990:322; Davidson, 1998:268).

The heading provides a musical instruction, *According to The Gittith* (Pss 8; 84), possibly "upon the harp of Gath" or "according to the Gath tune," though the meaning is not known *[Asaph; Musical; Superscriptions]*.

OUTLINE

Summons to Celebration of a Festival, 81:1-5b
The Prophetic Oracle, 81:5c-16
    81:5c-10   God Addresses Israel
    81:11-16   Admonition to Listen and Obey

Kidner (1975:293-295) gives a three-word thematic outline: Rejoice (vv. 1-5), Remember (vv. 6-10), and Repent (vv. 11-16).

EXPLANATORY NOTES

Summons to Celebration of a Festival   81:1-5b

In joyful praise, the people offer up to God singing, shouting, and instrumental music (vv. 1-2). The trumpet's sound may signal the beginning of a festival (v. 3), but it was also a way to honor a king, either human (1 Kings 1:34, 39) or divine (Pss 47:5; 98:6).

What may we know about the festival mentioned in this psalm? At the sanctuary on Mt. Zion, the covenant people celebrated three great annual pilgrim festivals: Passover and Unleavened Bread in early spring (start of barley harvest), Feast of Weeks (called Pentecost in NT) in late spring (end of wheat harvest), and Tabernacles/Booths/Ingathering in the fall (grape harvest; Exod 23:14-17). The major feature was the offering of sacrifices (1 Kings 9:25). Reference in Psalm 81 to the *new moon* and *full moon* suggests the Feast of Tabernacles, a harvest thanksgiving festival that featured the building of temporary booths to remember the wilderness experience and God's providence (Lev 23:34-36, 39-43; Num 29:12-38). An important feature of the Feast of Tabernacles was "the Joy of the Law" and the beginning of the cycle of *Torah* reading (vv. 9-10; cf. Deut 16:13). Celebration of the God of Jacob was not optional, but mandatory (vv. 4-5). The people may have added other celebrative days to this festival, such as the New Year (Weiser: 553).

The Prophetic Oracle   81:5c-16

In the sanctuary, a cultic priest or prophet communicated the message (Pss 50:1, 7; 110:1). The last line of verse 5 is usually joined to the following verses, the *I* as the Levitical priest claiming to be the mouthpiece for God, with the divine message (vv. 6-11; 2 Sam 23:1-2; Jer 1:9).

The oracle itself has two parts. It begins with a description of what God has done for his people and God's appeal to the people to listen: *Hear* and *obey* (vv. 5-10). The final section acknowledges Israel's unfaithfulness, but promises a better future if the people return to the ways of God (vv. 11-16) *[Oracle]*.

In reviewing the relationship God established with Israel, the prophetic oracle recalls the exodus (vv. 6, 10), the giving of the law on Sinai (vv. 7, 10), and the wilderness wanderings (v. 7). The theme is the divine deliverance from Egyptian servitude (Exod 6:6-7). *The secret place of thunder* may recall the cloud engulfing the mountain (19:16). *Meribah* was a place of testing when the Israelites were in a waterless wilderness (17:2, 7; Num 20:13). *Selah* may provide an opportunity for the worshippers to pause and reflect (v. 7) *[Selah]*.

In a heartbroken rebuke, God uses the term *admonish* (v. 8) to mark the address as a warning. The admonition calls for return to the commandments given at Sinai (vv. 9-10; Exod 20:2-4; Deut 32:12). The LORD and his name are symbols of liberation and deliverance (v. 10; Pss 78:12; 80:8; 135:8-9). The Feast of Tabernacles commemorated the wilderness experience, which included forty years of wandering and not listening. The call to listen at such an event is poignant. In the context of Tabernacles, *Open your mouth wide . . .* may be seen as an invitation for the community "to put its continuing trust in the God who can provide for all its needs" (Davidson, 1998:270).

The shocking fact of Israel's history is that the people did not listen to the LORD's voice or hearken to him (v. 11; 78:17, 40). Since they chose to disobey, God did not force them, but allowed them to go their own way (v. 12). But despite falling back into the bondage of their *stubborn hearts* and *own counsels* (v. 12) and the threat of *enemies* (v. 14), there is yet good news! The invitation remains open. The LORD addresses his words in the first person, in an urgent and almost begging plea (v. 13). The present generation can yet listen and change their ways. Amid the reality of disobedient covenant people, God's yearning for them is clear. The choice belongs to the people.

Some commentators suggest placing verse 10c after 16 for the best sense, but 10 anticipates the intent of 16. Moreover, upon hearing verse 10ab anticipating a warning against idolatry (Exod 10:2-3), the Hebrew listener would be startled to hear instead an invitation to enjoy God's goodness. God promises and wants the best for his people. So verses 10 and 16 express the great invitation: "Ho, everyone who thirsts, come to the waters" (Isa 55:1).

THE TEXT IN THE BIBLICAL CONTEXT AND LIFE OF THE CHURCH

The Need for Festival

Festivals are important. They imply community. This festival psalm reminds the people of God that they need to meet together (Heb 10:25). Matthew Henry commented: "No time is amiss for praising God. . . . But some are times appointed, not for God to meet us (He is always ready) but for us to meet one another, that we may join together in praising God" (via Kidner, 1975:294).

There is more to festivals, however, than fellowship and praising God. Festivals and services of worship can also be times for decision making, when people of God consider the story of God's way with them and their way with God. The failure of the people of God, as told in Psalm 81, was their choice to go their own way, which God allowed (vv. 11-12). We can also find the consequences of such behavior in the NT (Acts 7:42-43; Rom 1:24, 26). When people do not make God their guide and strength, their own lusts and passions doom them. Those whom Christ has set free from the bondage of sin ought not submit again to a yoke of slavery (Gal 5:1). Festivals with God's people can be occasions to make new choices.

That makes listening (hearing) so crucial. "What Israel missed by refusing to listen is parallel to my own loss if I miss God's cues for my life" (Wyrtzen: 229). Psalm 81 speaks of a dynamic relationship between God and his people. The psalm can function as a call to commitment at all times and in all places. Worship is celebrative; at the same time it should lead to deeper obedience. Jesus proclaimed the reign of God and invited people to enter it with the invitation "Follow me" (Mark 1:14-17). Jesus ended the Sermon on the Mount by appealing, "Everyone then who hears these words of mine and acts on them will be like a wise man" (Matt 7:24). That is the marvelous glory of preaching. Through very human words, the living word of God can confront people! Even when they have messed up, God still invites them to listen—and to choose life!

Psalm 82

Rise Up, O God, and Judge the Earth!

PREVIEW

Psalm 82 appears to be a prophetic liturgy of God's judgment upon pagan gods; it declares the rule of God's justice on the earth. This brief psalm asserts the uniqueness of the God of Israel, who has compassion for victims of injustice and rules the nations and the cosmos with justice and righteousness.

Initially, the psalm describes the scene of the heavenly council, composed of the gods of the nations, with Israel's God as head of the assembly (v. 1). The judgment speech of God begins with the complaint, *How long will you judge unjustly?* (v. 2). The criteria for administering justice is given in the assessment that the gods have favored the wicked and failed the poor, the orphan, the afflicted, and the destitute (vv. 3-4). God's indictment of the unjust gods follows (vv. 5-7): They have no understanding. They are in darkness. Their inability to do justice threatens the very foundations of the earth. The gods have failed their God-given charge. They are useless. They will *die like mortals* (v. 7). Psalm 82 ends with an appeal by the narrator (or congregation) for God to intervene as judge and ruler over all. Verses 1 and 8 frame the main part of the psalm, God's indictment and sentence upon the unjust gods. For the heading see the essay on *Asaph*.

OUTLINE

Presentation of God as Judge, 82:1
Indictment and Sentence upon the Unjust Gods, 82:2-7
Plea for God to Exercise Justice upon the Earth, 82:8

EXPLANATORY NOTES

Presentation of God as Judge 82:1

Recurring word clusters in this psalm include *God, gods*; and *judge, justice, judgment*; and secondarily, *earth, weak, wicked*. An initial question for interpreters has to do with the implication of the word 'ĕlōhîm (gods), which occurs four times. In verses 1a and 8, the word 'ĕlōhîm refers to God (or Israel's God, the LORD). In verses 1b and 6, does it refer to divine beings, either gods or angels? Or is the reference to human beings, such as Israelite judges, Jewish kings, or foreign rulers? While 'ĕlōhîm (vv. 1b, 6) refers to "gods" or "divine beings" other than Yahweh (LORD), there are also clear implications for how human leaders should judge (vv. 2-7).

The picture of God in the midst of the assembly of gods recurs often in the OT (1 Kings 22:19-23; Job 1:6-12; 2:1-6; Ps 29:1-2; Isa 6:1-13; Zech 1:7-17; 3:1-5). The psalm draws on the imagery of the ancient Near East. Israel lived in a world that had gods of the nations (Pss 86:8-9; 95:3; 96:4; 97:7). Now Israel's God is presented as having displaced the Canaanite high god El to convene a council of the gods and put them on trial (76:9; Isa 3:13-14). In this psalm, the God of Israel will render that divine world impotent and powerless (Miller, 1986:122).

Indictment and Sentence upon the Unjust Gods 82:2-7

The indictment, in the form of a question, implies that the gods (and so also human rulers) are making decisions that favor wicked persons (v. 2). The marginal note *Selah* may emphasize the indictment in the psalm's liturgical use *[Selah]*.

As chief justice, God hands down his verdict on the basis of the test for true justice, defense of those who cannot defend themselves (vv. 3- 4). Responsible justice must be evenhanded and not use power for self-interest, but for the protection of the poor and needy (Job 20:12-16; Ps 72:4, 12-14). Amos testifies to how rare such justice was in the ancient world (Amos 5:7, 12; 6:12).

The center of the psalm continues the indictment of those who disregard the commands of God in relation to justice, which includes care for the marginalized people in society (v. 4). The speaker may be the narrator of verses 1 and 8, offering the judgment that these gods are not only stupid; they also threaten the very order of creation. The connection between injustice and the physical world is often expressed (Pss 75:3; 96:10; Isa 24:1-6, 18-20; Hos 4:1-3; Amos 1:2). Failure in the moral realm has destructive effects in the physical world.

The trial continues as God pronounces the sentence (vv. 6-7). All the *gods* are *children* or *sons* (NIV) of the Most High and thus stand in the service of God. The divine name *Most High* is an epithet of kingship and indicates the exalted status and power of God (Pss 47:2, 6-7; 83:18; 91:1; 97:9). However, the gods have failed to do justice in caring for those whom society has shoved to the edges. They are not gods. Stripped of their divinity, they are condemned to the human fate of death.

Plea for God to Exercise Justice upon the Earth 82:8

The concluding prayer by the narrator or congregation calls on God to replace the false gods and set things right in the world by his rule, claiming all nations as his patrimony (v. 8). *Rise up, O God . . .* may have been an ancient prayer that Israel used on other occasions to plead for the LORD's intervention in the affairs of earth (Num 10:35; Pss 74:22; 132:8).

THE TEXT IN THE BIBLICAL CONTEXT AND LIFE OF THE CHURCH

Monotheism and the Place of Justice in Human Life

Beyond the description of a trial in the heavens, we can read Psalm 82 as a poetic expression of faith. The psalm asserts the clear conviction that injustice destroys the world, but that at the heart of life is a God of compassion and righteousness, whose purposes will prevail. Psalm 82 deals with two basic themes in the Judeo-Christian tradition: monotheism and the place of justice in human life.

The Hebrews lived in a world that accepted many gods. This prophetic oracle asserts that the gods are out to exalt themselves. Consequently, the true cosmic ruler, the LORD, the God of Israel, has done away with the divine beings that figured so prominently in the worldview of the ancient Near East. The implication (alongside Gen 1:26-28, "have dominion") is that God has chosen to assign to human beings a significant role to exercise authority (Guthrie: 35-37).

However, true divinity, whether in the person of God or among God's representatives, is ultimately decided by concern for the weak and the destitute. When the powerful trample over those on the margins, the foundations of human society crumble. Such behavior must stop! Justice is the cornerstone of the universe: justice and righteousness have to do with how the community distributes power and the matter of who has access to life. Justice is the issue on which the claims of deity are settled (Miller, 1986:122-24) *[Judge]*.

This psalm addresses the problem of why those in power continually deprive the weak and defenseless of justice, an ongoing problem in every generation. It is the rare person who really shows compassion for needy, hurting people. Nor can we count on governments and their leaders to place the needs of marginalized people as their highest priority. Psalm 82 is a reminder that religion needs to be grounded in the earthly needs of people. When the powerless are cheated or abused or have to suffer, the foundations of society are dangerously shaken (Matt 25:31-46; James 1:26–2:26). "True evangelical faith cannot lie dormant: . . . it clothes the naked, . . . it feeds the hungry, . . . it comforts the sorrowful, . . . it shelters the destitute" (Menno: 307).

The prayer to God as judge of the earth and all nations finds its fuller expression in the words "Your kingdom come. Your will be done, on earth as it is in heaven" (Matt 6:10). According to the NT message of fulfillment, Jesus Christ, through his death on the cross, is over "thrones or dominions or rulers or powers" (Col 1:16) and has become Lord of the universe (1 Cor 8:5-6; Col 2:15)!

Psalm 83

Prayer Against the Enemies of God

PREVIEW

This community lament is a prayer song on behalf of the nation, for deliverance from the surrounding enemies who threaten its existence. After the opening for God to intervene (v. 1), the psalmist describes the conspiracy of Israel's neighbors, backed by Assyria, the current world power (vv. 2-8). The petition, in the form of imprecations (vv. 9-18), is the wish that God's judgment upon the present enemies of Israel be the same that befell enemies in the period of the judges (vv. 9-12). May God mobilize nature's forces against the enemies of his name (vv. 13-18). An ultimate hope is for even the enemies to know Israel's LORD as God.

In spite of naming ten enemies, it is not possible to identify the specific date for the composition of the psalm. Situations suggested include the time of Jehoshaphat, in mid-ninth century BC (2 Chron 20:1-30), Nehemiah (ca. 444 BC), or the Maccabean period (second century BC). The mention of Assyria (v. 8) suggests a time between the ninth and seventh centuries, since the Assyrian empire fell in 612 BC. At no known time were all nations named united against Israel. Most commentators view the roll call of nations as a summary of names for liturgical purpose rather than as historical data. Israel has rarely been without hostile neighbors, so on numerous occasions the Israelites likely uttered this poetic prayer for God's intervention when they were threatened by foreign invasion. The petitions invoke the LORD's power to break in to protect the existence of Israel. The conclusion also states the hope that all nations might come to know the LORD as *Most High over all the earth* (vv. 16-18).

This is the last in the series of Asaph psalms (50; 73–83) *[Asaph]*. It is also the final psalm in the collection of psalms from 42 to 83, the Elohistic Psalter, so called because of the preference for the more general name *'ĕlōhîm,* or *God,* rather than *Yahweh (LORD,* NRSV), the specific name of the God of Israel *[Superscriptions; Composition].*

OUTLINE

An Urgent Cry to God, 83:1
Description of the Distress, 83:2-8
Petitions Interlaced with Imprecations, 83:9-18

EXPLANATORY NOTES

An Urgent Cry to God   83:1

An opening plea urges that God not remain an inactive onlooker as God's people are threatened with annihilation (v.1; Pss 28:1; 109:1). The psalmist contrasts the silence of God with the enemies' tumult and speech against Israel and her God. The implication is that a God who does not intervene is either powerless or indifferent. Both urgency and confidence are conveyed in the chiastic structure of the verse, with *God* as first and last word *[Hebrew Poetry].*

Description of the Distress   83:2-8

The complaint describes the threat to the community as coming from God's enemies (v. 2). Their intent is to obliterate God's people (vv. 3-4; Jer 11:19). In describing the conspiracy, the psalmist uses the term *covenant (alliance,* NIV, NJPS; *league,* NEB), perhaps to denote solidarity on the part of those plotting together to do away with God's covenant people (v. 5). Even more than God's people, however, God's name and cause are at stake. God cannot afford to ignore this threat!

The ten enemies named include some with close relationships to Israel: *Edom*, the people of Esau, Jacob's brother, living southeast of the Dead Sea (Gen 25:30; 36:9); *the Ishmaelites,* descendants of the half-brother of Isaac, nomads of desert areas (16; 37:25-28); and *Moab* and *Ammon,* the *children of Lot,* in territories east of the Jordan River (vv. 6-7; 19:36-38; Deut 2:9). Using the literary device of inclusio, the psalmist moves from north (*Gebal*, identified with the Phoenician city Byblos) to south (*Amalek*), and then from south (*Philistia*) to north (*Tyre;* Sabourin: 310) *[Hebrew Poetry]*. Behind the alliance stands the world power of Assyria, completing an "axis of evil" arrayed against the people of God (v. 8). Assyria, a persistent enemy of the Israelites, continued as a symbol of a world power even after its fall (Ezra 6:22; Lam 5:6; Zech 10:10) *[Enemies]. Selah* at the end of verse 8 may signal an outburst of music leading into the imprecations that follow *[Selah]*.

Petitions Interlaced with Imprecations 83:9-18

Next, the psalmist appeals to the great deeds of God in times past, representing examples of powerful intervention for the praying community (vv. 9-11). Here are cited the stories of Gideon's decisive victory over Midian (Judg 6–8) and Deborah and Barak's defeat of Sisera and Jabin (4–5). The psalmist includes reference to the hideous picture of rotting bodies of the invaders remaining unburied, scattered like dung on the field (Ps 79:3; Jer 8:2; 9:22). The text mentions other defeated enemies (Judg 7:25; 8:21) and appeals that God would do to present enemies as he did to those earlier ones. The cry for vengeance proceeds from the fact that God is being treated with contempt and his name is defiled, for it is God's own land that the opponents wish to conquer (v. 12; Ps 79:10-12).

From the past, the psalmist turns to the present, unleashing vivid metaphors for God's annihilation of enemies. Let them be like *tumbleweed* (NIV, NRSV n) and *chaff* driven by the *wind*, consumed as by a blazing forest *fire*, and pursued relentlessly as by a driving rainstorm or devastating *hurricane* (hurricane only here in NRSV; vv. 13-15). This language, drawn from the destructive forces of nature, is associated with God's coming in power and judgment (Isa 17:13-14) *[Imprecation; Theophany]*.

At the end, expressed hope mediates this fierce prayer somewhat: even the enemies may seek the LORD's name and come to know that the LORD is *the Most High over all the earth* (vv. 16-18). But the contradictory petitions remain—that the enemies be *put to shame* and *perish in disgrace,* and that they may *know . . . the LORD.* To "know" the LORD is to recognize his name and submit to his will (Ezek 7:2-4; 28:25-26). One cannot both destroy and convert opponents. Yet both of these wishes are present.

THE TEXT IN THE BIBLICAL CONTEXT AND LIFE OF THE CHURCH

When God's People Are Threatened

This psalm is so contemporary at the beginning of the twenty-first century AD that it is frightening. Jewish people in the modern nation of Israel read verse 4 with understandable horror: *Come, let us wipe them out as a nation; let the name of Israel be remembered no more.* The threat of annihilation is real. Unfortunately, when threatened with annihilation, the common human response is to wish and pray for revenge, and worse yet, to strike out to annihilate the enemies.

When a nation knows its cause to be at one with God and regards the activity of its enemies to be directed against God, it is usually the result of faith's simplifying outlook (Weiser: 563). The danger with "God is on our side" thinking is the expectation that God will reveal himself as savior by clubbing the enemy. But that is not necessarily the case. People are more likely to find God when they do not expect God to wield the big stick (Knight, 2:59). God is present in every human failure, in ugliness, in heartbreak, in the groaning of the oppressed (Exod 2:23-24). God is present even at the cross (1 Cor 1:17-18; Phil 2:8-11). It is better to leave vengeance to God than to tell God how to punish evildoers (Rom 12:19-21) *[Vengeance].*

The psalm's conclusion points to an openness to the nations of the world. Let them know that you alone *are the Most High over all the earth.* The gate is always open. Even God's worst enemies may come in and acknowledge God as Savior and Lord (Knight, 2:60).

Reardon (164), seeing the inclusion of Tyre in the psalm's list of foes, calls attention to the fact that enmity is more than physical and military. The biblical record shows no evidence of military hostility from Tyre. Yet the Phoenician capital's influence through political and economic alliances undermined Israel's faith and fidelity to God. Reardon contends, "There is more than one way for the people of God to be destroyed." The real threat to God's people may come through the subtle paths of syncretism, materialism, idolatry, and compromise (Isa 23; Ezek 28:1-19; Eph 6:12).

Christian Responses and Use of Psalm 83

Christian interpreters, seeking to soften the harshness of the psalm, have sometimes spiritualized it by viewing the psalmist, surrounded by enemies, as a type of Christ on the cross. Psalm 83 has been included in liturgies for Good Friday, though we should recognize that the words of the psalm (vv. 16-17) convey a different spirit than Jesus' words from the cross, "Father, forgive them" (Luke 23:34; Davidson, 1998:276).

On first publication the Roman Catholic Liturgy of the Hours, a guide to recitation of the full Psalter during four weeks, completely omitted three psalms (58; 83; 109). The papal explanation stated, "Some few of the psalms have been omitted, especially because of the difficulties that were foreseen from their use in vernacular celebration" (Holladay: 304). For many, the harsh imprecatory tone of Psalm 83 is troubling.

On the positive side, Psalm 83, a prayer of God's people in a time of trouble, illustrates one of their great resources. When surrounded by hostile forces, people of faith can cry out to God for intervention and deliverance on the basis of God's acts in the past. The prayer is an expression of trust in the fulfillment of God's reign over all the earth (v. 18).

Psalm 84

How lovely Is Your Dwelling Place, O LORD of Hosts!

PREVIEW

This hymn, a favorite among songs of Zion, is also a pilgrim song, closely connected to the psalms of Ascents (120–134). Zion songs (Pss 46; 48; 76; 84; 87; 122) focus on the choice of Zion, with its city and temple, as the mountain of God *[Zion]*. Psalm 84 begins a second series of psalms (84–85, 87–88) from the Levitical clan of the Korahites. These Korah psalms delight in the praise of God as the King who sits enthroned in Jerusalem, and express joy in the service of the temple *[Korah]*.

The psalm's structure includes three stanzas (vv. 1-4, 5-9, 10-12), separated by the liturgical notation *Selah* (vv. 4, 8). Three beatitudes (*happy,* or *blessed,* or *O how fortunate,* vv. 4, 5, 12; cf. NIV) identify the themes: those who find refuge in the LORD's sanctuary, the pilgrims to Zion, and those whose trust in the LORD has been renewed. The psalm glorifies the Zion sanctuary (vv. 1, 7). At the center of the psalm stands the divine name *O LORD of hosts* (vv. 1, 3, 8, 12). Only with the LORD can one find protection, security, satisfaction, and good fortune—life in the fullest (Kraus, 1989:171).

The prayer for the king (vv. 8-9) suggests a preexilic date for com-

Psalm 84

position. Goulder (37-43) has proposed that Psalm 84 was originally a tenth- or ninth-century pilgrimage psalm for the sanctuary at Dan. If so, in its present form it has been fashioned into a Zion psalm, with the speaker a faithful Israelite on pilgrimage to Jerusalem. Later generations, even after the postexilic sanctuary was built, could once more glory in the sight of the temple and sing the pilgrim songs (Pss 84; 122).

Psalm 84 is placed after the harshness of Psalm 83, with its plots to wipe out nations and crush enemies. It is a joyous psalm, delighting in God's dwelling and reign on Mt. Zion. After the Elohistic Psalter (Pss 42–83), which preferred use of the generic name *God*, the psalms that follow predominantly use the divine name *Yahweh* (*LORD*) *[Names of God]*. The heading provides the notation *According to The Gittith* (Pss 8; 81), possibly a music instruction, though the meaning is not known *[Superscriptions, Musical]*.

OUTLINE

Longing for God's House, 84:1-4
Pilgrimage to Zion, 84:5-9
Meditation on Blessings of Trust in the LORD, 84:10-12

EXPLANATORY NOTES

Longing for God's House   84:1-4

For this psalm's setting, imagine the end of a long, hot summer. Families of Israel leave their scattered villages and make their way to the hills of Jerusalem for the Feast of Tabernacles (Zech 14:16-19). They come to the sanctuary to pray for rain upon the parched land, and for the blessing on the king and his people, as the cycle of the agricultural year begins again.

Psalm 84 illustrates the OT's devotion to the house of God, the Jerusalem sanctuary as the place where one can meet God. The mood of intense longing centers on the pilgrimage to the temple as God's dwelling place (vv. 1-2; Pss 42:1-2, 4; 43:3; 63:1-2). Four times the name *LORD of hosts* is used (vv. 1, 3, 8, 12), a title associated with the ark, symbol of the LORD's presence with his people (1 Sam 4:3-4). This title for God has royal and military overtones (1 Sam 17:45), but also refers to the God who controls all the forces in the natural world (Deut 4:19; Amos 4:13; 9:5). The name points to God's sovereignty. The importance of this cultic ritual was that people somehow encounter the living God (vv. 2, 7, 11-12).

The birds living in the shelter of the sanctuary represent the life, freedom, and joy of those who dwell close to God (v. 3). The poetic illustration of how sparrows and swallows find protection for their nesting young within the temple is seen by Delitzsch as symbol for the psalmist himself, flitting from place to place, but now finding himself at home (Kidner, 1975:304). The pilgrim lauds the blessing bestowed by the holy place (v. 4; Ps 34:8), but expresses envy toward those who are fortunate enough to live and work in the temple, and thus continually enjoy this place of God's praise (Pss 26:8; 27:4). *Selah* could signal the joyous sound of instruments, or simply a break in the liturgy (vv. 4, 8). *[Selah]*.

Pilgrimage to Zion 84:5-9

The transformational power of Jerusalem is evident as the religious pilgrimage is recounted (vv. 5-7). Again, "how fortunate" are those who can set out on such a journey of faith! The place name *Zion*, as supplied by NRSV, is lacking in the Hebrew (v. 5). *Baca* may allude to some arid valley leading to Jerusalem and the miraculous transformation brought by autumn rains on the parched land (v. 6; Isa 41:17-18). Dahood sees this psalm as a prayer for rain (vv. 6, 11), along with Psalm 85. Since *Baca* (*bākā'*) is similar in sound to the verb "weep" (*bākāh*), some have translated it as *Valley of the Weeper/Weeping* (JB), implying that those whose strength is the LORD will find that the place of sorrow can become, by divine transformation, a source of encouragement and energy. The strength of the pilgrims was renewed in anticipation as they neared Zion (v. 7).

Prayers for the king, *our shield* and *your anointed*, were a regular feature of the festival (vv. 8-9). The prosperity of the people depended on the welfare of the king. The king as *shield* was protector of the people, and the channel of divine power and blessing (v. 9; Pss 47:9; 89:18). The petition asks that the LORD might look with mercy upon the king. In the postexilic era, the *anointed* could also refer to the high priest (Num 3:3).

Meditation on Blessings of Trust in the LORD 84:10-12

The third stanza describes a longing fulfilled, the joy and privilege of arriving at the sanctuary and sharing in worship (vv. 10-12). *A day in your courts* and *a doorkeeper* are word pictures emphasizing the supreme blessing of this pilgrimage to the temple (v. 10). Time spent in the holy precincts, "in the presence of the living God, is a new time, qualitatively filled" (Kraus, 1986:77). The comparison (v. 10) suggests, "I'd rather be just on the fringes of your domain than at the heart of another." *Tents of wickedness* is "any place characterized by self-serving rather than the service of God" (McCann, 1996:1014) *[Wicked]*.

The pilgrim affirms the LORD God for providing *favor and honor* (v. 11; Prov 3:34-35). True contentment is rooted in his experience of the LORD as giver and sustainer of life (*sun*) and as protector from danger (*shield*, here used for God, in verse 9 for the king). This is the only place where the Psalter actually says that *God is a sun* (a metaphor, v. 11), though God is asked to *shine forth* (Pss 4:6; 80:1, 3, 7, 19; 94:1; etc.; cf. Isa 60:1; Mal 4:2). The OT usually avoids calling God *a sun* because of the sun's association with the sun god in Egypt, or with Shamash, a highly popular sun god in Mesopotamia in Akkadian times. Elsewhere, the psalmist calls attention to the constancy represented by the sun (Pss 19:4-6; 72:5, 17; 89:36).

The psalm ends by underscoring the joy of placing one's confidence in the LORD: *O how fortunate, all those who trust in you!* (JW). This final verse extols the blessedness of the pious and becomes an invitation for all to make the LORD their refuge (v. 12; Pss 1:1, 6; 34:8; 40:4).

THE TEXT IN THE BIBLICAL CONTEXT AND LIFE OF THE CHURCH

Places of Worship

Psalm 84 begins with *place* (v. 1), but moves quickly to God's presence (v. 2). The place (temple) is a symbol of God's dwelling among his people. So in the life of the church, congregations have often used this psalm in dedicating sanctuaries built for God's people to gather and worship. Worship places become sacred by what happens within and beyond the walls, as the gathered people meet in God's presence.

For the church, Psalm 84 finds its fulfillment not in a church building, but in Christ. In Jesus of Nazareth, life with God was revealed (1 John 1:2). Here among humanity, God makes his residence (John 1:14). The congregation of Jesus Christ, in which the exalted Lord is present, is the counterpart of the OT sanctuary (Kraus, 1989:171). Christians celebrate that divine presence in the communion service and acknowledge it in "the living stones . . . built into a spiritual house" (1 Pet 2:4-5).

The joys of shared worship are no less today than for those who first sang this psalm: the granting of rest and a hearing in God's presence, receiving forgiveness, and fellowship with God and other worshippers. People of faith go to the gathered assembly to profess that their lives are not their own, but are lived under God's sovereign claim. What might be expected in and through worship? What does it demand from the worshipper? The psalm promises that God *bestows favor and honor. No good thing does the LORD withhold from those who walk uprightly* (v. 11). O, how fortunate, those who can come and worship!

Prayers and Songs for the Journey

A theme of this psalm is pilgrimage. John Bunyan drew on images from the psalm for his classic *Pilgrim's Progress*. All life is a journey, with valleys, peaks, forks in the road, fellow travelers, discouragement, and anticipation. While God comes to meet people, the faithful also seek God. Every visit to a church or meeting of believers is, in a profound sense, a pilgrimage (Mays, 1994b:275). Prayers and songs are part of the pilgrimage of faith.

Christians can take courage in the image of Jesus as God's true temple. God abides in Jesus. Believers are invited to abide in God through Jesus (John 15:4, 10; 1 John 2:23-25). Jesus prayed: "I ask not only on behalf of these, but also on behalf of those who will believe in me through their word, that they may all be one" (John 17:20-21). A prayer by Anselm of Canterbury (1033-1109) expresses the believer's longing for God's presence on the pilgrimage in this life and beyond:

> My God, I pray that I may so know you and love you
> > that I may rejoice in you.
> And if I may not do so fully in this life,
> > let me go steadily on
> > to the day when I come to that fullness. . . .
> > Let me receive
> That which you promised through your truth,
> > that my joy may be full. (via Appleton: 66)

Johannes Brahms drew on Psalm 84 for the wonderful chorus "How lovely is thy dwelling place, O Lord of hosts," in *A German Requiem* (1866–68). Hymns based on Psalm 84 include Isaac Watts' "Lord of the worlds above" (1719), Horatius Bonar's communion hymn, "Jesus, sun and shield" (1861), and Jean Janzen's "How lovely is your dwelling" (1991).

Psalm 85

Surely His Salvation Is at Hand

PREVIEW

Psalm 85 is a community lament. After looking back to God's saving deeds in the past (vv. 1-3), the people describe their distress and make their petitions (vv. 4-7). The answer comes in an oracle of salvation (vv. 8-13).

If Psalm 126 is a companion to Psalm 85, the most likely setting for composition is the return of Jewish exiles from Babylon following the edict of Persian King Cyrus in 538 BC (Ezra 1:1-4). The people's return demonstrated divine forgiveness, as the prophets had promised (Isa 40:2; Jer 31:31-34). However, the conditions they encountered— ruined cities, wasted fields, and drought—fell far short of the glorious and happy state foretold by the prophets (Hag 1:5-11; 2:16-17; Zech 1:12-17). The plea to God (vv. 4-7) is that since he assured them of pardon by letting them return, he might now demonstrate that further by fully accepting them into blessing, prosperity, and joy (White: 132).

The salvation oracle (vv. 8-13), spoken by priest or temple prophet, declares that God's *salvation is at hand* (near) and points to a vision of reconciliation and harmony hardly found elsewhere in Scripture. The oracle portrays salvation as the uniting of four characteristics of the way of the LORD: *steadfast love* (ḥesed), *faithfulness* ('ĕmet), *righteousness* (ṣedeq) and *peace* (shalom, šālôm). Sky and earth combine as God bestows *what is good* and makes the land productive (vv. 11-12).

Alternative settings and interpretations include Mowinckel's suggestion that Psalms 85 and 126 belonged to the festival of harvest and new year (v. 12, as well as the psalm's focus on "turning"). Dahood interprets Psalm 85 as a prayer for rain, translating *good* (*haṭṭôb*, v. 12) as *his rain*. Goulder, who assumes that the Korahite psalms came from festival celebrations in the Northern Kingdom, connects Psalm 85 with the story of apostasy, judgment, and forgiveness in Exodus 32–34, which might have been recited along with the reading of Psalms 44 and 85 (Goulder: 98-107; Tate: 368-69) *[Korah; Superscriptions]*.

OUTLINE

Recalling the LORD's Favor in the Past, 85:1-3
An Urgent Plea for Present Help, 85:4-7
God's Answer to the Plea, 85:8-13

EXPLANATORY NOTES

Recalling the LORD's Favor in the Past   85:1-3

In recalling the LORD's former deeds, Israel is not recounting past glories, but remembering past mercies. Description of God's saving acts is a feature of community laments (Pss 44:1-8; 74:12-17; 80:8-11; 83:9-12).

The immediate "turn of fortune" may well have been the permission Cyrus gave for those in exile to return to their homeland (v. 1). The idiom *restored the fortunes* (deriving from *šûb šĕbût*) means (lit.), "to restore the restoration," in the sense of "to bring about a change" (Ps 126:1-3; see comments on 14:7; Jer 31:23; Westermann, 1989:47). Generally the reference is to the restoration following the catastrophe of 587 (or 586) BC, though the phrase can refer also to spiritual renewal. The people related restoration to God's forgiveness of their guilt (v. 2). Hence, their unrepentance and unforgiven sin could hold back the winter rains (Deut 11:17; Jer 5:24-25). God's past favor shown to the land, making it fertile and productive, was manifest in removal of sin guilt (Isa 40:2). The liturgical note *Selah* could suggest a pause for reflection or emphasis *[Selah]*. God's wrath has been withdrawn (v. 3; cf. Amos 1:3, 6, 9, 12, where God's wrath is not withdrawn) *[Wrath]*.

An Urgent Plea for Present Help   85:4-7

Although the return announced in Isaiah 40–55 has taken place (Isa 40:1-11), people see themselves in great distress. Deliverance did happen: the exiles returned. But *glory* did not *dwell in [the] land*, and the powers of salvation did not prevail (v. 9; Isa 60:2; 62:2; Mays, 1994b:276). So the community pleads, *Restore us again* (v. 4), in the sense of "Turn again to us" as in former days! The series of questions probing the mystery of God's inaction assumes that the present crisis cannot be God's final word. Thus, the extended request is framed by key words about the known character of God: *salvation* (vv. 4, 7) and *steadfast love* (v. 7) *[Steadfast].*

The reader needs to recognize repetition of key words in this psalm: *Return* or *restore* (*šûb*, vv. 1, 3, 4, 6, 8); *salvation* (*yeša'*, vv. 4, 7, 9); *peace* (*shalom, šalôm*, vv. 8, 10) and the covenant virtues of *steadfast love* (*ḥesed*), *faithfulness* (*'ĕmet*), and *righteousness* (*ṣedeq*, vv. 7, 10, 11, 13).

God's Answer to the Plea   85:8-13

Let me hear . . . introduces the oracle (v. 9) *[Oracle].* In Israelite worship, great significance was placed upon the LORD speaking through priest or temple prophet (Pss 50:7-15; 81:8-10). Kraus (1989:176) suggests that this speaker may have been a peace prophet (Isa 57:19-21; Jer 6:14; 8:11), announcing peace that will bring healing "to the far and to the near," though not to the wicked. Tate questions whether there is a change of speakers in Psalm 85; he suggests that the message may be the psalmist's interpretation of what the LORD has to say in order to encourage and build hope (Tate, 1990:370).

The message is that *salvation is at hand,* for the LORD is near (v. 9; Isa 45:13; 51:5). Those who *fear* the LORD live in obedience to God's will, with attentiveness and submission (v. 9; Pss 22:23; 66:16; 103:11, 13). With the temple's destruction and the exile, many believed that the *glory* had left (Ezek 10:1-19). While God's dwelling *in our land* had its location in the Jerusalem temple (1 Kings 8:10-11; Ps 26:8), God would be, or is, present again with his people.

The remaining verses amplify the oracle, stating how the LORD's powers of salvation are at work creating peace (*shalom*). They portray *steadfast love, faithfulness, righteousness,* and *peace* as personifications of the divine attributes and the LORD's servants (A. Anderson, 2:612). The focus is on God's character and activity. *Steadfast love* and *faithfulness* convey the elements of loyalty and community. In the partnership of sky and earth, the time of blessing will come when the land will enjoy spiritual well-being and material prosperity (Matt 6:33). Psalm 85 thus begins and ends by speaking of the *land* (vv. 1, 12).

Translations of the final verse vary, usually with reference to the LORD's way. It may reflect the idea of the theophanic coming of the LORD, with *righteousness* going before the LORD as a herald to prepare the way for his journey across the land (Isa 40:3-5; Tate, 1990:372). It can also imply "his footsteps a way to walk in" (Kidner, 1975:311; Knight, 2:68).

THE TEXT IN THE BIBLICAL CONTEXT AND LIFE OF THE CHURCH

A Vision of Shalom

The biblical word *shalom*, often translated *peace*, conveys a comprehensive concept of well-being, peace, and welfare that includes love, faithfulness, righteousness, prosperity, and glory. Shalom is the hope the psalmist holds out to God's people living in dark and depressing times. It is the hope kindled and sustained by worship.

Psalm 85 speaks to the mystery of God's reconciliation and the partnering of heaven and earth. The ultimate revelation of God's glory in the midst of his people would come in the incarnation. The church believes the attributes of God were present and active in Jesus Christ. As God in human flesh, he "lived among us, . . . full of grace and truth" (John 1:14; 2 Cor 4:6). In and through him are grace and truth and righteousness (John 1:17; Rom 1:16-17). In him the fullness of God was pleased to dwell (Col 1:19; 2:9; Mays, 1994b:278). Christ "is our peace" (Eph 2:14), our righteousness, our sanctification, and redemption (1 Cor 1:30).

What is the result of this union of partners to the covenant? The psalm suggests that *faithfulness* will spring up from the ground, from human beings who live on earth, in response to the grace (*righteousness*) that comes from above. Isaiah 45:8 pictorially describes this two-way movement of grace and love (Knight, 2:67). Paul writes about it in Romans, using the word *justification*, how God acts in grace to make people *right* with himself (Rom 5:1-10), allowing love and faithfulness to spring up in people of God's peace (Rom 12:1-21). The hymn "We are people of God's peace" (Menno, 1552; trans. Esther Bergen, 1990) gives powerful expression to this union of partners to the covenant.

The Psalm's Liturgical Use

We may know Psalm 85 primarily for its striking portrayal of God's promise of peace and salvation (vv. 8-13). This psalm's preservation for liturgical use by the Jewish people is a reminder that the words apply also to situations other than the time of composition. It can speak to all time. How do God's people continue to live in hope in a world where so much seems meaningless?

The Book of Common Prayer lists Psalm 85 as an appropriate psalm for Christmas Eve. The church has found this a good song for Advent with the announcement, *Surely his salvation is at hand . . .* (v. 9). As the people first hearing Psalm 85 stood between "salvation at hand" and a vision of "salvation yet to be," so the church always stands between "already" and "not yet." Advent invites the Christian to celebrate salvation, and at the same time to pray for salvation. That is the tension of all genuine faith. In faith we believe, yet we wait for God's grace (Mark 9:24). True worship points God's people toward the ultimate hope of a new heaven and a new earth (Rev 21:1-4).

Psalm 86

Incline Your Ear, . . . for You Alone Are God

PREVIEW

A lament, this prayer song of one beset by foes (vv. 14, 17) is a cry to God for help (vv. 1-7). The lament is interrupted by a confident hymn (vv. 8-11) and vow of thanksgiving (vv. 12-13), to affirm the awesome and unique power of God. The final verses renew the complaint, and the psalm ends with petition for a *sign* from the LORD (vv. 14-17).

The setting may be that of a poor petitioner waiting in the sanctuary for word of the LORD's help, and perhaps a verdict of acquittal (v. 1). The phrases *devoted to you* and *your servant* (v. 2) can also point in the direction of pious believers in the postexilic community (Tate, 1990:379-80). Commentators generally agree that this psalm's composition is postexilic, for it uses the liturgical language of the times. The title in the heading, *A Prayer of David*, is likely a scribal ascription to give the psalm Davidic authority *[Superscriptions]*.

In Psalm 86 readers have identified no less than forty quotations from other psalms and other OT writings. Some have labeled this borrowing as unimaginative, repetitive, and mechanical. On the contrary, the psalm must be seen in the liturgical setting in which the concern of the petitioner is placed in the larger context of the worshipping community. Psalm 86 is a complex prayer song, drawing on Israel's creeds and prayer language to give powerful witness to the great and wondrous God who continues to help and comfort.

Psalm 86

OUTLINE

A Desperate Cry for Help, 86:1-7
Celebration of the Incomparable Sovereignty of God, 86:8-13
The Supplication Renewed, 86:14-17

EXPLANATORY NOTES

A Desperate Cry for Help 86:1-7

This prayer of supplication opens with typical lament language conveying desperation (Pss 17:6; 31:2; 88:2; 102:2). The petitioner identifies himself with the *poor and needy* (v. 1) and with those who belong to the LORD as his servants (v. 2; 31:16; 69:17; 116:16; 143:2). The psalmist's identity is bound up with God's identity.

The cry for help is characterized by a series of reasons, each introduced with the little word *for* (*kî*), to show why God should help the afflicted petitioner (vv. 1-7). Initially, the motivation is based on the psalmist's attitude toward God (vv. 1-4). Subsequent reasons *for* God to intervene are on the basis of God's character (vv. 5, 7, 10, 13). Significant features of this psalm include the names of God, words used to describe God, and the direct use of *you* (*'attâ*, as in v. 2), the nominative pronoun for God.

As for the names of God, *'ădōnāy, Lord*, indicating sovereignty or absolute lordship, is used seven times (vv. 3, 4, 5, 8, 9, 12, 15). *Yahweh, LORD,* the covenant God as helper, appears four times (vv. 1, 6, 11, 17). Five times the psalmist addresses God as *'ĕlōhîm*, revealing his consciousness of the divine might (vv. 2, 10, 12, 14, 15). In use of these terms, the combined sense is that of divine authority (Morgan: 71) *[Names of God]*.

Words used to describe God's character and activity include *gracious* (v. 3), *good, forgiving, abounding in steadfast love* (v. 5), *great, do wondrous things* (v. 10), *great, steadfast love, delivered* (v. 13), *merciful, gracious, slow to anger, abounding in steadfast love* and *faithfulness* (v. 15). The psalmist has taken many of these attributes from Israel's early creeds (Exod 34:6-7; Num 14:18; Ps 103:8). The first section of the lament closes as the praying person voices a traditional confessional statement about the character of the LORD (v. 5).

Celebration of the Incomparable Sovereignty of God 86:8-13

The central section of the psalm focuses even more clearly on God's identity by emphasizing God's incomparability (vv. 8-10). Elements of the literary structure likewise confirm the psalm's theological center. Psalm 86 has an unusual number of second-person pronouns, such as *your ear* (v. 1), *to you, your servant,* and *in you* (v. 2). These suggest that the situation of trouble is the LORD's problem as well as the psalmist's. But even more remarkable is the direct use of *you* (*'attâ,* six times), the nominative pronoun used for emphasis and urgency in addressing God. Brueggemann points to a possible intentional chiastic order, with the psalm framed by the confessional statements of verses 2 and 17 (Brueggemann, 1984:62):

> A *You are my God.* (v. 2)
> > B *For you, O Lord, are good and forgiving.* (v. 5)
> > > C *For you are great.* (v. 10)
> > > C´ *You alone are God.* (v. 10)
> > B´ *But you, O Lord, are a God merciful and gracious.* (v. 15)
> A´ *Because you, LORD, have helped me.* (v. 17)

This diagram centers on the God who does *wondrous things* (*niplā'ôt*), such as the exodus, the paradigmatic demonstration of God's rule (v. 10; Exod 3:20; 34:10). Though other gods are mentioned (v. 8; Ps 82:1), they serve as foil for the incomparability of Israel's God (Exod 15:11; Ps 77:13-15; Isa 40:18-25). A further theme is that of God as creator of all the nations, and how one day they will bow before him in worship (v. 9, Pss 22:27-28; 66:4, 8; 67:1-7; Isa 45:22-23; 66:23). Thus, this hymn at the psalm's center proclaims, *You alone are God* (v. 10).

The core of the psalm's instruction follows: *Teach me your way, O LORD* (v. 11). Walking in God's truth (*'ĕmet,* Pss 25:5; 26:3) calls for single-hearted reverence of God's *name* (Ps 119:2, 10; Jer 32:33-41; Ezek 11:19-20). The psalmist's response is a vow of thanksgiving and praise for the *steadfast love* through which God has delivered him from Sheol, the abode of the dead (vv. 12-13) *[Sheol].*

The Supplication Renewed 86:14-17

The lament resumes, echoing the psalm's opening section (vv. 1-7). The wicked are characterized as *insolent,* people who, in their arrogance, are oblivious to God's instruction and will use their power to destroy those who stand in their way (v. 14; Pss 54:3; 86:14). In contrast, God is *merciful, gracious,* and *abounding in steadfast love* (v. 15; Exod 34:6; Num 14:18; Pss 103:8; 145:8) *[Steadfast].*

The prayer *Be gracious to me* (v. 16) joins with the prayer at the psalm's beginning (v. 3). The psalmist appeals to God as *your servant, . . . the child of your serving girl.* A maidservant's child is born in the master's house and thus belongs to the master. The term indicates complete devotion (Murphy: 114). The ending request is for some *sign* of God's *favor,* some favorable demonstration of God's action so that his foes may *be put to shame [Enemies].* He concludes, trusting in the LORD's help and comfort. The verbs imply that God has already acted in deliverance (vv. 13, 17). This certainty permeates the psalm's petitions.

THE TEXT IN THE BIBLICAL CONTEXT AND LIFE OF THE CHURCH

The Language of Creed and Liturgy

Psalm 86 draws attention to the significance of liturgy and the power of language drawn from the creeds of faith. In worship, the Jewish people turned to the stories of the covenant God, the God of wonders, the helper and deliverer, as based on their early creeds (Exod 15:13; 34:6; Deut 26:5-10a). This covenant (fidelity) relationship of God and Israel is important. In distress, suffering people must find a voice. The creedal claims are still credible in the darkness (Brueggemann, 1984:63). Jewish people chant Psalm 86 on the penitential Day of Atonement (Yom Kippur, cf. Lev 16:1-34).

Formulaic summaries from the ancient church—the Lord's Prayer (Matt 6:9-13; Luke 11:2-4) and the Apostles' Creed—remind Christians Sunday after Sunday of realities that are not dependent on how the worshipper feels at the moment. They provide tools to help people of faith experience the world in relationship to the creating, saving God. They offer words and a voice to God's people at all times.

Suggestions for Prayer

This psalm also illustrates the power of memorized Scripture texts for personal prayer. To give expression to faith for present needs, spirituality always draws upon the tradition that has nurtured it. Biblical texts of comfort and hope committed to memory cannot be taken away from people of faith. These texts also provide a vast resource for voicing prayers to God. Mays outlines Psalm 86 as a guide to prayers of supplication by identifying prayer as the cry of a *servant* to his *Lord,* made in confidence that God *can* and *will* help, and as the utterance of an identity that is lived out. "Prayer is the voice of commitment" (Mays, 1994b:279-90).

Far from making prayers hackneyed and monotonous, the rich language of the psalms can become a tool for Christians to address God with their deepest needs and longings.

Psalm 87

Zion, Glorious City of God

PREVIEW

The words of John Newton's majestic hymn "Glorious things of thee are spoken" (1779) spring to mind on reading Psalm 87. This short song of Zion is similar to Psalms 46; 48; 76; 84; 122; and 137 in expressing deep love for Jerusalem.

Though the text appears damaged and commentators have attempted rearranging verses (e.g., Kraus; Weiser), most versions and commentaries follow the verse sequence of the Hebrew text. The major interpretive issue focuses on verses 4-6. Is the reference to Jews living outside Palestine? To converts from non-Jewish faiths? Or to the consummation of the kingdom of God, when all nations shall be adopted into the family of God (Rhodes: 124)?

The psalm's setting appears to be a processional dance (v. 7). The psalm portrays Zion as seen during a feast attended by pilgrims from many nations (as later on Pentecost; Acts 2:5-13). Goulder (170-74) suggests that the psalm originated in Dan before the fall of the Northern Kingdom, with the references to Zion (vv. 2, 5) added to adapt it for use in Jerusalem. However, it was likely a Zion hymn from the beginning, perhaps from the monarchy, though Assyria is not mentioned among the nations (Isa 19:25). Assyria had fallen to Babylon in 612 BC. Persia then absorbed the Babylonian Empire in 539 BC. Many commentators believe the present psalm is exilic or postexilic. The universal mission theme suggests a late date. For the heading, see the essays *Korah* and *Superscriptions*.

Psalm 87 deals with the glory and surpassing importance of Zion. As the center of the community of God on earth, Zion is the mother of all members of the people of God (Isa 54:1; 62:1-12). The psalm illustrates Psalm 86:9: *All the nations you have made shall come and bow down before you, O Lord.*

OUTLINE

Hymn in Praise of Zion, 87:1-3
The Joy of All Who Claim Birth in Zion, 87:4-7

Mark Smith has offered another outline of the psalm's structure as a chiasmus, to illustrate the role of Zion as the universal spiritual center of the world (via McCann, 1996:1023):

> A *in you* (v. 3; NIV, NRSV: *of you*)
>   B *there* (v. 4; NIV: *in Zion*)
>   C *in her* (v. 5; NRSV: *in it*)
>   B´ *there* (v. 6; NIV: *in Zion*)
> A´ *in you* (v. 7)

EXPLANATORY NOTES

Hymn in Praise of Zion   87:1-3

To the psalmist, Zion was the center of historical meaning that God had disclosed to Israel, and through Israel to the whole world. The choice of Zion is important to OT belief and frequently rehearsed (Pss 78:67-72; 132:13) *[Zion]*.

With transfer of the ark, Zion became the LORD's holy mountain, the holy place of the holy God (v. 1; 2:6; 15:1; 43:3; 48:1; 99:9). The *gates of Zion*, center of economic and social life, represent the whole city (v. 2). *Dwellings of Jacob* are the other towns and cities of the land, but could also represent the northern sanctuaries at Bethel and Dan, replaced by Zion (v. 2). The *glorious things* spoken of Jerusalem include her destiny as a city of compassion and love (v. 3; Isa 14:32). Ultimately all nations will make pilgrimage to Zion (2:2-4). The liturgical note *Selah* breaks the psalm into two stanzas (vv. 3, 6) *[Selah]*.

The Joy of All Who Claim Birth in Zion   87:4-7

The second part of the psalm has the sound of a prophetic oracle. One can imagine the pilgrim at the temple festival, as in a vision seeing people from all over the known world pass by. The pilgrim-poet overhears the divine counsel regarding God's people, as the LORD records: *"This one was born there. . . . This one and that one . . . This one . . .* (vv. 4-6). A "book of life" was well-known in OT times (Exod 32:32; Ps 69:28; Isa 4:3; Ezek 13:9; cf. Rev 20:12). The speaker (vv. 4-5) appears to be God, probably through the voice of a prophet *[Oracle]*.

The list of nations is surprising (v. 4). *Rahab*, a poetic name for Egypt, suggests a monster who repeatedly devoured Israel (Isa 30:7). *Babylon* was another great power that invaded Israel. Then are mentioned nearby neighbors, *Philistia*, the enemy Israel never dislodged; and *Tyre*, the affluent merchant city (Ezek 28:1-19). After naming world powers to the south and north, and next-door neighbors, *Cush* (Nubia or Ethiopia; NRSV n) is named, representing the nations at the margins of the known world.

Who are those *born there*? With the exile and other dispersions of the people of Israel, many members of Israel lived in foreign lands. Some were born in other lands and thus citizens of foreign nations. But these verses assert, "Zion is the mother of all Israelites living in the Dispersion." Hence, Zion becomes more than a geographical location; it is a spiritual reality, a people of God scattered as well as gathered. This likely included proselytes. So people have read the psalm as part of the OT hope that all nations would be drawn to the LORD (Pss 22:27; 48:10; Isa 2:2-4; 45:22; Zech 2:10-11). This spiritual citizenship does not depend upon the fact that one happened to be born in Zion, but rather upon one's obedience to the LORD (A. Anderson, 2:622). The psalm has a universal range that includes all humanity. The nations call Zion their home (v. 4) because the Most High (v. 5) claims them as God's own people (v. 6).

Religious dancing, as well as singing and instrumental music, was an expression of Israel's worship (v. 7; Exod 15:20; 2 Sam 6:5, 16; Pss 30:11; 149:3; 150:4). Such joyful praise marked the entry of processions of worshippers, coming to the chosen city at festival time (2 Sam 6:21; Ps 122). From the festival dance, a song rises: *All my springs are in you* (v. 7). In Zion (and in the LORD) are the waters of life, the sources of blessing, the creative energies, welfare, and joy (Pss 36:8; 46:4; Isa 12:3; Ezek 47:12; Rev 22:1-2).

THE TEXT IN THE BIBLICAL CONTEXT AND LIFE OF THE CHURCH

A Grand Vision of the People of God

Psalm 87 declares that eventually people of all nations shall be called by God and proud to reckon themselves as citizens of God's kingdom. What a grand vision! Such a universal mission had its roots in the political empire of David. It was reinterpreted when the empire fell apart and was spiritualized when the dynasty collapsed (Isa 2:2-4; 49:6). However, such openness to the Gentile world did not become central to Judaism. Is this why Psalm 87 was neglected textually and somewhat of an embarrassment (Stuhlmueller, 1983, 2:54)?

Since the psalm makes it clear that Zion gives its name to a community, not a place, the Christian church has been drawn to it as an expression of the catholic, universal character of the people of God. Here is the foundation from which Christianity has set out in mission. "The whole drama of God's dealings with the people leads up to the appearance of the Messiah in Jerusalem, and to his death and victory there—the crucial event which is reenacted in Christian worship. Zion is the historical center around which is gathered the people of God, whose membership is determined by God's choosing, not by human standards" (B. Anderson, 1983:195).

Through the passionate work of Paul, the Christian church took up the universal mission of Judaism (Eph 3:3, 6, 9). Paul declared free entry to Jerusalem. He declared that the city had been waiting to adopt all people as her children (Gal 4:21-31). The church was now the heir of the promises God had bestowed, even while the Jewish people also continued to be heirs of God's promises (Rom 9:4-5; 11:1; Knight, 2:74). For Paul, this mystery is linked with Jerusalem and to Jesus, "the mediator of a new covenant" (Heb 12:22-24). So Christians read and sing Psalm 87 in light of these and other NT texts (Eph 2:19-20; Phil 3:20). Christians can count themselves as citizens of "the holy city, the New Jerusalem" (Rev 21:2).

Psalm 87:3 became the text of Augustine's monumental work *The City of God*, though subsequent reform movements have rightly challenged Constantinian and other state-church understandings of the people of God. The church does not conquer by force. The church can carry out its evangelical mission to "make disciples of all nations" (Matt 28:19) only in loving compassion for God's orphans near and far, embracing them with their cultural richness and religious insights as brothers and sisters for whom "there is no longer Jew or Greek, . . . slave or free, . . . male and female; for all . . . are one in Christ Jesus" (Gal 3:28).

The implications of such a vision are immense. If all people are God's children and have access to what Zion represents in terms of God's kingdom, why should Jew, Christian, or Muslim fight over the city of Jerusalem? What right does any nation have to dehumanize others as "enemies" and wage war against them? Jesus wept over the holy city, saying, "If you, even you, had only recognized on this day the things that make for peace!" (Luke 19:41-42; Matt 23:37-39). How God who loves the whole world must grieve over all his children, who do not yet know "the things that make for peace."

Psalm 88

Like One Forsaken Among the Dead

PREVIEW

The saddest of all laments, this psalm is by one critically ill or in some other life-threatening situation; it ends with *darkness*. The Job-like lament describes death (*Sheol, the Pit*) as *the land of forgetfulness* (vv. 3, 4, 12), where it is too late for the miracle of God's *steadfast love* and *saving help*. Feeling victimized by God's wrath, the psalmist complains directly to God about his situation (vv. 6-8, 14-18). Yet, in affirmation and trust, the psalmist cries out in prayer. Three different Hebrew verbs for "cry" or "call" are used: *ṣā'aq* (v. 1), *qārā'* (v. 9b), and *šāwa'* (v. 13), perhaps indicating that the psalmist has exhausted every approach. These words also mark the psalm's points of division.

See Psalms 6; 22; 38; and 41 as other laments of the sick. In mood and the sense of forsakenness, it is akin to Psalms 38 and 41, or the book of Job. The dark character of Psalm 88 stands in sharp contrast to the preceding celebrative Psalm 87.

Regarding the heading, this is the last of the psalms of the *Korahites [Korah]*. *Mahalath*, a term of uncertain meaning found also in the title to Psalm 53, could suggest "according to a sad tune or melody." A *Maskil* may have to do with "instruction." Heman appears as one of the singers appointed by David to serve in the temple (1 Chron 6:33; 16:41-42). He is named alongside Ethan the Ezrahite among the famous sages of Solomon's court (1 Kings 4:31).

Psalm 88

The marginal note *Selah* (vv. 7, 10) suggests adaptation of this psalm for temple use *[Superscriptions; Musical; Selah]*.

OUTLINE

Cry to God for Help, 88:1-2
Lament of One Afflicted, 88:3-9a
Questions of Desperation, 88:9b-12
Cry for Help Renewed in Face of God's Wrath, 88:13-18

EXPLANATORY NOTES

Cry to God for Help   88:1-2

The introductory petition reveals the spiritual tension underlying the psalm. The *cry* (*ṣāʻaq*) is one of anguish or distress (v. 1; Ps 107:6, 28). Yet the psalmist, who keeps praying day and night, can still address the LORD as *God of my salvation* (v. 1).

This psalm may reflect the agonizing cry of a person near death who, through life, has struggled with isolating and debilitating illness (vv. 8-9, 15, 18). Might this have been a person in the final stages of leprosy (Lev 13:1-8, 45-46; 2 Chron 26:20-21)?

Lament of One Afflicted   88:3-9a

Whatever the affliction, the psalmist is on the brink of death. The fear of death, which cannot be banished from his mind (vv. 3-6, 10-12), gives rise to a powerful description of *Sheol* as *the Pit* (vv. 4, 6), and *regions dark and deep* (vv. 6, 12) *[Sheol]*. Sheol was the abode in the underworld to which the dead were consigned. Hebrews thought of death as greatly diminished vitality, almost to the point of extinction. In that shadowy existence (cf. v. 10, *shades*), there was praise neither of God nor of God's saving help (vv. 10-12). This *Pit* is the final destiny or fate of the lamenter if God does not come to the rescue (vv. 4-5; Pss 28:1; 30:3; 69:15; Isa 38:18).

From this description of Sheol, the psalmist moves to address his complaint directly to God as *You* (vv. 6-8). As with Job, the psalmist's troubles come from God: *You have. . . , your wrath. . . , you overwhelm . . .* (v. 7). The imagery is that of being in the depths and drowning under an overwhelming flood (Pss 42:7; 69:1-2). The liturgical marker *Selah* is perhaps for emphasis *[Selah]*.

As the result of sickness, isolation from the community was common (v. 8; Lev 13:45-46; Job 19:13-22; 30:9-23; Ps 31:9-13). The plaintive statement describes the psalmist's loneliness and personal affliction (vv. 8c-9a).

Questions of Desperation   88:9b-12

The psalmist's prayer is nonending (v. 9b). In four desperate questions, the praying person is trying to convince the LORD to let him live. Are the LORD's *wonders* (*pele'*) known in death (vv. 10, 12)? Is the LORD's *steadfast love, faithfulness,* and *saving help* known in Sheol? *Abaddon* derives from the verb "perish" (*'ābad*), is a synonym for Sheol, and is the name given the abyss in Revelation 9:11. The *land of forgetfulness* is the ultimate in being cut off (v. 12). These descriptions of Sheol are similar to those in the book of Job (7:9, 21; 10:21; 14:18-21; 16:22). To each of the four questions (vv. 10-12) the implied answer is "no," although we can find a different point of view elsewhere (Pss 49:15; 73:24; 139:8).

Cry for Help Renewed in Face of God's Wrath   88:13-18

The emphatic *But I . . .* focuses attention on the psalmist's plight and the renewed cry for help (v. 13). The complaints include unanswered prayer and spurning by God (v. 14), long-term affliction (v. 15), the terror of God's wrath (vv. 16-17), and shunning by others (v. 18). The psalm ends with the grim prospect of darkness (Job 17:13-16; 18:18). An alternative reading for the final line is NIV's *Darkness is my closest friend* (19:14).

In everything the psalmist discerns God's wrath directed against him (vv. 7, 14-18) *[Wrath]*. He can only cry out in the dark to a hidden God who remains a complete mystery. Afraid of death, he has come to death. The psalmist can only protest against being erased!

THE TEXT IN THE BIBLICAL CONTEXT AND LIFE OF THE CHURCH

Face to Face with Death

Psalm 88 vividly describes the Hebrew understanding of death. "The realm of the dead was thought of as an expansion of the grave. Its name was Sheol, the Pit, Abaddon. It was deep and dark and silent" (Mays, 1994b:282).

This grim picture of the end of human life has shaped the imagination of many people, who come to regard death as a most terrifying prospect. Death's reality ought not to be minimized. C. S. Lewis (1967:81) in his *Letters to an American Lady* observed that people basically have three different attitudes with respect to death: to desire

Psalm 88

it, to fear it, or to ignore it. The last, which he calls the worst, is the most common. Psalm 88 can serve persons who pass *through the valley of the shadow of death* (Ps 23:4 KJV) by preparing their way for divine comfort. Despite its gloom, the psalm is a unique dialogue with an absent God. Perhaps leprosy gave rise to this appeal. In the generations since then, how many have cried out because of debilitating illness or physical or emotional disability? They cried to a God who seems not only silent or absent, but who is even interpreted as capricious. Here is the "cry of absence" for the winter of the heart (Marty, 1983:68-72).

"The Unhappy Cry of an Existentialist" is the title given this psalm by Knight (2:72-78). This is a reminder that death can also be experienced in this life, that to be cut off from hope is a death in itself. All other laments in the Psalms, it is said, include somewhere a note of praise; but not this psalm.

Yet we know that Psalm 88 is not the last word about death or darkness. *Even the darkness is not dark to you*, wrote one psalmist (139:12). The NT speaks of how "the light shines in the darkness" (John 1:5; 9:5; 1 Pet 2:9; 1 John 1:5-10). This psalm reminds Christians of our groaning as we "wait for adoption, the redemption of our bodies" (Rom 8:22-25). In gratitude we ponder a resurrected Christ who "abolished death and brought life and immortality to light through the gospel" (2 Tim 1:10).

Interpretation and Use of Psalm 88

Goulder holds that the Korahite psalms have a northern origin and has proposed an alternative origin and purpose for this psalm. His thesis is that Psalm 88 was spoken by a representative of the nation, perhaps a priest, who was ritually made a scapegoat and driven from the community for a day, shut up in a watery pit near the sanctuary at Dan. While no one can prove this interpretation, the ritual and pathetic plea in Psalm 88 may suggest an innocent person's redemptive suffering as needed to heal the sins of society (Isa 53; Lam 3; Goulder: 200-10).

In the history of interpretation, readers have understood Psalm 88 as an exilic or postexilic prayer to articulate the plight of the whole people. The experience of the exile and its aftermath has shaped the character of book III of the Psalter. Thus, Psalm 88 becomes a fitting anticipation of Psalm 89, which extols the LORD's power and faithfulness (McCann, 1996:1027) *[Ways of Reading].*

Christian interpreters have seen in Psalm 88 a picture of Jesus, who was afflicted with scourging and crucifixion and was *counted among those who go down to the pit* (Ps 88:4, 8; Luke 23:49). The Book of Common Prayer lists Psalm 88 for evening prayer on Good Friday.

Brueggemann (1984:81) suggests that Psalm 88 shows what the cross is about: "*faithfulness* in scenes of complete *abandonment.*" The cross shows how much God loves the world. Psalm 88 is a reminder that despite the sense of abandonment, prayer remains an option. The psalmist could still cry out of the darkness. Jesus could cry out from the cross, "My God, my God, why . . . ?" (Matt 27:46). Thomas Merton (149) commends this psalm for "a day on which we seem to be buried alive under an inhumane burden of temptation."

Psalm 89

Where Is the Steadfast Love You Swore to David?

PREVIEW

Book III of the Psalter closes with an elaborate psalm centering on the Davidic dynasty. Psalm 89 is founded on the great prophecy of 2 Samuel 7:4-17, the promise of a throne to David forever and ever. Present reality, a military defeat of a Davidic king, appears to contradict God's faithfulness (v. 43). The psalm ends with a desperate prayer for deliverance or restoration in face of taunting enemies.

Three different forms are used in the makeup of this psalm: a hymn in praise of the LORD's power and faithfulness (vv. 1-18), an oracle of God's covenant with David (vv. 19-37), and a lament over the defeat of the Davidic king, ending in prayer for the LORD's intervention (vv. 38-51). Although earlier commentators saw Psalm 89 as a composite of diverse psalms, the tendency today is to consider the psalm as a unit. We can also regard Psalm 89 as a royal psalm because of its focus on the Davidic dynasty.

Readers offer various suggestions as to setting and date of composition. These include a time as early as 701 BC. More likely are the proposals of events following the death of King Josiah (609 BC; 2 Kings 23:29-30), or the exile of Jehoiachin (597 BC; 24:8-17), for they fit allusions to the king and the nation's plight (vv. 38-45). Some even propose a time as late as 520 BC, the background of the hope that the Davidic kingdom might be restored (Hag 2:20-23; Zech 4:6-14; 6:9-15). Nevertheless, the psalm gives no hint of the exile, though it presupposes the end of the Davidic dynasty. The speaker may be one of the LORD's faithful servants who struggled to maintain faith during a desperate time for God's people (v. 50; Tate, 1990:417). Some scholars dismiss historical references and even suggest that the king represents a dying and rising Canaanite nature deity in a cultic renewal ceremony.

Key words of the Mosaic covenant (Exod 34:6-7; Hos 2:19-20), *steadfast love* (ḥesed) and *faithfulness* ('ĕmet/'ĕmûnâ), knit the psalm together (vv. 1, 2, 5, 8, 14, 24, 33, 49; cf. vv. 5, 8, 28). Verse 49 asks the central question: *Lord, where is your steadfast love of old, which by your faithfulness you swore to David?* Present reality (vv. 38-45) starkly contrasts against the promises to David *forever* (*forever* reiterated nine times), thus giving rise to this sad lament. The chosen one has become the rejected one. Yet the LORD's deeds are not ended. A blessing closes book III of the Psalter (v. 52).

The heading identifies the psalm as a *Maskil* (used also for Pss 32; 42; 44; 45; 52–55; 74; 78; 88; 142), which appears to mean an "instructional song" or "artistic song." *Ethan the Ezrahite* was noted for his wisdom (1 Kings 4:31) and identified as a Levitical musician (1 Chron 15:17, 19) *[Superscriptions]*.

OUTLINE

Hymn Extolling the LORD's Power and Faithfulness, 89:1-18
    89:1-4   Prelude Introducing the Themes
    89:5-18   Hymnic Description of the Exalted Majesty of the LORD
Oracle on the LORD's Promises to David, 89:19-37
    89:19-27   The King as God's Chosen Representative
    89:28-37   Divine Promise of the Throne Forever
Lament on Rejection of the Dynasty, 89:38-51
    89:38-45   Complaint: The Plight of the King
    89:46-51   Prayer for the LORD's Intervention and Deliverance
Doxology Concluding Book Three of the Psalter, 89:52

EXPLANATORY NOTES

Hymn Extolling the LORD's Power and Faithfulness 89:1-18

The hymn begins with the confession of the inviolability of the mercies promised to the house of David. It places the LORD's *steadfast love* and *faithfulness* in juxtaposition to a statement of God's covenant with David. The theme of God's *steadfast love* (ḥesed, vv. 1, 2, 14, 24, 28, 33, 49) and *faithfulness* ('ĕmet/'ĕmûnâ, vv. 1, 2, 5, 8, 14, 24, 33, 49) is developed in verses 5-14. The theme of God's covenant with David as God's *chosen one* and *servant* (vv. 3-4) is developed in verses 19-37. The *forever* of this "everlasting throne" (vv. 1, 2, 4; 2 Sam 7:16; Pss 45:6; 61:7) becomes the critical term of the hymn, oracle, and petition. The liturgical notation *Selah* appears at the end of the prelude (also at vv. 37, 45, 48), perhaps to give the congregation time to pause for reflection *[Selah]*.

Rather abruptly, the psalmist praises the LORD for his incomparability and his creative power in the establishment of the ordered world. He lauds God for his *wonders* (*pele'*) and *faithfulness* (vv. 5-8; cf. Ps 88:10). The LORD is without comparison in his glory and loftiness (Exod 15:11; 2 Sam 7:22; Ps 18:31). The LORD has no peers in the divine assembly (vv. 6-7; 82:1). The widespread idea of human affairs controlled by a council of gods was adapted in Israel, with the LORD seen as leader over all gods (Caird: 232).

The poet draws on imagery from ancient Near Eastern mythology in reviewing God's conquest of hostile, chaotic forces, bringing secure peace and fertility on the earth (vv. 9-13; Ps 74:12-17; Isa 51:9-10). The account of the LORD subduing chaos alludes to a Ugaritic/Canaanite myth in which Baal conquers Yam, the sea god (v. 9; "Ugaritic Myths, Poems About Baal," *ANET* 130-35). *Rahab*, the name of a mythological sea serpent, refers to the dragon Tiamat, whom the Babylonian god Marduk overcomes (v. 10; "Akkadian Myths, Creation Epic," *ANET* 60-72). The psalmist uses these stories metaphorically to celebrate the sovereignty of the LORD's reign (Rhodes: 127). Even the lofty mountains, as home of the gods and centers of worship in ancient Palestine, extol the might of the LORD (v. 12). The LORD's arm and hand are declared to be strong as those of a mighty warrior (v. 13). Yet not might, but *righteousness and justice, . . . steadfast love and faithfulness*, the personified attributes, form the basis of the LORD's sovereignty (v. 14; Ps 85:10-11). So the hymn connects creation and history. The creator God is not just any supreme being, but the LORD of Israel's history, the God who has chosen and entered into community with his people.

In some way the king embodies or represents the LORD's reign upon earth (vv. 15-18). Filled with awe, a cultic prophet accords the king the divine designation *shield* to demonstrate who stands behind the chosen king (v. 18; Ps 84:9, 11). *Happy, blessed*, or *fortunate* are the people of God, who extol such kingship as belonging to the LORD (v. 15, 18).

Oracle on the LORD's Promises to David 89:19-37

The oracle proclaims the terms of the covenant with David (vv. 19-37) *[Oracle]*. The psalm presents the oracle as a vision revealed to a cultic priest or prophet (v. 19). The words gather up prophetic promises made to the Davidic dynasty. Based on prophecies of Nathan, these verses become a liturgical reformulation of 2 Samuel 7 and assume an eternal, unbreakable Davidic covenant. The oracle highlights the prerogatives assured by the LORD: anointing (v. 20), protection (v. 21), victory (vv. 22-25), adoptive sonship (vv. 26-27), and personal and dynastic security (vv. 28-37). The attributes of the king are those acclaimed of the LORD.

David is divinely chosen and anointed with holy oil (vv. 19-20; Ps 45:7). Anointing placed the ruler under the LORD's protection and signaled that his person was not to be violated (1 Sam 24:6; Ps 105:15; Kraus, 1986:109). Taking someone by the hand is a way of transferring the power of God to the ruler (v. 21). Regarding the promise of victory over enemies, the decisive factor is not trust in one's potential for waging war, but invoking the LORD's involvement and aid (vv. 22-24; Ps 20:7-8). *Horn* is a metaphor for strength (vv. 17, 24). The king shares in the divine task of controlling the primeval forces of watery chaos (v. 25). A father-son relationship exists between the LORD and his chosen king (v. 26; 2 Sam 7:14). In Israelite society the firstborn received the parental blessing, including succession to the authority of the father (Gen 27). *Firstborn* and *highest of the kings* describes the privileged position of the king and the people of Israel (v. 27).

The second part of the oracle sets forth the promises and conditions incumbent on successors within the Davidic dynasty (vv. 28-37). It repeats the pledge of an endless dynasty. Some have understood the frequent use of *forever* (vv. 28, 29, 36, 37) to point to the unconditional character of the promise to David. However, use of the word *if* does imply conditions to the covenant (vv. 30-31). Unfaithfulness on the part of David's descendants will bring punishment but will not void the divine promise. God remains faithful even though the people are unfaithful (vv. 34-35). The LORD cannot deny his oath to David, which should endure like the sun and the moon (vv. 36-37). Note again the use of *Selah*, perhaps an emphatic pause.

Lament on Rejection of the Dynasty 89:38-51

Here the mood of the psalm changes abruptly. With *But now . . .* (v. 38) the reality of the king's defeat and humiliation contrasts sharply with the picture of the promises to the LORD's anointed. Contrary to the covenant, God has *rejected* his *anointed*. The covenant was broken and the crown defiled (v. 39). God has laid the city in ruins (v. 40). The everlasting monarch suffers the frailty of all human existence (vv. 41-44; Kraus, 1989:210). Defeated in battle, he is now prematurely old and sterile (v. 45, 2 Kings 24:8-15; Ps 102:23). The complaint repeats the accusation over and over: *You have. . . , You have. . . .* All of this is spoken of as the work of the LORD (vv. 38-45; cf. v. 46).

The prayer of intercession comes in two sets of questions: *How long, O LORD, . . . will your wrath burn?* (vv. 46-48). *Lord, where is your steadfast love of old?* (vv. 49-51). Behind the complaint lies the question: "Has God abandoned us, his people?" The tragic loss of the nation is personalized by the speaker, who now focuses on the fragility of human life and the prospect of death as due to the wrath of God (vv. 46-48) *[Sheol; Wrath]*. Yet, the LORD is reliable, and for the sixth time in the psalm, the speaker appeals to the LORD's *steadfast love* and *faithfulness* (v. 49; Ps 132:11). The psalm ends with a petition for the LORD to *remember* and intervene (vv. 50-51). There is closure, but there is no resolution. Psalm 89 stands as a counterpart to royal Psalms 2 and 45, with their portrayal of the glory and majesty of the anointed monarch. Kraus (1986:123) points out how in Psalm 89 the deeply human side of the king becomes evident. The anointed one becomes one of the poor. Total helplessness now characterizes the ruler.

Doxology Concluding Book Three of the Psalter 89:52

A brief doxology closes book III of the Psalter, in which national suffering has played a large part. An individual lament and a communal one (Pss 73; 74) open book III; an individual lament and a communal one bring closure (Pss 88; 89). Book III leaves unanswered some searching questions about God's way with his people. Book IV of the Psalter will make clear that despite all, the LORD still reigns (Pss 93; 95–99).

THE TEXT IN THE BIBLICAL CONTEXT AND LIFE OF THE CHURCH

The Role of Psalm 89 in the Psalter

The covenant with David introduced in Psalm 2 has come to an end, and David's descendants wait for a restoration. *How long, O LORD?*

they pray (Ps 89:46). When the Psalter was compiled, Psalm 89 apparently was deliberately chosen to end book III. Books I and II view the psalms through the interpretive perspective of David as the LORD's chosen one.

Wilson (1985:214-15) sees Psalm 89, in recalling the covenant between the LORD and David, as representing a theological reevaluation of this relationship as it is reflected in Psalms 2–72. While books I and II of the Psalter have a more positive and hopeful view of the Davidic kingship, the extension of Psalms 73–89 modifies these hopes in the light of the exilic experience. The Psalter's book IV (Pss 90–106) then appears to set forth answers to the problem of the failed covenant in Psalm 89. Wilson summarizes these: the LORD is king; the LORD has been our refuge in the past and will continue to be our refuge without the monarchy; blessed are those who trust in the LORD [Composition].

Another Messianic Psalm

The last verses of Psalm 89 point toward *your servant* (v. 50) and *your anointed* (v. 51). While it would be too much to assume that the psalmist was foretelling Christ, it is understandable why early Christians read this as a messianic psalm. People gave messianic meaning to the royal psalms only after the disappearance of the Davidic dynasty, when the role of that dynasty had ceased to be a political reality (Westermann, 1989:59).

Laments over the decline of the monarchy and dissolution of the covenant with David (Ps 89:38-45; Lam 4:20) show the true situation more clearly than Psalm 2 or Psalm 45. Emptiness and death cast their shadow over the oft-acclaimed long life of the ruler. The deeply human side of the king and the dynasty becomes evident as the psalmist is looking for one whom death will not overcome and whose office will not become prey to decay (Ps 89:45-48). Kraus calls attention to how, in this psalm, the *anointed* one, the king, is now characterized by total helplessness, and how this picture of the anointed one's glorification and abasement became prophecy and promise of the messianic king (Kraus, 1986:122-23) [Anointed].

Christians believe that the Davidic promises have found a fulfillment in Jesus. The NT proclaims Jesus as the offspring of David, and that in Jesus all the promises of God are fulfilled (Acts 13:22-23, 32-39). Christians answer the strong challenge of Psalm 89:49 by pointing to Christ. The NT quotes or alludes to this psalm, particularly with reference to Christ's suffering and rejection and then his kingship

(Matt 27:44; Luke 18:32; Acts 2:30; 13:22; Rev 1:5; 19:16).

In the Book of Common Prayer, the Christian church has identified Psalm 89 as a proper psalm for Christmas Day. It is also appropriately read as a text for Advent.

Lament as Open-Ended Prayer

The lament is a prayer voiced in troubled times. These laments reveal the temptation to wonder whether God has forgotten his people. Both God's creation and his covenant appear under threat throughout history. Psalm 89 focuses on the question of whether God keeps his promises and whether God ultimately reigns. At the psalm's conclusion, that question is not resolved. In this sense, the lament is an open-ended prayer.

So people continue to lament and pray. Such prayers, in the face of God's apparent absence, witness to the fact that no present defeat can dim the glory of past history. No present reality can take away the will to keep on praying and hoping. Can believers see meaning in all of God's dealing with the people of faith? Thomas Chisholm's gospel hymn based on Lamentations 3:22-23 comes to mind as an expression of trust in a compassionate and faithful God:

> Great is thy faithfulness, O God my Father.
> There is no shadow of turning with thee.
> Thou changest not, thy compassions, they fail not.
> As thou hast been thou forever wilt be.

Book Four
Psalms 90–106

Psalm 90

Our God, from Everlasting to Everlasting

PREVIEW

In this psalm, the eternity of God stands in solid contrast to the brevity and misery of human existence. Human life is unspeakably short. While the memory of the God of all the generations may be fading away, the people still plead to the God of their forebears, asking him to bathe them in *steadfast love* (*ḥesed*, v. 14) and bless the *work* of their hands.

The psalmist does not identify the specific trouble out of which the community pleads to God. Following the opening vow of trust in the Creator God (vv. 1-2), a general lament follows about the tragic predicament of human life (vv. 3-12). The prayer for a *wise heart* (v. 12) then leads to the petitions on behalf of the community (vv. 13-17). The use of plural speech throughout suggests that the congregation is addressing its Lord.

This community lament opens book IV of the Psalter (90–106). Book III included prayers of lament over the destruction of Jerusalem, concluding with the announcement of God's rejection of the covenant with David (Ps 89). The ascription of the prayer to Moses, likely by later scribal editors, incorporates the authority of the LORD's servant

Psalm 90

par excellence and the ancient cultural feature of grounding statements in antiquity (Tate, 1990:440). This is the only psalm ascribed to Moses *[Superscriptions]*. This psalm (echoing Gen 1–3; Exod 32:12b; Moses' Song and blessing: Deut 32–33) takes the reader back to the time of Moses, when there was no land, temple, or monarchy. Some have characterized book IV, framed by Psalms 90 and 106 presenting Moses as intercessor, as "a Moses-book." In responding to the cries of exile and its aftermath, it offers the "answer" that pervades the Psalter and "forms its theological heart: God reigns!" (McCann: 1996:1040).

OUTLINE

Hymnic Introduction: Confidence in the Everlasting God, 90:1-2
Wisdom Reflection and Teaching, 90:3-12
    90:3-6   The Frailty of Human Existence
    90:7-11   Human Sin and the Wrath of God
    90:12   Prayer for Perspective
Communal Lament and Fervent Petitions, 90:13-17
    90:13-15   Steadfast Love and Gladness
    90:16-17   Prosper the Work of Our Hands

EXPLANATORY NOTES

Hymnic Introduction: Confidence in the Everlasting God 90:1-2

The psalm portrays God, the addressee, as timeless. But the God of all generations is also *our dwelling place* (origin, home, shelter, refuge, and goal). The verbs *brought forth* (born, NIV) and *formed* (v. 2) convey the image of God giving birth to the earth, and the world as evidence of his creative power. Human life and the life of the world find their origin and identity in God. The TEV translates verse 1: *Lord, you have always been our home.* There is "no moment in all of our time that we have not been in God's hands" (Miller, 1986:127).

Wisdom Reflection and Teaching   90:3-12

The word *turn*, used three times in two verses (vv. 3, 13), introduces a reflection on the brief and sin-marred existence of humanity, which deserves the wrath of God, and the fervent petitions to a compassionate God, who can yet bless our fleeting days. As mortals, God turns us *back to dust* (Gen 3:19). All the metaphors of verses 3-10 speak of brevity, insecurity, and imperfection: dust, a sentry's brief vigil, a flash flood, a dream that evaporates, grass that withers, a short story, a passing bird. Similar descriptions of human life are found in Psalms 102:3-11, 23-24; 103:15-17; and Isaiah 40:6-8. Though the tone of verses 3-12 is akin to the skepticism of Ecclesiastes, the outcome of Psalm 90 is far different from that most pessimistic of the OT writings. *Turn back, you mortals* expresses God's invitation to come back home (v. 3), because sin has separated mortals from God. For the psalm writer, God's wrath and the guilt of human beings in their sin are the causes of life's brevity *[Sin; Wrath]*.

We find the goal of this psalm in verse 12. A heart of wisdom comes in being realistic about the brevity and sinfulness of human existence, and in knowing that humanity's true home rests in God's governance. Many of the stories in Genesis 1–11 deal with mortals pushing the limits set for them (Gen 3; 4; 6:1-8; 9:20-27; 11:1-9). A wise heart is "the prize of the one who knows his own limits because he is aware of the limits of human existence" (Westermann, 1989:163). By reflecting on death, one can learn how to live.

Communal Lament and Fervent Petitions   90:13-17

With *Turn, O LORD!* the lament becomes fervent petition for God to forgive human sinfulness, which alienates us from God (v. 13). God's *steadfast love* is such turning toward humans that can satisfy and make glad (v. 14). God's *steadfast love* can bless *the work of our hands* (v. 17) and even provide majesty, power, and hope to the next generation! *[Steadfast]*. Although Psalm 90 ends with a plea, the implication is that God will turn, satisfy, make glad, manifest God's own work, and establish humanity's work, as God did in answer to Moses' intercession in Exodus 32–34 (McCann, 1996:1044).

The psalm uses three names for God: *Lord* ('ădōnāy, v. 1), *LORD* (*Yahweh*, v. 13) and *Lord our God* ('ădōnāy 'ĕlōhîm, v. 17). Brueggemann observes: "The repetition of Lord at the beginning and at the end is qualified by the covenantal term, 'our God.' . . . The psalm moves from a God who is outside human circumstance to a God now deeply drawn into our paths" (1984:114). So the psalm ends as it began, with God.

THE TEXT IN THE BIBLICAL CONTEXT AND LIFE OF THE CHURCH

A Healthy Dose of Realism

Psalm 90 is often read together with 1 Corinthians 15 at the time of burial. However, in public reading certain verses (vv. 7-9, 11-12) are frequently omitted. Perhaps in a setting of grief, such omission is justified. Yet if divine wrath is the result of human sin, full appreciation of reality and of the psalm requires that we do not gloss over difficult verses.

For people who tend to forget that the days on earth are not forever, the psalm brings a healthy dose of realism. The average life span in the psalmist's time, common until several generations ago in most cultures, was only twenty-six to thirty years. At most, a person today might hope for eighty, ninety, or perhaps a hundred years—not much beyond that. Death is still the lot of every person. How brief earthly life is—especially in comparison to God's time! Thus, 2 Peter 3:8 quotes Psalm 90:4 to remind readers that God is not confined to human understandings of time.

In seeing human finitude under the sign of God's wrath, this psalm stands with Genesis 3 and Romans 1–2. Although verse 12 suggests that life's brevity should help people become wise and more judicious in their living, the prayer does acknowledge that if life will count for anything, it is God's gift (vv. 14-17). The point of Psalm 90 lies in the prayer that the eternal God not overlook the short life of a person and let it pass away in misfortune, but to have mercy on his congregation, his servants. People of faith thus have found courage to live each day by the grace of God, and work and pray that God will use their labors and life for eternal purpose. In the Western monastic tradition, verses 13-17 came to be associated with the beginning of the day and were chanted just before going out to morning labor.

Isaac Watts' great hymn "O God, our help in ages past" (1719) is based on Psalm 90. So is the second stanza of Henry F. Lyte's "Abide with me" (1847): "Swift to its close ebbs out life's little day. . . . O thou who changest not, abide with me." The *German Requiem* of Johannes Brahms (1866–68) somberly reflects on human frailty, "All flesh is as grass," and the need to "know the measure of my days" (v. 12), but then broadens into praise, "How lovely is thy dwelling place, O Lord of hosts," from 84:1-2.

Psalm 91

Abiding in the Shadow of the Almighty

PREVIEW

This psalm of trust in the wisdom tradition has become a classic on the sure promises of God *[Psalm Genres]*. Despite frightful images of life's risks (vv. 3-10), a protective calm permeates the psalm. The theme is God as refuge of those who know the name of the LORD. Security comes by abiding in the shadow of the Almighty.

Together with Psalm 46, this psalm points to the strength that springs from trust in God. We can also find parallels in thought and imagery between verses 3-12 and the didactic wisdom of Psalm 34. Commentators identify connecting themes in the placement of this psalm. Psalm 90 extended the lament at the end of Psalm 89. Psalm 91 ends by answering the fear voiced in Psalm 90 about the fragility of human existence. Both psalms refer to the LORD as a *dwelling place* (90:1; 91:9). This psalm also introduces the pilgrim to the temple, with Psalms 92–100 providing liturgical celebration (Stuhlmueller, 1983, 2:72).

Dating Psalm 91 is not possible. Suggested settings include a royal psalm in which the king is addressed by a court priest, a personal confession of faith by a convert, fragments from liturgies on entrance to the temple (Pss 15 and 24), or address to a person who has taken refuge in the sanctuary. Kraus suggests that Psalm 91 may belong to psalms of sickness and healing. Composed of two parts, the psalm may have served the purpose of both instruction and blessing. Verses 1-13 provide instruction about the divine protection, with verses 14-16 reporting the divine oracle of assurance spoken by the temple priest. The language and imagery of Psalm 91 are open-ended enough to be relevant in many situations.

OUTLINE

Introductory Invitation to the Sanctuary and Refuge in God, 91:1-2
Instruction and Encouragement, 91:3-13
    91:3-4   Refuge in God's Faithfulness
    91:5-6   No Need to Fear the Terror of Night or Day
    91:7-8   Deliverance as the Wicked Are Punished
    91:9-10   Security in the LORD as Refuge
    91:11-13   Protected by Guardian Angels
Divine Oracle of Assurance, 91:14-16

EXPLANATORY NOTES

Introductory Invitation to the Sanctuary and Refuge in God 91:1-2

The change in pronouns is noteworthy: *you/who/my/I* (vv. 1-2), *you/your* (vv. 3-13), and the divine *I* (vv. 14-16). Four metaphors for security and four Hebrew titles for God are used in verses 1-2. *Most High* names the God exalted above the earth and above all the gods (v. 9; Pss 18:13; 47:2; 83:18; 97:9). The *Almighty* (Shaddai, šadday), the name that sustained the landless patriarchs (Exod 6:3), appears elsewhere in the Psalter only in 68:14. The possessive *my God* makes the LORD (Yahweh) intimate. To know the name indicates a deep knowledge of and special relationship to the person (v. 14) *[Names of God]*. *Abide* (v. 1) means "to spend the night," as in a room in an inn or home. Thus, the introduction welcomes the pilgrim to the sanctuary and into the secret intimacy of trust and refuge in the LORD.

Instruction and Encouragement 91:3-13

Graphic images of dangers in life dominate the psalm's instruction and encouragement: the hunter's trap and pit (v. 3); the terrors of night and day (vv. 5-6), which may refer to demonic forces believed especially active in the dark and at midday; military defeat or plague (vv. 7-8; 1 Sam 18:7; 2 Kings 19:35), and ravenous animals and poisonous reptiles (v. 13).

Yet, whatever threatens, the one taking refuge in God *will not fear* (v. 5). The emphatic pronoun, *For he will deliver* (v. 3), suggests God alone as the effective helper. Refuge *under his wings* (v. 4) calls forth the image of the protective mother bird (Deut 32:11; Matt 23:37). Even demonic forces, superstitions, and irrational fears of *night/day* and *darkness/noonday* are no match for God's refuge (vv. 2, 4, 9). The thoughtful reader is troubled by the hyperbolic word picture that the God-fearing person will be delivered no matter what the numerical strength of the adversaries, while the wicked will be punished (vv. 7-8). Here the psalmist affirms the traditional view of retribution (cf. Ps 125:4-5). Such a faith seizes on the God who saves.

The introductory invitation to find security in the LORD, the *Most High* (vv. 1-2), is later reaffirmed, using similar language (vv. 9-10). Over against the destructive demons, ministering angels are sent by God to protect the faithful, who will be carried carefully and protectively (vv. 10-13). The word *angel* is used in the OT of both human and heavenly messengers (Gen 24:7; Exod 23:20; Ps 34:7), and here specifically as guardians. The humanly impossible is possible to faith (v. 13).

Divine Oracle of Assurance   91:14-16

The oracle that the priest recites in the temple begins with *Because* (NIV; Heb.: *kî*, "for") *[Oracle]*. Now, in direct speech, the LORD speaks comfortingly to those who *love* and *know* his *name* (vv. 14-16). In a decree of assurance, responding to the trust of verses 1-13, God promises an eightfold blessing: *I will deliver, I will protect, I will answer, I will be with, I will rescue, I will honor, I will satisfy them*, and I will *show them my salvation*! For one who has likely faced death (vv. 3, 5-6, 7, 10, 13, 14-15), *long life* is promised (Pss 21:6; 23:6; Isa 53:10). The LORD's response is overwhelming. The security of which this psalm speaks lies in a continuing relationship with God.

The oracle to close Psalm 91 parallels the oracle to close Psalm 95. Introduced by the Moses-psalm (90), this psalm recalls the early days of Israel's history (95:8-11). Psalms 90–99 acclaim the LORD's kingship under the rubric of Moses, who proclaimed the LORD's reign in the deliverance from the sea (Exod 15:18). In the postexilic period, with the Davidic monarchy ended, these psalms proclaim that the LORD, *a great God, and a great King above all gods*" (Ps 95:3), reigns with might and power (Tate, 1990:458).

THE TEXT IN THE BIBLICAL CONTEXT AND LIFE OF THE CHURCH

Reassuring Words

The Jewish Prayer Book recommends reading Psalm 91 before retiring at night. The church has recited this psalm as both morning and evening prayer, at funerals, for casting out demons, in healing services for the sick, and as invocation for travelers.

The reference to guardian angels found its way into the liturgy and prayers. A Greek Orthodox Church litany urges: "For an angel of peace, a faithful guide, a guardian of our souls and bodies, let us beseech the Lord." Sabine Baring-Gould's evening hymn, "Now the day is over" (1865), contains similar lines: "Through the long night watches, may thine angels spread their white wings above me, watching round my bed."

Questions Raised

This psalm also raises questions. The psalmist offers no hint of the complex problem of evil, which certainly has been a prominent feature in many of the psalms from 1–89. The psalm's assurance of security is comprehensive and confident. Can one honestly believe in the promise of impunity (e.g. v. 7)? It seems much like Romans 8:31, "If God is for us, who can be against us?" (NIV). Perhaps we need to see the concluding oracle (vv. 14-16) as a corrective to the preceding verses. The godly person may not be immune to, untouched by, or insulated from the ills that affect others, but in the end the believer is not abandoned and is enabled to face destructive forces without fear (White: 143).

The other problem arises in the misuse of such Scripture. People have sometimes worn bits of this psalm text in amulets as a kind of magical protection for the wearer. Satan used verses 11-12 to tempt Jesus to jump from the pinnacle of the temple (Matt 4:5-7; Luke 4:9-12). However, Jesus refused to claim God's promise of protection for his own benefit. Quoting Deuteronomy 6:16, Jesus reminded his adversary that it is a mistake to try to force God's hand. "Real trust does not seek to test God or to prove his faithfulness" (Mays, 1994b:298).

Addressing Fear

Since security in the face of terror is a main theme of the psalm, it is helpful to recognize that the opposite of fear is not courage, but faith. Carl Jung declared, "Patients are far more dangerous when suffering from fear than when moved by wrath or hatred." J. B. Priestly stated, "Heads of governments know that a frightened people is easier to govern and will agree to millions and millions being spent on 'defense'" (Knight, 2:95-96). After the terrorist attacks on the Pentagon and the World Trade Center in 2001, it was much easier for the American nation to respond with "war on terror" than to ask, "Why these attacks?" This psalm in effect asks: "Will I choose to trust the LORD to deliver me from fear, or will I be victimized by it?" Brueggemann comments regarding Psalm 91: "The use of the psalm of trust while still in the pit is an act of profound hope which permits new life" (1982:47).

Psalm 92

Praise for the LORD's Righteous Rule

PREVIEW

With exuberant song to the accompaniment of stringed instruments, the psalm praises the LORD for his works in creation and history. The song of thanksgiving declares the LORD's judgment on the wicked, even as the righteous are exalted. The psalmist likens the community of faith to a flourishing tree, with roots deep in the living water, bearing fruit in testimony that *the LORD is upright*!

Psalm 92 provides a bridge from the "refuge" psalms (90 and 91) to "the LORD is king" psalms that begin with Psalm 93. *The LORD is Israel's rock* (v. 15) and refuge, and at the same time *on high forever* (v. 8). The writer may have experienced deliverance from certain personal enemies (vv. 10-11). The psalm arises from a concern to nurture and develop the faithfulness of the congregation. This may have been a royal thanksgiving psalm (like 18 and 138). It contains wisdom teaching elements (vv. 6-7, 10-11), suggesting a postexilic time for composition, at least in its present form *[Psalm Genres]*.

OUTLINE

Introduction: Joyous Exultation, 92:1-3
Thanksgiving for the LORD's Works in Creation and History, 92:4-11
    92:4-7   The LORD's Works and Wisdom Reflection
    92:8   Declaration Exalting the LORD
    92:9-11   The LORD's Re-creating Work and Wisdom Reflection
Exaltation of the LORD in the Rewards of the Righteous, 92:12-15

EXPLANATORY NOTES

Introduction: Joyous Exultation   92:1-3

As a *Song for the Sabbath Day* (title), the thanksgiving begins with declaring praise as right and good (v. 1; Ps 33:1) *[Superscriptions]*. Instruments accompany joyful morning and evening celebrations of the LORD's *steadfast love* and *faithfulness* (33:2-3) *[Steadfast]*. The technical word *higgaion* (*higgāyôn*), translated *melody* (v. 3; 9:16), may be a call for an instrumental interlude, but can also mean "meditation" (Holladay: 76). In this first stanza, the psalmist conveys exquisite delight in exultation before the LORD Most High.

Thanksgiving for the LORD's Works in Creation and History   92:4-11

For you, O LORD (v. 4) introduces the motive for the joyful song of thanksgiving, reaffirmed with *but you, O LORD . . .* (v. 8). An allusion to God's victory over the gods of chaos (vv. 8-9) reinforces mention of God's mighty *works* in creation and history (vv. 4-5). The reference may be to Israel's redemption from bondage in Egypt (Exod 15), or may draw language from an ancient victory liturgy about Baal's defeat of the Sea (v. 9; "Ugaritic Myths, Poems About Baal," *ANET* 130-35). However, the central verse of the psalm (v. 8) pointedly asserts that it is the LORD, not Baal, who triumphs and is *on high forever*, and who will rid the world of evil (Kidner, 1975:336).

In the wisdom reflections (vv. 6-7, 9-11), the psalmist wrestles with the problem of evildoers who flourish. The wicked sprout and *grow like weeds* (v. 7 TEV), though they ultimately are doomed to destruction. Fools do not understand this truth of divine retribution (v. 6). But in the end, the righteous will see the downfall of the wicked (v. 11; Pss 37:34; 91:8) *[Righteous; Wicked]*. Both deliverance of the righteous and destruction of the wicked, as evidence of the LORD's righteous rule, are grounds for exultant thanksgiving. Verse 10 gives striking metaphors for the righteous person (v. 10). *Exalted my horn*, as in the horn of an animal, symbolizes strength and restored vitality (75:4-5; 89:17; 112:9; 132:17). *Fresh oil*, as in anointing, suggests renewal, well-being, and prosperity (23:5; 133:2).

Exaltation of the LORD in the Rewards of the Righteous 92:12-15

New vitality and hope spring forth for the whole community of *the righteous*. So the psalmist ends with a clinching declaration that *the righteous flourish*, too (vv. 12-15)! But this is no short-lived prosperity ending in doom (cf. 73:18-20). The psalmist lists seven positive qualities of the righteous: *flourish like the palm tree, grow like a cedar, planted in the house of the LORD, flourish in the courts of our God, produce fruit, always green,* and *full of sap* (vv. 12-14). The palm tree embodies grace and erectness; the cedar, strength and regal magnificence (1 Kings 6:29; 7:2, 7; 9:11; Pss 80:10; 104:16; Jer 17:8). The righteous, pictured as trees planted in the sacred soil of the LORD's house, are granted a richness of life that bears *fruit*, even into *old age*. The final verse returns to the keynote of the psalm, *showing that the LORD is upright* (v. 15).

In addition to striking metaphors (*grass, horn, oil, tree, rock*), we see other literary devices *[Hebrew Poetry]*. The psalm has a chiastic structure, framed by the *declare* or *show* theme (vv. 2, 15), and the exultation *But you, O LORD, are on high forever* (v. 8) at the psalm's center. Corresponding and contrasting motifs abound. The enemies of the psalmist fail because the enemies of the LORD will perish (vv. 9, 11). The wicked briefly flourish, like grass (90:5-6), but the righteous flourish like the palm and cedar (vv. 7, 12). The wicked are doomed forever, because the LORD is on high forever (vv. 7-8). Praise declares the *steadfast love* of the LORD, and the lives of the righteous declare that the LORD is *upright* (vv. 2, 15; Mays, 1994b:299). *Upright* (v. 15) and *righteous* (v. 12) form the rhetorical figure of inclusio, highly appropriate in the definitive answer to the psalm's central question about the destinies of the wicked and the righteous.

THE TEXT IN THE BIBLICAL CONTEXT AND LIFE OF THE CHURCH

A Psalm for the Sabbath

Psalm 92 acquired a prominent place in the Sabbath liturgy of the temple as indicated by the title: *A Song for the Sabbath Day.* Psalm 92 is the only psalm so designated, though Greek texts also cite Psalms 24;

48; 81; 82; 93; and 94 for use on the other six days of the week. The psalm may have had an earlier history unrelated to Sabbath worship, perhaps in thanksgiving services during festival times to commemorate the mighty works of the LORD (Tate, 1990:465). The Mishnah (ca. AD 200) recalls Levites reciting Psalm 92 on the Sabbath (*Tamid* 7:4; Holladay: 139). Jews may have sung it daily during the libation that accompanied the morning sacrifice of a lamb. As the priest poured the drink offering of wine into the fire (Exod 29:39-40), the choir chanted, "It is good to give thanks to the LORD, . . . to declare your steadfast love in the morning . . ." (Reardon: 181).

Sabbath comes as the climax to the creation story in Genesis 1:1-2:4. The weekly rhythm of Jewish worship was built around the Sabbath. This day was hallowed and was to be consecrated to God by turning away from the business pursuits of the working day, and by tending to the praise and adoration of God (Isa 58:13-14). This psalm is a reminder of the significance of worship to shape and direct life (Ps 1). An ordered life that will show vitality into *old age* (v. 14) must be deeply rooted in God (vv. 5, 13). Commenting on the title, the Mishnah calls this also a psalm for "the era to come, for the day that will be entirely Sabbath, for eternal life" (*Tamid* 7:4; Mays, 1994b:300).

The traditional use of this psalm in Christian worship included chanting it at daybreak on Friday, in remembrance of the Lamb of God who took away the sins of the world (Reardon: 181). Psalm 92:1-2 are verses often used as a call to worship. Hymns of the church connecting with Psalm 92 include Amos Herr's morning hymn, "I owe the Lord a morning song" (1890), and John Ellerton's evening hymn, "The day you gave us, Lord" (1870). Christopher Idle's "Make music to the Lord most high" (1981) is based specifically on Psalm 92, and connecting in a more general way is the well-known "Great is thy faithfulness" (Thomas Chisholm, 1923).

The Prosperity of the Wicked and the Justice of God

In wrestling with the problem of the prosperity of the wicked, the psalm touches on an important issue, the apparent injustice of God. As in Psalms 37; 49; and 73, as well as Job and Habakkuk, Psalm 92 places this problem into the context of faith in God's sovereignty. In addition, values other than material prosperity, such as a close connectedness with God, address what at first seems imbalance, if not injustice (cf. Ps 73:23-26 with 73:3-12). Although the wicked might prosper for a time and the righteous be temporarily afflicted, there is no unrighteousness in God. Paul wrestles with this question in Romans, affirming that God is just and right (Rom 9:14; 11:33) *[Judge]*.

Psalm 93

The LORD Reigns!

PREVIEW

This significant psalm roars with the energy of crashing sea waves to proclaim *The LORD reigns!* (v. 1 NIV). In bold language, the hymn celebrates the everlasting kingship of the LORD. Victor over the primordial chaos and over all tumult, the LORD has established his throne over the world. Creator and lawgiver, the LORD is a present reality.

Psalms 93 and 95–99 are a series of psalms exalting the LORD as king. This collection appears at a crucial point in the Psalter, in response to the theological crisis articulated by book III. These so-called "enthronement psalms" include Psalm 47, on which I comment about a possible liturgy of enthronement as part of the New Year Festival. Though earlier proposals of the enthronement festival have been modified, the psalm's likely setting instead was a Jerusalem festival, such as the Feast of Tabernacles (Deut 31:9-13; Zech 14:16). *The LORD is king* psalms characteristically glorify God as king of the nations and his royal dominion over them. This became particularly important with the end of the monarchy, when the old royal psalms began to be interpreted messianically (Westermann, 1989:5) *[Psalm Genres]*.

OUTLINE

Acclamation of the LORD's Reign, 93:1a
Declaration of the LORD as King over the Raging Tumult, 93:1b-4
Conclusion: The LORD's Decrees and Temple Are Holy, 93:5

EXPLANATORY NOTES

Acclamation of the LORD's Reign   93:1a

The introductory acclamation *The LORD is king* also opens Psalms 97 and 99. In Hebrew, the verb usually precedes the subject. Here the order is reversed, appearing to emphasize *the LORD:* "The LORD, and no one else is king!" English has no verb meaning "to king." *To reign* (NIV) or "to rule" fails to convey the image as adequately and forcefully.

In language, Psalm 93 resembles Psalm 29, one of the earliest hymns in the Psalter, with similar motifs of victory, kingship, and praise of the LORD by his heavenly court. The use of doubled and tripled expressions are features of early biblical and Canaanite poetry (Ps 92:9; Exod 15; Judg 5). Speech *about* the LORD (vv. 1, 4) transitions to direct address *to* the LORD (vv. 2-3, 5). Psalm 93 "belongs to the long tradition, reaching back most probably to the reign of Solomon, when it absorbed many Canaanite/Ugaritic expressions and motifs, and yet was much at home in the exile and postexilic age, when an archaizing tendency revived many of these same expressions" (Stuhlmueller, 1983, 2:79). The style is concise, repetitive, and forceful. The psalm conveys confidence, wonder, awe, and joyful exultation.

Declaration of the LORD as King over the Raging Tumult   93:1b-4

At once the psalmist moves to the consequences of the LORD being king. The LORD's reign established the world and his throne. *Robed* and *girded* (v. 1) is military language, though here the focus is not on garments but on the LORD as clothed with *majesty* and *power*. As a result, the LORD has assured the stability of all things. The reference is to God's work in creation, but also to sovereignty manifested in a stable control of the world. The LORD's throne, established from the beginning to "end of days" (Dan 10:14), provides the unifying motif for the psalm (v. 2).

Now with the churning word picture of crashing waves from a storm at sea, the psalm declares that all the raging of the world will not destroy God's reign (vv. 3-4). God's rule is based upon his control over the powers of chaos, symbolized by the water of the sea (Job 38:8-11; Pss 74:12-17; 104:7-9). The imagery is borrowed from Ugaritic or Babylonian myths of the combat of the gods, Baal struggling with Yam (the Sea; "Ugaritic Myths, Poems About Baal," *ANET* 130-35), or Marduk's victory over Tiamat (the primeval deep;

"Akkadian Myths, Creation Epic," *ANET* 60-72). But how much more majestic is *the LORD* on high! These verses are pregnant with double meaning. Humanity is ever in turmoil (Ps 46:2-3, 6). The *floods* can represent hostile nations such as Egypt, Assyria, and Babylonia (Isa 8:7; 17:12-13; 27:1; 51:9-10; Jer 46:7-8). *Floods* generate fear. But *more majestic* is *the LORD!* The LORD on high calms floods and fear (Ps 92:8)!

Conclusion: The LORD's Decrees and Temple Are Holy 93:5

The psalm declares the reliability of the LORD's decrees, the holiness of the temple, and dominion *while time shall last* (v. 5 NEB). *Decrees* or *statutes* (NIV) refer to the covenant as a whole, the law (*torah*), which includes the mighty works of the LORD and his promises and commandments (Pss 19:7-14; 25:10; 119:1-2; 132:12). These decrees solicit obedience to the norms of justice, compassion, and equity within the community. Because of the LORD's presence, the temple where this word is proclaimed and heard is holy, beyond the human, and inviolable.

THE TEXT IN THE BIBLICAL CONTEXT AND LIFE OF THE CHURCH

Everything Centered on God

"A Psalm for the Eve of the Sabbath" was the title given Psalm 93 by the LXX. Jewish liturgical tradition has always regarded Psalms 92; 93; and 95–100 as Sabbath Psalms. The Mishnah (ca. AD 200) places the singing of this psalm on the eve of the Sabbath. It celebrates, "The LORD is king, and has put on glorious apparel," and anticipates the time "that shall be all Sabbath and rest in the life everlasting" (*Tamid* 7:4). Such an eschatological understanding was likely a later interpretation of the psalm (A. Anderson, 2:665). Christians have used the psalm at Epiphany and weekly at vespers.

Application of the psalm's theme in the life of the church might focus on "God as Lord of all!" The psalm centers everything on God and on obedient, loving response to God. The decrees of God are sure, reliable, and trustworthy (v. 5). This presupposes a view of the world in which creation and society are directly connected. If people confess that the LORD reigns, they believe that the divine decrees are as much a part of reality as the very continuity and stability of the world (Mays, 1994b:302). Then it does make a difference as to how we use or abuse creation. Concerns about the environment and the earth's ecology take on sacred significance.

Though the psalm opens with military terms (*robed, girded*), it ends with decrees and holiness. God's true holiness is not mere strength, but also character. God's holiness is the temple's inner glory (v. 5), a point echoed in Paul's comment about the living temple, the church (1 Cor 3:16-17).

The Tumult of the Nations

Every generation lives with the reality of unsettled areas of chaos not completely abolished in creation. Tumult and the raging of nations surround every attempt at an ordered world, such as the Pax Romana of NT times, the British Empire of the nineteenth century, or American efforts to "police" the world at the beginning of the twenty-first century. What may such a psalm be saying to the human temptation to respond to terror with military might?

In Psalm 93, the majestic LORD on high stands above and subdues the floods and tumult. In Mark 4:35-41, Jesus calms the raging sea with the words, "Peace! Be still!" comforting the terrified disciples (Ps 46:10).

What is comparable to Psalm 93 in a Christian worship setting? The most similar event may be Easter and the celebration of the resurrection, which declares that the Lord reigns. Worship can thus continue to shape the reality by which people choose to live. Jesus announced the presence of God's reign and invited people to enter it (Mark 1:14-15). That summons calls for denial of self and taking up a cross (8:34). Appropriate hymns include "The Lord is king" (Nicolaus von Zinzendorf, 1742) and "Great God, how infinite art thou" (Isaac Watts, 1707).

Psalm 94

Rise Up, O Judge of the Earth

PREVIEW

Psalm 94 wrestles with the dilemma posed by the evident power of the wicked in the world, which faith claims to be under God's sovereignty. The perversion of justice and judicial murder threaten to destroy the people of God. The psalm begins with an urgent plea for God to come forward to defend and vindicate the defenseless and innocent faithful. It ends in confident assurance that God will not forever tolerate the injustice of scheming and avaricious judges, who manipulate the law for themselves and their friends. The wicked will be wiped out, even as the righteous find in God their rock of refuge. The psalm relates in theme and language to Psalms 37 and 73.

Even though Psalm 94 is identified as a lament of the nation, elements of a thanksgiving hymn ring forth in the last part (vv. 16-23). The testimony from personal experience conveys confidence in describing divine intervention on behalf of the psalmist and his people (vv. 17-19). Placed within the series of psalms exalting the LORD as king (Pss 93; 95–99), Psalm 94 reverts to the problem that prevents Israel from recognizing the reign of the LORD: "How long will the wicked prevail?" (v. 3). Yet the LORD is *the rock of my refuge* (v. 22).

The situation of the poor, oppressed by wickedness in high places (vv. 5-6, 20-21), echoes the setting for prophetic pronouncements from Isaiah in the eighth century BC (Isa 1:17, 23) to Malachi in the fifth century BC (Mal 3:5, 13-15). The psalm uses many literary forms: invocation, question, lament, narrative, imprecation, instruction, and confidence. A wisdom instruction style appears in verses 8-15. Contrasts abound: wicked/righteous, fools/wise, evildoers/the LORD, empty breath/rock of my refuge. The beatitude (v. 12) introduces another way, that of instruction in the *law* (torah, *tôrâ*), connecting this psalm also with Psalms 1 and 119 *[Torah]*.

OUTLINE

Complaint Against the Wicked, 94:1-7
    94:1-3   Appeal to the LORD to Judge the Wicked
    94:4-7   The Arrogance and Violence of the Wicked
Rebuke to the Foolish, 94:8-11
    94:8-9   The Creator Is Greater Than the Creature
    94:10-11   The LORD Is Wiser Than the Fool
Commendation of Those Who Hold to the LORD's Instruction, 94:12-15
    94:12-13   Respite for the Righteous
    94:14-15   Justice Will Return
Confession of Confidence in the LORD, 94:16-23
    94:16-21   The Righteous Upheld by the Steadfast Love of the LORD
    94:22-23   Refuge and Divine Retribution

EXPLANATORY NOTES

Complaint Against the Wicked   94:1-7

The opening cry for divine intervention addresses the LORD twice as *you God of vengeance* (v. 1). This title, unique to Psalm 94, needs further explanation lest we think of God in terms of human vengeance. In the OT, vengeance was an act to restore justice where the regular legal processes were not competent or had failed (Mays, 1994b:302). The Hebrew word *nĕqāmâ* described the exercise of sovereign power on behalf of the disadvantaged. A better English translation would be "vindication." To the oppressed, God brings deliverance, but to the oppressors, punishment (Deut 32:35, 41, 43; Isa 35:4; 47:3; Ezek 25:14-17; Mic 5:15). The psalmist asks the *judge of the earth* (v. 2) to *give to the proud* [arrogant, wicked] *what they deserve*. They have trampled on the rights of humble, innocent people. It is time for the sovereign God to intervene (Holladay: 321) *[Judge; Vengeance; Wicked; Wrath]*.

    To emphasize the point, the psalm repeats the question *"How long?"* (v. 3). How long can the wicked be so successful? It faults the evildoers, among other things, for their presumption that the LORD will not right injustice (vv. 4, 7). The arrogant, confident in their hubris, fancy that they can do anything they please. Yet protecting the weak is precisely the privilege and duty of the strong and those in judicial office (Jer 7:5-7; Mic 3:1-4). The LORD's words specifically addressed to kings give direction to "execute justice . . . and deliver from the hand of the oppressor. . . . Act with justice and righteousness" (Jer 21:12; 22:3). Not only are they trampling on the marginalized; they also perceive God as a remote deity who neither knows nor cares.

Rebuke to the Foolish   94:8-11

The rebuke to the foolish and arrogant comes in the style of wisdom instruction. In a series of rhetorical questions, the psalmist presents the LORD as Creator and clearly superior to the creature (vv. 8-11). Those who do not take God seriously are blind *fools* (v. 8), their thoughts but *empty breath* (v. 11). Yet the purpose of these questions is to call the wicked to their senses. Thus, the psalmist plays a pastoral role, encouraging and supporting the discouraged and hurt as the people of God (Mays, 1994b:304).

Commendation of Those Who Hold to the LORD's Instruction   94:12-15

The sharp contrast between *an empty breath* (v. 11) and *Happy are those* . . . (v. 12) points to another way, much as Psalm 1 does. Quite different from the arrogant fool is the one whom God instructs out of his law. *Discipline* or "chastening" echoes Job 5:17 and Proverbs 3:11-12. The psalmist may be suggesting that the troubles the people have been experiencing are the LORD's ways of exercising discipline (vv. 10, 12). Teaching *out of [the] law* included instruction that God is the Judge (vv. 1-2) and will eventually punish the wicked (v. 23). It also included teaching about God's people who presently experience suffering (vv. 4-7), but that God will never abandon them (v. 14). Through the divine instruction, these know that the *days of trouble* will pass and the wicked will be destroyed. The LORD does *not forsake his people* (vv. 5, 14). Justice will return.

Confession of Confidence in the LORD   94:16-23

In what now appears as a personal testimony (vv. 16-23), the psalmist asks, *Who rises up for me . . . ?* He knows the answer: In *steadfast love* the LORD holds him up. In that certainty he finds consolation. So the personal witness extends the certainty of the LORD's judgment to the community. Though wicked rulers, under pretense of carrying out God's law oppress the innocent weak (vv. 20-21), *the LORD our God will wipe them out* (v. 23). In contrast, the psalmist will take refuge in the LORD, his *stronghold* and the *rock of refuge* (v. 22; Pss 19:14; 61:2; 92:15; 95:1).

THE TEXT IN THE BIBLICAL CONTEXT AND LIFE OF THE CHURCH

The Real World

"The powerful wicked oppressing the innocent poor" describes the real world in all generations and places (1 Kings 21:1-14; Job 13:4-7; Luke 19:1-8; 20:45–21:4). We think of petty officials who exact bribes from simple people lacking influence, and loan sharks, who prey on the poor. The Latin-American poet Ernesto Cardenal paraphrased Psalm 94: "How much longer are you going to let the party stay in power? . . . Don't you care now about victims of exploitation? Are you happy seeing the masses oppressed?" (Cardenal: 17).

But the real world of Psalm 94 comes closer home. It is found in the slums of our cities, with their inadequate schools and medical facilities. It is seen as modern agriculture forces many off the land. Corporate greed allows executives to walk away with millions while company workers lose their pensions. After decades of appealing to divine law to prop up a segregated society, sections of the United States continue to find it difficult to move out of the shadow of Jim Crow. Worldwide, refugees and displaced persons comprise a growing population.

To these issues of injustice, God's *vengeance* is addressed. That God practices vengeance is one way the Bible has of speaking about moral coherence and moral order. However, the Bible is clear that vengeance belongs to God (Deut 32:35; Isa 63:4; Rom 12:19; Heb 10:30). Vengeance is not human business (Brueggemann, 1982:72-73). Yet the LORD as Judge does not abandon his people (Deut 4:21-24). The motif of vengeance on behalf of the poor appears in the NT where the powerful are brought down (Luke 1:51-53; 4:18-19). Jesus' parables of judgment convey the same theme (Matt 25:31-46; Luke 16:19-31).

Our humanity is not complete without a strong ethical component. It is this sense of moral truth fixed eternally in the structure of reality that provides a fundamental hope. To that end, the Christian church prays in the language of the historic creeds: "He shall come again in glory to judge" (as in the Nicene Creed).

Psalm 95

O That Today You Would Listen!

PREVIEW

This hymn and prophetic admonition is related to Psalms 50 and 81, the other great festival psalms. The psalm extols God as supreme monarch over all so-called deities, over the cosmos itself, over all humankind, and specifically over the faith community. The vocabulary has similarities to Psalm 100. Whereas Psalms 50; 81; and 100 end with a promise, this psalm abruptly ends with a curse. Yet the key line (v. 7b) invites revival: *O that today you would listen to his voice!* The emphasis is on *today* as the time to *listen*. In the setting of worship, the temple prophet or priest cites the rebellion of past generations. The psalm appeals to covenant people: The God of creation and of covenant expects the obedience that comes from hearing!

Psalm 95, grouped with psalms celebrating the LORD as king (Pss 93; 96–99), may have been another of those sung at the Feast of Tabernacles. The language, with emphasis on *today*, echoes Deuteronomy 4:40; 5:3; 6:6; 7:11; 9:3; and 11:2. The oracle (vv. 7b-11) corresponds to the oracle of Psalm 91:14-16 to frame Psalms 92–94. It is also possible that Psalms 95 and 100 are intended to serve as a frame around Psalms 96–99, the core of "the LORD is king" collection (McCann, 1996:1061).

OUTLINE

Double Hymn, 95:1-7a
    95:1-5   Praise the Creator
    95:6-7a   Praise the Covenant God
Prophetic Warning Against Disobedience, 95:7b-11
    95:7b   Urgent Appeal to Listen (and Obey)
    95:8-11   Warning: Example of the Ancestors in the Wilderness

EXPLANATORY NOTES

Double Hymn   95:1-7a

Imagine a group of worshippers approaching the temple in Jerusalem (v. 1). The priest meets them at the entrance and invites them to *come*. They sing their way into the temple precincts: joy characterizes worship in Israel (vv. 1-2). In the words of the theologian Ludwig Koehler (51), "There is hardly a word so characteristic of the OT as the word *joy*." The songs of praise are addressed to the LORD, the *rock of our salvation* (v. 1; Ps 89:26).

A confessional statement (vv. 3-5) tells the reason for this rejoicing in song: *The LORD is a great God, and a great King above all gods* (Exod 15:11; Pss 96:4; 97:9; 136:2). Writing in a polytheistic culture, the psalmist does not deny the existence of the beings whom the nations worship, but does stress their weakness when compared to the LORD God (cf. comments on 96:5; 97:7). He cites the work of creation (vv. 4-5) to declare the *LORD* as a God whose power knows no limits (cf. Isa 40:26, 28-29).

Now inside the temple, the people in procession are invited to *bow down* (v. 6). They fall down on their knees before the LORD, the King. This is the way one approaches and, with face toward the ground, offers obeisance to a king (1 Kings 1:23). During festival weeks, bowing in worship must have taken place again and again. This time the creedal statement focuses on the God of the covenant: *He is our God, and we are . . . the sheep of his hand* (v. 7). This image of the shepherd and the flock reflected also the concept of the king and his people. The *LORD* rules his people because they owe him their existence. The metaphor of shepherd and flock (vv. 7, 10), prominent in the Bible, illustrates the care of God for his people (Pss 23; 77:20; 78:52; 80:1; 100:3; Isa 53:6; Ezek 34:11-16; John 10:14).

Prophetic Warning Against Disobedience   95:7b-11

Now, perhaps before the offering of sacrifice, comes a warning (vv. 7b-11). Remember the past! The priest (or prophet) reminds the worshippers of how the people of Israel rebelled in the wilderness at *Meribah* and *Massah*, names that mean "contention" and "testing" (Exod 17:1-7; Num 20:8-13). In God's displeasure over their disobedience, he did not allow these "wandering of heart" people to enter the land of promise. In this context, *My rest* (v. 11) means the Promised Land, in which the people would find rest and safety from their enemies (cf. Deut 12:9-10; 25:19; Josh 1:13; 21:44; 23:1). Here, God says through the speaker, is the story of a people on pilgrimage through the wilderness, a rebellious people who never reached their desired destination. Do not be like them, or you will suffer a similar fate. The oracle (vv. 7b-11, esp. v. 8) contributes to the character of book IV as a Moses book (Ps 90) *[Oracle]*.

The psalm's abrupt ending, with the oath of an imploring God, heightens the warning against hardening the heart. Psalms 50 and 81 point to the first commandment, "I am the LORD your God; . . . you shall have no other gods before me" (Exod 20:2-3), as what must be heard. In similar fashion, this psalm emphasizes that *today, today* in the proclamation of worship, one can yet *listen* (šāmaʻ) and turn and become obedient, resting on God and trusting God's promises. The bad news: If you don't obey, you shall not enter God's *rest*. The good news: Obedience is possible!

THE TEXT IN THE BIBLICAL CONTEXT AND LIFE OF THE CHURCH

With Receptive Hearts

The church uses this psalm widely. For many centuries, it was one of the psalms used to begin the Christian's day. The Anglican Morning Prayer Service calls it the *Venite* (Latin for *O come*). The opening verses serve as a popular call to worship (vv. 1-7a), though rarely is the second part of the psalm read in public worship. Judging by the arrangement of this psalm, a worship service, such as one conducted on a Sunday morning, is truncated if limited only to adoration. Words of exhortation are also in place. But if, on the other hand, the service is chiefly given to exhortation and warnings, then an important aspect of adoration is neglected. How can one enter into worship except with integrity of mind and spirit? Jesus asked: How honest is it to come to worship unless you have first forgiven your brother or sister and learned to love with your whole heart (Matt 5:22-24)?

Jesus refused to test God in the wilderness by resorting to wonders. Instead, he relied on the word of God (Matt 4:1-11). The psalm suggests that rest in God always depends on hearkening to his voice with receptive hearts, not given to wandering (v. 10). Hebrews 3:7-11 quotes the psalm's warning and then comments further on it in 3:12–4:13. The Christian writer urges believers under persecution not to cave in to unbelief. To turn away from the living God will prevent entry into God's rest, God's goal for life. The psalm stands as a warning that all persons are capable of similar infidelity and hardening of heart. But the writer of Hebrews, convinced that "a Sabbath rest still remains for the people of God" (4:9), appeals that *today* is the day of decision.

The line *O that today you would listen to his voice!* (7b) announces a new grace for each day, week, or season of the year. Festivals of worship provide the grace of recall and the possibility of new beginnings. So at Christmas believers rejoice, "Christ is born today! . . . Christ was born to save!" ("In dulci jubilo," 14th century; trans. J. M. Neale, 1853, "Good Christian friends, rejoice"). At Easter they sing, "Christ the Lord is ris'n today! Alleluia!" (Charles Wesley, 1739). Each Sunday morning the church celebrates the presence of the living Lord. But each day, *today*, now, is the acceptable time. "Now is the day of salvation!" (2 Cor 6:2).

Hymns based on Psalm 95 include Nahum Tate and Nicholas Brady's well-known "O come, loud anthems let us sing" (1696) and J. Harold Moyer's opening "O come, let us worship" (1964).

Psalm 96

Proclaim Among the Nations, "The LORD Reigns!"

PREVIEW

Intense joy pervades this new song, which asserts, "The LORD is king!" (v. 10). This hymn invites all the nations, indeed, the whole universe, to praise the LORD, its creator and king, as well as its judge. The psalm touches on many themes: worship, God's sovereignty over all, the mission imperative, justice with equity, and the rejoicing of nature. With praise for the great acts of the LORD in creation and history, the psalm looks forward to the further coming of the LORD, when all will be judged with *righteousness* and *truth* (v. 13).

Psalm 96 connects with the other so-called enthronement psalms (Pss 47; 93; 95; 97; 98; 99). It expresses concepts and images found in Isaiah 40–66 (Isa 40:18-26; 41:23-24; 44:6-8; 56:6-8; 60:1-4). In 1 Chronicles 16:23-33 the psalm is abridged and joined with parts of Psalm 105 (in 16:8-22) and 106 (in 16:34-36) as part of a thanksgiving meant to celebrate the arrival of the ark of God in Jerusalem. Most commentators agree the Chronicles version is dependent on Psalm 96. Yet the psalm is likely postexilic, since the theme of God-who-comes has its natural setting in a period when the temporal monarchy had disappeared in Israel. The expression *a new song*

(v. 1) has an eschatological ring (Pss 33:3; 40:3; 98:1; 144:9). The psalm was likely sung at the Feast of Tabernacles and celebration of the Israelite New Year. See comments on Psalms 46 and 93.

Repeated words and phrases in stairlike sequence give the psalm an insistent vigor. In addition to the tricola *sing to the LORD* (vv. 1-2) and *ascribe to the LORD* (vv. 7-8), other series appear (*bless/ tell/declare* [vv. 2-3], *come/worship/tremble* [8-9], *heavens/earth/sea* [v. 11], *judge/judge/judge* [vv. 10, 13], *all the earth/nations/all the peoples* [vv. 2-3, 9-10]), with the final verse repeating *for he is coming, for he is coming*. With the literary device of inclusio, *all the earth* ties together verses 1-9; *equity* and *righteousness* links verses 10-13 [Hebrew Poetry].

OUTLINE

Summons to Praise, 96:1-3
Reasons for Praise, 96:4-6
Renewed Introduction, 96:7-9
Universal Call to Worship, 96:10-13
    96:10a   Key Declaration: "The LORD Is king!"
    96:10b-13 Description of the LORD's Reign

EXPLANATORY NOTES

Summons to Praise   96:1-3

Psalm 96 highlights God's reign over the earth with righteousness (justice). The psalm begins with a summons to praise in the imperative mood. The *new song* (v. 1) contains the new future deeds and miracles of the LORD (Isa 42:10). It is filled with the newness that God will bring when he comes (Pss 98:1; 149:1; Isa 43:19). The hope in the new song is rooted in a fresh appreciation of the LORD's control of the world.

Tell of his salvation. . . . Declare his glory . . . , his marvelous works not only to the people of Israel, but also to all the nations, all the peoples (vv. 2-3). The substance of the good news is *his salvation*, which may refer to some recent deliverance of Israel, such as the return from Babylon. It could also refer to the LORD's triumph in the creation of the world, and God's victory over chaos and all the destructive forces. *Tell* is a translation of the Hebrew word *baśar*, often rendered "announce the good news" (Isa 40:9; 52:7), and its translation into Greek leads to our English word "gospel." *Declare his glory* (v. 2), a parallel to *his marvelous works*, may refer to both creation and deliverance. The content of praise is that the LORD has entered upon his rule, a life-giving message to all peoples!

Reasons for Praise   96:4-6

The hymnic main section of the psalm opens with *for* (*kî*), providing the reasons for joyful praise (v. 4). It describes the LORD as the powerful one enthroned *above all gods*. The gods of the nations are mere *idols*, *'ĕlîlîm*, a pun and parody of the word *'ĕlōhîm*, meaning *God* (v. 5). The former word is translated *worthless* in Job 13:4 and Jeremiah 14:14. In contrast to these useless idols made by human hands (Isa 40:18-19), the LORD made the heavens, which stretch over the whole earth (v. 5)! For this reason, the LORD is to be *feared* (v. 4 NIV) or *revered*. The LORD's attributes, *honor and majesty, . . . strength and beauty* (v. 6), can be compared to personified attendants, as in Psalm 85:10.

Renewed Introduction   96:7-9

In the renewed introduction (vv. 7-9), the psalmist repeats almost exactly the opening of Psalm 29. But here, instead of appealing to the heavenly council (as in Ps 29:1-2), the psalm extends the missionary invitation for all the nations to worship the LORD as king (Isa 45:20-25; 60:1-3). They are to recognize the LORD, as revealed in his acts of blessing to Israel. The psalm invites the creature to bless the Creator in thanksgiving. In worship, giving praise with offerings and trembling in the holy presence expresses awe and wonder in the *splendor of his holiness* (v. 9 NIV). The psalmist assumes the temple's existence and restoration of offering sacrifices (vv. 6, 8).

Universal Call to Worship   96:10-13

At the high point of the ceremony, a cultic cry is uttered: *The LORD is king!* or *The LORD reigns* (v. 10b NIV). The gospel to be announced to the nations is that the LORD's reign brings a reliable and equitable order to creation (v. 10). *The heavens, earth,* and *sea* constitute the universe. The whole world, and all that is in it, are invited to glorify their creator, sustainer, and vindicator (v. 11; A. Anderson, 2:685). Indeed, the psalm summons all nature to join in joyful celebration of the LORD who comes in judgment (Ps 98:4-9; Isa 44:23; 49:13; 55:12) *[Judge]*.

God's reign is a judgment of recompense and restoring harmony where there is disharmony (vv. 10-13). The LORD will set things right in affairs of both humans and nature, and between humans and nature. God will intervene to look after the rightful claims of the weak, who have no power to make their own claim (Pss 72:1-4; 82:2-4, 8; Isa 1:16-17).

Repetition of the phrase *for he comes* suggests that God keeps on coming, creating something new each time. Whatever *he is coming* may have meant in context of the liturgy in the temple, or as specific historical context in Israel's life, *he is coming* also points forward from the past into the future. Each New Year's Festival reminded Israel that the declaration of the LORD's kingship was not just a relic from the past as a hope deferred, but also a present reality. "Such a psalm is always an act of profound hope, . . . making the future momentarily present now through word, gesture, practice" (Brueggemann, 1984:145).

THE TEXT IN THE BIBLICAL CONTEXT AND LIFE OF THE CHURCH

Retelling the Story

The title that the LXX gives this psalm reads: "When the house was built after the captivity." In the bleak days of the postexilic age, psalms such as 96–99 enabled the people not just to survive and keep faith until the Messiah came, but also to anticipate the wonder of that great moment (Stuhlmueller 1983, 2:88). A later Christian accommodation appears in the old Latin version of verse 10: *Say among the nations, "The Lord reigns from the cross,"* a phrase suggesting the reign of the crucified Christ.

The Christian church has used Psalm 96 on Christmas Eve and Christmas Day, the Sunday after Epiphany, and for vigils on Trinity Sunday. Great festivals in the church year, such as Advent, Easter, and Pentecost, are times when the biblical story is told again. The significance of the liturgy lies in retelling the story and thus reenacting God's power over the forces of chaos and death. Through such speech the world of the worshipper is changed, even as Israel in worship could claim that the gods are defeated in the LORD's decisive defeat over the forces of injustice (Pharaoh and Babylon). In more recent times, African-Americans, facing incredible oppression, have found courage to confront injustice and gain a new solidarity in the songs of faith and such freedom songs as "We shall overcome" (developed from gospel songs, 1903–59).

Proclaiming the Message of God's Reign

The mission thrust of this psalm is striking. It insists that the sovereignty of the LORD is universal in scope and should bring forth the conversion of every being to the worship of Israel's God. This call to the nations and peoples to praise the LORD is pervasive in the psalms (33:8; 66:1; 67:2-4; 98:4; 100:1). All peoples are called to praise and bless the LORD again and again. In the Christian church, the reign of the risen Christ becomes the root of the church and its mission to all nations (Matt 28:18-20).

Psalm 96 offers rich preaching ideas, beginning with the word *tell* (v. 2), proclaiming the message that God has entered upon his rule. Psalm 96 articulates the good news that forms the theological heart of the book of Psalms: God reigns! Every day we must proclaim the new song. Preaching can bear witness to the great joy pervading Psalm 96. In spite of the gods of human making, the world over which God reigns *shall never be moved* (v. 10). God will never liquidate his creation. Verses 11-12 also claim the joy of the nonhuman part of creation, for now the world, as creation, once again comes into a right relationship with God and returns to his hands (Rom 8:22). God's justice is not a punitive judgment, but rather a "settling," a "helping one gain one's rights" (Rad, 1977:81). Injustice for sea, field, and forests may be in the form of ecological abuse and exploitation. What might it mean for how we live now, in light of God's reign, restoring beauty and order to the heavens and the earth?

An additional NT connection with Psalm 96 is in Jesus' words to Pilate, "You say that I am a king" (John 18:33-37). The book of Revelation acclaims a new song that embraces "every tribe and language and people and nation" (5:5-10) and climaxes in the words of the risen Christ, "Surely I am coming soon" (22:20).

Psalm 97

Rejoice in the LORD's Reign of Righteousness and Justice!

PREVIEW

The first verse proclaims the theme of the LORD's rule. As in the other "The LORD is king" psalms (Pss 47; 93; 95–99), it heralds his throne of righteousness and justice. The psalm invites obeisance not only from God's people Israel, but also from all the earth, as well as all gods. It describes the coming of the LORD as king and judge in terms of a theophany, a visible manifestation of God (vv. 2-5). The rule of justice makes its way to all lands. The effects of the LORD's sovereignty are described (vv. 6-9). The final stanza focuses on the relationship of the LORD to his *faithful*, the *righteous*. Themes of righteousness (righteous) and justice (judgments) bind the stanzas together, as does the call to *rejoice*. The psalm begins and ends with the invitation to rejoice (vv. 1, 12).

This enthronement psalm expands the theme of justice in Psalm 96. A celebration in Zion, such as the Feast of Tabernacles, is a possible setting (v. 8). The psalm draws freely on other psalms (18:7-15; 50:1-6; 77:16-20) and Isaiah (40:5; 42:10, 13, 17, 25; 45:16; 49:13; 51:5; 58:10; 60:1). Stereotypical forms of liturgy may account for borrowing and adaptation to form the mosaic of Psalm

Psalm 97

97. Focus on the coming of the LORD as judge of all peoples and God's future final victory gives the psalm an eschatological tone.

OUTLINE

Call to Rejoice in the LORD's Reign, 97:1-5
    97:1   Cultic Cry and Invitation for All to Respond
    97:2-5   Theophanic Description of the LORD's Majesty
Effects of the Theophany, 97:6-9
Hortatory Reflection: God's Care for the Righteous, 97:10-12
    97:10-11 The LORD Loves the Righteous
    97:12   Call to Rejoice and Give Thanks

EXPLANATORY NOTES

Call to Rejoice in the LORD's Reign   97:1-5

The initial verse invites the whole earth to rejoice at the LORD's coming and reign. The *many coastlands* (*distant shores*, v. 1 NIV) represent a worldwide thrust (vv. 4-7, 9). Immediately the psalm presents a verbal portrait of *the Lord of all the earth* in the form of a theophany, to take singers and hearers imaginatively into the royal presence (vv. 2-5) *[Theophany]*. The poetic description of God's intervention to deliver his people draws on images and literature from Israel's past. God appeared as mysterious, one veiled and hidden in *clouds and thick darkness* (v. 2; Exod 13:21-22; Deut 4:11; Isa 6:1-4). In OT theophanies fire appears to consume or refine (Exod 3:2; 19:18; Ps 50:3). Thunderstorms, lightning, and earthquakes show that God is drawing near (Judg 5:4-5; Pss 18:7-15; 29:1-11; 68:7-9, 33; Hab 3:6-16). Erupting volcanoes, when *mountains melt like wax* (v. 5), describe God's awesome power (Mic 1:3-4; Nah 1:5).

Effects of the Theophany   97:6-9

At the foundation of the LORD's majestic reign lie *righteousness* and *justice [Judge; Righteous]*. This aspect of the LORD's sovereignty is emphasized, as stanza 2 describes the effects of the LORD's appearing on heavens and peoples, on idol worshippers and deities, on Judah and on the poet (vv. 6-9). The *heavens* and all peoples proclaim it. However, those who worship *images* and *idols* will realize their folly (v. 7; see comments on Ps 96:5). *All gods bow down* (v. 7) may allude to the LORD's victory over the gods of the nations. It is a statement of faith, for throughout Israel's history, the Israelites had witnessed the victories of nations worshipping such idols (A. Anderson,

2:689). The psalmist's witness once more affirms the LORD's supremacy as *most high* over *all gods* (v. 9; Ps 96:4-5).

All this is bad news for those who organize life around idols and exploitative symbols that reduce people to things; but it is good news to trampled Judah (v. 8). This verse is almost identical to Psalm 48:11, where the LORD demonstrates his reign by defending his people against all threatening forces. The good news is that the LORD is ruling as king (v. 1). Zion (Jerusalem) and the towns of Judah respond in jubilation to God's *judgments*, likely referring to the overthrow of the enemies of the *righteous* (cf. vv. 10-11).

Hortatory Reflection: God's Care for the Righteous 97:10-12

The reigning LORD's care for the *righteous* is the theme of the final stanza. These are *his faithful* (v. 10), who keep the covenant. The NIV translation, *Let those who love the LORD. . .* , seems directly to address the worshippers, as Psalm 97 speaks to readers in every generation. They *hate evil*, love good, and work toward justice (Amos 5:15). The psalms of enthronement "express the grand claim of majesty, which concerns world sovereignty, smashing the idols, elimination of other gods, subjugation of other peoples. . . . The psalms express the dialectic of majesty and mercy" (Brueggemann, 1988:65). So the psalm ends with the promise of light for the *righteous* as blessing to enlighten the heart and enhance life (Ps 36:9). The appropriate response is to give thanks with joy!

THE TEXT IN THE BIBLICAL CONTEXT AND LIFE OF THE CHURCH

Rejoicing in God's Righteousness

As an eschatological psalm in which the LORD who has appeared is also yet to come, Psalm 97 is sometimes identified with NT predictions of Christ's coming, when "all the tribes of the earth will wail" (Matt 24:30; Rev 1:7). Here is a vision of the Lord's glorious coming for all the nations. However, first and primary, we must see the psalm as a call to righteous living and faithfulness. The psalm contrasts the wicked and the righteous. In the normal course of public life, the unresponsive wicked are in control. But the kingdom of God represents an inversion. The high and mighty are brought low, and the lowly lifted up (Luke 1:51-53; 4:18-19). Jesus entreated his hearers to "strive first for the kingdom of God and his righteousness" (Matt 6:33).

These psalms connect the issue of idolatry with justice. In biblical times idols were usually physical objects made with hands. How might we define idolatry in contemporary terms? Idolatry, referring to anything or anyone that "comes between God and me," takes many subtle forms. Getting carried away with one's own gifts, personal status symbols, education, or expertise all reflect the story of Genesis 3 and the temptation to "be like God." God's majesty and mercy are both aspects of his judgment.

The theme of *light* dawning to scatter the encircling darkness is a message of hope (v. 11). Hope is waiting in the darkness for the light (Isa 58:8; 60:1-3; John 1:4-9; 9:5; 2 Cor 4:6). Other NT allusions appear in Romans 12:9, "Hate what is evil" (cf. Ps 97:10) and Hebrews 12:29, "our God is a consuming fire" (cf. v. 3). Hebrews 1:6 quotes Psalm 97:7 from the LXX. Where the psalm mentions *gods* (*'ĕlōhîm*) in the context of idols and worshippers, the LXX interprets that to be "angels." In the period of this ancient Greek translation, it is understandable that an expression such as "gods" would be softened (Holladay: 125).

This psalm, about the whole earth rejoicing in the Lord's coming and reign of righteousness, is the second of three psalms (Pss 96; 97; 98) assigned by the church as lectionary readings for Christmas Day. Christmas, as the festival of the incarnation, celebrates God's involvement in the world when "the Word became flesh and lived among us" (John 1:14). It is also appropriate to use Psalm 97 during the season of Easter, a time to reflect on the transformation wrought by God. In Christian hymnology, Charles Wesley's "Rejoice, the Lord is King!" (1744) expresses trust in God's righteousness and justice reaching out in caring protection.

Psalm 98

A New Song to the LORD as Savior, King, and Judge

PREVIEW

In approaching such an exuberant hymn of praise as Psalm 98, it is helpful to ask, "What inspired this explosion of joy?" The reasons for the *new song* and summons to *make a joyful noise* are introduced by the little word *for* (kî, vv. 1, 9). The declarations *The LORD . . . has done marvelous things* and *He is coming to judge the earth . . . with equity* frame this joyous psalm (vv. 1, 9). The deliverance that the LORD has wrought for his people Israel (vv. 1-3) is also relevant for all the earth (vv. 4-6), and indeed, for all creation (vv. 7-9). In a time when the monarchy has ended, the psalm points to the future and the LORD's universal reign of justice.

Like the two preceding psalms, Psalm 98 acclaims the LORD as king over the universe. In style, language, and theme, it relates to the other so-called enthronement psalms (47; 93; 95–99). The beginning and ending connects directly with Psalm 96, and almost all that lies in between is influenced by the other "The LORD is king" psalms or the second part of Isaiah, the book of consolation for exiles. Worshippers likely used the psalm in ceremonies celebrating the New Year in the postexilic period.

OUTLINE

Invitation to Sing the LORD's Marvelous Deeds of Salvation, 98:1-3
    98:1a   Call to a New Song
    98:1b-3   Reasons for the Song of Praise
Summons to Praise the LORD as King with Voice and Instrument, 98:4-6
All Nature Summoned to Jubilation for the LORD Coming to Judge, 98:7-9
    98:7-8   The Summons to All and Everything
    98:9   Reason: The Coming LORD Will Judge with Righteousness and Equity

EXLANATORY NOTES

Invitation to Sing the LORD's Marvelous Deeds of Salvation 98:1-3

The summons to sing a *new song* (v. 1) may imply that the old song, based on what God has done in the past or even in the present, no longer suffices. The *new song* of these psalms answers to the newness that God will bring when he comes (Pss 96:1; 149:1).

What are the *marvelous things* (v. 1) the LORD has done? The LORD's *victory*, or *salvation* (NIV), is declared three times (vv. 1, 2, 3). The Hebrew noun *yĕšû'â* can have the sense of "rescue, salvation" as well as "victory." The name "Jesus" is based on the Greek form of the word and conveys the sense of salvation (Matt 1:21). The image of the LORD as a victorious warrior, overcoming with *his right hand and his holy arm* (Exod 15:6; Pss 20:6; 44:3), describes the divine intervention that transcends human expectation and opens up new possibilities. References to deliverance may refer to the exodus, the return from exile, or both. Repeated emphasis on *victory* (or *salvation*) places the LORD at center stage. The word *reveal* (*gālāh*, v. 2) designates self-revelation and occurs only at this place in the Psalter; it speaks of the LORD's revelation of righteousness (NIV; *vindication*, NRSV) before the eyes of all the peoples (Isa 40:5; 53:1; 56:1). These verses match the warrior language with words out of Israel's covenant tradition: *righteousness* (v. 2 NIV), *steadfast love,* and *faithfulness* (v. 3). The basis for exaltation of the LORD is the LORD's intervention on behalf of Israel. In the unfolding of history, the people experience God's presence.

Summons to Praise the LORD as King with Voice and Instrument 98:4-6

The second stanza is the summons to a full orchestra of temple singers and instrumentalists: *Make a joyful noise to the LORD* (Pss 66:1; 95:1-2; 100:1). But in addition to the temple musicians, the psalm invites the whole earth to join in the music acclaiming the LORD as *King*. The flourish of *trumpets* and the *sound of the horn* remind us of coronation ceremonies for the kings of Israel (2 Sam 15:10; 1 Kings 1:34, 39).

All Nature Summoned to Jubilation for the LORD Coming to Judge 98:7-9

The psalmist invites nature to join in jubilant praise of the LORD (Ps 96:7-13). The psalm's climactic line appears in verse 9, *at the presence of the LORD, for he is coming to judge the earth*. It directs all jubilation for the one coming to judge. The righteous judgment of the LORD rules the entire created world (9:8; 58:1; 75:2; 96:10; 99:4). These verses point to a messianic era of worldwide justice. The faithful await such judgment with joy rather than fear, for it will be characterized by righteousness and equity (truth and fairness, as in Ps 96:10-13; Isa 33:15) *[Justice; Righteous]*. The hymn celebrates that the LORD has become king and has thus redefined the world. Under the LORD's sovereign reign, the world's inequities will give way to what is morally right and fair for all.

Psalm 98 calls for praise because of what God has done in the past (vv. 1-3), encourages praise to the Lord in the present (vv. 4-6), and looks forward to the coming of the Lord, when all nature will join in the celebration (vv. 7-9).

THE TEXT IN THE BIBLICAL CONTEXT AND LIFE OF THE CHURCH

The New Song of God's Arm in History

This psalm illustrates how worship keeps hope alive, provides a foretaste of the future, and enables persons to persevere in justice. The latter part of Isaiah, in which the dominant theme is Israel's return from captivity in Babylon, speaks of God's "arm," a metaphor used in conjunction with the noun "salvation" and the adjective "holy" (Isa 40:10; 51:9; 52:10; 53:1; 59:16; 63:5). As in the account of the exodus from Egypt (Exod 6:6; 15:16), the deliverance of the oppressed was ascribed to the holy flexing of God's muscle on their behalf (Reardon: 193). Isaiah 52:7-10 is the prophetic counterpart of Psalm 98, the belief that God had been shaping Israel's particular history to establish and reveal his rule over all history. The psalm claims that the savior of Israel is the creator of the world, and also its final judge (Mays 1994b:313).

The new song has an eschatological character. It is the revelation of God's holy arm taking charge of human history. The NT writers saw in Jesus the continuation and climax of God's saving appearance. Echoing verse 3, Mary called her unborn child a marvelous deed in which God remembered his mercy to Israel and "has shown strength with his arm" (Luke 1:49-54). Paul saw in the gospel of Jesus Christ the salvation that reveals God's righteousness to the nations (Rom 1:16-17). The NT also speaks of a time of final judgment, as in Jesus' parable "When the Son of Man comes in his glory, . . . all the nations will be gathered before him . . ." (Matt 25:31-46). At the heart of that parable of judgment is the issue of equity and of making right, and for the righteous, the promise of eternal life.

Sing to the LORD a new song is one of the most repeated lines in the Psalter. Something has happened or is about to happen, and the only way to respond is in praise and thanksgiving. With the appearance of God in human history, music finds its place. Psalm 98 serves as the OT text for Isaac Watts' "Joy to the world" (1719), sung to Mason's arrangement from Handel. This joyous hymn puts the NT gospel into the psalm and makes it a hymn of Advent and Nativity. It interprets the Advent as decisive event in the reign of God, something that changes history for the nations. Also, it maintains the connection between salvation and rule: "The Savior reigns!" (Mays 1994b:314).

Psalm 99

A Hymn to the God of Holiness

PREVIEW

This song of praise to the God of holiness completes the series of "The LORD is king" (enthronement) psalms (Pss 47; 93; 95-99). As another version of the festival theme in the preceding psalms, there are noticeable differences. References to history replace the effect of God's work upon nature. The word *rejoice* becomes *extol* and *worship* (v. 9); instead of Psalm 99 calling people to *ascribe glory* (96:3, 7-8; 97:6) to the LORD, here it bids the earth to tremble and quake.

Holy becomes the key word, directing attention to the essential nature of the reigning LORD. It appears in a refrain to each of the three stanzas (vv. 3, 5, 9). The holiness of God points to awesome majesty and mystery. Yet the content given holiness in the second stanza (vv. 4-5) acclaims the *Mighty King* as *lover of justice*. After appeal to Israel's intercessors of old, Moses, Aaron, and Samuel, the psalm ends with a focus on the answering and *forgiving God,* in whom is also judgment against wrongdoing (v. 8). The psalm is further bound together by the Hebrew word *rûm,* meaning "to be high" and "lifted up," translated as *exalted* (v. 2, *rām*) and *extol* (vv. 5, 9). Psalm 99 provides an awed exclamation that the God of all peoples works justice and answers prayer.

The references to *cherubim, in Zion, his footstool,* and *holy mountain* point to the psalm's use in the temple (vv. 1, 2, 5, 9). The psalm, perhaps from the time of the monarchy, represents a period of political stability; the divine presence in Zion is celebrated. In contrast to other "The LORD is king" psalms, there are few similarities to Isaiah 40–66. Psalm 99 places emphasis on God's relationship to the people who present themselves before the LORD as king. In its focus upon the holiness of God, the psalm appears to connect with the eighth-century prophet Isaiah (Isa 1:4; 5:19, 24; 6:3).

In style, Psalm 99 appears as a series of short cries and exclamations. The structure is complex, with uneven stanzas and expanded refrains. Contrasts are blended: awesome holiness alongside a forgiving God; liturgical acts alongside the daily practice of justice; Israel's particularity as God's chosen people alongside God's relating to other peoples; and sanctuary alongside world (Stuhlmueller, 1983, 2:94).

OUTLINE

Praise the Ruling, Highly Exalted LORD, 99:1-3
    99:1-2   Enthroned on Cherubim in Zion
    99:3   Invitation to Worship and Refrain: "Holy Is He!"
Extol the LORD for His Justice, 99:4-5
    99:4   Equity, Justice, Righteousness in Jacob
    99:5   Invitation to Worship and Refrain: "Holy Is He!"
Extol the LORD for Grace and Judgment in History, 99:6-9
    99:6-7   Citation of Moses, Aaron, and Samuel as Intercessors
    99:8   God's Forgiveness and Judgment
    99:9   Invitation to Worship and Refrain: "For the LORD Our God Is Holy"

EXPLANATORY NOTES

Praise the Ruling, Highly Exalted LORD   99:1-3

The opening contrast is of people trembling and the earth quaking while the LORD *sits enthroned . . . in Zion*. *Cherubim* (v. 1), sometimes regarded as personifications of wind or storm clouds (2 Sam 22:11-13; Ps 18:10), are also depicted as winged creatures with an animal body and with a human or animal face (Ezek 41:18-20). These stand as wings of the throne, accenting the power of God (1 Sam 4:4; 2 Sam 6:2; Ps 80:1). *His footstool* (v. 5), at the base of the throne, may refer to the ark of the covenant (1 Chron 28:2; Ps 132:7). This poetic way of dealing with the transcendence and presence of God indicates the point of contact between earth and heaven. The psalm's concluding appeal to *worship at his holy mountain* (v. 9) reinforces the claim of the LORD's reign as emanating from Jerusalem. God's divine presence represents stability and order over human weakness and uncertainty, a claim encompassing all peoples and inviting their praise.

Extol the LORD for His Justice 99:4-5

In worship, people come face-to-face with awesome mystery. Stanza 2 declares that the divine mystery has a human face. The *Mighty King*, who has all kingly power at his disposal, is a *lover of justice* (v. 4; Pss 11:7; 97:2, 6; Isa 61:8) *[Justice; Righteous]*. The term *holy* directs attention to the essential nature of God as being different from human beings (vv. 3, 5, 9). *Holy* emphasizes the distance between God and humanity. It connotes wonder (Isa 6:3). Though holiness implies perfection, it is also a statement of the divine power that shines forth (as *glory*; Ps 96:7; 97:6) and permeates the world. *Holy* is a statement about the LORD's name (Pss 33:21; 103:1; 111:9; 145:21), about his word (105:42), his arm (98:1), his way (77:13), and all his works (145:17). Thus, God is not simply "wholly other," but also persistent in self-expression. This psalm leaves no doubt that an important aspect of God's holiness is his love of justice, equity, and righteousness *[Holiness]*.

Holiness means compassionate and creative love (33:5; 37:28; 93:5; Isa 5:16). As a Davidic king is celebrated for the exercise of justice, for heeding the petitions of the helpless (Ps 72:1-2), so the sovereign LORD's strength is manifested in equity and righteousness. If there is no justice, there is no God (Ps 82). Justice questions are foundational to Israel's world. The LORD notices injustice and acts to right it (Pharaoh, Babylon). This psalm brings together the Mosaic tradition of liberation and social transformation with the Jerusalem tradition of presence and establishment (Brueggemann, 1984:148).

Extol the LORD for Grace and Judgment in History 99:6-9

The final stanza draws on Israel's history in calling on the LORD's name and how God has answered. It seems as if Psalm 99 intentionally recalls Exodus 15:1-18 as a way of affirming for a later generation—discouraged by events like those described in book III—that God still reigns (McCann, 1996:1075). The psalm names three heroes from the past as intercessors who were favorably answered: Moses (Exod 14:15-18; 32:30-35), Aaron (Num 16:41-50), and Samuel (1 Sam 7:8-9; 12:19-25). They may be named here as guardians of the statutes of God's justice which they had received. As part of the annual festival in later years, the worshippers recalled the names of these three persons with reverence as source of authority in the Jewish community. God had spoken to Moses and Aaron out of the "pillar of cloud" (Exod 33:9; Num 12:5), and to Samuel from above the sacred ark (1 Sam 3:3-14). Samuel had vigorously resisted the establishment of kingship (1 Sam 8:4-18; 12:15, 25). His inclusion in this liturgical psalm, focusing on the LORD's presence from Jerusalem, underlines the emphasis on justice and God's responsiveness to the community in need (Brueggemann, 1984:149).

The coexistence of God's judgment and grace, so incomprehensible to human minds, is vigorously affirmed (v. 8). The LORD's self-revelation had already expressed forgiveness in tension with God's severity (Exod 34:6-7). God forgives and God punishes. The tension reminds the hearer that forgiveness is not leniency, nor is one to take it for granted. Here are the two sides of the LORD's awesome kingship.

The stanzas end with the exclamation *Holy is he!* (vv. 3, 5), with the final refrain underscoring the reason to praise and extol: *for the LORD our God is holy* (v. 9).

THE TEXT IN THE BIBLICAL CONTEXT AND LIFE OF THE CHURCH

Holy Is the Lord!

God is the Holy One, as affirmed throughout the OT (Lev 19:2; 1 Sam 2:2; 2 Kings 19:22; Pss 71:22; 78:41; 89:18; Isa 1:4; Jer 51:5; Ezek. 39:7; Hos 11:9; Hab 1:12). Holy is a statement about his name (Pss 33:21; 99:3-4; 103:1; 111:9; 145:21), his action (Pss 33:5; 99:4; 129:4), and especially about his quality of being God.

An important biblical theme is God's demand for holiness in his people (1 Thess 4:7). In the book of Exodus, the LORD forms his people and gives the first call for holiness, as in the Song of the Sea, where the LORD is said to bring his people ultimately to his "holy dwelling" (Exod 15:13 NIV). The mountain where the delivered people gather, Sinai, is described as a holy mountain (19:23), before which are those destined to be "a holy nation" (19:6). The tabernacle to be erected has a holy place and also a most holy place (26:33). The covenant code states, "You are to be my holy people" (22:31 NIV). For Israel, "holy" means more than that which is unapproachable. It becomes a goal associated with God's nature and his desire for humans: "You shall be holy; for I . . . am holy" (Lev 19:2). A series of ethical and ritual commands follows, with the commandment to love all persons, including aliens (19:18, 34). Deuteronomy repeats a similar refrain and also ties it to God's election: "For you are a people holy to the LORD your God; it is you the LORD has chosen out of all the peoples on earth to be his people, his treasured possession" (Deut 14:2). Repeatedly the election is affirmed: Israel is to be a treasured people and thus be given an elevated position; they are to be a holy people (26:19). Isaiah, whose favorite designation for the deity is the Holy One (30 occurrences), envisions a time when the exiles have returned and they shall be called "The Holy People" (62:12). Ezekiel, in portraying a future time when "I will be their God, and they shall be my people," follows this announcement with "I the LORD make Israel holy" (Ezek 37:28 NIV). In sum, the God who is marked by holiness establishes a people who are to be marked by holiness.

Such a focus on God's holiness as characterized by justice continues through the NT (Luke 4:18-19; Rom 12:1; Heb 10:19-25; 1 Pet 1:15-16; 2:5, 9; Rev 15:3-4). Christians express it as adoration in the opening lines of the Lord's Prayer, "Our Father, . . . hallowed be your name." Hymns about the holiness of God include Reginald Heber's "Holy, holy, holy" (1826); Johann Philipp Neumann's text sung to Franz Shubert's melody, "Heilig, heilig, heilig" (in the *German Mass*, 1826–27); and Guillermo Cuellar's liberation hymn from Nicaragua, "Santo, santo, santo" (1986).

The book of Hosea, drawing on the illustration of unfaithfulness in marriage, provides further commentary on the *forgiving God* (v. 8), acknowledging cost for both the one who forgives and the one who needs to be forgiven. So also Jesus' parable of the father and his two sons conveys the powerful gift of grace in forgiveness (Luke 15:11-32). The forgiveness offered by God's grace is never cheap grace; instead, it is the deepest expression of God's holiness.

Psalm 100

Make a Joyful Noise to the LORD

PREVIEW

Psalm 100 is a simple and beautiful hymn inviting God's people everywhere to enter into worship with thanksgiving and praise. The whole psalm speaks of joyful response to life, seeking to praise God for all God has done and is. It serves as a doxology to conclude the psalms of "enthronement" (Pss 93; 95–99), or the larger collection of liturgical psalms (Pss 91–99). In tone and wording, it is similar to Psalm 95:1-7a. Thus, Psalms 95 and 100 form a frame around the core collection of "The LORD is king" Psalms 96–99.

The psalm consists of two hymn parts, with the summons to worship (vv. 1-2, 4) and the motivation (vv. 3, 5). Pilgrims approaching the gate of the temple may have sung the first part, with a choir within the temple courts chanting the second part. There the procession is to offer the LORD thanksgiving (*tôdâ*) and praise (*tĕhillâ*). The word *thanksgiving* in a psalm heading occurs only here. Words such as "psalm" or "song" to describe poetic genres are more common [Superscriptions].

OUTLINE

First Summons to Praise (with Motivation), 100:1-3
Second Summons to Praise (with Motivation), 100:4-5

EXPLANATORY NOTES

First Summons to Praise (with Motivation) 100:1-3

Imperative verbs invite adoration of the LORD by all the earth: *Make a joyful noise, worship, come!* The word *worship* can also be translated *serve* (v. 2 NIV; *'ābad*). It is used in Deuteronomy to mean walking in the LORD's way, loving him, and keeping his commandments (Deut 6:13; 10:12).

The fourth imperative verb, *know* (v. 3), states the reason for worship. *Know that the LORD is God* takes on additional meaning when the title *LORD* is understood from the Hebrew to be a name (*Yahweh*) with the connotation "present to act in salvation." Older versions, such as KJV, read verse 3b following one ancient text (MT): *It is he that hath made us, and not [lō'] we ourselves*. The preferred text, following other ancient manuscripts, renders the last phrase *and we are his [lô]* (NRSV, NIV, NJPS). Though only a brief summary of Israel's faith, Psalm 100 is a gem in its succinct expression of the creed: *the LORD is God* (cf. Deut 6:4); he is our creator, we are his people, the LORD is good, his steadfast love is everlasting, his faithfulness endures to all generations. Many other passages cite this covenant faith (Deut 4:35, 39; Josh 24:17; 1 Kings 18:39) and affirm that the LORD created Israel (Deut 32:6, 15; Isa 43:1, 21; 44:2). God's covenant people are the flock of God's *pasture* (Pss 23; 74:1; 79:13; 95:7).

Second Summons to Praise (with Motivation) 100:4-5

With *thanksgiving* and with *praise* the people are to honor and exalt the God of Israel (v. 4). The motivation is *steadfast love* and *faithfulness*, characteristics that make God the *good* (v. 5; 106:1; 118:1; 136:1) to be celebrated with joy (34:8). *Steadfast love* (*ḥesed*) is love that loves no matter what *[Steadfast]*. To speak of God as *good* is to affirm that the LORD of Israel is the source of all that makes life possible and worthwhile, often experienced specifically in God's deliverance of persons from distress (Miller, 1986:71).

THE TEXT IN THE BIBLICAL CONTEXT AND LIFE OF THE CHURCH

Call to Worship and to Witness

The opening invitation to *all the earth* to join in praise of God reminds us of the missionary purpose in some of these psalms (66:1; 67:2-3;

98:4). If God is God of all the world, then to him is due the praise of all lands. God's people are called to worship and also to witness.

Herein lies the claim of Psalm 100. When the community praises, it submits and reorders life. When the Hebrews proclaimed that *the LORD is God* (v. 3), they asserted that the God of the exodus is the sovereign of all of life. That is a broad claim, encompassing all peoples.

The other dimension of such a claim is personal. To submit to God as Lord means that a person no longer grounds life in oneself. Rather, life is rooted in the steadfast love and faithfulness of God. Even more, God is *our God* (99:5, 8, 9) and *we are his people* (v. 3), a belonging together in covenant relationship (Jer 31:33, a verse later quoted in Heb 8:10 to affirm the fulfillment and superiority of the new covenant). In summary, God rules the world, and we belong to God.

The NT echoes of Psalm 100 are many (Eph 2:10; Phil 4:4-7; Col 3:16-17). At Lystra, Paul and Barnabas refer to God "doing good," reject worship of themselves, and exalt the living God (Acts 14:15-17).

Through the centuries, Jewish and Christian liturgies have used Psalm 100 as a call to worship, carrying the thanksgiving of God's people. As a psalm for the thank offering (Lev 7:11-20), it is appropriate for the communion service.

Well-known hymns are based on Psalm 100. William Kethe's "All people that on earth do dwell" has been sung to L. Bourgeois' tune "Old Hundredth" since 1561. Isaac Watts' "Before Jehovah's aweful throne" (1719) is a free paraphrase. A more recent musical setting of the text, "Jubilate Deo omnis terra" ("Rejoice in the Lord, all lands. Serve the Lord with gladness"), is in Jacques Berthier's canon (1980), as sung by the Taizé community in France.

Praise as the Enjoyment of God

From human experience we discover that what is admirable is deserving of praise. The enjoyment of anything spills over into praise—praise of people, favorite books, favorite games, "praise of weather, dishes, actors, motors, horses, colleges, countries, historical personages, children, flowers, mountains, rare stamps, rare beetles, even sometimes politicians or scholars" (C. S. Lewis, 1961:80).

The psalmists, in telling everyone to praise God, are doing what people do when they speak of what they care about. God is the Object to admire, to appreciate, to receive, and to enjoy. Older catechisms stated that the chief purpose for people is "to glorify God, and to enjoy him forever" (Westminster Shorter Catechism, 1). This call to praise invites us to enjoy God!

Psalm 101

A King's Vow to the Way That Is Blameless

PREVIEW

In a series of assertive *I will* . . ." declarations, the king pledges the desire to walk in *the way that is blameless* (v. 2). Composed for use at the inauguration of the king or an annual celebration of his kingship, the psalm proclaims commitment to rule according to the statutes of the covenant (2 Kings 23:3). The king celebrates the LORD's commission of *ḥesed* (*loyalty* or "love") and *mišpāṭ* (*justice*) and promises to take the royal duties with utmost seriousness. The psalm ends with the guarantee that his administration will ensure the community's welfare. Beginning with integrity of heart (v. 2), the ruler's pledge offers a moral code for all persons in positions of authority.

In book IV, David's name reappears in the titles only here and in Psalm 103. This royal psalm initiates a new series of "Psalms of David" that extends into book V (Pss 108–110; 138–144) *[Superscriptions]*. Following a series of "The LORD is king" psalms, featuring the LORD's reign in holiness, Psalm 101 describes the true attitude of the earthly ruler who recognizes the sovereignty of God. The declaration of the king may have originally been the vow of moral purity on his coronation day, as a response in the judicial transfer of power.

The psalm appears to draw on the wisdom tradition (Kenik: 391–

403). The contrast between those who seek the LORD and those who do not recalls the language of Psalm 1.

Certain features of style are interesting: *No one . . . shall remain; . . . no one . . . shall continue . . .* (v. 7) is similar to the structure of verse 3, to which it is connected as an inclusio. So also the divine name, *LORD* (vv. 1, 8), encloses the intervening lines. The first part of the psalm focuses on the king's personal integrity; verses 5-8 tell how that integrity is reflected in the life of the community governed (*within my house* [v. 2] / *the city of the LORD* [v. 8]). These parts are bound together by a series of words: *the way that is blameless* (vv. 2, 6), *my house* (vv. 2, 7), and *my eyes* and *I will look* (vv. 3, 6) *[Hebrew Poetry]*.

OUTLINE

Introduction and Vow to Walk in the Way of Integrity, 101:1-3a
Specific Norms About Character and Behavior, 101:3b-7
Conclusion: Justice Shall Prevail, 101:8

EXPLANATORY NOTES

Introduction and Vow to Walk in the Way of Integrity 101:1-3a

The psalm begins with the king praising the LORD's *ḥesed* and *mišpāṭ* (v. 1, *loyalty* or "love," NIV, and *justice*). These are the basic divine qualities stressed in the Mosaic covenant (Exod 34:6-7) and source of the king's ethics and administration. The king, as head of the corporate body of Israel, is to walk in the LORD's steadfast love and justice (Pss 72:1; 132:12). Psalm 136 provides an example of what it means to sing of steadfast love or loyalty. Justice entails right relationship among persons *[Steadfast; Judge]*.

The psalm's organizing terms, *blameless* (*tāmîm*) and *integrity* (*tōm*), occur in verse 2. These words also describe the king's righteousness in Psalms 18:20-30 and 78:72. Synonyms include sincerity, single-mindedness, honesty, and humility. The antonym in Psalm 101 is *perverseness of heart* (v. 4; Prov 10:9; 11:20), suggesting that which is twisted and inconsistent (Mays, 1994b:321).

The puzzle for interpreters is the nature of the answer to the question posed in verse 2: *When shall I attain it?* or *When will you come to me?* (NIV). If the verbs that follow are to be taken in past tense, we could read the psalm as the king's complaint that the LORD has not adequately responded to his devotion and blameless conduct (Dahood,

3:4). Then Psalm 101 would be a royal complaint, and we could read it as response to the destruction of the monarchy, like Psalms 90–100. In verse 1, however, the king has expressed his intention to celebrate the LORD's love and justice. The verbs that follow the question, *I will walk. . . , I will sit. . .* , can also be taken as vows.

The promises that follow pledge a godly morality from the inside out. Meanings for *my house* (v. 2) can include family and household, the royal court, the temple, or the whole land; here it likely means the royal court. *House* is used of the Davidic dynasty upheld by God (2 Sam 7:13-16; Ps 127:1). Integrity begins from within. The private life affects the public life. The king's personal integrity must be reflected in the life of the community that he governs.

Specific Norms About Character and Behavior 101:3b-7

As the king describes his administration, he identifies expectations for those who minister on his (and the LORD's) behalf. As guardian of the gate, the obedient king sets up a standard of purity (Pss 15; 24). Zero tolerance is granted those who are perverse of heart, slanderers, haughty and arrogant, deceitful and liars (vv. 4-5, 7). The king receives justice from the LORD (72:1-4). He is therefore the representative and enforcer of the LORD's justice and judgment. The concern of the just king is care for *the faithful in the land* (v. 6; 35:20). The character of those who govern determines the effect of their governing. "Conduct depends on character and character is shaped by ultimate commitments" (Mays, 1994b:322).

Conclusion: Justice Shall Prevail   101:8

The king's vow ends with the promise that he will exercise the office of judge (72:2; Prov 20:26; Isa 11:4). Morning was the preferred time for administering court justice (2 Sam 15:2). The *city of the LORD* is parallel to *the land*, suggesting that what is done in Jerusalem affects the whole land (v. 8).

THE TEXT IN THE BIBLICAL CONTEXT AND LIFE OF THE CHURCH

Guidelines for Those Who Govern

Psalm 101 expresses high ideals, but these promises are repeatedly broken in the abuse of royal power. The tragic story of David illustrates how personal failure of the king poisons the whole kingdom

(2 Sam 11–12). The tone of Psalm 101 sounds like promises heard from politicians before election. White comments on these guidelines for those who govern: "The expressed intentions are admirable; the anticipations of temptation are shrewd—if only the personal manifesto did not sound so self-assured!" (White: 154).

It is not surprising that readers have given the psalm a future messianic interpretation. Early Christians read these words as Jesus' charge to all who belong to the faithful. "In Christ God was reconciling the world to himself" (2 Cor 5:19). In the NT, the exalted Christ is the judge among his chosen people (Rev 1:16; 2:1–3:22).

This psalm speaks to the issue of personal and public ethics. The pledge to lead a blameless life affirms how one's heart dictates actions. The psalm tolerates no shady deals and under-the-counter maneuvers. Here it connects with ethics of the Sermon on the Mount, that if the whole person is good, then his deeds will be good as well (Matt 7:15-20). Consequently, attention must be given to "secret sins." Psalm 101 provides a format for an examination of conscience. Interior wholeness and external justice go hand in hand. Thus, the psalm roots political ethics in religious commitment and is applicable to all persons in authority in any age.

Delitzsch relates the story of Ernest the Pious, Duke of Saxe-Gotha in the seventeenth century, who sent an unfaithful minister a copy of Psalm 101. It became a proverb in the country: when an official does wrong, he will certainly soon receive the prince's psalm to read (Delitzsch: 107).

Psalm 102

Prayer to the Everlasting God by One Afflicted

PREVIEW

The title ascribed to this lament suggests the theme: *A prayer of one afflicted*. In this prayer song, the troubles of the person afflicted (vv. 1-11) are related to, and set against, the background of the destruction of Jerusalem and its hoped-for restoration (vv. 12-22). The psalmist concludes with further lament over the brevity of life, yet finds comfort and hope in contemplating God's unchangeable and enduring presence (vv. 23-28).

Psalm 102 is the only psalm of lament so described in its title *[Superscriptions]*. When sufferings ravage body and mind, the *afflicted* (or *lowly*, NJPS; *'ānî*) confides in God with deep emotion. The opening mood is reminiscent of Job 7:16.

Several interpretive questions arise: Who is speaking? Is it the king or some other representative of the community, or an unidentified individual pleading because of terminal illness? Do verses 14-15 suggest the time of exile or the early postexilic period, before the temple was rebuilt? How do the laments (vv. 1-11, 23-24) relate to the hymnic praise and prophetic hope (vv. 12-22, 25-28)? Is this a composite psalm or a single composition? The following comments view the psalm as an individual lament, in which the psalmist sees the plight of the community mirrored in his own suffering (Davidson, 1998:333-34). The psalm also illustrates how an individual lament can become collective when the community adapts it for liturgical purpose. In the literary setting of book IV, Psalms 101-102 together address the three key elements of the crisis of exile—loss of monarchy, Zion/temple, and land.

The motif of time provides a compositional unity in that God's everlasting reign (vv. 12, 24b-27) is set in contrast to the brevity of human life (vv. 3, 11, 23-24). The psalm asserts that an appointed time has come for the LORD's compassion in Zion (v. 13). The psalm looks forward to a future time when coming generations will praise the LORD and dwell in security (vv. 18-20, 28; Mays, 1994b:323).

OUTLINE

Individual Lament of One Afflicted, 102:1-11
   102:1-2   Introduction: Cry for Help
   102:3-11   Description of the Psalmist's Illness, Loneliness, Godforsakenness
Hymn of Praise and Prayer to God to Restore Zion, 102:12-22
   102:12-17 Appeal to the God Enthroned Forever to Rebuild Zion
   102:18-22 Vow of Praise and Appeal to the Certainty of the LORD's Future Deeds
Lament on the Brevity of Life, 102:23-24
Praise to the LORD as Creator, Unchanging, Everlasting, 102:25-28

EXPLANATORY NOTES

Individual Lament of One Afflicted   102:1-11

The psalm opens with a cry to God, echoing many other psalms (27:9; 39:12; 69:16-17). Now it puts into words the bodily and psychic deterioration (vv. 3-11). Images of *fire* (fever?) and *smoke*, a heart dried up like withered grass, loss of appetite, *loud groans,* and "skin and bones" depict the body's deterioration (vv. 3-5). References to the unclean *owl of the wilderness* (v. 6, vulture?) and solitary sparrow *on the housetop* (v. 7) underscore loneliness and desolation. Sleeplessness (v. 7) and taunting enemies (v. 8, accusations of guilt or death itself?) fill moments of consciousness. *Ashes* and *tears* become food and drink in the recognition that God's *indignation* and *anger* cause the suffering (vv. 9-10). Here appears the common understanding of sickness as the result of sin and God's punishment for sin (22:7-8; 42:10). Other understandings are possible: suffering is future oriented (e.g., Joseph, Gen 50:20); suffering is educative (Elihu's speech, Job 36:5-23); and one may suffer on behalf of others (Isa 53). As *smoke* (v. 3) symbolizes the fleeting character of life (Pss 37:20; 68:2), so the *evening shadow* (v. 11) represents the evening of life, though the psalmist is only at the midpoint (vv. 23-24). The outlook is bleak indeed.

Hymn of Praise and Prayer to God to Restore Zion 102:12-22

Yet even as despair abounds, the writer rebounds with an emphatic *But you, O LORD, are enthroned forever* (v. 12). This abrupt vocative (*O LORD*) contrasts the majestic, eternal God with the supplicant's sense of rejection. However, it is also a word of praise. God enthroned in eternal majesty can turn away in wrath, but God can also turn back to the supplicant. The LORD is still king. He will *rise up and have compassion on Zion* (v. 13). The juxtaposition of lament and praise highlights the contrast between the finite and the infinite, perhaps to elicit God's compassion. Was this written during the exile, or just afterward? Reference to the *stones* and *dust* (v. 14) suggests that the temple still lay in ruins. Biblical scholar Claus Westermann, who saw the destruction of Berlin in World War II, comments: "All who have experienced their city's destruction understand such phrases as 'hold her stones dear' and 'have pity on her dust'" (Westermann, 1989:114).

However, that early postexilic period was also a time of hope. The love for the sanctuary in Jerusalem has not disappeared despite its destruction. Prophets hope for the *glory* of the LORD to return to Zion (Ezek 43:2-5). The LORD will build up Zion, and nations will revere and praise the LORD because of his self-manifestation in the restoration of Jerusalem, marking a new era for all nations (Ps 105:14-15). The LORD will do this in response to *the prayer of the destitute* (v. 17), but also for his name's sake (vv. 12-13). Thus, the psalmist comforts himself and those who hear his prayer, not with God's deeds in the past, but with those anticipated in the future. Two occurrences of *prayer* in verse 17 recall the superscription and verse 1, suggesting that the hope expressed (vv. 12-16) is related to verses 1-11.

The psalmist moves from prophecies about the rebuilding of Zion to a focus on the coming generation; he records a statement of confidence for everyone to see (Job 19:23-24; Jer 30:2-3). The theme of the congregation's hymn in worship is how God reveals his name and manifests his saving rule (vv. 18-22). *Prisoners* being released and *peoples* and *nations* flocking to Zion to pay homage to the LORD will be the fulfillment of ancient prophecies and hopes (Pss 22:27; 47:9; 67:7; 96:7; Isa 2:2-4; 60:3-7; Mic 7:12; Zech 14:16).

Lament on the Brevity of Life 102:23-24

Now the lament arises again as the psalmist brings before the LORD the prayer for rescue from death (vv. 23-24). The poignancy of his suffering is brought out by the thought of *'ēlî, O my God,* as the one who might *take me away* at the midpoint of life. Yet that same God has no end (v. 24b).

Praise to the LORD as Creator, Unchanging, Everlasting 102:25-28

Quickly the psalmist regains confidence, not by thinking of his own brief life, but of the greatness of God the LORD, the everlasting one, the creator (vv. 25-26; Isa 44:24; 48:13). Though the heavens and the earth should wear out like clothing, and be replaced by new heavens and a new earth (65:17; 66:22), the LORD will endure (vv. 26-27). *But you are the same* (v. 27), the emphatic contrast to what precedes, as in verse 12: God always is, and is always adequate to the situation (Isa 43:10, 13; 48:12). The psalm climaxes in affirmations: *You endure, you are the same, your years have no end* (vv. 26-27). The one approaching death can know that he is secure, and that the eternal God will be the security of future generations (v. 28).

THE TEXT IN THE BIBLICAL CONTEXT AND LIFE OF THE CHURCH

The Cry of the Afflicted as the Prayer of God's People

Psalm 102, which places the everlasting God in juxtaposition with transient human beings, is reminiscent of Psalm 90. The psalm is the prayer of one who finds hope for existence under the wrath of God in the kingdom of God.

In the Mishnah (ca. AD 200), Psalm 102 was listed with Psalms 120; 121; and 130 for days of fasting (*Ta'anit* 2:3). In early Christian usage it was designated one of the seven Penitential Psalms, along with Psalms 6; 32; 38; 51; 130; and 143 *[Penitential].* The psalm does not specifically mention penitence or confession. Rather, it conveys acceptance of suffering as justified, and submission to God's judgment (vv. 9-10, 23).

The hymnic verses 25-27, that God outlasts what he has created, are quoted in Hebrews 1:10-12 in reference to Christ. This quotation comes from the LXX, in which the first line reads, "In the beginning, you, O Lord, laid the foundations of the earth," though the Hebrew text lacks "O Lord." The writer of the book of Hebrews has taken the

"O Lord" as an address to Jesus Christ. It was not uncommon for NT writers to take OT expressions referring to God and apply them to Jesus Christ (Holladay: 125, 129). This identification of the psalm with Jesus Christ, as well as the focus on time, including the future, has led to messianic understandings of the psalm: the Messiah's suffering and dereliction (vv. 1-11), and then his eager anticipation of the kingdom in its worldwide glory (vv. 12-22; Kidner 1975:363) [Anointed].

Other NT allusions to themes in Psalm 102 include: the brevity of life (James 4:14), recording God's mighty deeds for the instruction of the next generation (1 Cor 10:11), transformation of the peoples into God's people (1 Pet 2:9-10; Rev 15:4), and new heavens and new earth (2 Pet 3:7, 10; Rev 20:11; 21:1).

The cry of the afflicted applies to the experience of any individual or nation, ancient or modern. We hear the cry in the experience of millions of refugees. In this prayer, the needy see their own image. The prayer of an individual also becomes the prayer of God's people. What finally gives hope is that God does not change. So God shares his permanence with his people. In their song based on Psalm 102:1-2, the Taizé community has given musical expression to this cry of the afflicted: "O Lord, hear my prayer. . . . When I call, answer me. . . . Come and listen to me" (Les Presses de Taizé, 1982).

Throughout the generations God's people have found hope and strength in the conviction that because God reigns, we can entrust the future to God. This psalm's lament over the brevity of life and the proclamation of God's unchangeable enduring presence makes it appropriate for funerals. The final verses offer a strong promise for the future (Ps 102:25-28), which finds affirmation in the words of Jesus, "I am with you always, to the end of the age" (Matt 28:20).

Psalm 103

Praise to the God Abounding in Steadfast Love

PREVIEW

In Psalm 103 we find a hymn of pure praise. Beginning with the individual consciousness of God's gracious gifts of forgiveness and healing (vv. 1-5), the psalmist proceeds to declare the LORD's abounding steadfast love to the covenant people (vv. 6-18) and ends with an invitation for the whole universe to bless the LORD (vv. 19-22).

A theme throughout the psalm is the relationship of the LORD to sinners. The LORD's abounding steadfast love, so much greater and longer lasting than his anger at sin, provides the foundation and hope of forgiveness for the sinner. The psalm is close in theme to psalms of sickness and healing; worshippers may have used it as a prescribed form in the sanctuary. In this psalm, petitioners with a variety of problems and afflictions could find a place before God to express their gratitude for forgiveness and healing. The psalm warns against accepting life as a matter of course and invites acknowledgment of the incredible grace by which we live. *Bless the LORD, . . . and do not forget all his benefits* (vv. 1-2).

The editors of the Psalter may have placed Psalm 103 right after 102 because they saw God's forgiveness as the answer to the horrors the people of God had suffered in the Babylonian exile (102:13-14). This psalm is given the title *Of David,* as also for Psalm 101, the other such ascription in book IV *[Superscriptions].* However, most commentators consider Psalm 103 to be postexilic, recognizing allusions to Isaiah 40–66 (v. 9 and Isa 57:16; vv. 15-17 and 40:6-8). Yet the reverse is a possibility; perhaps Isaiah was dependent on the Psalms. Psalm 103 also picks up themes from Psalm 90: forgiveness of sin (vv. 3, 10, 12; Ps 90:7-8), the LORD's steadfast love and mercy (vv. 4, 8, 11, 17-18; 90:14), human beings as transient as grass (v. 15-16; 90:5-6), and the LORD's rule over all (v. 19; 90:1-2).

Examining the psalm's structure and style reveals a carefully formed work of poetic art. The psalm opens and closes with the same line, an inclusio defining the whole as praise with thanksgiving. The imperative *bless* (*praise,* NIV) introduces two lines at the beginning and four lines at the end, emphasizing declarations that exalt the LORD. The psalm uses twenty-two lines (verses), the number of letters in the Hebrew alphabet, suggesting comprehensiveness. In verses 11-14 the poet has composed a chiasmus of *for, as, as, for* sentences, each of which in Hebrew begins with a *k* sound. We see repetition not only in the pairing of *steadfast love* with *mercy* and *compassion* (vv. 4, 8, 11, 13, 17), but also in the emphasis on *all* (five times in the first six verses and four times in the last four verses), giving a sweeping and inclusive tone to the whole (Mays, 1994b:326-27) *[Hebrew Poetry].*

OUTLINE

Introduction: Praise for Forgiveness and Healing, 103:1-5
God's Gracious Love to the Covenant People, 103:6-18
    103:6-7   In the Days of Moses
    103:8-13   For His Saving Deeds in Patient Forgiveness
    103:14-18   Reasons for the LORD's Mercy
Conclusion: Invitation for the Whole Universe to Bless the LORD,
    103:19-22

EXPLANATORY NOTES

Introduction: Praise for Forgiveness and Healing
103:1-5

The psalmist initially calls for an inward focus. In this dialogue with oneself, a person is invited to *bless* or *praise* so that God is not forgotten. Forgetting and turning away from God begins when we no longer praise.

Five benefits of God's grace are now enumerated: forgiveness, healing, redemption (rescue), crowning of life with mercy, and renewal (vv. 3-5). Life's terrifying contrasts are listed, with focus on the One who alone has power to make life new from sin, illness, or despair. One view, among others held in the OT, saw illness as the result of some offense (Ps 32:3-5; see comments on Ps 102:9-10). The singer can announce personal sins forgiven, personal infirmities healed. *The Pit* refers to the place of the dead. The *eagle*, while easily and freely soaring aloft, symbol of youth and renewed strength, was also thought to live a long life (Isa 40:31).

God's Gracious Love to the Covenant People 103:6-18

From personal benefits of God's grace, the psalmist moves to praise for God's steadfast love in history. Verses 6-7 refer to the exodus, the wandering of the children of Israel in the wilderness and before God at Mt. Sinai. Verse 8, almost word for word the portrait of God in Exodus 34:6, reminds us of the story of Israel's golden calf and of God's amazing mercy despite human inconsistency (Num 14:18; Ps 86:15; Jon 4:2). This focus on God's mercy stands at the center of the psalm. In no way does it do away with God's wrath, but it limits it. God's anger is his reaction to all that threatens life; the very force of his wrath upholds life. Yet the psalm extols God's mercy as yet more powerful and more permanent, knowing no bounds (Ps 30:5; Westermann, 1989:240) *[Wrath]*.

The psalm has a great deal to say about the patience of God (vv. 8-13). Verse 10 recalls the question of Psalm 130:3: *If you, O LORD, should mark iniquities, Lord, who could stand?* But there is forgiveness! Drawing on metaphors of distance (heaven/earth, east/west) and the love and pity of a father for his child, the psalmist describes the limitless love of God (ḥesed) toward *those who fear him,* a phrase repeated three times (vv. 11, 13, 17). *Steadfast love* also occurs four times (vv. 4, 8, 11, 17). This is a love that bridges the great chasm between the divine and the human *[Steadfast]*.

Now follow the reasons for the LORD's mercy (vv. 14-18). The LORD knows *how we were made* and *that we are dust* (v. 14). Human life is so utterly brief and transient (vv. 15-16; Pss 90:5-6; 102:11). *But* there is also *the steadfast love of the LORD!* The *but* (v. 17) that introduces the contrast between God's everlasting goodness and human transitoriness makes clear that human transience and vulnerability still remain in God's embrace (Westermann, 1989:242). After reflecting on the brevity of life and God's covenant-keeping love without limits, the psalmist appeals to people to keep covenant and do the commandments. Remembrance and praise of God's grace must lead to obedience. The ultimate aim of God's redemptive work is that it would lead the individual and community to worship, to serve and fear the LORD.

Conclusion: Invitation for the Whole Universe to Bless the LORD   103:19-22

The conclusion praises the LORD for his dominion over all (vv. 19-22). All God's messengers and works are called to join the praise! With the final line, the psalmist invites his own soul, as at the beginning, to *Bless the LORD!*

THE TEXT IN THE BIBLICAL CONTEXT AND LIFE OF THE CHURCH

A World Saturated with God's Steadfast Love

This much-loved and much-read psalm extols the *steadfast love* of God. Its appeal begins with recognition of pain in life, acknowledged in those *who* phrases of verses 3-5. The community brings that pain before the God who has power to transform. So the praising community (and the individual) proclaims a world that is saturated with God's steadfast love (*ḥesed*)! The old creation is guilt and death. But in death, as in life, what's real is *ḥesed*! No wonder Psalm 103 has stimulated many hymns of praise, of which Henry F. Lyte's "Praise my soul, the King of heaven" (1834) is a prime example.

Psalm 103 illustrates that in the OT God is not simply a God of wrath and judgment, as some contend. The opening verses declare that God's recompense is first of all forgiveness and redemption, steadfast love and mercy (Ps 103:1-5). Yet the psalmist acknowledges the tension between God's justice and mercy. Steadfast love or compassion is for those who fear God (vv. 11, 13, 17), and righteousness is for those who are obedient (v. 18). God wills and demands justice and righteousness, yet loves and is committed to relationship with sinful people, a tension that is present in Genesis 6–9 and clearly expressed in Exodus 34:6-7. Psalm 103 proclaims God's universal sovereignty as well as compassionate love, which is embodied in forgiveness (Ps 103:6-18; McCann, 1996:1092-93).

In the NT, God's *ḥesed* has become manifest in Jesus Christ (John 1:17; 3:16). In Mary's Magnificat, the line "His mercy is for those who fear him from generation to generation" (Luke 1:50), connects with Psalm 103:17. The illustration of God's love as parental (Ps

103:13, 17; Isa 49:15) brings to mind Jesus' teaching about God's loving care for all his children (Luke 11:11-13), as well as the parable of the father and the two sons (15:11-32). In Christian theology, the cross of Jesus Christ indicates the great cost to God of forgiving love (Rom 5:8). To the world, the miracle of grace looks like weakness, but it is in truth the power of God (1 Cor 1:25; 2 Cor 12:9).

The Versatility of Psalm 103

Use of Psalm 103 includes not only its recitation for the Jewish Sabbath, but also by all Christian traditions for worship, celebration of communion, and funerals. The faithful often draw on the psalm for individual reflection, to address one's own soul. The story of God's dealings with his people is also the history of our own souls. In Psalm 103, the soul is called to contemplate God's infinite, forgiving mercy.

Do not forget all his benefits (v. 2) is a pivotal sentence in this psalm. If we forget the benefits, "we are only aware of our own efforts, our puny self-help efforts at making the best of a bad deal, our haphazard attempts at capitalizing on the chances available to us. . . . Most of our life consists in what God has done—creating us, speaking to us, loving us" (Peterson, 1989:116). *Bless the LORD, O my soul!*

Psalm 104

O LORD, How Manifold Are Your Works!

PREVIEW

This great praise hymn of creation relates in theme to Psalms 8; 19:1-6; and 29. It celebrates the Creator's glory and worth as seen in the beneficent providence, the grandeur and order of God's created world.

Readers have often made attempts to correlate Psalm 104 with the days of creation in Genesis 1. This poetic exclamation of wonder confirms Genesis 1:31: "God saw everything that he had made, and indeed, it was very good." Genesis 1 declares *what* God was making. Psalm 104 focuses on *why* and *how* the Creator acts. The psalm praises God the Creator rather than the creation. It sees the world as a continuing event, a continuing creation.

This hymn may belong to the liturgy of the great New Year Festival in the autumn. It is enclosed, as is Psalm 103, by a self-exhortation: *Bless the LORD, O my soul* (vv. 1, 35). At the end, *Praise the LORD! (Hallelujah!)* may well belong to the beginning of Psalm 105, framing that psalm even as Psalm 106 is enclosed by the exclamation *hallelujah!* These three hymn psalms (Pss 103; 104; 105) provide a sequence of praise liturgies for God's providence in human life (forgiveness of sins), in the world of creation (order and harmony), and in history (God's deeds on behalf of Israel).

Psalm 104

OUTLINE

Call to Praise: The Heavens (God Above All Worlds), 104:1-4
The Earth (God's Conquest over Chaos), 104:5-9
The Water (God as Sustainer Through Water and Food), 104:10-18
The Moon and the Sun (God of Time and Seasons), 104:19-23
The Sea (God of All Creatures, Great and Small), 104:24-26
Life (God as Master of Life and Death), 104:27-30
Doxology: Joy and Wish for Perfect Harmony, 104:31-35

EXPLANATORY NOTES

Call to Praise: The Heavens (God Above All Worlds) 104:1-4

The call to praise begins with God as *wrapped in light* (vv. 1-2; Gen 1:3-4) and as set above all worlds, but acting. The verbs show movement: *You stretch, set, make, ride* (vv. 2-4; Gen 1:7-8). They depict the one addressed as *O LORD my God* as *very great*, royally clothed, and dazzlingly resplendent. This portrayal of the LORD as a royal deity (v. 1b) shifts to the warrior image, using the thunderstorm as chariot (v. 3bc) and its winds and lightning as his cohorts (v. 4). These images correspond to the traditional description of the king of heaven's theophany (Pss 29; 114; cf. Ps 102:19-22) *[Theophany]*.

The Earth (God's Conquest over Chaos)   104:5-9

God's conquest over chaos in subduing the primeval flood and establishing the earth is the subject of verses 5-9 (Gen 1:1, 9-10; Ps 89:9-10; Isa 51:9-10). In the theme of conflict between the forces of chaos symbolized by *the deep* and *the waters* (v. 6), we meet imagery not only from Genesis (1:1; 7:17–8:5), but also from a mythical battle, as found in the Babylonian creation story (Job 38; Ps 77:16; "Akkadian Myths, Creation Epic," *ANET* 60-72). Such forces proved powerless to stand in the way of the creative purposes of the LORD, who laid the unshakable foundations of the earth (Pss 24:2; 46:2-3; 102:25). Rebuked, the waters fled to become mountain springs and rivers in the valleys, recognizing the boundaries set by God (vv. 7-9; Davidson, 1998:340).

The Water (God as Sustainer Through Water and Food) 104:10-18

Stress falls on the beneficent use of water. The watering of the earth by rain and irrigation canals, of extreme importance in Palestine and

Mesopotamia, receives significant attention (vv. 10-13). With the presence of water comes all vegetation (vv. 14-18; Gen 1:11-12) and food for all creatures, the beasts, birds, goats (even the "nonessential" rock badgers, *coneys*, v. 18), and humans (Murphy: 124)! The psalmist sees the created world as a single all-embracing organism based on a divine and meaningful world order.

The Moon and the Sun (God of Time and Seasons) 104:19-23

God's creation presents not only *space* but also *time* (vv. 19-23; Gen 1:5, 14). So God made the *moon* and the *sun*. Here moon and sun are not deities, as claimed by early pagan cults (Deut 4:19; 17:3; Jer 19:13), but essential timekeepers for nomadic people, and important for God's people in setting festival times. Darkness, too, is a part of God's providential ordering. Even at night all life is dependent on the Creator. In this quaint picture from an agrarian society, night is for the beasts and day is for humans to work. This hymn of praise to the Creator sees the human species simply as one of the creatures dependent on God, the Provider. With respect to existence and dependency for life, we are one among many (Mays, 1994b:334).

In the language of verses 19-24, readers have observed similarities to the Egyptian hymn to the sun by Akhenaton (Amenhotep/Amenophis IV, ca. 1379-1362 BC; "Hymn to the Aton," *ANET* 369-71; http://www.wussu.com/poems/akhnaton.htm). This influence likely reached Israel by way of the Phoenicians and Canaanites. One major difference is that the Egyptian hymn depicts the sun itself as the creator; in Psalm 104, the sun is but the handiwork of God. The Egyptian hymn to the sun and other nonbiblical creation accounts represent the learning and worldview of cultures neighbor to Israel. In this psalm, the poet may well have adapted external sources for praising the LORD according to Israel's knowledge of God (Mays, 1994b:332; Holladay: 40).

The Sea (God of All Creatures—Great and Small) 104:24-26

At this point (v. 24) the psalmist pauses for reflection and adoration, admiring the divine wisdom in creation (Prov 8:24-31), especially as exhibited by the sea. The sea, including man-made *ships* and *Leviathan* (Ps 74:12-17; Job 3:8), is further symbol of God's creativity. Often the sea implies threat. Here the sea is God's plaything, in which the great sea monster serves for God's amusement. The infinitely great and the infinitely small—all of them are God's handiwork!

Life (God as Master of Life and Death)   104:27-30

Verses 27-30 speak to how totally dependent all life is upon the continuing daily providence of God. *These all* (v. 27) refers back to *your creatures* (v. 24). This section of the psalm adds the rhythm of life and death to the rhythm of day and night (Westermann, 1989:250). All creatures are dependent upon God's *breath*, God's *spirit,* for the vital spark of life (vv. 29-30; Gen 1:2; 2:7; Job 12:10). The world is well-ordered and reliable. But on its own, it has no possibility of survival or well-being. *When you hide your face* (v. 29; Ps 10:1), the gift of life is withdrawn, and only death remains (103:14). Renewing of life lies entirely in God's hands and depends on God's continuing grace (v. 30).

Doxology: Joy and Wish for Perfect Harmony 104:31-35

The psalm concludes with a series of wishes and vows: that the LORD endure forever (v. 31), that the LORD himself rejoice in his works (v. 31b), and that this meditation (psalm) will be a pleasing offering to the LORD (v. 34). However, in a reference to earthquake and volcano, the final verses acknowledge also God's awesome power to destroy (v. 32; 144:5; Amos 9:5). And finally, the psalmist blurts out the one sour note in God's created world—human sin and wickedness (v. 35). The wicked do not fit into the vision. In praying *Let sinners be consumed from the earth* the psalmist longs for restoration of the original intended harmony of creation. The prayer stems from a desire to see a perfect world, in which divine justice will be manifested *[Imprecation; Wicked]*.

THE TEXT IN THE BIBLICAL CONTEXT AND LIFE OF THE CHURCH
Life as a Gift of God

Belief in God as Creator has far-reaching implications. This claim invalidates the solar deity, the reigning god in the Egyptian hymn to the sun. The belief that creation is an expression of God's grace, that the Creator provides food as a parent provides for the household (Pss 104:27-28; 145:15-16), means that no one can lay claim to anything as a right. Life is a gift of God. Our life is interrelated with all of creation.

Such a faith has implications for how we live and act toward the earth's resources: air, water, land, plants, animals, and other human beings. Marya Mannes (41), referring to a generation of wasters, asks:

> What kind of people are these—people who discard a million tons of metal, who demand that forests be cut down to wrap and seal what they eat and smoke and drink, who need thirty feet of steel and two hundred horsepower to take them to their small destinations? Destroying beauty with their hideous signs, they leave the carcasses of cars to rot in heaps, spill their trash into ravines, and choke off the life in the rivers and lakes with the waste of their produce. . . . Who is so rich that he can squander forever the wealth of earth and water for the trivial needs of vanity or the compulsive demands of greed?

Psalm 104 affirms a cooperative relationship between God's work and human endeavor (vv. 14, 23, 26). That is possible only if we do not see ourselves as autonomous from the world, its creatures, and our Creator.

We hear some NT echoes to Psalm 104 in words about God's providential care in the Sermon on the Mount (Matt 6:25-31), Jesus' comment about God's continuing work (John 5:17), and the reference to God's ministering servants (Heb 1:7, 14). Hymns based directly on the psalm include "I sing the mighty power of God" (Isaac Watts, 1715) and "O worship the King" (Robert H. Grant, 1833). Francis of Assisi's famous song of thanksgiving for all his brothers and sisters, "Canticle of the Sun" (1225; http://www.webster.edu/~barrettb/canticle.htm), and the hymn "All creatures of our God and King" (1225) have their home in Psalm 104.

Liturgically, Jewish people have chanted Psalm 104 on *Yom Kippur* (Day of Atonement, providing a pledge that new life will emerge out of penance and sorrow), on the evening of the new moon (to consecrate another month of life), and as praise throughout the winter season, that spring rains will bring new life. The Greek Church sings Psalm 104 daily in its vesper service (vv. 19-20). Churches have also given the psalm a prominent place at Pentecost, to celebrate the gift of God's Spirit to renew life (v. 30) (Stuhlmueller, 1983, 2:112; Reardon: 205).

Psalm 105

Remember the Wonders God Has Done

PREVIEW

Psalms 105 and 106 are storytelling psalms. Psalm 105, in hymnic mood of thanksgiving, recounts the marvelous works by which the LORD has demonstrated his faithfulness to the covenant he made with Israel in promising the land to Abraham. From beginning to end, the story is that of a gracious God, caring for his chosen people, no matter how grim the circumstances. The narrative touches on the patriarchs, the sojourn in Egypt, the exodus, and wilderness wanderings. From worshipful beginning to abrupt but praiseful end, from the promise of the land (v. 11) to its possession (v. 44), all is of God.

Noticeably absent in Psalm 105 is the account of the people's response, particularly their faithlessness. Psalm 106, a psalm of penitence, tells that story, reciting Israel's disobedience. In telling these two strands of sacred history, God's faithfulness and human disobedience, Psalms 105 and 106 relate to the other historical psalms (Pss 78; 135; 136).

Psalm 105 presents a view of history about how, in the great events of Israel's past, a guiding hand has been at work. The purpose of reciting God's covenantal dealings seeks to awaken and produce a new obedience to the commandments of God (v. 45). The psalm provides encouragement to the community of Israel to trust in the faithfulness of God.

The covenant has a fundamental place in Israel's theology and self-understanding. Ancient summaries of the story of God's involvement with Israel appear in the credo of Deuteronomy 26:5-9 or Joshua 24:2-13. Psalm 105, as an historical poem, is such a recital of the credo. Israel defined the theological significance of its life by reciting its story according to a set pattern in an interpretive way (Guthrie: 44).

This psalm, for a recital of basic events that created the nation of Israel, was almost certainly composed for use at one of the major festivals. The absence of reference to David points to a time when the monarchy was no longer relevant to the nation's life. The land, however, is still valued. The people need assurance that this is the land promised by God to his people (Davidson, 1998:342). This promise is closely associated with Abraham (Gen 12; 15:18). The promise of the land, grounding the story of Israel's trek from Egypt to Canaan, was a theme of Deuteronomy (Deut 1:8; 4:31; 8:1). Psalm 105 is certainly connected with Deuteronomy (v. 1 with Deut 32:3; v. 4 with 12:5; v. 5 with 7:18 and 1:16; v. 6 with 7:7; v. 8 with 7:9; v. 11 with 32:9; v. 24 with 6:3). This psalm, perhaps from the early postexilic period, was in existence when the Chronicler worked: verses 1-15 appear as verses 8-22 in the composite poem of 1 Chronicles 16. The intent of Psalms 105-106, to address the crisis of exile, is in keeping with the apparent purpose of book IV as response to the theological crisis of exile elaborated in book III (McCann, 1996:1104).

OUTLINE

Introduction: Summons to Thanks, Praise, and Remembrance, 105:1-6
    105:1-4   Invitation to Joyful Worship
    105:5-6   Remembrance of God's Wonderful Works to His Children
The LORD's Faithfulness to His Covenant and Promise, 105:7-11
    105:7-10   The Covenant with Abraham, Isaac, and Jacob
    105:11   The Promise of the Land
God's Providence Through the Wanderings of His People, 105:12-42
    105:12-15   The Patriarchs Protected
    105:16-22   Joseph in Egypt (Prisoner Yet Released)
    105:23-38   Israel in Egypt (Oppressed Yet Freed)
    105:39-42   Israel in the Wilderness (Protected and Fed)
Conclusion: Possession of the Land and Admonition, 105:43-45

EXPLANATORY NOTES

Introduction: Summons to Thanks, Praise, and Remembrance 105:1-6

The hymnic introduction addresses the covenant community and calls on the people to participate in the cultic ceremony through prayer and hymns (v. 1; Isa 12:3-4). In addition to the call to sing, verse 2 invites recall and exploration of the great wonders of the LORD in the history of his people. The section urges with imperatives: *give thanks, call, make known, sing, sing, tell, glory, rejoice, seek, seek, remember* (vv. 1-6). While referring to the Lord, already in these opening verses the pronoun *he/his/him* predominates, pointing to the activity of God in all the experiences through which his people have passed. God's acts are identified here as the *wonderful works, miracles,* and *judgments* spoken by the LORD (v. 5).

Here the psalm introduces key words and themes: *servant* or *chosen one* (vv. 6, 9-10, 15, 17, 25, 26, 42-43) and *remembrance* (vv. 5, 8, 42). The pairing of *servant* and *chosen* means that the ancestors and their descendants came into such a relationship to the LORD by the LORD's initiative (Mays, 1994b:338).

The LORD's Faithfulness to His Covenant and Promise 105:7-11

The psalmist now does what the introduction invites. The LORD is Israel's God. *He is the LORD our God* (v. 7a) sounds like the opening line of the Ten Commandments (Exod 20:2). Verse 7b recalls the world-penetrating power of the God of judgment. The *judgments* here are part of his saving miracles, as in the judgment on the Egyptian oppressors in the exodus. The psalm states its main theme: the LORD remembers his covenant *forever* (v. 8). This covenant made with Abraham, and confirmed to Isaac and Jacob, is mentioned often (Gen 50:24; Exod 2:24; 6:3-5; Num 32:11; Deut 1:8).

According to Psalm 105, a strong feature of the covenant is the way it promises to give *the land of Canaan* to Israel (v. 11). Verse 11, a quotation of God's promise, introduces a key cluster of words: *land, earth, portion* (vv. 7, 11, 12, 16, 23, 27, 30, 31, 32, 33, 35, 36, 41, 44). *The word that he commanded, for a thousand generations* (v. 8) denotes the promise of the land as the inheritance of God's people. *Canaan,* perhaps initially the Phoenician coastal plain, came to refer to the whole of Palestine (A. Anderson, 2:729).

God's Providence Through the Wanderings of His People 105:12-42

The reference to the patriarchs tells of seminomads, strangers, aliens who lack security and yet are providentially safeguarded (vv. 12-15). *Rebuked kings* (v. 14) may refer to the episode of Pharaoh and Sarah (Gen 12:14-17). Only here are the patriarchs—Abraham, Isaac, and Jacob—given the title *my anointed ones*, perhaps in the sense of being called by God and equipped for a special task (v. 15; cf. Gen 20:7, Abraham as a prophet; 1 Kings 19:16, a prophet anointed). From small beginnings, God carries his plan of salvation forward.

In the story of Joseph's rise to power and Israel's sojourn in Egypt, the psalmist again makes it clear that this is a story of God's providence (vv. 16-22; Gen 37; 39–50). God *summoned famine*. God *sent* Joseph as a slave. God made Joseph *lord* (*'ādôn*) of Pharaoh's house. When the Israelites lived in *Ham* (a poetic name for Egypt: Gen 10:6; Ps 78:5), God *made his people very fruitful* and caused the Egyptians to hate them (vv. 24-25). God sent Moses and the plagues to rescue them. Here the sequence of the ten plagues differs from the Exodus account (Exod 7–11). In the psalm, the order of the plagues from Exodus is 9, 1, 2, 4, 3, 7, 8, and 10, with no mention of the fifth or sixth plagues (cf. comments on Ps 70:40-64). This poetic account does not present the plagues to trace the progress of Pharaoh's hardening; he is not even mentioned. Instead, the plagues illustrate the decisive and versatile power of God: *He sent, he spoke, he gave, he struck*. In Egypt, God protected his people so marvelously that the Egyptians were *glad when they departed* (v. 38). A striking literary feature in these verses is the chiasmus: v. 25: whose hearts he *turned*; v. 26: He *sent* . . . Moses; v. 27: They performed his signs; v. 28: He *sent* darkness; v. 29: He *turned* their waters (Stuhlmueller, 1983, 2:117) *[Hebrew Poetry]*.

The psalm deals more briefly with the miracles during the wilderness wanderings. The focus is on the manna from heaven and other provisions through which God sustained the people in that hostile environment (vv. 39-42). The recital of the wanderings of God's people comes to a climax in verse 42, with God's remembrance of his holy promise to Abraham. This verse forms an inclusio with verse 8, beginning and ending the main body of the poem with reference to Abraham and the eternal covenant with him. The exodus is confirmation of the LORD's keeping covenant with the patriarchs.

Conclusion: Possession of the Land and Admonition 105:43-45

The psalm concludes with God's people pictured in possession of the Promised Land; there is great joy. Once more, the psalm rehearses key words: *remember, promise, servant, chosen ones, land* (vv. 42-44). The end of the psalm finally relates to the Sinai tradition and the giving of the *statutes* and *laws*. All this has happened so that Israel may walk according to the LORD's commandments (Exod 19:6; Deut 4:1, 40; 26:17-18; Ps 78:7). The final verse reaffirms the purpose of the psalm: to evoke praise and obedience (vv. 1-6, 45). And if, as some commentators suggest, *Praise the LORD!* (*Hallelujah!*) at the end of Psalm 104 should be shifted to the beginning of Psalm 105, then the final exclamation of *Hallelujah!* forms an inclusio with the *Hallelujah!* that begins this psalm of praise for the LORD's mighty works.

THE TEXT IN THE BIBLICAL CONTEXT AND LIFE OF THE CHURCH

The Purpose of Knowing History

Psalm 105 ends with an admonition. The purpose of knowing history is that people may know God. Israel's historiography was all theology. The unifying theme was God's governance of events through various interventions, miracles, and direct speech, or the more subtle influence of divine activity called God's providence. Paul expresses such an understanding in Romans 8:28: "We know that [God makes] all things work together for good for those who love God, who are called according to his purpose" (NRSV n).

Such a storytelling psalm as Psalm 105 is a reminder that the past must become present to every generation if the God of Abraham, Isaac, and Jacob is to be their God. Each generation must make a fresh discovery of God's faithfulness. "A healthy respect for the past is a necessary ingredient for a healthy future" (Stevens: 189).

Several NT references connect to Psalm 105, such as Luke 1:72-73, Zechariah's reference to God's covenant with Abraham; John 6:31 and 1 Corinthians 10:4, about manna in the wilderness and the spiritual rock; Romans 4 and Galatians 3:6-14, references about Abraham's seed; and Luke 12:48, about privilege enjoining responsibility. The church has been identified as Abraham's offspring through Jesus Christ (Gal 3:29), and has understood itself to be a people who live by his rule in the midst of the nations (Matt 5–7; 1 Pet 2:9-10).

The opening verses of Psalm 105 invite God's people to *seek the LORD* (vv. 2-3). To seek the LORD can be a onetime incident, as when an individual or community is experiencing distress (2 Sam 12:15-16). More frequently, it refers to an ongoing relationship with God (Isa 55:6). Prayer and worship cultivate such an affinity, but obedience and righteousness are the fruits of such a God-person relationship. The psalm emphasizes that without God we wander hopelessly, but under God's basic law or promise (v. 10), our wandering leads to a promised land (Stuhlmueller, 1983, 2:117).

The Promise of the Land

An ongoing issue presented by this psalm has to do with God promising Israel the land of Canaan. To Israel, the land is a gift of God's promise (Deut 6:10-11). It is a good land and place in which to serve the LORD (Josh 23:14-16). The land is not only giver of nourishing gifts and place of satisfaction, but also bearer of historical words and a place for listening, for hearing the word of the LORD (Brueggemann, 2002:45-50).

During the exile, Israel lost the land for fifty years. Israel lost the land again in AD 70, when the Romans destroyed Jerusalem, and again later to people of Christian and Islamic faiths. In the past century, renewed Zionist hopes, on the basis of God's promise of the land to the Jews (as well as political decisions and wars), helped establish the new nation of Israel. However, questions still remain: Whose land is it? Can it be a "holy land" to people of the three major faiths, whose spiritual leaders were nurtured by its soil? A view of divine election must always be tempered by the admonition of verse 45, to obey God's statues and laws. That sense of being "chosen" dare not give way to the temptations of empire-building and imperial abuse of power.

Biblical understandings of the land include awareness that God bestows it as gift. God remains the owner, and the inhabitants are but sojourners. God provided laws concerning the rights and treatment of the alien and foreigner in the land (Exod 22:21; Lev 19:33; Num 15:14-16; Deut 24:17-21). God intended for Israel to be a light to the nations, a quite different understanding of the covenant and promise of the land than the present prevailing pattern of acquisition of territory by violence and force.

Marlin Jeschke explores this theme in *Rethinking Holy Land*, a study in salvation geography. Jeschke (149-56) invites us to read the biblical story in its entirety, from the garden of Eden, through the promise to Abraham and Sarah, through the experiences of Israel in the land and in exile, to Jesus repeating the Psalm 37:11 declaration that the meek shall inherit the land, to Paul's claim that God promised Abraham and his descendants the cosmos. Jeschke concludes that "God intends every person on earth to find a home where he/she may dwell in peace and security," and that involves a different way of relating geographically to peoples of the world than seizing territory. The new way is "to present the gospel to all peoples of the world and . . . to live as salt and light, to live in the world as followers of the way of Jesus."

Psalm 106

Both We and Our Ancestors Have Sinned

PREVIEW

In contrast to Psalm 105, which emphasized the LORD's faithfulness to his covenant, Psalm 106 tells the story of the ingratitude and disobedience of the Israelites, from the time of the exodus to the present. The theme of this national penitential lament is found in verse 6: *Both we and our ancestors have sinned.* Whatever God has done, Israel has been unfaithful (vv. 7, 13-14, 19, 21, 24-25, 28-29, 32, 34-39, 43). Nevertheless, God has shown mercy and forgiveness (vv. 8, 15, 23, 30, 44-46).

This theme of God's extraordinary long-suffering overrides the story of human rebellion. The psalm expresses an attitude of hopeful sorrow over sin. Through this tale of Israel's apostasy shines a theology of hope based on the character of a gracious God. The story told is similar to that of the didactic Psalm 78. Psalm 106 uses the language of worship, and the mood is praise and penitence.

This storytelling psalm appears to have been written for public confession of sin and used during the annual renewal of the covenant, or at some other great festival. Factors in dating include the reference to a people scattered *among the nations* as in the exile (v. 47) and the quotation of verses 1 and 47-48 in 1 Chronicles 16:34-36. The psalm generally follows the Pentateuch in outlining Israel's story, suggesting its composition and use after return from the exile (537 BC),

Psalm 106

and before 1 and 2 Chronicles appeared (ca. 450 BC). Psalm 106 concludes book IV and further responds to the theological crisis of exile that is presented in book III.

Structurally, the main body of the psalm, Israel's confession of sin (vv. 7-46), is framed by an introduction (vv. 1-6) and ends with a petition and doxology (vv. 47-48). A notable feature of the framework (vv. 1-7, 47) is how it directly addresses the LORD in the second person (*you*). The psalm's recital of Israel's story (vv. 8-46) speaks of the LORD in the third person.

OUTLINE

Introduction: Thanksgiving and Petition, 106:1-6
    106:1-3   Summons to Praise
    106:4-6   Petition and Confession
A Confessional Recital of Israel's Sin, 106:7-43
    106:7-12   The Exodus Story
    106:13-18   The Wilderness Period
    106:19-23   The Golden Calf Incident
    106:24-27   Report of the Spies
    106:28-31   Baal of Peor Incident
    106:32-33   At the Waters of Meribah
    106:34-39   The Sins in Canaan
    106:40-43   Cycles of Rebellion, Judgment, and Deliverance
God's Mercy and Concluding Petition for Restoration, 106:44-48

EXPLANATORY NOTES

Introduction: Thanksgiving and Petition   106:1-6

The entry chant of thanksgiving for the LORD's goodness and eternal *steadfast love* (*ḥesed*) follows the opening *Hallelujah!* (NJPS). These or similar words also appear at the beginnings of Psalms 107 and 136, calling the community to testify to the everlasting goodness of God. Yet human speech is unable or unworthy to adequately express the power and praise of the LORD (v. 2). The blessing (v. 3), which sounds like a congratulation conveyed upon the righteous, is also exhortation for the worshipper to obey the divine commandments (Ps 105:45).

In the petition, the community appeals to the LORD's power and grace (vv. 4-5). Scattered (v. 47), the people long for the good fortune of the *chosen ones*. God's heritage is his people (v. 5). These verses convey the intimate tone of personal prayer: "This includes me,

Lord!" The petition illustrates how, in approaching God, the individual can use a national psalm designed for public worship (Knight, 2:159).

Verse 6 sounds like a liturgical formula of confession (1 Kings 8:47; Lam 3:42). Three words are used for sin: *ḥāṭā'â*, missing the mark; *'āwôn*, perverseness; and *rāšā'*, act wickedly (see comments on Ps 51:1-4). *Both we and our ancestors have sinned* may also imply that "we have sinned in the sinning of our ancestors." Jeremiah and Ezekiel saw the guilt of their contemporaries as rooted in the conduct of Israel's earlier generations (Jer 2; Ezek 16). Israel had learned that sin is intergenerational and social (Mays, 1994b:342) *[Sin]*.

A Confessional Recital of Israel's Sin   106:7-43

The guilt that separates the people from God must now be removed. Thus, the main part of the psalm, Israel's confession of sin, reflects upon the acts of grace that God in his mercy has continually wrought on behalf of his people, in spite of their ingratitude and disobedience. That is why a religious community keeps retelling its story. The past is the present (Davidson, 1998:348).

The catastrophe had its beginnings already in Egypt (vv. 7-12). In spite of being delivered from their bondage and led to the Egyptian frontier, the people failed to grasp the marvelous deeds of the LORD and *rebelled* when trapped between the Egyptian army and the sea (v. 7; Exod 14:10-12). The LORD *rebuked the Red Sea* (vv. 7, 9, 22), likely the *Sea of Reeds* (NRSV n, NIV n), a marshy stretch of water ringed with reeds in the eastern Nile delta; the Hebrew word *sûp* means "reed." The psalmist pictures the sea as transformed into land as dry as a desert (Exod 14:21-22). At the miracle of Israel's deliverance from the Egyptian pursuers, *they sang his praise* (v. 12; Exod 15:1-18).

This first of eight incidents, in which the people responded to God's gracious act by rebelling, reveals their unbelief. *They soon forgot his works* (v. 13) is a repeated word of warning in Deuteronomy (Deut 4:9, 23; 6:12). From the wilderness period, the psalm alludes to the people's impatient murmuring for food (Num 11:4-6, 31-35) and expresses irony in verses 13-15. The people were looking for a demonstration of God's gracious favor. They received the food they craved, but with it a *wasting disease* (v. 15).

The psalm flags Dathan and Abiram's jealousy as an illustration of insurrection against superiors (vv. 16-18, Num 16). Korah, also a part of the rebellion, is not mentioned. Might this omission be in deference to the part the descendants of Korah played in the collection of the

Psalms? *[Korah]*. The incident is a reminder that God meant Israel to be a company, a community, but now envy had destroyed that fellowship.

The psalm cites Israel's third sin as the worship of the image of the calf (Exod 32:1-35; Deut 9:8-21). Horeb serves as another name for Mt. Sinai, especially in Deuteronomy. The psalm accentuates the irony. They exchanged *the glory of God* (*their Glory*, NIV) for a cast *image of an ox that eats grass* (v. 20; Jer 2:11). The Israelites shifted from worshipping the great God of wondrous saving deeds to worshipping an inanimate idol, nothing more than a metal image of an ox that eats grass! Upon this ingratitude and apostasy, God's judgment of destruction would have come, *had not Moses . . . stood in the breach* (v. 23). This military metaphor depicts Moses as a fearless warrior standing in the breach of the city wall and facing the enemy (Ezek 22:30). He exercises the role of intercessor, appealing to God to turn away his justified anger (Exod 32:11-13, 31-32; Deut 9:25-29). Moses seems to perform the role of intercessor within the Psalter itself, since the majority of laments appear in Psalms 1–89, with Psalm 88 (individual) and Psalm 89 (communal) providing the crescendo of hopelessness and despair echoed in Psalm 90, ascribed as *A Prayer of Moses*.

The exaggerated report of the spies (Num 13:25-29) disheartened the people so that they had no faith in the LORD's promise to give them the land (vv. 24-27). They even planned to return to Egypt (Num 14:4). The punishment that God *would disperse their descendants among the nations* (v. 27), not threatened in Numbers 14, appears elsewhere (Lev 26:33; Deut 4:27; Ezek 20:23). To people in exile, this story from the past had direct contemporary meaning.

Numbers 25 tells the story of Israel's apostasy by intermarrying and worshipping Baal at Mt. Peor in Moab. A plague broke out. Phinehas arrived as a judge and slew an Israelite and his Midianite wife. *The plague*, an expression of God's anger, *was stopped*, but only after 24,000 Israelites had died (Num 25:9). God's accolade for Phinehas' zeal and atonement, summarized in verse 31, is given in full in Numbers 25:11-13.

Reference to the insurrection of the people against Moses and Aaron at the waters of Meribah stresses the seriousness of failure to respond in obedience to God (vv. 32-33). At Meribah, both the people and Moses sinned. Moses was forbidden entrance to the Promised Land (Exod 17:1-7; Num 20:1-13; Deut 32:51-52). Moses' fault is never fully described, but the psalmist suggests a frustration so deep that Moses *spoke words that were rash*.

The story moves on to the settlement of Canaan (vv. 34-39). The

Israelites failed to exterminate the Canaanites (Deut 7:2, 16; 20:16-18; Judg 1:21–2:5). Instead of opposing their evil practices, God's people just joined in with them. The people intermarried (v. 35) and worshipped pagan gods (v. 36), even to the point of practicing child sacrifice (v. 37; Lev 18:21; Deut 12:31; 18:9-10; 2 Kings 16:3-4; Jer 7:31). *Innocent blood* (v. 38) may refer to legal murders of an unjust judicial system (2 Kings 21:16; Isa 1:15-26; Jer 22:3; Mic 3:1-3). Their idolatry became a form of prostituting themselves (v. 39; Hos 1–3).

Six hundred years of apostasy followed their entrance into the land (vv. 40-43). The inability of the people to conquer the inhabitants of the land is explained by their disobedience to God's command (Exod 23:32-33; 34:11-17). On style, verses 41 and 42 are arranged as a chiasmus. Verse 42 also includes a play on words. The Hebrew verb *yikkānĕʻû, brought into subjection*, contains the same root (*kānaʻ*) as *kĕnāʻan, Canaan* (v. 38). In using the verb, the psalm may allude to the subjection/humiliation of the Israelites as due to their humbling themselves before the idols of Canaan.

God's Mercy and Concluding Petition for Restoration 106:44-48

With *nevertheless* or *but* (v. 44 NIV), the psalmist returns to the infinite patience of God. God *heard* their cry. God *remembered* his covenant. Israel's unfaithfulness does not annul God's faithfulness. God expresses his judgment, not as wrath, but as *compassion* in an outpouring of his *steadfast love* (*ḥesed*, v. 45).

The concluding petition for restoration (v. 47) picks up themes from the beginning of the psalm (vv. 4-5). As the congregation's response to the recital of Israel's sin and God's mercy, the people pray that God bring them back together from the just punishment of their exile so that they might again give praise. The final verse, marking the end of book IV of the Psalter, appropriately crowns a psalm whose theme has been God's steadfastness alongside human perversity. Doxologies also end the other books within the Psalter (41:13; 72:18-19; 89:52; 150:1-6).

THE TEXT IN THE BIBLICAL CONTEXT AND LIFE OF THE CHURCH

Taking Inventory

The main body of Psalm 106 is Israel's confession of sin (vv. 7-43). The confessional recital begins with recognition that the people of

God have not observed justice at all times (v. 3). It recounts many times when they forgot and did not remember the LORD's wonderful saving works, or they put God to the test through their cravings or deliberate rebellion by worship of idols.

Such "transgression lists" appear in other passages of Scripture. Jeremiah calls the people to amend their ways by acting justly one with another, including an end to oppression of the alien, orphan, and widow (Jer 7:5-7). Ezekiel provides an extended list, beginning with the shedding of blood and ending with oppression of the poor and needy (Ezek 22:3-13, 23-29). Jesus identified evil acts that come from the human heart: "fornication, theft, murder, adultery, avarice, wickedness, deceit, licentiousness, envy, slander, pride, folly" (Mark 7:21-23). Such lists can aid God's people to take inventory and lead to confession and repentance.

Hope Based on the Character and Action of God

In theme and tone, Psalm 106 can be connected with the sermons in the book of Deuteronomy, the autobiographical writing of Nehemiah, or the call to repentance and prayers in the last chapters of Isaiah (Isa 59; 61:1-3; 63:7–64:12). In spite of human perversity, the psalm's theology of hope is based on the character and action of God.

We can read Psalm 106 in light of Zechariah's prophecy on how the Lord God "has looked favorably on his people and redeemed them" (Luke 1:68). We can also read the psalm as an exhibit of "the kindness and the severity of God" (Rom 11:22), with the recital functioning "to serve as an example" (1 Cor 10:11-13). In many ways the psalm portrays a negative moral example, conveying the implication, "Don't let this happen to you." The writer of the book of Hebrews took the period of the wilderness wanderings as exemplifying the danger of apostasy; the author warns believers: "It is a fearful thing to fall into the hands of the living God" (Heb 10:31). On rebels not entering the rest, see also Hebrews 3:11-18.

Paul found in Psalm 106:20 the clue to the fundamental error that underlies all sin in the human race: "They exchanged the glory of the immortal God for images" (Rom 1:23). Paul knew that humankind is fundamentally sinful (1:18-28; 3:9-20; 7:14-25). Yet believers are justified by God's grace (3:24-26; 5:1-2, 8). Other NT allusions to Psalm 106 include Jesus' lament, "How often have I desired to gather your children together, . . . and you were not willing!" (Luke 13:34). And the NT agrees with Psalm 106:36 against idolatry (1 Cor 8; 10:14-21; Rev 2:14).

The references to Moses and Phinehas (vv. 23, 30) call attention to the role of the intercessor. The gory account of Phinehas' action (Num 25:7-8), as well as the violence commanded in verse 34, do not reflect the psalm's overriding tone and message of compassion. Indeed, the psalm "in its closing petition is such a cry of an intercessor on behalf of his congregation and people" (Mays, 1994b:343).

Mysteries of Grace and Judgment

What might people who are part of any dispersion learn from Psalm 106? During the nineteenth and twentieth centuries, large numbers of ethnic and sectarian groups migrated from Europe to the United States and Canada. For some—including many Mennonites leaving Russia in the 1870s, the 1920s, and the 1940s—migration was driven by issues of conscience and the longing for freedom of worship and the life of faith. Through these wilderness wanderings, it was easy to identify with the people of Israel in their exodus deliverance from Egypt. For others, disrupted by war and scattered as refugees, the experience seemed more like that of the exile. Thinkers have considered issues of judgment and of mercy in trying to understand these experiences and how God works in human affairs. In retrospect, there is often a sense of deep gratitude for God's compassion and leading in spite of the judgments of suffering and sorrow experienced. Even in the darkness, some remnant of hope prevails. When it seems humanly impossible, the *LORD our God* can yet *gather us from among the nations* (Ps 106:47), that we may give thanks and praise!

Book Five
Psalms 107–150

Psalm 107

Let the Redeemed Thank the LORD for His Steadfast Love and Wonderful Works

PREVIEW

This thanksgiving liturgy of the redeemed community opens book V of the Psalter. The psalm exalts the steadfast love (ḥesed) of the LORD as the creative rule that spawns new beginnings.

The opening summons to give thanks (vv. 1-3) leads to a litany of thanksgiving by four groups of redeemed pilgrims: desert travelers, prisoners, sick people, and seafarers (vv. 4-32). After experiencing deliverance from distress, these persons are to bring forward the sacrifice of thanksgiving with shouts of joy, proclaiming the wonderful works of the LORD (v. 22). They are to narrate the wonders of God in the assembly of the people and council of the elders (v. 32).

The four illustrations of deliverance from homelessness, bondage, affliction, and storm witness to the steadfast love and wonderful works of God. Such interventions, in response to the cry of those in trouble, are consistent with how God works in nature and in society (vv. 32-43). God can turn a fruitful place into a wilderness or a wilderness into a fruitful place. The LORD dethrones the high and exalts the lowly.

The upright are delighted and the wicked silenced. The *wise* will take note, reflecting much upon the LORD's *steadfast love* (v. 43) *[Steadfast]*.

Although this remarkable psalm about God's steadfast love opens book V of the Psalter, we also should recognize its association with Psalms 105 and 106. These three tell the story of God's choice and nurture of Israel (105), God's forbearance in spite of Israel's sinful ways (106), and God's redemption of the people out of exile and all kinds of distress (107). Connecting the three psalms is the expression *the lands* (105:44; 106:27; 107:3). A further bridge is in the theme of gathering the exiles (106:47; 107:2-3). All three share themes with Isaiah 40–66 and the book of Job. Thus, book V begins in a manner suggesting that the editors of the Psalter intended it, like book IV, to serve as a response to book III and its elaboration of the theological crisis of exile and its aftermath (McCann, 1996:1117). The key words *trouble, distress, steadfast love,* and *wonderful works* (vv. 6, 8, 13, 15, 19, 21, 28, 31) remind us of the mood expressed in Psalm 90, which opens book IV *[Composition]*.

OUTLINE

Introduction: Summons to Give Thanks, 107:1-3
Litany of Thanksgiving by Four Groups of the Redeemed, 107:4-32
    107:4-9   Those Who Wandered Desert Wastes
    107:10-16 Those Who Were Imprisoned
    107:17-22 Those Who Needed Healing and Forgiveness
    107:23-32 Those Who Experienced the Perils of the Sea
Closing Hymn on the Providence of God, 107:33-42
    107:33-38 God's Power over Nature
    107:39-42 God's Care for the Afflicted
Wisdom Reflection, 107:43

EXPLANATORY NOTES

The Literary and Social Setting

As a litany of thanksgiving, worshippers may have used this psalm as a communal thank offering, with various groups of people presenting their thanksgiving sacrifice and grateful praise. Captives returning from Babylonian exile or pilgrims to Jerusalem may have sung it. The examples of distress (vv. 4-32) illustrate the kinds of dangers people experience; they can also be metaphors of the experience of the whole community in exile. Some commentators propose that the earliest form of the psalm contained only verses 1 and 4-32 (or perhaps only 4-22) as a traditional thanksgiving litany from before the exile. To this were added verses 2-3 in light of the experience of the people in the exile, and verses 33-43 as a hymn celebrating the awesome power of God (Davidson, 1998:354). This psalm illustrates how the prayers of persons in diverse situations can be brought together to become the prayer of the worshipping community.

The final form of this psalm exhibits a remarkable unity evident in the repetition of patterns and key words. The summons to thankful praise (v. 1) is repeated in verses 8, 15, 21, and 31, with the hymn (vv. 33-42) expressing such thanksgiving. In the four groups of the redeemed (vv. 4-32), the pattern describes distress (vv. 4-5, 10-12, 17-18, 23-27), prayer refrains (vv. 6, 13, 19, 28), deliverance (vv. 7, 14, 20, 29-30), and thanksgiving refrains (vv. 8-9, 15-16, 21-22, 31-32). In each group repetition of the double refrain is clear (vv. 6 and 8, 13 and 15, 19 and 21, 28 and 31). The two sets of key words in these refrains are *trouble* and *distress,* and God's *steadfast love* and *wonderful works.* The psalmist may also intend the four groups of the redeemed to illustrate all those who have experienced the redemption of the LORD, since the number four in the ancient Near East suggested totality (v. 3). Features of style include the use of chiasmus (often more apparent in Heb.: vv. 4, 9, 11, 14, 16, 19, 32), and the wordplay in the expression *himrû 'imrê, they rebelled against the words* (v. 11). Finally, the inclusio formed by use of *steadfast love* (ḥesed) at the beginning and end attests to the further unity of the psalm, as well as its message (vv. 1, 43) *[Hebrew Poetry].*

Introduction: Summons to Give Thanks 107:1-3

The opening call is a frequent exclamation of praise in the liturgy of the temple (1 Chron 16:34; Pss 106:1; 118:1; 136:1; Jer 33:11). *The redeemed of the LORD* may refer to those delivered in the exodus (v. 2) or those gathered in from the exile (v. 3). Other texts refer to those whom God calls and delivers being gathered out of all nations (Isa 43:5-6; 49:12; 62:10-12). The motif of the four cardinal points of the compass appears in verse 3 (Ps 75:6).

Those Who Wandered Desert Wastes 107:4-9

The psalm declares its schema in the first group of the redeemed identified. Desert wanderers or leaders of caravans often lived in great danger. The Israelites of the exodus from Egypt experienced hunger and thirst (Exod 16:3; 17:3). In desperation they cried to the LORD and were led out of the desert. *Let them thank the LORD . . .* (v. 8).

The refrain emerges as summons to a vertical dialogue with God and horizontal proclamation of the LORD's *wonderful works* (*niplā'ôt*), the extraordinary deeds the LORD wrought in the course of Israel's deliverance from Egypt (Pss 9:1; 40:5; 78:11). After the exile worshippers may have understood this reference to lost travelers as a description of the exiles' homecoming.

One can read the four scenes of the redeemed at different levels, literally of persons lost in the wilderness, of the Israelites in the exodus or exile, but also metaphorically. A wanderer in *desert wastes* can refer to anyone struggling through the desert of life to reach the city of God. Let them thank the LORD for his *ḥesed*, which does not fail when his people are hungry and thirsty and lost (Knight, 2:166).

Those Who Were Imprisoned   107:10-16

Prisons were damp and dark places, such as a cistern or pit (Jer 38:6; Zech 9:11). This passage relates imprisonment to rebellion against God's words (v. 11). In the OT, people often view misfortune and sickness (v. 17) as the consequence of sin (e.g. 2 Kings 17). Yet, the LORD in his *steadfast love* and by his *wonderful works* (*niplā'ôt*) can shatter *doors of bronze* and *bars of iron* (v. 16; Acts 16:25-40). Returnees from Babylon could rejoice and give thanks for freedom from imprisonment in a strange land.

Those Who Needed Healing and Forgiveness 107:17-22

Verse 17 emphasizes the connection between illness and sin (Pss 32:1-5; 38:2-5); several translations read *some became fools* (NIV, NEB, NJPS, NRSV n). The sinner is a foolish person who defies instruction (Prov 1:7). The picture here is that of God healing and forgiving some who are ill and close to death (vv. 17-18, 20). The psalmist sees the LORD's word as a divine agent at work in human life (v. 20; Ps 147:15, 18; Isa 55:11). Those delivered are to offer *sacrifices* of *thanksgiving* (v. 22) for the divine help received (Lev 7:11-15; 22:29-30).

Those Who Experienced the Perils of the Sea 107:23-32

Merchants and travelers who escaped perils of the sea, particularly the vicious storms, have seen the awesome power of the LORD that can churn mighty waves or bring calm and lead to a safe haven (vv. 24-

26, 29-30; Jon 1:4-6; Mark 4:35-41; Acts 27:6-44). With few natural harbors, the Hebrews were generally not seafaring people, though during the reigns of Solomon and Jehoshaphat, Israel had a fleet of ships at Ezion-geber (1 Kings 9:26-28; 22:49). *Elders* (v. 32), representatives of the tribes and families, were prominent from the time of Moses to Ezra (Exod 3:16, 18; 12:21; Ezra 10:8, 14).

Closing Hymn and Wisdom Reflection   107:33-43

The closing hymn glorifies the providence and sovereign power of the LORD with allusions to the preceding verses. It clearly reflects the situation of the postexilic community (Isa 41:18; 50:2). In verses 33-38 the hymn proclaims the LORD's unlimited control of nature. God responds to human need by providing richly watered land suitable for cultivation. By God's providence the Hebrews exchanged the desert for "a land flowing with milk and honey" (Exod 3:8; Deut 26:9).

This special care extends to the poor and needy (vv. 39-42). *Princes* may refer to Canaanite leaders driven out of the land (v. 40; Job 12:21, 24), here contrasted with how the LORD lifts the *needy* (Israel) out of distress to flourish (v. 41). So this hymn of praise exalts the power of God to create a new reality, in accord with the LORD's purpose, by putting down the mighty and the powerful and raising up the lowly and the weak (Pss 75:7; 113:7-9; 147:6; Job 5:11-16; 12:17-25).

The wisdom reflection (v. 43) can be paraphrased: "If you are wise, think about these word pictures that illustrate the enduring steadfast love of the LORD!" The *wise* describes the persons for whom the fear (reverence) of the LORD is the basic principle of life (Hos 14:9). In this opening psalm of book V, we see the wisdom theme of two ways, good and evil, and reversal of situations (vv. 33-43), as in other psalms that stand at the beginning of collections (Pss 1; 73; 90).

THE TEXT IN THE BIBLICAL CONTEXT AND LIFE OF THE CHURCH

Stories of God's Wonders

Human destiny is not inevitably set. If the status quo is not in accord with God's righteous rule, it can be turned upside down (Luke 1:46-55). The OT stories of God's wonders (*pĕlā'ôt, niplā'ôt*, vv. 8, 15, 21, 24, 31) deal with "impossibilities" that are still open, since conventional definitions of reality do not contain or define what God will yet do. This Hebrew term occurs 27 times in the Psalter, out of 45 occurrences in the OT. These "songs of impossibility" become a central part of Israel's doxology (Pss 9:1; 78:11; 106:7; 136:4; 145:5).

In Israel's expression of praise and thanksgiving, Psalm 107 illustrates the movement from the cry for help in distress, to deliverance, and then human response of praise. We can see this in each of the four examples: exile to place, hunger and thirst to sufficient food and drink, prison to liberation, and sickness to healing. The climax comes in announcing the LORD's turning things around on behalf of the weak, the troubled, and the needy. The final verses extend the hymn given us for praise and instruction, and to magnify God. The psalm serves as a paradigm for the Psalter: the first half is dominated by laments, and the second half moves to thanksgiving and praise. Praise is the final word (Miller, 1986:66). In the NT we can also see this movement toward the glorification of God (Phil 2:5-11).

The Totality of Life Embraced by God's Steadfast Love

Psalm 107 embraces the totality of life. Contrary to the prevalent view of human self-sufficiency, the psalm affirms that human life depends on God. Reaching into the most desperate moments of our existence, it enables us to realize that God's steadfast love embraces and cares for us. The examples in Psalm 107 find their parallels in the NT. Jesus compassionately provides bread in the wilderness (Matt 14:13-21), releases the chains of prisoners (Luke 4:18), heals and forgives (Mark 2:1-12), and calms the sea (4:39).

This psalm has enriched the hymnody of the church through Isaac Watts' "Come, we that love the Lord" (1707), based on the refrain in verses 8, 15, 21, and 31. Verse 16 (as well as Ps 24) has inspired James Montgomery's "Lift up your heads" (1843). The fourth stanza of Charles Wesley's "And can it be" (1739) proclaims verses 10-16. Finally, the mariner's hymn, "Eternal Father, strong to save" (William Whiting, 1860), is based on verses 23-32.

Appropriate circumstances for use of this psalm include travel and near accidents, famine, illness, epidemic, and threats of terror. What if persons in danger cry out and are not delivered, sick and not healed, starving and not fed? That also is reality, though the testimony of Psalm 107 is clear. At its center lies the word *ḥesed*, translated *steadfast love*. This amazing grace of God surrounds us in all distress (vv. 1, 8, 15, 21, 31, 43).

Psalm 108

Liturgy of Thanksgiving and Petition

PREVIEW

Psalm 108 splices parts of two psalms into one, and so combines thanksgiving (vv. 1-5; 57:7-11) with an oracle and a lament (vv. 6-13; 60:5-12). We can only conjecture why these fragments were brought together. In a time of defeat, as after the exile, people might appeal to the oracle (vv. 7-9) preserved in 60:5-12 for reassurance. Here it has a new introduction, the thanksgiving of 57:7-11.

The heading identifies this song as a *Psalm of David*, the first in a series of three psalms so designated in book V. Psalms 57 and 60 are both ascribed to David [*Superscriptions*].

OUTLINE

Hymn of Praise to the God of Steadfast Love, 108:1-5
Petition for Deliverance, 108:6
Divine Oracle of God's Dominion, 108:7-9
Petition for God's Help and Assertion of Confidence, 108:10-13

EXPLANATORY NOTES

For Psalm 108:1-6, see the explanatory notes on Psalm 57:7-11; for Psalm 108:7-13, see the comments on Psalm 60:5-12. Only minor variations are found in the use of those verses here. The term *God* ('ĕlōhîm) is frequently used by itself in this psalm, but in only one other place in book V of the Psalter (144:9). That may be why Psalm 108 borrows from Psalms 57 and 60, which are in the Elohistically revised Psalter, book II *[Composition]*.

What was the purpose of combining these two psalms for later use? The clue might lie in verse 10 and the unresolved conflict of the postexilic community with Edom, whose treachery contributed to the fall of Jerusalem (Ps 137; Obadiah; Mays, 1994b:348).

THE TEXT IN THE BIBLICAL CONTEXT AND LIFE OF THE CHURCH

Reusing Psalms

Psalm 108, in combining earlier psalms for a new time, suggests a pastoral need to meet new expectations and demands. Psalms 57 and 60 may have been brought together to form Psalm 108 as a response to the postexilic situation.

Regarding the use and reuse of the psalms, Allen (1983:70) comments: "The combination of earlier psalms illustrates the vitality of older scriptures as they were appropriated and applied to new situations in the experience of God's people." Modern hymnbooks include hymns from all centuries in the past. Such a psalm invites us to make the whole book of Psalms contemporary with ourselves (Knight, 2:174).

Psalm 109

Accusations, Curses, and the Steadfast Love of the LORD

PREVIEW

This prayer song of an individual expresses the raw rage of an innocent person on trial for his life. The psalm focuses on the difficulty of loving someone who seems beyond love, and articulates a yearning for retaliation and vengeance. As one of the most vehement of the imprecation psalms, it is rarely used in public worship. However, Psalm 109 deserves a rereading and a serious attempt to understand its place in the life of faith *[Imprecation; Vengeance]*.

Following an opening petition for God's intervention, the psalm describes the enemies as persons who slander, lie, hate, and accuse (vv. 1-5). The extended imprecation (vv. 6-19) raises the key issue for interpretation: By whom and against whom are the curses? (See Explanatory Notes, below.) The psalmist prays that these words be applied to the accusers (v. 20) and then pleads for God's action (v. 21). After the psalmist describes his condition (vv. 22-25), he renews the plea (vv. 26-29). The psalm ends with a vow of thanks and praise, in confidence that the God of steadfast love *stands at the right hand of the needy* (vv. 30-31).

As a literary work, Psalm 109 reflects excellent poetic qualities, with examples of chiasmus (v. 2), congruency of metaphors (vv. 2-3,

Psalm 109

13-14), inclusios (vv. 1 and 30, 7 and 31, 21 and 26, 26 and 31), as well as connecting motifs (*ḥesed*, translated *kindness* and *steadfast love*, vv. 12, 16, 21, 26; and *the poor and needy*, vv. 16, 22, 31) *[Hebrew Poetry]*. The theme of God's *steadfast love* and *kindness* connects Psalm 109 to 107 (vv. 1, 8, 15, 21, 31, 43) and to 108 (v. 4). Placement of this psalm of vengeance, grounded in God's love for the poor and needy (vv. 21-22), may relate to the mention of Edom (108:10) as a way of addressing the postexilic situation. The heading identifies the psalm with *David*, the second in a series of three "David" psalms at the beginning of book V *[Superscriptions]*.

OUTLINE

Prayer of Lamentation, 109:1-5
    109:1   Plea for God's Intervention
    109:2-5   Complaint About the Accusers
Imprecation: An Extended Curse, 109:6-20
    109:6-7   The Juridical Setting
    109:8-15 The Hoped-for Sentence
    109:16-19 Reasons for the Curse
    109:20   The Reward: The Curse upon the Accusers
Prayer of Trust and Petition, 109:21-29
    109:21-25 Grounds for Appeal to the LORD
    109:26-29 Imprecation That the Accusers Be Punished
Vow of Thanks and Praise, 109:30-31

EXPLANATORY NOTES

Prayer of Lamentation   109:1-5

This lament suggests a court trial after the author has been accused of sorcery and held responsible for the death of a poor man (v. 16), presumably caused by magically effective curses (v. 17). The picture of the court, with the prosecutor/adversary/*accuser/s* and (*I/me/my*) the defendant/accused (vv. 4, 6, 20, 29; *śāṭān,* to *attack*; *śāṭān, accuser*), resembles Job 1:6-7; 2:1-2. The psalmist is facing accusers bringing false charges. The penalty could be death.

The psalm begins with an urgent appeal to God to remain inactive no longer (v. 1). God being *silent* contrasts with the deceiving and maligning *mouths* of the *wicked*, as well as the psalmist's own mouth singing God's praise (vv. 1, 30; Deut 10:21; Jer 17:14). In describing his accusers, the psalmist points to an underlying conflict of words with no less than thirteen references to malicious speech. The problem is a breakdown of equity (vv. 4-5). Good should evoke a responsive good. Love should receive a responsive love. Instead, evil and hate are returned.

Imprecation: An Extended Curse   109:6-20

The crux for interpretation lies in identifying the speaker in verses 6-19. Traditionally, readers have taken this section as the words of the psalmist calling down curses upon his accusers. In recent years, some translators and commentators have read these verses as a quotation of the curse placed upon the psalmist by his accusers. Hence, NRSV (and NIV n) introduces verse 6 with the words, *They say* (lacking in Heb.), with quotation marks placed around verses 6-19. One can find reason for this in the psalmist's use of the plural in speaking of his *accusers* (vv. 1-5 and vv. 20-29), whereas verses 6-19 use the singular, *he/his/him*. Such an understanding of verses 6-19 is attractive in "softening" the imprecation. However, it does not change the central spiritual issue raised by the psalm. In verse 20, the psalmist insists that the charges brought against him should rightly fall upon his accusers. There is no turning of the other cheek (Luke 6:29).

It is possible that the words of rage are indeed the prayer (and curse) of the psalmist addressed to the chief accuser or a corrupt judge. The psalmist's closing prayer (vv. 26-29) has a parallel in Jeremiah 17:14-18.

In the extended imprecation (vv. 6-20), the psalmist pleads for a role reversal, that the wicked accuser may find himself on the receiving end of the perjury (Davidson, 1998:361). In a juridical setting, the accuser usually stood on the left, with the accused and his defender on the right (v. 31; Pss 110:5; 121:5). Does verse 6 suggest appointment of a special prosecutor, one who knows evil and will look into every wrongdoing without fear or favor (Brueggemann, 1984:83)? Or is the *accuser* standing on the defendant's *right*, so that the psalmist refers to a corrupt judge who should have thrown out his case in the first place (Dahood, 3:110)? If the first scenario is right, verses 7-19 seem to shortchange the investigation with a pronounced verdict of "Guilty!" If the second scenario is right, the curse appears directed at the accuser-judge.

The hoped-for sentence (vv. 8-15) begins with a wish for premature death, that the guilty one's family and property be taken, and his *name be blotted out* and *memory be cut off from the earth*. May the guilty receive no kindness for *he did not remember to show kindness* (vv. 12, 16). Instead of blessings, curses saturated his whole life (vv. 17-19). *May that . . .* (v. 20) refers to verses 6-19. As the curses work their way into the life of the accuser, he is receiving the due reward for his malicious and false slander against the psalmist. The verse expresses the law of "an eye for an eye" and hope for the LORD's strong retribution.

Prayer of Trust and Petition 109:21-29

The forces aligned against the psalmist are malicious and powerful. Yet there is a counsel for the defense who can be trusted: *But you, O LORD my Lord* (v. 21). With this pivotal point the mood of the psalm changes: the psalmist appeals to the LORD on the basis of his name (Yahweh, which means "present to act for salvation") and *steadfast love (ḥesed) [Steadfast Love]*. Nothing less than a miracle of God's intervention will save the psalmist. God is the only power capable of breaking the curse. The psalmist appeals on the basis of his frailty and need by identifying himself with the *poor and needy* (vv. 22-25). He expresses frailty by the metaphors of the fading evening *shadow*, and the *locust*, which one can brush off a garment with the flick of a finger (v. 23). In scorn the accusers *shake their heads*, a sign of derision and hostility (v. 25; Matt 27:39).

Following repetition of the plea for deliverance (v. 26), the imprecation is resumed in the prayer that the accusers be punished in a reversal of fortune (vv. 27-29). The psalmist attributes deliverance of the afflicted and punishment of the accusers entirely to God (v. 27). No longer disturbed, the psalmist is confident that the LORD's blessing will offset the curse of the enemy (v. 28; Num 23:11).

Vow of Thanks and Praise 109:30-31

Looking to the future, the psalm ends by expressing confident hope and joy in the promise of affliction ending (vv. 30-31; Pss 22:29-31; 69:30-36). The psalmist anticipates his deliverance or has received some reassurance. Possibly the rage is being transformed by the double step of owning and yielding (Brueggemann, 1982:71). In any case, it is not the accuser (*Śāṭān*) but the LORD who will stand at the right hand of the needy (16:8; 35:9-10; 86:1). So the LORD's vindication will be celebrated within the assembly (v. 30).

THE TEXT IN THE BIBLICAL CONTEXT AND LIFE OF THE CHURCH

Dealing with a Vengeful Psalm

In the prayer books of the church, Psalm 109 (along with 58 and 83) is usually omitted because of its vindictive language (Holladay: 304,

309; Reardon: 215). It is not surprising that interpreters of the Scriptures consider this a challenging psalm. How do we mesh the diatribe of verses 6-19 with other OT passages about God as *merciful and gracious, slow to anger and abounding in steadfast love* (Ps 103:8), or with the NT imperative to "turn the other cheek" (Matt 5:38-39)? Though commentators have sought to rebuff or soften the "unchristian" imprecatory psalms, it is not enough to say that the spirit of love overpowers the wrathful spirit in the NT: requests for vengeance do not disappear in the NT (cf. Rom 12:19-20; Rev 6:7-11). Nor can we simply dismiss these words as "impossibly unpreachable." What might we learn from such psalms that can be helpful to the life of faith? *[Imprecation].*

In the story of the disciples after Christ's resurrection and ascension, they set to the task of choosing a successor to Judas Iscariot (Acts 1:15-26). Peter quotes Psalm 109:8b with reference to the fallen Judas, "Let another take his position" (Acts 1:20). As told in all four Gospels, the story of Judas is unsettling, but it is a sober reality that one of the twelve could be cut off from the fellowship of the community. More encouraging is the confidence with which the psalm ends. The *accuser*, who appears as the "satanic power," is not able to separate the servant of God from the LORD. Psalm 109:31, about the LORD who *stands at the right of the needy*, finds a strong echo in Romans 8:31-34: "Who will bring any charge against God's elect? It is God who justifies. . . . It is Christ Jesus, . . . who is at the right hand of God, who indeed intercedes for us." Small wonder that sixteenth-century Anabaptist martyrs quoted Psalm 109:31 for their comfort and as witness to their accusers (Braght: 951, 956).

An Alternative Reading

Brueggemann has articulated a helpful reading of Psalm 109 (1985:144-54; 1995:268-82). Focusing on the *ḥesed* motif (vv. 12, 16, 21, 26) and the situation of the psalmist as from *the poor and needy* (vv. 16, 22, 31), he writes about "steadfast love and social solidarity." Brueggemann recognizes this psalm's juxtaposition of the two sections, the human juridical process (vv. 1-20) and the theological language and powerful fidelity of God (vv. 21-31). He sees this psalm as dealing with the need for due process in society (vv. 1-19), but also with the symbolic underpinnings of legitimacy (here expressed by *ḥesed*), without which the weak and powerless have no source of appeal. Brueggemann suggests that in the prayer of imprecation, the speaker submits his problem to God in a bold act of faith, for it insists that such wrongs belong in the scope of God's governance.

Furthermore, when we are well-off, we cannot understand the depths of such rage, but oppressed peoples can (victims of rape, refugees, the dispossessed and powerless). The voice of this psalm is the voice of the poor, who insist that human solidarity (*ḥesed*) matters to the quality of our common life. Such an appeal to God comes out of the memory that God hears the cry of the exploited and intervenes on their behalf (Exod 2:23-25; Ps 82) *[Steadfast Love]*.

Difficult as they may be, these psalms thus provide an important theological resource for all who live in a world of terrorism, crime, and violence. The strong language reflects grappling with the issue of God's sovereignty even when many are questioning that. In addition, these difficult psalms (including 22 and 69) provide background for the Gospels' presentation of the passion story. "Like Psalm 109, Jesus' life and death are testimony to the good news that God stands with the poor and needy" (McCann, 1996:1128).

Psalm 110

The Priest-King at the Right Hand of God

PREVIEW

This royal psalm reflects a festival ceremony of ancient times, likely the coronation of a Davidic king. The divinely appointed king sits beside God in honor, under God's protection, exercising God's authority on earth (v. 1). To military authority is added priestly authority (v. 4). The psalm is structured around two oracles (vv. 1, 4), with commentary on the nature of the king's rule (vv. 2-3, 5-6). The psalm ends as it began, with the new king exalted, confident, and triumphant (v. 7) *[Oracle]*.

This appears to be a very old psalm, perhaps from the early years of the monarchy, with a recent memory of the Jebusite priest-kings of Jerusalem (v.4; Gen 14:18-24). The superscription attributes the psalm to David. Holladay (23-24) articulates the plausibility of royal Psalms 2 and 110 and the thanksgiving Psalm 18 all originating during David's reign. Whether composed by David or a court poet, the people may have used it at coronations or enthronement festivals.

In the psalm one can trace an outline of a coronation ceremony for the Davidic king: the crown prince is led to the royal throne in the temple (v. 1), presented with the scepter as symbol of authority (v. 2), and anointed with oil; he hears the consecratory formula (v. 3). The people acclaim the new king according to the titles of the ancient Jebusite royalty (v. 4) and consider him to be the LORD's representative (vv. 5-6). He drinks of the sacred life-giving water from the Gihon spring in the Kidron valley (v. 7; Stuhlmueller, 1983, 2:129).

Kraus (1986:111-12) suggests that Psalm 110 contains the most clearly recognizable description and texts of an enthronement festival. Though not the complete ritual, the psalm begins with a message proclaimed as the decree of the LORD. Psalm 110 commands the king to *sit at [the] right hand* of the LORD (v. 1). The king is the son of God (v. 3; Ps 2:7) and legitimate heir of the royal tradition of Jerusalem (the Melchizedek tradition, v. 4). In time, people came to believe that the king of Israel sat on the throne of the LORD as the visible representative of the invisible LORD (1 Chron 28:5; 29:23).

The Hebrew text of the psalm is difficult, and the footnotes in the NRSV and NIV show that it has been disputed. Verses 3 and 7 are particularly obscure, evoking a wide variety of translations and interpretations. A curious feature is the frequent reference to parts of the body. The poet mentions *right hand* (vv. 1, 5), *feet* (v.1 NIV), *his wrath* (v. 5, from "his nostrils/nose"; cf. 18:8), *corpses* (v. 6), and *head* (vv. 6-7).

OUTLINE

A Divinely Appointed Ruler, 110:1-3
    110:1   The Oracle: Installation of the King
    110:2-3   Commentary on the King's Rule
A Divinely Appointed Priest-King, 110:4-7
    110:4   The Oracle: Conferring the Office of Priesthood upon the Ruler
    110:5-6   Commentary: Protection and Judgment
    110:7   Empowerment and Promise of Triumph

EXPLANATORY NOTES

A Divinely Appointed Ruler   110:1-3

The psalm opens with the LORD speaking an oracle to the king through a priest or temple prophet. These divine sayings in verses 1 and 4 are the crucial word by which God bestows office through the prophet. To *sit at my right hand* (v. 1) is the highest place of honor (1 Kings 2:19; Ps 45:9). It implies, "Rule in confidence, for I am the strength of your arm" (v. 5). The military metaphor of making *enemies your footstool* conveys the image of complete domination (Josh 10:24; Isa 51:23; comments on Ps 21:12).

The description of the king's rule further expresses the oracle's meaning (vv. 2-3) *[Zion]*. The king is backed by the effective power of God, symbolized by the scepter as emblem of authority and might. Under the outstretched scepter, the land becomes the arena of the king's authority. Now follows a picture of the people offering themselves willingly, as hosts of volunteers rally to their leader in time of war. Or is this an admiring reference to the splendor of the ceremony (Kraus, 1989:350)?

The second part of verse 3 gives rise to many interpretations. The dawn of the morning, shattering the darkness of night, symbolizes hope and a turn for the better. *Your youth will come to you* (NRSV) or *You will receive the dew of your youth* (NIV) could mean a host of young recruits for the king's army, or restoration of the king's youthful vigor in the rebirth of coronation. Kraus (1989:346, 350) sees in Psalm 110 the possibility of three oracles, with the second reading: "On holy mountains, from the womb of the rosy dawn, have I begotten you like the dew." Many interpreters see the focus on the king as God's son (2 Sam 7:14; Ps 2:7), with emphasis on the mystery, like the dew (Job 29:22; 38:28). The glorious birth theme is featured in the NEB translation: *At birth you were endowed with princely gifts and resplendent in holiness. You have shone with the dew of youth since your mother bore you.*

A Divinely Appointed Priest-King   110:4-7

A solemn irrevocable oath of the LORD introduces the second oracle and focuses on the king's priestly function. Kings such as David, Solomon, and Ahaz performed priestly rites on occasion (2 Sam 6:12-19; 1 Kings 3:4; 8:14, 55-56, 62-63; 9:15; 2 Kings 16:12-15). David did not come from the family of Aaron or Levi. His legitimacy for exercise of priestly functions is drawn from the Abraham traditions in Genesis 14:18-19, where Melchizedek, the pre-Israelite king of Salem (Jerusalem), appears not only as king but also as priest of the Canaanite god El Elyon (*'ēl 'elyôn*), "God Most High." The name Melchizedek means "(My) king is righteous." It is a lineage of priesthood alternative to the Aaronic (purely Israelite) line. Israel came to separate the royal and priestly offices. The first office was reserved for descendants of David (of the line of Judah), and the second for the descendants of Aaron (of the line of Levi). The Davidic king now claims this priestly role in the manner of Melchizedek (Davidson, 1998:366).

After this linking of throne and altar, the scene changes from throne to battlefield, and the psalm's commentary (vv. 5-6) reverts to the context of the first oracle. According to the psalm, the king, with his host of warriors, is to be God's intermediary for matters of earth. The enthroned king is the instrument for carrying out the final divine intention. The LORD is at the king's right hand as his protector

(Pss 16:8; 109:31; 121:5). The jarring military metaphors portray an ugly picture of *wrath* and *judgment*, with *corpses* strewn over the earth *[Wrath]*. Thus, verse 7 seems to be an inconsequential end to the psalm if it simply refers to the king refreshing himself at a brook along the way to further conquests (v. 7). More likely, the reference is to a royal ritual, a rite of empowerment, such as drinking from the spring of Gihon (1 Kings 1:38). The last line, *He will lift up his head*, is a promise of triumph (Pss 3:3; 27:6). Verse 1 has a portrayal contrasting with 7. In the first verse, the LORD promises to abase the king's enemies, making them the stool for the king's feet. The ending pictures the Israelite king with head lifted high in triumph.

THE TEXT IN THE BIBLICAL CONTEXT AND LIFE OF THE CHURCH

A New Hymn to the Coming Kingdom of God

Though we can read Psalm 110 as a royal nationalistic psalm because of its message to its age, many phrases and symbols are open to wider application. As with other royal psalms (notably Psalm 2), this poem took on messianic meaning when Judah no longer had kings of her own. Prophets, in light of the failures of contemporary kings, began to speak of an ideal king of the future who would fill the messianic office. By the time Psalm 110 was incorporated into the book of Psalms, and placed in book V following psalms that bemoan the exile, it likely no longer represented the relation between God's sovereignty and the nation. Instead, readers took it as an eschatological vision of God's kingdom. Mays (1994b:353) suggests that Psalm 110 is "a sequel to Psalm 89 and its lament over the rejected Messiah. It is a prophetic voice repeating and affirming the promises of Psalm 2 that the LORD will claim the nations through the Messiah."

In its setting within the Psalter, following Psalms 107–108, Psalm 110 would have been understood as an affirmation of God's reign and as expressing hope for the future. By the first century AD, Jewish messianic hopes took a variety of forms, including a Messiah who would arise to throw off Roman oppression. Followers of Jesus were convinced that Jesus of Nazareth embodied God's sovereign claim upon the world, and they hailed him as Messiah.

The Christian Church and Psalm 110

The early Christian church interpreted Psalm 110 christologically, as David speaking to Christ. In the NT, royal Psalms 2 and 110 are quoted and alluded to more than any other psalms. The NT writers took these metaphors from their context of nationalism and militarism and composed a new hymn of the coming kingdom of God and the priest-king Jesus Christ at the right hand of God. To understand this psalm for the life of faith today, we need to explore how they did this.

The psalm blends three major forms of leadership: the prophetic (oracles of vv. 1, 4), the royal (in functioning as a coronation hymn), and the priestly (v. 4). The psalm was at the center of conflict between Jesus and the Jewish leaders, as Jesus quoted Psalm 110:1 in controversy with his rabbinical opponents in the context of the question about the Lord's identity (Matt 22:41-46; Mark 12:35-37; Luke 20:41-44). Is Jesus, as the Messiah, David's son or David's Lord? Was Jesus here raising the issue of the kind of Messiah he was—not a royal figure at all, as thought by the scribes and Pharisees, but a Messiah of a different sort, a poor outcast with a supernatural origin (V. Taylor: 540; Holladay: 119)? At the end, Jesus completely disowned the nationalistic and militaristic sides of the "Son of David" messianic hope and reinterpreted messiahship as service through suffering. In the NT, the messianic king is crowned with thorns, given a reed scepter for his right hand, and mocked (Matt 27:27-30).

Psalm 110:1 is quoted in the Pentecost sermon (Acts 2:34-36) to affirm the crucified Jesus as both Lord and Messiah; it becomes the foundation of important christological statements of the NT (Rom 8:34; Eph 1:20; Col 3:1; Heb 1:3; 8:1; 10:12; 12:2). The NT sees the resurrection of Jesus Christ from the dead as the fulfillment of Psalm 110:1. The same verse is also used to speak of those who oppose the triumph of Christ (1 Cor 15:25-26; Eph 1:20-23; Heb 10:12-13).

Hebrews 7 draws on the Melchizedek tradition and combines Psalm 110:1 and 110:4 in the concept of Jesus as high priest, who sits at the right hand of God in heaven (Heb 8:1) and waits for his foes to be defeated (10:12-13). Written to Judeo-Christians who may have had an attachment to the idea of an exclusive Levitical priesthood, the epistle to the Hebrews exhorts them to recognize that Jesus is a priest despite his non-Levitical ancestry. The argument presents a qualification of the priesthood, that it was obtained not by inheritance but by oath (7:15-22).

With such an extraordinary role for Psalm 110 in the early church, we should not be surprised to hear echoes in the words of the Apostles' Creed: "I believe in Jesus Christ, . . . who sits at the right hand of God." Liturgically, the Western church has had a long tradition of reciting Psalm 110 as the first psalm of vespers on Sundays. It is also a favorite reading for Ascension Day.

Psalm 110

Psalm 110, as testimony to the national religion of Israel, also presents a danger—the danger of degrading God into a partisan of national arrogance. Such is the temptation for rulers in every generation, be they kings or presidents, particularly during wars. However, no claims to "divine right" by any ruler are valid. For this reason we need the prophetic voice to call to account a ruler who seeks to abuse his position in pursuit of personal aggrandizement (Jer 22:13-19). The NT's use of Psalm 110 proclaims the crucified and risen Jesus as the one for whom and through whom God is working out his purpose in the world.

Psalm 111

Great Are the Works of the LORD

PREVIEW

Psalm 111 is a hymn in praise of the works and goodness of the LORD, recited or sung by an individual during worship at one of the annual festivals (v. 1). From the opening ritual cry of *Hallelujah!* (NJPS) and the vow to give thanks, the psalm moves to the main theme, the steady goodness of God displayed in his works, with allusions to the deliverance from Egypt, the wilderness journey, and the gift of Canaan (vv. 2-6). The LORD's *precepts* are further proof of God's working in covenant for the redemption of his people (vv. 7-9). The psalm concludes with a wisdom saying about the understanding that comes from revering the LORD (v. 10).

As an acrostic, the psalm is limited to twenty-two short lines, each beginning with the next letter of the Hebrew alphabet. With only three or (at most) four words per line (in Heb.), this is a remarkable poetic feat. The acrostic form accounts for the stringing together of stereotyped statements and maxims. Most commentators date the psalm as postexilic because of the acrostic form and the wisdom theme *[Psalm Genres]*.

Psalm 111 and 112 are twin psalms in form and content. In Psalm 111 those who fear God praise the works of the LORD. Psalm 112 commends the way and life of those who fear the LORD. If we read the opening psalms in book V sequentially, 111–112 puts the return

Psalm 111

from exile (107–108) in line with all God's saving work on behalf of the oppressed (109; McCann, 1996:1133). Psalm 113, then, initiates a series of psalms celebrating God's saving work in general, and the exodus in particular. The ritual cry *Praise the LORD! (Hallelujah!)* may have been added to Psalms 111–112 to introduce the Egyptian Hallel (113–118; Stuhlmueller, 1983, 2:133).

OUTLINE

Introductory Declaration of Thankful Praise, 111:1
Reason for Praise, 111:2-9
    111:2   Theme: The Great Works of the LORD
    111:3-6   Brief Rehearsal of the LORD's Deeds in Israel's History
    111:7-9   Grounds for Trusting and Obeying the LORD
Concluding Wisdom Saying About a Good Understanding, 111:10

EXPLANATORY NOTES

Introductory Declaration of Thankful Praise   111:1

The opening *Hallelujah!* (v. 1a) is not part of the acrostic form. The psalm begins with an introductory, unreserved declaration of thankful praise offered in the setting of the *congregation* as response to the ritual cry. The psalm's concluding line, *His praise endures forever*, connects with the opening cry as an inclusio and emphasizes the psalm's function as praise (Mays, 1994b:356). The poet may use the acrostic form because the theme is so large that he draws on all the tools at his disposal, the entire alphabet.

Reason for Praise   111:2-9

The body of the psalm extols *the works of the LORD*. Verse 2 clearly expresses that theme, with thematic words repeated: *his work* (v. 3), *his wonderful deeds* (v. 4), *his works* (v. 6), and *the works of his hands* (v. 7). Indeed, the LORD's *works* are also topic of the divine action in the other verses of the psalm (*food* and *covenant*, v. 5; *his precepts,* v. 7; *redemption,* v. 9). The psalmist refers to those who study (*ponder,* NIV) the works of the LORD (v. 2). The Hebrew word *dāraś* suggests those who "seek, search out, inquire of God" (Pss 9:10; 119:45, 94, 155). From it comes the later word "midrash," the detailed investigation into and exposition of the text (*midrāš,* "commentary," 2 Chron 24:27; Davidson, 1998:369).

    In this compact version (vv. 4-6) of the traditional recital of the

LORD's wonderful deeds and providential acts (Pss 78; 105; 106; 136), one can find allusions to the exodus (v. 4), manna in the wilderness (v. 5), Sinai (v. 7), and the conquest of Canaan (v. 6). Although several Hebrew words refer to the acts of God in this psalm, *niplā'ôt, wonderful deeds*, carries this meaning in verse 4. These are the "impossibilities" of God's power (Gen 18:14), as seen in the deliverance from Egypt, when God put down a mighty pharaoh and lifted up a powerless oppressed people (Exod 15:11; Miller, 1986:78).

God's *precepts* (v. 7), the laws of the code as found in the Pentateuch, are also God's work. The work of God and the law of God belong together (vv. 7-9). God's laws are essentially a gift to his people and not a burden (Ps 19:7-10). They are a part of the covenant relationship through which God *sent redemption* (v. 9), deliverance to his chosen people. Israel's life in the land is the fulfillment of the promise and the reality of redemption (vv. 6, 9). In telling the story, the psalmist extols the character of the LORD with words like *righteousness, gracious, merciful, mindful, faithful, just, trustworthy, faithfulness,* and *uprightness*. Thus, God's holy name inspires awe (v. 9).

Concluding Wisdom Saying About a Good Understanding   111:10

The fear of this holy and terrible God is the beginning of wisdom (Job 28:28; Prov 1:7; 9:10). *Fear of the LORD*, revering God's name, meant worship, law, and life (Pss 19:9; 34:11). *Wisdom* has to do with the practical knowledge of the divine laws governing the relationships in life. *A good understanding* of life comes to those who recognize the parameters within which the good life must be lived (1:1-3).

THE TEXT IN THE BIBLICAL CONTEXT AND LIFE OF THE CHURCH

Confident Living in a God-ordered World

The acrostic form is not a neutral poetic device. It provided an ideal medium for the psalmist to convey the message that God rules the world and it therefore has moral symmetry. Psalms 111 and 112 express "serene, acrostic comprehensive confidence in a well-ordered world, in which God rules and we benefit" (Brueggemann, 1984:45; 1988:110). The same can be said of Psalm 145.

The church has used these *hallelujah* psalms, as evidenced in writings of Hippolytus (about AD 210), Augustine (354-430), and Benedict (480-543), who prescribed the psalm for Sunday vespers. The practice has continued to the present as churches celebrate the redemption that God has sent to his people (Reardon: 219). Luther looked on this psalm as "composed for the festival of Easter." Many churches use Psalm 111 in connection with the Lord's Supper (v. 5).

In his treatise "The True Christian Faith" (ca. 1541), Menno Simons (337) quoted Psalm 111:10 as he appealed to believers to receive and impress the Word upon the heart: "It is impossible to become righteous without the fear of God. . . . It really is the power which expels, buries, slays, crushes, and destroys the sins of believers; it is the first part of true repentance." Psalm 111:10 was also a favorite verse quoted by Anabaptist martyrs, as in the letter that Soetgen van den Houte left her children at Ghent, Flanders, in 1560, or the 1576 letter that Hans Bret wrote to his brother in England (Braght: 646, 1041).

One can summarize the enduring lesson of Psalm 111: In a world where God is continually working, the common sense of wisdom invites reverence of his holy name. To recognize God's relating and activity in the world about us is the beginning of intelligent living (White: 170).

Psalm 112

The Blessedness of Fearing the LORD

PREVIEW

As Psalm 111 declares the praise of God, Psalm 112 praises the blessedness of the God-fearing person. This didactic wisdom psalm's identical acrostic structure, similarity of vocabulary, and common emphasis on *the fear of the LORD* (111:10; 112:1) suggest the same poet as writer. Some of the words used to describe God in Psalm 111 are boldly transferred to 112 and applied to the godly person: *righteousness* (111:3; 112:3), *remembered* (111:4 NIV; 112:6), and *established* (111:8; 112:8, *steady*, NRSV; *secure*, NIV). The words translated *forever* ring through the psalm (vv. 3, 6, 9), as they do in Psalm 111 (vv. 3, 5, 8, 10).

Psalm 112 develops the last verse of Psalm 111, declaring that the righteous, the godly who *fear the LORD* and *delight* in his commandments (v. 2), have a great future (v. 9). The psalm ends with a reminder of the bleak prospect for the wicked (v. 10). This contrasting destiny of the godly and the wicked relates this psalm in theme also to Torah Psalms 1; 19:7-14; and 119. Psalm 112, celebrating the blessings of *righteousness* (vv. 3, 4, 6, 9), seeks to inspire covenant fidelity *[Psalm Genres; Righteous; Torah]*.

Psalm 112

OUTLINE

Introduction: Affirmation of the Life Rooted in Joyful Obedience, 112:1
Description of the God-fearing Person, 112:2-9
    112:2-3   The Fruit of Family Continuity and Prosperity
    112:4-5   Qualities of Character That Reflect God's Character
    112:6-9   Integrity and Security in the LORD
Contrasting Conclusion: The Destiny of the Wicked, 112:10

EXPLANATORY NOTES

Introduction: Affirmation of the Life Rooted in Joyful Obedience   112:1

Following the opening ritual cry, *Hallelujah!* (v. 1a; also 111:1a, NJPS), verse 1 sets forth the theme. *Those who fear the LORD* and *delight in his commandments* are the same *upright* who in Psalm 111 *delight* in the works of the LORD (111:2) and do his *precepts* (111:7, 10). The righteous stand in a living relationship to God and take pleasure in the direction and commandments of their God (1:2; 119:24, 77, 92, 143, 174). The rest of Psalm 112 expands the congratulatory word *Happy* (Heb.: *'ašrê*) by listing ways in which the life of the upright is blessed. Psalm 112 begins as does Psalm 1: *Happy are those* or *Happy is the man* (NIV). The NRSV, in order to be gender inclusive, renders the singular as plural.

Description of the God-fearing Person   112:2-9

The list of promises heaped upon the one who fears the LORD begins with family continuity (v. 2) and material prosperity (v. 3). In the OT days, people saw wealth as a symbol of divine bestowal of blessing and salvation (1 Kings 3:13; Prov 3:10, 16; 13:18; 22:4). *Righteousness* (v. 3) is the state of being in proper relationship with God and of possessing happiness that flows from it. *Righteousness* denotes the behavior that is in keeping with the covenant. According to Psalm 112, this relationship is indissoluble (v. 3b).

The psalm lists the righteous person's qualities of character that reflect God's character (vv. 4-5). Like God, the just person is a shining light (v. 4; Ps 27:1; Prov 13:9). The subject in the clause of verse 4b is uncertain. The RSV inserts "the LORD" as the subject of 4b, though NRSV and NIV continue the portrait, with the righteous person as the subject, as *gracious, merciful, and righteous.*

The God-fearing person is generous, lends to others, and conducts his affairs so as to injure no one (v. 5). He acts with justice (*mišpāṭ*), dealing according to the demands of God's law. Material prosperity (v. 3) is not the prerogative for abusive misuse of money, nor for miserliness, but for sharing in mutual aid (v. 9).

Other characteristics of the righteous include their integrity and the confidence that comes from hearts *secure in the LORD* (vv. 6-9). The expression *never be moved* (v. 6, *môṭ* with a negative) is characteristically used in contexts of pious obedience and devoted trust (Pss 15:5; 16:8; 21:7; 30:6; 62:6; Prov 10:30). Grounded on trust in the LORD, they can handle bad news and in the end will witness the downfall of enemies (vv. 7-8; Pss 54:7; 118:7). Having lived justly and shared liberally (v. 9), their *horn*, their strength and dignity, will be *exalted in honor.*

Contrasting Conclusion: The Destiny of the Wicked 112:10

Anything but honor is the destiny of the wicked. *Gnash their teeth* provides a word picture of envy and powerless rage (35:16; 37:12). So evildoers will become unhinged and perish. The opening and closing words of Psalms 1 and 112 are identical (*'ašrê*, *blessed*; *tō'bēd*, *perish*, KJV). In these psalms the two ways are starkly set before every person so as to elicit a choice *[Wicked]*.

THE TEXT IN THE BIBLICAL CONTEXT AND LIFE OF THE CHURCH

Reverence That Leads to the Obedience of Faith

The opening verses present an idyllic picture of piety and prosperity, calling to mind the beginning of the book of Job. This acrostic poem, in which everything is ordered and in place, absolutizes the arrangement with no harsh tales of intrusion or ambiguity. But what do verses 1-3 mean to persons who are still "on the way" (Knight, 2:187)? The psalm seems smug and overly optimistic. Many find the ways of the wise and upright to be less serene than here described. Disruption and suffering, as well as benevolence, is the lot of the just and unjust alike (Matt 5:45). Perhaps the psalm can point to the truth articulated in 1 Timothy in the appeal to "lead a quiet and peaceable life in all godliness" (2:2), since "there is great gain in godliness combined with contentment" (6:6).

The psalm invites persons to *fear the LORD* (v. 1), having the attitude of reverence that leads to the obedience of faith. Here there are many NT connections, as in Jesus' words in the Sermon on the Mount: "Let your light shine before others" (Matt 5:16); "Be perfect, therefore, as your heavenly Father is perfect" (5:48); "Strive first for the kingdom of God and his righteousness" (Matt 6:33). The early church urged persons to the obedience of faith (Acts 6:7; Rom 5:1; 16:26). Teachings about the judgment recognize there will be "weeping and gnashing of teeth" for those who have not been faithful and find themselves on the outside (Ps 112:10; Matt 8:12; 25:30; Luke 13:28).

A direct quote of Psalm 112:9 appears in one of Paul's letters (2 Cor 9:9). The psalm praises the godly person's righteousness and compassion toward the poor as the meaning of a life blessed by God, honored among humans, and lived in full strength. Paul draws on these words about generosity as he appeals to the Corinthians to contribute to the Jerusalem collection.

The psalm conveys several enduring insights:

1. Satisfaction and life fulfillment come from trusting the generosity of God, not from greed and self-sufficiency.

2. The fear of the LORD engages us in the needs of others. We do not live as isolated individuals.

3. Social justice and political questions saturate the literature of the Bible. God will not put up with injustice.

4. The liturgy of worship is important to energize the justice and righteousness issues. Psalm 112 is an example of psalms of instruction and their use as praise.

Psalm 113

God's Majesty in Mercy

PREVIEW

This simple, pleasing hymn of praise celebrates the majestic LORD, both as sovereign of the cosmos and as helper of the lowly. The climax of the psalm comes in the two illustrations of how the LORD raises the poor and needy to sit with princes, and how the barren woman becomes a mother through divine intervention (vv. 7-9). Two ideas form the nucleus of the psalm: the incomparable majesty of God, and God's mercy on those who are often despised and on the margins of society.

The psalm begins and ends with *Praise the LORD! (Hallelujah!)*. Psalms 113–118 are often called the Egyptian Hallel, from the reference in Psalm 114:1 and the use of these psalms with the Passover. Worshippers also used them at the other great pilgrimage festivals, Pentecost and Tabernacles. In the temple worship, a solo voice may have offered verse 1, followed by antiphonal choir responses (vv. 2-4 and vv. 5-9).

OUTLINE

Summons to Praise, 113:1-3
The Majestic God over the Heavens and the Earth, 113:4-6
God Cares for the Lowly, 113:7-9

Psalm 113

EXPLANATORY NOTES

Summons to Praise   113:1-3

The psalm begins with a vigorous call to praise *the name of the LORD*. The *servants* may be priests or Levites on duty in the temple, or more likely, a reference to the whole congregation of God's people (Pss 69:35-36; 90:13, 16). The summons to praise focuses on *the name of the LORD* and is for all time (v. 2) and in all places (vv. 3-4), for the LORD's activity is all-encompassing. God inhabits the universe; he is present in the nursery.

The Majestic God over the Heavens and the Earth 113:4-6

God's majesty, theme of the second stanza, is focused with the question *Who is like the LORD our God?* The God "so high" as beyond reach, comes "so low" as to live in our midst (Ezek 48:35). Indeed, what is lowly is the special object of God's attention and mercy. We can find the heart of the psalm in this two-member sentence (vv. 5-6), in which the praise of God as *high* and *far down* is supremely concentrated. The wonder of Psalm 113 lies in this recognition of God's incomparability. The question of God's incomparability is also raised elsewhere (Exod 15:11; Ps 35:10) and answered (Isa 46:9; Jer 10:6).

God Cares for the Lowly   113:7-9

Two illustrations follow. The *ash heap* (*dunghill*, v. 7 NEB) was the city dump. Here the poorest of the poor scavenged for sustenance, as homeless and hungry persons hunt for discarded food in the garbage cans and dumpsters of our cities. In ancient Israel the importance of large families encouraged the belief that the *barren woman* (v. 9) was cursed by God (Gen 16; 1 Sam 1; 2:5). A wife who had no children had no position in relation to her husband.

With these two illustrations, asserting that God lifts the lowly *from the dust* and allows the barren woman to become *the joyous mother of children*, the psalm comes to its climax. What is impossible by human custom or effort is made possible by God (1 Sam 2:8; 1 Kings 16:2; Job 5:11)! The two illustrations of distress typical of a man and of a woman in those days can represent all humanity. Psalm 113 knows of no boundaries to God's mercy (Westermann, 1989:206). The faithful can also reapply these illustrations of change in human circumstances: upon the return from Babylon, Judah looked back on the humiliation and barrenness now left behind (Isa 54:1-5; 61:3; 66:8).

THE TEXT IN THE BIBLICAL CONTEXT AND LIFE OF THE CHURCH

The High God Lifts Up the Lowly

The message of Psalm 113 is similar to that of Isaiah 57:15. God's majesty and might appear in history, but especially as God bends to the helpless and poor (Ps 18:6-19). Israel's hymns of praise exalt the power of God to create a new reality that is in accord with the LORD's just and loving purposes, by putting down the mighty and raising up the lowly and weak (75:7; 107:33-42; 146:9; 147:6). This divine behavior is evident in the advent and ministry of Jesus (Matt 1:23; Phil 2:7-9). Indeed, one may use Luke's Gospel to illustrate Psalm 113, starting with the story of Elizabeth's conception (Luke 1:5-25, 57-58) and Mary's Magnificat (1:46-55). After Jesus' ministry begins (4:18-19), he challenges with such parables as the return of the prodigal (15:11-32), the rich man and Lazarus (16:19-31), and the publican and the Pharisee (18:9-14).

However, this psalm connects not only with the incarnation. Its message about God's majesty and greatness, manifested precisely in his compassion on those suffering miseries of human life, points also to Jesus' death on the cross as the sacred place where the ultimate depth of God's nature was revealed (1 Cor 1:18-31).

Jews and Christians alike have given this psalm a special place in their repertoire of praise. At Passover, Psalms 113–114 are recited or sung before the meal, and Psalms 115–118 afterward. Jesus likely used this psalm before the Last Supper (Matt 26:30; Mark 14:26). In Christian tradition, Psalm 113 is one of the psalms for evening worship on Easter Day.

Psalm 114

When Israel Came Out of Egypt

PREVIEW

This brief, exuberant hymn of praise proclaims the powerful appearance of the God of Israel. It recalls the birth of the nation, from the exodus to the entrance into Canaan (vv. 1-4). From being aliens in a strange land (v. 1), the children of Israel became God's sanctuary and kingdom (v. 2). The foundation of that new beginning was laid amid majestic wonders (vv. 3-4). Between a sea that opened and a river that closed was the mighty wonder of the giving of the law (v. 4).

In the second half of the psalm, the poet mockingly questions nature's response (vv. 5-6). The psalm's concluding answer calls on all the earth to tremble at the presence of the Lord, awesome in might and grace (vv. 7-8).

People often cite this remarkable poem for its high artistic quality—regular parallelism, beauty of expression, imaginative figures, surprise and wonder, strength and power—all within eight verses (Stuhlmueller, 1983, 2:136). The use of twin phrases is striking: *Israel/Judah, Egypt/people of strange language, sanctuary/dominion, sea/Jordan, fled/turned back, mountains/hills, rams/lambs, Lord/God of Jacob, rock/flint.* The mood is exuberant, almost playful.

The date of composition is uncertain. Suggestions offered range from the ninth–eighth century BC, on the basis of the terms *Israel* and

Judah (v. 2), to the time of King Josiah (640–609 BC). Worshippers likely used the psalm at the Passover ritual to aid them in visualizing the miracle at the sea and the marvelous passage through the Jordan (Josh 3). In its setting in the Psalter, it serves to put the exodus and entry into the land in sequence with the return from exile (Pss 107–108) and other divine acts of deliverance (109; 115–116).

OUTLINE

The Exodus and Birth of the Nation Recalled, 114:1-2
Wondrous Events at the Sea, Jordan, and Sinai, 114:3-4
The Psalmist's Mocking Questions and the Answer, 114:5-8

EXPLANATORY NOTES

The Exodus and Birth of the Nation Recalled   114:1-2

History for Israel as God's people begins with the exodus. The miracle of the departure from Egypt, the revelation of the LORD at Sinai, and entrance into the Promised Land are combined into one mighty event. The psalm begins with the central theme: God's wonder in transforming *sanctuary* and *dominion* (vv. 1-2). The *strange language* (Egyptian, with hieroglyphic writing, by 7th century BC simplified in demotic) tended to isolate the Hebrews. *Sanctuary* may allude to the Jerusalem temple or may imply that the whole nation of Judah has become the people of God and holy to the LORD. Even as *God's sanctuary . . . his dominion* are rhythmical rather than logical, so *Judah . . . Israel* likely refer to the whole of God's people rather than political terms for Southern Kingdom and Northern Kingdom. We see a dramatic change of status between verses 1 and 2. From the life of aliens, isolated by a strange language, they have now become God's holy people and abode.

Wondrous Events at the Sea, Jordan, and Sinai 114:3-4

The psalm briefly refers to three key incidents, from the exodus to entering Canaan; it presents God's activity as much more than history. Israel was, in fact, a miracle. These verses celebrate the wondrous deeds of God with delightful poetic imagination and embellishment. The people cross the Reed Sea (Exod 13:18 n; 14:21; Ps 77:16, 19) as the water *fled* (NIV) in the face of God's mighty act. The Jordan River, the last barrier before entering the land, *turned back* (Josh 3:16). The *mountains* and *hills* skipping is usually seen as a reference to the giving of the law at Mt. Sinai (Exod 19:18; Judg 5:5; Ps 68:8), though it could also refer to the mountains and hills of Canaan, startled at the coming of the awesome God of Israel (Ps 29:6; Davidson, 1998:375).

The Psalmist's Mocking Questions and the Answer 114:5-8

Now the psalm becomes a series of mocking questions that the psalmist addresses to the forces of nature. Why did the sea and the Jordan turn back and flee? Why did mountains and hills skip like lambs? Why did they behave so strangely? The questions are rhetorical, asked in a teasing and taunting manner. The psalmist knows the answer. The reaction of the sea is due to the theophany (v. 7). The sea, the personification of chaotic powers, flees without fighting. In the background of this imagery lies the Ugaritic/Canaanite myth of a battle between a god and the sea (Pss 24:1-2; 46:1-3; 65:7; 77:16-18; 89:9-11; 93:3-4; 104:7; Hab 3:8; "Ugaritic Myths, Poems About Baal," *ANET* 130-35). The mountains, symbol of all that is solid and durable, quake before the presence of God (v. 7; Hab 3:10) *[Theophany].*

So the conclusion gives the answer (vv. 7-8). The mood changes from playfulness to utmost seriousness as the psalm invites the earth to *tremble . . . at the presence of the Lord. Tremble* suggests "twisting" or "writhing" before the majestic God. The exodus is so momentous, claims the psalm, that even the fixtures of the cosmos are unfixed. Now the humble God is exalted. The exalted elements are humiliated. "Nothing is secure when the God of liberation begins to make his move" (Brueggemann, 1984:142).

The final verse speaks of a God awesome not only in might but also in grace. *Turns . . . rock into . . . water* (Exod 17:6; Num 20:11), an allusion to God's care for the Hebrews in their wilderness wandering, points to the wonders of a God who can convert death into life. Thus, the psalm ends on a note of the quiet creativity and care of God.

THE TEXT IN THE BIBLICAL CONTEXT AND LIFE OF THE CHURCH

Rehearsing Sacred History

Psalm 114 invites each new generation to participate in this world-transforming memory, to identify themselves with the tradition and receive life through it. The children of Israel certainly must rehearse their history, remember God's covenant, and instruct future generations in that heritage. It is hardly surprising that so many psalms recount this history (Pss 78; 105; 106). In the experience of the exodus and entrance into the Promised Land, God was making a new world. But worshippers must remake it again and again through the liturgy. "If the world is not remade, it will disappear and we will settle for the world of tyranny and despair that is so much with us" (Brueggemann, 1984:142; 1988:45).

The LXX and the Latin versions treat Psalms 114 and 115 as one psalm. Psalm 114 is about the power of the LORD to transform, and Psalm 115 dismisses other gods, who are powerless. Hence, it is similar to the enthronement psalms (Pss 29; 47; 93; 95–99), which acknowledge the power of the LORD and delegitimize the other gods as powerless (Brueggemann, 1988:172).

Psalm 114, the second of the Egyptian Hallel songs (Pss 113–118), was sung on the eighth day of the Passover, according to Jewish tradition. Not only does verse 1 connect directly with the exodus celebrated at Passover; its assurance that rain would fall again (v. 8) also was all-important at the beginning of the dry season. Dante (203: "Purgatorio" 2.45-48) used Psalm 114 as the hymn sung by the spirits in the boat that brings human souls to the shore of purgatory. The words are taken to represent mystically the exodus of the soul from this world to the next. Christians use the psalm during the Easter season, celebrating the new Passover from death to life (Stuhlmueller, 1983, 2:138).

Psalm 115

Not to Us, O LORD, but to Your Name Give Glory

PREVIEW

Psalm 115 is a liturgical prayer-song with a strong note of assurance. The liturgy begins with a plea for God's aid in face of the nations' taunt (vv. 1-2). The answer through hymnic satire mocks the gods of the nations as impotent in contrast to Israel's omnipotent God (vv. 3-8). The psalm exhorts Israel to *trust in the LORD,* who is mindful, will bless with enhancement of life, and increase progeny (vv. 9-15). In conclusion, the hymn reaffirms the LORD's sovereignty in heaven and on earth, and asserts that to live is to praise God (vv. 16-18).

The taunt suggests a crisis situation: *Where is their God?* (v. 2). The psalmist pleads for the LORD to restore the honor of his name and bless the scattered and decimated community. Though we cannot rule out a preexilic date of composition, most commentators consider this psalm as speaking to the postexilic community. To that dispersed and oppressed flock in need of encouragement, Psalm 115 provides assurance of the mercy and constancy of the LORD. Psalm 115 is congruent with the apparent purpose of book V: to address the crisis of exile and its aftermath.

As used in the temple worship, the psalm may have accompanied the offering of a sacrifice after verse 11, with verses 12-18 expressing the joyous conviction that God has accepted the sacrifice. Although we cannot reconstruct the precise liturgical service, the outline proposes a possible pattern (Davidson, 1998:376).

In the LXX, Psalm 115 is joined with Psalm 114 to make up a psalm of twenty-six verses. Then the LXX divides Hebrew Psalm 116 into two. Psalm 115, as the third psalm in the Egyptian Hallel (Pss 113–118), belongs to the cycle of psalms used in the liturgy of the joyous festivals and Passover. The psalm celebrates the living, active God, who hears the cry of his oppressed people (Exod 2:23-25). At the Passover Seder, Psalms 113–114 are recited before the meal and Psalms 115–118 after the meal (Matt 26:30).

OUTLINE

Lament Prayer for Restoration, 115:1-2 (Congregation)
    115:1   Appeal to God's Name, Steadfast Love, and Faithfulness
    115:2   Ridiculed by the Nations
Hymnic Satire Against the Gods of the Nations, 115:3-8 (Solo)
    115:3   God Does What He Will
    115:4-7   Idols Are Impotent
    115:8   The Fate of Idol-Makers and Idol-Worshippers
Exhortation to Trust in the LORD, 115:9-11 (Temple Singers)
Assurance and Blessing, 115:12-15 (Priest)
    115:12-13   Affirmation of God's Care
    115:14-15   Promise of Posterity and Blessing
Conclusion: Praise Through Commitment, 115:16-18 (Congregation)
    115:16   The LORD of Heaven and Earth
    115:17   No Praise from Sheol
    115:18   The Time for Blessing and Praise Is Now

EXPLANATORY NOTES

Lament Prayer for Restoration   115:1-2

The lament begins, not with words of self-deprecation, but with a protest: "We do not ask for our own sake, O LORD!" The appeal is to the honor of the LORD's name, and to the divine attributes of *steadfast love* (*ḥesed*) and *faithfulness* (*'ĕmet*; v. 1). The phrase *give glory* (v. 1) is often associated with the total community's confession of sin and a new consecration to the LORD (Josh 7:19; 1 Sam 6:5). In the taunting question *Where is their God?* what is at stake is the LORD's name (v. 2; Pss 42:3, 10; 79:10; Joel 2:17; Mic 7:10). God needs to protect his honor.

Hymnic Satire Against the Gods of the Nations 115:3-8

Now a solo voice, probably that of a priest, answers the plea of the community. *Our God*, invisible in the heavens, *does what he pleases. Our God* does what he will. *Our God* is absolutely unlimited! That is the point of the ridicule heaped upon the idols of the heathen nations (vv. 4-7). Their gods *do not speak, do not see, do not hear, do not smell, do not feel, do not walk, make no sound!* (cf. vv. 5-7). Using the mystical number seven, a biblical symbol of perfection, the indictment is complete. These idols, *the work of human hands*, are decidedly imperfect. They are dead; they are nothing (Reardon: 228). And those who trust in them become like the gods of their making—nothing (v. 8). This malediction may be a prediction or a prayer, "Their makers will end up like them," or "May their makers end up like them" (Kidner, 1975:405).

Ridicule and curse of an enemy's gods was a common practice. The Assyrians made sport of Israel's God (2 Kings 18:33-35). Elijah mocked the god Baal (1 Kings 18:27). Many texts satirize or ridicule idolatry (Ps 135:15-18; Isa 40:18-20; 44:9-20; Jer 10:1-5, 8-9, 11; Wisd of Sol 13:10-19; Bel and the Dragon; Rom 1:22-23; Rev 9:20). For people feeling the sting of oppression, the pastoral poetry of Psalm 115 uses irony to confirm the congregation's confidence in the LORD and the LORD alone (Davidson, 1998:377).

Exhortation to Trust in the LORD 115:9-11

The summons to *trust in the LORD* is now addressed to three groups: *Israel*, the congregation; *house of Aaron*, the priests; and *you who fear the LORD*. In postexilic time "God-fearers" described proselytes (Acts 13:16, 26). In the context of the psalm, the term may mean no more than all who truly worship the LORD, the people in general and the priests (Davidson, 1998:378). The temple singers declare the antiphonal response three times: *He is their help and their shield*, their protector!

Assurance and Blessing 115:12-15

We find the psalm's turning point in the assurance of the LORD being *mindful of us* (v. 12). The priest may have performed the sacrifice and then offered the blessing (vv. 12-15). The word *bless* or *blessed*, used five times in four verses, implies God's saving presence bestowing the things and conditions that work for the good of the ones blessed. The LORD's blessing upon *both small and great* (v. 13), meaning everyone, includes enhancement of life and increase of progeny (vv. 14-15).

Conclusion: Praise Through Commitment   115:16-18

The hymnic conclusion begins with emphasis on the creator God's work (v. 15-16). The LORD of both *heaven* and *earth* has given life as a special gift, in contrast to dead idols, which are merely the work of human hands and can do nothing (vv. 3-8). Can the dead, those who have gone down *into silence* (*Sheol*), praise the LORD? Since the Hebrews believed the essential content of life was praise, to be cut off from life also ended praise of the LORD (Pss 6:5; 30:9; 88:10-12). *But we . . .* identifies the congregation with "the living." Now is the time for blessing and praise, as long as there is life! The LXX transfers the liturgical cry *Praise the LORD!* (*Hallelujah!*) to the beginning of Psalm 116.

THE TEXT IN THE BIBLICAL CONTEXT AND LIFE OF THE CHURCH

Faith in Face of Trial

Psalm 115 deals with the problem of faith, with how the community of faith bears up in face of the trials of the world. The enduring message resides in the summons to *trust in the LORD* (vv. 9-11) in the confidence that *the LORD has been mindful of us* (v. 12; Pss 4:5; 37:3, 5; Prov 3:5; Isa 26:4). According to Allen (1983:11), "Psalm 115 is a stirring lesson to the people in every age concerning survival in an alien, hostile environment."

Paul and Barnabas, confronted in Lystra with the charge that they are gods in human form, appeal that they are only mortals. However, they also seek to persuade the crowd to turn from the worship of idols, "from these worthless things to the living God, who made the heaven and the earth and the sea and all that is in them" (Acts 14:15). What is *the work of human hands* (Ps 115:4) that becomes contemporary idolatry, drawing persons away from the living God? What are the technologies and ideologies that become today's idols? The automobile and oil? Television? The computer? Education? A political system? George Knight (2:195) illustrates this with how humans make a war, but it soon is out of control and escalates beyond the intention of either side. The result is that we fear the creation of our own hands and brains and become slaves (Rom 1:25). Or as David Baken suggests, in a complacent science, idolatry is being rigidly stuck on one answer, rather than restlessly pursuing the search (via Brueggemann, 1988:181).

An enduring truth from Psalm 115 is that we grow into what we worship (v. 8). We tend to become like the people we idolize, or the environment we live in. Like a sponge, we absorb the personalities and the mannerisms of the people we admire. Mentors and models dramatically alter and influence our lives. When people or possessions become more important to us than God, we become idolaters.

Finally, this psalm touches on death and life. The psalm proclaims an early biblical understanding: *The dead do not praise the LORD, but we, the living, shall praise the LORD from now and forevermore. Hallelujah!* (cf. vv. 17-18 NEB). Judaism's skepticism about life after death may be connected to its passion for justice. The important thing in this life was to create justice and love in this world. The expression of praise was a way of offering up that commitment to work for what gives life here and now (Marty, 1992:6).

Psalm 116

Thank You, God!

PREVIEW

With a deep sense of gratitude, an individual has come into the temple in Jerusalem (v. 19) to offer a sacrifice of thanksgiving (v. 17) for deliverance from an illness that brought him to the brink of death (v. 3). Before the worshippers in the temple, he recites his testimony to God's gracious love and vow of devotion.

This song of thanksgiving is similar to Psalms 113; 115; and 117 in ending with *Praise the LORD!* (*Hallelujah!*), and it forms part of the ancient Hallel (see Psalms 113 and 118). Most commentators consider it postexilic on the basis of Aramaisms in verses 7, 12, and 16. The psalm's theme of deliverance is in keeping with the main thrust of book V *[Composition; Psalm Genres]*.

OUTLINE

Profession of Faith amid Distress, 116:1-7
Praise and Confidence for the Gracious Deliverance, 116:8-11
Sacrifice of Thanksgiving, 116:12-19

EXPLANATORY NOTES

Progression in the Psalm

Readers have variously analyzed the movement in Psalm 116. The psalm begins with words recited or sung before the congregation (vv. 1-6). The psalmist dialogues with his soul (vv. 7-11) before addressing the religious assembly (vv. 12-15). Then the psalmist utters a prayer (vv. 16-17) and turns again to the congregation (vv. 18-19).

From a literary viewpoint, we see three parts in the psalm (vv. 1-7, 8-14, 15-19), with each part ending with a refrain-like repetition (vv. 7, 13b-14, 17b-18). Each part concludes with a performance statement: going to the house of the LORD (v. 7), offering the *cup of salvation* (v. 13), and offering a *thanksgiving sacrifice* (v. 17; Mays, 1994b:369).

The words of Psalm 116 move from distress (vv. 1, 3-4, 6, 8, 10-11), to deliverance (vv. 1-2, 5-6, 7-8), to devotion (vv. 12-19). For the psalmist, who had been in the grasp of *Sheol*, the abode of the dead (vv. 2, 8), deliverance has come through God's gracious action. The LORD has overcome the power of both death and evil. There is nothing left for the psalmist to do but to offer *a thanksgiving sacrifice* (vv. 12, 17). The nature of *thanksgiving* (*tôdâ*) is the narration of a witness and proclamation of great trust *[Sheol]*.

Profession of Faith amid Distress 116:1-7

Why should God answer a distress call of one near death (vv. 1-4)? Because that is what the LORD is like: *gracious, merciful,* and one who *protects the simple* (vv. 5-7; Exod 34:6). The verb *protects* (*šāmar,* "watch over") describes a basic activity of God, a theme that runs throughout the psalms (Pss 25:20; 34:20; 86:2; 97:10; 121). In identifying with *the simple* or vulnerable, the psalmist admits that he had been *brought low* and near the end of his ability to cope.

Praise and Confidence for the Gracious Deliverance 116:8-11

In praise for the bounty of God's deliverance, the psalmist now describes the physical and mental turmoil experienced (vv. 8-11). Yet with confidence he walks in the presence of the LORD *in the land of the living* (v. 9). Verses 10 and 11 appear to reflect his earlier distress. In this retrospective narration, the psalmist admits despair in the face of slanderous accusations. Illness or deep hurt can skew the perspective, often generating blame upon others.

Sacrifice of Thanksgiving 116:12-19

In gratitude, the psalmist responds to God rescuing him from the clutches of death and despair (vv. 3-4, 10-11), knowing that in *return* he can never match what the LORD has done for him (vv. 12-19). As the LORD's *servant* (v. 16), he appeals to the bond between master and servant, for the master protects and provides for his servant (Gen 24). As servant he will offer a *thanksgiving sacrifice* in return (v. 17). Leviticus 7:11-15 and Numbers 15:1-10 describe the thank offering. Later, in the temple at the ritual of the thanksgiving feast, the psalm is sung before the assembled congregation. Before the sacrificial act, the one bringing the offering would appear with the *cup of salvation* (v. 13), emptying the wine as a drink offering upon the altar, while calling *on the name of the LORD*. Then one of the temple servants would sing the song of thanksgiving (Sabourin: 293) *[Psalm Genres]*.

The preceding notes assume the text of Psalm 116 as we have received it. Westermann (1989:196-97), observing disruptions in the text, has proposed a reconstruction of Psalm 116 as follows, to produce a psalm in which every sentence makes sense in its position within the structure of the individual psalm of praise:

Introductory Summary (vv. 14, 1, 2)
Narrative of Distress and Deliverance (vv. 3, 10, 11, 4, 16, 8, 9)
Praise of God (vv. 15, 5, 6, 7)
Renewal Vow of Praise (vv. 12, 13, 17, 18, 19)

THE TEXT IN THE BIBLICAL CONTEXT AND LIFE OF THE CHURCH

The Thankful Heart

The opening words, *I love the LORD, because he has heard,* express the thankful heart. The question *What shall I return . . . for all his bounty to me?* (v. 12), invites thanksgiving. We can never repay. But we can pray, praise, and offer our life "as a living sacrifice" (Rom 12:1). Some churches (as in India) customarily provide space and time for people to step to the altar with their gift/offering and give testimony of God's healing. This is in keeping with what apparently was Israelite practice, and we might well emulate it.

The Value of Human Life

Verse 15, *Precious in the sight of the LORD . . .* speaks to the value of human life. Nothing that happens is a matter of indifference. In the light of Christ's resurrection, we take the statement that God puts great value on the death of his faithful ones to mean that God will take them to himself when they die (cf. Rev. 14:13). First Corinthians 15:54-57 well expresses this ultimate act of faith, that God overcomes even death. Many worship leaders have appropriately used Psalm 116:15 at funerals.

The identification of the *cup of salvation* (v. 13) as the cup of martyrdom is found in the writings of Origen in the third century as well as other patristic and medieval writers (Reardon: 232). When Thieleman J. van Braght (5) wrote an invocation to preface the *Martyrs Mirror* in 1659, he quoted Psalm 116:15, declaring that the Christian martyrs about whom he writes "gave their precious lives and bodies as a sacrifice to Thee." He expresses profound thanks to God for sparing his own life when "snares of death had compassed me, keeping me bound nearly six months, . . . so that I often thought I could not survive." Nevertheless, "Thy hand rescued me and by Thy grace was I led safely through, so . . . I wrote and finished the greater part of this work."

Later Jewish practice included reading Psalm 116 during the course of the Passover meal. The psalm speaks to people celebrating the God who had answered their cry born of oppression, who delivered them from the death of Egyptian slavery, and who set them free to become a people obedient to the law, in thankful response for all that God had done for them (Davidson, 1998:382). Christian liturgy often uses Psalm 116 in celebration of communion on Holy Thursday, inviting Christians to hear the psalmist's experience as an anticipation of Jesus' faithful suffering (v. 10) and ultimate deliverance from death in the resurrection (vv. 3-4, 8-9, 16). Verses 12-14 are common words of invitation to receive the bread and the cup of communion.

Psalm 117

Let All People Praise!

PREVIEW

This shortest of all the psalms portrays a grand worldwide outlook. In abbreviated form, the hymn of praise invites all people to praise God for *steadfast love* and *faithfulness*. Indeed, it stands as a classic example of the hymn form [Psalm Genres].

Some see these two verses as a psalm fragment that might have been part of Psalm 116; 118; or 148. Yet the verses can stand alone, proclaiming a message akin to Isaiah 40:3-5, where "all people shall see . . . the glory of the LORD."

OUTLINE

Call to Praise (addressed to all nations),   117:1
Reason for Praise: God's Steadfast Love and Faithfulness
   (as Experienced by Israel), 117:2ab
Renewed Call to Praise, 117:2c

EXPLANATORY NOTES

Praise for God's Steadfast Love and Faithfulness 117:1-2

Following the summons for all nations to *praise the LORD*, the psalmist states the reason: God's steadfast love (*ḥesed*) and faithfulness (*'ĕmet*) to Israel. By recalling Exodus 34:6, this psalm settles the reasons for praising the LORD in God's fundamental identity. It invites the nations to praise because of what Israel knows and has experienced about the steadfast love and faithfulness of God.

While Psalm 117 simply appeals to *praise the LORD* for ḥesed and 'ĕmet, other psalms make God's steadfast love and faithfulness much more specific. Thus, we have Psalm 30:1-3, or 40:2, "He drew me up from the desolate pit" *[Steadfast]*.

Observe the use of *you* in verse 1 and *us* in verse 2. This shift leads us to look at how Israel can be a blessing for all nations (Gen 12:1-3).

THE TEXT IN THE BIBLICAL CONTEXT AND LIFE OF THE CHURCH

Summons for All to Praise God

Other psalms invite the nations to praise the God of Israel (Pss 22:27-31; 47:1; 100:1; 113:2-4). These and other passages do not see Israel as the end of the OT revelation, but as the instrument God has chosen to manifest his glory also to others.

Paul quotes Psalm 117 in Romans 15:11, sharing the psalmist's assumption that *the LORD* is highest God, to whom all the world is subject. Thus, Paul argues that the inclusion of the Gentiles in God's salvation is not a divine afterthought.

Paul's reference to Psalm 117 has fostered its mission use. Isaac Watts' hymn "From all that dwell below the skies" (1719) is based on it, as is the Taizé chant *Laudate Dominum* ("Praise the Lord, all you nations"). The psalm is appropriate for Worldwide Communion Sunday. Its wide use as a call to worship summons people of all nations to praise God within the particularities of their own history, culture, and language (Dan 7:14; Rev 14:6; 15:4).

Psalm 118

A Processional Liturgy of Thanksgiving

PREVIEW

The psalm is in the form of a thanksgiving; it is the sixth and last of the Hallel Psalms and one of the great hymns of the Psalter *[Psalm Genres]*. All the Hallel Psalms, customarily connected with the Passover observance, include divine help as a theme. Psalm 113 centers on praise of the LORD, who lifts up the lowly, needy, and helpless. Psalm 114 recalls the story of the exodus. In Psalm 115, the LORD, as Israel's help, is contrasted to the impotent gods of the nations. Psalm 116 thanks the LORD for deliverance from death, and Psalm 117 calls on the nation to praise the LORD. Psalm 118 provides a powerful testimony to the strength of faith that flows from the direct experience of God's help.

Following the antiphonal call to worship and thanksgiving to the LORD for his *steadfast love* (vv. 1-4), an individual who has survived a distressing crisis comes to the temple to express thanksgiving for the LORD's answer to his cry for help (vv. 5-21). The last part of the psalm reflects the community's praise through ritual interaction within the sanctuary (vv. 22-29). We cannot reconstruct the literary history of the psalm, though it appears to be an individual's thanksgiving set within the context of the community's worship. While elements of the psalm may come from preexilic times (vv. 14-16), Psalm 118 was likely used in the period of the second temple, for joyous ceremonies such as described in Nehemiah 12:27-43. The psalm appears suitable for the Feast of Tabernacles (v. 15, *tents*; v. 24, *the day*; v. 27, *light, branches*). People also recited it at the Feast of Passover, during which the Hallel Psalms have been used for centuries.

Prior to verse 19, the festive procession takes place outside the temple. Upon entry to the temple area, participants are to give a declaration of loyalty. Thus, Psalm 118, along with Psalms 15 and 24, provides an entrance liturgy on the occasion of solemn thanksgiving to God (vv. 19-21).

A major question for interpretation of this complex psalm centers on identity of the singer in verses 5-21, and how the individual's song of thanksgiving came to be anchored in the liturgy of the entire assembly (Kraus, 1989:395). Some interpreters see the individual as the king or the king's representative, and thus interpret the psalm as a thanksgiving for victory in battle (Davidson, 1998:383). Others suggest that the key question focuses on identity of *the one who comes in the name of the LORD* (v. 26; Mays 1994b:375-76). We also recognize the psalm's reinterpretation by the rabbis and NT writers and the prominent attention the church has given to it.

OUTLINE

Antiphonal Call to Thanksgiving, 118:1-4
An Individual Psalm of Thanksgiving, 118:5-21
    118:5-9   Narrative of Distress and Cry for the LORD's Help
    118:10-14 Description of the Individual's Plight and the LORD's Intervention
    118:15-16 Citation from a Victory Psalm
    118:17-18 Testimony about Life
    118:19-21 Thanksgiving in the Sanctuary
The Community's Praise in the Inner Court, 118:22-29
    118:22-25 Jubilant Praise for What the LORD Has Done
    118:26-27 Festal Procession to the Altar
    118:28   Personal Thanks
    118:29   Doxology: Call to Thanksgiving for the LORD's Steadfast Love

EXPLANATORY NOTES

Antiphonal Call to Thanksgiving   118:1-4

Psalm 118 opens and closes with the same verse: *O give thanks to the LORD, for he is good; his steadfast love endures forever!* (vv. 1, 29). This inclusio by the traditional liturgical formula reverberates throughout Psalm 136, occurs widely (Ezra 3:11; Ps 100:5; 106:1; 107:1; Jer 33:11), and introduces the theme: God's *steadfast love* (*ḥesed*). With deliberate emphatic use of repetition, each verse announces the theme of the introduction. This psalm testifies to the abiding goodness and grace of God *[Steadfast]*. Since Psalm 118 begins and ends with the same verse that opens book V (Ps 107:1), Psalms 107–118 together offer a perspective from which to face the reality of continuing oppression: recollection of God's past activity as a basis for petition and grateful trust in God's future activity on behalf of the people (McCann, 1996:1154).

The antiphonal verses 2-4 connect with Psalms 115:9-11 and 135:19-20, inviting the congregation, the priests, and all *who fear the LORD* to praise the LORD of covenant faithfulness. This declarative act, telling abroad God's great deeds, is a call to the nations and all peoples to praise the LORD (Pss 33:8; 66:1; 96:1; 98:4; 100:1; Miller, 1986:13).

An Individual Psalm of Thanksgiving 118:5-21

The main body of the thanksgiving opens with the singer declaring the deeds of the LORD (v. 5). In distress, he calls on the LORD, who answers by setting him in *a broad place*. God's help gives him room so that he no longer feels trapped. These verses contrast *refuge in the LORD* as over against *confidence in mortals* (vv. 5-9). In Hebrew, the poet places the name *the LORD* at the beginning of the sentence and *mortals* (*man*, *'ādām*) at the end, accentuating the contrast (v. 6).

In describing his oppression by enemies (vv. 10-14), the psalmist borrows metaphors from royal psalms (Ps 18:29-30, 36-39). *Surrounded, surrounded, surrounded, surrounded!* But with the help of the LORD (v. 13) and *in the name of the LORD, I cut them off* (vv. 10-12). This could be an allusion to 1 Samuel 18:25-27, which narrates David's hunt for Philistine foreskins (from circumcision). It could also mean "resist" or "ward off." The decisive conjunction *but* (v. 13) signals the dramatic change brought about through the LORD's intervention. *The LORD is my strength and my might* (v. 14) echoes an early Hebrew victory song (Exod 15:2).

The citation of victory at the exodus is followed by the threefold repetition of *the right hand of the LORD* (vv. 15-16; Exod 15:6, 12). The *right hand* is God's instrument of victory and a figure of speech for the intervening action of God in human affairs. *Tents* (v. 15) may refer to dwellings or booths for the festival. The *righteous* (v. 15) are the covenant people whose life matches their profession.

The psalmist's declaration, *I shall not die, but I shall live* (vv. 17-18), refers to being delivered from imminent death rather than to belief in immortality or resurrection, though the new life is more than simply renewal of vital breath. The essence of living is to declare the saving deeds of the LORD. The LORD has chastened him sorely, but as a discipline for good (v. 18; Prov 3:11-12). Death does not hold the sufferer in its power. Throughout these verses, the theme is about life engendered not by human strength, but by action and intervention of the LORD.

To this point the thanksgiving has been recited outside the temple. Now the singer moves into the sanctuary. *The gates of righteousness* are the gates of the temple (v. 19). The response of the gatekeeper is spoken by the priest (v. 20). The condition for entry into the temple calls for righteous living (Pss 15; 24:3-6). With verse 21, the worshipper is now inside, with all God's people. He must show his gratitude.

The Community's Praise in the Inner Court   118:22-29

With happy shouts and dancing, the procession moves into the inner courts of the temple, and the congregation respond as a choir (vv. 22-25). *The stone that the builders rejected has become the chief cornerstone* (v. 22), perhaps a proverb, suggests that what appears worthless has now taken the place of honor. The one earlier cast into the realm of death, like a stone rejected, now has been given life. For the community, in the context of the exodus festivals, Israel was the stone rejected by the great empire builders, but the LORD has given his disciplined remnant an honorable and important place in the building of his kingdom. This is from the LORD (v. 23), God's wonderful work (*niplā'ôt, marvelous,* "extraordinary"; Ps 107). Thus, the choir (or congregation) joyously chants what God has done.

This is the day when the LORD acted, a time for joy and gladness in God's mighty works (v. 24). *Save us, . . . give us success* (v. 25) is a cry for deliverance and a petition for blessing. By the time of Jesus' entry into Jerusalem, "Hosanna," from this Hebrew term *hôšî'â nā,* had become not only a cry for deliverance, but also an expression of praise (Matt 21:9).

As the festal procession to the altar begins (vv. 26-27), the supplicant is admitted with a priestly benediction (Num 6:24-26). God has given his people *light* (v. 27): he has shown them favor (Num 6:25; Pss 67:1; 80:3, 7, 19; 119:135). Verse 27 is usually interpreted in the light of the Mishnah, which describes how, at the Feast of Tabernacles, the worshippers went in a procession around the altar, carrying branches of palm, myrtle, and willow (*Sukkah* 4:2-7; Lev 23:40; A. Anderson, 2:804).

As the psalm concludes, an individual (the supplicant, king, or representative of the nation) expresses personal thanksgiving (v. 28). A poetic feature of verse 28 is that every word begins with the first Hebrew letter, *'ālep* א, as also in Exodus 15:2b, perhaps symbolizing a new beginning. The choir's doxology completes the inclusio, repeating the psalm's first verse (v. 29) *[Hebrew Poetry]*.

THE TEXT IN THE BIBLICAL CONTEXT AND LIFE OF THE CHURCH

Psalm 118 in Judaism

The importance given Psalm 118 in the NT is due in part to the fact that this psalm had great significance in Judaism. The petition, *Save us, Hosanna* (v. 25), was a cultic cry used at the Feast of Tabernacles. The Hallel, Psalms 113-118, was a fixed part of the Jewish cycle of autumn feasts and of Passover, a recollection of the exodus and an anticipation of God's continuing presence and ongoing help (Matt 26:30; Mark 14:26). In Judaism, Psalm 118:22-23 was interpreted as referring to Abraham, David, and the Messiah (Kraus, 1986:193). The Targum, the ancient Aramaic translation of the OT, recognized the psalm as one for worshippers to recite antiphonally in the liturgy. In contemporary Jewish liturgy, Psalm 118 also has a place in the celebration of Hanukkah, the Feast of Lights, commemorating the rededication of the temple in Maccabean times (1 Macc 4:52-59; John 10:22).

Psalm 118 in the New Testament

The NT, however, gives special attention to Psalm 118 and applies individual verses to Jesus Christ, his suffering and resurrection. Nevertheless, the *stone . . . rejected* becoming *the chief cornerstone* (v. 22) became a key verse in the apologetic for Jesus as the long-expected Messiah, along with Isa 8:14-15 and 28:16 (Matt 21:42; Acts 4:11; Rom 9:33; Eph 2:20; 1 Pet 2:6-8). Jesus cited Psalm 118:22-23 to close the parable of the vineyard (Mark 12:1-11), told during his last week in Jerusalem.

The synoptic Gospels differ in the words shouted by the crowd on Jesus' entry into Jerusalem, but all draw on material from Psalm 118:25-26. According to Mark, the onlookers shouted, "Hosanna! Blessed is the one who comes in the name of the Lord! . . ." (11:9-10). Matthew has "Hosanna to the Son of David! Blest is the one who comes. . . !" (21:9). Luke reports the shout as "Blessed is the king who comes in the name of the Lord! . . ." (19:38). The evangelists all imply that Jesus accepted identification with the figure in Psalm 118:26 (Holladay: 117).

Regarding the identity of *the one who comes in the name of the LORD* (v. 26), we observe development. The tradition of the exodus informs the language of the psalm (Exod 15:1-18). The psalm's language can also include the whole history of the LORD's preservation of Israel in the midst of the nations, especially the exile and the return. The prophets had announced the death of Israel as the LORD's judgment (Amos 5:2; Hos 13:1; Ezek 18:31). But the LORD did not give Israel over to death. At every festival the people could recount the deeds of the LORD (v. 17; Mays, 1994b:378-79).

The NT identifies Jesus as "the one who comes in the name of the LORD." He is acclaimed as "Son of David" (Matt 21:9; Mark 11:9-10), and as "king" (Luke 19:38; John 12:13), a representative in the Davidic succession to the messianic promise. In his crucifixion and resurrection, Jesus is the rejected stone that has become the chief cornerstone (Acts 4:11).

Early Christian believers had no difficulty reading *This is the LORD's doing; it is marvelous in our eyes* (Ps 118:23) as applying to the resurrection, or to associate *This is the day . . .* (v. 24) with the resurrection. In verse 24, the subject is not *the day*, but rather, the LORD and what he has done today. When we experience a wonder as God's work, all that we can say of it is that it is "wonderful," or a "marvelous" change has occurred (Westermann, 1989:107).

The Church's Use of Psalm 118

The church's use of this psalm has focused on Palm Sunday (vv. 25-27) and Easter (vv. 22-24). Leaders have often used *This is the day . . .* (v. 24) as a call to worship on Sundays, reminding us of God's resurrection victory over the power of death. Believers have often applied *This is the day . . .* to the "day of salvation" (Luke 19:9; 2 Cor 6:2).

Among citations from Psalm 118 in church history, we flag four, representing a wide range of use. The *Didache* (12.1), a short church manual from the second century, applies "who comes in the name of the Lord" (v. 26) to visiting teachers and prophets. The word "Lord" is understood as referring to Jesus, in whose name the visitor comes and should be welcomed as such (Holladay: 163).

Martin Luther wrote that Psalm 118, his favorite psalm, had helped him "out of troubles out of which neither emperor nor king, nor any other man on earth could have helped him." Luther recalls that Christ alone has entered the holy place as our high priest, so that as a result, we dare to grasp the horns of the altar, but only through his doing so first by ascending the cross (Knight, 2:213).

Before the Battle of Coutras in southwestern France in 1587, Henry of Navarre's Huguenot army sang Psalm 118 as a battle hymn. The Calvinists won the battle but ultimately lost their struggle (Holladay: 209).

In letters written from prison, Anabaptist martyrs quoted Psalm 118:6, *With the LORD on my side I do not fear*. They took comfort that present sufferings are "not worth comparing with the glory about to be revealed" (Rom 8:18; Braght: 517, 817).

Psalm 119

How I Love Your Word, O LORD!

PREVIEW

Extolling the Word of God

With exhausting completeness, the psalmist praises the *law* (*torah, tôrâ*) of the LORD in the longest of all the psalms. In this magnum opus extolling the word of God, nearly every verse uses the term *law* (*torah*), or a synonym for it. The psalmist desires to make God's *law* the governing principle of his conduct and every sphere of life. This divine instruction represented by *torah* is no burden to the psalmist, but a means of joy, refreshment, and life in communion with God. God's word and revelation of his will are a demonstration of grace. The psalmist exclaims, *Your word is a lamp to my feet and a light to my path* (119:105; Job 29:3; Isa 2:5), and declares God's word to be *sweeter than honey* (119:103; 19:10; Ezek 3:3; Rev 10:9-10) *[Torah]*.

An alphabetical acrostic is the form chosen for this meditation (see Psalms 9–10; 25; 34; 37; 111; 112; 145). However, Psalm 119 has twenty-two stanzas, one for each letter of the Hebrew alphabet. *Each of the eight verses* in a stanza begins with *the same Hebrew letter* until the whole alphabet is completed, from *'ālep* א to *tāw* ת, or as we would say, from A to Z. The use of the entire alphabet signals completeness, and the whole vocabulary represents comprehensiveness. The structural use of the alphabet may also assert that the word and law of God is the inner core and essential substance of human language *[Hebrew Poetry]*.

In content, Psalm 119 is anthological in style, drawing on language of the other psalms, Deuteronomy, Proverbs, Job, Jeremiah, Ezekiel, and Isaiah. Examples include Psalm 19:7-10; Deuteronomy 4:29 (Ps 119:2); Jeremiah 18:20 (v. 85); Isaiah 40:8 (v. 89). The mood is meditative and reflective, with openness to God's ongoing instruction and further revelation. The word *meditate* (*śîaḥ*, vv. 15, 23, 27, 48, 78, 148) suggests that one ought to go over in thought, muse on, linger upon, and even to mumble the sound repeatedly (Stuhlmueller, 1983, 2:153). Elements of lament are also evident, as from one who is persecuted for his faith, or who decries the apostasy of the times (vv. 8, 21, 51, 61, 84, 115, 126, 136). While the acrostic pattern makes for much repetition, Will Soll (90-111) has detected an overall movement in Psalm 119—from complaint and petition (vv. 17-24) to praise and assurance (vv. 169-176), with the turning point at verses 89-96 (McCann, 1996:1168).

There is little agreement on dating Psalm 119. One suggestion is to date it as early as the Deuteronomic reform in the late-seventh century BC. Many commentators consider the psalm postexilic, perhaps from the time of Ezra, around 400 BC. According to Deuteronomy 31:9-13, Levites were obligated to preserve the law, read it before the people, and explain its impact upon their daily lives, so that the people and their children "may hear and learn to fear the LORD your God." However, because Psalm 119 ignores the stipulation of the covenant law and never quotes from it, it is possible that the poem was composed among disciples of the wisdom writers (Stuhlmueller, 1983, 2:153). Increased devotion to the revealed word from the past was a product of the Babylonian exile. Kraus (1989:414) is typical: "Psalm 119 is a collection of statements of the individual Torah piety of postexilic times that originated from the study of Scripture, of Deuteronomic theology, of cultic Torah instruction of an individual, and of the stimulus of wisdom teaching."

Synonyms for Law

Since primarily eight synonyms for *law* appear throughout the psalm, one in each verse (except none in v. 122 and two each in vv. 15, 16, 48, and 160), here we briefly examine each. I present them in order of their first entry, as translated by the NRSV:

Law (*torah, tôrâ,* v. 1). *Torah*, as also in Psalms 1 and 19, refers to the divine instruction, the teaching and revelation of God, rather than the more narrow meaning of the Roman *lex* (law), which formed the basis of our Western legal system. The divine instruction as the guide of life was codified for future use in the form of a law code (Deut 4:44; 17:18-20; Josh 8:31-35), and eventually the *Torah* (capitalized) denotes the whole Pentateuch. *Torah* implies that revelation is for obedience.

Decrees (*'ēdôt*, v. 2). Traditionally translated "testimonies," *'ēdôt* belongs to the terminology of the covenant (Exod 31:18; Deut 31:26). It points to a divinely instituted standard of conduct (Deut 6:17, 20; Ps 99:7). The NIV translates this word *statutes*.

Precepts (*piqqûdim*, v. 4). This word is synonymous with *law* as that which is "appointed or charged."

Statutes (*ḥuqqim*, v. 5). The emphasis is on something prescribed, an enactment (Ps 105:10; Isa 30:8). The NIV translates this word *decrees*.

Commandments (*miṣwôt*, v. 6). This word denotes commands or decrees issued by a person in authority (1 Kings 2:43).

Ordinances (*mišpāṭîm*, v. 7). These are the "judgments," the decisions of the all-wise Judge about human situations (Exod 21:1; Deut 17:8a, 9b), and denote the standard given for fair dealing between persons. The NIV translates the term *laws*.

Word (*dābār*, v. 9). *Word*, a more general term, usually refers to an utterance of men or of God. In Psalm 119:9 it is the divine word which proceeds from the mouth of God. *Dābār* may indicate not only a particular message of the LORD (Jer 7:2), but also the sum total of his revealed will (Deut 4:2).

Word or *promise* (*'imrâ*, v. 11). This is similar to the previous term. In Psalm 119 it often means the law of God in general, or his promises in particular (v. 140).

In addition to these eight terms, the psalm uses several others to explain God's self-revelation: *ways* (vv. 3, 15, 37, 59), *judge/judgments/just/justice* (vv. 75, 84, 120, 121, 137, 149, 156), *name* (vv. 55, 132), *faithfulness* (vv. 90, 138), and *appointment* (v. 91). Even verse 122, the one verse not containing a synonym for *law*, may have originally read "pledge thy word as surety" (White: 180).

Translators are not consistent in rendering the eight main expressions used for *law*. We do well to look at the whole psalm as a mosaic, treating the theme of a life dedicated to God's word. C. S. Lewis speaks of Psalm 119 as literary "embroidery," in which stitch by stitch the whole is crafted, "the order of the Divine Mind, embodied in the Divine Law" (1961:52-53).

OUTLINE AND EXPLANATORY NOTES

Here we identify each of the twenty-two stanzas with a brief theme statement, followed by explanatory notes, without attempting to comment on each verse.

In Praise of Fidelity to the Word of God
119:1-8   'ālep (א)

The Psalm begins with a twofold *'ašrê*: *Happy* (*blessed*, NIV) are the *blameless*, and *happy* (*blessed*) those who keep the LORD's *decrees* (vv. 1-2). The theme is familiar, the claim that the source of happiness and the fulfilled life is to be found in obedience to the law (*torah*) of the LORD (Ps 1:1). Following this greeting to those seeking to live a life of obedience to God's will, the psalmist shifts to petition of an individual lament and confession of need for divine help (vv. 5-8).

Storing the Treasure of God's Word in the Heart
119:9-16   Bêt (ב)

Stanza 2 begins in the style of wisdom inquiry (v. 9). Interest in the welfare of youth was characteristic of the wisdom writers (Prov 1:4, 8, 10, 15; 2:1; 3:1). The psalmist's response about the way to purity calls for hiding the word in the heart as inward motivating power (vv. 9b-11). Does this suggest memorizing the word, so mastering the word that it will exercise control over the person? The NEB translates verse 13a, *I say them over, one by one*. The word dwelling in the heart produces joy: *Blessed are you, O LORD* (v. 12). The psalm frequently mentions a note of *delight* or *joy* in observing God's law (vv. 14, 16, 24, 35, 47, 70, 92, 111, 174). The comparison with riches is characteristic of the sages (v. 14; Prov 22:1, 4). The stanza declares this *word* (vv. 9, 11, 16) as antidote to sin (v. 11).

Solace in Suffering
119:17-24   Gîmel (ג)

Lament and petition dominate. The psalmist prays for the grace of enlightenment and revitalization (vv. 17-18) in the midst of persons who scoff and persecute (vv. 21-23). He prays, convinced that the law (*torah*) contains an abundance of *wondrous things* (*niplā'ôt*), miracles that can bring life (v. 18). As an alien (*gēr*), he is but a stranger in God's world, in need of guidance (v. 19). He longs not for the land, but for the instruction of the LORD (vv. 20, 24). In face of *the insolent* (v. 21), including *plotting princes* (v. 23, *the powers that be*, NEB), he appeals to God to *deal bountifully* with him, so that he *may live* (v. 17). In doing the will of God, he finds solace and delight (v. 24).

Revive and Strengthen Me!
119:25-32   Dālet (ד)

Description of the psalmist's plight continues in stanza 4. This passage, rich in contrasts, displays the positive against the negative. The mournful tone is heard in *My soul clings to the dust* (v. 25), *My soul melts* (v. 28), *Put false ways far from me* (v. 29), and *Let me not be put to shame* (v. 31). Yet the psalmist realizes the possibilities available through God's word—revival, understanding, strength, truth, freedom. Life may be collapsing, but God renews hope through the wonders (v. 27) of the connection between word and life (vv. 25, 28, 107). The psalmist focuses comfort in the statutes, precepts, ordinances, decrees, commandments of God. Through them the *understanding* is enlarged (v. 32) in the sense of *You gave me room . . . in distress* (Ps 4:1). Here is a contrasting and progressive use of *cling*: *My soul clings to the dust* (v. 25), and *I cling to your decrees, O LORD* (v. 31)!

Teach Me, O LORD!
119:33-40   Hê (ה)

Petitions predominate in verses 33-40. Observe the series of requests beginning each verse: *Teach me, give, lead, turn my heart, turn my eyes, confirm, turn away the disgrace.*

The stanza closes with the plea *Give me life* (v. 40). The petitions focus on God's work within as the psalmist prays for instruction and guidance, that he may escape the bypaths of selfish gain and worthless things (vv. 36-37). *Teach* (*yārāh*, v. 33) is the verb from which *torah* comes. Verse 33 sets forth the theme: God's reward of obedience to the *torah* stands in contrast to all vain things. *Understanding* (v. 34) has a religious rather than an intellectual sense, like "fear of the LORD" (vv. 38, 74). *Fear* and *dread* show some wordplay (vv. 38-39). The psalmist dreads that he may experience disgrace or scorn (v. 22). In belonging to *those who fear you*, he finds the antidote to that kind of oppressive fear (v. 38; Ps 19:9; Davidson, 1998:393).

Passion to Speak the Word
119:41-48   Wāw (ו)

From confinement and oppression, obedience to the LORD's word and instruction brings the persecuted person to the wide-open realm of freedom. The stanza begins with the LORD's *steadfast love* (*ḥesed,* first of seven uses in Ps 119) and *salvation* (first of six uses; v. 41) as answer to those who taunt (v. 42). Now follow bold assertions in progression: *I trust in your word* (v. 42). *My hope is in your ordinances* (v. 43). *I will keep your law continually* (v. 44). *I shall walk at liberty* (v. 45). *I will also speak . . . before kings* (v. 46). Here is a portrait of those with passion for God's word, because they love God's commandments (vv. 47-48).

Comfort in Affliction
119:49-56   Zayin (ז)

While lament appears to dominate this stanza (vv. 50-51, 53), the psalmist's theme is the comfort found in God's word (vv. 49-50, 52, 54-56). He opens with a prayer, *Remember your word to your servant* (v. 49), and closes with *I remember your name, . . . O LORD* (v. 55). Quickened by God's word (*law, torah,* vv. 51, 53, 55), the psalmist describes experience of comfort as loyalty in the presence of reproach (v. 51), *hot indignation* at those who forsake God's law (v. 53), and making God's decrees the theme of his songs and the LORD's name object of his prayers (vv. 54-55). There is no comfort equal to the certainty of the soul obedient to the revealed will of God (v. 56; Morgan: 105).

Fellowship in the LORD
119:57-64   Ḥêt (ח)

Loyalty to God is not only comfort in sorrow; it is also the medium of fellowship. So the opening words of this section declare the theme: *The LORD is my portion* (v. 57). The LORD as the people's portion may have its roots in the experience of the Levites, who were excluded from owning land. The LORD was their *portion* of land and livelihood (Num 18:20; Deut 10:9; Josh 13:14; Ps 16:5). This confession is later transferred to the mouth of the pious. Only to the LORD's word do they feel bound, and here they seek to meet his *steadfast love* (vv. 57, 64). The psalmist fosters this fellowship in the LORD by imploring God's favor *with all my heart* (v. 58), by turning his feet with haste to God's *decrees* (vv. 59-60), by not forgetting God's *law* even when threatened (v. 61), and by praise at all times (v. 62). People often regard *midnight* as a time of judgment and lament; in contrast, one may identify it as a time to praise God (Acts 16:25). Such fellowship with the LORD means fellowship with *all who fear* and keep the precepts of the LORD, whose *steadfast love* embraces all the earth (vv. 63-64).

The LORD's Instruction as Highest Good
119:65-72   Ṭêt (ט)

Beginning with a song of thanksgiving (v. 65), the psalmist moves immediately to petition (v. 66) and concludes with a wisdom saying (v. 72). Five verses begin with the Hebrew word *ṭôv* (*good*, vv. 65, 66, 68, 71, 72). This stanza declares that the good word of the gracious God is the fountain of all good, and one learns it in lowliness. The psalmist accepts lessons of affliction (vv. 67, 69) as the LORD's chastening (vv. 71, 75). He concludes that the law of the LORD's mouth is better than all material wealth (v. 72).

Complete Your Work in Me
119:73-80   Yôd (י)

The theme of the LORD humbling the psalmist continues in this stanza, with chastening affliction justified as an expression of the LORD's faithfulness (vv. 67, 71, 75). The LORD is creator, but also guide. So the declaration and prayer with which this section opens conveys a plea: "Complete your work in me." Yet the vision goes beyond personal perfection to the hope that others may see and profit (v. 79). The psalmist again acknowledges his total dependence upon the LORD. He offers five petitions in verses 76-80, each beginning with the word *Let*. These petitions are for *comfort* in the LORD's *steadfast love* (v. 76), life-giving *mercy* (v. 77), vindication that *the arrogant* may be *put to shame* (v. 78), the power of witness to others who *fear* the LORD (v. 79), and fidelity in living in God's will and way (v. 80).

Cry from the Darkness
119:81-88   Kâp (כ)

Hear the sobbing in each of these verses. The obedient servant of God, persecuted by enemies, is facing the end of life. The circumstances are all darkness, and worst of all is the apparent abandonment by God. Lament follows upon lament: *My soul languishes*, or "is wasting away" (v. 81). *My eyes fail*, or "I am worn out" (v. 82). *I have become like a wineskin* alludes to old leather wineskins, which shrivel up in the smoke of a primitive house, becoming black and unsightly (v. 83). The persecution by foes continues (vv. 84-87). The questions (vv. 82, 84) are connected, implying: "How many (really, how few) are my days—help me in time!" Yet in the darkness the psalmist finds glimmers of light: *I hope, I have not forgotten, Your commandments are enduring, I have not forsaken your precepts* (vv. 81, 83, 86, 87). The stanza ends with the psalmist's appeal to God's *steadfast love* (ḥesed, v. 88).

The Foundation of Faith
119:89-96   Lāmed (ל)

In Hebrew, this stanza opens with (and thus stresses) the word translated *forever*. The psalmist reaches out for stability and finds it in the LORD's word (v. 89; Isa 40:8). As an example of divine reliability and loyalty, the psalmist cites the creation of the earth and the LORD's care of it (vv. 89-91; Ps 89:2). All creation stands in the relation of servanthood and obedience to the Creator (v. 91). So imperishable is the consoling word of God that the psalmist *would have perished* without it (v. 92). He now affirms his new determination: *I will never forget your precepts. . . . I am yours* (vv. 93-94). At this point, lament and petition again break in (v. 95). The stanza ends with an insight: *I have seen a limit to all perfection, but your commandment is exceedingly broad* (v. 96). Use of *perfection* here may be in the sense of wholeness, completeness. The psalmist contrasts the limitation of all earthly things with the unlimited nature of the divine commandment, or perhaps recognizes that fulfillment of God's commandment falls short of what it should be.

Oh, How I Love Your Law!
119:97-104   Mêm (מ)

These verses reflect the psalmist's delight of life through the *law* (*torah*). The stanza contains no petition, but it joyously declares the heart's delight in the superior wisdom that comes from *meditation* on the law (vv. 97, 99). Observe the threefold comparison. Through the divine law, he is wiser than his enemies (v. 98), has more understanding than his teachers (v. 99), and understands better than those with a lifetime of experiences (v. 100). All this, because *you* (emphatic) *have taught me* (v. 102). Intimate acquaintance with the word of the LORD produces a careful walk (v. 101) and delightful enjoyment (v. 103; Ps 19:10; Jer 15:16; Ezek 3:3). *I love your law!* (vv. 97, 113, 163) stands in sharp contrast to what the psalmist hates or rejects (vv. 104, 113, 163).

Light upon the Way
119:105-112   Nûn (נ)

Here the psalmist uses the image of a pilgrim passing through a world of darkness, in which it would be easy to lose one's way. The *word is a lamp* to show the way, proclaims this most frequently quoted verse of Psalm 119 (v. 105). The *oath* (v. 106) may originally have been rooted in a ceremonial. Lament and petition return as the darkness of living in constant danger is described: *Severely afflicted* (v. 107, "at low ebb"), *I hold my life in my hand* (v. 109; Judg 12:3) and dodge the *snare* of the wicked (v. 110). Yet as the darkness closes in, the enlightenment of the word keeps him from straying (vv. 105-106, 109-110). Amid the threatening darkness, there is joy (v. 111) and renewed commitment (v. 112). The stanza closes with complete abandonment to the will of God. When the possession of the land was lost, the heritage of the law became all-important (vv. 111-112).

In Awe of God's Judgments
119:113-120   Sāmek (ס)

In this stanza, the psalmist contemplates the course of the wicked. After declaring hatred for the *double-minded*, those who "ride the fence," he asserts his love and single-minded devotion to God's *law* and *word* (vv. 113-114). Indeed, his shelter and strength is in the LORD (v. 114). Now he addresses the *evildoers* (v. 115)—the only verse, in addition to verses 1-3, not addressing God. He calls the LORD *my God*, whose promise he believes will sustain him in the difficulties he faces. Petitioning God to *hold* him up (vv. 116-117), he reflects on the fate of the wicked (vv. 118-119). Such contemplation of God's judgments *makes my flesh creep* (v. 120 NEB). Love for the LORD's decrees (v. 119) creates, in the obedient person, an overwhelming reverence for the awesome God (v. 120).

Hope for God's Servant in Distress
119:121-128 'ayin (ע)

The stanza opens on a despairing note. Even though the poet has *done what is just and right*, oppressors are ever present (vv. 121-122). He pleads for the LORD's intervention to protect him on the basis of his integrity to the divine law (v. 121), but especially because of the LORD's *promise* and *steadfast love* (vv. 123-124). Three times the psalmist refers to himself as the LORD's *servant* (vv. 122, 124, 125), indicating his dependence upon God and his claim of personal relationship based on covenant. He asks for the mercy of learning and understanding (vv. 124-125). Tired of waiting (v. 123), he declares his conviction that *it is time for the LORD to act*, to administer justice by saving the oppressed and punishing the wicked (v. 126; Pss 7:6; 17:13; 102:13; Jer 18:23). The stanza ends with a declaration of certainty that the precepts of the LORD are right, indeed, more to be desired *than gold* (vv. 127-128; Pss 19:10; 119:72; Prov 8:10, 19; 16:16).

Your Word Is Wonderful!
119:129-136 Pê (פ)

The psalmist begins the next stanza with enthusiastic appreciation for the divine instruction (v. 129). The LORD's *words* illumine the inner life so that the soul longs for more (vv. 130-131). The prayer contains a series of requests (vv. 132-135; Davidson, 1998:401). Be true to your *gracious* character (v. 132). *Steady* me when the going gets rough (v. 133). *Redeem me* when I am up against the wall (v. 134). Turn your face toward me and *teach me* (v. 135). The stanza ends with an expression of sorrow, *streams of tears because your law is not kept* (v. 136). Implied is the psalmist's grief for those who seem oblivious to the wonder of life in God's marvelous will.

You Are Righteous, Your Word Is Righteous
119:137-144 Ṣādê (צ)

The words *right, righteous,* and *righteousness* dominate this stanza (vv. 137, 138, 142, 144), likely because the first letter of each line must begin with *ṣādê*, the first letter of the Hebrew word translated *righteous* (*ṣadîq*). The psalmist affirms that the LORD is righteous, so his word is also fully trustworthy. His promises are reliable because they have been tested and found genuine (v. 140). After opening affirmations (vv. 137-138) is a description of experiences through which the psalmist has come to his conclusion (vv. 139-144). The writer's self-portrait (vv. 141, 143) expresses lament in feeling insignificant and vulnerable. Yet he has a burning passion centered on the LORD's instruction and promises (vv. 139-143). At the end he prays for still further understanding (v. 144) *[Righteous]*.

Sustained by Memories of God's Faithfulness in the Past
119:145-152   Qôp (ק)

I cry, I cry to you, I . . . cry for help. So the stanza opens (vv. 145-147). The psalmist, under threat by persons of *evil purpose* (v. 150), is sustained by memories of God's faith in times past (v. 152). Anticipating the set times and seasons for prayer, his whole life revolves around a daily pattern of devotion (vv. 147-148). Relying on the LORD's *promise, steadfast love,* and *justice,* he dares to cry out to the LORD: *Preserve my life* (vv. 148-149). Even though his persecutors are near, there is a greater reality: *You are near, O LORD* (vv. 150-151). In the dark days it is good to strengthen the heart by remembering (Morgan: 112).

The Plea for Life
119:153-160   Rêš (ר)

As the psalm draws toward its close, the psalmist's plea for life becomes more urgent (vv. 154, 156, 159). This repeated appeal emphasizes the extent to which the petitioner feels under threat of the wicked. Hostile surroundings are evident by use of the first-person possessive pronoun: *my misery, my cause* (as of a suit at law), *my persecutors, my adversaries* (vv. 153, 154, 157). In contrast, the psalmist asserts his fidelity (vv. 157, 159) and pleads with the LORD to be his advocate (v. 154). He rests his case on the LORD's *promise* (v. 154), *mercy* (v. 156), *justice* (v. 156), and *steadfast love* (v. 159). The stanza ends on the certainty of the LORD's word as dependable truth (v. 160).

Peace in Love of God's Law
119:161-168   Śîn (שׂ), šîn (שׁ)

This stanza, in common with verses 97-104, contains no petition. After the opening lament about powerful persecutors, the psalmist moves into a hymn of thanksgiving and praise for God's law (*torah*). Verses 161-162 show the tension between awe and joy, with the metaphor of finding *great spoil*, precious treasure in God's *word*. He affirms his intense love for God's law (vv. 163, 165, 167). *Seven times* (v. 164), rather than the literal number, suggests praise continually. *Great peace* (shalom, *šālôm,* v. 165) is a comprehensive term, meaning welfare, well-being, health, rather than only an inner peace. The psalmist describes the marks of the pious person's commitment as love for and obedience to the *torah* (vv. 167-168). The NEB translates the last line: *All my life lies open before thee.*

Teach Me, Help Me, Seek Me
119:169-176   Tāw (ת)

In this stanza, unlike the previous one, petitions predominate. All of them convey the earnest desire to know and do the will of God. They reflect the sense of need, but also a profound conviction of the sufficiency of God's will. Six of the verses begin with *let* or *may* (vv. 169-173, 175, NIV, NEB, NASB), but even verses 174 and 176 convey petition. The last verse sounds the note of urgency: *I have gone astray like a lost sheep* (v. 176). This could be the psalmist's confession of a sense of failure in keeping all of God's law. Or the metaphor may depict defenselessness, that like a lost sheep, the writer needs the protection of the shepherd (Ps 23; Isa 53:6; Jer 50:6; Ezek 34:16). Yet the final word is not that of failure, but the affirmation of loyalty of intention and purpose: *I do not forget your commandments!*

THE TEXT IN THE BIBLICAL CONTEXT AND LIFE OF THE CHURCH

Placing the Psalm

In the development of the Psalter, Psalm 119 may at one time have served as conclusion to an earlier collection comprising Psalms 1–119, framed by the two psalms that express devotion to the *torah* (Pss 1; 119; Westermann, 1989:294). Placed after the *Hallel* collection (113-118) in book V, Psalm 119 further responds to the crisis of exile and its aftermath by proclaiming God's sovereignty, by recalling past deliverance, and by praying for future deliverance. Psalm 119 is prominent in the Qumran discoveries, with 114 of its verses preserved in the *Psalm Scroll* labeled 11Q5 (11QPs^a). The Qumran sect was preoccupied with the Law of Moses, with frequent references to Psalm 119, with (e.g.) the phrase, *those whose way is blameless* (v. 1; Holladay: 109) *[Composition].*

In Psalm 119 (as in Ps 19), *torah* implies the body of legal formulations that comprise the instruction of the LORD. These psalms are products of a period when the community was making written legal collections and shifting to a concern for the precise memory of those written collections. Ezra the scribe came from Babylon to Jerusalem in the second half of the fifth century BC with a copy of the *Torah* of Moses (Ezra 7:1-26, esp. 14; Neh 7:73–8:18), which he read and taught to the assembled people in Jerusalem (Holladay: 63).

Psalm 119 reflects devotion to the received tradition (vv. 97-98, 103-104), but illustrates openness to new experiences of the divine word (vv. 97-98, 103-104). Torah is not a set of rules, but a mode of God's life-giving presence. Torah obedience is a starting point for a life of utter trust and submission. The psalm shows how obeying the law as God's instruction emanates from a deep and loving relationship with the Lawgiver.

Fostering the Life of Faith

The psalm has had wide use in both Jewish and Christian faith communities as a document fostering faith rooted in the word of God. Mays (1994b:384-85) summarizes values of such scriptural piety. God's instruction in all forms is important because it is God's. The word of God calls for both obedience and faith. The word of God is given but never possessed. The instruction comes from God, yet it must infill the life of the servant of God.

As we *meditate* (vv. 15, 23, 27, 48, 78, 148), go over these words in thought and linger upon them, we allow God to speak in the silence of our hearts. The repetition of letter by letter, line by line, quiets our hearts and allows the present moment to be filled with the LORD's presence. Praying this psalm can lead us into hidden depths of meaning, not only about God as the center of life, but also about relationships, forgiveness, and obedience.

Since Psalm 119 focuses on God's word, Christians will remember the NT declaration of Christ as the Word (John 1:1-18; Rev 1:8; 19:13; 21:6; 22:13). So one might pray Psalm 119 as a psalm about Jesus, with each of the psalm's testimonials to the law, the precepts, the commandments referring to the One of whom the law prophesies and in whom it is fulfilled (Reardon: 238). Or the Christian might think of being open to God's instruction in terms of what Paul calls "maturity," of reaching "the measure of the full stature of Christ" (Eph 4:13). This does not come about simply by obeying a set of rules. Becoming "like Christ" means to depend on God at all times, to be dedicated and open to God's guidance and instruction (McCann, 1993:37).

Of many NT allusions to verses in Psalm 119, we cite only one: 2 Corinthians 6:11 and Psalm 119:32. Paul historicizes the acrostic by altering the petition of the lament, *I run in the path of your commands, for you have set my heart free.* He turns it into an accomplished fact: "and opened wide our hearts to you" (NIV). Yet now the object of enlargement is not the pursuit of Torah piety, but rather the reconciliation between Paul and his congregation. What the psalmist wished for, what for him lay in the future, was for Paul a present reality (Harrisville: 175).

Above all, Psalm 119 deals with a place to stand. J. Clinton McCann Jr. (1993:36) tells a story of Nathan Sharansky, a dissident Jew jailed in 1977 for his opposition to the Soviet Union. He was subjected to harsh treatment, at times put in solitary confinement, and left almost to starve. When freed from prison, he had one thing in his possession, a Hebrew copy of Psalms, which his wife had given him. Two things saved him in prison. One was an awareness of his wife's persistent efforts to obtain his release. The other was his reading, memorizing, and reciting of psalms. Once, before he was released, the prison authorities seized his Hebrew Psalter and would not give it back to him. He lay down in the snow and refused to move unless they did so. McCann comments that this had nothing to do with naive optimism or self-righteous legalism. "It has everything to do with delighting in and meditating on *torah*; it has everything to do with being open to God's instruction; it has everything to do with being open to God's presence in the face of unimaginable opposition and open to God's power to transform the most hopeless of situations. In short, it has everything to do with having a 'place to stand.'" Psalm 119 offers a place to stand.

Psalm 120

People of Peace in a World of War

PREVIEW

Psalms 120–134 represent a collection of psalms within the Psalter with each entitled *A Song of Ascents [Composition]*. Commentators are not certain what "ascents" refers to, but the traditional explanation takes it as a song sung when ascending to Jerusalem, because Jerusalem is elevated above the surrounding countryside (except Bethlehem, to the south). Interpretations given the title, *A Song of Ascents,* include the steplike repetition of certain words and phrases within a psalm (Ps 121:1 and 2, 3 and 4, 4 and 5); the fifteen steps in the temple from the Court of the Women up to the Court of Israel, where the Levites were said to have sung these psalms (so the Mishnah, ca. AD 200: *Sukkah* 4:4; *Middot* 2:5); psalms sung on the return to Jerusalem from Babylonian exile (Ezra 2:1; 7:7-9); and a collection of psalms chanted by pilgrims coming up to Jerusalem to celebrate one of the major festivals (Deut 16:16). The last is the most prevalent view, giving rise to understanding the Songs of Ascents as the pilgrims' song and prayer book.

Though we find a variety of psalm types and themes in this collection of fifteen, common to all is their brevity and felicity. They reflect a communal orientation and joy in Zion as God's chosen abode. Liturgical phrases are frequent. Two major concerns are protection and blessing (with frequent use of the words *bless, peace,* and *good*). They relate to issues of everyday life that might occupy the minds of lay pilgrims: neighborhood (Ps 120:5-6), daily routine (121:8), relatives and friends (122:8), work and families (127; 128), kindred living together (133:1). Psalms 120–134 thus reflect a pattern of convictions and concerns appropriate for a pilgrim piety (Mays, 1994b:386).

In Psalm 120, a pilgrim living in an alien environment has returned home to the sanctuary and cries to God for deliverance, or has returned to the temple to give thanks to the LORD for answered prayer in deliverance (Explanatory Notes on vv. 1-2). The call for God's judgment upon the enemies continues (vv. 3-4). He describes his predicament as a sojourner committed to peace, living among a people of violence. Psalm 120 reflects relief from the constant friction of life in hostile surroundings, which a sacred pilgrimage could offer.

Psalm 120 follows naturally upon the conclusion of 119, whose writer, surrounded on all sides by apostasy and persecution, compares himself to a sheep that is easily lost and in danger of perishing (119:176). In Psalm 120, the speaker has suffered from being among a people who did not observe the LORD's precepts. In the Songs of Ascents, those who know the instruction of the LORD turn their faces toward the temple to worship.

OUTLINE

Confident Appeal for Deliverance or Thanksgiving for Answered Prayer, 120:1-2
Retribution upon the Enemies, 120:3-4
The Psalmist's Predicament: A Sojourner Among People of War, 120:5-7

EXPLANATORY NOTES

Confident Appeal for Deliverance or Thanksgiving for Answered Prayer   120:1-2

The NRSV's wording of verse 1 assumes Psalm 120 as a lament. However, the verbs in past tense (NEB, NASB, NIV implied) may be more accurate. Then, as many commentators suggest, this becomes a psalm of thanksgiving for an answered lament. The cry of distress recalled (v. 1) and the cry for help (v. 2) show that the petitioner has experienced persecution and threats from *lying lips* and *a deceitful tongue* (Pss 5:9; 57:4; 64:2-4).

Retribution upon the Enemies   120:3-4

The psalmist is confident of the LORD's retribution upon the enemies. *What more* (v. 3) calls to mind the formula used for an oath or curse: "May God do so to you and more also . . ." (1 Sam 3:17; 25:22; 2 Sam 3:9; 1 Kings 2:23). If someone has made such slander under oath, the perjury will bring a quick end. Malice will receive its recompense (Pss 5:6; 28:4). The slanderous tongue, likened to *sharp arrows* and *glowing coals* (v. 4), will be destroyed with God's *arrows* of truth (64:7-8) and *coals* of judgment (140:9-11).

The Psalmist's Predicament: A Sojourner Among People of War   120:5-7

The pilgrim, an alien (sojourner), refers to *Meshech* and *Kedar* (v. 5). Meshech is the name of an ancient people of northeast Asia Minor (Gen 10:2; Ezek 27:13). Kedar refers to a desert tribe from north Arabia (Isa 21:16-17; 42:11). These two places are so far apart geographically that they likely are metaphorical for "barbarians." The names imply the alien company in which the pilgrim lives, as foreign as the remotest peoples and hostile enemies (Ezek 38:1-4).

In these verses the pilgrim laments that though he seeks to foster caring relationships, those around him sow the seeds of conflict (vv. 6-7). With the shrill dissonance of *peace* and *war*, the psalm ends. Psalm 120 reflects the homesickness of those who live among strangers and enemies. Living in a foreign land and with no legal rights and protection, these people of faith could only take refuge in the LORD. This is reason for the pilgrimage to Jerusalem, center of peace, for such a weary, longing pilgrim (Ps 122:6-9).

THE TEXT IN THE BIBLICAL CONTEXT AND LIFE OF THE CHURCH

Living in a Violent World

The motif of the *deceitful tongue* (vv. 2-3) punctuates the Scriptures (Prov 17:20; Jer 9:8; Zeph 3:13). The letter of James provides striking commentary on the dangers of the untamed tongue—"a restless evil, full of deadly poison" (James 3:8). Persons, communities, and even nations pay a heavy price for the conflict and division sown by *lying lips* and *deceitful tongues*. James 1:19 gives sound advice, as paraphrased by Peterson: "Lead with your ears, follow up with your tongue, and let anger straggle along in the rear."

In Psalm 120 the pilgrim prays against the atmosphere of antagonism in which he constantly dwells. He is weary of living among those who will not even return the friendly greeting *peace (shalom)*, but whose response is uncivil hostility. The people of God have to live within an antagonistic world and try to love it. Jesus reminded his followers, "If the world hates you, be aware that it hated me before it hated you" (John 15:18). The epistle of 1 Peter provides commentary with reference to the "sojourn" of the church in the world. Peter exhorts "the exiles of the Dispersion in Pontus, Galatia, Cappadocia, Asia, and Bithynia" (1 Pet 1:1), beset by various trials (1:6) and maligned by evildoers (2:12, 20), to live as God's people. He holds out to them the model of the suffering Christ: "When he was abused, he did not return abuse; when he suffered, he did not threaten; but he entrusted himself to the one who judges justly" (2:23). Believers are not ultimately "at home" in this world (John 18:36).

That is particularly true for those who seek to follow Jesus Christ as the Prince of Peace. The NT portrays Jesus not only as a teacher or example of what peace means, but further, as the letter to the Ephesians declares, "He is our peace" (2:14), creating a new reconciled humanity. Following the LORD as peacemaker is by traveling the costly path of service and sacrifice. Psalm 120 poses the question for every generation: How do we speak for peace when the society in which we live chooses war? Where and how do people of peace find renewal of conviction and courage in a world of war?

Psalm 121

The LORD Is Your Keeper

PREVIEW

In Psalm 121 we come to one of the best-known psalms in Christian liturgy, hymnody, and piety. As the second *Song of Ascents*, it reflects the experiences, both the anxiety and trust, of pilgrims who came up to the temple in Jerusalem for the great festivals (Deut 16:16). The declaration, *My help comes from the LORD* (v. 2), answers the question with which the psalm opens (v. 1). The psalm develops this response in a series of assurances about the LORD as *your keeper* (vv. 3-8). This sixfold focus on the LORD who *keeps* (šāmar) the pilgrim on his way (vv. 3-4), protects day and night (vv. 5-6), and watches over all of life (vv. 7-8)—this has made it a psalm of trust and comfort to people of faith in all generations.

Questions about the origin and setting of Psalm 121 focus on the use of first-person speech (*I*) in verses 1 and 2, and second-person address (*you/your*) in verses 3-8. This suggests dialogue, but dialogue with whom? Is the psalmist conversing with himself, a father speaking with his son, or a worshipper with the priest? Furthermore, is the pilgrim setting out on the journey to Jerusalem? Has the pilgrim just arrived in the temple? Or is this a liturgy of blessing before returning home? Many commentators have come to understand the psalm in the latter sense, as a priestly blessing as the pilgrim is departing the temple for the hazardous journey home. The psalm is an appropriate farewell liturgy, suited for the beginning of a journey to or from Jerusalem.

OUTLINE

The Inquiry and Confession of Trust (First Person), 121:1-2
The Blessing and Promises (Second Person), 121:3-8
    121:3-4   The Attentive LORD Guards the Pilgrim on the Way
    121:5-6   The LORD Protects by Day and Night
    121:7-8   The LORD Watches over All of Life

EXPLANATORY NOTES

The Inquiry and Confession of Trust   121:1-2

Pilgrims en route to Jerusalem, especially from the north and east via Transjordan and Jericho, would face the wilderness hills, an ascent of nearly 4,000 feet (from 1,300 below sea level to 2,600 above) and dangerous because of beasts and bandits. In this situation, the question was pressing: From what quarter might one seek help? Or, about to return home from Jerusalem, the people look anxiously at the hills. Danger lies along those roads, and protection is a burning issue for travelers through lonely country (Luke 10:30). From where will protective help come (v. 1)? Though *the hills* may also be the hills of Jerusalem on which the temple stood, or the hilltops around Jerusalem where shrines of other gods were located (2 Kings 23:5; Jer 3:23), the hills are not the travelers' surety. It is *the LORD* who is their help, *the LORD, who made heaven and earth* (v. 2; Pss 124:8; 134:3). The doctrine of creation is one of the basic facts of faith, vitally relevant to one's daily life (Pss 65:6; 115:15; 146:5-6).

The Blessing and Promises   121:3-8

In the pilgrim's moment of anxiety, the priest gives the blessing (vv. 3-8), committing into God's protecting care the traveler about to embark on the perilous journey. Behind these words we can recognize the blessing as given in Numbers 6:24-26.

    The verb *keep* (šāmar, vv. 3, 4, 5, 7, 8), "watch over" or "guard," describes a basic activity of God. Psalm 121 is centered entirely on the expression of confidence in the LORD's "keeping watch," yet that theme runs throughout the psalms (Pss 25:20; 34:20; 86:2; 97:10; 116:6; 127:1). Furthermore, the mighty creator God watches over *you*. The LORD does not *slumber nor sleep*, in contrast to the vegetation gods of Israel's neighbors, who "slept" during winter months and were revived in seasons of growth and harvest, or had to be awakened by intense cajoling (1 Kings 18:27-28).

The rest of the psalm swells the note of confidence sounded in verses 2 and 4. The LORD guards every step (vv. 3-4), and protects day and night (vv. 5-6). The possibility of sunstroke in Palestine is real (Isa 49:10), and superstitions have abounded for centuries about the moon causing illness and affecting behavior (Ps 91:5-6; Matt 17:15, Greek word translated "epileptic" means "moonstruck"). The LORD as *shade* (v. 5) also has metaphorical meanings associated with the safety of the temple (Pss 17:8; 36:7; 61:4; 91:1).

Finally, the blessing moves to the promise that God will keep the pilgrim from every kind of danger (vv. 7-8). The LORD will watch and protect *from all evil*, from all misfortune, even *your going out and your coming in*. That could mean "your departure and return home," or "your return to the sanctuary next time," or "all your undertakings and affairs" (Deut 28:6). Out of this psalm's vision of God that embraces creation, history, and eternity "has grown that unshakable strength springing from trust in God which has caused this song to become a source of comfort that even today does not cease to flow" (Weiser: 749).

THE TEXT IN THE BIBLICAL CONTEXT AND LIFE OF THE CHURCH

A Farewell Liturgy for Many Occasions

The personal reception of a blessing forms the subject matter of both Psalms 91 and 121. In both, the avowal of trust precedes the bestowal of blessing. The recipient does not passively accept the blessing, but receives it with a trusting heart.

In Jewish worship, Psalm 121 is one of the psalms of confidence recited for the morning services of the Sabbath and of the great festivals. Family members also refer to Psalm 121:8 daily on entering or exiting the home, as they touch the mezuzah fastened to the doorframe. This small metal cylinder contains a piece of parchment on which are written the words of Deuteronomy 6:4-9 and 11:13-21.

The NT recognizes the assurance of God's help and protection, particularly in passages that refer to the protective care offered in Jesus to those who belong to him. Jesus is the Good Shepherd (John 10:11-15, 27-30), "the shepherd and guardian" of souls who trust in him (Phil 4:7; 1 Pet 2:25). The church came to understand Psalm 121 as a testimony to God's providence in the life of believers through Jesus Christ (Mays 1994b:390). In the Apostles' Creed, the church continues to voice the ancient confession: "I believe in God the Father Almighty, maker of heaven and earth" (Ps 121:2).

Christian liturgy has used Psalm 121 widely, including services for baptism, comforting the bereaved, and burying the dead. It has been used in ministering to those addicted, and the last verse is part of an order for the blessing of a dwelling (Limburg, 1985:180). The lectionary places Psalm 121 in the period immediately before Advent. The psalm may help prepare for Advent during a time of "pilgrimage" to that season of the church year. Two widely used hymns based on this psalm are "I to the hills will lift mine eyes" (*Scottish Psalter,* 1650; music, 1615), and "Unto the hills around" (John Campbell, 1866). In these hymns, "hills" is taken as a metaphor for God and not as symbol of danger. Two of the songs in Mendelssohn's oratorio, *Elijah,* draw on Psalm 121, "Lift thine eyes" and "He, watching over Israel."

The Traveler's Psalm

As a psalm for travelers, it is well-suited for reading or reciting at the beginning of a journey. But in embracing the whole of life, Psalm 121 also serves the sojourner. The metaphor of journey or sojourn, favorite for the religious mind, comes from biblical examples. We think of Abraham and Sarah, Israel's sojourn in Egypt and exodus to Canaan, the exile and return, Jesus' ministry and calling of people to "follow me" in the way of discipleship, and Paul's mission travels and the life of the early Christian church. Paul could testify that no perils along the way, "neither death, nor life, nor angels, nor rulers, nor things present, nor things to come, nor powers, nor height, nor depth, nor anything else in all creation, will be able to separate us from the love of God in Christ Jesus our Lord" (Rom 8:38-39).

When viewed as a psalm for the journey of life, it is helpful to reflect on the extravagant claim of Psalm 121 that the LORD will keep *from all evil* (v. 7). Nevertheless, there are perils along the way (cf. Job, Ecclesiastes, or Paul's testimony, above). That may be precisely the reason for affirming such confident assurance in worship, even when there appears to be disjunction between faith affirmations and the realities of life. The *help* that comes from the Lord is help to face the evils, not simply to avoid the evils, for God's keeping is "more than all" (Ps 87:2), more powerful than all evil.

The use of Psalm 121 for personal piety and in corporate worship has an astonishingly wide focus. It sends us forth with a benediction resounding in our ears.

Psalm 122

Pray for the Peace of Jerusalem

PREVIEW

This pilgrim psalm, one of the Songs of Zion (Pss 46; 48; 76; 84; 87), provides a religious tourist's description of coming to the Holy City *[Zion]*. On arriving in Jerusalem, feelings of joy and wonder dominate (vv. 1-2). The splendor of the city lay not in its great buildings; rather, Zion stood for all that was central to the life of the people: security, worship, and justice (vv. 3-5). Patriotic and pious, the pilgrim prays for the peace of Jerusalem and prosperity for all who love the city (vv. 6-9).

Attention focuses on the temple (vv. 1, 4, 9). Pilgrimages to the three major festivals, Passover, Weeks, and Tabernacles, were rooted in the decrees of Exodus 23:14-17 and Deuteronomy 16:16-17. The occasion for this group pilgrimage may have been the celebration of the Feast of Tabernacles, to *give thanks to the name of the LORD* for the bounty of harvest (v. 4).

OUTLINE

The Pilgrim's Joy on Arriving in Jerusalem, 122:1-2
Reasons for the Praise of Jerusalem 122:3-5
Prayer for the Peace of Jerusalem, 122:6-9

EXPLANATORY NOTES

The Pilgrim's Joy on Arriving in Jerusalem 122:1-2

This psalm appears to be the joyous exclamation of a pilgrim who has just arrived within the city gates (vv. 1-2). It mentions *Jerusalem* three times (vv. 2, 3, 6). Psalm 84 expresses the same sense of joy at being in the Jerusalem temple. Use of *house of the LORD* (vv. 1, 9) forms an inclusio.

Reasons for the Praise of Jerusalem 122:3-5

After reference to the fortified city with its protecting walls (v. 3), Jerusalem is praised as the center for worship of the LORD (v. 4; Exod 34:23). People feel a sense of overwhelming unity in this city, where all the tribes gather. It is also the ancient seat of government where the kings of David's line had reigned and judged (v. 5; 2 Sam 8:15; Isa 16:5; Jer 21:12). The reference to *the house of David* (v. 5) may be the reason *Of David* appears in the psalm heading [Superscriptions].

Prayer for the Peace of Jerusalem 122:6-9

The prayer for the *peace of Jerusalem*, a form of blessing on the city, begins thus: ša'ălû šělôm yěrûšălāim. In Hebrew, the alliteration of the words—*pray, peace* (*shālôm* used three times in vv. 6-8), *Jerusalem*, and *prosper*—reminds us that in this case Jerusalem is more than a name and more than a city. The psalm sees the city of God, and the house of God within the city, as a place where peace reigns and from which salvation springs to transform the people of God.

THE TEXT IN THE BIBLICAL CONTEXT AND LIFE OF THE CHURCH

Peace for Jerusalem?

The invitation to pilgrimage, with which the psalm begins, ultimately became the invitation to many peoples to come to Jerusalem in order to receive instruction in the LORD, in the ways that make for peace (Isa 2:2-4; Mic 4:1-4). The psalm reminds us of Jesus' pilgrimage to Jerusalem with his parents (Luke 2:41-51), and Jesus' later entry when he wept over the Holy City, "If you, even you, had only recognized on this day the things that make for peace" (Luke 19:41-42).

But can there be peace for Jerusalem? Peace for the city David fortified in (ca.) 1000 BC and Nebuchadnezzar destroyed in 587 (or 586) BC? Some Jews returned from exile in 537 BC and rebuilt the city and temple by 515 BC. The Syrians invaded Palestine and profaned the temple in Maccabean times, 169–142 BC. In 63 BC Pompey captured Jerusalem for Rome, in AD 70 the Roman legions of Titus destroyed Jerusalem and its temple, and in 135 the Romans again leveled the city center. The Byzantines controlled the city in 324 to 638. In 614 the Persians destroyed most churches and expelled Jews. In 638 Muslim Crusaders took Jerusalem, in 1099 Christian Crusaders, in 1517 the Turks, and 1917 the British. The war of 1948 divided the city, and in 1967 the Six-Day War was in the streets. At the beginning of the twenty-first century, violence continues to rock this "city of peace." *Pray for the peace of Jerusalem* are words that Jews, Christians, and Muslims urgently speak.

The Holy City

Jerusalem is a Holy City for three of the world's great religions. This city—where for centuries shrines hallowed by the feet and prayers and tears of pilgrims have expressed the highest aspirations of people—continues as symbol of hope and peace. A vision of God's "holy city" as center of unity, law, peace, and worship appears in the closing verses of the Bible (Rev 21:2-4).

Focus on Jerusalem should not, however, diminish a Christian application of this psalm drawn from what verse 8 expresses: *For the sake of my relatives and friends I will say, "Peace be within you."* The assembled community, the friends who have come together in the name of Jesus Christ, understand themselves as the Jerusalem of the new covenant and as belonging to the Israel of God (Gal 6:16; Kraus, 1989:435). Consequently, believers have also used Psalm 122 as a prayer that the church on earth will enjoy tranquility, in which to serve God toward the peace of the whole world and the unity of all peoples (Reardon: 244).

During Advent one could base preaching on Psalm 122. What the psalmist experienced in Jerusalem was a sign that "the Lord is here" amid the dark realities of a world filled with danger (cf. Ezek 48:35). Eli Wiesel's *A Beggar in Jerusalem* says of Jerusalem that "no one can enter it and go away unchanged." During Advent we wait, experience, proclaim, and work for the justice and peace that God intends for the world. The affirmation that "the LORD is here" makes all the difference in the world (McCann, 1992:13).

Psalm 123

Our Eyes Look to the LORD Our God

PREVIEW

In Psalm 123, a petitioner speaks for the community. The lament of an individual (v. 1) moves to the lament of a group (vv. 2-4). The psalm is an upward look of expectant faith to the LORD amid tyrannical oppression (vv. 1, 4). The supplicant voices the people's dependence on the LORD (v. 2), pleads for grace toward their humiliation (v. 3a), and in the description of trouble, provides motivation for divine action (vv. 3b-4).

Ridicule and mockery prompt the prayer (vv. 3-4). These might be foreign oppressors during the exile and postexilic dispersion, when the nation was exposed to the *contempt* and *scorn* of arrogant adversaries (Ps 80). A setting of distress, as in the time of Nehemiah, is plausible (Neh 2:17-19; 4:1-8). Psalm 123 is consistent with the character of book V, which appears to be a response to the theological crisis and the need for help that persisted even after the return from exile (Ps 107:2-3; McCann, 1996:1187). Or the psalm could point to conflict within Israel, between the rich and the poor (Amos 6:1). Usually classified as a community lament, the simile of *the eyes* at the center of the text (v. 2) makes this also a psalm of trust (Westermann, 1989:43).

Poetically, the psalm is a gem of repetitive parallelism. Note the stairlike pattern in verses 2-4: *eyes* (vv. 1, 2a, 2b, 2c); *mercy* (vv. 2,

3a, 3b); *had more than* (vv. 3, 4); *contempt* (vv. 3, 4) *[Hebrew Poetry]*.

OUTLINE

Gesture of Obedient Trust and Hope, 123:1-2
Plea for Grace and Motive for Divine Action, 123:3-4

EXPLANATORY NOTES

Gesture of Obedient Trust and Hope   123:1-2

The psalm begins by speaking of *eyes*, a word occurring four times in verses 1 and 2. To lift up the eyes, a gesture of yearning and longing, also expresses trust (Ps 121:1). The heavenly throne (v. 1) is an image that represents the LORD's transcendent, unlimited sovereignty over earth (2:4; 11:4; 115:3).

As the servant looks to the hand of his master or her mistress for everything good (v. 2), so God's people are dependent upon the LORD (104:27-30; 145:15; Isa 30:18). As an expression of humble dependence, Psalm 123 is like 131. People rediscover their dignity and strength when they look to the Lord, their God.

Plea for Grace and Motive for Divine Action   123:3-4

The fervent petition, *Have mercy upon us, O LORD* (v. 3), can also be translated *Be gracious to us* (NASB), *Show us favor* (JNPS), or *Deal kindly with us* (NEB). Laments flow from the lips of those who have had their fill of *contempt* and *scorn* (vv. 3-4; Job 31:34; Pss 42:3, 9-10; 115:2). The similarity of the complaint (vv. 3-4) to Psalms 44:13 and 79:4 would support the hearing of Psalm 123 in a postexilic context. The sense is, "Enough! LORD, we've had it! Help!" Here the cry is directed at the nonchalant, those *at ease* in their privileged position and oblivious to the social implication of their arrogance (Isa 32:9-14; Amos 6:1-7; Zech 1:1-15).

THE TEXT IN THE BIBLICAL CONTEXT AND LIFE OF THE CHURCH

Lament in the Transformation of Bitterness

In this lament, the psalmist heaps no imprecation upon his adversaries, even though their *contempt* is the worst kind of human behavior. Being treated with contempt means being viewed as less than a person, not even as a servant or worker, but as a dog. In this *Song of Ascents*, the pilgrim in his heart brings up to Jerusalem all the bitterness and degradation he and his people have suffered under the Babylonians. Prisoners of war and refugees can be emotionally distraught and embittered for years. Is this a pilgrim's prayer for "peace of heart" (Knight, 2:271)?

God can transform bitterness. Nelson Mandela, who served twenty-seven years as a political prisoner in South Africa, was released in 1990. When inaugurated as president of South Africa in 1994, he introduced three of his former jailers from Robben Island. As a young man with a quick temper, he had time in prison to look deeply into his own heart. When he walked out of prison a free man, he said, "I knew if I didn't leave my bitterness behind, I'd still be in prison" (Clinton: 206).

Worship often plays a powerful role in such freeing of the heart. The "Kyrie eleison" ("Lord, have mercy," a Greek refrain) has a central place in liturgies of Eastern, Roman Catholic, and some mainline churches. Such a plea for mercy echoes the NT story of the blind men crying out to Jesus, "Have mercy on us, Son of David" (Matt 9:27).

This psalm reminds us of the irony that the high and mighty (*at ease*), whom people often look up to with respect and even servility, too often look down in indifference and contempt. Yet the Lord *enthroned in the heavens* looks down in mercy. The trustful raising of the eyes to heaven is certainly a component of prayer in the book of Psalms (25:15; 141:8). It is also the opening expression in the prayer of our Lord: "Our Father in heaven" (Matt 6:9).

Psalm 124

Deliverance from a Close Call

PREVIEW

In this *Song of Ascents*, the psalmist calls on all Israel to join in thanksgiving for the removal of a serious obstacle that would have blocked their coming to Jerusalem. Psalm 123 was a prayer for help in the face of hostility and opposition; Psalm 124 reports deliverance of the nation from its foes. In this hymn of thanksgiving, the community acknowledges that the LORD alone saved them from impending destruction.

Four dramatic metaphors convey strong emotion about the miraculous escape from near disaster: the monster that swallows whole (v. 3), a raging torrent of floodwater (v. 4), a wild beast stalking its prey (v. 6), and the snare of the fowler (v. 7). But the LORD's sovereignty holds the waters within their bounds and permits the bird in the trap to fly free. A concluding confession affirms the miracle of help in the LORD's name (v. 8).

Traditionally, readers classify this as a song of thanksgiving. Kraus (1989:441-42), however, views Psalm 124 as a prayer instruction to help people gain a new insight into God's never-ending assistance. Westermann (1989:51-54) identifies the shout of praise, *Blessed be the LORD* (v. 6), as the kernel of the psalm and calls this "a communal psalm of praise." The heading ascribes this as a psalm *Of David* (along with 122 and 131 of the fifteen *Songs of Ascents*) *[Superscriptions]*.

The psalm's development shows poetic art. The opening line, *If it had not been the LORD. . .* , is repeated (vv. 1-2). The contrast is set by three statements of *then* to describe the close call (vv. 3-5), and God's saving, liberating intervention (vv. 6-8). The psalm's liturgical use is evident from the invocation, *Let Israel now say* (v. 1; Ps 129:1); the praise formula *Blessed be the LORD* (v. 6); and the closing confessional sentence (v. 8).

OUTLINE

Description of What Might Have Happened, 124:1-5
Grateful Praise for the LORD's Deliverance, 124:6-8

EXPLANATORY NOTES

Description of What Might Have Happened   124:1-5

The psalm opens with reflection on what might have happened without the LORD's intervention. The *enemies* who *attacked* are likened to beasts who swallow their victims alive or rip them to pieces (vv. 3, 6). This is the language used of Death, described as a devouring monster (Pss 55:15; 69:15; Prov 1:12). The other image is that of a raging torrent of water, which destroys everything in its path (vv. 4-5; Pss 18:4; 42:7; 69:2). The psalm does not identify the *enemies*. Perhaps it was a military operation, as suggested in verses 1-3 and 6, or the threat of complete annihilation as the people of God (83:1-8) [*Enemies*].

Grateful Praise for the LORD's Deliverance   124:6-8

But in fact, the LORD did not allow his people to be wiped out (vv. 6-7). The exclamation *Blessed be the LORD* corresponds to "Thank God!" The utterance voices the sigh of relief from people who have found deliverance and safety. The simile of the bird escaping from the snare highlights the issue of freedom. The image denotes defenselessness. Israel is like a bird freed from the trapper's snare (91:3). Israel is ever a liberated people—set free originally from the clutches of Pharaoh, and now from the clutches of the current enemy (the Babylonians, or later oppressors). Note the chiasmus in verse 7: *escaped, snare, snare, escaped*.

The psalm closes with a liturgical confession (v. 8) answering the question implied in verses 1-2: Where or who is our help? Trust in God is based on the LORD's power as creator (115:15; 121:2; 146:5-6). The conclusion affirms the LORD's sovereignty over all he has made, heaven and earth, water and snares. The *enemies* (*'ādām*, v. 2) are men who are weak and vulnerable. Israel knows its help is *in the name of the LORD, who made heaven and earth*!

THE TEXT IN THE BIBLICAL CONTEXT AND LIFE OF THE CHURCH

If God Is for Us

At the heart of Psalm 124 lies the claim that God is *on our side*. The psalm does not blame God for war, human wickedness, and cruelty. Rather, the psalm shouts for joy that God takes sides, that God comes down on the side of the weak and the poor and the suffering masses who live in constant danger (Exod 2:23-25). God helps those who cannot help themselves. When God's people pass through the waters, God is in the flood or in the horrors of the exile along with his people (Isa 43:1-2). God shares the pain and contempt of his servants.

But God is also the God of deliverance who rescues his servants from a great variety of perils (Exod 15:1-18; 2 Cor 11:21-33; Rev 22:1-5). Most important of all for Christians, God "has rescued us from the power of darkness and transferred us into the kingdom of his beloved Son, in whom we have redemption, the forgiveness of sins" (Col 1:13-14). In this sense Menno Simons (57) quotes Psalm 124:7 in his 1536 essay on "The Spiritual Resurrection." That same verse is quoted in *Martyrs Mirror* (Braght: 835) by a sixteenth-century imprisoned Anabaptist, Jan Quirijnss, before he was burned at the stake: "For this reason we may well be glad in our hearts and rejoice, and say with David: 'The snare is broken and we are escaped. . . ,' that is, in this dismal, abominable, subtle, wicked world."

Drawing on Psalm 124's assertion that God is for us, with us, and on our side, it was the custom in Scotland to sing this song in its metrical version on occasions when God had reversed some crisis in national or local history. Claims that God is on one side or another fill human history—as for recent wars in the Middle East. Rather than "God is for us" and against all who oppose us, this psalm of thanksgiving recognizes the limitations of all human power; it grounds faith and hope in the LORD alone. Paul wrote to the Christians at Rome: "If God is for us, who is against us? . . . Who is to condemn? . . . Who will separate us from the love of Christ? . . . In all these things we are more than conquerors through him who loved us" (Rom 8:31-39).

For preaching, this psalm illustrates proclamation of the good news: God's saving deed and word. It affirms that in the difficult times of life, *our help is in the name of the Lord.* For private devotions, the psalm shows that we can always begin by gratefully acknowledging what God has done. "Count your blessings, name them one by one" (Johnson Oatman Jr., 1897).

Psalm 125

Protector of Those Who Trust in the LORD

PREVIEW

The sixth in the *Songs of Ascents* collection (Pss 120–134) is a community song of confidence. A steady, calm faith lies beneath this psalm about those who *trust in the LORD* (v. 1). Other designations for the community of God include *his people* (v. 2), *the righteous* (v. 3), the *good* (v. 4), those *upright in their hearts* (v. 4), and *Israel* (v. 5). These trusting souls are as unshakable as *Mount Zion* (v. 1) because the LORD *surrounds* (*enfolds*, NEB) them with protective care as the *mountains surround Jerusalem* (v. 2). The psalm announces the end to external and internal forces of wickedness (v. 3). It ends with prayer for the LORD's blessing on the faithful and expects him to *lead away* the wicked (vv. 4-5ab). A final liturgical refrain pleads for the salvation of the covenant community (v. 5c).

Regarding its setting, Psalm 125 focuses on Jerusalem and concludes with petitions aimed at the establishment of peace. Like Psalms 123 and 124, the people live under foreign domination. The psalm could be a response to postexilic anxieties about whether God will honor the ancient promises of restoration. What about the promise in Isaiah 57:13? "Whoever takes refuge in me shall possess the land and inherit my holy mountain." The return of the exiles under the leadership of Ezra and Nehemiah provide possible examples; they had conflict with the lax and antagonistic "people of the land" led by

Sanballat, governor of Samaria (Ezra 4:1-5; Neh 2:10, 19; 5:1-5).

Yet, the language about the *scepter of wickedness* (v. 3), those who *turn aside* (v. 5), and *evildoers* (v. 5) is indefinite. It allows for various possibilities, such as foreign occupation, Israelites compromising their faith, or internal divisions within Israel. For pilgrims coming up to Jerusalem, the psalm would speak of the LORD's protective power. The pilgrimage itself served as an enactment of trust.

OUTLINE

Expression of Confidence in the LORD's Protection, 125:1-3
Petition for Recompense to the Just and the Unjust, 125:4-5

EXPLANATORY NOTES

Expression of Confidence in the LORD's Protection 125:1-3

The pilgrim psalms use picturesque figures of speech drawn from everyday life. Here, *those who trust in the LORD* are likened to Mount Zion, the rock on which the temple was built (v. 1) *[Zion]*. Ancient traditions proclaim the stability of Zion, the mountain of God deeply rooted in the womb of the earth (Pss 46; 48; 78:68-69; 87:5; Isa 14:32). As the mountains surround Jerusalem, *so the LORD surrounds his people* with his protective power *forevermore* (v. 2; Ps 34:7; Zech 2:7-12).

That power even affects the situation of internal or external oppression symbolized by the *scepter of wickedness* (v. 3). The seductive inducement to apostasy is subject to God's power. The description of *the land allotted to the righteous* refers back to the time after the conquest when Joshua cast lots for dividing the land among the tribes (Num 26:55-56; Josh 18:6). The land was a gift to those who had committed themselves to the LORD. Stuhlmueller (1983, 2:164) calls attention to the careful nuances in verse 3: "Because the Lord is round about his people, THEN the scepter of the wicked shall not rest upon the land, AND SO the righteous will not put forth their hands to do wrong."

Petition for Recompense to the Just and the Unjust 125:4-5

On the basis of the strong faith expressed (vv. 1-2) and the hope declared (v. 3), the psalmist offers petition that the LORD would bestow the desired blessing of freedom upon the faithful and remove the cowardly and apostate from the community. Those who *are good and upright in their hearts* (v. 4; Pss 7:10; 119:7) are loyal to the LORD. They are his people and will inherit his land (Prov 2:21). Those who *turn aside* (v. 5), the apostates and renegades, the unfaithful among the people of God, will be exiled and forfeit their share in the religious community (Prov 2:22).

Following this psalm's contrast of "two ways"—the wavering end for those who worship false gods and have *crooked* conduct, and the solidity of those who *trust in the LORD* (as in Ps 1)—the final line is a liturgical blessing and prayer for Israel's peace (*shalom, šālôm,* v. 5c). No prayer is uttered with so much anguish and longing as *Peace be upon Israel!* (Pss 29:11; 122:6-9; 128:6).

THE TEXT IN THE BIBLICAL CONTEXT AND LIFE OF THE CHURCH

Probing Implications of Peace Through Trust

If peace (*shalom*) is the end of tyranny, hostility, unrest, and terror; if peace is freedom, harmony, security, and blessedness; then such prayers are not only appropriate but necessary. However, we dare not base security on the relative stability of life's circumstances. Protection and peace are essentially matters of the spirit, not necessarily a deliverance from those who can kill the body.

Reflection on verse 3 of this psalm of trust is intriguing. The people were under domination of a *scepter of wickedness*, under oppression cruel and prolonged. Perhaps the danger was that the righteous might, through loss of faith and in desperation, be tempted to avenge themselves by wrong deeds. What do people show about trust when they take into their own hands the prerogative of God? Is a declaration of war and the ensuing violence defensible for God's people? Is a preemptive strike to depose another national leader morally acceptable? Is defensive killing the appropriate way for God's people?

During the Russian Revolutions (from 1917), nonresistant Mennonite colonies in the Ukraine faced a dilemma: marauding bandits pillaged their defenseless villages. In response, some young men organized a *Selbstschutz* (self-defense) and gave armed resistance to Machno and his ruthless bands of robbers (in 1918–19). How do such acts square with Psalm 125? How does Psalm 53 (the fool saying, "There is no God") and the story of Nabal (taking matters into his own hands and refusing to return favors for aid received; 1 Sam 25) relate to these questions? How do Jesus' words (Matt 20:28) and Paul's (Rom 12:19-21) relate to the temptation to avenge oppressive evil?

Maillot-Lelierre describes this psalm as "a chant of subversion" secretly gathering strength against an oppressive government (via Stuhlmueller, 1983, 2:164).

This psalm assumes that God will do good to the upright and punish the wicked. Psalm 73 sounds another note: this confession of God doing the good is problematic since the wicked prosper and are not destroyed. Experience can call into question the received tradition. Psalm 125:4-5 represents the traditional orthodox doctrine; Psalm 73 cites reasons to question that tradition, yet ends with a redefinition of the *good* (73:28). In this way we not only probe the tradition but also retain and affirm it.

In the NT, the Christian community is designated "the Israel of God" (Gal 6:16), so that wishes for peace such as those expressed in the psalms for Israel (Pss 125:5; 128:6) are extended or transferred to the new people of God (John 14:27). The reformer John Calvin took the identity of Israel and the church so much for granted that he regularly used the word "Church" for the nation Israel. Similarly, the psalm-prayer for Psalm 125 in the Liturgy of the Hours of the Roman Catholic Church reads: "Surround your people, Lord, within the safety of your Church, which you preserve on its rock foundation. Do not let us stretch out our hands to evil deeds, nor be destroyed by the insidious snares of the enemy, but bring us to share the lot of the saints in light" (Holladay: 332).

Psalm 126

Joy Remembered and Joy Anticipated

PREVIEW

As the seventh *Song of Ascents* (Pss 120–134), Psalm 126 voices the pilgrim's remembrance of the LORD's restoration of Zion and pleads for the LORD's intervention once again. Beginning with historical retrospection on how *the LORD has done great things* in the past (vv. 1-3), the plea for God's miracle yet again (v. 4) leads to the consoling promise that those who sow in tears will reap in *shouts of joy* (vv. 5-6).

The psalm's setting appears to be Cyrus' edict of release from Babylonian exile in 538 BC, a miracle that must have seemed unreal to the soon-returning refugees (v. 1). But now, God's people are still in trouble (v. 4). In Israel's frequent experiences of national distress, such a psalm served to keep hope alive in the hearts of the people. Most commentators classify Psalm 126 as a community lament (like Ps 85). Westermann (1989:47) sees in this community lamentation also a psalm of trust based on certainty from earlier experience (vv. 1-3) and the confidence expressed for the future (vv. 5-6).

A striking literary feature is the deliberate echoing of words and phrases: *restore our fortunes* (vv. 1, 4); *then, then* (v. 2); *The LORD has done great things* (vv. 2, 3); and *shouts of joy* (vv. 2, 5, 6). This is a song about joy remembered and joy anticipated.

OUTLINE

Remembering the LORD's Saving Help in Restoring Zion, 126:1-3
Petition for the LORD's Intervention for a New Restoration, 126:4-6

EXPLANATORY NOTES

Remembering the LORD's Saving Help in Restoring Zion   126:1-3

The community's hope lies in reminiscence of previous experiences when divine intervention restored the fortunes of Zion (vv. 1-3) *[Zion]*. The verbs refer to the past. We see a similar structure in Psalm 85: historical retrospect, petition, and promise.

In *restored the fortunes, šûb . . . šĕbût,* (lit.) "to turn a turning" (v. 1), the psalm uses a Hebrew idiom. It suggests "bringing about a change," restoration of an earlier situation between God and people (Pss 14:7; 53:6; 85:1; Jer 29:14; 30:3, 18; 31:23; Hos 6:11; Amos 9:14; Zeph 2:7; 3:20). An earlier understanding of the phrase *šûb . . . šîbat/šĕbût* took it to mean "bring back the captivity," taking the second word in the phrase to derive from "captive." Scholarly consensus now is to see the two words as cognates, "turn the turning" = "restore fortunes" or "bring about a restoration." When the liberated refugees returned from Babylon, they had to remind themselves they were not dreaming. In their changed circumstances, they could express joyous hearts only through laughter and singing (cf. Ps 137). Indeed, the transforming power of God's saving word and deed would even invoke the wonder, praise, and confession of others (vv. 2-3; 98:2; Isa 52:10; Ezek 36:36).

Petition for the LORD's Intervention for a New Restoration   126:4-6

The second part of the psalm, rooted in these memories of the past, is a prayer for the present and the future. The people are still in trouble. Return from the exile was not all it was envisioned to be (see Ps 125). The LORD's continuing intervention was needed. Nothing short of God's miracle would suffice, as declared in the image, *like the water courses in the Negeb* (v. 4). *Negeb* (or *Negev*) means "dry" or "parched" and is the name given the southernmost part of Judah, extending down toward the Sinai peninsula. In the summer heat, life withers until the winter rains return to replenish the dry wadis (streambeds), whose banks swiftly flourish again with green (Isa 35:1).

The consoling words of promise, possibly uttered by a priest

(vv. 5-6, though v. 5 can be legitimately translated as a wish form) may have been inspired by an old proverb (Job 4:8; Prov 22:8; Hos 8:7). Sowing with tears leads to a joyful harvest (Ps 30:5). This reference may allude to an ancient custom that considered sowing a mournful time. Practically, sowing in an arid region meant doing so with little prospect of harvest. All depended upon God sending the life-giving rains. These images of the winter rain in the Negeb and the farmer's life of sowing and harvesting illustrate what God has done, does, and will do for his people. These comparisons are more than illustration or poetic decoration. They proclaim the certainty that God's intervention is real and life-producing (Westermann, 1989:35).

THE TEXT IN THE BIBLICAL CONTEXT AND LIFE OF THE CHURCH

Sowing in Tears—Reaping in Joy

Psalm 126 proclaims God as the One who brings good out of evil. God is the God of hope, for the future lies in his hands. God can resurrect what is past and can give renewal and life to his faithful people. Also, every calamity can be a sowing time if, remembering God's past goodness, we have patience to await his season. In this sense there are similarities between Psalm 126 and the book of Joel. In addition to references about "restoring the fortunes" (Ps 126:1, 4; Joel 3:1), Joel moves from articulation of need (1:2–2:17) to the promise of God's response (2:18–3:21).

Jesus' Sermon on the Mount echoes Psalm 126:5-6: "Blessed are those who mourn" (Matt 5:4). Even more directly, Jesus speaks about sowing, death, resurrection, and fruit-bearing: "[If] a grain of wheat falls into the earth and dies, . . . it bears much fruit" (John 12:24-25), or tells of rejoicing following weeping (John 16:20). Paul also refers to sowing in speaking about death and resurrection (1 Cor 15:35-38, 42-44).

The psalm's reference to harvest has led to its use for Thanksgiving Day. Psalm 126 is listed in lectionary readings for Advent and Lent. It reflects a mood that surfaces in celebration of New Year's Day. Henry Downton's hymn (1841) expresses it in the words, "For thy mercy and thy grace, constant through another year, hear our song of thankfulness."

Sixteenth-century Anabaptists imprisoned for their faith quoted Psalm 126 in writing about their sure hope and joy in believing. For example, Jacob the Cobbler of Antwerp, on the eve of Whitsuntide in 1575, was burned alive with his tongue screwed fast. He had written from prison in testimony of his faith, quoting Psalm 126:2; Matthew 5:10; and 1 Peter 1:6; 4:14 (Braght: 1008). Dorothy Day (1897–1980), pioneer of the Catholic Worker movement in the United States, wrote about how the Psalms nourished her. When jailed for demonstrating on behalf of women's suffrage, she read Psalm 126, commenting, "If we had faith in what we were doing, making our protest against brutality and injustice, then we were indeed casting our seeds, and there was the promise of the harvest to come" (80-81). Psalm 126:5-6, about sowing in tears and reaping in joy, has become a popular proverb in Israel's agricultural settlements (Holladay: 154).

Psalm 127

Everything Depends on God's Blessing

PREVIEW

This wisdom psalm joins two proverbs to teach how human beings live exclusively because of the LORD's intervening, protecting, and giving. Fruitful work and strong family are the blessing of the LORD, the theme and subject also of Psalm 128. These psalms proclaim trust in the providence of God as the decisive factor in all of human life.

Most commentators understand Psalm 127 as focusing on the family or household. As a *Song of Ascents,* it speaks to the issues of daily life, particularly work and family (see comments on Ps 120). A pilgrimage to Jerusalem usually included members of the family (Luke 2:41-42) and represented an exercise in household building.

Though possibly written, as some suggest, after the returnees from the Babylonian exile rebuilt Jerusalem and the temple, about 520 BC, the title calls this a song *Of Solomon.* Reasons suggested include the words *his beloved* (v. 2), a name given to Solomon (2 Sam 12:25 NRSV n). The psalm speaks of many children, which Solomon certainly had! More likely, the title ties this psalm to Solomon because of its proverb style and wisdom content, though Solomon's vital connection to *house* should not be overlooked (v. 1; 1 Kings 3–10; Prov 9:1; 14:1; 24:3). House-building/keeping demonstrates "administration," an essential aspect of the kingly metaphor of which Solomon was considered the wise example par excellence *[Superscriptions].*

Notable literary features are the inclusio begun by *city* and ended with *gate* (vv. 1, 5), the alliteration in the Hebrew of *b* sounds (e.g., *yibneh bayit*, "build house"; *bônāyw bô*, "the ones building it," v. 1; and *lō'-yēbōšû . . . 'ôyĕbîm bašā'ar*, "unashamed . . . enemies in the gate," v. 5b) and the repetition of *sh* (š) sounds (vv. 1, 5a). The two proverbs are also united by a deliberate pun in use of the Hebrew words *bānāh*, *build* (v. 1), and *bānîm*, *sons* or *children* (v. 3 TEV) *[Hebrew Poetry].*

OUTLINE

The Futility of Work Apart from God, 127:1-2
Children Are the Blessing of God, 127:3-5

EXPLANATORY NOTES

The Futility of Work Apart from God 127:1-2

The psalm begins with an underlying theme of the vanity of human efforts without God (vv. 1-2; Prov 11:4-11; 16:1, 9; 19:21). More positively, the LORD is giver of all gifts (Pss 104:27-30; 145:15-16). Note the threefold repetition of *in vain* (šāwĕ'), which is the very opposite of *shalom*.

In Hebrew, "to build a house" (v. 1) means both to "construct a dwelling" and to "raise a family" (Deut 25:9; Ruth 4:11; 1 Sam 2:35; 7:5, 11; 1 Kings 11:38). Here it could mean temple, palace, David's line, or any family or household. *House* may also serve as metaphor for administrative leadership with justice (1 Sam 2:35; 2 Sam 7:26-29; Pss 101:2, 7; 132:3-5, 13-17). *Keeps watch* (šāmar, v. 1) describes a basic activity of God (Ps 121).

Anxious toil (v. 2) portrays a frantic, ceaseless involvement in work. The psalm does not belittle industry, but clearly repudiates the enslavement of the workaholic (Gen 3:17-19). Other translations for the word *sleep* (v. 2) include "prosperity" or "honor," suggesting that the LORD supplies the need of those he loves. If *sleep* is correct, it could mean that God gives sleep as rest to the weary, or that while nonanxious laborers are sleeping, God provides for them (NJPS, NRSV n, NIV n, JB n: perhaps as in the dream of 1 Kings 3:5-14; Mark 4:26-29; Miller, 1986:133; Mays, 1994b:402).

Children Are the Blessing of God 127:3-5

In Hebrew, the second stanza begins with an emphatic *indeed*, meaning "look" or "listen," to introduce the assertion that *sons* or *children* (TEV) are the gift and blessing of God. "Inheritance" (*heritage*, v. 3) traditionally describes the holy land given to the people Israel. Like the land, children are God's gift. A large family, particularly sons, would inherit family property and continue the family name. In that culture, the gift of many stalwart sons made a father feel secure in the protection and defensive power they represented (v. 4). Or at the city gate (v. 5), where judicial proceedings took place, a man with many sons would not be wrongly deprived of his rights, as often was the case with widows, orphans, and aliens, who had no family to protect their interests (A. Anderson, 2:869).

THE TEXT IN THE BIBLICAL CONTEXT AND LIFE OF THE CHURCH

God's Blessing on Work and Family

This psalm's insistence on how everything depends on God is a theme stressed by Jesus (Mark 4:26-29). Jesus warned against fretting anxiously (Matt 6:25-31; Luke 12:22-31; 1 Pet 5:7). Sleep, by contrast, is one of God's gifts (Eccles 5:12).

The second stanza, focusing on *sons* and fathers, requires cultural awareness of an ancient time: it paints a picture of the family far removed from cultural and social assumptions in the Western world today. The stanza conveys a male perspective, with no reference to daughters, or to family responsibility for the mother. Though mothers and daughters are not specifically mentioned, in poetic fashion, *the fruit of the womb a reward* need not be limited to sons, and it clearly affirms the indispensable role of the mother. Some cringe at the phrase *quiver full*, regarding large families as irresponsible in a world of finite resources.

On the other hand, does society undervalue children today, too often viewing them as an inconvenience and liability rather than an asset? Whatever form the family may take, and whatever problems arise out of the act of procreation, children are one of the richest manifestations of the blessing of God. Parents can find both joy and security in their children. A society that fails to cherish family values and celebrate the family will find itself significantly impoverished (Davidson, 1998:420; Miller, 1986:135).

Lessons and applications suggested by Psalm 127 include the following. No human work can survive if it ignores God. Missiles and bombs in and of themselves are inadequate protection (v. 1; Ps 121). In vain is anxious toil by those who believe it all depends on them. The psalm challenges each family to reconsider its values and the source of strength and continuity. The health of both church and community rests on the family life practiced in them. Even the work of the church depends fully upon the grace of God (Acts 2:47; 1 Cor 3:6-9).

Psalm 128

Blessed Are Those Who Fear the LORD

PREVIEW

Psalm 128 begins in the same way as the final verse of Psalm 127, with *Happy* or *Blessed* (NIV; *'ašrê*, Pss 1:1; 119:1). Psalms 127 and 128 support each other as companion psalms, both dealing with the blessing of productive labor and gift of family.

This wisdom psalm teaches that those who worship the LORD and obey his commandments will enjoy the fruit of their labor and be blessed with a prosperous family (vv. 1-4). Hence, every blessing the individual enjoys comes from God. Mortals work and marry, but it is the blessing of God that brings such activity and relationship to fruition.

The psalm ends with a benediction (vv. 5-6), possibly spoken by the priest, reminding the pilgrim that the life of the individual and family is related to that of the community. If pilgrims used Psalm 127 on arrival in Jerusalem for a festival, Psalm 128 may have been the blessing upon them before they departed for home.

OUTLINE

Beatitude: Fruitful Labor and Family for Those Who Fear the LORD, 128:1-4
Benediction: The LORD's Blessing Goes Forth from Zion, 128:5-6

Psalm 128

EXPLANATORY NOTES

Beatitude: Fruitful Labor and Family for Those Who Fear the LORD   128:1-4

The psalm is addressed to *everyone who fears the LORD* (v. 1; Pss 34:7, 9; 85:9; 102:15). *Fear of the LORD* does not mean craven fear or mere obedience to a set of commandments, but a way of life (v. 1b) that follows the LORD's direction (91:1-16; 112:5; 119:1).

One could not take for granted being able to *eat the fruit of the labor of your hands* (v. 2) in a region and time where wars, drought, and insects often destroyed the crops that represented people's livelihood. A more holistic view of work is presented here than in Psalm 127:2: this is the positive kind of labor that is blessed by God.

That God blesses the faithful with a devoted family is a frequent theme of wisdom teaching. Verse 3 presents an idyllic picture of the family, with the wife *like a fruitful vine* and children *like olive shoots*. People viewed the *vine* and *olive*, both basic to the economy of the land (Ps 52:8) and here as symbols of life and fertility, as blessings bestowed by God. This psalm does not deal with exceptions, and the perspective is that of a paternalistic society.

An emphatic *Thus* or "behold" opens verse 4 to echo and form an inclusio with verse 1.

Benediction: The LORD's Blessing Goes Forth from Zion   128:5-6

The opening line of the liturgical benediction may be the heart of the psalm. It is *the LORD* who blesses from Zion (132:13-16; 133:3; 134:3). The blessing is a free gift, not just a reward. The family does not live in isolation: the fortunes of the individual and family are bound up with the future of all. *Children's children* (v. 6a) means "may you live a long life" (Gen 50:22-23). The final prayer, *Peace be upon Israel!* (v. 6b; Ps 125:5), recognizes that the family's future rests upon Zion's welfare and that of Israel.

THE TEXT IN THE BIBLICAL CONTEXT AND LIFE OF THE CHURCH

Walking in the Way of the Lord and Family Solidarity

As *A Song of Ascents* for pilgrims, Psalm 128 asserts that pilgrimage is always to walk in the ways of the LORD. It also speaks to the interdependence of the individual, family, civic, and social aspects of life, characteristic of Hebrew thinking, and challenging the individualism characteristic of our day.

A strong NT echo appears in Galatians 6:15-16, where Paul appeals that God's people should not put up barriers against each other, but show themselves true citizens of "the Jerusalem above" (Gal 4:26; Kidner, 1975:444). The church came to see itself as the new Israel of God. Hence, Christian believers are not bound up with an old Zion, but rather with Christ, who bestows spiritual blessings (Eph 1:3), and with "the new Jerusalem, coming down out of heaven from God" (Rev 21:2).

Psalm 128 can help us reflect on issues of family solidarity. In the pilgrimage to Jerusalem, whole families went up together to worship God. God's blessing is on families who worship together. The psalm can speak to the vital and positive role both fathers and mothers play in teaching children the way of life. Though we often stress the effect of parents' iniquity upon following generations (Exod 20:5), we fail to speak enough of the blessings of the righteous filtering down through the generations. Finally, the image of eating together *around your table* (v. 3) continues as a powerful sign and symbol, not only of loving and joyous fellowship in the family, but also of the essence of the divine fellowship (Ps 23:5; Luke 22:30).

Parents in Jewish and Christian homes have appropriately read Psalm 128 at the birth of a child, using *children* (NRSV) instead of *sons* (v. 3 NIV; Holladay: 146).

Psalm 129

Often Have They Attacked Me, . . . Yet They Have Not Prevailed

PREVIEW

Psalm 129 begins with a dismal description of Israel's history. From the beginning, Israel's life has been that of oppression and suffering. The oppressor's plow has raked over the nation, and like oxen the people were even hitched to draw that plow. But God has cut the harness and set Israel free (v. 4).

The second part of the psalm voices confident prayer that those who hate Zion will be punished (vv. 5-8). Like grass that withers in the scorching sun, they will know no harvest nor receive the blessing of the LORD.

This community prayer song has aspects of a national lament, though the expression of confidence predominates. Written in the first person, the psalm conveys a personification of Israel (v. 1b). In style, subject matter, and purpose, it is a companion to Psalm 124.

OUTLINE

Summary of Israel's History of Oppression and Deliverance, 129:1-4
Confident Prayer That Those Who Hate Zion Will Be Punished,
    129:5-8

EXPLANATORY NOTES

Summary of Israel's History of Oppression and Deliverance 129:1-4

Repetition of the opening clause (vv. 1-2) emphasizes the conflicted character of Israel's story. *Let Israel now say* (v. 1b) suggests that the community is gathered for worship (Pss 115:9; 118:2; 124:1; 149:2) and invites thankful recall of the lessons of history. *From my youth* (v. 1a, 2a) refers to Israel in Egypt (Exod 1:11-14; Hos 11:1). But after the Egyptians, oppression came from the Moabites (Judg 3:14), Canaanites (4:2-3), Midianites (6:6), Ammonites (10:9; 1 Sam 11:2), and other nations until the Babylonian exile, and beyond. Israel was not only used as a beast of burden; the nation itself was trampled upon and "plowed up" (Isa 51:23; Mic 3:12), until the LORD broke the cords that enslaved her (vv. 2-4). Verse 4 begins emphatically: *Yet the LORD in his justice has cut me loose* (NEB).

Confident Prayer That Those Who Hate Zion Will Be Punished 129:5-8

After the look backward over Israel's story (vv. 1-4), the psalm seeks a word of reassurance for the present (vv. 5-8). The tone of the prayer expresses confidence that the just judgment of the LORD will confound Israel's enemies *[Judge]*. Those *who hate Zion* may be foreign enemies or Israelites who rejected the claims of Zion. For such, there will be no harvest (vv. 6-8). Like the stray blades of grass on the roof sod that shoot up and die quickly, may the wicked never know the joy of harvest (Pss 90:5-6; 103:15-16; Isa 40:6-7). Indeed, may the blessing, such as that for or by the harvesters (Ruth 2:4), be withheld from the enemy. Both RSV and NIV assume that the closing words, *We bless you in the name of the LORD!* (v. 8) are part of the blessing the people *who hate Zion* will never hear (Davidson, 1998:424). We can infer that the priest blesses the assembled congregation of those who truly trust in the LORD (Pss 115:12-15; 118:26; 134:3).

THE TEXT IN THE BIBLICAL CONTEXT AND LIFE OF THE CHURCH

Remembering Past Deliverances

As another *Song of Ascents* (Pss 120–134), Psalm 129 illustrates how the people of God are sustained by memory of the LORD's help in the past. Such is the purpose of a pilgrimage. For healing, they may offer up suffering and humiliation, a horrid memory. Now, at last, ascending the hill of the LORD, the pilgrim anticipates the priest's welcome: *We bless you in the name of the LORD!* In times of peril, it is good to strengthen the heart by looking back and remembering past deliverances.

This psalm, with its focus on a history of oppression and suffering, brings to mind modern pilgrimages to the Western Wall in the old city of Jerusalem. Part of the retaining wall of the Temple Mount, for Herod's temple, it has become a holy place, where devout Jews pray. It is the tears of generations of such worshippers, grieving for the lost temple, to which the name Wailing Wall refers. They stuff the cracks between the stones with slips of paper carrying petitions. The swaying and praying of the devout attests to the powerful hold the place still has on the minds and hearts of many Jews, who lament their history as a suffering people.

We can read Psalm 129 in conjunction with the litany of Israel's martyrs and saints in Hebrews 11. Jesus invited his followers to enter God's reign by taking up their cross (Mark 1:14-15; 8:34). Persecution of God's people continued through the NT (Matt 23:34; 1 Pet 1:1-9; Revelation). Yet Paul could write of affliction and repeated experiences of deliverance (2 Cor 4:8-9; 2 Tim 3:11). Sixteenth-century Anabaptist martyr Maerten van der Straten wrote a farewell letter to his wife from prison: "'My enemies ploughed upon my back, and made long furrows' [Ps 129:3]. But I console myself . . . that God, as Paul says, 'chasteneth whom he loveth [Heb 12:6], . . . and with the temptation also makes a way to escape, that one may be able to bear it' [1 Cor 10:13]" (Braght: 956).

Psalm 130

Out of the Depths

PREVIEW

Psalm 130, an individual lament, begins with the petitioner's cry to the LORD from great distress. Knowing that he has no claim upon the LORD, the desperate prayer and expectant waiting on the LORD is his only hope. At the end of the song the horizon is enlarged as the supplicant remembers his people and the common need. Thus, personal poems become corporate.

Classified with the Penitential Psalms (Pss 6; 32; 38; 52; 102; 143), Psalm 130 has had wide use in the church *[Penitential]*. Here there is no mention of atoning sacrifices. The sense of sin is too deep for the old concepts. Face-to-face with God, all creatures are unclean and sinful (v. 3). If God were not merciful and forgiving, nobody could stand. For this reason God will show mercy. When God in mercy forgives sin, the result will be a restoration of the relationship between God and the penitent. Hence, the soul is silent before God, the source of hope.

OUTLINE

The Cry from the Depths, 130:1-4
Waiting and Hoping, 130:5-8

EXLANATORY NOTES

The Cry from the Depths 130:1-4

The psalm is a personal cry from *out of the depths* (vv. 1-2). The image is that of one drowning in deep water. The *depths* are the watery deep, chaos, the sphere of death and Sheol, the place of separation from God (Ps 69:2, 14-15; Isa 51:10; Ezek 27:34; Jon 2:2-3, 5-6). The slang expression "That's the pits" suggests the worst sort of situation imaginable. The way out begins with the possibility of prayer to the God who can draw us from the depths (Exod 22:27; Amos 7:1-3; Miller, 1986:140).

This psalm reflects a deep consciousness of personal sin (vv. 3-4). Offense against God affects the whole being, body and soul, and a person's life in community with others. But when life in alienation seems hopeless, there is the LORD, and one can still cry to the LORD. The answer to the rhetorical question (v. 3) is, "No one." If the LORD dealt with us according to our sins, no one could stand in his presence. *But there is forgiveness with you* (v. 4). The LORD forgives, and the forgiveness of the LORD is fearful indeed, calling forth awe.

Waiting and Hoping 130:5-8

This leads to a sense of expectant waiting (vv. 5-6). More eagerly than the watchman on lookout (Isa 21:11-12), the psalmist looks for the word of the LORD. The psalmist can *watch* (v. 6bc) with anticipation, because God does not watch for or *mark iniquities* (v. 3; McCann, 1996:1205). For with the LORD is *steadfast love (ḥesed)*, and in him is redeeming grace (v. 7). The term *ḥesed* describes God and the kind of love that never gives up (Exod 34:6-7; Hos 3:1-5; Luke 15:20-23) *[Steadfast]*.

However, salvation is more than an individual matter. The psalmist's hope for personal salvation merges into hope for the salvation of the whole community (vv. 7-8). Verses 7a and 8 may have been added to this individual lament later (as also in Ps 131:3). As *A Song of Ascents*, such pilgrimage songs may have received this kind of appendix to give them a community reference (Westermann, 1989:121).

THE TEXT IN THE BIBLICAL CONTEXT AND LIFE OF THE CHURCH

The Cry from the Depths as an Act of Faith

Martin Luther called Psalms 32; 51; 130; and 143 "the Pauline Psalms" because of their description of sin and forgiveness. Yet we must take them for what they are, not didactic treatises, but poetic testimonies. They are forerunners of the Christian experience of salvation by grace through faith (Rom 3:10-18, 20; Gal 2:16). Common with the NT message is the fact that for and in our deepest need, God acts (Rom 5:6-8, 20-21). So also, the act of God's forgiveness in the cross is a fearful (awe-filled) event (1 Cor 1:18-25).

The expectant waiting suggests the believing, trusting, staking one's life on God implied in the NT's use of the word *believe* (faith). Salvation, though personal, has the corporate concern, as in the witness of the early church in Acts, or as in the invitation of John 20:31 or 1 John 1:1-4.

The influence of Psalm 130 on Luther appears in one of his finest hymns, "Aus tiefer Not schrei ich zu dir" (1523; trans. E.T. Horn III, 1909, "Out of the depths I cry to you"). John Wesley reports in his *Journal* how the Aldersgate conversion experience was preceded by hearing the anthem based on Psalm 130 at the afternoon service at St. Paul's in London. Modern pastoral handbooks recommend the psalm for the most difficult times: stillbirth, death shortly after birth, burial (Limburg, 2000:447).

This intensely personal psalm sets to sound the depths of human existence in terms of guilt and forgiveness. Life goes on in the face of the destructive forces of human inadequacy and sinfulness because God is a God of forgiveness. Our cry can become a profession of reliance. Faith in God is that attitude of waiting in the midst of darkness, in that precarious balance of hope and fear, with hope ultimately prevailing.

My paraphrase can serve as an example of using Psalm 130 for personal prayer:

> Out of the depths, I cry out to you, LORD.
> Do you hear me?
> Open your heart to me,
> I am begging for mercy.

Psalm 130

If you, LORD, should preserve the burden of our guilt,
Who could stand and face it?
But with you there is forgiveness.
You are to be taken seriously.

I look eagerly for the LORD.
I wait with all my heart.
For his word I wait.
I look for the LORD
    just as one on guard
    looks out for the morning.
Hope in the LORD
For with the LORD there is mercy.
With him is pardon.
He will set us free from the burden of our guilt.

Palm 131

Calmed and Quieted Like a Weaned Child

PREVIEW

This beautiful psalm declares the contentment of a restless soul in submission to the will of God. Trust and confidence characterizes this prayer song of an individual. The first two verses contrast the proud and arrogant self with the soul that is patient and composed. The dominant image is that of the child, quieted with its mother, and completely trusting.

The liturgical addition (v. 3) transforms an individual psalm of confidence into a song of the community, fitting for this collection of the *Songs of Ascents* (Pss 120–134). The psalm repeatedly calls pilgrims who gather in worship to place their hope in God (115:9; 130:7). The heading ascribes Psalm 131 to be *Of David* (as Psalms 122 and 124 are also titled in the *Songs of Ascents* collection). However, that does not necessarily imply authorship, as acknowledged below, in the comments regarding the psalm's feminine images *[Superscriptions]*.

OUTLINE

Declaration of Humility and Limitation, 131:1
Image of Childlike Trust, 131:2
Call for the Community to Hope Confidently in the LORD, 131:3

EXPLANATORY NOTES

Childlike Trust   131:1-3

The psalm opens with a repudiation of pride. In address to God, the psalmist vigorously rejects haughty ways (Ezek 28:2, 17; Prov 16:5). Note the repetition of *not, not, not* (v. 1). *Marvelous* (v. 1, *niplā'ôt*) refers to what is beyond human understanding because it reveals the mystery of the divine love (Pss 9:1; 78:11). The psalmist rejects the temptation to venture into the mysterious ways of God so as to understand or control them (Job 42:3; Isa 40:12-14). This psalm's attitude of humility and limitation contrasts with Isaiah 2:6-22, where Israel is accused of being proud, haughty, and lifted up. Humble trust in God was a major element in the inner life of the poor (*'ănāwîm*) and righteous (*ṣaddîqîm*). The psalm may have come from the circles of the righteous of the postexilic community (Kraus, 1989:470).

The second verse opens with a contrasting *But* or *No* (NEB). *I have calmed*, or (lit.) "leveled," as if preparing the ground to allow God to sow the seed, and *quieted my soul* (v. 2a). Now the psalm's dominant image appears—that of the child with its mother. Translations and interpretations vary. The RSV pictures a baby pacified at its mother's breast. More accurately, NRSV and NIV translate *like a weaned child with its mother* (v. 2b), suggesting the trusting content of a three-year-old (2 Macc 7:27), old enough to be accustomed to a mother's care and no longer clamoring to be nursed (White: 194). This picture of the child with its mother illustrates hope in the LORD, as do other biblical images comparing the parent-child relationship to God and his people (Deut 1:31; Isa 46:3-4; Hos 11:4). Notable is the clear "mothering" image of God.

On the basis of the psalmist's experience of the "mothering" God, the congregation is called to hope confidently in the LORD (v. 3). So Israel is to live in trust and fix all expectation on the LORD (Ps 130:7).

THE TEXT IN THE BIBLICAL CONTEXT AND LIFE OF THE CHURCH

Contentment in God

Psalm 131 aligns with Jesus' teaching about becoming like a child in order to enter the kingdom of God (Matt 18:1-5; Mark 9:33, 37; 10:13-16). The psalm's focus on humility and quietness of soul brings to mind Paul's warning "do not become proud" (Rom 11:20) and "not to think of yourself more highly than you ought to think" (12:3). We hear further echoes in Paul's words about "the peace of God, which surpasses all understanding," learning "to be content with whatever I have" (Phil 4:7, 11), and letting "the peace of Christ rule in your hearts" (Col 3:15).

Psalm 131 cultivates contentment in the knowledge that God holds life in his embrace. It encourages a patient, trusting lifestyle that is not preoccupied with status, peer approval, or material gain (Matt 16:26). In this sense the piety of Psalm 131 runs counter to modernity with its drive toward independence, self-sufficiency, and autonomy. Modernity believes that real maturity is to be free of every relationship of dependence. Psalm 131 promotes childlike trust, including submission to the trustworthy will of the LORD (v. 3). Such submission makes it possible to hope rather than to rely only on one's own resources (Brueggemann, 1984:49).

Might a woman have written Psalm 131:1-2? Gottfried Quell has proposed that thesis on the basis of the statements of modesty and serenity, and the self-quotation *My soul is like the weaned child that is with me* (v. 2b). Quell speculates that the poem might have been deposited in the temple at the time of a thank offering (Lev 7:12-13), found later by the compiler of pilgrim songs, and with the addition of verse 3, accepted into the collection of Psalms 120–134 (Quell: 173-85; Holladay: 40-41). Speculation aside, Scriptures attribute the psalmlike *Song of Hannah* (1 Sam 2:1-10) to a woman. Psalm 131 clearly portrays a picture of God as mother, and the psalmist as child (Num 11:11-15; Deut 32:18; Isa 49:15; 66:13; Luke 15:8-10). Like a child, the trusting soul is sheltered in the nearness and tender loving-kindness of God.

Psalm 132

God's Choice of David and Zion

PREVIEW

Since Jerusalem was identified as the LORD's residence forever, pilgrims made journeys to the city year after year, decade after decade (vv. 13-14). This psalm, for a festival celebrating both the place (*Zion*, vv 8-9, 13-16) and person (*David*, vv. 11, 17), fits well into a collection of psalms for a pilgrimage to Jerusalem.

This thirteenth *Song of Ascents* (Pss 120–134) differs noticeably from the others in language and length. However, it provides opportunity for pilgrims to retell dramatically the story of David's bringing the ark of the covenant to Jerusalem (2 Sam 6) and of Nathan's promise to the Davidic dynasty forever (2 Sam 7:5-16). As the pilgrims remembered King David in the context of the temple, they prayed that the LORD would do so too (v. 1).

Two themes dominate this royal psalm, which is similar to the Songs of Zion and also a liturgical procession hymn. The themes highlight the election of Zion as God's dwelling place and God's choice of the Davidic family (1 Kings 8:16). Coordination between Zion as the LORD's habitation and David as the LORD's anointed provides the structure of the psalm. The narrative theme begins with the line to *find a place for the LORD* (v. 5). Intricately crafted, the psalm takes the form of a prayer (vv. 1-10) and its answer (vv. 11-18). Within those two broader parts we find David's vow to the LORD (vv. 3-5) and the LORD's oath to David (vv. 11-12). As David thought to build God a house (*bayit*, v. 3; 2 Sam 7:2), God would build David a *bayit* in the sense of a household dynasty (2 Sam 7:11; Reardon: 264).

How was Psalm 132 used? Proposals include a processional ceremony to commemorate the finding of the ark, anniversary of the temple's dedication at the Feast of Tabernacles, and a royal Zion festival.

The psalm is composed of various materials, including quotations from older sources. Notable literary features include the fourfold reference to David (vv. 1, 10, 11, 17) and the steplike progression in verse after verse, coming back to what has been said and carrying the idea forward.

Suggestions for the date of composition range from the tenth century BC, during or after Solomon's reign (Holladay), to the late preexilic time, and even as late as the second temple, when the Davidic kings were no more and the *place* God had chosen had been obliterated by Nebuchadnezzar (Knight, 2:293). Basic elements may be from the era of Solomon, with the present form of the psalm receiving modification in the course of its history. After the Davidic dynasty disappeared and the priesthood absorbed its powers (Zech 6:9-14), the faithful would have reinterpreted the psalm with a focus on the temple. The psalm has numerous synonyms for temple or dwelling place. Yet hopes for a new, messianic heir to David's throne were not abandoned (Stuhlmueller, 1983, 2:174-75).

Helpful background to understand Psalm 132 will come from reading about what happened when David brought the ark to Jerusalem (2 Sam 6), and Solomon's prayer at the dedication of the temple (1 Kings 8; 2 Chron 6).

OUTLINE

An Appeal to the LORD, 132:1-10
    132:1-5   Prayer for David and His Oath Regarding the LORD's Dwelling
    132:6-10   Description of the Ark's Procession to Zion
The Divine Promise Prevails, 132:11-18
    132:11-12 The LORD's Oath to David
    132:13-18 The LORD's Presence in Zion

EXPLANATORY NOTES

An Appeal to the LORD   132:1-10

The psalm begins with a petition asking God to remember David's fidelity in finding a suitable house for the LORD (vv. 1-5). These words point back to the loss of the ark of the covenant (1 Sam 4:1–6:21). In spite of *hardships* (v. 1; 2 Sam 6:6-15), David had vowed its recovery (vv. 3-6). His oath, not to rest until his purpose was accomplished, draws on a hyperbolic proverb (v. 4; Prov 6:4). *The Mighty One of Jacob* (vv. 2, 4) is an ancient divine title (Gen 49:24). Who is the speaker in these verses? It could be the king, a descendent of David, or a priest.

Now follows a description of the ark's procession to Zion (vv. 6-10). The words suggest a liturgical reenactment, the worshippers perhaps led by a choir. Verse 6 begins with the Hebrew interjection *hinnēh*, not translated into English, but meaning "Look!" or "Behold," and suggesting the changing fortunes for the ark. These verses also imply that past and present merge as the congregation relives the story in worship. *Ephrathah* (v. 6) refers to Bethlehem, David's birthplace, and *Jaar* was a poetical designation of Kiriath-jearim, where the ark had been kept (1 Sam 5:1–7:2; 2 Sam 6:1-15). *Footstool* (v. 7) refers to the ark (1 Chron 28:2).

The liturgical cry *Rise up, O LORD* (v. 8) draws on the exclamation used in the days of Moses, when the ark set out to protect or deliver God's people (Num 10:35). The *ark of your might* (v. 8) represented the might and power of the LORD, and in the midst of the congregation, guaranteed military victory (1 Sam 4:3-5). In the book of Psalms, this is the only explicit mention of the ark (v. 8), though it is implied in other passages (Pss 78:60-61; 99:5; 105:4). The ark, a box the size of a child's coffin, was housed in the most holy place and functioned in the nature of a divine throne room (Exod 25:10-22). Containing the Ten Commandments, it came to be understood as the place where God met his people in special ways—in mercy as well as in judgment. David transferred the ark from Kiriath-jearim to Jerusalem. A tent shrine was erected for the purpose, and the ark was brought with great ceremony and rejoicing (2 Sam 6). Verse 9 suggests a rubric for the priests to put on sacred vestments and for people to meet the ark with shouts of joy. This section closes with intercession for the king (v. 10). When the king is called *servant,* he is accorded a place of honor and a role of servant (v. 10; Pss 78:70; 89:3; 144:10). The plea is that the *anointed one,* the ruling Davidic king, not be rejected. Verses 8-10 reappear in the 2 Chronicles 6:41-42 account of Solomon's prayer.

The Divine Promise Prevails   132:11-18

The answer to the prayer of verses 1-10 comes as an oracle uttered by temple prophet or priest (vv. 11-18), declaring that the divine promise prevails. The LORD has chosen David (vv. 11-12), and the LORD has chosen Zion (vv. 13-18). The promise is that of permanence (*forevermore*, v. 12) and abundant blessing (vv. 15-18) *[Oracle]*.

The LORD's oath to David (vv. 11-12) echoes David's oath to the LORD (vv. 3-5). This foundational promise of the LORD to David appears elsewhere, though unconditionally (2 Sam 23:5; Ps 89:3-4, 28-37; Isa 55:3). Here the psalm identifies covenant fidelity as the prerequisite for fulfillment of the promise: *If your sons keep my covenant* (v. 12). The dynasty will be eternal, provided that the descendants are faithful to the covenant and decrees.

The psalm's final section tells of the LORD's choice of Zion and the blessings that flow from his presence (vv. 13-18). God has chosen to reveal himself to his people through Zion (vv. 13-14; Pss 33:12; 65:4; 100:3) *[Zion]*. The LORD's governing presence among his people is the guarantee that their needs will be met (v. 15). Verses 13-16 parallel verses 8-9. The psalm ends with the metaphors of *horn, lamp,* and *crown* as endorsement of the Davidic king (vv. 17-18). *Horn* refers to David's strength and his descendants, and so does *lamp*, symbol for the preservation of the dynasty (1 Kings 11:36; 15:4; 2 Chron 21:7). The language also implies that the monarchy no longer exists, since the image of a *horn* sprouting may suggest the restoration of something that has been destroyed (Ezek 29:21), and *lamp* represents the possibility of a future (2 Sam 21:17; McCann, 1996:1212)

THE TEXT IN THE BIBLICAL CONTEXT AND LIFE OF THE CHURCH

The Hope of Messiah

Psalm 132 declares that the city and the throne shall stand forever. What happened to the promise, in light of the Babylonian invasion, that ended the Davidic monarchy and left Jerusalem and the temple in ruins in 587 (or 586) BC? The answer given was that Zion and the Davidic monarchy were destroyed because the people had broken the covenant. Kings and people alike had failed to establish the justice to which the prophets pointed (Lam 1:8, 18; Hab 1:12–2:4). As a pilgrim song, even after the end of the monarchy, Zion was there, and so the psalm could still serve as a liturgy of prayer and promise, and as a proclamation of hope.

Psalm 132, as with the other royal psalms, underwent changes in interpretation after the Davidic dynasty ended. Original descriptions of the ruling kings were projected into the future to provide a portrait of a great king, the anointed one (Messiah) who would come from the line of David. "This great king would rule with righteousness and justice, would bring peace, and would rule forever" (Limburg, 2000:454). The place of Psalm 132 in the Psalter appears to be significant. Psalm 89, the final psalm in book III, tells of the rejection of the Davidic dynasty. Books IV and V seem to be shaped to respond to the crisis of exile and its aftermath. In the context of the postexilic realities, the *Songs of Ascents* articulate the subjugation of God's people by their enemies (Pss 123:3-4; 126:4-6; 129:1-2). The placement of Psalm 132 encourages the reader to hear it as articulation of the hope called for (130:7; 131:3). Thus, one needs to hear the references to David messianically, as a way of symbolizing the hope for the future (Allen, 1983:209; McCann, 1996:1211). Psalm 132 was part of the seedbed from which would develop Israel's expectation of Messiah.

The hope of the Messiah as a light to the nations (Isa 42:6-7; 49:6) underwent further transformation in the NT (Luke 2:32). The church came to see such texts as prophecies, and found the fulfillment of the promise to David in Jesus Christ (Matt 16:13-20; Luke 1:69-79; Acts 2:30-36; 2 Cor 1:19-22). So also the promise regarding Zion came to be seen as fulfilled in the church (1 Pet 2:4-10). Christians pray this psalm with reference to its fulfillment in Jesus, "*the* Anointed One and *the* Temple" (Rev 21:3, 22; Reardon: 264) *[Anointed]*.

Dimensions of Leadership

Psalm 132 emphasizes David's leading role in establishing Zion as the place of worship and the abundant blessings that flow from such fidelity to the LORD. As a royal psalm, it speaks to dimensions of leadership as represented by prophet, priest, and king. Issues of justice are at the heart of leadership (vv. 12, 15). But so also is the priestly role of representing the love and grace of God to the people in worship (vv. 9, 16). However, leadership also needs the dimensions of administration as represented here by David's vision, commitment, and action (vv. 1-5), and by the ark of the covenant in the midst of the congregation (v. 8).

In considering leadership in the church, is it possible to reclaim the kingly metaphor—not with its paternalistic, military, and autocratic corruptions, but as embodying the essential function of administration? Here again, the NT reinterprets with more kindly metaphors of teacher (John 13:13-14), shepherd (10:11-16), and master (Luke 9:33). In Jesus, these characteristics are combined to provide a model for leaders of God's people.

Psalm 133

When Sisters and Brothers Live in Unity

PREVIEW

This delightful three-verse psalm begins with a wisdom maxim extolling the joy of peaceful coexistence with brothers and sisters (v. 1). The psalmist compares the reality of kindred unity to the sweet fragrance of the anointing oil confirming the blessing of the priesthood, and to the welcome dew that refreshes a thirsty land (vv. 2-3a). The conclusion asserts that the reward of fraternal harmony will be *life forevermore* (v. 3b).

Psalm 133 praises unity without specifying whether in a family or a larger group. We can interpret the psalm in both ways. In ancient Israel, when brothers lived together and one of them died and left no son, the surviving brother was supposed to marry the widow, to perpetuate his brother's name and (likely) inheritance (Deut 25:5-10; cf. Ruth 3–4). Younger brothers' families then came under the headship of the eldest brother. Such customs of family solidarity provided well-being and order for the society of that day. Exceptions to family harmony are recorded in the biblical story—Abram and Lot (Gen 13), Jacob and Esau (27:41-46; 32:3–33:16; 36:6-8) and Joseph and his brothers (Gen 37). This psalm exalts family solidarity.

Read as a *Song of Ascents* (Pss 120–134), a pilgrim song for the festivals at Jerusalem, Psalm 133 is an exclamation of delight at the goodness the pilgrims experienced in assembly as one family in Zion. They come from near and far, and the LORD's covenant binds them together.

Psalm 133 "celebrates the goodness of the life with which the LORD blesses those who are assembled by his Presence" (Mays, 1994b:414).

OUTLINE

Opening Affirmation: The Goodness of Kindred Living in Unity, 133:1
Two Metaphors Describing Unity, 133:2-3a
Conclusion: Place of the LORD's Blessing, 133:3b

EXPLANATORY NOTES
Two Metaphors Describing Unity 133:1-3

The psalm begins with the attention-getting Hebrew word *hinnēh*, *Behold!* which does not appear in English translations. It may suggest surprise that any *kindred live together in unity*. Or perhaps, in the context of the pilgrim festival, it means, "Look at what we are experiencing!" The NRSV translates the Hebrew word for "brother" with the term *kindred*. "Brother" and "sister" have also taken on the broader connotation of members of the faith community.

Two words provide pictures of what unity is like (vv. 2-3a). Unity is like the pleasant fragrance and refreshing liquid used as a body *oil* (Ps 23:5; Amos 6:6; Mic 6:15) and poured on the head at installation of the high priest (Lev 8:12). The breast portion of the priest's robe featured two precious stones, which bore the names of the twelve tribes of Israel. When the anointing oil flowed down upon the garments and over these stones, it represented God's blessing upon the twelve tribes and the unity of the tribes in the high priest's consecration.

Unity is also like the dew of Hermon (v. 3a). The ancients believed that this snow-covered peak, at an elevation of 9,232 feet (2814 m) fifty miles northeast of the Sea of Galilee, was the source of the refreshing *dew* that settled on the parched countryside to the south. Dew is symbol of God's mysterious life-giving blessing (Gen 27:28; Deut 33:28; Ps 110:3; Hos 14:5).

The threefold use of the Hebrew word *yōrēd*, translated as *running down* (v. 2) *running down* (v. 2) and *falls* (v. 3), helps the hearer visualize the descent of the divine blessing. Now appears the motif of *Zion* as a blessing and the place from where the people have received the blessing from the LORD (v. 3; Pss 132:13-15; 134:3). Mention of Zion shifts the focus from the local family to the whole people, and may be an appeal for national unity. *For there* (v. 3b) points back to Zion, but also beyond, to the achievement of unity as what is blessed (v. 1) *[Zion]*. With use of the name of *the LORD* in the last sentence, the psalmist leaves no doubt that true unity, like all good gifts, is from above, bestowed rather than contrived. While the Israelites understood *life forevermore* as the preservation of earthly life (Pss 21:4; 61:6; 91:16) or the ever-continuing vitality of the community, it is capable of a fuller application in light of the gospel (Ps 16:11; Davidson, 1998:433).

THE TEXT IN THE BIBLICAL CONTEXT AND LIFE OF THE CHURCH

Unity in the Family and the Faith Community

This brief wisdom psalm reflects Israel's capacity to appreciate the common joys of life, which are attributed to the well-ordered generosity of the LORD. This includes how people relate to each other, an area of human life touched by the saving power of God (2 Cor 13:11; Phil 4:9).

The theme of unity in family and faith community relationships receives high priority in the NT. Jesus' parables include the story of a father and his two sons (Luke 15:11-32). He admonished persons at odds, "Be reconciled to your brother or sister" (Matt 5:23-24). Jesus promised, "Where two or three are gathered in my name, I am there among them" (18:20). He spoke of his followers as branches connected through the vine (John 15:1-12) and prayed "that they may all be one" (17:21). Paul wrote of the church as one body in Christ, with many members (1 Cor 12:12-13), and appealed for unity in the church (1 Cor 3; Phil 2). Admonitions to mutual love are many (Rom 12:3-13; Heb 13:1; 1 John 4:11-12).

Gossip, backbiting, and nasty criticism do not foster unity. Positively, unity entails interest, care, and concern for one another within the group. Harmony in relationships gives life and empowers all. Indeed, unity signifies the miracle of God's blessing.

Psalm 133 has stimulated hymns on unity, such as Charles Wesley's "All praise to our redeeming Lord" (1747) and J. E. Seddon's "How good a thing it is" (1982). Other uses of the psalm include its reading for celebration of the Lord's Supper and for services of Christian unity. The psalm anticipates the solidarity and harmony of all humanity, and witnesses to God's work at building a family that transcends all barriers separating and diminishing life. The psalm reminds us of the importance of family and community. It can point to the significance of family reunions, church conferences, or homecoming celebrations.

Psalm 134

To Bless and to Be Blessed

PREVIEW

This brief liturgy of blessing closes the *Songs of Ascents* collection (Pss 120–134). It summarizes the major concern of the "pilgrimage to Zion" psalms: to praise the LORD and receive blessing from the LORD.

The liturgy may be a farewell blessing, as the pilgrims ask the priests and Levites to continue praising the LORD (vv. 1-2). Verse 3 is then the answering blessing from the priests to the people as they depart for home. Or the psalm may have belonged to the pilgrimage Feast of Tabernacles, which included night vigils. In that case, the priest might have addressed the words to the pilgrims, calling on all the assembled people (Ps 113:1) to acknowledge their dependence upon the LORD, with verse 3 as a pronouncement of blessing upon the worshippers.

The psalm's keynote word is *bless*, which appears in each verse, twice to *bless* or "praise" the LORD, and then to receive the LORD's blessing (v. 3). The LORD is named five times in this three-verse psalm.

OUTLINE

Hymnic Introit: Invitation to Bless the LORD, 134:1-2
Benediction: May the LORD Bless You, 134:3

EXPLANATORY NOTES

Invitation to Bless and Be Blessed   134:1-3

Psalm 134 begins with the Hebrew word *hinnēh*, as does the previous psalm. Usually translated "behold," here it is an invitation, *Come* (NRSV, NEB). *Bless* means to praise with words that declare the greatness and goodness of God (Ps 66:8). The Hebrew root *bārak*, translated *bless*, originally meant more literally "to kneel," as in paying homage to a superior (cf. 2 Chron 6:13; Ps 95:6). *Servants of the LORD* may denote the priests or the whole congregation (Ps 135:1). *Stand* is a word used for the service of the priests and Levites (Deut 18:7; 1 Chron 23:30; 2 Chron 29:11). *By night* suggests that the praise of God knows no limits of time. The Levitical singers were on duty day and night (1 Chron 9:33). To *lift up hands to the holy place* was a gesture of adoration and prayer (Ps 28:2).

The benediction *May the LORD . . . bless you* (v. 3), draws from priestly blessings (Lev 9:22; Num 6:22-26). To bless in the name of the LORD is one of the priestly functions (Deut 10:8; 21:5). The priest mediates God's blessing but does not bestow it himself. Calling upon the Creator stresses the validity and power of God (Pss 121:2; 124:8). *Zion* is emphasized as channel of the divine blessing (Ps 133:3). The psalm proclaims the mutuality of blessing between God and the people.

THE TEXT IN THE BIBLICAL CONTEXT AND LIFE OF THE CHURCH

A Benediction for the Journey

This finale to the *Songs of Ascents* collection reminds us of what worship meant for those who journeyed to Jerusalem for the great festivals of the religious year. These joyful celebrations focused on Jerusalem/Zion as the place where God dwells among his people. Worship provided the context for celebrating the joys of family life and affirming the unity that binds together the larger family of God. These became occasions to voice expectancy and trust, joyful thanksgiving and praise (Davidson, 1998:434).

Public worship usually concludes with a benediction, which is the invocation of a blessing upon the people. Here the prayer is, *May the LORD . . . bless you*. We might read this psalm not only as a blessing upon the pilgrims ready to leave the temple, but also as a blessing upon the reader of the Scripture. In this sense, Psalm 134 came to be used in the daily office of the Catholic Church as the Compline, the last liturgical prayer of the day, spoken after nightfall. The Psalms used were 4; 91; and 134, in that order. The psalm breathes the spirit of rest, of the One who is *maker of heaven and earth* watching over us. This pilgrim song is a fitting benediction not only for the day, but also for the journey of life.

Psalm 135

Hallelujah to the LORD Above All Gods!

PREVIEW

This liturgical hymn invites priests and laity to offer praise for the goodness and greatness of the LORD. The psalm praises the God of creation and redemption by whose favor the election of Israel became a central element of salvation history. Themes include the LORD's special relationship to Israel and the LORD's supremacy over all gods. This storytelling psalm, like Psalms 105 and 136, praises God's mighty acts.

Reasons to praise the LORD make up the body of the psalm (vv. 5-18), which is framed by the introductory call to praise (vv. 1-4) and the concluding call to praise (vv. 19-21). The psalm begins and ends with the liturgical shout *Praise the LORD!* (*Hallelujah!* vv. 1, 21 NJPS), forming an inclusio.

In anthological style, the psalm draws on other psalms and OT passages to form a musical mosaic of praise. Readers can identify many parallels: v. 1//Ps 113:1; vv. 1-2//Ps 134:1; v. 3a//Ps 136:1; v. 4//Exod 19:5; Deut 7:6; v. 5//Exod 18:11; Ps 115:3; v. 7//Jer 10:13; 51:16; vv. 10-12//Ps 136:17-21; v. 13//Exod 3:15; v. 14//Deut 32:36; vv. 15-18//Ps 115:5-8. Drawing on some fixed and stylized worship forms, the psalmist likely designed this hymn for antiphonal use at one of the major festivals. The emphasis on the exodus from Egypt and entrance into Canaan suggests the Passover.

Psalm 135

Scholars often link Psalms 135 and 136 as partner psalms, following the collection of praise in Psalms 111–118 and 120–134. Whether intended or coincidental, Psalms 135–136 form an appendix to the Songs of Ascents, articulating the praise invited by Psalm 134:1-2 and use of the key word *bless* (Pss 134:2-3; 135:19-21).

OUTLINE

Invitation to Praise, 135:1-4
Motivation for Praise, 135:5-18
    135:5-7   The LORD's Mighty Deeds in Creation
    135:8-12   The LORD's Mighty Deeds in Exodus and Conquest
    135:13-14   The Permanence of the LORD's Name
    135:15-18   The Powerlessness of Idols
Concluding Call to Praise, 135:19-21

EXPLANATORY NOTES

Invitation to Praise   135:1-4

Psalm 135 opens with an extended summons to praise the LORD. It sounds the call to *praise* four times and mentions *the LORD* six times in these opening verses. The summons is directed to all the people who have gathered for worship (vv. 1-2). The *name* (vv. 1, 3, 13) symbolizes the nature of God, here identified as *good* and *gracious*, in keeping with the essence of *Yahweh*, a name that means "present to act in salvation" (v. 3). The *house of the LORD* (v. 2) expresses the mystery and wonder of revelation, the object of all prayer, praise, and reflection.

Verse 4 introduces the psalm's theme, the historical experience of Israel as the LORD's *own possession*. The Hebrew word *segullâ* is used to convey that the LORD chose "precious treasure" in claiming Israel as his "prized possession" (Exod 19:5; Deut 7:6-7; 14:2; 26:17-19; 1 Chron 29:3; Eccles 2:8; Mal 3:17). Emphasis is on the divine graciousness that called Israel into being as the people of the LORD.

Motivation for Praise   135:5-18

Motivation for praise, already introduced with the opening *for* (*kî*, v. 4), is now carried further with another *for* (*kî*, v. 5) to open the body of the hymn celebrating the LORD's power and greatness as the creator and deliverer of his people.

A solo voice gives personal witness to the LORD's omnipotence

(v. 5; Exod 18:11; Ps 115:3). *All deeps* (v. 6) may refer to the subterranean supply of water, source of springs and rivers, or the phrase might allude to the story of the defeat of the sea and its deeps. The allusion to *clouds, lightnings, rain, wind* (v. 7), four components of a Palestinian storm, suggests to some that this psalm may have been used at the harvest Feast of Tabernacles and the beginning of the rainy season. Verse 7 may have been part of the common stock of liturgical material (Jer 10:13; 51:16).

Following this account of the LORD's mastery over chaos by means of his mighty deeds in creation, the hymn appeals to history as evidence of the greatness of God (vv. 8-12). Three deeds are mentioned: plagues in Egypt (vv. 8-9; Ps 78:51), victory over Pharaoh and the nations and kings who stood in the way of Israel's entry into Canaan (vv. 9-11; Num 21:21-35; Deut 2:26—3:11), and bestowal of the land as inheritance to Israel (v. 12; Ps 105:11).

The *LORD* and his *name* are symbols of liberty and deliverance, as people remember the saving acts in the past (103:7). The congregation now joins in a choral refrain to celebrate the LORD's *name* and *renown*, affirming again how, in compassion, *the LORD will vindicate his people* (vv. 13-14).

The LORD's defeat of hostile powers means that images representing those powers are worthless (vv. 15-18). The psalm heaps scorn upon idols as a reminder to unconditional faithfulness and renunciation of foreign gods (Ps 115:4-8; Isa 44:9-20). The contrast between the powerlessness of idols and the might of the LORD is clear. The LORD made Israel, but the nations made their gods (Mays, 1994b:416).

Concluding Call to Praise   135:19-21

Against the background of the greatness of the LORD, the psalm closes much as it began, with a renewed invitation to *Praise the LORD!* It repeats *Bless the LORD* four times. Blessing is a form of praising in the sense of "Let God be worshipped, adored." The threefold call to *bless the LORD* (Ps 115:9-11; 118:1-3) becomes fourfold by mentioning the *house of Levi* (v. 20). In the postexilic time, Levites formed a subordinate order of temple officials in charge of various minor tasks, while the priests (*house of Aaron*) performed all the important duties (A. Anderson, 2:893). With this concluding call to praise, the psalm addresses the community, the priests, Levites, and God-fearers, or proselytes.

THE TEXT IN THE BIBLICAL CONTEXT AND LIFE OF THE CHURCH

God in History

Jewish worship uses this psalm, with its brief rehearsal of the great historic creed of Israel, as the morning psalm for Passover. It is also one of the psalms recited for the Sabbath morning services of the great festivals (Holladay: 142). Psalm 135 has also had a long history of use by the church. Traditional monastic practice was to sing Psalms 135 and 136 on Wednesdays. The Eastern Orthodox Church uses these two psalms on solemn feast days (Reardon: 269).

The psalm proclaims God's redemptive interventions in the history of ancient Israel. God is sovereign. God reigns, and therefore our hope is not in ourselves, but in God. The church has come to view the LORD's election of Israel (Exod 19:5; Deut 7:6) as a foreshadowing and firstfruits of the church (1 Thess 1:4). Christian use of this psalm connects it with the calling out of a people through Jesus Christ (Titus 2:14; 1 Pet 2:9-10). The psalm is an appropriate hymn of praise for all who believe that by grace they belong to the people of God. Psalm 135 sees God at the heart of all human experience.

Historians today tend to assume that God is to be excluded from history writing. Not so in the OT. According to the biblical record, an event in history is something transparent, something that offers a glimpse "of the sphere of the sole Power" (Martin Buber, via Knight, 2:305). History, as it appears in these psalms, is not a critical reconstruction of the past. It is a "liturgical use of tradition whose interest is the way the past impinges on the present and shapes the future" (Mays, 1994b:418). Such reviews of history (Pss 78; 105; 106; 135; 136) draw attention to the role of grateful, factual remembering in worship. Christian creeds have a similar pattern and role in worship, moving from creation to redemption to consummation. Hallelujah! (Rev 19:1-6).

Psalm 136

Litany of Thanksgiving: "For His Steadfast Love Endures Forever"

PREVIEW

Hear the sound of thanksgiving and joy as the reader voices the first line, and the choir of Levites and all the people join in the refrain *kîlĕ-'ôlām ḥasdô! For his steadfast love endures forever!* As the reader recites line by line the wonders of God, a burst of music comes from the stringed instruments, cymbals clash, and the masses shout, *For his steadfast love endures forever!*

This litany of thanksgiving, used at festivals in the temple, is a hymn constructed so the recital of God's wondrous deeds becomes an exposition of the refrain. God's *steadfast love* (*ḥesed*), God's mercy, is his oath and action on behalf of Israel. God's eternal grace is the motivating power of the wondrous works of his creation and ordering of the universe (vv. 4-9), as well as the saving deeds he has wrought on behalf of his people Israel, from deliverance in exodus to inheritance of the land (vv. 10-22). This mighty God continues to care for his people (vv. 23-25). The summons to thankful praise frames the hymn (vv. 1-3, 26).

Psalm 136 resembles Psalm 135 in structure and subject matter. If the responses are removed, the recital sounds much like that of the

Psalm 136

preceding psalm. Psalm 135 contrasts the LORD and his people with the nations and their idols. Psalm 136 expounds the steadfast love of the LORD. Both psalms may be drawing on common oral worship traditions. A clue to the psalm's use in the postexilic assembly may be found in 2 Chronicles 7:1-6.

OUTLINE

Introductory Summons to Thankful Praise, 136:1-3
Motivation: The LORD's Great Wonders, 136:4-25
    136:4-9   The LORD's Majesty in Creation
    136:10-22   The LORD's Wonders in the History of Israel
    136:23-25   The LORD's Continuing Care for His People
Concluding Summons to Give Thanks, 136:26

EXPLANATORY NOTES

Introductory Summons to Thankful Praise   136:1-3

This hymn begins with a summons to give thankful praise to the God whose stature and power are unique and without challenge. The first line sets the theme of the hymn (1 Chron 16:34; 2 Chron 7:1-3). To give thanks is to confess, to acknowledge and tell publicly what God has done.

The response line *for his steadfast love endures forever* often occurs in other passages (2 Chron 5:13; 20:21; Ezra 3:11; Pss 89:2; 100:5; 106:1; 107:1; 118:1-4; 138:8). The term *hesed, steadfast love*, is the most basic characteristic of God toward his people and is variously translated: love, mercy, grace, kindness, fidelity, loyalty. It implies a pledge, a covenant love, love that is boundless, love that loves no matter what the circumstance or response *[Steadfast].* Versions render the idea of the word *endures* in a variety of ways: forever, everlasting, eternal, never fails, never quits. The refrain claims that the origin and history of Israel and of the world are inextricably tied to the love of God.

The psalm uses several divine titles: LORD, *God of gods, Lord of lords,* and *God of heaven* (vv. 1, 2, 3, 26). *God of gods* and *Lord of lords* (Deut 10:17) suggests, "God, who is God indeed!" The God of Israel is the Lord and Master in unlimited sovereignty and freedom.

Motivation: The LORD's Great Wonders   136:4-25

Verse 4 states the subject of the body of the hymn, the *great wonders* of the LORD, as reason for thankful praise (vv. 4-25). According to

Clifford (1986:73), these verses should not be divided into deeds of "creation" (vv. 4-9) and deeds of "redemption" (vv. 10-22), for the actions constitute a single process. "God makes the environment for human community by arranging heaven and earth, and makes the community itself by freeing the people from Pharaoh and giving them their land." The LORD who made Israel a people continues to rescue that people from foes and gives them the produce of the land (vv. 23-25).

Recital of the LORD's *great wonders* (*niplā'ôt*) begins with recognition of his majestic deeds in creating the universe (Gen 1). God's *wonders* are great acts on behalf of the people that evoke awe (Pss 78:4, 11-12; 105:2, 5; 106:2, 7, 22). These "songs of impossibility" become part of Israel's doxology. *Wonders* (*niplā'ôt*) is a confessional term for special happenings enacted by the divine power and purpose. The hymn claims that the *LORD* is not only the God who has done the creative work *alone*, but also the only one who could do it (v. 4). *By understanding* (v. 5) refers to the wisdom motif of *understanding* at the LORD's side during creation (Job 38:4; Ps 104:24; Prov 3:19).

Crucial to this recital of the LORD's wonders are the verbs: *made, spread, made, rule, rule* as relating to creation (vv. 5-9). Striking verbs tell of the exodus and entry into the land: *struck, brought, divided, overthrew, led, struck down, killed,* and *gave* (vv. 10-22). These verbs suggest identifiable moments in the life experience of Israel (Brueggemann, 1988:96).

The history of God's people in verses 10-22 is similar to Psalm 135:8-12. When the psalms speak of Israel's beginnings, the basic event is always the exodus and deliverance from Egypt (Pss 105:43; 114:1; 136:11, 14, 21). *Red Sea* (v. 13, *yam sûp*) may be *Sea of Reeds* (NRSV n, NIV n, NJPS). Verse 16 refers to Israel's experience of divine guidance during the wilderness period (Deut 8:15-16; Jer 2:6; Amos 2:10). Events of the entry into the land of Canaan are once again described, with clear focus on the LORD as giver of the land (vv. 17-22; Num 21:21-35; Ps 135:10-12).

With the shift from third person to first person (vv. 23-25), the recital brings the story to the present. The majestic God of creation and of history *remembered us, rescued us,* and *gives food to all flesh.* We can read these verses as God's remembrance of Israel from the days of its settlement in Canaan (Judg 3:7-9; 6:1–8:32), onward through the distresses suffered at the hands of Arameans, Assyrians, and Babylonians. These verses sound like the confession of the post-exilic community as to how they are beneficiary of the LORD's ḥesed.

How the Creator and Lord of the universe stooped down in loving-kindness to them in their *low estate* (v. 23) never ceased to be a wonder! The daily *food to all flesh* (v. 25; Ps 104:27-29) is no less a wonder! *All flesh* is a metaphor for human frailty in its terrifying vulnerability. However, the LORD God cares and provides, *for his steadfast love endures forever.*

Concluding Summons to Give Thanks   136:26

The final verse completes an inclusio by repeating the opening theme (vv. 1-3, 26). *God of heaven* is a title used only this one time in the Psalms, but is found in other late writings of the OT (2 Chron 36:23; Ezra 1:2; Neh 1:4-5; Dan 2:18; Jon 1:9).

THE TEXT IN THE BIBLICAL CONTEXT AND LIFE OF THE CHURCH

The Great Hallel

Psalm 136, by itself or with Psalm 135, constitutes the Great Hallel (Song of Praise) sung on the morning of every Sabbath, on Passover night, and for the feast of Hanukkah. The psalm's connection with Passover is clear because of its recital of the exodus story. Some have also suggested that the psalm connects to the Feast of Tabernacles, the fall harvest festival, because of verse 25 (A. Anderson, 2: 893). Psalm 136 anticipates Psalm 145, which also speaks of the LORD's wonders and of his sustenance to all creatures (Ps 145:15-21).

Repetition of the refrain in each verse conveys a sense of peaceful serenity in the constant, abiding love of God. Therefore, it is jarring to recognize that the history recited is marked with violence, such as the slaying of firstborn in Egypt, the fate of Pharaoh and his armies, and the killing of famous kings (vv. 10, 15, 17-20). When Psalm 136:1 was spoken before a military campaign against Moabites and Ammonites (2 Chron 20:21), the phrase *for he is good* was struck out, explained the rabbis in the midrash, because there would be "no rejoicing before Him on high over the destruction [even] of wicked people" (Stuhlmueller, 1983, 2:185-86). The stark realism of this psalm's language indicates that God's love is not simply sentimental. God's creational purposes, "God's will to grant life to the threatened and dispossessed (vv. 23-24), cannot finally be opposed with impunity" (McCann, 1996:1225). Yet, the psalm can utter deeds of violence, whether the slaying of firstborn or famous kings, in the same breath with *His steadfast love endures forever*; this contrast should cause sensitive people of faith to take an agonizing pause.

The church's worship often uses Psalm 136 as a litany of thanksgiving (sometimes in edited versions omitting the "violent" verses). The psalm has served as a model for many other litanies. It has also been a source of hymnody, including "Let us, with a gladsome mind" (John Milton, 1623), "Give to our God immortal praise" (Isaac Watts, 1719), and "We give thanks unto you" (Marty Haugen, 1986).

Acclaiming God's Love at Every Moment

Whether for public worship or for personal meditation, Psalm 136 enables us to acclaim God's love at every moment of our existence. This psalm, with mercy defining God in relation to everything, fits all contexts as it moves from creation to deliverance to being given a place. We can identify our own individual story with the psalm's movement. The psalm illuminates our redemption and the meaning of our baptism and faith pilgrimage (1 Cor 5:7; 10:1-13). The *wilderness* (v. 16) is a reality metaphorically, if not literally, for all of us. Only by the gracious leading of God do we find our way through and out of the wilderness to the place God has for us.

As part of *all flesh* we share the frailty of humanity in our daily dependence upon food for sustenance. The Lord's Prayer (Matt 6:9-13) combines prayer for the reign of God and the gift of daily bread. Giving thanks over a plate of food acknowledges the wonder that the gift of daily food is on the same level as the great acts of creation, exodus, and entry (place). We can find an appropriate mealtime prayer in Psalm 136:1 or 136:2.

Psalm 137

By the Rivers of Babylon

PREVIEW

This community lament is easiest of all the psalms to date. It comes from the time of the exile, after the Jerusalem temple was destroyed (587 or 586 BC), and likely before the temple was rebuilt (515 BC). Psalm 137 is also the most difficult of the psalms to read and accept because of the raw hate and vengeance voiced in verses 7-9.

The psalm begins with the refugee experience of Israelites in Babylonia after the fall of Jerusalem. The author describes how he and his fellow exiles in grief *remembered* Jerusalem (vv. 1-4), how he was ready to be cursed if he were to *forget* Jerusalem and if he did not *remember* her (vv. 5-6). Therefore, God simply must *remember* the *day of Jerusalem* against the foes (vv. 7-9). From silent mourning and homesickness, the psalm moves into self-cursing if he does not keep the vow and becomes a prayer of bitter imprecation toward the enemy.

The psalm is characterized by an envelope construction in which the outer sections fold around the inner ones (Freedman: 203). The opening and closing sections (vv. 1-2 and 8-9) form an inclusio (with *Babylon* in vv. 1 and 8). The body of the psalm consists of an outer shell (vv. 3 and 7) and an inner core (vv. 4-6), with verses 5-6ab serving as center of the psalm. Thus, the focus is on Jerusalem, now in ruins, but a powerful symbol of faith in God's power to control history.

Perhaps when the psalm was written, its author was no longer in Babylon (vv. 1, 3), but he may well have seen the ruins of the Holy

City, stirring in him the grief-stricken anger and vitriolic utterance against Edom and Babylon.

OUTLINE

Community Lament: Silent Mourning in Remembering Zion, 137:1-4
The Writer's Vow to Remember Zion, 137:5-6
Petition for the LORD to Remember Against Zion's Enemies, 137:7-9

EXPLANATORY NOTES

Community Lament: Silent Mourning in Remembering Zion   137:1-4

Uprooted from their homes, the exiles could only sit in silence and mourn with tears. Their musical instruments hung undisturbed in the trees along the irrigation canals. Another account of the plight of such refugees is given by Ezekiel (3:15), who sat for seven days with those distraught at Tel-abib by the river Chebar (*Canal*, NJPS).

When taunted by their captors to sing happy songs, these refugees refused. Songs of Zion (Pss 46; 48; 76; 84; 87; 122) tell of Jerusalem as impregnable and its inhabitants as happy and safe. But in this foreign land, separated from Zion, songs of praise for the amusement of their captors would have been a desecration. The crisis provoked by the destruction of Jerusalem and the temple was more than geographical separation from their homeland. This was a crisis of faith, and the medium of the LORD's presence, singing songs of thanksgiving, was no longer there for them. That is the deep sense of despair in which Israel found herself in exile (Guthrie: 111-12). Thus, the psalm's central question can be found in verse 4: Can we worship our God in *a foreign land? [Zion]*.

The Writer's Vow to Remember Zion   137:5-6

Voicing a firm vow, the psalmist responds with a resounding "Yes!" It comes in the form of a solemn oath resembling a self-imprecation. Jerusalem, *my highest joy*, dare never, never be forgotten! Ironically, having asserted the impossibility of singing *songs of Zion* in the foreign land of Babylon, the vow is precisely to continue doing so.

Petition for the LORD to Remember Against Zion's Enemies   137:7-9

Interpreters of Psalm 137 find difficulty in the curses uttered upon Edom and Babylon (vv. 7-9). The Edomites, a nomadic people who lived southeast of Judah, allied with the Babylonians in plundering Jerusalem (2 Kings 25:8-12; Ezek 35:1-5; Obad 8-14; cf. 2 Kings 24:2, similar raids; 2 Chron 28:17, earlier raid). According to tradition, they were descended from Esau, Jacob's brother, and so were distant cousins of the Israelites. That made their cheerleading for the Babylonian invaders all the more abhorrent. *Remember, O LORD* (v. 7) is the imprecatory plea for divine retribution upon them.

However, the harshest words demanding payback are directed toward Babylon, as evil personified (v. 8). *Happy* (*Blessed*, NASB) will be those who *take your little ones and dash them against the rock!* Sadly, killing the children, seeking to wipe out the next generation, was normal practice in warfare of those days (Deut 20:16; Josh 6:21; 2 Kings 8:12; Hos 9:16; Nah 3:10). The prayers appear as a naked appeal for retribution in the context of other prophecies that look for punishment of Edom and Babylon (Isa 34; 47; Jer 49:7-22; 51:1-58; Ezek 35; Obad 1-21). In these prayers, victims give voice to exasperation. Moreover, through the confidence gained by remembrance, the people pour out their petitions, beseeching the LORD to intervene once again for his defeated and scattered people. They call on the LORD not to allow his enemies free reign, or to let their rage go unanswered (Pss 79:10-12; 83:9-12). They call on God to remember and act with judgment against those who had destroyed the place that he had chosen as his *resting place forever* (132:13-14). Nevertheless, these words of verses 8-9 are appalling to the modern reader and stir images of gas chambers and other forms of ethnic cleansing. What is their place in the Bible and in the life of the church? *[Enemies; Imprecation; Vengeance; War].*

THE TEXT IN THE BIBLICAL CONTEXT AND LIFE OF THE CHURCH

Faith Shaped by Exile and Suffering

In contrast to the protest in verse 4, Israel did learn to sing *the LORD's song* in a foreign land. From the experiences of suffering in exile, the nation brought back the synagogue, its Scriptures, and these psalms. The exile shaped Israel's life and faith, as did the exodus out of Egypt. In the sequence of the Psalter, following the Hallel collections of Psalms 113–118 and 120–136, Psalm 137 introduces the last set of Davidic and Hallelujah psalms. The plaintive cry of the exiles is answered by the sequence of Davidic psalms that offer praise to the LORD. Jewish practice is to recite Psalm 137 on weekdays, at the beginning of the blessing after meals. The meal is a reminder of the altar of sacrifice in the temple. Recitation of the lament offers remembrance of the loss of the temple (Holladay: 80, 145).

The lectionary readings for the Christian Church Year include Psalm 137. Most church hymnals include songs based on this psalm, such as the traditional canon "By the waters, the waters of Babylon, we sat down and wept, and wept for thee, Zion. We remember thee, we remember thee, remember thee, Zion." Many Christians wonder, however, whether they should be reciting or hearing these imprecations in public worship, lest they incite feelings of hatred and vengeance. How do we respond to the white-hot imprecation of Psalm 137, especially verse 9?

Dealing with Rage

As we ponder the appropriateness of celebrating the brain-bashing of Babylonian babies (v. 9), one can make a case for omitting certain psalm verses in Christian worship. On the other hand, we should not dismiss Psalm 137 too readily. By legitimizing rage, it can speak for us and for all people who experience massive upheaval in life. It is a prayer that we are fed up! It is a prayer that the wrongs we or others experience are an assault on God! (cf. Rev 6:9-11). This psalm reminds us not to gloss over rage, but to take it seriously. So it speaks for many victims of abuse, oppression, and violence today.

Second, it is a prayer that can help us relinquish rage. In prayer we can offer up our most entrenched hatreds to God, and then let them go. This is the prayer of trusting that the sovereign God will, in good time and in God's own way, be faithful. Eugene Peterson writes about human hurt not being a promising step to the accomplishment of wholeness, but human hurt prayed is a step into the presence of God. "Hate, prayed, takes our lives to bedrock where the foundations of justice are laid" (Peterson, 1989:101). Pouring out bitterness and hurt can be the beginning of healing.

Breaking the Cycle of Violence

This passage confronts us again with the cruel aspects of warfare. In war, "eye for eye" (Exod 21:24) is never enough. The cycle of violence widens in acts of retaliation. Warring parties think that they must always develop greater weapons. So they add nuclear bombs, napalm, chemical and biological weapons to the arsenal. Smart bombs do not assure that innocent children will not die. War is barbaric in every age.

We may find a further clue to appropriating Psalm 137 in the psalm's keyword, *remember*. Our remembering needs to include other biblical words about the attitude toward enemies. The OT itself gives witness to an alternative and humane way of treating prisoners of war (2 Kings 6:20-23; 2 Chron 28:8-15), and of thinking the unthinkable, of praying for the peace and welfare (*shalom*) of Babylon (Jer 29:7) *[War]*.

To the harshness of this psalm we must also bring the teaching of Jesus about another way: "Love your enemies" (Matt 5:38-48). Paul follows Jesus' words with "Do not repay anyone evil for evil, and if your enemies are hungry, feed them . . ." (Rom 12:17, 20), as he quotes a text from Deuteronomy (32:35): "Vengeance is mine, I will repay, says the Lord." Is it legitimate for Christians to wish for commensurate hurt on their enemies, or wish death on their enemies? The Scriptures point to another way for people of faith, who trust in the God whose *steadfast love endures forever* (Pss 136:26; 138:2).

Psalm 138

I Give Thanks, O LORD, with My Whole Heart

PREVIEW

Psalm 138 is a song of thanksgiving (*tôdâ*) for a specific deliverance from trouble (vv. 3, 7). In the temple, the worshipper praises the LORD for his steadfast love and faithfulness (vv. 1-3, 8). The second stanza (vv. 4-6) expands the invitation to praise the LORD to *all the kings of the earth* (v. 4), for the LORD's *glory*, for he *regards the lowly* (vv. 5-6). Rescued, the psalmist trusts that the LORD will always be there in moments of danger, continuing the earlier protection (vv. 7-8).

The question for interpreters of Psalm 138 focuses on identification of the speaker. Is it the king or an unidentified individual who offers this song of thanksgiving? Most commonly, readers interpret this psalm as coming from an individual in the court of the temple (v. 2), expressing gratitude for some deliverance, perhaps healing from sickness (vv. 3, 7). The comments that follow take this approach. One can also understand the psalm, in later use, as a song of praise by the restored community in the postexilic period (Isa 40–66). To the title *Of David*, some Septuagint manuscripts add "of Haggai and Zechariah," possibly from a tradition that the psalm belonged to the period of the Restoration. This is the first in a group of eight psalms titled *Of David [Superscriptions]*.

Other individual songs of thanksgiving include Psalms 30; 32; 34; 40; 41; 92; and 116. Psalms 138 and 145 frame a group of individual laments. While these psalms may have originated as individual prayers, they were capable of speaking to the crisis of the exile and its aftermath in keeping with the response of book V.

OUTLINE

Wholehearted Thanksgiving for an Answered Prayer, 138:1-3
Expectation of Universal Homage to the LORD of the Lowly, 138:4-6
Confession of Trust and Petition for Continuing Help, 138:7-8

EXPLANATORY NOTES

Wholehearted Thanksgiving for an Answered Prayer 138:1-3

The first Hebrew word, *yādāh* (*give thanks,* related to *tôdâ,* "thanksgiving"), determines the character of the psalm. A member of the community comes into the presence of the LORD with a song of thanksgiving offered *with my whole heart* (vv. 1-3). The heart was considered the center of human life (Pss 9:1; 86:12; 119:2, 7, 10, 34). Praise is sung *before the gods* ('*ĕlōhîm*: "godlike beings," "angels," "kings," or "judges"; *divine beings,* NJPS). Here it could mean "heavenly beings" portrayed as surrounding the throne of God and serving him (Pss 29:1; 58:1), or it could refer to the gods of the foreign peoples who powerlessly watch the praise of the Most High God (A. Anderson, 2:901-2).

The worshipping community bows down before the temple to address prayers to the LORD, because in the inner sanctuary, the LORD is present (v. 2). The psalmist may be speaking from the forecourt of the temple. He looks toward the sanctuary, where he will bow down and worship (Ps 5:7). The psalmist finds motivation for thanksgiving, first of all, in the LORD's *steadfast love and faithfulness.* The LORD's *steadfast love* (*ḥesed*) involves a community relationship and expresses the element of loyalty (Pss 25:10; 40:11; 61:7; 89:14). *Exalted . . . above everything* or *made thy promise wide as the heavens* (v. 2c NEB) suggests that God offers everything to human beings, including himself *[Steadfast].*

Verse 3 summarizes the LORD's saving intervention. The motive for thanksgiving is specific. God has been faithful to me. The speaker knows when and where, and on which day. Verse 3b has variant translations, from *You increased my strength of soul* (NRSV) to *You made me bold and stouthearted* (NIV, cf. NEB). Whatever the distress, a song of thanksgiving is testimony to a lament resolved.

Expectation of Universal Homage to the LORD of the Lowly 138:4-6

In *tôdâ* (thanksgiving), the individual praying wants the kings of the nations to join in offering thanks. This idealistic and enthusiastic appeal reminds the earthly kings of the LORD's ways (fidelity to his promises and saving deliverance), and of the LORD's great glory (v. 5; Pss 24:7-10; 29:1-3, 9-11). Kings can understand regal power and splendor. However, now comes the surprise in the pivotal point and central testimony of the psalm: *The LORD is high,* but *he regards the lowly* (v. 6). That is unlike the other *gods* and unlike conventional *kings* (vv. 1, 4). The miracle of the divine condescension is that the exalted LORD is not too proud to help the least of his creatures (113:4-9; Isa 57:15; 66:2). Glory is not only power, but also magnanimity. God chose Israel to be a light to the nations. God chose Israel to identify with the underprivileged (Knight, 2:318). As for the kings of the earth, they should take note that the LORD may be *far away,* but the LORD sees (v. 6; Pss 10:14; 11:4; 14:2; 33:13-15; 35:22; 94:9; 102:19-20; 113:5-7; 139:3, 16, 24).

Confession of Trust and Petition for Continuing Help 138:7-8

Psalm 138 concludes with a confession of trust and petition for continuing help. The oppressed receive help and assistance from the LORD. The worshipper knows himself to be safe in the LORD's everlasting grace (Ps 23:4-6). The psalm ends as it began, with the affirmation of *steadfast love, ḥesed* (vv. 2, 8). The last line voices a petition, but in words of quiet trust, that the LORD is at work in and through the psalmist's life in the past and will be there to continue that work into the future. When applied to the community, Israel is *the work of your hands* (Isa 60:21; 64:8), and in submission to the LORD finds her purpose and confidence (Stuhlmueller, 1983, 2:193).

THE TEXT IN THE BIBLICAL CONTEXT AND LIFE OF THE CHURCH

Thanksgiving as Testimony to God's Steadfast Love

In Psalm 138, the psalmist acknowledges deliverance (v. 3a), but continues to pray for liberation. With gratitude the psalmist trusts that God's character is to manifest *steadfast love* and *faithfulness* (v. 2). The two words became part of the basic confession of Israel's faith

(Exod 34:6-7) and are frequently paired in appeals to God for help (Pss 40:11-12; 115:1-2).

Several themes in Psalm 138 connect directly with themes and passages in the NT. One of these is the LORD's exaltation of his name and word *above everything* (vv. 2, 8). That God shows himself more than we could ever have known or imagine appears in the blessing "to him who by the power at work within us is able to accomplish abundantly far more than all we can ask or imagine . . . " (Eph 3:20).

Expressions of God's steadfast love (vv. 2, 8) are found in John 3:16 and Philippians 2:5-11. The divine condescension in the incarnation of Jesus Christ connects with Psalm 138:6, a verse with many NT allusions. These include Mary's Magnificat, "For he has looked with favor on the lowliness of his servant" (Luke 1:48). In his parable about the Pharisee and the tax collector, Jesus says, "All who exalt themselves will be humbled, but all who humble themselves will be exalted" (18:14). We also find divine condescension in two quotations of the saying "God opposes the proud, but gives grace to the humble" (cf. Ps 138:6; James 4:6; 1 Pet 5:5). We find the theme of God fulfilling his purpose in us again in Paul's declaration, "I am confident of this, that the one who began a good work among you will bring it to completion by the day of Jesus Christ" (Phil 1:6).

In the worship of the church, Psalm 138:1-3 is appropriate as an invocation for a service of thanksgiving. The psalm provides a guide to the meaning and practice of thanksgiving. Salvation is not primarily for our sake; instead, it is foremost about the coming kingdom of God. Thanksgiving is testimony, inviting others to join in praise of *the glory of the LORD,* whose *steadfast love . . . endures forever* (vv. 5, 8).

Congregations can use the psalm in celebrating the Lord's Supper. One of the names given that ritual of celebrative remembrance is "Eucharist," a Greek word meaning "gratitude" and "thanksgiving." The bread and cup is our way of giving thanks for how our Lord comes to us and how we are embraced and lifted up in the fellowship of God's community.

A Model for Prayer

As an example of prayer, Psalm 138 begins with the psalmist's assertion of prayer *with my whole heart* (v. 1). Too often contemporary claims of "praying from the heart" identify sincerity with emotional spontaneity. Biblically, prayer from the heart refers to the core of our being, the context of decision and resolve, a region vastly deeper than our feelings and emotions. The most fundamental confession we can make in our hearts is, "Jesus is Lord!" In his name we pray (1 Cor 12:3; Reardon: 275-76).

As a model for prayer, Psalm 138 begins with adoration, in thankful praise of God Most High for an act of personal deliverance (vv. 1-3). The prayer then broadens to a global perspective and mission thrust on behalf of God, who in mercy condescends to the lowly and helpless (vv. 4-6). It concludes with trusting personal confession, accepting the divine purpose for one's life, and the petition for God's continuing help to fulfill that purpose (vv. 7-8).

Psalm 139

O LORD, You Have Searched Me and Know Me

PREVIEW

This reflective meditation on the LORD as the total environment of life has become a devotional classic. Its intimate exploration of the relationship between the sensitive soul and the all-encompassing God has universal appeal to every generation.

The psalm is a prayer addressed to the God who searches and knows the human being. God knows everything (omniscience, vv. 1-6), is present everywhere (omnipresence, vv. 7-12), and as creator, can do anything (omnipotence, vv. 13-16). God's thoughts and designs defy human understanding (vv. 17-18). God can destroy the wicked (vv. 19-22) and provide guidance into *the way everlasting* (vv. 23-24).

The theme, God and self, is introduced and reaffirmed by the opening and closing verbs: *search* (vv. 1, 3, 23), *know* (vv. 1, 2, 23), *discern* (v. 2), and *test* (v. 23). These verbs belong to vocabulary describing the LORD's activity as a divine judge who discerns and assesses the human heart (Job 7:17-18; 13:9; Ps 11:4-7; Jer 9:7; 17:10). As used in every verse, the second- and first-person pronouns, *you, your, I, me, my,* point to how God and self are inextricably the subject of the psalm; they give an intimacy to this dialogical prayer.

The inclusio formed by verses 1-3 and 23-24 affirms the psalm's unity in spite of the sharp break in thought by the imprecation of verses 19-22.

As to setting, Psalm 139 is often interpreted as a protestation of innocence by one accused of being an idolater. In that scenario, the psalmist asks the omniscient God to probe him and testify to his innocence (vv. 23-24). Or the psalm may be the prayer of a sensitive person meditating on the meaning of life. The word translated *search* (*ḥāqar*, vv. 1, 23) occurs most frequently in the wisdom literature (Job 5:27; 13:9; 28:3, 27; Prov 18:17; 25:2). One may read the psalm as an individual's reflection on his intimate relationship with God. Consequently, readers have variously classified Psalm 139 as the prayer of an accused person (lament and imprecation), a wisdom reflection on God's active presence, or a hymn expressing thankful praise for God's wonders (vv. 6, 14).

Psalm 139, the second in a series of eight psalms given the ascription *Of David* (138–145), is the first of six laments, prayers for deliverance from enemies *[Superscriptions]*. While one of the most appealing and prayerful poems, it is also one of the more complex psalms because of uncertain text, as shown in the variety of translations and footnotes to several verses.

OUTLINE

Prayer Extolling the All-knowing, Ever-present, and Wonder-creating God, 139:1-18
    139:1-6   You Have Searched Me and Know Me
    139:7-12   There Is No Escape from Your Presence
    139:13-18   I Am Fearfully and Wonderfully Made
Prayer for Vindication and Deliverance, 139:19-24
    139:19-22   Imprecation for Destruction of the Wicked
    139:23-24   Petition: Search Me and Know My Heart

EXPLANTORY NOTES

Prayer Extolling the All-knowing, Ever-present, and Wonder-creating God   139:1-18

This hymnic prayer begins with affirmation of God's intimate acquaintance with all our ways (vv. 1-6). *Search* and *know* implies knowledge of the intimate, personal, private affairs of human beings. To *sit down* and *rise up* encompasses all of a person's activities, one's whole life (vv. 2-3). This description of the LORD's knowledge emphasizes God's ability to *see* and *discern* from afar. Not only actions and words are well known, but also human thoughts (v. 4). You *hem me in* and *lay your hand upon me* may appear confining, though they can also mean protection and blessing in the sense of being held close (v. 5). The initial response to being known by God so intimately and fully is wonder and reverent awe at the mystery of such an all-knowing God (v. 6; Isa 55:8-9).

Since God is ever-present as well as all-knowing, escape from the LORD is impossible (vv. 7-12). These verses do not say that the psalmist wished to escape, but imply the positive reality. There is no place where he finds himself beyond God. As for descending to Sheol (v. 8), one tradition held that the LORD was absent from Sheol (Ps 88:3-12). But another tradition confessed the LORD's presence even in the realm of the dead (Job 26:6; Ps 23:4; Prov 15:11; Amos 9:2). The horizontal dimensions of life are covered by reference to the four points of the compass (vv. 9-10). The poetic expression *wings of the morning* refers to the east, where the sun rises at dawn and rapidly spreads the light of day. The *sea* (Mediterranean) represents the farthest limits to the west. *Your right hand* would be south, and *your hand* (the left), the north. Even the mystery of *the darkness* is no cover for the eyes of the LORD (vv. 11-12). God is everywhere (Jer 23:23-24).

Why can there be no escape from the LORD? The LORD is the creator and author of every detail of the human being (vv. 13-18; Job 10:8-12). While the psalms say little about the beginning of life, in critical situations the writer reminds himself and his God of his birth (Ps 22:9-10). Here the psalmist praises God that he was created so wonderfully and formed so perfectly that nothing unknown to God can have any place in him (vv. 13-16).

The ancients viewed the development of the child in the womb as one of the great mysteries (Eccles 11:5). As the psalmist thinks of himself developing in his mother's womb, he uses not only the metaphors of knitting and weaving, but also that of a clay figure taking shape under the knowing hand of the sculptor (vv. 13, 15-16; Caird: 151). Egyptian mythopoetic texts present the notion that during pregnancy the individual fetus is fashioned by the deity (Khnum) as on a potter's wheel (*ANET* 32, 431n; Morschauser: 731-33). *The depths of the earth* (v. 15) may also allude to the mythological notion that all things come from the cosmic womb of the earth (Gen 2:7; Job 33:6; Eccles 3:20). So intricately and carefully formed, the psalmist praises God, *for I am fearfully and wonderfully made* (v. 14)!

Your book (v. 16) brings to mind other references to a divine register (Exod 32:32-33; Pss 40:7; 56:8; 69:28; Dan 12:1; Mal 3:16; Rev 21:27). On the basis of creation, all human life is open to the Creator. God's foreknowledge is accepted (v. 16; Jer 1:5), though this is not basis for a doctrine of predestination. Patrick Miller refers to predestination as "a theological claim that works better as a personal conviction about one's own destiny's being set in the purpose of God than as an effort to work out logically the mystery of God's purpose for others" (Miller, 1986:147).

Another exclamation of wonder follows (vv. 17-18) to sum up verses 1-16. Contemplating the immeasurable greatness of the LORD's knowledge and thoughts, the only human response can be thanksgiving and astonishment. As the psalmist tries to tally the uncountable wonderful works of God, he acknowledges his human limitations. The psalmist's knowing lies in trust and praise: *I am still with you* (vv. 18; cf. 6, 14).

Prayer for Vindication and Deliverance   139:19-24

As this hymnic prayer extolling the omniscient and omnipresent creating God concludes (v. 1-18), the mood shifts to a vehement imprecation upon the wicked (vv. 19-22). The *wicked* (*rāšā'*) are viewed as the enemies of the LORD. The *bloodthirsty* are those prepared to commit any violent deeds or resort to any form of deceit; they are malicious and arrogant (v. 20). In the first line of verse 24, the phrase about *wicked way* can also be translated "way of an idol" (Isa 48:5), suggesting that this psalm was originally by someone who had been falsely accused of idol worship and was making a public declaration of innocence (Holladay: 44). The psalmist looks upon those who defy the LORD with disgust (v. 21), expressing *perfect* ("whole-hearted," "undying") *hatred* for them (v. 22) *[Wicked]*.

Although the vehemence of these verses causes great difficulty for interpreters and is reason for their omission in most liturgical readings of Psalm 139, we cannot ignore them. The hatred spoken is not spite, but zeal for the LORD. The enemies of the LORD are the psalmist's enemies, and the psalmist puts himself at all possible distance from them. Vengeance is clearly left in the hands of God. The psalmist hates the evildoers for God's sake (Deut 32:35; Ps 104:35) *[Imprecation; Vengeance]*.

We should recognize the dangerous temptation to self-righteousness. In the final two verses, the psalmist confesses that he himself needs examination; he ends with the petition *Search me, O God, and know my heart* (vv. 23-24). The prayer reflects the possibility of wrong in the self. Pondering the imprecation (vv. 19-22), the poet uses language from the earlier part of the psalm about God's all-encompassing knowledge. He invites God to probe even more, as if saying, "I need to know that you know that I am not among the wicked against whom I have prayed." *Any wicked way*—literally, "a way of pain," "hurtful" (NRSV n), or "offensive" (NIV)—is reminiscent of the two ways, one leading to destruction, the other to life (Ps 1:6; Matt 7:13-14). Psalm 139 illustrates how a psalm with strong language (vv. 19-22) cannot only begin with self-critique, but also end with it.

THE TEXT IN THE BIBLICAL CONTEXT AND LIFE OF THE CHURCH

Common Themes

We have acknowledged some phraseology that Psalm 139 has in common with Job, Proverbs, and Jeremiah. Compare Job 10:8-11 with Psalm 139:13-16, and Job 17:12-13 with Psalm 139:8, 11-12.

Passages touching on themes in Psalm 139 abound in the NT. Matthew 5:44 offers a contrasting approach regarding enemies (Ps 139:19-22). Romans 8:28-30 and Ephesians 2:10 touch on God's foreknowledge and foreordination (Ps 139:16), and Romans 8:38-39 tells of nothing being able to separate us from the love (and presence) of God. Paul in Romans 11:33 speaks of God's vast knowledge, judgments, and ways, and in 1 Corinthians 13:12 he refers to knowing only in part until we have been fully known (Ps 139:6, 14, 18). God's testing of our hearts (Ps 139:23) appears in 1 Thessalonians 2:4. Hebrews 4:13 declares that no creature is hidden before the eyes of God. First John 1:3, 5, 7 proclaims how God is light and in him there is no darkness at all (Ps 139:11-12).

Liturgical Use and Model for Prayer

In ancient liturgies, Psalm 139 was sung or recited during Friday afternoon vespers, uniting an individual's prayers with the peaceful sleep of Jesus, when night was to become bright as day (v. 12) in the Lord's resurrection (Stuhlmueller, 1983, 2:200). An ancient prayer of invocation, widely used in churches at the communion service, conveys the dominant sense of Psalm 139: "Almighty God, unto whom all hearts are open, all desires known, and from whom no secrets are hid, cleanse the thoughts of our hearts. . . ."

Psalm 139 has also influenced the hymnody of the church, as in Isaac Watts' hymns "I sing the mighty power of God" (1715) and

"Lord, thou hast searched and seen" (1719), and the folk hymn from the *Psalter Hymnal* (1927) "Lord, thou hast searched me."

Psalm 139, as a hymnic declaration of innocence, affirms that God knows the inner life of the one who prays. Thus, the psalm has had strong appeal as a model for personal prayer. People sensitive to God's unrelenting Spirit have used it autobiographically, as Francis Thompson (1859–1907) did in authoring the well-known poem "The Hound of Heaven" (1893). Others have found repeated reading and reflection on the words to be a means for personal orientation. We are rooted when we know where we belong and to whom we belong.

The psalm reminds people of the necessity of perseverance in trust, of seeing by faith the strong love of God, particularly in life's darkest moments. The images of the *womb* and the *depths of the earth* (vv. 13, 15) have become metaphors for those who pray out of earthly trials, disappointment, sickness, and death. "Within each of these 'wombs' the Lord is knitting each one of us together" (Stuhlmueller, 1983, 2:199).

The devout have offered many paraphrases of Psalm 139. Kathleen Henry, a spiritual director, employed the enneagram, which identifies personality types, to adapt Psalm 139 as a prayer for persons with different personalities (Henry: 108; Holladay: 301). Her paraphrase for perfectionists begins thus:

> Spirit-Source of All Life and All Truth,
> I come from You.
> All that I am is known to You.
>
> Even if I bury, in the soil of resentment,
>   the seeds of my anger, deep,
> Even then,
> You are there—
> Seeing through to my inmost self,
> Claiming me as Your own.

Human Dignity in God's Creating Presence

Psalm 139 provides every person a remarkable basis for self-worth. Emphasis on the prenatal fashioning by God (vv. 13-16) provides a powerful reminder of the value God places upon human beings. Sophisticated modern medical technology such as the sonogram may reveal what is happening in the womb, but it cannot demystify the wonder of emerging life. In the debate regarding abortion, people often cite these verses with reference to God's activity in the formation of life in the womb, and how God knows the individual even before birth. Such affirmation can inform the discussion of abortion, though we must not read too much into the text. We must interpret the psalm within the poetic genre to which it belongs, not as a scientific or propositional statement (Hays: 446-47).

The psalmist's confession about God's divine foreknowledge and care affirms our human dignity. What a marvelous creature I am! The psalm declares that even unimportant "little me" is part of God's good and wondrous creation. God, who is everywhere present, knows me, so that at the end, *I am still with you* (v. 18)!

Although the psalm speaks about the character of God, people often use the theological terms omniscience, omnipresence, and omnipotence to describe the three sections of part one (vv. 1-18); yet the psalm's language is much more intimate. The psalm describes God as known from experience. "Devotion and confession must not be reduced to metaphysics" (Mays, 1994b:427).

Psalm 140

Protect Me from the Violent

PREVIEW

This individual lament, the prayer of an accused man who is tormented by insidious slander, cries out for God's protection from the violent (vv. 1, 4). The psalmist describes the conduct of his adversaries in images of war, poisonous snakes, and the hunter's trap (vv. 2, 3, 5). Addressing the LORD as *my strong deliverer* (v. 7), the petitioner appeals for God's justice to thwart the evil scheming of the wicked (v. 8), and to punish them with the very mischief they have plotted upon others (vv. 9-11). After the rage is spent, the psalm concludes with cheerful thanksgiving (vv. 12-13). *I know* expresses confidence in the LORD's protection for the hurting (v. 5) and justice for the poor and needy (v. 12). The psalm concludes with the certainty that the righteous will dwell in the land and give thanks to the LORD (v. 13), in contrast to the fate of the wicked (vv. 9-11).

Psalm 140 has similarities in language and content to Psalms 58; 64; and 109. This psalm introduces a series of four laments (Pss 140–143) that traditionally have been associated with difficulties David faced and the revolt led by his son Absalom (2 Sam 15–18). *[Superscriptions]* The term *Selah*, possibly a signal for a musical pause (vv. 3, 5, 8), serves as reminder of the psalm's later use in public worship *[Selah]*. Since Psalms 139–143 are framed by psalms that make sense as testimony and petition offered by the postexilic community, these individual laments and prayers for deliverance can also be heard as pertinent to the whole community.

OUTLINE

Prayer for Deliverance from the Attacks of the Wicked, 140:1-5
Plea for God to Deal with the Wicked, 140:6-13

EXPLANATORY NOTES

Prayer for Deliverance from the Attacks of the Wicked 140:1-5

The opening cry, *Deliver me, O LORD* (v. 1), suggests the long tradition of requests for rescue (Pss 6:4; 119:153) and reports of such deliverance (18:19; 34:7; 116:8). The psalm doubles the plea *Protect me from the violent* (vv. 1, 4). *Stir up wars*, from the Hebrew *yāgûrû*, "stirring strife," suggests language for a king or language borrowed from royal psalms for metaphorical use. The devising of schemes is referenced often (10:2; 35:4; 41:7; Jer 11:19). Allusion to the forked tongue of the snake (v. 3) may imply a curse upon the psalmist (Pss 58:4-5; 109:28).

The renewed appeal for protection from the violent draws on metaphors taken from the life of the hunter seeking prey (vv. 4-5; 7:15; 9:15; 31:4; 35:7-8; 57:6; 64:4-5).

Plea to God to Deal with the Wicked 140:6-13

The confession *You are my God* (v. 6) offers the psalmist's first basis of appeal. The term *My strong deliverer*, literally, "the strength of my salvation," appears only here in the OT (v. 7). The worshipper relies on his previous experience of God's help: *You have covered my head in the day of battle.* Such language normally refers to protective armor (Isa 59:17). Slander is a vicious form of violence. The appeal comes to the righteous judge for judgment upon the slanderers (vv. 8-11).

Verses 8 and 9 are difficult to interpret because of uncertain text. After the words *Do not further their evil plot,* an NRSV footnote indicates that the Hebrew reads, *They are exalted* (v. 8). The NIV translates, *or they will become proud* (v. 8c), and NJPS similarly, *else they be exalted* (v. 8c, note: "Meaning of Heb. uncertain"). The NRSV appears to transfer *They are exalted* to the beginning of verse 9: *They lift up their heads* (Davidson, 1998:452). Verses 9-11 focus on the inevitable punishment that will overtake the psalmist's slanderers, for evil signs its own death warrant (Pss 7:14-16; 9:15-16). Those who reject a person's covenantal right to the land—they themselves have no place in that land (vv. 11, 13).

With an emphatic *I know* the psalmist now asserts certainty of vindication (v. 12). God cares about the needy and the poor. Experiences of deliverance bring knowledge and a clear recognition that the LORD maintains the cause of the afflicted. The righteous will go to the temple to offer thanksgiving for deliverance. Their blessing of being able to *live in your presence* (v. 13) contrasts with the fate of the wicked in Sheol (v. 10; Pss 9:17) *[Wicked]*.

THE TEXT IN THE BIBLICAL CONTEXT AND LIFE OF THE CHURCH

Psalms as a Witness to Human Depravity

The NT draws on the psalms as a witness to human depravity. Paul quotes Psalm 140:3 in Romans 3:10-18 to illustrate the universality and deadly power of sin. However, Paul also asserts how God justifies (Rom 3:24; 8:33-35), even as Psalm 140 affirms the LORD's justice (vv. 12-13). Romans 12:20 echoes words from Psalm 140:10 and 12, but conveys a quite different attitude toward enemies, though both psalm and epistle affirm vengeance and retribution as God's prerogative.

The epistle of James (3:5-8) expands the psalm's emphasis on evils of the tongue (vv. 3, 9, 11). Jesus echoes the concluding promise about the upright living *in your presence* (Ps 140:13) as his words close the Gospel of Matthew: "I am with you always, to the end of the age" (Matt 28:20).

Prayers for Use by the Victimized and the Abused

Violence plagues the beginning of the twenty-first century. With conflicts in the Middle East, the terrorist attack on New York's World Trade Center (September 11, 2001), and wars on terrorism in Afghanistan and Iraq—violence has risen to new levels. News reports include daily death tolls, though selective reporting shields us from the real toll on all of humanity. Violent people make war on society. The use of violence is accompanied by hatred, fear, and cruelty. Victims include not only those who make up armed forces. Families, women, children, the old and frail often suffer the most. Underlying violence is arrogance, the outer sign of the sin of egotism run rampant (Knight, 2:328-29).

Unfortunately, violence takes many forms. Families are not immune to domestic strife resulting in battered spouses and physically, emotionally, and sexually abused children. Nor is the church safe from such problems. Religious strife brings out the unscrupulous worst in people. Poisoned and malicious talk, arrogance, and attempts to ensnare and trip up opponents are not reserved for the international or political arena; they are all too common even in the life of the church. The life of God's people has no place for the violence of slander (2 Cor 12:20; Eph 4:31; 1 Tim 6:4).

More positively, we should not miss the basic theological assertion of Psalm 140: the LORD preserves justice for the hurting (v. 5), the poor and the needy (v. 12). James 1:27–2:7 clearly spells out God's care for the powerless and implications for God's people. The concern for the poor and the needy is a golden thread that runs through the Scriptures (Gen 18:19; Exod 23:6, 9-11; Deut 10:17-19; Ps 10:17-18; Prov 22:22-23; Amos 5:24; Mic 6:8; Mal 3:5; Matt 25:31-46; Acts 2:43-47; Gal 2:10). In the sixteenth century, Menno Simons (307) asserted that the sharing of economic resources is as much, perhaps even more, a "sign of true Christianity" as the Lord's Supper. Without a corresponding economic practice, breaking bread in the Lord's Supper is an empty ritual. "True evangelical faith . . . cannot lie dormant; . . . it clothes the naked; it feeds the hungry; it comforts the sorrowful; it shelters the destitute."

The church has used readings from Psalm 140 for vespers on Maundy Thursday, with repetition of verse 4. In the liturgy for Good Friday, Psalm 140 is read before recital of the passion from John 18–19 (Holladay: 221).

Psalm 141

With Hands, Heart, and Eyes Toward You, O God

PREVIEW

In this individual lament, the psalmist pleads for deliverance from temptation (vv. 3-5) and divine protection from his enemies (vv. 8-10). In face of enticement and persecution by the wicked, the righteous person takes refuge in prayer (vv. 1-2, 5, 8). The psalmist confesses a need for the LORD to watch over his lips and heart (vv. 3-4) and others to give him appropriate correction (v. 5). The psalm acknowledges that the faithful life depends on the faithfulness of God (v. 8), by whose divine judgment the wicked will receive their recompense (vv. 6-7, 10).

As laments, Psalms 140–143 are interwoven and form the core of the *David* collection (Pss 138–145) *[Superscriptions]*. Psalm 141 is similar to Psalm 1 in the contrast between the wicked (vv. 4, 10) and the righteous (v. 5), and the need to say "no" to the wicked and "yes" to God (vv. 4, 8). As a teaching prayer, the psalm's piety appears to be influenced by the wisdom writers. Since the text of verses 5-7 is uncertain, a variety of translations appear. The ideas seem to focus on the fate of the wicked.

Psalm 141

OUTLINE

Call for Help and Strength to Withstand Temptation, 141:1-5
Petition Regarding the Wicked and Confession of Refuge in God, 141:6-10

EXPLANATORY NOTES

Call for Help and Strength to Withstand Temptation 141:1-5

Give ear is a cry for the LORD's attention. The psalmist describes his prayer as rising up to God like sweet-smelling smoke of incense (Lev 2:1-2; 6:14-15; 16:12-13; Jer 41:5), and as hands stretched up in supplication (Pss 28:2; 63:4; 134:2). The *evening sacrifice* in the temple was well-known (Exod 29:38-42; Ezra 9:5; Dan 9:21). Some suggest that verse 2 spiritualizes sacrifices (Pss 40:6; 51:16-17; 69:30-31; Isa 1:13; Amos 5:21-25), though it is doubtful that the psalmist intended to replace sacrifice with prayer. Rather, the images of ascending smoke of incense and uplifted hands illustrate prayer (cf. Heb 13:15).

The petition is for the grace of silence, lest the worshipper fall into the sins of speech (v. 3; Pss 34:13; 39:1; Prov 13:3). Yet the battleground is the *heart* (v. 4), and so he prays that he may not be seduced by those *who work iniquity* (v. 4). Designation of the enemies as doers of *iniquity* emphasizes their uncanny powers to subvert others (Ps 73:3, 12). He prays that the LORD keep him from temptation to attend their feasts (*eat of their delicacies*, v. 4), or accept their hospitality (v. 5c). Anointing with *oil* signified prosperity and festivity (Ps 23:5; Ezek 16:9). Though the text of verse 5 is uncertain, the NRSV reading suggests that it is better to be reproved by the righteous than feted with the perfumed oil of the wicked. The NEB adds, *For that would make me a party to their crimes* (v. 5d).

Petition Regarding the Wicked and Confession of Refuge in God 141:6-10

While the Hebrew text of verses 5-7 is uncertain and translations differ, NRSV, NIV, and NEB point to the ghastly end to which the wicked are destined. *Bones scattered at the mouth of Sheol* symbolizes a shameful death (v. 7). God is often called the rock on which the wicked founder and come to naught (Ps 18:2). Difficulties of interpretation continue. For example, should we take verse 7 as introducing the psalm's final section? If so, it may describe the faithful community, broken by Death, who leaves victims and their bones strewn on the ground at the entrance to his abode, Sheol (Davidson, 1998:456).

The conclusion offers greater clarity: *But my eyes are turned toward you, O God* (v. 8). The antidote to temptation lies in prayer (v. 2), in inner purity (v. 4), in the strong support of good friends (v. 5), and in taking constant refuge in God (v. 8). The psalmist prays for protection from the traps of the wicked and that their plans may boomerang (vv. 9-10; Pss 7:15-16; 9:15-16; 35:8; 140:9). The psalm ends in confidence that evil is self-defeating *[Wicked]*.

THE TEXT IN THE BIBLICAL CONTEXT AND LIFE OF THE CHURCH

Deliver Us from Evil

In the prayer for deliverance from the temptation represented by the existence of the wicked and their apparent prosperity (vv. 3-5), this psalm shows affinities to Proverbs 15:26-32, as well as to Psalms 1; 73; and 119. NT connections include the line in the Lord's Prayer, "Lead us not into temptation, but deliver us from evil" (Ps 141:4; Matt 6:13 KJV). In correspondence to the Corinthians, Paul quotes a proverb, "Bad company ruins good morals" (from Menander, *Thais*, a lost comedy), to warn of the danger that evil associates may corrupt a believer (Ps 141:4-5; 1 Cor 15:33). The prayer of Psalm 141 stands in relation to the wisdom law-theology of the letter of James (James 1:12-16, 19-26). The rising incense smoke, symbolic of prayer, is portrayed in the vision of the heavenly throne room in Revelation (Ps 141:2; Rev 8:3-4).

Throughout the centuries, worshippers have heard or recited Psalm 141 at evening worship (v. 2). To this day, they regularly use it at vesper services, as well as for Maundy Thursday.

Fostering the Piety of Prayer

Psalm 141 reflects a sincere piety and provides sound advice in spite of some uncertain text (vv. 5-7). In danger and temptation, people of faith find refuge in God. The guarding of the lips and heart is crucial. The enticement of wickedness is seductive. The psalmist warns against compromise. Strike no bargain with evil!

Psalm 141 also teaches about prayer. A prayer is more than a text. It is spoken, and in this psalm, with raised hands (v. 2; Ps 28:2). The psalm appears preoccupied with the psalmist's person—voice, hands, mouth, lips, heart, head, and eyes. Sincere prayer does that. It involves the whole being. When Christian believers raise hands in prayer (1 Tim 2:8), it can symbolize that their prayer, their entire relationship to God, is founded on the power of Christ's cross, "that true evening sacrifice" through which we draw near to God (Reardon: 282).

Psalm 142

Cry to the LORD, My Refuge and My Portion

PREVIEW

This brief prayer song of an individual reflects the strain of being hated, hunted, and hurting. Persecuted by enemies, exhausted, imprisoned, and forsaken, the psalmist cries out in desperation to the LORD. His only hope lies in the LORD, who knows his path (v. 3) and who alone will care and provide refuge and life (v. 5). The psalm ends with a final petition for release and the vow to give thanks in the community of the faithful (v. 7). Thus, the prayer of desolation and isolation ends, confident of the LORD's bountiful gift of deliverance.

Interpretation of Psalm 142 depends on the meaning of *prison* (v. 7). Taken literally, the psalm may be the prayer of one falsely accused and detained until the time of trial, a prayer likely spoken in the temple, where the LORD's verdict will be made known (Lev 24:12; Num 15:34). *Prison* may also be used as a synonym for death or the abode of the dead. If so here, this could be a deathbed lament. Or *prison* may be a metaphor for deep distress, including the experience of exile (Pss 88:8; 107:10; Isa 42:7; Lam 3:6-9). The psalm can speak to a variety of oppressive situations in which people long for liberation.

We do not know the setting and date of composition. The title given Psalm 142, *A Maskil of David. When he was in the cave,* may have been an editor's attempt to provide an appropriate setting for the psalm by alluding to David's flight from Saul, either at Adullam (1 Sam 22:1-2) or En-gedi (24:1-7). We should not take the superscription as a secure historical reference, but as illustrative of a narrative context for hearing the psalm. The Davidic collection (Pss 138–145) in book V reinforces the necessity to reinterpret the traditional Davidic theology, as Psalm 144 seeks to do (McCann, 1996:1246). *Maskil*, a literary or musical term (NIV n), could suggest a didactic or artistic song (Holladay: 73) *[Superscriptions]*.

OUTLINE

Complaint Describing the Psalmist's Plight, 142:1-4
Petition for Deliverance and Vow of Thanksgiving, 142:5-7

EXPLANATORY NOTES

Complaint Describing the Psalmist's Plight   142:1-4

Energetic complaint characterizes the urgent cry of the psalmist. Repetitions appear: *voice, voice, cry, make supplication, to the LORD, to the LORD, pour out, tell, my complaint, my trouble* (vv. 1-2). *Voice* (*qôl*) is the term also used for *thunder* (Ps 29). *Supplication* (v. 1) implies "to seek" or "to implore" (1 Kings 8:59; Job 8:5; Ps 30:8). *Complaint* (*śîaḥ*) often expresses plaintive musing or meditation. While the psalmist cries out with urgency, the appeal is to the LORD's gracious nature. The invocation ends in a trusting confession. *When my spirit is faint*, when anything physical or spiritual undermines vitality, *you know my way* (v. 3a). The pronoun *you* is emphatic, underscoring the emphasis of the first two lines on *the LORD*.

In distress, the psalmist points to hidden traps (v. 3c; Ps 141:9). Looking to *my right hand*, where protector or advocate should stand (v. 4; Pss 16:8; 109:31; 110:5; 121:5), there is none. No one notices. No way of escape is open. No one cares (v. 4). The lament bemoans the loss of every human comfort and aid, expressing complete abandonment (Job 11:20; Jer 25:35; Amos 2:14).

Petition for Deliverance and Vow of Thanksgiving 142:5-7

A second cry opens the petition portion of the psalm. But now the cry begins with a declaration of trust: *You are my refuge and my portion* (v. 5). The psalmist has one last refuge and place of security, the LORD (Ps 91:2, 9; Jer 17:17). *Portion in the land of the living* refers to the tradition about the tribe of Levi, whose inheritance was the LORD himself, but not a portion of the Promised Land (Num 18:20; Deut 10:9; Pss 16:5, 11; 27:13; 73:26; 119:57).

The petition points to exhaustion of body and spirit (v. 6). The persecutors are too strong. The LORD needs to intervene. *Prison* (v. 7) is a symbol for helplessness or wretchedness. The motivation given for liberation is the opportunity to praise God along with the community of the righteous (Ps 22:22-25). The closing verse looks to the future with calm confidence in the LORD's goodness (13:6; 119:58).

THE TEXT IN THE BIBLICAL CONTEXT AND LIFE OF THE CHURCH

Prisoners

As a "prison psalm," we have already recognized the association of Psalm 142 with David *when he was in the cave* (1 Sam 22:1-2; 24:1-7). Many biblical stories deal with persons in prison. Potiphar cast the falsely accused Joseph into prison (Gen 39:20–41:14). The forces of Jezebel pursued Elijah, who hid in the desert and fled to the mouth of the cave (1 Kings 19:1-18). Jeremiah was cast into the cistern and drawn out of it only to be imprisoned until the fall of Jerusalem (Jer 37:11–38:28). Daniel was cast into a lions' den, and his three friends were cast into a fiery furnace (Dan 3:19-23; 6:16-26). These stories, and others, tell of fervent prayer while in prison, and of deliverance by God's intervention.

The NT has similar stories of imprisonment and of persons who might have prayed Psalm 142: John the Baptist (Matt 11:2-6; Mark 6:17-29), Peter (Acts 5:12-26), Paul and Silas (16:16-40), and John, writer of Revelation (1:9). Perhaps most of all, adding dignity to those falsely accused and imprisoned, there is Jesus. Taken prisoner in the garden, he was abandoned by his closest friends, betrayed by one of them, and denied by another, but he found his sole refuge in God (Reardon: 284).

Prison psalms and prayers abound in the history of the church. Many can be found in the stories from sixteen centuries of Christian martyrs as compiled by Thieleman J. van Braght in *Martyrs Mirror*. John Bunyan, arrested for preaching without a license in Bedford, England, in 1660, spent the next twelve years in prison, where he wrote many religious works. After a brief release, he was imprisoned again and began writing *The Pilgrim's Progress*. The letters and diaries German theologian Dietrich Bonhoeffer (1906-1945) wrote in a Nazi prison, before being executed, were published after his death under the title *Prisoner for God* (1951). Baptist minister and Nobel Peace Prize recipient Martin Luther King Jr. (1929-1968) was arrested and jailed numerous times while protesting injustice and discrimination. From a Birmingham jail, he wrote: "Injustice anywhere is a threat to justice everywhere."

The church's worship uses Psalm 142 along with 141 at vespers on Maundy Thursday. Often believers repeat Psalm 141:9 and 142:5 as reminders of Jesus' imprisonment. The psalm can help anyone going through "the dark night of the soul." In the dark times, repeating verse 5 can affirm that "God is my judge and advocate."

Persons facing death have found comfort in Psalm 142. Francis of Assisi recited this psalm while dying on October 3, 1226. The psalm enables persons of biblical faith to walk confidently into eternal rest as they declare, *You are my refuge, my portion in the land of the living.*

Although the mood of Psalm 142 is akin to modern-day blues tunes, which articulate sadness and loneliness, the psalm ends on a strong note of confidence. Henry Frances Lyte's familiar hymn "Abide with me" (1847) articulates such trust in the line, "When other helpers fail, and comforts flee, Help of the helpless, O abide with me."

Psalm 143

Prayer of a Penitent in Distress

PREVIEW

This prayer song of the individual in distress has similarities to the preceding psalm (Pss 143:4, 8; 142:3, 7). As the lament's unique feature, the psalmist does not protest that he is innocent. Instead, the petitioner cites the predicament of all mortals: *For no one living is righteous before you* (v. 2). Thus, he pleads that God let mercy, rather than judgment, have its course with him. The prayer appeals to the LORD's attributes of *faithfulness, righteousness,* and *steadfast love* (vv. 1, 11-12).

Composed as a prayer for deliverance from enemies (as are Pss 139–144), the note of penitence (v. 2) has led to including this psalm in the church's list of seven penitential psalms, to direct the practice of repentance (Pss 6; 32; 38; 51; 102; 130; 143) *[Penitential]*. The psalm's purpose is repentance, turning all of life over to the LORD. Implicit in the confession that no one is righteous before God (v. 2) is also the awareness that everyone needs divine guidance (vv. 8, 10). A final plea for deliverance on the basis of the LORD's *name, righteousness,* and *steadfast love* expresses petition for extermination of the enemy; the prayer ends with the psalmist's firm statement, *I am your servant* (vv. 11-12).

Though we cannot determine the specific setting, the petitioner may be in the darkness of prison or at the point of death (v. 3). Or someone accused might have been reciting the psalm in the temple (v. 9) the evening before the expected divine decision (v. 8). With its placement in the Psalter, Psalm 143 participates in the response of book V to the exile and its aftermath. It is the sixth in this *Of David* group of psalms *[Superscriptions]*.

OUTLINE

Lament Appealing to the LORD's Faithfulness and Righteousness, 143:1-6
Petitions for the LORD's Intervention, 143:7-12

EXPLANATORY NOTES

Lament Appealing to the LORD's Faithfulness and Righteousness   143:1-6

The psalmist's cry is urgent: *Hear, give ear, answer me* (v. 1). The poet pleads two motives, the LORD's *faithfulness* and *righteousness* (v. 1). He begs not to be put on trial on the basis of what he deserves, but throws himself before the LORD, whom he believes to be gracious. *No one living is righteous* is a common biblical idea referring to the power of evil to corrupt human beings from the beginning (Gen 8:21; Job 4:17-21; 9:2; 14:4; 15:15-16; 25:4; Pss 14:3; 130:3). Verse 2 implies that salvation is by the grace of God; the psalm contrasts God's righteousness with the ineffectiveness of human power.

Description of the crisis in the psalmist's life begins with focus on *the enemy* (vv. 3, 9, 12), whose identity is not clear *[Enemies]*. However, the writer is affected by being pursued, trampled upon, and consigned to the darkness of Sheol. The spirit *faints*; the heart is *appalled* (*dismayed*, v. 4 NIV; *dazed with despair*, NEB; *numbed with horror*, NJPS). Does *darkness* suggest prison (Pss 107:10-15; 142:7) or the realm of the dead (88:6)? *Those long dead* may refer to those whose names and memory have ceased to exist. The picture is that of one physically, psychologically, and spiritually broken, at the end of his rope (vv. 3-4).

However, there is still ground for trust—remembering what the LORD has done in the past (vv. 5-6; 77:1-3). *I remember* (*zākar*, "to relive and experience anew"), *meditate* (v. 5 NIV, *hāgāh*, "to mumble, quietly repeat, and absorb"), *muse* or *ponder* (JB, *śîaḥ*, "meditate or consider") God's saving acts on behalf of Israel, which include exodus and conquest, David and Zion. "You saved Israel before; now *I stretch out my hands to you.*" The extended hands in prayer symbolize the supplicant's dependence on God (28:2; 44:20; Lam 1:17). With this gesture of prayer, the psalmist illustrates his need for God's help, much as the parched earth urgently cries out for revitalizing rain (Pss 42:2; 63:1). The first half of the psalm ends with this prayer posture, thus connecting with the desperation of the opening cry (v. 1). The marginal note *Selah* further confirms the end of part one (v. 6) *[Selah]*.

Petitions for the LORD's Intervention   143:7-12

A series of petitions fill the second part of the psalm. A twice-repeated thought sequence, appealing for the LORD's deliverance and guidance, characterizes verses 7-10. *Do not hide your face* (v. 7) suggests that only a God who reveals himself can hide his face. Without the presence of God, there is death, *the Pit* (28:1; 30:3; 69:15; 88:4, 6). Sunrise symbolizes joy and hope (5:1-3; 30:5; 90:14). *Let me hear . . . in the morning* may express hope for an oracle of deliverance, usually made known in the temple liturgy at the break of day (v. 8). Yet the psalmist prays for more than deliverance. He also seeks instruction in God's will and way. *Teach me . . .* (vv. 8, 10), *for you are my God* (v. 10) affirms the essence of the LORD's covenant promise (31:14; 40:5; 86:3; 118:28; 140:6). Prayer for the LORD's *good spirit* to lead (v. 10) contrasts with the weakness of the psalmist (vv. 4-7).

In a final appeal for the LORD's intervention, the petitioner identifies four reasons for God to act on his behalf: *For your name's sake, your righteousness, your steadfast love, for I am your servant.* In repeating these motives and the claim *I am your servant*, the conclusion affirms the introduction (vv. 1-2, 11-12). With this distinctive framing of the psalm, the speaker focuses on how the needy person dare make supplication to the awesome God (Brueggemann, 1984:103).

Christian readers find the harshness of the final verse troubling in light of mediating passages, such as Luke 23:34 and Philippians 2:1-11. Jesus' parable in Matthew 25:31-46 expresses an outcome more in line with Psalm 143:12. We need to see this verse in the context of the contrast between blessings and curses (Deut 27–28). The petitioner prays that God's life-giving breath would inspire the psalmist's life and give protection from enemies. The psalmist's plea is not for personal revenge but for God's righteousness and justice.

THE TEXT IN THE BIBLICAL CONTEXT AND LIFE OF THE CHURCH

The Righteousness of God and Repentance

The church's inclusion of Psalm 143 in the list of penitential psalms rests on verse 2. The NT prominently uses this verse. From the Greek version of the OT, Paul freely quotes the line *For no one living is righteous before you* in Romans 3:20 and Galatians 2:16. Paul draws on these words to illustrate his argument that neither Jews nor Gentiles can put themselves in the right with God. No one living is in a right relationship with God. Only through the cross do we now possess God's own sacrificial love in our heart, with the result that Christ calls upon us in our turn to take up our cross and follow him (Knight, 2:337). Psalm 143:2 is quoted in the writings of the reformer Menno Simons (506, 568) and the *Martyrs Mirror* (Braght: 270, 699, 850, 959, 1043) as testimony to the need for God's grace and the plea that God not judge on the basis of human standing before the Holy One.

As a penitential psalm, these verses begin and end with the confession *You are my God* and *I am your servant* (vv. 2, 10, 12). Repentance responds to grace (Rom 2:4). The prayer appeals to the faithfulness and righteousness of God (v. 1). Repentance is in order because of what we are, not because of what we have done. In repentance, we turn from the darkness and death that is our lot to God's love for our salvation (v. 8). It is a move of hope (v. 6). The prayer seeks divine instruction and guidance for living (vv. 8, 10; Mays 1994b:434-35).

Resources for Comfort and Guidance

The church has used Psalm 143 widely to begin the day. The Eastern Church reads it with Psalms 3; 37; 62; 87; and 102 as a daily morning prayer. The Western Church prays it on Saturday. Other liturgical uses have included the psalm as a prayer of absolution at burial, on Passion Sunday, and during Holy Week (vv. 9-10). Except for parts of verse 12, some use Psalm 143 as a prayer applying to the suffering Christ (Sabourin: 263; Reardon: 285).

This psalm draws on verses of many other psalms and illustrates the value of memorizing texts that come to the aid of persons in distress. Remembering God's acts of deliverance in the past and naming them can bring comfort, with a sense of the divine presence. Spiritual distress often leads to change and growth. When at the end of one's limited resources, the penitent can reach out for the infilling of God's Spirit (v. 6).

Psalm 143 is concerned with the governance of God's Holy Spirit (v. 10). In the NT, walking under guidance of the Spirit is contrasted with walking "according to the flesh" (Gal 5:16-25). Praying for God's will and the Spirit's guidance becomes necessary, as articulated in these two prayers by Thomas à Kempis (1380-1471) in *The Imitation of Christ*:

Teach me to do thy will, for thou art my wisdom. Thou didst know me before the world was made, and before I was born into the world. (3.3.7; via Knight, 2:338; cf. http://www.bartleby.com/7/2/)

Let thy will be mine, and let my will ever follow thine, and fully accord with it. Let there be between thee and me but one will, so that I may love what thou lovest, and abhor what thou hatest; and let me not be able to will any thing which thou dost not will, nor dislike any thing which thou dost will (3.15.3; via Appleton: 95).

Psalm 144

A New Song to the God Who Rescues and Blesses

PREVIEW

Diverse elements are incorporated into this royal lament, centering on the king's plea for deliverance. The psalm begins with a liturgical exclamation of praise (vv. 1-2), confesses human frailty (vv. 3-4), and then moves to petitions for a theophany of deliverance from the peril of deceitful aliens (vv. 5-8). A vow of thanksgiving follows (vv. 9-10), with refrain-like verse 11 restating verses 7-8. The psalm ends with a prayer or statement of prosperity for the nation (vv. 12-15).

Commentators have often identified the first part (vv. 1-11) as a royal psalm, like other psalms that celebrate the king (Pss 2; 18; 20; 21; 45; 72; 89; 101; 110; 132). The second part (vv. 12-15) appears as a psalm of blessing (like 127 and 128), with the two disparate psalms brought together to form Psalm 144. However, readers have long recognized that verses 1-11 also draw widely on other psalms, especially 18 and 33. Many commentators today view Psalm 144 as a literary unit, acknowledging that the writer has leaned heavily upon older traditions to compose *a new song* (vv. 9-10).

What might have been the setting? The petition for deliverance names deceitful *aliens* (vv. 7-8, 11). In a time when the welfare of the community was threatened by treacherous reports and action of aliens (Neh 9:2; Isa 56:3; 60:10; 61:5; 62:8; Ezek 44:7, 9), the writer draws on earlier psalms to compose a song for his own time, likely the postexilic community. In drawing on Psalm 18, the thanksgiving of a warrior king, this psalmist reshapes material to make it relevant to the realities of the exile and the disappearance of the Davidic monarchy. It speaks of the LORD, who rescued *his servant David* (v. 10; Ps 89:3, 35). Psalm 144 keeps alive the postexilic community's hope for the coming of a future Davidic king, or it helps the community see itself as the heir to the promises in the LORD's "steadfast, sure love for David" (Isa 55:3; Davidson, 1998:463). By recycling Psalms 18 and 33 into a new version, the psalmist is appealing to the LORD to do for his people what the LORD had done for his servant David (Mays, 1994b:436).

OUTLINE

Royal Lament Centering on the King's Plea for Deliverance, 144:1-11
    144:1-2   Liturgical Exclamation of Praise
    144:3-4   Confession of Human Frailty
    144:5-8   Petition for a Theophany and Deliverance
    144:9-11   Vow of Thanksgiving and Refrain
Communal Prayer for Peace and Prosperity, 144:12-15

EXPLANATORY NOTES

Royal Lament Centering on the King's Plea for Deliverance   144:1-11

The psalm opens with a liturgical exclamation of thanksgiving, *Blessed be the LORD* (v. 1; Pss 66:20; 68:19; 72:18). The ruler confidently praises the LORD as protective power, to which he feels completely entrusted (vv. 1-2; 2 Sam 22:2-3; Ps 18:1-2). God intervenes for the king and aids him (Pss 2:5-6; 21:8-9; 110:2-3, 5). A striking term for God in place of *rock* (NRSV) is found in verse 2, where the Hebrew *ḥesed* appears. NIV translates *my loving God*, and NEB *my help that never fails*. *Fortress* suggests stability and security (9:9; 18:1-2; 46:7; 48:3; 59:9, 16-17; 94:22). In addition to the defensive idea referring to Yahweh war, verse 2 also conveys the concept of an offensive subjugation of the nations. See comments on Psalm 20 and the essay *War.*

Now follows a confession of the insignificance, fragility, and transience of human life (vv. 3-4; Job 7:7, 17; Pss 90:5-6; 146:3-4; contrast 8:4-6). The confession appeals to the magnanimity of God, recognizing that humanity is the object of God's care. This has significance for kings: their authority and power do not reside in their own strength. All is from the LORD (see comments on Ps 33:13-19).

In the petition for a theophany and deliverance from deceitful aliens, the crisis is identified (vv. 5-8). The psalmist appeals to the LORD, the Divine Warrior, to come and vanquish both cosmic (*mighty waters*) and historical (*aliens*) foes. The call for a theophany, as at Sinai, is the petition for the LORD's powerful intervention from on high (18:7-19; 29; 50:3-6; 68; 77:11-20; 97:1-6) *[Theophany]*. *Mighty waters* is a metaphor for peril, chaos, and death. The situation is reminiscent of exodus from Egypt, but also of exile in Babylon. *Aliens whose right hands are false* may refer to deceitful deeds, or the making of false oaths by raising the right hand toward God (vv. 8, 11; Deut 32:40; Ezra 10:3, 19; Ezek 17:18; Dan 12:7).

The vow to sing a *new song* of praise follows the deliverance sought (vv. 9-11). The new song of celebration will reflect the victory, the surprise in the new reality and relationship (Pss 33:2-3; 40:3; 96:1-3; 98:1; 149:1). The LORD bestows *victory* or *salvation* (v. 10 NASB; *těšû'â*). *Kings* refers to rulers from the dynasty of David (v. 10). *David* may also denote the reigning king of the house of David. Calling the king *servant* of the LORD accords him a place of honor and of service (78:70; 89:3; 132:10). While communal lament appears to dominate verses 1-11, sorrow is softened by a messianic hope.

Communal Prayer for Peace and Prosperity 144:12-15

Although the psalm's first part is spoken in first-person singular, verses 12-15 are in the plural, giving voice to the community. The question about the psalm's second part is whether these verses are a prayer (NRSV) or a statement of present blessing or hope (NIV, NEB). In the Hebrew, verse 12 begins with a relative particle *'ăšer*, often translated "that," but amended in NEB to *'ašrê*, "happy" or "blessed." As prayer or statement, the focus is on prosperity and *blessings* for the people *whose God is the LORD* (v. 15). Themes include the blessing of human progeny, filled granaries, and increasing herds (vv. 12-14a). Then, in a psalm that opens with military imagery, comes this striking appeal: *May there be no breach in the walls, no exile, and no cry of distress* (v. 14b). Let there be no invasion, no exile, no outcry! In other words, no war! In an ideal society under the reign of God, rags and hunger and war are banished! That new song needs yet to be sung!

THE TEXT IN THE BIBLICAL CONTEXT AND LIFE OF THE CHURCH

New Songs and New Prayers

Psalm 144 illustrates the practice of using earlier biblical materials to compose new songs and prayers for use in a later time. That custom continues to this day. Psalms of David as king, but also as poet and musician, were particularly useful to the community that looked back on God's promises to David. So these psalms, later given the title *Of David*, helped the community pray "as David prayed" (Mays, 1994b:437). In hymnody, poetry, and sermon, many of these psalms are recast to speak to our day.

Paraphrasing is another example of how leaders transform the word for a later generation. For example, Leslie F. Brandt's *Psalms Now*, initially written by a parish minister for the church bulletin, opens Psalm 144 with this wording:

> O God, it is difficult to understand
> how You can regard man with such high regard
> and show him so much concern.
> His years upon this earth are so few. . . .
> You created him as the object of Your love—
> only to see him turn from You
> to play with his foolish toys.
> You tried to teach him to love his fellowman—
> only to see him express his fear
> and suspicion and hate
> through cruel acts of violence and war. (Brandt: 217)

Other helpful contemporary paraphrases of psalms include Ernesto Cardenal's *Psalms*, recasting psalms to reflect the struggle of oppressed peoples in Latin America, and Eugene Peterson's *The Message: Psalms*, paraphrasing the message of the psalms into today's language.

How Shall the Church Use Psalm 144?

The church has not widely used Psalm 144, perhaps because of the jarring militarism of verse 1 (common in royal psalms). When it has done so, for example in the Liturgy of the Hours, the Catholic Church has understood the speaker in Psalm 144 to be Jesus Christ and the warfare to be spiritual. This was John Calvin's interpretation, and also the understanding behind a quotation of verse 1 by Calvin's contemporary Menno Simons: "Blessed be the Lord my strength, which teacheth my hands to war and my fingers to fight" (Holladay: 333; Menno: 57). However, such an understanding of Psalm 144 as a description of the present reign of Jesus "teaching us to do battle and our fingers to make war" appears inappropriate language in a day when the horrors of war display human madness. Even such a marching hymn as Sabine Baring-Gould's "Onward, Christian soldiers" (1865; music, A. S. Sullivan, 1871) stirs up images of crusades that seem improper in light of the Christian gospel and the message of the Prince of Peace.

How does the church read and use Psalm 144? Is the image of verses 12-15 a place to begin? How does that image of "no war" (v. 14b) speak to current international debates over "just war," "defensive war," and "preemptive war"? What might persons who have been sheltered from war's devastation learn from speaking with veterans who have returned from war zones? With families whose lives have been disrupted by war and the loss of loved ones? With refugees whose families and communities have been torn apart by the violence and chaos of war? With relief workers who have lived and worked among the victims in war's aftermath? Can we hear the prayers of the people? "God send that there may be an end at last; God send that there may be peace again. God in heaven, send us peace" (diary of Hartich Sierk, a peasant, 1628). Or, "Lord, make this world to last as long as possible" (prayer of 11-year-old child on hearing of Sino-Indian border fighting). Christians would do well to join with the multitudes around the world to "pray for peace in our hearts, in our homes, in our nation, in our world, the peace of your will, the peace of our need" (Appleton: 78-79).

Two themes of Psalm 144 are God's deliverance and God's blessings. Not only does life hold dramatic moments of divine intervention and deliverance that call forth a new song of celebration. There is also God's blessing in everyday gifts such as family, food, health, the beauty of the earth, and for many, communities that allow people to live and work in peace. All the blessings, dramatic and daily, may tempt us to worship God for what God does. Psalm 144 proclaims that God is, and that we human beings, insignificant as we are, are also the object of God's care and magnanimity (v. 3). What a song to sing!

Psalm 145

In Praise of God's Greatness and Goodness

PREVIEW

Following six laments, Psalm 145 moves the Psalter toward its hymnic conclusion by extolling the LORD as king and celebrating the everlasting kingdom (vv. 1-2, 11-13). With the invitation for *all flesh* to praise the LORD (v. 21), Psalm 145 becomes the bridge from lament over the crisis of exile and its aftermath, to a resounding doxology of hallelujahs (Pss 146–150).

In this alphabetical acrostic, structure and content combine for a comprehensive declaration celebrating the greatness and goodness of God, which embraces every living thing. To illustrate God's majestic greatness, the psalm draws on the LORD's mighty acts in creation and history (vv. 4-7). Rooted in Israel's oldest confession of God's fidelity (vv. 8-9; Exod 34:6-7), the psalm then testifies to God's enduring and reliable providential care for all (vv. 10-20). Recognizing the LORD's kingly position and royal power, the hymn emphasizes the LORD's merciful compassion and attentive concern for all, particularly for those burdened down and who cry out for help.

The acrostic structure, in which every verse begins with a succeeding letter of the Hebrew alphabet, is a literary device conveying completeness. The verse beginning with *nûn* is missing in the Hebrew text. However, NRSV supplies it as verse 13b on the basis of other supporting manuscripts (NRSV n). Every verse is a sentence of praise.

So, from א to ת, from A to Z, this is a psalm of praise. Beginning with verse 9, the word *all* appears nineteen times in the final thirteen verses, emphasizing the unlimited comprehensiveness of the praise of the LORD and reasons for praise. The inclusio formed by vows to praise frames the psalm, as well as repetition of *name forever and ever* (vv. 1-2, 21) *[Hebrew Poetry]*. The title later given this psalm, *Praise*, is found only here. Its plural form, *tĕhillîm*, "Praises," became the title of the Hebrew Psalter.

Many commentators see Psalm 145 as belonging to the postexilic period because of its acrostic structure, dependence upon other psalms, late Hebrew vocabulary, and concept of the LORD's kingship. The psalm concludes the final *Of David* collection (Pss 138-145) and explicitly addresses God as *King* to affirm God's sovereignty amid the realities of the postexilic time.

OUTLINE

Introductory Doxology, 145:1-3
Israel's Praise of the Divine Deeds, 145:4-9
    145:4-7   The LORD's Mighty Acts
    145:8-9   The LORD's Loving-Kindness and Compassion
Proclamation of the LORD as King, Provider, and Savior, 145:10-20
    145:10-13a The LORD's Glorious Kingdom
    145:13b-20 The LORD's Providential Care
Concluding Doxology, 145:21

EXPLANATORY NOTES

Introductory Doxology   145:1-3

The singer's inclusio formed by verses 1-2 and 21 states the psalm's purpose, to praise the name of the LORD by reciting the attributes and actions that comprise the character of the LORD. The singer's goal is to encourage all human beings to praise God (v. 21). The opening vocative should be translated *my God the King* (NIV) rather than *my God and King*. This doxology recalls psalms that celebrate and praise God as king (Pss 93; 95–99). The identity of those who *bless* progresses from the psalmist (vv. 1-2), to *your faithful* (v. 10), to *all flesh* (v. 21). Verse 3 responds to verses 1-2, celebrating the greatness of the LORD in familiar words (48:1; 96:4).

Israel's Praise of the Divine Deeds   145:4-9

Israel's praise of the divine deeds begins with reference to the LORD's activity (vv. 4-7). *Your works, your mighty acts, the glorious splen-*

dor of your majesty, your wondrous works, your awesome deeds are general descriptions to affirm what was central to Israel's faith: God's deeds in creation and history. Reciting the stories from generation to generation gave occasion to sing aloud praises for the LORD's greatness and goodness.

The central focus comes into view with the listing of the LORD's attributes: *gracious, merciful, slow to anger* or *forbearing* (NEB), *steadfast love, good,* and *compassion* (vv. 8-9). Verse 8 recalls the creedal confession of the LORD's self-disclosure as faithful (Exod 34:6-7; Num 14:18) and is quoted elsewhere (Pss 86:15; 103:8; Jon 4:2). Proclaiming the life-giving power of the LORD's steadfast love and mercy (v. 9; Pss 79:8; 119:77, 156), Psalm 145 asserts the congruence between God and God's world.

Proclamation of the LORD as King, Provider, and Savior 145:10-20

The LORD's compassion shall evoke *thanks* (v. 10). The created world is not silent; it has a message reaching out to all lands as all the works of God testify to God's greatness (19:1-4; 97:6). The message is about a glorious kingdom and the rule of the LORD forever (vv. 11-13). Here the word translated *kingdom* (*malkût*) appears four times at the center of Psalm 145, but only once more in the book of Psalms (103:19). Elsewhere in the OT it appears more commonly in the late books of Chronicles, Esther, and Daniel. The emphasis is on the sovereignty and power of the LORD's rule.

However, the majestic LORD's power expresses itself in compassion and in providential care for all (vv. 13b-20). As the ideal king, God sustains the oppressed and starving (vv. 14-16; Pss 104:27-28; 146:7-9). God's presence is promise and assurance to the poor and the helpless (34:18). As *just* and *kind in all his doings,* the LORD also gives watchful attention to the needs of the faithful (vv. 17-20). Verse 20 conveys a covenantal dimension and note of realism: "The equilibrium of the world is experienced best by those who live contentedly with Yahweh's expectations. . . . Creation does work within the boundaries of obedient responsibility" (Brueggemann, 1984:31). The happiness or prosperity of the righteous (1:1-3) is not so much a reward as it is their experience of being connected to the true source of life—God. In like manner, the destruction of the wicked is not so much a punishment as it is the result of their own choice to cut themselves off from the source of life (1:4-6; McCann, 1996:1260).

Concluding Doxology   145:21

Psalm 145 ends as it began, with the promise to praise the LORD and an invitation for *all flesh*, especially all people, to join in praise (v. 21; 65:2; cf. 136:25). The call to all nations to praise the LORD is pervasive in the Psalms (33:8; 47:2; 66:1; 67:4-5; 96:1; 98:4; 100:1; 148:7-12, including animals). *Holy* is a statement about the LORD and his name (33:21; 99:3; 103:1; 111:9). In the promise to *speak the praise of the LORD*, the last verse of Psalm 145 leads into the five *Hallelujah!* psalms that bring the Psalter to a resounding conclusion of praise. To praise God is to acknowledge one's own insufficiency and the sovereignty of God's loving purposes.

THE TEXT IN THE BIBLICAL CONTEXT AND LIFE OF THE CHURCH

Foreshadow of the Kingdom of God

The emphasis of Psalm 145 on the glorious and everlasting kingdom (vv. 11-13a) foreshadows the NT's proclamation of the kingdom of God (Matt 6:33; Mark 1:15; Luke 4:43; John 3:3). The book of Revelation begins with a greeting to those called into the *kingdom* of God (1:6). The writer continues, "The kingdom of the world has become the kingdom of our Lord and of his Messiah, and he will reign forever and ever" (11:15). Later we hear the judgment doxology (15:3; 16:5), "Just and true are your ways, King of the nations!" Christians pray in the words of Jesus, "Our Father in heaven, hallowed be your name. Your kingdom come. Your will be done" (Matt 6:9-10).

The Eternal Truths of God's Compassionate Generosity

Psalm 145, as an invitation to live in the world of God's reign, has had a prominent place in Jewish liturgy, being recited three times daily in the synagogue by pious Jews. The Dead Sea Scrolls' version of the psalm adds a refrain after each verse, "Blessed be the LORD, and blessed be his holy name." From the time of the ancient church, people have used verses 10, 15, and 16 as a mealtime prayer. Luther suggested use of these words, followed by the Lord's Prayer and then the words, "Lord God heavenly Father, bless us and these your gifts, which we receive from your bountiful goodness through Jesus Christ our Lord" (Limburg: 2000:492). The psalm's inclusion in most lectionaries and hymnals assures its wide use for reading, prayer, and song in public worship by all the Christian traditions. Based directly on Psalm 145 is the praise hymn "We would extol thee," from the *Scottish Psalter* (1650), altered by Nichol Grieve (1940).

Christian readers have found verses 8-9 splendid in their breadth and universality. God's compassion knows no bounds. It embraces all catastrophes, without exception. We can say the same of Jesus' compassion for the suffering and the outcast. Here is an appropriate preaching text. God's awesome power becomes compassionate generosity to care for those otherwise uncared for.

Though Psalm 145 throughout is a celebration of praise, verse 20b sounds a warning. What might that mean for our day and culture? The psalm declares that humans live by gift and not by greed (vv. 15-16). In a secular consumer society, people do not hope for God to satisfy their desires, but they do expect their desires to be satisfied even if they do the taking. Declaring our independence and frantically trying to prove ourselves, we lose sight of the truth that self-sufficiency will leave us wanting. Gathering with God's people in worship to praise God's greatness and goodness is a reminder that no one can lay claim to anything as a right. The gifts of life come because God is good and *his compassion is over all that he has made* (v. 9).

Psalm 146

Praise the LORD, the One True Helper

PREVIEW

Psalm 146, a statement about God's powerful purpose for human well-being, echoes Psalm 145. It recalls both the beginning of the Psalter (Pss 1—2) and its theological center (Pss 93, 95—99), that we are not to place trust in mortals but in the sovereign LORD, who reigns over all. On that basis, Psalm 146 introduces the series of doxologies. Psalms 146–150 all begin and end with *Praise the LORD!* (transliterated *Hallelujah!* as in NJPS) to form a Hallel (praise piece) that concludes the book of Psalms with resounding praise.

Psalm 146, the hymn of an individual, is composed as a teaching psalm. The hymn celebrates the power and beneficence of God, which contrasts with the frailty and transience of human beings. Following the opening call to praise (vv. 1-2) and an exhortation against trust in mortals (vv. 3-4), it lists reasons for putting trust in the LORD alone (vv. 5-9). Alluding to Israel's experience in the exodus, the psalm praises the LORD as creator (v. 6) and redeemer (vv. 7-9). Five sentences, beginning with *the LORD* and the unmistakable emphasis upon the LORD's special care for the powerless, answer the underlying question of the psalm: "In whom shall we trust?" The psalm concludes by asserting, *The LORD will reign forever* (v. 10).

The anthological style of quoting or alluding to earlier psalms, a number of Aramaisms, and the organization of the psalm (vv. 7b-9) suggest a postexilic time for composition. Psalm 146 appears to draw from Hannah's thanksgiving song in style and content (1 Sam 2:1-10).

OUTLINE

Call to Praise, 146:1-2
Exhortation Against Trust in Mortals, 146:3-4
Motivation for Trust in the LORD, 146:5-9
    146:5   Priestly Blessing
    146:6-9   The LORD as Creator and Liberator
Concluding Doxology, 146:10

EXPLANATORY NOTES

Call to Praise   146:1-2

The call to praise parallels the opening and closing words of Psalms 103 and 104, though instead of *bless*, the psalmist says *praise*. The vow of praise for a lifetime anticipates the psalm's theme of trust and allegiance that will not disappoint.

Exhortation Against Trust in Mortals   146:3-4

The warning about placing trust *in princes* is based on knowledge of human transitoriness (Gen 3:19; Pss 90:3-6; 103:15-16). Even influential persons will not be able to save or provide deliverance, since their planning and projects are temporary (33:16-17; 118:8-9). The divine breath that enters into the material world makes the human a living being. When his breath departs, he returns to the earth (104:29). The warning about placing one's trust in mortals serves as a foil to the following verses about the all-powerful God.

Motivation for Trust in the LORD   146:5-9

In contrast to *no help* (v. 3), *help* can be found in *the God of Jacob, . . . the LORD* (v. 5). Indeed, there is only one who can help, the Creator and liberator as experienced by the people Israel (vv. 6-9). This section of the psalm, listing reasons for praise, begins with *Happy are those* ('ašrê, "blessed," the word that opens the book of Psalms). As the Psalter comes to an end, this assertion is repeated: How fortunate are those whose trust and hope is in the LORD. The LORD as creator refers to the unlimited, absolute power of God (v. 6). This is a faith-keeping God, a compassionate God, who offers justice to the oppressed, as symbolized by the provision of food to the hungry (Exod 14–16; Isa 49:8-12).

Psalm 146

As the psalm spells out the character of God, it uses a fivefold utterance of the divine name (*LORD*) to dismiss all other gods or mortals who might claim saving powers. It is the LORD, none other, who can bring the afflicted out of distress (vv. 7b-9; Ps 107). The *blind* were often considered the most helpless. The *strangers* were resident aliens in Israel who did not enjoy the rights of citizenship. Along with widows and orphans, they were protected by law, but often neglected (Exod 22:21-22). The LORD exercises sovereignty through loving service on behalf of those in need. The LORD is to be praised and trusted, because the LORD has done justice. This section, about the LORD's saving help for the hurting, ends with a reminder that the door is closed against the wicked (v. 9). Might this suggest that celebrating a compassionate God is meaningful only to those who show a like compassion (Deut 24:19-22; Davidson, 1998:471)?

Concluding Doxology 146:10

The doxology declares the LORD's reign forever (Exod 15:18; Pss 29:10; 145:13). The main functions of the king were justice-bringing and tending to the welfare of the people (Ps 72; Jer 21:11-12; 22:3, 15-16). The psalm affirms that this concern is at the heart of God's character and kingdom. *Praise the LORD!* forms an inclusio with verse 1.

THE TEXT IN THE BIBLICAL CONTEXT AND LIFE OF THE CHURCH

In Praise of God, the Compassionate Liberator

Jewish usage described Psalms 145–150 as the Hallel (praise) hymns, forming part of the daily morning prayers in the synagogue. We can not only assume that Jesus and the disciples sang psalms; the narrative of the Last Supper also attests to it (Mark 14:26). Later, when Peter and John were released from prison, "they raised their voices together," saying, "Sovereign Lord, who made the heaven and the earth, the sea, and everything in them . . ." (Ps 146:6; Isa 37:16-17; Acts 4:23-24). Isaiah 40:26-29 joins a similar mention of God's creation work with his accessibility to the weak.

The psalm's theme of God as compassionate liberator is the message of Jesus' ministry when he begins reading Isaiah 61 in the synagogue at Nazareth and declares: "Today this scripture has been fulfilled in your hearing" (Luke 4:16-21). Many other parallel passages appear in both the OT and the NT (Isa 35:4-6; 49:8-9; Matt 8:16-17; 11:5; Luke 1:53; 7:18-23).

Like Psalm 145, Psalm 146 points to the future "kingdom of God" proclaimed in the NT (Ps 145:11-13; Mark 1:15; Rev 19:6). The church has given expression to the Lord's reign particularly through its hymnody. Hymns specifically based on Psalm 146 are numerous and include "Praise to the Lord, the Almighty" (Joachim Neander, 1680), "Praise thou the Lord, O my soul" (Johann Herrnschmidt, 1714), and "I'll praise my Maker" (Isaac Watts, 1719).

In Whom Shall We Trust?

By focusing on the issue of trust, this psalm touches human life directly in every generation. What are the temptations regarding our allegiance? Where will we place our trust? In democracy? In the president? In the promise of science and technology to solve our problems? In military might? In ourselves? In the financial security we build up? From the perspective of the psalm, to be *wicked* means to be self-ruled. In contrast to the self-centeredness of our culture, the psalms and the gospel challenge us to be God-centered. To be *righteous* means that one's life fundamentally depends on God.

That makes worship so critical. This psalm confronts an affluent North American society beset with self-sufficiency. These songs of praise declare the radical transforming power of God at work on behalf of the weak, the innocent, and the righteous, and against the powerful and the wicked. True worship always serves to remind people that they cannot abuse and exploit others. Praise exalts the power of God to create a new reality by putting down the mighty and the powerful and raising up the lowly and the weak (Job 5:11-16; 12:17-25; Pss 75:8; 107:38-42; 113:7-8; Miller, 1986:77). At its best, worship seeks to persuade people that their lives are not their own, and that happiness and blessing belong to those who know their help and hope is in God, their Lord.

Psalm 147

How Good It Is to Sing Praises to Our God

PREVIEW

The exclamation *Praise the LORD! (Hallelujah!)* frames this song of praise (vv. 1, 20). The psalm is composed of three parts, each in the form of an imperative hymn with an opening summons to praise, followed by reasons for praise (vv. 1-6, 7-11, 12-20). Recurring themes are the power of God and God's compassionate grace in creation and election.

The first part praises the LORD because he restores Israel (vv. 2-3, 6) and *determines* the stars, forces that the ancients thought were controlling history (vv. 4-5). The second part thanks the LORD because he provides food for his creatures (vv. 8-9) and prefers the dependence of people upon his steadfast love rather than trusting in military might (vv. 10-11). The third part exalts the LORD for providing security and well-being for his people (vv. 13-14), the coming and passing of winter (vv. 15-18), and the revelation of his word to Israel (vv. 19-20; Mays, 1994b:442).

Written for the Jerusalem congregation (v. 12) in the period of the restoration after the exile (vv. 2-3, 13-14), the psalm may have been used at the Feast of Tabernacles, when people were thinking of God's great providence. References to rebuilding Jerusalem suggest a possible date sometime after 445 BC, when Nehemiah dedicated the city walls (vv. 2, 13; Neh 12:27-43; Stuhlmueller, 1983, 2:214). In vocabulary and ideas, Psalm 147 relates to Psalms 33 and 104 and Isaiah 40-66. Parallel passages abound (v. 6//Ps 146:9; v. 9//Ps 104:21; Job 38:39-41; v. 10//Ps 33:16-17; v. 14//Ps 81:16; vv. 16-17//Job 38:29-30).

The LXX and the Latin Vulgate divide Psalm 147 into two psalms. Verses 1-11 appeared as Psalm 146 and verses 12-20 as Psalm 147. Since the Greek and Latin versions counted Psalms 9–10 as a single psalm, the Hebrew numbering of the psalms was one ahead of the Greek-Latin traditions. From Psalm 148 on, the numbering is once more the same in all the traditions.

OUTLINE

Praise God as Lord of the Universe and Helper of the Downtrodden, 147:1-6
    147:1   Invitation to Praise
    147:2-3, 6   Building Up Jerusalem and Gathering the Outcasts
    147:4-5   God's Greatness in Naming the Stars
Thank God for Sustaining the World, 147:7-11
    147:7   Invitation to Thanksgiving
    147:8-9   Providential Care over Nature
    147:10-11   God Delights Not in Strength but in Trust
Praise God for the Gift of Shalom and the Life-giving Word, 147:12-20
    147:12   Invitation to Praise
    147:13-14   Protection and Blessing
    147:15-18   God's Word Orders the Seasons
    147:19-20   Privilege and Responsibility in the Ordinances

EXPLANATORY NOTES

Praise God as Lord of the Universe and Helper of the Downtrodden   147:1-6

After the opening *Praise the LORD!* the rest of verse 1 focuses on the beauty and delight of the song of praise, for God is *gracious.* God shows his compassion in gathering the exiles (Neh 1:9; Isa 56:8), here referred to as *outcasts of Israel, brokenhearted,* and *downtrodden* (vv. 2, 3, 6). The compassionate LORD *heals, binds,* and *lifts up* (vv. 2, 3, 6). Jerusalem, once in ruins, has been rebuilt (vv. 2, 13).

Verses 4-5 tell of the great power of the LORD. As the God who creates and names the stars, as God of the constellations, the LORD is supreme over all gods (Isa 40:26). Thus, as also envisioned by Isaiah, nothing can hinder the people's return from exile (40:1, 3,

28-31). The LORD's understanding is *beyond measure*. How does God show his power? By lifting up the downtrodden, providing for those who have lost their rights, and condemning the wicked (v. 6; Pss 113:7-9; 145:14; 146:8-9; Isa 40:29).

Thank God for Sustaining the World 147:7-11

With a renewed call to thank the LORD with grateful songs, the second part of the psalm lauds God for sustaining the world. It praises God for rain and vegetation, for food for beast and bird (vv. 8-9). Not the gods of Baal, but the God of Israel is the one who brings the rain (Job 5:10; 36:27-31). Why does the psalm single out God's care for the *young ravens*? An ancient belief held that ravens left their young to fend for themselves, and their cry was a sign that they were neglected (Job 38:41). But the LORD provides even for them (v. 9; Luke 12:24). The cry of the young ravens may be used here as an analogy for Israel's cry for help.

The military imagery of the war horse (Job 39:19-25) and the strong trained legs of the infantry may be an allusion to the Yahweh war tradition, in which the LORD fought the battle on behalf of the people (vv. 10-11; Josh 6; 2 Kings 19:32-36). God does not like war *[War]*. God is not favorably impressed with those who put their trust in military might, but desires people to turn to his steadfast love for their hope and help (Pss 20:7; 33:17; Amos 2:14-16). The LORD's pleasure is in those who *fear*, who revere and are faithful to the LORD (Pss 19:9; 22:23; 25:12, 14; 31:19; 34:7, 9; 61:5; 66:16; 85:9; 103:11, 13; 112:1; 128:4; 130:4).

Praise God for the Gift of Shalom and the Life-giving Word 147:12-20

The third part of the psalm exhorts the worshipping community to praise God for the gift of *shalom* (šālôm, v. 14) and the life-giving word (v. 15). In what may have been a period of relative peace and prosperity, the blessing of God again rests upon the children of the sacred city (vv. 12-14). This is the primary blessing that Israel hoped for (Pss 72:3, 7; 85:10-13; 127–128). The last five verses of the psalm describe the exercise of God's sovereignty (vv. 15-20). Using the language of Genesis 1, the psalm represents God's word as a messenger and active power in the world (Gen 1:9-11, 14). The word of God is responsible for the cycle of the seasons (vv. 16-18).

However, the climax of the psalm comes in the last two verses.

The *statutes* and the *ordinances*, the gift of torah, was Israel's unique heritage to shape the people's life and history (vv. 19-20; Pss 1; 19; 119). For Israel, the law of the LORD became the most significant form of the word (Deut 4:1-8; 32:8-9). The word came in mighty acts of mercy and judgment, such as no other nation had experienced [*Torah*]. Thus, the psalmist invites Zion to sing and praise the LORD for his sovereignty and providential care in creation, in liberation, and ultimately as a light to the nations (Ps 148:7-12; Isa 49:6). With this exclamation of wonder, the psalm ends. *Praise the LORD!*

THE TEXT IN THE BIBLICAL CONTEXT AND LIFE OF THE CHURCH

Placement of Given Psalms

Reflecting on the sequence of psalms in the Psalter, one can observe how this collection is roughly chronological. In the earlier sections we find more psalms of David and psalms from the period of the Kings. Psalms from the exile and restoration are much more numerous toward the end. The placement of Psalm 147 reinforces the conclusion that book V was shaped in response to the ongoing crisis of the postexilic era. Even as the prophets proclaimed the sovereignty of God amid the loss of the Davidic monarchy (Isa 52:7), so the Psalter appears to be shaped to offer the same response. Following this psalm of thanksgiving to God for restoring Jerusalem are psalms of thanksgiving for the unique mission of God's people (Pss 148; 149) [*Composition*].

Songs of Praise and the Transforming Power of God

Songs of praise declare the transforming power of God at work on behalf of the weak and oppressed, and against the powerful and the wicked. The LORD's compassionate power can reverse the human situation. Songs of praise exalt the power of God to create a new reality by putting down the mighty and the powerful and raising up the lowly and the weak (Job 5:11-16; 12:17-25; Pss 75:7; 107:33-42; 113:7-9; 146:9). Israel's worship is supposed to result in justice and righteousness (37:28; 50:16-21; 82:3-4; 98:9; 99:4; 103:6; 119:5-7; 146:7). Yet when doxologies focus on the abundance and goodness of the present order, awareness about social realities and existing needs may be diminished (Brueggemann, 1984:164).

We should not overlook this psalm's clear criticism of reliance on military might. We may compare the war horse and infantry of OT days to killing technology in our own day: tanks, stealth bombers, and smart bombs. God has less regard for such weapons of violence than for establishing relationships of trust. Care for outcasts, the brokenhearted, the wounded, the downtrodden seems far more significant to God than enthrallment with the mass killing of modern warfare. Wherein lies the gift of a nation? Is it in its laws and commitment to humanity, or in military might that can wreak unimaginable havoc, but is unable to "win the hearts and minds" of people?

The Intervening, Comforting Word of God

The NT takes the message of Psalm 147 about the living and intervening word of God, unique to Israel among ancient peoples, and underlines it as fulfilled in the NT, in the incarnation of God in Christ. Jesus is proclaimed as the Word incarnate, who dwells among us (John 1:14; 14:6). Behind Jesus' parable of the grain as a symbol of God's word (Mark 4:3-9) is the imagery of the bread from heaven in the desert (Deut 8:3; Matt 4:4; Luke 4:4; John 6:1-14, 48-51). In like manner, the early Christian church drew on OT images of God's word in celebrating the abundance of God's grace (Isa 55:10-11; 2 Cor 9:8-15). The NT proclaims that God has now granted to the church his blessing of the revealing and reconciling word (Eph 2:4-22).

Appealing in Psalm 147 is the cry of the young ravens (v. 9) and the assurance that God hears their cry for food. Jesus quoted this verse about the God who controls wind and rain caring also for helpless baby birds, to illustrate how God cares for his own (Matt 6:26; Luke 12:24). This text of God's compassion for the helpless provided comfort to the martyrs. So Hendrick Verstallen, sixteenth-century martyr in the Netherlands, wrote to his wife just before his death: "The LORD shall care for you; He . . . who feeds the young ravens that cry unto God, as David says [Ps 147:9], will also feed you, my dear lamb, when you, my widow, . . . shall with my young orphans cry to God" (Braght: 879).

Psalm 148

Let All Praise the Name of the LORD

PREVIEW

As the Psalter comes to its climax and close, the final three songs (148–150) heighten the crescendo of praise. Hallelujahs again frame Psalm 148. It calls on all creatures in the heavens (vv. 1-6) and on the earth (vv. 7-10) to join in the hymn of praise that all humanity, and especially Israel, should sing unto the LORD of all (vv. 11-14).

Structurally, the psalm is an imperative hymn in two parts, summoning praise of the LORD from the heavens (vv. 1-6) and from the earth (vv. 7-14). Each section concludes with a summary sentence *Let them praise the name of the LORD* (vv. 5a, 13a). The psalm introduces motivation or reason for praise with *for* (*kî*) or "indeed" (vv. 5b, 13b). The word *all* appears ten times, thus insisting that the list of those summoned to praise is inclusive, representative of everything that is.

The psalm comes to a climax with the emphasis that the LORD's name alone is to be exalted, that his glory is above earth and heaven, and that he has restored his covenant people to dignity and vitality (vv. 13-14). This hymn for public worship summons the people's praise of the exalted name on behalf of all creation.

Psalm 148

OUTLINE

Praise the LORD from the Heavens, 148:1-6
    148:1-4   Summons to Celestial Praise
    148:5-6   Motivation: He Commanded and They Were Created
Praise the LORD from the Earth, 148:7-14
    148:7-12   Summons to Terrestrial Praise
    148:13-14 Motivation: His Name, His Glory, a Horn for His
                People

EXPLANATORY NOTES

Praise the LORD from the Heavens   148:1-6

The first summons to praise is addressed to the celestial world. The *heavens, angels,* and *host* bring to mind the heavenly council (Pss 2; 8; 29; 82). *Heights* (*mārôm*) is the place of transition between heaven and earth, where what is heavenly becomes earthly. Here it designates the heavenly height (v. 1; 102:19). The *angels* belong to the circle of heavenly powers around the LORD, who praise and honor him, serving as messengers and representatives (v. 2; 103:20-21). Now the psalm names *sun, moon,* and *stars* (v. 3). The psalmist's cosmology follows the ancient oriental concept of the world as a storied structure, with the heavens above the earth, and waters above the visible vault of heaven (v. 4; Gen 1:6-8; Ps 104:3). But though others in the ancient world worshipped the luminaries as deities, the psalmist counts them as the creation of the one God (147:4).

The LORD's creative word in calling forth the heavenly beings—and fixing the heavens, sun, moon, and planets in their stations—is reason for prompting them to praise (vv. 5-6; Ps 33:9; Prov 8:27-29). The Hebrew of verse 6b, as an NRSV footnote says, uses two words with double meanings: *ḥoq*, both "limit" and "law"; and *'ābar*, "pass." So one could read: God established the heavenly bodies forever; "he fixed their limit, which cannot be passed," or "he fixed their law, which cannot pass away." The implication is both of a limit that the created heavenly bodies cannot cross and of a law that will never cease (Holladay: 325).

Praise the LORD from the Earth   148:7-14

The second part of the hymn directs attention to all of creation on earth, beginning with *sea monsters* and *all deeps, fire, hail, snow,* and *storm*, creatures and elements that are terrible and frightening (vv. 7-8). Is the psalm suggesting that even the *sea monster,* the object of fearful battles (Pss 74:13-14; 89:9-10; Isa 51:9-10), is now tamed into being the LORD's obedient and worshipping creature? Are such awesome forces of nature as fire or lightning, hail, snow, and storm not also at God's command?

Mountains and all hills represent the whole earth (v. 9). *Beasts and all cattle* represent the wild and domesticated animals (v. 10). One might ask, how does all creation praise the LORD? Obviously, praise need not be limited to words (Ps 150). Yet, praise comes to a climax with the mention of humankind (vv. 11-12; Ps 8:6). Along with all creation, humanity is summoned to praise God. The psalm calls praise forth from leaders and all people, young and old, women and men alike! We are all God's creatures, and "life in community can only be healthy when ordinary people, as well as kings and presidents, are conscious of this and act accordingly" (Westermann, 1989:259).

As the psalm moves toward its climax, it specifies the reason for praise (vv. 13-14). Though verse 5 calls celestial bodies to praise God simply for the fact of their existence, humanity is to praise God consciously, for God has revealed himself in his name (v. 13). In the Psalms, *the name of the LORD* expresses all the mystery and wonder of revelation, the object of all prayer, praise, and reflection (7:17; 20:7; 103:1; 113:1-3; 116:4, 13, 17; 118:10-12; 122:4; 124:8; 129:8; 135:1). The name makes one present to another. Among all the "gods," only the LORD is truly present on earth, and hence only the LORD deserves acclaim (72:18; Isa 2:17; Clifford, 1986:84). By his name the LORD has declared himself to be Creator and King of the universe. Thus, *his glory is above earth and heaven* (v. 13c).

The final verse reflects on the relationship between the LORD of the universe and his people, Israel. *He has raised up a horn for his people* (v. 14). Raising up a *horn* means bestowing dignity, honor, and strength (Pss 75:4-5, 10; 89:17, 23-24; 92:10; 112:9). Israel of the exile had lost its horn. The psalm proclaims that God has helped Israel again to attain a place among the nations that commands respect. This likely was not a military or political independence. Might the use of this idiom in Psalm 148 suggest new vitality and strength, in that the life of his *faithful* people would be characterized by praise? God's creation of a people *close to him* and restoring them after exile were acts no less wondrous than the other acts of creation. Thus, the psalm ends in awe that, of all the peoples on earth, God has chosen Israel to render special thanks and praise. The precise meaning of the phrase *praise for all his faithful* (v. 14b) is unclear, but in the context of the psalm it may suggest that God's people are called upon to continue showing forth the praise of God because of what they have been made by God. The line (v. 14b) appears to form an inclusio with the praise summoned in verses 1 and 7. *All his faithful ones* will play a key role in the following psalm, which reserves for them the role assigned to the king in Psalm 2 (Ps 149:1, 5, 9).

THE TEXT IN THE BIBLICAL CONTEXT AND LIFE OF THE CHURCH

Inclusive Praise

The organization of Psalm 148, listing category by category all creation, suggests a kind of systematic pondering of the universe that was part of wisdom. We find this pattern also in Job 38 and in the Song of the Three Jews, inserted (with The Prayer of Azariah) after Daniel 3:23 (LXX) in the Apocrypha. Though Psalm 148 shows similarities with an ancient Egyptian compendium, the "Onomasticon of Amenemope" (1100 BC), scholars have challenged that association in favor of its rootage in ancient Near Eastern hymnic traditions (Kraus, 1989:256; Miller, 1986:73).

In Psalm 148, human beings, the people of God, are partners in praising God with a multitude of other living beings, and inanimate things as well. Other hymns that proclaim God's reign also invite heaven and earth, and all beings and objects therein, to praise God (Pss 29:1-2, 9; 96:11-12; 97:1; 98:4, 7-8; Luke 2:13-14).

Liturgical Use of Psalm 148

Psalm 148 has enjoyed wide use in the weekly morning service of the Jewish liturgical tradition, and in the Christian church, which has often used the last three psalms as a unit. The psalm's focus on creation allows its use as Genesis 1 adapted to the form of praise. However, its widest influence may come through hymnody. Francis of Assisi (1182-1226) based his *Canticle of the Sun* (1225) upon this psalm, which many know through the hymn "All creatures of our God and King." Of the many other hymns inspired by Psalm 148, we mention "Oh, that I had a thousand voices" (Johann Mentzer, 1704), "All things bright and beautiful" (Cecil F. Alexander, 1848), "Praise the Lord, sing hallelujah" (William J. Kirkpatrick, 1871), "Let the whole creation cry" (Stopford A. Brooke, 1881), "This is my Father's world" (Maltbie B. Babcock, 1901), "Joyful, joyful, we adore thee" (Henry van Dyke, 1907), and "Earth and all stars" (Herbert Brokering, 1964).

In Psalm 148, the church has found significant suggestions for its own life as *people close to his heart* (v. 14 NIV). Sometimes readers interpret the *horn* (v. 14) as a king, the messianic king fulfilled in the coming of Jesus Christ. The church confesses that the name to which all creation is related is Jesus Christ (Col 1:15-20; Heb 1:2-4). God's purposes for the church and the world are closely related, and in Christ the created order is rectified and set on the path to transformation (Rom 8:18-25; Rev 5:13; 21:1-5; 22:1-5).

This Is God's World

Psalm 148 serves as a reminder that this is God's world. The theology is akin to Genesis 1. The world is good. In focusing upon the environment in which humans live, the psalm clearly challenges the secular worldview in which humanity (since the Enlightenment) has been set over against nature. Viewing nature as an object to investigate and exploit leads to destruction of the very environment needed for survival of life. Psalm 148 contends that all that exists is one in creatureliness. God is the Creator, and the whole created order derives its existence from him (Westermann, 1989:259). Appropriate praise includes joy and delight in the existence of life and beauty in nature's pulsing world. Our praise should include a kinder, gentler treatment of the environment.

Praise echoes God's creative work. The praise of God unites human beings with the rest of creation. This call to praise is pervasive in the psalms (33:8; 47:2; 66:1, 8; 67:4-7; 96:1-4; 97:1; 98:4-6; 100:1-2; 145:21). However, it is well to remember that when praise becomes primarily a repetition of thanks for a glorious, well-ordered, and king-ruled world (vv. 11, 14), people become complacent. Resounding doxologies like Psalm 148 are best paired with songs that acknowledge the reality of a human world of hurt, need, and injustice (such as Ps 146).

Psalm 149

Glory for All His Faithful Ones

PREVIEW

Psalm 149, again an imperative hymn framed by hallelujahs (vv. 1, 9), follows the same structural form as Psalm 148 *[Psalm Genres]*. In the two parts of the psalm, the faithful ones are summoned to praise the LORD (vv. 1-4, 5-9), with the motivation identified at the end of each part (vv. 4, 9b). What is different and jarring, however, is the content of the second part. The unrestrained joy of God's people (vv. 1-4) turns to the execution of vengeance upon their enemies (vv. 6-9) *[Vengeance]*.

Interpretation of Psalm 149 is difficult. In the attempt to make sense of the psalm's contrasts, readers have suggested many settings: worship and vengeance, praise and power. Possible historical settings for this hymn, sung on the eve of battle or to celebrate a military victory, have included early conflicts with Canaanite kings (Num 31:8; Josh 10:24-27; Judg 1:6-7), Nehemiah's triumph over hostile neighbors (Neh 4:10-23), or the Maccabean revolt against the Seleucid domination in the second century BC (1 Macc 2:42; 4:24, 33; 7:46-49).

Unable to associate Psalm 149 with a specific historical event, some consider Psalm 149 as looking toward the final judgment of God. Thus, the psalm celebrates the day in the future when Israel will fulfill the written promise of the prophets (v. 9) and execute judgment on kings and nations who have oppressed them (vv. 7-8). Others view Psalm 149 as drawing on the cultic traditions of Jerusalem in a reenactment of the salvation history of the nation. The praises of the people and the shouting of the warriors (v. 6) report past events, yet look to the future. As the LORD has acted in the past, so he is involved in the present situation, and will bring to a glorious completion all his purposes (A. Anderson, 2:952).

It will be helpful to hear Psalm 149 and its martial language in the context of ancient times, when people's hope was sustained by eschatological visions of God's final victory and sovereignty. Also important is the placement of this psalm in the sequence of the Psalter [Composition]. Psalms 1 and 150 show how torah obedience leads to praise. Psalm 149, as next to the last psalm, may be paired with Psalm 2, which concerns the anointing of a king in defiance of the nations. Both Psalms 2 and 149 affirm God's sovereignty. Both assert that those who try to exercise their own sovereignty will be brought to account (Pss 2:8-12; 149:7-9). In Psalm 149, kings are the powers to be overthrown in praise of the LORD (vv. 8-9). And again, "the human instrument is the assembly of the faithful, who seem in their service to be a messianic community through whom the LORD achieves what was assigned the vocation of the Davidic king" (Mays, 1994b:448; Brueggemann, 1984:167).

OUTLINE

Sing to the LORD a New Song, 149:1-4
    149:1-3   Summons to the Faithful to Praise the LORD
    149:4   Motivation: The LORD's Care of the Humble
A New Call to Praise in the Wake of Judgment, 149:5-9
    149:5-9a   Summons and Action to Complete Praise
    149:9b   Declaration About the Meaning of the Action

EXPLANATORY NOTES

Sing to the LORD a New Song 149:1-4

Psalm 149 begins with the closing thought of Psalm 148:14, the special privilege of the people of Israel. The psalm is centered and framed by reference to *the faithful* (*ḥăsîdîm*, vv. 1, 5, 9). The community assembled in Zion represents a group of dependent but God-fearing people who put their trust in the LORD (v. 4). *A new song* suggests a new situation, a new reality, a new reliability (v. 1; Pss 33:3; 40:3; 96:1; 98:1; 144:9; Isa 42:10). The song praises the LORD as their Maker and King (v. 2). In the hymns of praise, we find explicit declarations of the kingship and sovereignty of the God of Israel (Exod 15; Deut 33:1-5, 26-29; Pss 29; 47; 93; 95–99; 145; Isa 52:7-10). Music and dance to express joy in the LORD were important elements in the worship of Israel and her neighbors (Exod 15:20; Judg 11:34; 2 Sam 6:14-15; Pss 68:24-25; 150:4; Jer 31:4).

The basis for praise is the LORD's care for his people, and particularly the *humble*, those who, in desperate need, cry out for help (v. 4). The language about *victory, salvation* (NIV), and "liberation," may be drawing on early memories of Israel's victories in the days of Moses and David.

A New Call to Praise in the Wake of Judgment 149:5-9

The psalm's central verse renews the summons to praise in songs of joy (v. 5). *Couches* or *beds* (NIV) may suggest praise in private along with public praise. Or it may have reference to prayer mats or reclining at mealtime. This renewed summons turns to the judgment on the nations and is a call to action on the basis of praise (vv. 6-9). *High praises . . . in their throats* and *two-edged swords in their hands, vengeance, punishment, fetters, chains*—all this is martial language that jolts. Is this a lust for revenge? Is it an association with Yahweh war? *[War].* Is the opposite aspect of salvation the judgment upon the other nations? Does not victory and deliverance for the people of God mean defeat for the enemies? Does *the judgment decreed* (v. 9) refer to extermination of pagan nations of Canaan (Deut 7:1-6; 20:10-18)? Or is it an allusion to prophetic oracles against the nations (Ezek 25:14; Mic 4:13; Zech 12:6)?

The language of *vengeance, punishment,* and *judgment* suggests that the battle was the LORD's, and victory is God's favor to Israel. On the other hand, *glory for all his faithful ones* (9b) suggests that Israel's true glory lies in executing the LORD's decree regarding the nations. But is that decree extermination of the nations or telling the LORD's salvation to all peoples and all nations (Pss 96; 145; 148; 150)? In these verses, so difficult for us (vv. 5-9), the psalmist may simply be saying in his own way, "Your will be done" (Matt 6:10), not dreaming of a national war of conquest, but of the establishment of divine justice (A. Anderson, 2:954).

THE TEXT IN THE BIBLICAL CONTEXT AND LIFE OF THE CHURCH

Praying Psalm 149

The church cannot pray Psalm 149 as the people of Israel in OT times might have prayed it. Unfortunately, some have enlisted it as a war prayer with disastrous consequences. Psalm 149 became Thomas Müntzer's battle hymn to stir up the Peasants' Revolt (War) of 1524–1525 in Germany, and Caspar Scloppius (Scloppe) used it (in his *Classicum belli sacri*, 1619) to inflame the Roman Catholic princes to fight in the Thirty Years' War (1618–1648). To those who would launch wars in the name of God, Jesus' warning stands: "Put your sword back into its place; for all who take the sword will perish by the sword" (Matt 26:52).

In the psalmist's day, the Israelites envisioned the kingdom of God in nationalistic and militaristic terms. The NT sets this framework aside. Jesus said to Pilate, "My kingdom is not from this world. If my kingdom were from this world, my followers would be fighting" (John 18:36). Paul wrote that "the weapons of our warfare are not merely human" (2 Cor 10:4); Christian warfare is "not against enemies of blood and flesh, but against . . . spiritual forces of evil" (Eph 6:10-17). This NT passage describes "the whole armor of God" by drawing on metaphors of the soldier's battle equipment, ending with the "helmet of salvation, and the sword of the Spirit, which is the word of God" (for background, see Isa 59:16-17). The comment about being "ready to proclaim the gospel of peace" is insightful (Eph 6:15).

We may be averse to the warlike metaphors, though they are used in both the OT and NT. Judgment is much a part of the biblical revelation (Deut 30:15-20), including on Israel, God's own special people (Amos 3:1-2; 8:1-3). In the book of Psalms, vengeance always serves the purpose of justice (94; 109). The two-edged sword (149:6) is used metaphorically in the NT for the fierce justice of God (Heb 4:12-13; Rev 1:16; 2:12). However, it is not the NT way for God's own to be applying violent force (Rom 12:19-21; Heb 10:30-31), nor is it necessarily the OT way (Deut 32:35) *[Imprecation]*.

Praise and Public Policy

Observing how Psalm 149 moves from a lyrical remembering of the exodus to a powerful resolve for the conquest of the land, Brueggemann sees in the psalm an example of how praise engenders public policy (1995:124-25). Songs of praise can reinforce public resolve and action. In the 1960s songs and prayers were driving forces for the protests of the civil rights movement. Brueggemann points out how the action of Psalm 149 is aimed at kings and merchant-lords (v. 8), against those who control a social monopoly, depriving others of their legitimate goods for life. Thus, we can also read the psalm as illustrating how the praise of God can mobilize people for righting social wrong. Depending on who is singing, doxology can lead to action or reinforce complacency about the status quo.

The Psalter is the soil from which the language of the Spirit-inspired hymns and prayers of the early Christians sprang. The "new song" raised in the NT (Eph 5:19-20; Col 3:12-17; Rev 5:9-10; 14:3) has its prototype in the psalms of the OT (Pss 33:3; 40:3; 96:1; 98:1). However, the content is different: these songs point to a new reality and reliability—ransom rather than destruction of "every tribe and language and people and nation" (Rev 5:9-10; 15:3-4).

Psalm 150

Praise the LORD!

PREVIEW

The Psalter concludes with a mighty crescendo of praise. This final hymn begins and ends, as do Psalms 146–149, with an emphatic *Praise the LORD!* Different in this psalm, however, is the sustained summons to praise with ten successive imperatives: *Praise God/him . . . !* (vv. 1b-5). The psalm needs to give no reason for praise beyond *his mighty deeds* (v. 2).

Some commentators have seen in the ten imperatives an allusion to the ten words of creation (Gen 1), or to the Ten Commandments (Exod 20), or that the number ten represents for the poet a complete and inexhaustible whole. The word *praise* is used thirteen times in all. The focus is on the praise of *the LORD* (*hallelu-Jah* or *Praise Yah*). At the end, with the help of the entire temple orchestra, the psalm invites everything that has breath to praise the LORD.

We should recognize its significance as the final psalm. Four other hallelujah psalms are inserted in front of it, so that the Psalter concludes with five hallelujah psalms, one for each "book of the Psalms," with the 150th doing double duty as the conclusion to the fifth book and to the five books altogether (Peterson, 1989:127).

OUTLINE

Introduction: Praise the LORD! 150:1a
Ten Imperatives to Praise, 150:1b-5
Conclusion: Praise as God's Ultimate Purpose for All Creation, 150:6

EXPLANATORY NOTES

Ten Imperatives to Praise   150:1-6

Answers to four questions—Where? (v. 1), Why? (v. 2), How? (vv. 3-5), and By whom? (v. 6)—allow us to look at the thrust of this final doxology. After the introductory call to *praise the LORD*, the imperatives identify *his sanctuary* and *his mighty firmament* as places of praise (v. 1). The temple and the heavens are God's dwelling. The implication is that heaven and earth meet, and that praise is fitting for everyone everywhere.

God is to be praised *for his mighty deeds* (v. 2). No other reasons need to be added. His acts of creation, deliverance, and preservation have already been stated throughout the psalms (Pss 71:16; 106:2; 145:4, 11-12). God's sovereignty is the fundamental affirmation that pervades the Psalter (Pss 2; 93; 95-99; 145-149).

Musical instruments enlisted for praise are cataloged (vv. 3-5). The *trumpet* (*šôpār*) was made from a hollowed ram's horn and used to signal the parts of the worship service, the Sabbath hours, and the beginning of religious feasts. The *lute* (*nēbel*) and the *harp* (*kinnôr*) were stringed instruments used to accompany singing by individuals or small groups (1 Sam 16:16; 2 Sam 6:5; 1 Chron 15:16). The *tambourine* (*tōp*) was a hand drum used to accentuate the beat of a tune. It is mentioned in connection with a whirling dance (Exod 15:20-21; Ps 149:3). The *strings* (v. 4) may refer to other stringed instruments such as the zither, and *pipe* was a flute made from a reed. Here *cymbals* are mentioned twice (1 Chron 15:19). The loud sound of the cymbals accents the intensity of the praise. Though the psalmist's list of musical instruments is not exhaustive (cf. NJPS), it portrays worship as a lively, energetic, sound-filled experience! *[Musical].*

The final verse then broadens the call to praise to include all living things (v. 6). This verse matches verse 1, forming an inclusio. Psalm 150:6 also recalls Psalm 145:21 and thus provides an envelope around the final collection of doxology psalms. In praise, the congregation is moving toward the consummation of creation as the psalm calls upon all on earth to give praise. Praise is creation's most characteristic mode of existence. On that note the Psalter closes.

THE TEXT IN THE BIBLICAL CONTEXT AND LIFE OF THE CHURCH

Praise and the Life of Obedience

The Hebrew name for the book of Psalms, *tĕhillîm*, or "Praises," comes from the Hebrew verb *hillēl* (the *pi'ēl* form, from *hālal*), "to praise." This concluding doxology reminds us how Psalm 1 invites a life based on torah (*tôrâ*), God's instruction. Psalm 2 celebrates enthronement of the Davidic kings and points to the LORD's anointed. The first part of the Psalter is marked by anguish and repeated prayers for help. Book III laments the crisis of exile and loss of the Davidic dynasty (Ps 89). Books IV and V offer response about how the LORD reigns in steadfast love even during times of opposition and oppression. Now at the end, the Psalter concludes with overwhelming praise. The final word is *Hallelujah!* (*Praise Yah!*), as though all the complaint and the pain, the struggle and the doubt of the Psalter are now left behind in a glorious outburst of joy in God.

Brueggemann calls attention to the danger that people will sing a psalm like Psalm 150 too soon. "Israel can join God in God's full praise only at the end. . . . Such affirmation is not Israel's first song, but it is Israel's last doxology, which is a satisfied, obedient, delighted yielding" (Brueggemann, 1988:155). Thus, the outcome of life under torah is not simply obedience, but adoration.

The Psalter as Hymnbook

Psalm 150 leaves no doubt that the Psalter was Israel's hymnbook. Even prayers adapted as psalms were set to music. The Psalter was also hymnbook of the early church. Through the centuries of Christendom, singing of the psalms has continued.

The earliest known publication of a Protestant translation of the Psalms appeared in Strasbourg in 1539: the hymnal included 19 psalms, 13 rhymed by Clément Marot and six by John Calvin. In 1541 Marot, a Huguenot, published another 30 psalms in Paris, thus making 49 psalms in rhyme. The first complete Psalter in rhyme, translated by Théodore de Bèze and published in 1562 in Geneva (after publishing 34 there in 1551), became the hymnbook of many Reformed churches (http://spindleworks.com/library/deddens/psalmOrigins.htm). For two hundred years after Luther had inspired a rich treasury of poems for use in congregational singing, the Calvinistic churches were still using only psalms and paraphrases of Scripture. The early Anabaptists and Mennonites did not sing psalms, preferring the hymns composed by the martyrs and the songs dealing with their faith and suffering. However, by the early seventeenth century, psalm-singing became prevalent, and for a time in many of the Dutch Mennonite churches, it was the exception to sing any hymn other than a psalm (Geiser: 226-27; Zijpp, 1956:873-74; 1959:227). Many of the psalm-hymns have found their way into subsequent hymnals. The poetry of the psalms continues to be set to music in every age.

Music offers an experience of God, not an explanation of God. When words run out, music keeps going. By participating in the very act of creation, of making music, we discover another way to approach the one in whom we live and move and have our being.

The NT connects with this psalm in the words about singing "psalms and hymns and spiritual songs . . . and making melody to the Lord . . ." (Eph 5:19-20). The Bible's final book, the Revelation to John, tells of "thousands of thousands" singing with full voice, "Worthy is the Lamb" (Rev 5:11-13). That book, too, comes to a final crescendo: "Hallelujah! For the Lord our God the Almighty reigns" (19:6), a definitive exclamation of praise to the sovereign God made memorable through the "Hallelujah Chorus" in George F. Handel's oratorio *Messiah*.

Outline of Psalms

Book One: Psalms 1–41

Blessed—the Way of the Righteous	**1:1-6**
Portrait of the Righteous	1:1-3
Portrait of the Wicked	1:4-6
The LORD and His Anointed	**2:1-12**
Astonishment at the Rebellion of the Nations	2:1-3
The LORD's Response from the Heavens	2:4-6
The King's Report of the Decree of the LORD	2:7-9
Admonition and Invitation	2:10-12
How Many Are My Foes!	**3:1-8**
Invocation and Complaint	3:1-2
Affirmation of Confidence	3:3-6
Petition and Vow of Trust	3:7-8
Evening Prayer to the Giver of Peaceful Sleep	**4:1-8**
Plea to God, Who Hears the Cry of the Faithful	4:1-3
Exhortation to Honor the LORD	4:4-6
Statement of Trust	4:7-8
Morning Prayer to the God of Righteousness	**5:1-12**
Appeal to God to Hear the Petition	5:1-3
Praise for God's Judgment of the Wicked	5:4-6
Statement of Intention to Enter the Sanctuary	5:7-8
Description and Fate of the Accusers	5:9-10
Celebration of the Divine Presence	5:11-12
The LORD Has Heard My Weeping	**6:1-10**
Complaint and Petition for Healing	6:1-5

Description of the Psalmist's Plight	6:6-7
Declaration That the LORD Has Heard	6:8-10
Prayer to God, the Righteous Judge	**7:1-17**
Cry for Refuge and Declaration of Innocence	7:1-5
Petition for Personal Vindication	7:6-8
Petition for Public Vindication	7:9-16
Vow of Praise	7:17
The Wonder of Creation: Creature and Creator	**8:1-9**
An Ascription of Praise	8:1-2
Reflection on the Dignity of Humanity	8:3-8
An Ascription of Praise	8:9
Thanksgiving and Prayer for God's Justice	**9:1–10:18**
Thanksgiving for God's Judgment on the Enemy	9:1-6
Thanksgiving That God Does Not Forget the Oppressed	9:7-12
Petition for Deliverance and the Cry for Justice	9:13-20
Lament over the Prosperity of the Wicked	10:1-11
Petition That God Remember the Afflicted and Punish the Wicked	10:12-15
Praise That the LORD Is Judge of the Nations and Savior of the Poor	10:16-18
In the LORD I Take Refuge	**11:1-7**
Declaration of Refuge in the LORD	11:1-3
Confidence in the LORD's Judgment Throne	11:4-7
Destructive Words and the Saving Word	**12:1-8**
Cry for Help and Complaint About Destructive Speech	12:1-4
Oracle of Salvation and Statement of Trust	12:5-6
Petition for Protection from the Wicked	12:7-8
How Long, O LORD?	**13:1-6**
Invocation and Complaint	13:1-2
Petition and Motivation	13:3-4
Statement of Trust and Vow of Praise	13:5-6
Prayer for Deliverance in a Corrupt Age	**14:1-7**
Lament About the Depravity of the Wicked	14:1-3
Rebuke of the Wicked	14:4-6
Prayer for Deliverance of God's People	14:7
Admission to the Temple	**15:1-5**
The Question About Admission to Worship	15:1

Outline of Psalms

The Answer	15:2-5b
The Declaration	15:5c
The LORD, a Goodly Heritage	**16:1-11**
Confession of Faith: The Chosen Loyalty	16:1-6
Thanksgiving: Blessings of the Goodly Heritage	16:7-11
Plea of the Innocent to the Savior of Fugitives	**17:1-15**
Petition for a Fair Hearing and Declaration of Innocence	17:1-5
Petition for Refuge from the Wicked	17:6-12
Imprecatory Prayer for God's Judgment upon the Enemies	17:13-14
Expression of Confident Hope	17:15
A King's Thanksgiving Hymn for Deliverance and Victory	**18:1-50**
Introductory Hymn of Praise	18:1-3
Account of Peril and Salvation	18:4-19
Metaphors of Deliverance	18:4-6
Theophany	18:7-15
Report of Salvation	18:16-19
Confession of Praise	18:20-30
Righteousness Rewarded	18:20-24
God's Covenant Love	18:25-30
Thanksgiving to God as Source of the King's Victory	18:31-45
Doxology	18:46-50
In Praise of God's Creating and Redeeming Word	**19:1-14**
Hymn to Creation: God's Glory Through Nature	19:1-6
Hymn to the Torah: God's Will Through Law	19:7-10
Petition for Pardon and Reconsecration	19:11-14
Prayer for the King	**20:1-9**
Prayer for the King	20:1-5
Assurance of Victory	20:6-9
Thanksgiving Prayer for a King	**21:1-13**
Prayer of Thanksgiving for Blessings to the King	21:1-7
Commission of the King and Concluding Prayer	21:8-13
My God, My God, Why Have You Forsaken Me?	**22:1-31**
The Cry of Anguish When God Is Absent	22:1-21
Address, Complaint, Affirmations, and Petition	22:1-11
Description of the Psalmist's Plight and Petition	22:12-21
The Response of Thanksgiving and Praise	22:22-31

Praise in the Congregation	22:22-26
Proclamation of the Worldwide Sovereignty of the LORD	22:27-31

The LORD as Shepherd and Host — **23:1-6**
  The LORD Is My Shepherd — 23:1-4
  The LORD Is My Gracious Host — 23:5-6

The King of Glory — **24:1-10**
  Hymn Celebrating God the Creator — 24:1-2
  An Entrance Liturgy — 24:3-6
  Ceremony Welcoming the King of Glory — 24:7-10

To You, O LORD, I Lift Up My Soul — **25:1-22**
  Prayer of Trust and Petition — 25:1-7
  Celebration of the LORD's Dependable Friendship — 25:8-15
  Petition for Deliverance and Redemption — 25:16-22

To Walk in Integrity and God's Faithfulness — **26:1-12**
  Prayer for Vindication — 26:1-3
  Protestation of Innocence — 26:4-7
  Standing in the Temple and Petition Not to Be Swept Away — 26:8-10
  Reaffirmation of Innocence — 26:11-12

The LORD Is My Light and My Salvation — **27:1-14**
  The Confidence of Faith — 27:1-6
    Trust in the LORD as Refuge — 27:1-3
    Desire to Live in the House of the LORD — 27:4-6
  The Cry for Help — 27:7-14
    Plea for Deliverance from Enemies — 27:7-12
    Expression of Confidence and Exhortation — 27:13-14

Petition and Thanksgiving — **28:1-9**
  Petition for Deliverance and Retribution — 28:1-5
  Thanksgiving and Intercession — 28:6-9

The Voice of the LORD in the Storm — **29:1-11**
  Introduction: Summons to Praise — 29:1-2
  Reason for Praise: The Voice of the LORD in the Thunderstorm — 29:3-9
  Conclusion: The LORD's Enthronement as King — 29:10-11

You Have Turned My Mourning into Dancing — **30:1-12**
  Song of Praise for Deliverance — 30:1-3
  Invitation to the Congregation to Join in Praise — 30:4-5
  Narrative of the Crisis and Restoration — 30:6-12

Outline of Psalms

My Times Are in Your Hand	**31:1-24**
Prayer for Refuge and Confession of Confidence	31:1-8
Petition for God's Grace in Distress and Statement of Trust	31:9-18
Hymn of Thanksgiving for Deliverance	31:19-24
The Blessing of Confession and Forgiveness	**32:1-11**
The Blessedness of Forgiveness Through Confession	32:1-5
The Forgiven Sinner Teaches About Deliverance	32:6-11
Hymn to the LORD, Whose Steadfast Love Fills the Earth	**33:1-22**
Call to Worship: Praise with Instruments and Voices	33:1-3
The LORD's Praiseworthiness: His Word and Work	33:4-19
The Word of the LORD in Creation	33:4-9
The Counsel of the LORD and the Nations	33:10-12
The Eye of the LORD on All Humankind	33:13-19
Concluding Affirmation of Trust	33:20-22
O Taste and See That the LORD Is Good	**34:1-22**
Invitation to Praise	34:1-3
Testimony to the Goodness of the LORD	34:4-10
Narrative of the Psalmist's Experience	34:4-6
The LORD's Care for Those Who Seek Him	4:7-10
Instruction on How to Live a Long and Happy Life	34:11-21
Invitation to Learn About Life	34:11-14
The LORD's Face Toward the Righteous	34:15-21
Liturgical Conclusion: The LORD Redeems	34:22
Plea from One of the Quiet in the Land	**35:1-28**
Cry for Deliverance, Imprecation, and Promise	35:1-10
Cry of Innocence, Plea, and Vow of Thanksgiving	35:11-18
Complaint, Plea for Vindication, Imprecation, and Praise	35:19-28
With You Is the Fountain of Life	**36:1-12**
Complaint: Description of the Arrogant Wicked	36:1-4
Hymn: Praise of the Gracious Love of the LORD	36:5-9
Petition: Prayers for the LORD's Continuing Care and Protection	36:10-12
Commit Your Way to the LORD	**37:1-40**
Fret Not Because of the Wicked, but Trust in the LORD	37:1-11
The End of the Wicked and the Righteous Contrasted	37:12-22

The Blessings of the Faithful	37:23-29
The LORD Is the Helper of the Righteous	37:30-40

Do Not Forsake Me, O LORD! — 38:1-22
Opening Plea for Help	38:1-2
Description of the Psalmist's Illness	38:3-10
Abandoned by All	38:11-20
Final Plea for Deliverance	38:21-22

I Am Your Passing Guest — 39:1-13
Confession of Self-imposed Silence	39:1-3
Meditation on the Frailty of Human Life	39:4-6
Petition for Deliverance from Sin	39:7-11
Plea for God's Pity and Protection	39:12-13

The Lord Takes Thought for Me — 40:1-17
Description of Past Deliverance	40:1-4
The New Song	40:5-10
Plea for a New Deliverance	40:11-17

O LORD, Be Gracious to Me — 41:1-13
Didactic Introduction of Confidence in the LORD	41:1-3
The Psalmist's Prayer: *O LORD, Be Gracious to Me*	41:4-10
Concluding Statement of Confidence	41:11-12
Doxology Concluding Book One of Psalms	41:13

Book Two Psalms 42–72

The Cry of the Soul for God — 42:1–43:5
Homesickness in Exile	42:1-5
Despair in Abandonment	42:6-11
Hope for Vindication	43:1-5

Israel Cries Out for Help in a Time of National Crisis — 44:1-26
Hymn Reciting God's Mighty Deeds in the Past and Expressing Trust in God	44:1-8
Lament over the Nation's Defeat and Shame	44:9-16
Protestation of Innocence: Faith and Fact in Conflict	44:17-22
Desperate Petition for God to Act Again	44:23-26

Royal Wedding Song — 45:1-17
Dedication to the King	45:1
The King as Bridegroom Addressed and Praised	45:2-9
The Bride Addressed and the Procession Described	45:10-15
Concluding Promise of Progeny and Reign	45:16-17

Outline of Psalms

God Is Our Refuge and Strength	**46:1-11**
God, Our Refuge in the Midst of Chaos (Creation)	46:1-3
God, Our Help in the Midst of the City (History)	46:4-7
God, Our Hope in the Midst of the Warring Nations (Kingdom)	46:8-11
Call to Joyful Praise of the God Who Reigns over All the Earth	**47:1-9**
Summons to Praise of God, Who Has Subdued the Nations	47:1-5
Sing Praises, for God Is King of All the Earth	47:6-9
Zion, City of Our God	**48:1-14**
Call to Praise the LORD in Zion	48:1-3
Description of a Deliverance from Enemies	48:4-8
The Worshipping Pilgrims Ponder God's Steadfast Love	48:9-11
The Procession and Acclamation	48:12-14
Not Wealth, but God	**49:1-20**
The Wisdom Teacher's Introduction	49:1-4
Reflective Teaching on the Transitoriness of Wealth and Inevitability of Death	49:5-12
Lament for Those Trusting in Themselves; Comfort in God's Ransom	49:13-20
The Judge Speaks	**50:1-23**
The Coming of God, the Judge	50:1-6
Address to the Congregation: Judgment of Worship	50:7-15
Address to the Wicked: Judgment of Conduct	50:16-23
Have Mercy on Me, O God. . . . I Have Sinned	**51:1-19**
Plea for Mercy	51:1-2
Confession of Sin	51:3-6
Petition for Cleansing from Sin	51:7-9
Petition for Spiritual Restoration	51:10-12
Vow of Praise and Public Contrition	51:13-17
Prayer for Jerusalem	51:18-19
To Boast, or to Thank?	**52:1-9**
Accusation Against the Arrogant Wicked	52:1-4
Divine Judgment and the Response of the Righteous	52:5-7
Confession of Trust and Praise	52:8-9
God, the Deliverer, in a Corrupt World	**53:1-6**

Confidence in God's Name — 54:1-7
- Petition for Help and Complaint — 54:1-3
- Statement of Confidence and Vow of Thanksgiving — 54:4-7

Betrayed by a Friend — 55:1-23
- Desperate Cry for Help — 55:1-5
- The Temptation to Flee — 55:6-8
- Complaint: Violence in the City — 55:9-11
- Complaint: Betrayal by a Friend — 55:12-15
- The Psalmist Calls upon God — 55:16-19
- Reprise: The Unfaithful Friend — 55:20-21
- Confident Trust in God — 55:22-23

In God I Trust — 56:1-13
- Petition, Complaint, and Affirmation of Trust — 56:1-4
- Complaint, Petition, and Affirmation of Trust — 56:5-11
- Vow of Thanksgiving — 56:12-13

Be Exalted, O God — 57:1-11
- Lament, Refrain, and Transition — 57:1-6
- Hymn of Confidence and Refrain — 57:7-11

A God Who Judges on Earth — 58:1-11
- Complaint: Judgment upon the Wicked Leaders — 58:1-5
- Petition for God's Intervention: Sevenfold Curse — 58:6-9
- Declaration: Vindication of the Righteous — 58:10-11

Deliver Me, O God of Steadfast Love — 59:1-17
- Petition for Deliverance from Enemies and Refrain of Trust — 59:1-10
  - Plea for Help — 59:1-2
  - Lament and Declaration of Innocence — 59:3-4a
  - Appeal for the LORD's Intervention — 59:4b-5
  - Description of the Enemies — 59:6-7
  - Refrain: Trust in God's Steadfast Love — 59:8-10
- Petition for Judgment upon the Enemies and Refrain of Trust — 59:11-17
  - Plea for Judgment upon the Enemies — 59:11-13
  - Description of the Enemies — 59:14-15
  - Refrain: Trust in God's Steadfast Love — 59:16-17

With God, . . . for Human Help Is Worthless — 60:1-12
- Lament: National Distress — 60:1-5
  - The People's Situation Described — 60:1-3
  - Prayer for Deliverance — 60:4-5
- Divine Oracle: God Lays Claim to the Hebrew — 60:6-8

Outline of Psalms

Territories	
Lament and Prayer for Victory	60:9-12
God, a Refuge in Time of Trouble	**61:1-8**
Opening Plea for Refuge	61:1-4
Prayer for the King and Vow of Praise	61:5-8
For God Alone My Soul Waits in Silence	**62:1-12**
Avowal of Trust in God	62:1-7
Refrain-like Statement of Confidence	62:1-2, 5-7
Lament: The Psalmist's Situation	62:3-4
Instruction to the Community to Trust in God Alone	62:8-12
Summons to Trust	62:8
Admonition About Human Mortality and Greed	62:9-10
Prayer Addressed to God	62:11-12
Your Steadfast Love Is Better Than Life	**63:1-11**
The Soul's Thirst for God	63:1-4
Satisfied by God's Protective Help	63:5-8
Confident of Deliverance	63:9-11
Wicked Tongues and Tongues of Witness	**64:1-10**
Complaint About the Cutting Tongue	64:1-6
Confidence in God's Arrow of Recompense	64:7-10
Thanks for God-given Bounty	**65:1-13**
God of the Temple: Forgiveness and Blessing	65:1-4
God of the World: Awesome Stabilizing Power	65:5-8
God as Giver of Rain: The Bounty of the Land	65:9-13
Come and See. . . . Come and Hear!	**66:1-20**
Summons to Praise for God's Awesome Deeds	66:1-4
Thanksgiving for Past Deliverance	66:5-7
Summons to Praise for Present Deliverance	66:8-12
Vow of Thanksgiving Sacrifice	66:13-15
Testimony to What God Has Done for the Psalmist	66:16-20
The Blessing—for All Nations	**67:1-7**
Blessing upon an Assembled People and Petition for All Peoples	67:1-3
Petition for the Nations to Recognize God's Just Rule	67:4-5
The Universal Blessing and Mission of God	67:6-7
Procession Hymn of Praise to the Ascended God	**68:1-35**
Exultant Call to Praise God, Who Comes to Battle Injustice	68:1-6

Let God Scatter the Enemies	68:1-3
Praise for Protection of the Defenseless	68:4-6
Praise God for Past Deliverance	68:7-18
The Wilderness, Sinai, Abundant Rain	68:7-10
The Divine Word Scatters the Enemies	68:11-14
God's Ascension to the Holy Mountain	68:15-18
Praise God, Who Daily Bears His People Up	68:19-31
The God of Salvation	68:19-20
Assurance of Deliverance from All Enemies	68:21-23
Description of God's Entry into the Sanctuary	68:24-27
Petition for Display of God's Power to Defeat a Present Threat	68:28-31
Concluding Summons for All to Praise the Awesome God	68:32-35

The Desperate Cry of God's Suffering Servant — 69:1-36

Call for Help and Initial Lament	69:1-4
Confession, Petition, and Lament Resumed	69:5-12
Renewed Plea for Deliverance	69:13-18
Description of Disgrace Suffered and Petition for Punishment of the Enemies	69:19-29
Vow of Thanksgiving and Prayer for Zion	69:30-36

O LORD, Make Haste to Help Me! — 70:1-5

Petition for the Psalmist's Deliverance and Shaming of the Enemies	70:1-3
Petition for God-Seekers to Rejoice and Deliverance of the Psalmist	70:4-5

Do Not Cast Me Off in Old Age — 71:1-24

An Elderly Person Appeals for Help	71:1-13
Petition for Deliverance (from Position of Trust)	71:1-4
Declaration of Trust and Continuous Praise to God	71:5-8
Petition Not to Be Cast Off (by Age, Enemies, or God)	71:9-13
Song of Praise for God's Mighty Deeds	71:14-24
Declaration of Trust and Hope for Continuous Praise to God	71:14-18
Declaration of Confidence That the Prayer May Be Heard	71:19-21
Vow of Praise to God in Song and Word	71:22-24

Prayer for the King: May Righteousness Flourish and Peace Abound!	**72:1-20**
Introduction: Petition for a Just Reign	72:1-4
Petition for a Long and Beneficent Reign	72:5-7
Petition for a Worldwide Reign	72:8-11
Statement About the King as Deliverer of the Needy	72:12-14
Conclusion: Petition for the Fulfillment of the Patriarchal Blessing	72:15-17
Doxology and Compiler's Notation	72:18-20

Book Three Psalms 73–89

Nevertheless—the Great Affirmation	**73:1-28**
The Problem	73:1-12
Transition	73:13-17
The Resolution	73:18-28
Remember Your Congregation	**74:1-23**
The Complaint and Appeal to God	74:1-11
Lament of Abandonment by God	74:1-3
Graphic Description of the Temple's Destruction	74:4-8
Lament of Bewilderment at God's Silence and Inaction	74:9-11
Hymn to God's Power in History and Creation	74:12-17
Concluding Appeal for God's Intervention	74:18-23
God Executes Judgment, . . . Eventually	**75:1-10**
Introductory Statement of Congregational Praise	75:1
Oracle of Assurance and Judgment	75:2-5
Prophetic Exhortation	75:6-8
Vow of Praise and Closing Oracle	75:9-10
The Awesome God	**76:1-12**
God's Greatness Associated with Zion	76:1-3
Address to the God of Glory and Majesty	76:4-6
Address to the God of All Power and Saving Grace	76:7-9
Invitation to Make Vows to the Awesome God	76:10-12
Questions About the God Who Works Wonders	**77:1-20**
Individual Lament Also Representing the Community	77:1-10
The Cry of Distress	77:1-3
Questions in the Night	77:4-10
Hymn About the Mighty Acts of God	77:11-20
Meditation on the Wonderful Deeds of God	77:11-15
Description of God's Coming to Save His People	77:16-20

That the Next Generation Might Know — 78:1-72
- Introduction — 78:1-11
  - Listen to the Story of God's Wonders — 78:1-4
  - Teach the Next Generation — 78:5-8
  - Failure of the Ephraimites — 78:9-11
- Recital: The Wilderness Events — 78:12-32
  - God's Gracious Acts — 78:12-16
  - Israel's Rebellion — 78:17-20
  - God's Anger — 78:21-32
- Meditative Response: God's Restraint and Compassion — 78:33-39
- Recital: From Egypt to Canaan — 78:40-64
  - God's Gracious Acts — 78:40-55
  - Israel's Rebellion — 78:56-58
  - God's Anger — 78:59-64
- Meditative Response: God Chooses Judah, Zion, David — 78:65-72

Help Us, O God of Our Salvation — 79:1-13
- Complaint and Description of Distress — 79:1-5
- Petitions for God's Intervention — 79:6-12
  - To Turn His Anger on the Nations — 79:6-7
  - To Deal Compassionately with the Sins of His People — 79:8-9
  - To Make the Nations Know the Vindication of His People — 79:10
  - To Respond to the Afflicted — 79:11
  - To Deal with the Taunts Against the LORD — 79:12
- Vow of Thanks and Praise — 79:13

Restore Us, O God — 80:1-19
- Invocation and Petition—Refrain — 80:1-3
- Complaint Describing the Nation's Plight—Refrain — 80:4-7
- Parable of the Vine — 80:8-16a
- Petition and Vow—Refrain — 80:16b-19

If You Want to Live, Listen! — 81:1-16
- Summons to Celebration of a Festival — 81:1-5b
- The Prophetic Oracle — 81:5c-16
  - God Addresses Israel — 81:5c-10
  - Admonition to Listen and Obey — 81:11-16

Rise Up, O God, and Judge the Earth! — 82:1-8
- Presentation of God as Judge — 82:1
- Indictment and Sentence upon the Unjust Gods — 82:2-7

Outline of Psalms

Plea for God to Exercise Justice upon the Earth	82:8
Prayer Against the Enemies of God	**83:1-18**
An Urgent Cry to God	83:1
Description of the Distress	83:2-8
Petitions Interlaced with Imprecations	83:9-18
How Lovely Is Your Dwelling Place, O LORD of Hosts!	**84:1-12**
Longing for God's House	84:1-4
Pilgrimage to Zion	84:5-9
Meditation on Blessings of Trust in the LORD	84:10-12
Surely His Salvation Is at Hand	**85:1-13**
Recalling the LORD's Favor in the Past	85:1-3
An Urgent Plea for Present Help	85:4-7
God's Answer to the Plea	85:8-13
Incline Your Ear, . . . for You Alone Are God	**86:1-17**
A Desperate Cry for Help	86:1-7
Celebration of the Incomparable Sovereignty of God	86:8-13
The Supplication Renewed	86:14-17
Zion, Glorious City of God	**87:1-7**
Hymn in Praise of Zion	87:1-3
The Joy of All Who Claim Birth in Zion	87:4-7
Like One Forsaken Among the Dead	**88:1-18**
Cry to God for Help	88:1-2
Lament of One Afflicted	88:3-9a
Questions of Desperation	88:9b-12
Cry for Help Renewed in Face of God's Wrath	88:13-18
Where Is the Steadfast Love You Swore to David?	**89:1-52**
Hymn Extolling the LORD's Power and Faithfulness	89:1-18
Prelude Introducing the Themes	89:1-4
Hymnic Description of the Exalted Majesty of the LORD	89:5-18
Oracle on the LORD's Promises to David	89:19-37
The King as God's Chosen Representative	89:19-27
Divine Promise of the Throne Forever	89:28-37
Lament on Rejection of the Dynasty	89:38-51
Complaint: The Plight of the King	89:38-45
Prayer for the LORD's Intervention and Deliverance	89:46-51
Doxology Concluding Book Three of the Psalter	89:52

Book Four Psalms 90–106

Our God, from Everlasting to Everlasting   90:1-17
Hymnic Introduction: Confidence in the Everlasting God   90:1-2
Wisdom Reflection and Teaching   90:3-12
    The Frailty of Human Existence   90:3-6
    Human Sin and the Wrath of God   90:7-11
    Prayer for Perspective   90:12
Communal Lament and Fervent Petitions   90:13-17
    Steadfast Love and Gladness   90:13-15
    Prosper the Work of Our Hands   90:16-17

Abiding in the Shadow of the Almighty   91:1-16
Introductory Invitation to the Sanctuary and Refuge in God   91:1-2
Instruction and Encouragement   91:3-13
    Refuge in God's Faithfulness   91:3-4
    No Need to Fear the Terror of Night or Day   91:5-6
    Deliverance as the Wicked Are Punished   91:7-8
    Security in the LORD as Refuge   91:9-10
    Protected by Guardian Angels   91:11-13
Divine Oracle of Assurance   91:14-16

Praise for the LORD's Righteous Rule   92:1-15
Introduction: Joyous Exultation   92:1-3
Thanksgiving for the LORD's Works in Creation and History   92:4-11
    The LORD's Works and Wisdom Reflection   92:4-7
    Declaration Exalting the LORD   92:8
    The LORD's Re-creating Work and Wisdom Reflection   92:9-11
Exaltation of the LORD in the Rewards of the Righteous   92:12-15

The LORD Reigns!   93:1-5
Acclamation of the LORD's Reign   93:1a
Declaration of the LORD as King over the Raging Tumult   93:1b-4
Conclusion: The LORD's Decrees and Temple Are Holy   93:5

Rise Up, O Judge of the Earth   94:1-23
Complaint Against the Wicked   94:1-7
    Appeal to the LORD to Judge the Wicked   94:1-3

Outline of Psalms

The Arrogance and Violence of the Wicked	94:4-7
Rebuke to the Foolish	94:8-11
The Creator Is Greater Than the Creature	94:8-9
The LORD Is Wiser Than the Fool	94:10-11
Commendation of Those Who Hold to the LORD's Instruction	94:12-15
Respite for the Righteous	94:12-13
Justice Will Return	94:14-15
Confession of Confidence in the LORD	94:16-23
The Righteous Upheld by the Steadfast Love of the LORD	94:16-21
Refuge and Divine Retribution	94:22-23

O That Today You Would Listen! — 95:1-11

Double Hymn	95:1-7a
Praise the Creator	95:1-5
Praise the Covenant God	95:6-7a
Prophetic Warning Against Disobedience	95:7b-11
Urgent Appeal to Listen (and Obey)	95:7b
Warning: Example of the Ancestors in the Wilderness	95:8-11

Proclaim Among the Nations, "The LORD Reigns!" — 96:1-13

Summons to Praise	96:1-3
Reasons for Praise	96:4-6
Renewed Introduction	96:7-9
Universal Call to Worship	96:10-13
Key Declaration: "The LORD Is King!"	96:10a
Description of the LORD's Reign	96:10b-13

Rejoice in the LORD's Reign of Righteousness and Justice! — 97:1-12

Call to Rejoice in the LORD's Reign	97:1-5
Cultic Cry and Invitation for All to Respond	97:1
Theophanic Description of the LORD's Majesty	97:2-5
Effects of the Theophany	97:6-9
Hortatory Reflection: God's Care for the Righteous	97:10-12
The LORD Loves the Righteous	97:10-11
Call to Rejoice and Give Thanks	97:12

A New Song to the LORD as Savior, King, and Judge — 98:1-9

Invitation to Sing the LORD's Marvelous Deeds of Salvation	98:1-3

Call to a New Song	98:1a
Reasons for the Song of Praise	98:1b-3
Summons to Praise the LORD as King with Voice and Instrument	98:4-6
All Nature Summoned to Jubilation for the LORD Coming to Judge	98:7-9
The Summons to All and Everything	98:7-8
Reason: The Coming LORD Will Judge with Righteousness and Equity	98:9

A Hymn to the God of Holiness — **99:1-9**

Praise the Ruling, Highly Exalted LORD	99:1-3
Enthroned on Cherubim in Zion	99:1-2
Invitation to Worship and Refrain: "Holy Is He!"	99:3
Extol the LORD for His Justice	99:4-5
Equity, Justice, Righteousness in Jacob	99:4
Invitation to Worship and Refrain: "Holy Is He!"	99:5
Extol the LORD for Grace and Judgment in History	99:6-9
Citation of Moses, Aaron, and Samuel as Intercessors	99:6-7
God's Forgiveness and Judgment	99:8
Invitation to Worship and Refrain: "For the LORD Our God Is Holy"	99:9

Make a Joyful Noise to the LORD — **100:1-5**

First Summons to Praise (with Motivation)	100:1-3
Second Summons to Praise (with Motivation)	100:4-5

A King's Vow to the Way That Is Blameless — **101:1-8**

Introduction and Vow to Walk in the Way of Integrity	101:1-3a
Specific Norms About Character and Behavior	101:3b-7
Conclusion: Justice Shall Prevail	101:8

Prayer to the Everlasting God by One Afflicted — **102:1-28**

Individual Lament of One Afflicted	102:1-11
Introduction: Cry for Help	102:1-2
Description of the Psalmist's Illness, Loneliness, Godforsakenness	102:3-11
Hymn of Praise and Prayer to God to Restore Zion	102:12-22
Appeal to the God Enthroned Forever to Rebuild Zion	102:12-17
Vow of Praise and Appeal to the Certainty of the LORD's Future Deeds	102:18-22
Lament on the Brevity of Life	102:23-24

Outline of Psalms

Praise to the LORD as Creator, Unchanging, Everlasting	102:25-28
Praise to the God Abounding in Steadfast Love	**103:1-22**
Introduction: Praise for Forgiveness and Healing	103:1-5
God's Gracious Love to the Covenant People	103:6-18
In the Days of Moses	103:6-7
For His Saving Deeds in Patient Forgiveness	103:8-13
Reasons for the LORD's Mercy	103:14-18
Conclusion: Invitation for the Whole Universe to Bless the LORD	103:19-22
O LORD, How Manifold Are Your Works!	**104:1-35**
Call to Praise: The Heavens (God Above All Worlds)	104:1-4
The Earth (God's Conquest over Chaos)	104:5-9
The Water (God as Sustainer Through Water and Food)	104:10-18
The Moon and the Sun (God of Time and Seasons)	104:19-23
The Sea (God of All Creatures, Great and Small)	104:24-26
Life (God as Master of Life and Death)	104:27-30
Doxology: Joy and Wish for Perfect Harmony	104:31-35
Remember the Wonders God Has Done	**105:1-45**
Introduction: Summons to Thanks, Praise, and Remembrance	105:1-6
Invitation to Joyful Worship	105:1-4
Remembrance of God's Wonderful Works to His Children	105:5-6
The LORD's Faithfulness to His Covenant and Promise	105:7-11
The Covenant with Abraham, Isaac, and Jacob	105:7-10
The Promise of the Land	105:11
God's Providence Through the Wanderings of His People	105:12-42
The Patriarchs Protected	105:12-15
Joseph in Egypt (Prisoner Yet Released)	105:16-22
Israel in Egypt (Oppressed Yet Freed)	105:23-38
Israel in the Wilderness (Protected and Fed)	105:39-42
Conclusion: Possession of the Land and Admonition	105:43-45
Both We and Our Ancestors Have Sinned	**106:1-48**
Introduction: Thanksgiving and Petition	106:1-6
Summons to Praise	106:1-3
Petition and Confession	106:4-6
A Confessional Recital of Israel's Sin	106:7-43

The Exodus Story	106:7-12
The Wilderness Period	106:13-18
The Golden Calf Incident	106:19-23
Report of the Spies	106:24-27
Baal of Peor Incident	106:28-31
At the Waters of Meribah	106:32-33
The Sins in Canaan	106:34-39
Cycles of Rebellion, Judgment, and Deliverance	106:40-43
God's Mercy and Concluding Petition for Restoration	106:44-48

Book Five Psalms 107–150

Let the Redeemed Thank the LORD for His Steadfast Love and Wonderful Works — 107:1-43

Introduction: Summons to Give Thanks	107:1-3
Litany of Thanksgiving by Four Groups of the Redeemed	107:4-32
Those Who Wandered Desert Wastes	107:4-9
Those Who Were Imprisoned	107:10-16
Those Who Needed Healing and Forgiveness	107:17-22
Those Who Experienced the Perils of the Sea	107:23-32
Closing Hymn on the Providence of God	107:33-42
God's Power over Nature	107:33-38
God's Care for the Afflicted	107:39-42
Wisdom Reflection	107:43

Liturgy of Thanksgiving and Petition — 108:1-13

Hymn of Praise to the God of Steadfast Love	108:1-5
Petition for Deliverance	108:6
Divine Oracle of God's Dominion	108:7-9
Petition for God's Help and Assertion of Confidence	108:10-13

Accusations, Curses, and the Steadfast Love of the LORD — 109:1-31

Prayer of Lamentation	109:1-5
Plea for God's Intervention	109:1
Complaint About the Accusers	109:2-5
Imprecation: An Extended Curse	109:6-20
The Juridical Setting	109:6-7
The Hoped-for Sentence	109:8-15
Reasons for the Curse	109:16-19
The Reward: The Curse upon the Accusers	109:20

Outline of Psalms

Prayer of Trust and Petition	109:21-29
Grounds for Appeal to the LORD	109:21-25
Imprecation That the Accusers Be Punished	109:26-29
Vow of Thanks and Praise	109:30-31

The Priest-King at the Right Hand of God — 110:1-7

A Divinely Appointed Ruler	110:1-3
The Oracle: Installation of the King	110:1
Commentary on the King's Rule	110:2-3
A Divinely Appointed Priest-King	110:4-7
The Oracle: Conferring the Office of Priesthood upon the Ruler	110:4
Commentary: Protection and Judgment	110:5-6
Empowerment and Promise of Triumph	110:7

Great Are the Works of the LORD — 111:1-10

Introductory Declaration of Thankful Praise	111:1
Reason for Praise	111:2-9
Theme: The Great Works of the LORD	111:2
Brief Rehearsal of the LORD's Deeds in Israel's History	111:3-6
Grounds for Trusting and Obeying the LORD	111:7-9
Concluding Wisdom Saying About a Good Understanding	111:10

The Blessedness of Fearing the LORD — 112:1-10

Introduction: Affirmation of the Life Rooted in Joyful Obedience	112:1
Description of the God-fearing Person	112:2-9
The Fruit of Family Continuity and Prosperity	112:2-3
Qualities of Character That Reflect God's Character	112:4-5
Integrity and Security in the LORD	112:6-9
Contrasting Conclusion: The Destiny of the Wicked	112:10

God's Majesty in Mercy — 113:1-9

Summons to Praise	113:1-3
The Majestic God over the Heavens and the Earth	113:4-6
God Cares for the Lowly	113:7-9

When Israel Came Out of Egypt — 114:1-8

The Exodus and Birth of the Nation Recalled	114:1-2
Wondrous Events at the Sea, Jordan, and Sinai	114:3-4
The Psalmist's Mocking Questions and the Answer	114:5-8

Not to Us, O LORD, but to Your Name Give Glory — 115:1-18

- Lament Prayer for Restoration — 115:1-2
  - Appeal to God's Name, Steadfast Love, and Faithfulness — 115:1
  - Ridiculed by the Nations — 115:2
- Hymnic Satire Against the Gods of the Nations — 115:3-8
  - God Does What He Will — 115:3
  - Idols Are Impotent — 115:4-7
  - The Fate of Idol-Makers and Idol-Worshippers — 115:8
- Exhortation to Trust in the LORD — 115:9-11
- Assurance and Blessing — 115:12-15
  - Affirmation of God's Care — 115:12-13
  - Promise of Posterity and Blessing — 115:14-15
- Conclusion: Praise Through Commitment — 115:16-18
  - The LORD of Heaven and Earth — 115:16
  - No Praise from Sheol — 115:17
  - The Time for Blessing and Praise Is Now — 115:18

Thank You, God! — 116:1-19
- Profession of Faith amid Distress — 116:1-7
- Praise and Confidence for the Gracious Deliverance — 116:8-11
- Sacrifice of Thanksgiving — 116:12-19

Let All People Praise! — 117:1-2
- Call to Praise — 117:1
- Reason for Praise: God's Steadfast Love and Faithfulness — 117:2ab
- Renewed Call to Praise — 117:2c

A Processional Liturgy of Thanksgiving — 118:1-29
- Antiphonal Call to Thanksgiving — 118:1-4
- An Individual Psalm of Thanksgiving — 118:5-21
  - Narrative of Distress and Cry for the LORD's Help — 118:5-9
  - Description of the Individual's Plight and the LORD's Intervention — 118:10-14
  - Citation from a Victory Psalm — 118:15-16
  - Testimony about Life — 118:17-18
  - Thanksgiving in the Sanctuary — 118:19-21
- The Community's Praise in the Inner Court — 118:22-29
  - Jubilant Praise for What the LORD Has Done — 118:22-25
  - Festal Procession to the Altar — 118:26-27
  - Personal Thanks — 118:28

Outline of Psalms

Doxology: Call to Thanksgiving for the LORD's Steadfast Love	118:29

How I Love Your Word, O LORD! — 119:1-176

In Praise of Fidelity to the Word of God	119:1-8
Storing the Treasure of God's Word in the Heart	119:9-16
Solace in Suffering	119:17-24
Revive and Strengthen Me!	119:25-32
Teach Me, O LORD!	119:33-40
Passion to Speak the Word	119:41-48
Comfort in Affliction	119:49-56
Fellowship in the LORD	119:57-64
The LORD's Instruction as Highest Good	119:65-72
Complete Your Work in Me	119:73-80
Cry from the Darkness	119:81-88
The Foundation of Faith	119:89-96
Oh, How I Love Your Law!	119:97-104
Light upon the Way	119:105-112
In Awe of God's Judgments	119:113-120
Hope for God's Servant in Distress	119:121-128
Your Word Is Wonderful!	119:129-136
You Are Righteous, Your Word Is Righteous	119:137-144
Sustained by Memories of God's Faithfulness in the Past	119:145-152
The Plea for Life	119:153-160
Peace in Love of God's Law	119:161-168
Teach Me, Help Me, Seek Me	119:169-176

People of Peace in a World of War — 120:1-7

Confident Appeal for Deliverance or Thanksgiving for Answered Prayer	120:1-2
Retribution upon the Enemies	120:3-4
The Psalmist's Predicament: A Sojourner Among People of War	120:5-7

The LORD Is Your Keeper — 121:1-8

The Inquiry and Confession of Trust	121:1-2
The Blessing and Promises	121:3-8
The Attentive LORD Guards the Pilgrim on the Way	121:3-4
The LORD Protects by Day and Night	121:5-6
The LORD Watches over All of Life	121:7-8

Pray for the Peace of Jerusalem	**122:1-9**
The Pilgrim's Joy on Arriving in Jerusalem	122:1-2
Reasons for the Praise of Jerusalem	122:3-5
Prayer for the Peace of Jerusalem	122:6-9
Our Eyes Look to the LORD Our God	**123:1-4**
Gesture of Obedient Trust and Hope	123:1-2
Plea for Grace and Motive for Divine Action	123:3-4
Deliverance from a Close Call	**124:1-8**
Description of What Might Have Happened	124:1-5
Grateful Praise for the LORD's Deliverance	124:6-8
Protector of Those Who Trust in the LORD	**125:1-5**
Expression of Confidence in the LORD's Protection	125:1-3
Petition for Recompense to the Just and the Unjust	125:4-5
Joy Remembered and Joy Anticipated	**126:1-6**
Remembering the LORD's Saving Help in Restoring Zion	126:1-3
Petition for the LORD's Intervention for a New Restoration	126:4-6
Everything Depends on God's Blessing	**127:1-5**
The Futility of Work Apart from God	127:1-2
Children Are the Blessing of God	127:3-5
Blessed Are Those Who Fear the LORD	**128:1-6**
Beatitude: Fruitful Labor and Family for Those Who Fear the LORD	128:1-4
Benediction: The LORD's Blessing Goes Forth from Zion	128:5-6
Often Have They Attacked Me, . . . Yet They Have Not Prevailed	**129:1-8**
Summary of Israel's History of Oppression and Deliverance	129:1-4
Confident Prayer That Those Who Hate Zion Will Be Punished	129:5-8
Out of the Depths	**130:1-8**
The Cry from the Depths	130:1-4
Waiting and Hoping	130:5-8
Calmed and Quieted Like a Weaned Child	**131:1-3**
Declaration of Humility and Limitation	131:1
Image of Childlike Trust	131:2

Outline of Psalms

Call for the Community to Hope Confidently in the LORD	131:3
God's Choice of David and Zion	**132:1-18**
An Appeal to the LORD	132:1-10
Prayer for David and His Oath Regarding the LORD's Dwelling	132:1-5
Description of the Ark's Procession to Zion	132:6-10
The Divine Promise Prevails	132:11-18
The LORD's Oath to David	132:11-12
The LORD's Presence in Zion	132:13-18
When Sisters and Brothers Live in Unity	**133:1-3**
Opening Affirmation: The Goodness of Kindred Living in Unity	133:1
Two Metaphors Describing Unity	133:2-3a
Conclusion: Place of the LORD's Blessing	133:3b
To Bless and to Be Blessed	**134:1-3**
Hymnic Introit: Invitation to Bless the LORD	134:1-2
Benediction: May the LORD Bless You	134:3
Hallelujah to the LORD Above All Gods!	**135:1-21**
Invitation to Praise	135:1-4
Motivation for Praise	135:5-18
The LORD's Mighty Deeds in Creation	135:5-7
The LORD's Mighty Deeds in Exodus and Conquest	135:8-12
The Permanence of the LORD's Name	135:13-14
The Powerlessness of Idols	135:15-18
Concluding Call to Praise	135:19-21
Litany of Thanksgiving: "For His Steadfast Love Endures Forever"	**136:1-26**
Introductory Summons to Thankful Praise	136:1-3
Motivation: The LORD's Great Wonders	136:4-25
The LORD's Majesty in Creation	136:4-9
The LORD's Wonders in the History of Israel	136:10-22
The LORD's Continuing Care for His People	136:23-25
Concluding Summons to Give Thanks	136:26
By the Rivers of Babylon	**137:1-9**
Community Lament: Silent Mourning in Remembering Zion	137:1-4
The Writer's Vow to Remember Zion	137:5-6

Petition for the LORD to Remember Against Zion's Enemies	137:7-9

I Give Thanks, O LORD, with My Whole Heart — 138:1-8

Wholehearted Thanksgiving for an Answered Prayer	138:1-3
Expectation of Universal Homage to the LORD of the Lowly	138:4-6
Confession of Trust and Petition for Continuing Help	138:7-8

O LORD, You Have Searched Me and Know Me — 139:1-24

Prayer Extolling the All-knowing, Ever-present, and Wonder-creating God	139:1-18
You Have Searched Me and Know Me	139:1-6
There Is No Escape from Your Presence	139:7-12
I Am Fearfully and Wonderfully Made	139:13-18
Prayer for Vindication and Deliverance	139:19-24
Imprecation for Destruction of the Wicked	139:19-22
Petition: Search Me and Know My Heart	139:23-24

Protect Me from the Violent — 140:1-13

Prayer for Deliverance from the Attacks of the Wicked	140:1-5
Plea for God to Deal with the Wicked	140:6-13

With Hands, Heart, and Eyes Toward You, O God — 141:1-10

Call for Help and Strength to Withstand Temptation	141:1-5
Petition Regarding the Wicked and Confession of Refuge in God	141:6-10

Cry to the LORD, My Refuge and My Portion — 142:1-7

Complaint Describing the Psalmist's Plight	142:1-4
Petition for Deliverance and Vow of Thanksgiving	142:5-7

Prayer of a Penitent in Distress — 143:1-12

Lament Appealing to the LORD's Faithfulness and Righteousness	143:1-6
Petitions for the LORD's Intervention	143:7-12

A New Song to the God Who Rescues and Blesses — 144:1-15

Royal Lament Centering on the King's Plea for Deliverance	144:1-11
Liturgical Exclamation of Praise	144:1-2
Confession of Human Frailty	144:3-4
Petition for a Theophany and Deliverance	144:5-8
Vow of Thanksgiving and Refrain	144:9-11

Outline of Psalms

Communal Prayer for Peace and Prosperity	144:12-15
In Praise of God's Greatness and Goodness	**145:1-21**
Introductory Doxology	145:1-3
Israel's Praise of the Divine Deeds	145:4-9
The LORD's Mighty Acts	145:4-7
The LORD's Loving-Kindness and Compassion	145:8-9
Proclamation of the LORD as King, Provider, and Savior	145:10-20
The LORD's Glorious Kingdom	145:10-13a
The LORD's Providential Care	145:13b-20
Concluding Doxology	145:21
Praise the LORD, the One True Helper	**146:1-10**
Call to Praise	146:1-2
Exhortation Against Trust in Mortals	146:3-4
Motivation for Trust in the LORD	146:5-9
Priestly Blessing	146:5
The LORD as Creator and Liberator	146:6-9
Concluding Doxology	146:10
How Good It Is to Sing Praises to Our God	**147:1-20**
Praise God as Lord of the Universe and Helper of the Downtrodden	147:1-6
Invitation to Praise	147:1
Building Up Jerusalem and Gathering the Outcasts	147:2-3, 6
God's Greatness in Naming the Stars	147:4-5
Thank God for Sustaining the World	147:7-11
Invitation to Thanksgiving	147:7
Providential Care over Nature	147:8-9
God Delights Not in Strength but in Trust	147:10-11
Praise God for the Gift of Shalom and the Life-giving Word	147:12-20
Invitation to Praise	147:12
Protection and Blessing	147:13-14
God's Word Orders the Seasons	147:15-18
Privilege and Responsibility in the Ordinances	147:19-20
Let All Praise the Name of the LORD	**148:1-14**
Praise the LORD from the Heavens	148:1-6
Summons to Celestial Praise	148:1-4
Motivation: He Commanded and They Were Created	148:5-6
Praise the LORD from the Earth	148:7-14
Summons to Terrestrial Praise	148:7-12

Motivation: His Name, His Glory, a Horn for His People	148:13-14 |//

Glory for All His Faithful Ones	**149:1-9**
Sing to the LORD a New Song	149:1-4
Summons to the Faithful to Praise the LORD	149:1-3
Motivation: The LORD's Care of the Humble	149:4
A New Call to Praise in the Wake of Judgment	149:5-9
Summons and Action to Complete Praise	149:5-9a
Declaration About the Meaning of the Action	149:9b
Praise the LORD!	**150:1-6**
Introduction: Praise the LORD!	150:1a
Ten Imperatives to Praise	150:1b-5
Conclusion: Praise as God's Ultimate Purpose for All Creation	150:6

Essays

ANOINTED, ANOINTED ONE The word *māšîaḥ*, "anointed one," occurs thirty-nine times in the OT, primarily in 1 and 2 Samuel and the Psalms. It designates primarily and in most cases the king of Israel or of Judah who reigned at the time. The LXX employs *christos* as the Greek word to translate *māšîaḥ*. The NT uses the name "Messiah" for "the anointed one," but also the title "Christ" (from *christos*, meaning "anointed") for Jesus.

Anointing with oil was part of the investiture for kings, high priests, and prophets in Israel (Exod 28:41; Ps 105:15). Holders of these offices were regularly referred to as "anointed," with kings commonly referred to as "the LORD's anointed" or "his anointed" (1 Sam 16:6; Ps 2:2). The term is not used in reference to a future savior or deliverer. "Anointing," used of kings, emphasizes the exclusive, intimate relationship between the God of Israel and the king, to whom God has given power to reign in his name (Pss 2:2; 20:6; 89:38, 51; 132:10). Anointing placed the ruler under God's protection and signified that his person was not to be violated (1 Sam 24:6; Pss 89:20-28; 105:15).

In the "royal psalms" (2; 18; 20; 21; 45; 72; 89; 101; 110; 132; 144), the king as "the LORD's anointed" is described variously. The king is portrayed as God's son, and as king he will be victorious over God's opponents worldwide (2:7-9; 110:5-6). The king is the recipient of God's "steadfast love to his anointed, to David and his descendents forever" (18:50). Anointed "with the oil of gladness," the king will reign in equity and righteousness (45:6-7). The king's relationship to God is one of a firstborn to his father and is linked to the promise made to David (2 Sam 7:14-17; Pss 89:3-4; 132:10). The king's righteousness is extolled; when the king prospers, the people are secure in God's protection and will live in peace and prosperity (72:1-4, 12-14). See "Royal" in the essay *Psalm Genres* (below).

The royal psalms contain far-reaching assertions in their reference to the promises to David and his dynasty. Though initially related to the currently reigning king, their expansive claims remained largely unfulfilled. In a later time, these royal psalms were interpreted as referring to a future Davidic king anointed of the Lord, whose arrival Israel hoped for. This messianic hope came about through the prophets who announced a decisive change God would bring about for the people. In these prophecies, though the term "anointed" is not used, the central figure is a descendant of David who represents an ideal of kingship in the name of the Lord (Isa 9:1-7; 11:1-9; Jer 23:1-6; Mic 5:2; Zech 9:9-10). Thus, the themes of the royal psalms outlasted the age of the kings and took on new significance for God's people. No longer applied to earthly rulers, people came to understand them as prophecy and promise of the messianic king of the end time.

While in Jewish writings from 200 BC to AD 100 the term "anointed" (*māšiaḥ*) is used only infrequently in connection with the agent of divine deliverance expected in the future, the early Christian community used it freely. Many within Judaism interpreted Psalm 2 messianically, but the followers of Jesus of Nazareth regarded Jesus as the Messiah expected by Israel. Interpreting the OT prophecy of an ideal ruler descended from David, and a new reign of righteousness, justice, and peace on earth, these believers came to call Jesus the Messiah (Matt 1:16; Mark 8:29; Luke 2:11). They saw him as the anointed one, the Christ, primarily and above all the king, the new David expected at the end of the age, the one who fulfilled all that the kingship signified under the old covenant (Matt 2:2; 21:5; 27:11; Luke 23:2; John 12:13; Acts 17:7; Heb 1:5; 5:5). The Davidic motifs employed by the psalmist (Pss 89; 132) and the bold expression "son of man" used by Ezekiel were to find strong echoes in the interpretation of Jesus in the Gospels. In this sense Christians have also come to read the royal psalms as messianic—as underlining the just administration, the saving function, and the universal rule of Jesus Christ.

Other psalms were also interpreted messianically in the NT. Laments such as Psalms 22 and 69 provided the background for presentation of the passion story in the Gospels. The NT claims that the Messiah suffers and even prays a lament. Similarly, Psalm 102 came to be identified with Jesus Christ (Heb 1:10-12), the Messiah's suffering and dereliction (Ps 102:1-11), and his eager anticipation of the kingdom in its worldwide glory (102:12-22).

References: Jorge, *ABD* 4:777-88; Kraus, 1986:109, 123; Martens, 1988:530-31; Rivkin, *IDB* 5:588-91.

ASAPH Asaph is mentioned as a singer, cymbal player, and chief among David's musicians (1 Chron 6:31-32, 39; 15:16-19; 16:4-7). The name Asaph may represent a guild of temple singers. These singers participated in nearly every major celebration relating to the temple, both before and after the exile (1 Chron 25:1-2; 2 Chron 29:30). The prominence of this guild is apparent in the postexilic period with the designation of the Asaphite Uzzi as "the overseer of the Levites" over the house of God (Neh 11:22-24).

The twelve psalms of Asaph are Psalms 50 and 73–83. We cannot determine whether this collection of psalms originated with the singer Asaph himself or whether it is simply an "Asaphite" collection. All (except Psalm 50) are found as a subsection in book III of the Psalter, which has a dominant communal orientation. The community articulates its anxieties (Pss 74; 77; 79–80; 83) and hope (75–76; 78; 80). In these psalms, the individual is deeply rooted in community relations and aspirations. Usually the psalms of Asaph use the name *'Elōhîm* for God.

References: Gerstenberger: 38; Holladay: 32-34; Rogers, *ABD*, 1:471.

COMPOSITION OF THE BOOK OF PSALMS In its present form, the Psalter consists of 150 psalms divided into five books. Editorial work included

Essays

collecting and arranging individual psalms and subgroups, division into books, and supplying superscriptions or titles for 116 of the psalms. This gradual process lasted for centuries. Recent studies on the composition of the book of Psalms suggest that individual psalms were placed not arbitrarily but through intentional editorial shaping.

The composition of psalms began with the initiation of corporate worship in Israel and continued beyond the closure of the book of Psalms about 200 BC. Worship leaders collected prayers and sacred songs for liturgical reasons, not primarily for personal edification. In most cases, the personal identity of the authors is unknown *[Superscriptions]*. They commonly revised and adapted existing prayers and songs to new situations (Pss 18; 51; 68; 102). Psalms written for ceremonies centering on individuals came to be used by the community (25; 56; 66; 77; 130). The Levitical singers, including those of the guilds of Asaph and Korah, appear to have been most directly involved with the recital of psalms (1 Chron 16:7; 2 Chron 7:6; 20:19; Ezra 8:15-20) *[Asaph; Korah]*. After the exile, the scribes also were an influential group, copying and proclaiming the law (torah) in postexilic Jewish communities (Ezra 7:1-10; Neh 8:9). It may have been under the scribes that the book of Psalms received its final shape (Gerstenberger: 28).

The Psalter is divided into five "books" (Pss 1–41; 42–72; 73–89; 90–106; 107–150) by a series of doxologies (Pss 41:13; 72:18-19; 89:52; 106:48). Psalm 150 provides a concluding doxology for book V and for the Psalter as a whole. According to the *Midrash Tehillim*, this was to correspond to the five-part division of the Pentateuch: "As Moses gave five books of laws to Israel, so David gave five books of Psalms to Israel" (Braude: 5). In the compilation of the five books, I–III were stabilized before IV–V, where fluidity appeared, with more untitled psalms. We also see evidence of this in the variation in order and content of the Qumran psalms manuscripts (Wilson, 1985:120-38).

Book I (Pss 1–41) is made up almost entirely of psalms with titles associated with David. Psalms 1 and 2 are introductory, perhaps to the entire collection. Psalm 10 is joined to Psalm 9 through the acrostic pattern, and Psalm 33 is connected thematically to Psalm 32. The majority are psalms of the individual. Exceptions include hymns (19; 29), liturgy (24), and a lament of the community (12). Royal Psalm 2 may have been prefixed to this sequence of Davidic psalms (3–41), with the closing psalm (41) providing assurance of the LORD's continued protection to David against his scheming enemies. Later, Psalm 2 would introduce the full Psalter, giving the instruction in covenant norms (Wilson, 1985:173, 204-6). Psalms 1 and 2 provide a literary context for hearing 3-41. In the context of the whole Psalter, which was assembled after the exile, the laments of the individual may also be heard as expression of communal plight.

Book II (Pss 42–72) begins with psalms that express deep alienation from God and God's place (42–43), followed by a communal lament reminiscent of the destruction of Jerusalem and the exile (44). Psalms 42–49 are identified with the "Sons of Korah," members of a musical guild (2 Chron 20:19; cf. Pss 84–85; 87–88) *[Korah]*. Following an Asaph psalm (50), the second small collection is Psalms 51–72, bearing Davidic ascriptions (except for 66–67 and 71–72). In form and content, these are primarily individual laments (51–59; 61–64; 69–71), with only a few national (60; 65–68) or royal (72) psalms. Some texts reveal a Zion-Jerusalem piety (63; 65) already found in Psalms

42–49. Book II ends with a doxology (72:18-19) and with a further editorial note, *The prayers of David son of Jesse are ended* (72:20). This might suggest that books I and II are now completed with a psalm (72) ascribed to David's son Solomon, or might refer to the contents of books I and II, where the majority of Davidic Psalms (55 out of 73 so titled) are concentrated.

Psalms 42–83 are often called the Elohistic Psalter because of a preference for the divine name *'Elōhîm* (God) in contrast to Yahweh (LORD, as in NRSV, NIV). In the 41 psalms of book I, Yahweh appears about 275 times and *'ĕlōhîm* 50 times. In the 42 psalms of the Elohistic Psalter, Yahweh occurs 43 times and *'ĕlōhîm* just under 240 times. In Psalms 84–150, Yahweh again predominates. The production of this Elohistic Psalter may suggest an editor preparing a collection of psalms for use in the temple at a time when the name Yahweh was being used less frequently and was being replaced by the more general name *'ĕlōhîm* (Limburg, *ABD*, 5:526) *[Names of God]*.

In book III (Pss 73–89), the Elohistic Psalter concludes with the sequence of Asaph psalms (73–83) *[Asaph]*. As the book reverts to Yahwistic psalms, four Korahite psalms (84–85; 87–88) appear, interrupted by a psalm attributed to David (86) and closed by a psalm attributed to Ethan. This closing psalm (89) is explicitly concerned with the Davidic covenant. The covenant introduced in Psalm 2 has come to nothing, and David's descendants wait for a restoration: "How long, O LORD?"

Book III is pervaded by communal lamentations through which the community articulates its anxieties (74; 79–80; 83; 85; 89:38-51). The experience of exile appears to have decisively shaped the whole book: the people of God lost the temple, the land, and the monarchy. The progression in books I–III is revealing. Psalm 2 establishes the intimate relationship between God and the Davidic king. Psalm 72 reinforces this relationship, while Psalm 89 concludes with a wrenching description of God's rejection of the covenant with David. Thus, books I–III call out for a response—offered by the proclamation of God's reign, which is present in books IV and V (McCann, 1996:660).

Book IV (90–106) consists of 17 psalms, as does book III. This book appears to function as the "editorial center" of the Psalter, setting forth answers to the plaintive question raised in Psalm 89. The answer is that the LORD (Yahweh) is king. Wilson summarizes the claim of Yahweh's kingship: "He has been our 'refuge' in the past, long before the monarchy existed," and "he will continue to be our refuge now that the monarchy is gone" (1985:214-15; cf. Holladay: 78).

Book IV begins and ends with Moses, who led Israel before there was a monarchy (90; 105:23-45; 106:7-33). Psalm 91 continues the motif of God as refuge, and 92 transitions to "the LORD is king" psalms (Pss 93; 95–99), which Wilson calls "the theological heart" of the Psalter. Even 94, a communal lament, may be intended to bind these psalms about the LORD's reign more closely to 90–92. The psalms in praise of the LORD as king (96–99) are framed by the theme of Israel as the sheep of Yahweh's pasture (95:6-7; 100). Psalms 101–102 rehearse major elements in the crisis of the exile: loss of monarchy, Zion/temple, and land. Psalm 103 is a hymn of praise for God's steadfast love and mercy. Psalms 104–106, the first of the Hallelujah (*Praise the LORD!*) psalms, close book IV and serve as bridge to book V, as 105–106 revert to the theme of Moses and the people's plea to be gathered "from among the nations" (106:47).

Book V (107–150) has several clear subcollections within it: Davidic psalms (108–110; 138–145), Hallelujah psalms (111–117; 135; 146–150) and Songs of Ascents (Pss 120–134). Book V abounds in communal hymns and thanksgivings. Psalm 107, with six occurrences of *steadfast love* (*ḥesed*), suggests that book V picks up where book IV left off, continuing the response to the crisis of the exile (89:49; 106:47). Psalms 108 and 109 continue the focus on God's steadfast love. Royal Psalm 110 is followed by Hallelujah Psalms 111–117. This whole unit may be framed by 107 and 118, which appear to describe the return from exile, with 118 moving toward a petition for continuing help (v. 25). The impressive Psalm 119, an acrostic with eight lines for each letter of the Hebrew alphabet, is included here. Extolling the torah, God's instruction, it articulates the experience of the postexilic generations, scorned and persecuted, needing to wait upon God. Linked to Psalm 1 with the torah theme, 119 may have concluded an early form of the Psalter.

Psalms 120–134 are a collection of Songs of Ascents, pilgrim songs that do not ignore the suffering of the people as the dark background of joy and praise (120; 124; 126; 129–130). As a group, they affirm the necessity to rely on the LORD alone. Psalms 135–137 are the prelude to a final Davidic collection, which testifies to the theme of God's steadfast love. Psalm 135 reinforces the last ascent psalm. Psalm 136 opens with the same verse with which 107 and 118 open, and looks toward 145, which also celebrates God's steadfast love. Psalm 137 introduces the last set of Davidic and Hallelujah psalms. The plaintive cry of the exiles is answered by the sequence of psalms that offer David's praise of the LORD. Psalm 145 begins by addressing God as "King," thus recalling 93 and 95–99, the collection at the center of book IV. It responds to the royal lament of 144 by offering God's steadfast love. Book V concludes the Psalter with a series of five "Praise the LORD!" or "Hallelujah" psalms, carrying out the proclamation and praise of God's sovereignty as anticipated in 145:21. Book V appears to be a final answer to the plea of the exiles; as with books I to III, David is seen to model the attitude of reliance and dependence on the LORD (Holladay, 1993:80).

Taking account of the composition and current canonical ordering, scholars have discerned various "progressions." Westermann (1989:10) calls attention to the move *from lament to praise*. Forty-six of the eighty-nine psalms (52 percent) in books I–III are laments, but only sixteen of the sixty-one psalms (26 percent) in books IV–V are laments. Hymns praising and thanking God as creator and ruler of history abound in the second half of the Psalter. Brueggemann (1991:81, 88) calls Psalm 73 a pivot point in the Psalter, moving Israel *from obedience to praise* "by way of protest, candor and communion." McCann (1996:661-64) has shown that the intention of the last two books of the Psalter point postexilic Israel *away from reliance on human kings toward trust in the LORD*, who alone rules eternally. Wilson (1992:137-38) highlights the placement of Psalm 1 as introduction and the wisdom elements in the final shape of the Psalter; he points to the movement *from performance to meditation*. Thus, the psalms are no longer primarily for public performance in temple worship, but especially for use in the synagogues and to be meditated upon day and night as the divine word of life for faithful readers. One obvious movement is that *from the individual to the community*. Psalms that concern the individual dominate the first half of the Psalter; a communal voice is more pronounced in the last half. The central message of book IV (90–106) shows that praise is the final goal of the Psalter.

The God who comes in response to Israel's plea in Psalm 89, the God enthroned as king over the earth in 93–99, is the God who is worthy of praise. This call to praise draws the Psalter to a concluding crescendo in 146–150. Hallelujah!

References: Brueggemann, 1991:81, 88; Gerstenberger: 27-30, 36-39; Holladay, 1993:69-70, 76-80; Limburg, *ABD*, 5:526-27; Mays, 1994b:8-19; McCann, 1996:657-65; Stuhlmueller, 2002:3-6; Westermann, 1989:8-10; Wilson, 1985:120-38, 214-15, 231-35; 1992:129-42.

ENEMIES While "enemy" (*'ōyēb, ṣar/ṣār*) in the OT usually refers to the national enemies of Israel (Josh 23:1; 24:11), it is also used to designate personal enemies (Exod 23:4; Judg 16:23; 1 Sam 18:29; and especially in the psalms). An enemy is one who seeks to harm, steal from, or otherwise complicate the life of a person, including individuals or matters of concern to that person.

The community or national laments focus on threats by military foes, famine, drought, or some pestilence. Enemies threaten the city of God (Pss 46:6; 48:4; 76:5-6). These enemy powers are characterized as "kingdoms," "princes," or "kings." They are the people who wage war against God's people (2:2, 8, 10; 18:47-48; 45:5; 72:11; 110:5; 144:2). National laments portray catastrophe as having already struck (44:11). The city is sacked and becomes no more than a heap of stones (79:1; 102:14). The ravaging of the countryside is seen as an event of cosmic proportions (80:12-13).

God intervenes for his king and aids him to defeat and destroy the enemies (2:5, 8-9; 21:8-9; 110:2-3, 5; 144:1-2). Faith is expressed that the God of Israel reigns over the hostile powers in unchallenged sovereignty and strips them of all power (96:5; 135:15-18).

Regarding the enemies of the individual, the situation is more complex. The terms include "enemy" (*'ōyēb:* 3:7; 6:10; 7:5; 9:3, 6; 13:4; 17:9; 31:8, 15; 41:5; etc.), "foe" (*ṣar/ṣār:* 3:1; 13:4; 23:5; 27:2; 31:11; etc.), "evildoers" (*mĕrē'îm:* 26:5; 27:2), and "the wicked" (*rĕšā'îm:* 3:7; 9:17; 10:2-4; 11:2, 6; 12:8; 17:9; 26:5; etc.). The foes of the individual are the godless and the persecutors (5:9; 9:6; 14:1).

We cannot determine the particular identity of these enemies. Earlier attempts to identify the enemies in the psalms suggested false accusers (Hans Schmidt), sorcerers and demonic forces (Sigmund Mowinckel), foes of the king (Harris Birkeland), or party strife within the Israelite community. The opponents are described in stark terms, with strong and negative imagery.

Three common metaphors are used to illustrate the uncanny and gruesome assaults of the foes: wild beasts, hunters or trappers, and hostile armies. The enemies of individuals are often compared to ravenous beasts, which suddenly spring on a person (7:2; 22:12-13; 27:2; 35:21). The enemies are likened to a ravening lion, an aggressive bull, the venomous serpent, and a pack of wild dogs (10:9-10; 17:12; 58:4; 59:6-15; 74:4; 91:13; 92:10; 140:3). Or they are compared to hunters or trappers, who seek their prey with pits, nets, or arrows (7:15; 9:15; 31:4; 35:7-8; 57:6; 64:3-4; 140:5). The bow is not only a weapon of the hunter, but also of the warrior. Thus, the foes of the individual are often compared with a hostile army that attacks the helpless (3:6; 27:3; 55:18; 56:1-2; 59:1-3; 62:3).

Two areas where readers frequently meet the "enemies" in the psalms are in the institution of divine judgment and the cleansing of the sick. In judicial cases, the enemy powers appear as accusers and persecutors, using lies, slander, and false witness to accuse the victim of breaking the law. The one who is unjustly accused submits to the verdict rendered by God through the priest (7:8; 26:1-2; 35:22-24). By accusations and slander, the enemies of the sick person are eager to focus on a commonly held causal relationship between guilt and sickness (32:1-4; 38:3-11; 39:8, 11).

That the "enemies" of the individual cannot be identified more specifically allows these psalms to speak for persons who cry out to God in all kinds of situations of tension, hostility, and conflict. For example, reference to the "enemy" may even refer to death itself as a force hostile to life (31:7-8, 12). This poetic language is open and metaphorical and speaks to situations of distress in every generation (B. Anderson, 1983:82-90; Miller, 1986:50-51).

Before the LORD, the enemies stumble and vanish as the mischief they planned returns on their own heads (7:16; 9:3, 6). Those who have been persecuted can look back with thanks and joy at the defeat of the enemies when it occurs (33:4-5; 138:7). While one can find in the OT the spirit of goodwill and kindness toward personal enemies (Exod 23:4-5; 1 Sam. 24:17-19; Job 31:29), Jesus further clarifies the command of love for enemies (Matt 5:43-44). Paul, spelling out the meaning of loving one's enemy, quotes Proverbs 25:21-22 to make his point: "If your enemies are hungry, feed them; if they are thirsty, give them something to drink; for by doing this you will heap burning coals on their heads" (Rom 12:20).

References: B. Anderson, 1983:82-90; Keel: 78-109; Kraus, 1986:125-36; Miller, 1986:49-51. See essays on *Vengeance*; *War*; *Wicked*; and *Wrath of God*.

HEBREW POETRY The psalms are poetry. They are rhythmic and expressive. They require an imaginative, open, evocative reading that involves feeling as well as thoughts. The Western world has often identified classic poetic composition by rhyme, rhythm, and meter. In addition, vivid imagery and compression of words are notable. Hebrew poetry employs striking images and terse word usage but shows no evidence of a purposeful use of rhyme. The use of meter is evident in stressed syllables or in counting the syllables in poetic lines (in the Hebrew text), but is not easy to convey in translation. The following are characteristics of Hebrew poetry.

Parallelism. The most distinctive feature of Hebrew poetry is the terse two-part sentence style historically called *parallelism*. Robert Lowth (1753) observed that often the second line repeats the first line, either with synonyms or antonyms. However, the relationship between the two lines usually appears far more complex, and Lowth's term "parallelism" may have unduly prejudiced the discussion of the relationship between the two lines (Roop: 276; cf. Kugel; Alter). James Kugel proposes that a second line asserts, strengthens, or otherwise completes the thought in the first line, as expressed in the formula, "A, and what's more, B" (54).

The sum of the two parts is always more than mere repetition, as the following examples of affirming, opposing, advancing, and climactic parallelisms will illustrate (Wilson, 2002:48):

> Their mischief returns upon their own heads,
>   and on their own heads their violence descends. (Ps 7:16)

> The wicked borrow, and do not pay back,
>> but the righteous are generous and keep giving. (37:21)
>
> O sing to the LORD a new song,
>> for he has done marvelous things. (98:1)
>
> The floods have lifted up, O LORD,
>> the floods have lifted up their voice;
>> the floods lift up their roaring. (93:3)

The psalms are poetry of progression, with the above only a few of many variations possible in the highly sophisticated parallelism of Hebrew poetry (Berlin, *ABD*, 5:155-62).

Repetition. A very important poetic feature of the psalms is *repetition*, which provides emphasis (39:5-6), or invites the reader's attention to a key word or concept, such as "steadfast love" (103; 107; 136). The emphasis may take the form of a refrain (42:5, 11; 43:5; 46:7, 11). Another form of repetition is known as steplike or stairlike, since it involves repeating a word either in both parts of the same line or juxtaposed parts (124:1-5). A thematically central expression may recur throughout a psalm, such as the sevenfold occurrence of "the voice of the LORD" (29).

Inclusio (inclusion) is a technical term for a passage in which the opening expression, phrase, or idea is repeated, paraphrased, or in some other way returned to at the end, tying the whole together (as an envelope, bookends). This framing technique often identifies a crucial theological theme or concept and denotes unity and emphasis (8:1, 9; 103:1, 22; 118:1, 29).

Chiasmus (chiasm), named after the Greek letter *chi*, x) is a special form of repetition. In this literary device, words or ideas are listed first in serial order and then in reverse order, as in an ABBA or ABCBA pattern. The number of elements in a chiasmus may vary, but the effect is to provide a sort of multiple envelope structure that focuses attention on the center of the chiasmus. An example can be found in Psalm 103:11-14, where the verses begin with "for, as, as, for." Another chiasmus, stretching across three lines, is found in Psalm 90:1-2, with the opening vocative *LORD* standing outside the chiastic structure (Wilson, 2002:51):

> O Lord,
> A   you have been our dwelling place
>   B   in all generations.
>   C   Before the mountains were brought forth,
>   C′   or ever you had formed the earth and the world,
>   B′   from everlasting to everlasting
> A′   you are God.

Other examples of *chiasmus* can be found in the comments on Psalms 86 and 87.

A psalmist may also use repetition to create a sharp contrast in the mind of the reader, as in the fourfold use of the word "hand" (31:5, 8, 15). It may also create irony, as in the repeated use of the term *šûb*, "to turn, return" (90:3):

You *turn* us back to dust,
and say, *"Turn* back, you mortals."

Hebrew poetry utilizes word pairs, such as *wisdom* and *folly, wicked* and *righteous, heaven* and *earth*. Sometimes psalmists use merism, word pairs describing opposites or extremes yet including all that lies between. Some obvious examples include *great* and *small, rich* and *poor, near* and *far* (Wilson, 2002:50).

Metaphor and Simile. In a figure of speech called *metaphor,* a person speaks about one thing while using terms customarily appropriate for something else, as in "The LORD is my shepherd" (23:1). A *metaphor* involves the subject (what is being described), the image (the nonliteral, surprising element), and the meaning that the writer seeks to convey, often through clues given in the context. A *simile* is a comparison using "like" or "as" between the terms compared: "who whet their tongues like swords, who aim bitter words like arrows" (64:3). The psalms are filled with vivid images that provide a point of contact with human experience and add concreteness to illustrate a topic (1:3-4; 52:8; 74:1; 91:4).

Alphabetic Acrostic. Eight psalms are constructed on an acrostic pattern, the initial letters of each line following the order of the Hebrew alphabet (9-10; 25; 34; 37; 111; 112; 119; 145). Psalms 9 and 10 together constitute a broken acrostic, with some of the letters of the alphabet missing. Psalm 119 is an acrostic with eight lines built on each of the 22 letters of the Hebrew alphabet, for a total of 176 lines. The psalmist likely chose the acrostic form as an aid to memorization and perhaps also to convey comprehensiveness, as "from A to Z" (119). Alphabetic acrostics have enjoyed association with the wisdom tradition in ancient Israel.

Other Figurative Use of Language. In addition to literary features described above, the poetry of the psalms includes other traits not easily recognizable in English. These include Hebrew syntax and word order, alliteration (122:6-8), onomatopoeia (140:3), and wordplay (39:4-5; McCann, 1996:654).

Finally, there is also ambiguity, some perhaps intentional (51:14; 71:7; 87:4-5). However, all poetry is inevitably ambiguous, for it aims not so much at describing things objectively as it does at evoking the reader's imagination. Where ambiguity is perceived in the text, it may not be a matter of finding the "correct" meaning, "but rather may be a pointer to the richness of a text where dual or multiple meanings may truly present themselves to the reader" (Miller, 1986:43).

References: Alter; Berlin, *ABD*, 5:155-162; 1996:301-15; Caird: 152; Kugel: 54; Limburg, *ABD*, 5:528-31; Mays, 1994b:5-7; McCann, 1996:652-55; Miller, 1986:43; Tate, 2004:371-414; Wilson, 2002:39-57; Yoder: 3-15, 157-65.

HOLINESS, HOLY Reference to something as "holy" usually means it is set apart as belonging to God. It is sacred instead of profane. However, there are deeper meanings to "holiness." The word refers to the very nature and being of God. Thus, "holiness" and "holy" refer to the numinous (divine spirit), the imponderable and incomprehensible, a potent power removed and distant, yet at the same time near and present, the *mysterium tremendum* (Rudolph Otto).

The main Hebrew word denoting holiness is *qādôš*, "to be holy, sanctify," which appears as a verb, noun, or adjective over 800 times in the OT. The main Hebrew antonym is *ḥālal*, "to profane, desecrate." Although one strong idea behind the root *qdš* is "apart" or "separate," more central is the notion of purity and cleanness (Gammie: 9-32; Martens, 2002:201). Holiness has to do with wholeness and completeness and with a way of being. Holiness, it has been said, is the "godness of God."

The OT portrays God as holy, with the title *the Holy One of Israel* reflecting his supremacy (Pss 71:22; 78:41; 89:18; Isa 1:4 and thirty occurrences in Isaiah; Jer 50:29; 51:5). God is the source of holiness for creation. God sustains and displays his sanctity through miraculous acts and judgments (Ps 111:9; Isa 5:16; Ezek 28:22, 25; 38:23; 39:7, 25-27). Glory, the phenomenon of light that streams out as the majesty of God, is the manifestation of the LORD's holiness (Pss 19:1; 29:1-2, 9; Isa 6:3).

In the psalms, the holiness of God is given prominence in the collection celebrating the kingship of the LORD (93–100). The LORD's designation as holy is seen most clearly in Psalm 99. Holiness is his royal perfection as king worthy of adoration, with a divine power that permeates the world (99:1, 3, 5, 9). The LORD is a God of justice and not only a deity of being (99:4). The holiness of Israel's God is the power that makes justice and righteousness prevail (see comments on 99). Holy is a statement about the LORD's name (33:21; 103:1; 111:9; 145:21), about his word (105:42), his arm (98:1), his way (77:13), and all his work (145:1; Kraus, 1986:42). Thus, God is not simply "wholly other," but also persistent in self-expression.

God as holy is eternal, above any competitors, and is to be the sole object of Israel's devotion (Exod 15:11; 1 Sam 2:2; Pss 77:13; 89:6-8; 95:3; Isa 40:25; 57:15; Hos 11:9). The people are charged to emulate God's holiness by keeping the commandments (Lev 11:44-45; 20:26; Pss 16:3; 34:9). The biblical ideal is that all Israel shall be "a priestly kingdom and a holy nation" (Exod 19:6). Thus, for Israel "holy" means more than that which is unapproachable. It becomes a goal associated with God's nature and his desire for humans and so the basis for action: "You shall be holy; for I . . . am holy" (Lev 19:2). A series of ethical and ritual commands follow, with the commandment to love all persons (19:18), including aliens (19:34). Such love must be concretely expressed in deeds (19:9-10; Num 35:15; Pss 145:10-17; 146:5-9). God's people are to act a certain way because they are set apart.

More broadly, in addition to the holiness of God, the OT touches on holiness for humans (priests, Israelites, Levites, and prophets), objects (offerings, sanctuary furniture, priestly clothing, real estate, money, oil, incense, and water), places (sanctuaries, sites of theophany, land, heaven), and time (Sabbath, holidays, jubilee, and sabbatical year), as well as covenant and war (Wright, *ABD*, 3:238-44). However, it is not by cult, ritual, observance, or ceremony that holiness is imparted. All holiness derives from the personal God who is holy.

The NT borrows and reworks the material relating to God's holiness and that of his people. In the Gospels and Acts, the term "holy" is used to describe the Spirit of God at work in and through those who believe. In the Pauline writings, addressed to those "called to be saints," the status of God's people as holy is established more systematically. As Hebrews makes clear, it is by means of the holiness of Christ that the people of God are made holy (Heb 9:11-12). The final book of the NT pictures them at home in the worship of the holy God, fully belonging with him in the final fulfillment of the promise made through Moses at Sinai in Exodus 19:5-6 (Rev 4:8; 15:3-4; Wells: 239-40).

References: Gammie: 9-32, 104-6; Kraus, 1986:41-42; Martens, 2002:201; Milgrom, *IDB*, 5:543-44; Muilenberg, *IDB*, 2:616-22; Wells: 239-240; Wright, *ABD*, 3:238-49.

IMPRECATION The lament or complaint psalms often contain cries for elimination of the evil that is threatening the supplicant. Since evil is personalized, imprecation is directed against persons (evildoers, enemies, godless, criminals, beasts, even the demonic).

Examples of imprecatory or "cursing" prayers include verses in at least twenty psalms (3:7; 5:6, 9-10; 12:3-4; 17:13-14; 28:4-5; 31:17-18; 35:4-8, 22-26; 36:12; 58:6-9; 59:5-7, 11-13; 69:22-28; 70:2-3; 79:6-7, 12; 83:9-18; 94:23; 104:35; 109:6-19; 137:7-8; 139:19-22; 140:9-11). Some of these psalms place emphasis on annihilation of evildoers. Often hope is expressed that evildoers will receive the same suffering they have caused others under the law of equivalent retribution (28:4-5; 35:8; 57:6; 69:22-28). The language is harsh and bitter (109:12-13; 137:8-9).

These authentic prayers of biblical people are calling not for a personal fight but with concern about the adversaries of God's cause (5:5-6, 9-10; 139:19-22). In language of exasperation, this is human rage directed at injustice. The worshippers petition the LORD to do away with the wicked and thus establish justice. We may more readily understand Psalms of imprecation when we see them as the cry for justice by oppressed and powerless people. Thus, imprecation psalms are not "curse psalms" as much as prayers to God for vindication of the right in God's own way and time. They give voice to the psalmist's belief that God's right must prevail (35:24).

Yet the fiery imprecatory passages create a dilemma for the Christian reader in light of the NT call to love the enemy. One approach has been to assume that this is only an OT issue. But that is to forget that the NT also has its expressions of hostility and curse toward opponents who are seen as the enemy (Luke 19:44; Gal 1:8-9; Rev 6:9-11). Another solution has led to the censoring of "offensive" texts for public and private reading of Scripture, excising imprecations from lectionaries and prayer guides (Holladay: 304-15). However, faithful reading and interpretation of the Scriptures demands that we struggle with the meaning and value of all of these texts.

I offer the following suggestions to help us understand these prayers of imprecation and to encourage their appropriate use in the life of the church:

1. Yearning for vengeance is present in the psalms. It is part of the candor and honesty of the psalms to name the experiences of hurt, terror, and pain. Moreover, these texts touch something in us that we may not like—the recognition that the yearning for vengeance is here, among us and within us as well (Brueggemann, 1982:67-68).
2. We must not equate the speech of vengeance with acts of vengeance. In the psalms, the speech of vengeance is characteristically offered to God, not directly to the enemy (109:1, 21). When one is in the depths and besieged on every side, the only way out is to cry to God with thoughts and words of the moment. To pray at such times is both to let it (the anger) out and at the same time to hold it (the anger) back. The prayer becomes a vehicle for the inner fury of the oppressed, a way to deal with

one's anger. Recognizing that imprecations express rage by people who experience massive upheaval in life can help us legitimize rage. The prayer out of hatred that says, "I am fed up," can be a first step in relinquishing that hatred to God. Pouring out bitterness and hurt can be the beginning of healing.

3. Vengeance belongs to God, and the prayer of rage as voiced in psalms of imprecation finally leaves the matter where Moses (Deut 32:35) and Paul (Rom 12:18-21) both tell us it belongs—in the hands of God (cf. Ps 94:1; Isa 63:4; Heb 10:30). We may understand the vengeance of God as "the other side of his compassion—the sovereign redress of a wrong" (Brueggemann, 1982:73). That God practices vengeance is one way the Bible has of speaking about moral coherence (Ps 94:2-3, 23). An important feature of the imprecation prayers is that the one who prays for the defeat and destruction of enemies views them not only as *my* and *our* enemies, but also as *your* enemies, God's enemies (139:19-22). This is based on the claim that in God's creation is a moral order not to be ignored. The anger and judgment of God, therefore, are not manifestations of a divine arbitrariness nor pure retribution for misdeeds. Rather, God moves against people and evil forces in a way that is consistent with the divine character and thereby vindicates the purpose of God (Miller, 1986:151-53).

4. The prayers of imprecation are poetry in all its power and evocative potential. As poetic prayers, the psalms calling for vengeance are "a passionate clinging to God when everything really speaks against God" (Zenger: 79). The terrible image of babies being dashed against rocks is a picture of violence at its worst (137:8-9). The text lifts up this kind of act as the extreme form of the destruction of a community. Here the Scripture may serve not to perpetuate violence, as a surface reading might suggest, but rather to expose and unmask violence (Miller, 2004:196-98). Within Scripture there is explicit and implicit criticism of the inclination to violence (Pss 46:8-9; 122:6-9; Prov 25:21-22; Isa 2:2-5; 11:1-9; Mic 4:1-5). We also need to read the texts of imprecation in the light of other texts. The whole of the canon represents the larger picture of God's way and purpose.

5. These texts can help us hear the deep human pain in the cries of brothers and sisters in the faith, or others who may legitimately cry for vindication and even revenge. Those who pray the psalms of enmity are shouting out their suffering because of injustice and the hubris of the violent. Thus, the texts can draw us into solidarity with those who wept by the rivers of Babylon (Ps 137:1) and with countless refugees who have lost home and all else. These texts, about the memory of rage, are reminders to us all of a world that cries out for God's justice. Zenger summarizes: "These are poetic prayers that hold up a mirror to the *perpetrators* of violence, and they are prayers that can help the *victims* of violence, by placing on their lips a cry for justice and for the God of vengeance, to hold fast to their human dignity and to endure *nonviolently*, in prayerful protest against a violence that is repugnant to God. . . . The transfer of vengeance to God . . . implies renouncing one's own revenge" (Zenger: 92).

6. Finally, we read these texts also in the light of Jesus' words about enemies (Matt 5:43-45, 48), Paul's words about vengeance (Rom 12:14, 19), the meaning of the death of Christ and the way of crucifixion (cf. Luke 23:34), the experience of Christian martyrdom and the prayer of Stephen

(Acts 7:60). As Brueggemann contends, "There is a way *beyond* the Psalms of vengeance, but it is a way *through* them, and not *around* them. . . . Our rage and indignation must be fully owned and fully *expressed*. And then (only then) can our rage and indignation be *yielded* to the mercy of God" (Brueggemann, 1982:78-79).

References: Brueggemann, 1982:67-80; Holladay: 304-15; Miles: 151-75; Miller, 1986:150-53; 2004:193-202; Zenger, 1996:63-95. Also see the comments on Psalms 69; 109; and 137, and the essays *Vengeance* and *Wrath of God*.

JUDGE, JUDGMENT, JUSTICE "Moderns tend to equate justice with the application of the legal system. Such a view is too narrow an understanding of biblical justice. . . . In a court or legal setting, the primary import of justice is 'fair-ness.' The judge(s) shall be evenhanded, treating all alike with regard to the law . . . (cf. Exod 23:2-3, 6-8; Deut 17:8-13; Lev 19:15). . . . The meaning of justice . . . is not restricted to the role of the legal institutions [but] is concerned to restore harmony to the community. It consists of action for members of the community and against oppressors . . . (cf. Job 29:7-29). It [justice] is the responsibility of every member of the group, not merely the judiciary. It consists of concrete actions of caring. It moves beyond written codes to address weakness, poverty, and inequities of every kind" (A. Guenther: 390). Or, put another way, "doing justice" is seeing to "honorable relations" all around (cf. Martens, 1986:299-300).

The Israelites connected justice with their God, Yahweh. The LORD, called *lover of justice* (Pss 33:5; 37:28; 99:4; Isa 61:8), was regarded as the source and guardian of justice because justice (*mišpat*) and righteousness (*ṣĕdāqâ*) are his very nature and attributes (Pss 33:5; 72:2; 97:2; 99:4). These passages pair the terms justice and righteousness and use them synonymously. Yahweh, the Judge of the whole earth (Gen 18:25; Ps 94:2), is the righteous Judge (Pss 7:11; 9:8; 119:137; 145:17). The LORD created the world and established equity and justice (99:1-4).

The Hebrew word for "just" is used with reference to rulers, judges, and the LORD in the sense of seeing that people are treated fairly. A prominent OT use is the concern that justice is done to the accused (Pss 35:24-28; 40:9-17). This may take the form of punishment for sin (Isa 5:13-16; 10:22; 42:24), but is often used in the sense of deliverance and vindication of God's oppressed people (Ps 40:9-10; Isa 42:6; 46:13; 62:1-2).

When the Israelites summoned God to judge them, they were calling him to avenge them of their enemies as vindication for their own uprightness (Pss 17:2; 26:1-3; 28:3-4). Thus, they saw God's acts of helping, leading, and saving them as acquittals, since judgment is deliverance and victory (Ps 135:4; Isa 30:18). They summoned God to judge the nations for their disregard of justice in their social dealings with other people (Ps 9:7-9). It is not piety that God required of humans, but the practice of justice and righteousness (Amos 5:21-24; Mic 6:6-8).

God is portrayed as having a special concern for the poor, particularly the widow, orphan, foreigner, and oppressed (Pss 10:17-18; 82:1-4; 109:16; 146:7-9). God judges in order to restore the lost rights of the oppressed (76:9). He establishes justice in the world by eliminating inequalities (113:4-9), thus upholding the covenant by coming to the help of the weak and driving out the oppressor. Biblical justice actively pursues the welfare of the community and the individuals in it.

In addition, the temple festivals were associated with the king who played the role of judge. The object of these ceremonies was to renew the covenant and to strengthen justice, which was the condition of life and happiness (Pss 50:4, 7, 16-21; 81:5, 8-10). The LORD's judgments confirm the covenant and demonstrate his faithfulness.

References: Blackman, *IDB*, 2:1027; A. Guenther: 390-91; Kraus, 1986:92-93; Mafico, *ABD*, 3:1127-29; Martens, 1986:299-300; Pidoux: 209, 216. See also the essay *Righteous*.

KORAH Korah, a Levite, was head of a guild of psalm writers (Exod 6:18-21; 1 Chron 9:19; 2 Chron 20:19). The groups of Korahite psalms in the Psalter (42–49; 84–85; 87–88) attest to the early importance of the Korahites in Israelite worship. The Korahite collection apparently was used by this family of temple singers known from the books of Chronicles (1 Chron 15:17, 19; 16:5, 7; 25:1-2). These psalms differ widely in form, content, and setting. As a group, they convey delight in the praise of God (*'ĕlōhîm*) as the King who sits enthroned in Jerusalem; they express joy in the service of the temple (though Pss 44, 49 and 88 are not specifically temple oriented).

References to Korah suggest a demotion from an earlier prominent position (2 Chron 20:19) to "keepers of the entrance" and the "charge of making the flat cakes" (1 Chron 9:19, 31). An earlier narrative tells of a revolt of the Korahites against the Levites, with the Korahites losing the power struggle (Num 16:1-35; 26:9-11).

While most commentators identify the Korah psalms with Jerusalem, Goulder has proposed a northern origin of these psalms for use at the autumn Feast of Booths, perhaps at the Israelite sanctuary at Dan. He proposes that Psalms 84; 85; and 87 were early, joyful psalms in the sequence of the festival's week of liturgy, composed in the ninth century BC. Psalms 42–43; 44; and 48 were later replacements with a more anxious tone, at a time when the Northern Kingdom was facing military reversals, after 750 BC. Goulder suggests that for use in Jerusalem, the name "Zion" was later inserted (cf. Pss 48:2, 11, 12; 84:7; 87:2, 5).

References: Gerstenberger: 38; Goulder: 16-19; Holladay: 28-32.

MUSICAL TERMS In the early times of biblical history, the main functions of music were social merrymaking, martial noisemaking, magic incantation, and worship. Liturgical music became institutionalized with the establishment of the kingdom in David and Solomon's time. King David is credited with organizing temple music in 2 Chronicles 7, an account written many centuries later. The earlier historical accounts (2 Samuel) do not mention organized temple music.

While temple music may have begun with chants and dances and early pilgrimages, it began to be formalized as professional guilds were employed to form choirs and orchestras (1 Chron 6; 15–16; 25; 2 Chron 35:14-19). Their responsibility was to make constant praise to the LORD and "prophesy with lyres, harps, and cymbals" (1 Chron 25:1). They recited the epic history of the LORD's past victories at the major festivals and the coronation of kings (Pss 78; 81; 105). These Levitical singers, whose original leaders were said to be Asaph, Heman, and Jeduthun (1 Chron 25:1-8), were prominent in the worship of the second temple following the exile (Ezra 2:41, 65). Musical guilds such as the Korahites (1 Chron 9:19; 2 Chron 20:19) and the Asaphites (1 Chron 16:7; Ezra 3:10-11) have left their legacy through groups of psalms identified with their name in the Psalter [Asaph; Korah].

Many of the musical terms appear in the superscriptions, added by later scribes or collectors who sought to indicate the nature, authority, and use of psalms. These psalm headings list ancient categories of psalms, offer instruction for musical performance, refer to tunes, and identify occasions for a psalm's use in worship. Much of the information in these titles consists of specialized musical terms that readers no longer understand, such as *Shiggaion* (Ps 7) and *Gittith* (8). See the essay *Superscriptions* for a detailed listing of the musical terms.

One prominent liturgical notation not found in the superscriptions is *Selah*. It occurs 71 times in 39 psalms. *Selah* (selâ) may be an instruction to the conductor for a rise in the music, the cymbals to sound, or a pause in the chant for reflection. The specific purpose is no longer known [Selah].

The music of the psalms involves singing, chant, procession, and dance. Musical instruments are also a prominent feature. The two most frequently mentioned are the *harp* (33:2; 57:8; 71:22; 92:3; 108:2; 144:9; 150:3) and the *lyre* (33:2; 57:8; 71:22; 92:3; 98:5-6; 108:2; 147:7; 149:3). Other instruments include *cymbals* (150:5), *horn* (98:5-6), *lute* (92:3; 150:3), *pipe* (150:4), *tambourine* (149:3; 150:4), and *trumpet* (81:3; 98:5-6; 150:3).

References: Jones, *ABD*, 4:934-39; Matthews, *ABD*, 4:930-34; Werner, *IDB*, 3:457-76.

NAMES OF GOD Two names for God predominate in the book of Psalms: *Yahweh*, translated *LORD*, and *Elohim* ('ĕlōhîm), translated *God*. Yet other names are given the divine, including metaphorical designations to describe aspects of God's character. The Holy One addressed as *LORD* or *God* in the psalms cannot be reduced to any single conception.

Yahweh, the personal name for the God of Israel, appears more than 6,000 times in the OT. The book of Psalms has 803 occurrences, counting the shortened form *Yah* (yâ) and some form of the name 'ādôn (Lord), usually with a plural of excellence: 'ădōnāy ("my Lord"; often transliterated as *Adonai*) or 'ădōnênû (our Sovereign/Lord). As a title of courtesy, a form of 'ādôn is often substituted for the divine name. The name transliterated as *Yahweh* is always written with the four Hebrew consonants YHWH, called the Tetragrammaton (*LORD* in English Bibles). The pronunciation of YHWH as "Yahweh" is a scholarly guess, for the Tetragrammaton was not pronounced at all: the word 'ădōnāy (my Lord) was pronounced in its place. 'Elōhîm (God) was substituted in cases of the combination 'ădōnāy YHWH. When the Jewish scholars (Masoretes) added vowel signs to the biblical manuscript some time before the tenth century AD, the Tetragrammaton was punctuated with the vowels of the word 'ădōnāy or 'ĕlōhîm to indicate that the reader should read "Lord" or "God" instead of accidentally pronouncing the sacred name (Thompson, *ABD*, 6:1011). The form "Jehovah" results from reading the consonants of the Tetragrammaton (YHWH) with the vowels of the surrogate word 'ădōnāy. The hybrid form "Jehovah" comes from the early sixteenth century but was not widely accepted. It is found a few times in KJV, in the ASV, and in some hymns.

The meaning of the name YHWH is unknown, though it has long been thought to be a form of the Hebrew verb *hāwāy*, an older form of the Hebrew verb *hāyāh*, "to be." It is variously translated "I am who I am," "I am that I am," "I will be what I will be," "I will be present as I am present," and "I cause to happen what I cause to happen" (Exod 3:14; Craven: 88). Such understandings underline the creative activity of God. According to some suggestions, "I am that I am" is no name in the usual sense, and God did not reveal a personal name so that people could not manipulate the name. All expressions of who God is and how God acts can only be partial and incomplete expressions of the divine mystery.

Since the revelation of God's name as Yahweh occurs in the context of the exodus and the promise of deliverance, the name has come to signify a God who is present to save (Exod 3:6-17; 6:2-8). In the psalms, the *name of Yahweh [the LORD]* expresses all the mystery and wonder of revelation, the object of all prayer, praise, and reflection (Pss 7:17; 20:7; 103:1; 113:1-3; 116:4, 13, 17; 118:10-12; 122:4; 124:8; 129:8; 135:1; 148:5, 13). In the psalms those who pray and sing base what they do on the fact that the name is not meaningless; in this name everything is contained—"justice and salvation, deliverance and life, knowledge and wisdom" (Kraus, 1986:21).

'Ĕlōhîm/'ēl or some form of these names, translated into English as "God" or "god(s)," occurs 440 times in the book of Psalms, with 428 references to the God of Israel and twelve references to other gods. Most often *'ĕlōhîm, 'ēl*, and its inflected forms function as a synonym for *YHWH* (cf. Ps 68 with twenty-nine uses of some form of the name *'ĕlōhîm* or *'ēl*).

Why did this plural form *'ĕlōhîm* come to designate the one God of Israel? It is probable that this plural should be understood in the sense of intensification and eventually as an absolutization: "God of gods," "the highest God," "the only God who represents the divine in a comprehensive and absolute way" (Rose, *ABD*, 4:1006). In this sense, the term *'ĕlōhîm* appears to be used in a systematic way instead of the divine name *Yahweh* in Psalms 42–83, sometimes called the Elohistic Psalter. Note the two almost identical psalms (Ps 14 with *Yahweh* and 53 with *'ĕlōhîm*).

The psalms admit the existence of other divine beings, like those in the Canaanite pantheon. The Israelites did not question the existence of these gods, though they assigned such gods lower status than *YHWH*. They were rivals to whom the psalmists gave no allegiance (82:1, 6-7).

Distribution of the dominant divine names in the psalms may be charted as follows (Stuhlmueller, 1983:21):

		Yahweh	*'ĕlōhîm*
Book I	(Pss 1–41)	272 times	15 times
Book II	(42–72)	30 times	164 times
Book III	(73–89)	44 times	43 times
Book IV	(90–106)	103 times	0 times
Book V	(107–150)	236 times	7 times

Additional names appear, such as *'ēl-šadday* ("Almighty," 91:1; often transliterated as *El-Shaddai*) and *ăbîr* ("Mighty One," 132:2, 5). However, more common are the many metaphors used to describe the character of God. The biblical writers speak of God's presence and action in the world by using metaphors, terms, or images borrowed from human experience, to express something lying outside of direct human experience. Characterizations of God in the psalms fall into four categories of analogy: transcendent, human, animal, and inanimate likenesses.

"Most High" (*'elyôn*) is the dominant suprahuman designation of God, appearing in twenty-two verses (as in 7:17; 47:2; 97:9). This title for God makes the explicit claim that the covenant God is a God beyond all realities, human or divine (78:35, 56; Kraus, 1986:25-29). The God of Israel is the supreme God (86:8; 96:4-5; 135:5).

Human-like characterizations also serve as a conceptual basis in the psalms, with analogies that compare God's activities to those of a shepherd, a king, a judge, or a parent. God is likened to a shepherd in only three verses in the psalms (23:1; 28:9; 80:1), to a king in twenty verses (as in 29:10; 95:3), and to a judge fifteen times (as in 7:8; 82:1-2, 8). God is explicitly named father in the psalms (68:5; 89:26; 103:13). While YHWH *'ĕlōhîm* is never named mother in the psalms, six references explicitly connect God's relationship to the psalmist with actions associated with the birthing process or maternal activities (22:9, 10; 27:10; 71:6; 131:2; 139:13). Note also 123:1-2: "To you I lift up my eyes. . . . As the eyes of servants look to the hand of their master, as the eyes of a maid to her mistress, so our eyes look to the LORD our God." Psalm 103:13 is an example in which YHWH is named father and described with words that evoke maternal images. The word "pities" or "shows compassion" is *rāḥam*, a word related to the womb. God is a father who is compassionate like a mother (Craven: 109-10).

Animal analogies for God in the psalms refer to the protective concepts evoked by the eagle's wings (17:8-9; 36:7; 57:1; 61:4; 63:7; 91:4). Inanimate analogies are regularly employed. God is a fortress, a rock, a shield, water, and light (cf. 18:2, 10-15, 28).

In summary, God's name, whether *Yahweh* or *'ĕlōhîm*, describes God (99:6, 8). God's name saves and helps his people (54:1; 116:3-4). In response, they are enjoined to praise and glorify God's name (68:4; 86:12; 99:3; 105:3), trust and hope in it (33:21; 52:8-9), fear it (86:11), call on it (116:4, 13, 17), and declare it (22:22).

References: Craven: 82-113; Kraus, 1986:17-31; Rose, *ABD*, 4:1001-11; Scullion, *ABD*, 2:1041-48; Stuhlmueller, 1983, 1:21; Thompson, *ABD*, 6:1011-12; Trible, *IDB*, 5:368-69.

ORACLE An oracle is a pronouncement or utterance from God through a prophet or priest, often in the context of Israelite worship. In biblical studies, oracle has become a technical term implying literary structures recognizable by their standard form and content.

The basic experience of the psalms is that the LORD speaks in the sanctuary (60:6; 108:7). Psalm 35:3 asks for a divine response to be articulated in worship. The ones who transmit the divine word (cultic prophet or priest) seek to hear what God says (85:8). When the word is heard, the officiant can proclaim it (81:5).

The priestly salvation oracles found in the psalms provide assurance of divine grace. When in a prayer song an individual gave voice to his lament and petition, the response was delivered with divine authority, often with the characteristic introduction "Fear not . . ." (55:22; 91:14-16; Isa 41:14; 43:1; 44:2). While the following psalms do not explicitly contain the words of a spoken oracle, the abrupt change in mood to assurance may be response to an oracle of salvation (Pss 6:6-8; 13:5-6; 22:22-31; 69:30). Oracles offer assurance of God's intervention on Israel's behalf (60:6-8) and the promise of peace (85:8-13).

Prophetic oracles announcing divine judgment are also found in the psalms (12:5; 75:2-5; 81:5c-16; 87:4-7; 95:7b-11). An oracle may be specifically addressed to or prophesy about the king (Pss 89:19-37; 110:1, 4).

References: Gerstenberger: 253; Kraus, 1986:33-34; Martens, 1986:295, 299.

PENITENTIAL PSALMS In the liturgical tradition of the Middle Ages, seven psalms were identified as penitential (6; 32; 38; 51; 102; 130; 143). This classification is based on content rather than literary form. For example, Psalm 32 is a thanksgiving song with wisdom characteristics. The others are in lament form.

A common characteristic of the penitential psalms is the supplicant's plea for deliverance from a deep sense of guilt. The "enemy" is not "out there," but "here," in the depths of one's being. God is experienced as inescapable judgment and gracious acceptance (B. Anderson, 1983:93-94). Thus, these psalms give voice to contrite confession, an integral component of all prayer for forgiveness (32:5; 38:18).

The best known of the penitential psalms, Psalm 51, describes a true penitence consisting of the following elements. After calling on the mercy of God (vv. 1-2), the psalmist confesses his sin (vv. 3-6), then asks to be purified, healed, and restored (vv. 7-12). Finally, he promises to give thanks and work for the conversion of sinners (vv. 13-19). The prophets condemn rituals of penitence, weeping, fasting, rending clothes, and donning sackcloth and ashes if the heart is not involved (Ps 51:6, 10; Isa 1:15-17; 29:13; Hos 7:14; Joel 2:12-13). Furthermore, inner contrition must be followed by matching outward acts. Remorse must be translated into deeds and ceasing to do evil (Ps 15; Isa 33:15) must be followed by doing good (Isa 1:17; Jer 26:13; Amos 5:14-15). The Hebrew word for "repent" (šûb, "turn," "return") means "turn from evil and turn to good" (Healey, ABD 5:671-72).

In the penitential psalms, bodily sickness and spiritual affliction are inseparably fused (6:1-3; 32:3-4; 38:3-8; 102:3-11; 143:3-6). These graphic descriptions of physical illness can help us think of sin as an abscess, a malignancy that needs to be arrested and removed. The penitential psalms are reminders that only through the surgery and treatment of confession can healing come from the burden of guilt.

References: B. Anderson, 1983:93-102; Healey, ABD, 5:671-72; Milgrom, IDB, 5:736-38; Sabourin: 241-44. See also the essay Sin.

PSALM GENRES The reader of the book of Psalms encounters a wide variety of compositions reflecting diverse moods and situations. Yet many psalms belong together in distinct groups, such as those in which the psalmist pours out his distress to God and asks for deliverance, or those centered upon the theme "Praise the LORD."

Early attempts to categorize the psalms were made in the nineteenth century. However, the application of form criticism to the psalms is traced to the foundational work of the German scholar Hermann Gunkel (1862-1932). Form criticism seeks to identify the genre or type of literature to which a particular psalm belongs and the setting in life in which the genre functioned. Such scholars identify a psalm type by the presence of a set of features (elements of composition, expression, intention) common to the genre. They infer a setting in life by connecting the features with what is known about religious practices in Israel, and more broadly in the ancient Near East (Mays, 1994b:19-20). In his study of the psalms, Gunkel proposed that the present psalms derived from earlier prototypes that were liturgical texts used in the cultic life of Israel, not personal lyric poems.

Analyzing the psalms on the basis of formal or structural criteria, Gunkel identified five main types. *Hymns* are psalms of praise. Characteristically, they open with a call to praise, follow with the motivation for praise, and conclude with a renewed call to praise (as in Ps 117). They may extol God for his wonders in creation or acts in history. *Communal laments* are psalms in which the nation laments some public disaster, for example, the destruction of the Jerusalem temple (74). After addressing the complaint to God, the petitioner enters pleas for God's deliverance. *Individual laments*, the most common type found in the Psalter, express an individual's cry for help. Sometimes laments cry out in bitterness upon enemies (69). Sometimes the lament ends on a note of confidence (11). In *individual thanksgiving* psalms, the psalmist thanks God for deliverance from personal distress (30). Usually the psalm describes a previous distress and reports the prayer for deliverance and its fulfillment. *Royal* psalms center on the king, whom Gunkel understood to be the preexilic Israelite monarch (2). Royal psalms are identified not so much by a distinctive structure as by their content.

In addition, Gunkel recognized a number of less common types, such as *communal thanksgiving* (124); *psalms of trust* (23); *wisdom*, poems of a didactic nature (1; 37); *pilgrim psalms* (84; 132); *liturgies* (15; 75); and *mixed poems*, which draw on various other forms (119; J. Day: 11-13).

In broad terms, but with modifications, most subsequent scholars have followed the main outline of the psalm types as designated by Gunkel. A type or genre is constituted of standard elements that can be arranged, developed, and related in various ways. However, reading a psalm in terms of its typical element does not account for all the aspects of a psalm's composition. As Mays urges, further "literary analysis is crucial in discerning the individuality of a psalm. Form criticism looks for the typical. It is important to ask also what constitutes a psalm's individuality" (Mays, 1994b:20-21).

The following summary of Psalm genres lists the major types as well as the psalms within each genre. However, we can identify some psalms by several forms, in that several genres appear in a particular psalm (cf. 66; 75; 139). Hence, commentators' lists of psalms classified by type vary somewhat.

This commentary usually identifies the genre in the PREVIEW for each psalm. The OUTLINE is attentive to form in order to follow the movement of meaning, though one may also develop outlines on the basis of content. We must supplement genre considerations by giving attention to rhetorical criticism, which considers other literary features *[Hebrew Poetry]*. Another important consideration is canon criticism, which looks at a psalm in its place and relationship to other psalms and the purpose of the shaping of the Psalter *[Composition]*.

Lament. The lament is an individual or communal complaint song that specifically articulates the affliction threatening the worshipping group or individual. The lament focuses on a present distress that remains unresolved. Laments often articulate misery about one's own suffering or guilt, about enemy activities, and about God's negligence. Individual and community laments together comprise over 40 percent of the psalms. The lament of the individual is the most common form (3; 4; 5; 6; 7; 9–10; 13; 14; 17; 22; 25; 26; 28; 31; 35; 36; 38; 39; 42–43; 51; 53; 54; 55; 56; 57; 59; 61; 64; 69; 70; 71; 77; 86; 88; 102; 109; 120; 130; 139; 140; 141; 142; 143). Sometimes called a complaint or prayer for help, the lament usually contains these elements:

a. opening address,
b. description of the trouble or distress,
c. petition for God's response, often accompanied by reasons for God to act,
d. profession of trust in God, and
e. promise or vow to praise God or to offer a sacrifice.

Not all of these elements appear in every prayer. In some prayers, the psalmist claims innocence or admits guilt *[Penitential]*. Some prayers include the psalmist's plea for revenge against the enemies *[Imprecation]*. The question of life setting of the laments continues to be debated. Laments often speak of the distress in terms of *sickness* or *accusation* by ruthless enemies. Sometimes the images are those of *warfare*. Yet the language of the psalms is often metaphorical and open. Consequently, the laments become appropriate for persons who cry out in all kinds of situations in which they encounter opposition. The ambiguity of the psalms allows them to speak beyond their own time.

Laments of the community are prayer complaints in times of communal distress (12; 44; 58; 60; 74; 79; 80; 83; 85; 90; 94; 108; 123; 126; 129; 137). These laments contain the same elements as the lament of the individual. In addition, they usually include a reminder of God's relationship with the people and of God's mighty deeds in the past. The most dramatic communal disaster in the biblical period was the destruction of Jerusalem in 587/586 BC and then the exile. Psalms 44 and 74, the second psalms in books II (counting 42 and 43 as one) and III, are communal laments. Five laments of the community appear in book III, highlighting the theological crisis of the exile and its aftermath; they encourage reflection on what it means to continue to profess faith in God's sovereignty in situations of extreme distress.

Thanksgiving. These psalms originated as grateful response to God for a specific act of deliverance such as healing, liberation from enemies, or rescue from trouble (30; 32; 34; 40; 41; 92; 116; 138). Main elements of the thanksgiving song often include the following:

account of trouble and salvation,
praise of the LORD's saving work,
presentation of offering, and
blessing and exhortation.

These psalms assume the presence of the congregation gathered for worship or instruction. At the heart of these psalms is the story of deliverance so that the suffering and pain described lie in the past. The elements are similar to those of lament, the major difference being that the problems are resolved in thanksgiving psalms. Some psalms are controversial regarding genre because resolution may or may not have been accomplished (cf. 56; 57).

The grateful response to the experience of deliverance makes thanksgiving songs similar to the praise songs, for we can find elements of thanksgiving in general songs of praise, where the nation praises or thanks God for his deeds. This has led some scholars to question whether there is a separate category of thanksgiving psalms of the community. Nevertheless, some psalms show signs of specific thanksgiving rites of communal and national dimensions (65; 66; 67; 75; 107; 118; 124; 136).

Historical. Historical reviews with a teaching purpose may be found in Psalms 78; 105; and 106. These psalms express thanksgiving for the LORD's mercies to Israel, but also proclaim prophetic warnings on the basis of past history. Psalm 135, a hymn of praise, and Psalm 136, a community thanksgiving, also have a strong historical theme.

Hymns of Praise. These hymns give expression to praise as Israel's response to God (8; 19; 29; 33; 68; 100; 103; 104; 111; 113; 114; 115; 117; 134; 135; 145; 146; 147; 148; 149; 150). Most hymns begin with an invitation to praise, provide the reason for praise, and conclude with a renewed invitation to praise. These songs ordinarily refer to God in the third person rather than address God directly. The hymns celebrate God's work in both nature and history. They express an awe-filled confidence in God's power as "stabilizer of the universe—humanity's sole assurance of continued stability and reliability in a chaotic world" (Wilson, 2002:65). Most of the hymns of praise are found in books IV and V, a reminder that the hymns are to be heard as proclamation of the reign of God. Note the imperative "Praise the LORD" (146–150). Hymns of praise include the subgenre "hymns of creation" (8; 19:1-6; 104; 148).

Psalms of Trust. A group of psalms express trust (11; 16; 23; 27; 62; 63; 91; 115, 121; 125; 131). According to Gunkel, these psalms of confidence may have derived from the lament of an individual, when the "certainty of being heard" became detached from the elements of complaint and petition. Psalms of trust assert God's sovereignty and protective help in the face of potential danger (in contrast to actual danger, which calls for lament).

The LORD is King. Related to the royal psalms by their emphasis on kingship are psalms that proclaim the kingly reign of the LORD (47; 93; 95; 96; 97; 98; 99). The exclamation "The LORD reigns" or "The LORD is king" is characteristic (93:1; 96:10; 97:1; 99:1). These are sometimes referred to as "enthronement" psalms, though Mowinckel's proposal of an annual "re-enthronement" of Yahweh as king of the universe has been abandoned for lack of historical evidence (i.e., in Israel), as well as biblical evidence (Mowinckel, 1962, 1:106-92). Nevertheless, Mowinckel's work and subsequent proposals by Kraus (Royal Zion Festival) and Weiser (Covenant Renewal Festival) have emphasized the liturgical origins and use of the psalms, and especially the reign of God and the centrality of Zion (McCann, 1996:649).

The LORD's sovereign kingship is grounded in his creative power and authority. The LORD is also judge of the earth and all that lives in it (98:9; 99:4). These psalms play a significant role in the shaping of the whole Psalter "by providing a refocusing of emphasis from limited human kingship to the enduring divine sovereignty of Yahweh" (Wilson, 2002:71).

Songs of Zion. Six psalms celebrate the LORD's choice of Mt. Zion in

Jerusalem as the earthly center of the LORD's presence (46; 48; 76; 84; 87; 122). These psalms refer to Jerusalem as the city of God (46:4-5; 48:8; 76:2; 87:1-3) and point to the joy of pilgrimage to the holy city (48:12-14; 84; 122). Other psalms also refer to Jerusalem. Though not a distinct genre, a subcollection within the Psalter contains pilgrim songs concerning a trip to Jerusalem, the Songs of Ascents (120–134).

Liturgies. Entrance liturgies appear to have functioned as question-answer dialogue for entrance into the temple area (15; 24; 26). Psalm 68:24-27 refers to "solemn processions." Prophetic sayings or oracles are present in several psalms that may be called prophetic liturgies (12; 14; 50; 52; 53; 60; 75; 78; 81; 82). These psalms contain prophetic exhortations. The instructional intent is evident: these psalms challenge the reader to make a decision regarding God's sovereign claims.

Royal. Eleven psalms were likely composed for an event connected with the life of a king (2; 18; 20; 21; 45; 72; 89; 101; 110; 132; 144). This is a group based not as much on form-critical criteria as on content, since they could fit into common categories of complaint and thanksgiving (18; 89; 144) as well as hymns (2; 72; 110). The number and variety of these royal psalms signal the important role the Israelite kings played in religious life and temple worship.

These psalms originated and functioned during the period of the monarchy. After the fall of Jerusalem in 587 (or 586) BC, they took on additional significance through a change in interpretation, projecting descriptions of an ideal king to come. Gerald Wilson has observed that royal psalms occur at the "seams" of books I–III (2; 72; 89; Wilson, 1985:207-8). Book I begins with Psalm 2 as confident royal theology, and Book III ends with Psalm 89 as its demise. The failure of the monarchy is now replaced by a renewed emphasis on the LORD as king. The fact that the royal psalms are scattered throughout the Psalter gives the whole Psalter a messianic orientation. They are "not only poetic relics from the days of the Davidic dynasty, but are also expressions of the ongoing hope that God will continue to manifest God's sovereignty in concrete ways in the life of God's people and in the life of the world" (McCann, 1996:650).

Wisdom and Torah. A group of psalms is identified with wisdom poetry (32; 37; 49; 73; 112; 127; 128; 133; 139). These offer reflections on the possibilities and problems of life before God and give advice on how best to live that life in pragmatic terms. In so doing, they are linked with the biblical Wisdom literature (Proverbs; Job; Ecclesiastes). The material includes memorable proverbs and comparison and contrast to illustrate the consequences of wisdom and folly. The theme of retribution is prominent, as is the description of "two ways," with reflection on the blessings of those who fear the LORD and the emptiness of the life of the wicked. The use of the Hebrew term *'ašrê* (as in 1:1: "happy," NRSV; or "blessed," NIV) to describe the anticipated reward of the righteous/wise is common. Likewise, the phrase "fear the LORD" depicts the appropriate relationship of the wise to God (112:1). Several wisdom psalms deal specifically with theodicy questions (Pss 37; 73).

Occasionally the alphabetic acrostic form is used as a teaching device (111–112, though 111 is in the form of a hymn). Gerstenberger (20) suggests that the wisdom psalms were liturgical pieces from the beginning, as the scribes and Levites tried to gather members and proselytes around the written word of God during and after the exile. Teaching the revealed will of God became the backbone of communal and individual existence.

Closely related to wisdom psalms are the torah psalms, which focus on the importance of instruction (1; 19; 119) *[Torah]*. Psalm 1 introduces the entire Psalter by commending meditation on the teaching of the LORD as the way to a blessed life. Psalm 19 likewise revels in the desirability of the LORD's instruction. The expansive Psalm 119, in nearly every one of its 176 verses of the alphabetic acrostic form, offers some reflection on the divine torah. These three psalms, along with the wisdom psalms, give the whole Psalter an instructional orientation. The torah at the center is a reminder that "the primal mode of faithfulness and knowing God is obedience" (Brueggemann, 1982:56).

As with the royal psalms, the psalms reflecting wisdom themes and vocabulary appear at significant locations within the Psalter, suggesting purposeful placement to provide a structuring framework for the whole collection. Psalm 1 stands at the beginning of the Psalter as an introduction. "Neither is it coincidental . . . that wisdom concerns appear in Psalm 73, at the beginning of Book 3 of the Psalter, in Psalm 90 at the beginning of Book 4, and in Psalm 107 (vv. 41-43) and 145 (an alphabetic acrostic) at the beginning of Book 5" (Wilson, 2002:74). Does this suggest that "wisdom" interests had the upper hand in the final shaping of the Psalter? It appears Israel's sages came to equate the demands of wisdom with the covenant commandments of the LORD, and that they now present the Psalter as a book of instruction to guide the faithful into a life of obedience and praise.

For a list of the psalms arranged by literary genre and a listing of the psalms sequentially, with genre descriptions, see Appendix I and Appendix II.

References: Brueggemann, 1982:56; J. Day: 11-13; Gerstenberger: 20; Mays, 1994b:19-21; McCann, 1996:644-51; Mowinckel: 1:106-92; Wilson, 1985:207-8; 1992:129-42; 2002:57-75.

RIGHTEOUS, RIGHTEOUSNESS Righteousness, as understood in the OT, has to do with fulfillment of the demands of a relationship. Biblical righteousness is not simply behavior in accordance with an ethical, legal, or religious norm. Nor is it equivalent to giving every person one's just due. Biblical righteousness is rooted in the LORD's saving action (Pss 7:9-11; 33:5; 99:4). The righteous person in Israel was the one who related rightly to the LORD and preserved the peace and wholeness of the community by fulfilling the demands of communal living (15:1-5; 24:3-6).

Words deriving from the root *ṣdq* occur 523 times in the OT. The words *righteous* (*ṣaddîq*) and *righteousness* (*ṣedeq/ṣĕdāqâ*) occur 66 and 45 times respectively in the Psalms, for the most part in the context of God's saving action. The words *righteous* and *righteousness* are often used in parallelism or coordination with *justice* (*mišpāṭ*, 33:5; 37:6; 72:2; 97:2; 99:4; 106:3). Together they describe proper order in the life of the people put there and willed by God.

The word "righteous" defines the quality of a relationship, which for Israel was not legalistic but based on grace, on the LORD's loving choice of an oppressed Semitic tribe in Egypt to be his people, his peculiar treasure (Exod 19:4-5). Thus, the primary notes of Hebrew faith regarding this relationship are celebration, joyfulness, and praise. This response is rooted in an understanding of the LORD as righteous and into whose intimate fellowship the person who fears the LORD may enter and so also be called "righteous."

Throughout the OT, the LORD is proclaimed as righteous (Neh 9:8; Pss

7:8-9; 103:17; 111:3; 116:5; Jer 9:24; Zeph 3:5; Zech 8:8). The LORD is portrayed as righteous in his function as judge of the earth (Pss 9:4, 8; 50:6; 96:13; 99:4; Isa 5:16; Jer 11:20). He demonstrates his righteousness by displaying faithfulness to the community and by rescuing his people when they are threatened. The LORD is the restorer of social order, who will redress the affliction of the widow, the stranger, and the fatherless (Ps 94:6). The purpose of his judgment is the preservation of the community and of his covenant with Israel (89:1-18; 94:12-15). The LORD's righteousness is evident in his intervention for his people (22:31; 36:6; 40:10; 65:5). He acts in accordance with his name to preserve and display his glory (43:1). Therefore, those in peril can plead, "In your righteousness deliver me" (31:1; 71:2).

God's saving judgments on behalf of his covenant people point to a specific designation of "the righteous" as a group, defined over against "the wicked." Those called righteous are contrasted with oppressors, enemies, and wicked rulers (14:5; 69:28; 94:21; 140:12-13). The wicked put God at a distance. The "righteous" are those who walk in his way (1:1-6). Their hope is in the LORD to save them (116:8; 146:7-9; Amos 2:6-7).

The righteous person is the one whom the LORD's verdict has declared innocent and who is now upheld by the LORD (Pss 11:5; 17:3; 34:15; 37:17). This does not mean being without defect in the presence of God. All claim to righteousness is denied to every human being in the profound insight that all humans are fallen and guilty (14:3; 130:3). That is why the "righteous," the "faithful," the "innocent" can and need to pray the so-called penitential psalms (Pss 6; 32; 38; 51; 102; 130; 143). When people stand in a right relationship with God, that is, have a righteousness they cannot claim as a prerogative but which is granted them in the relationship of the covenant, then they can assert their innocence and plead for God's forgiveness (B. Anderson, 1983:102).

References: Achtemeier, *IDB*, 4:80-85; B. Anderson, 1983:98-102; A. Guenther: 390-91; Kraus, 1986:42-43, 154-57; Rad, 1962:370-83; Scullion, *ABD*, 5:724-36. Also see the essay *Judge*.

SELAH *Selah* (*selâ*), appearing 71 times in 39 psalms and three times in Habakkuk 3 as a marginal note, is likely a musical instruction. With few exceptions, the term is used in psalms that have titles. The majority of the titles identify the psalms containing *Selah* with David or the Levitical singers, and about 75 percent of the titles also make reference to the "musical director" or "choirmaster" *[Superscriptions]*.

Translated "interlude" in the LXX, the original meaning is unclear. The three basic interpretations focus on the root *sll*, "lift up"; *slh*, "repetition"; and the Aramaic root *şl'*, "to bow" or "to pray." Thus, interpreters have suggested that *Selah* might call for the instruments to enter, raise the pitch or volume, affirm what has been said, or serve as a breath marker.

In addition to suggestions that *Selah* might signal raising the voice, changing the voices, or increasing the volume, scholars have offered other possibilities. It could be a unit marker in some contexts, as in the paired Psalms 9 and 10. *Selah* appears at the ends of Psalm 9:16 and 20, marking off verses 17-20 as a unit, almost exactly in the center of the two psalms when they are read as one (Tate, 2004:410-11). Michael Goulder (103-5) has offered the suggestion that it means "recitative," marking a pause at which there should be the recitation of a prayer or story from Israelite tradition (68:7, 19, 32).

Martin Luther referred to *Selah* as a sign that we are to think more deeply and at greater length what the words to which it is attached mean to say. He called *Selah* "a punctuation mark of the Holy Spirit. Whenever we find it in the Psalter, the Holy Spirit wants us to pause and ponder; there he wants to touch and enkindle our heart for particularly deep meditation" (Luther, 1956:37).

References: Craigie, 2004:76-77; Goulder: 103-5; Luther, 1956:37; Tate, 2004:410-11.

SHEOL   *Sheol* (šĕ'ōl) is the most common word used in the Hebrew Bible to designate the abode of the dead. Of the 66 references, sixteen are in the psalms, three of these in Psalm 49:14-15. The term *Sheol* has been linked with the root š'l, "to ask, inquire," and may have originally meant "the place of interrogation." Common synonyms are *Pit*, used nine times in the psalms as referring to *Sheol*, and *Abaddon* (in 88:11 and six other places). *Death* is a synonym for *Sheol* 25 times in the psalms (three times in 116; twice each in 18; 55; and 109). *Grave* is another reference for *Sheol* (49:9, 14; 88:5, 11).

Sheol is described as a place to which one "goes down" (Num 16:30; Job 7:9; Ps 88:3-4). It is pictured as a vast cavern (Ezek 32:18-32) or stronghold (Pss 9:13; 107:18), but also as a dark wasteland (Job 10:20-22; Pss 88:12; 143:3), a place from which there is no return. It is characterized by dust (Job 17:16; 21:26; Ps 7:5) and silence (Pss 31:17-18; 94:17; 115:17). Some passages depict *Sheol* as a devouring monster (Ps 141:7; Isa 5:14; Hab 2:5). Affliction with a serious illness was viewed as being taken to the very gates of *Sheol* (Ps 6:2-5; Isa 38:10). In the Psalter, *Sheol* is a term frequently used to describe the plight of the psalmist while he is still alive (16:10; 18:4-5; 86:13; 88:3; 116:1-4).

The descriptive language is poetic and evocative. *Sheol* as the place far from God came to be viewed as the opposite of the life that has its source in the LORD (36:9, 12). The tragedy of death and *Sheol* lay in the silencing of praise in the realm of death (6:5; 30:9; 88:10-11; 115:17; Isa 38:18-19). Nevertheless, a few hints of an attitude other than fear point to the possibility of transformation (Pss 49:15; 73:24; 139:8). The prospect of greatly diminished human vitality and the lack of communication and worship remained daunting.

God's presence did not generally extend to *Sheol* (though note 16:9-11; 139:8). Apart from Job 19:25-26; Isaiah 26:19; and Daniel 12:2, the OT offers scant promise of liberation or resurrection from Sheol.

References: Kidner, 1973:61; Kraus, 1986:165-68; T. Lewis, *ABD*, 2:101-5.

SIN   The biblical writers label as sin the attitude that separates one from God and the actions that represent human failure; they make sin a major theme. The Bible takes sin seriously. Mortals find themselves in sin and suffer its painful effects. God graciously offers salvation from it. This is the story of the Bible. Here we consider the primary terms used for sin and reflect briefly on the nature, origin, and consequences of sin, and the remedy for sin in the OT, particularly in the Psalter.

Scholars have identified more than fifty words for "sin" in biblical Hebrew. The three most important terms are based on the Hebrew roots ḥṭ', pš', and 'wn. Of these, the root ḥṭ' (verb: ḥāṭā'), "to miss," "fail," or "sin," occurs 595 times in the OT. The word denotes a deviation from what is good and right. Sin as "missing a goal or way" means failing to do something in relation to man or God (noun: *ḥaṭṭā'â*, Pss 32:5; 51:2). The root *ps'* (verb: *pāša'*) occurs 135 times and signifies willful violation of a norm or standard. It is often translated "to revolt," "rebel," or "transgress," but it can also mean "breach." Not a mere failure or mistake (like *ḥt'*), it consists of willful disobedience (noun: *peša'*, 32:1; 103:12). The third Hebrew term for "sin" is *'āwôn*, used 229 times. Meaning perversity, "error," or "iniquity," it is almost always used to indicate moral guilt or iniquity before God (1 Sam 20:1, 8; Ps 36:2). These three common words characterize sin as failure, crookedness, and infringement of the soul (*nepeš*, the seat of longing and desire, the self). Additional words for "sin" provide a sampling of the wide range of expressions regarding human failure: *šāgāh*, "err"; *'ĕwîl*, "wicked/fool"; *rāšā'*, "guilty"; and *mārāh*, "contend, revolt, rebel."

The nature of sin suggests personal alienation from God. All life is upheld by covenant, and the essence of sin is breach of covenant, damaging the solidarity of the community. Thus, sin against another is also sin against God, for the life of the whole people is closely linked to God, who sustains that life (Gen 39:9; 2 Sam 12:13). The prophets saw sin as affecting one's personal standing with God. Thus, the sinner becomes aware of his sinfulness in the awesome presence of the holy God (1 Kings 17:18; Ps 51:4; Isa 6:5).

The Hebrews were not as concerned with the ultimate origin of sin as with its undeniable existence all around them. "I was born guilty, a sinner when my mother conceived me" (Ps 51:5) amounted to saying "like the rest of humankind, I have been a sinner from birth." Such a statement is not about biologically inherited sin or sexual morality. Rather, it recognizes the power of evil to corrupt humans from the beginning (Gen 3; 8:21; Job 14:4; 15:14-16; 25:4; Ps 143:2).

For the Hebrew writers, human sinfulness was related to creatureliness (Job 4:17-21; Pss 39:4-6; 89:46-48; 90:3-4; 102:3-4, 11; 103:14-16). Yet, more than frail creatureliness, sin was also identified with the heart as the seat of the human will (Isa 29:13; Jer 17:9). Because sin is rooted in the heart, all of human life is liable to its taint. All Israel needed to be warned: "Do not harden your hearts!" (Ps 95:8), and the psalmist prayed for a clean heart and a new and right spirit (51:10).

A consequence of sin is the rupture of the relationship between the Creator and the creature. The prophets preached the tragic reality of the nation's sins, which the people learned by experience in the events leading up to the exile and the years that followed. The troubles in which Israel found itself again and again, as described in the prayer songs of the people, are always the consequence of apostasy and disobedience. The prophets came to understand the LORD's punishment for the nation's sins in terms of divine wrath and vengeance. In polluting the land and defiling the temple, sin rendered the entire nation susceptible to disease and the direct punishment of God. The psalms show that Israel always had to receive its identity anew from the LORD and to be brought into being by him (78). When Israel's national security was threatened, "sinners" were identified as a class, the wicked who became the enemy of the king and of the LORD (69:22-28; 106:6-20; 137:7-9; 140:7-11).

For the individual, there was concern about sins committed in ignorance (19:12; 25:7; 90:8). The Israelites considered one's guilt a possible cause for all kinds of calamities. Often guilt and sickness were associated (32:1-4; 38:3-11; 39:8, 11). The enemies of the sick person focused on this connection by analyses, accusations, and slander. People accompanied restitution, the sacral cleansing of the sick, by acts of atonement. They believed that sin, guilt, and punishment would accumulate if not expiated and forgiven.

Sinners sought atonement through cultic rituals (51:18-19), and later, in attention to the commandments and laws as a joyful celebration of torah (119). They primarily found forgiveness, however, in casting themselves upon God's mercy in an act of confession and trust (3:8; 32:5; 38:18; 130:3-4). A common OT expression of guilt is the confession "I have sinned" (Exod 9:27; Deut 1:41; 1 Sam 7:6; Pss 41:4; 51:4; 106:6). Confession face-to-face with God gains forgiveness, so that the inward being and life itself is restored to wholeness (51). After the exile, communal confession played an important role in synagogue worship (Ezra 9; Neh 9; Ps 106). The writing prophets and psalmists nurtured this promise of forgiven sin as the basis of hope for permanent identity of the people of God long after national hopes were shattered.

References: Cover, *ABD*, 6:31-40; De Vries, *IDB*, 4:361-67; Grayston: 227-29; Kraus, 1986:61, 132, 156-57. Also see the essays *Penitential; Wicked*.

STEADFAST LOVE Among the Hebrew words for "love" in the OT, *ḥesed* is the most prominent to designate the unique character of divine love. In the Psalter, the term *ḥesed*, steadfast love (NRSV), is found 127 times of the 245 occurrences in the entire OT. The most basic characteristic of God toward his people, *ḥesed,* is variously translated: steadfast love, love, mercy, grace, kindness, loving kindness, fidelity, loyalty. No one English word adequately conveys the nuances of the Hebrew word *ḥesed*. Transliteration of the first letter in the word has varied: *k, kh, ch,* or a dot under the *ḥ* (as used here).

Understanding of this important biblical term has been enhanced by the study of Nelson Glueck (1927; English, 1967) and Katherine Sakenfeld's later work. Recognizing the covenantal nature of God's relationship to Israel, Glueck summarized the meaning of *ḥesed* as "conduct in accordance with a mutual relationship of rights and duties." By connecting *ḥesed* so closely to a legal covenant, Glueck emphasized the obligatory character of the word. Sakenfeld (1978:44-45, 78-82) has observed that earlier biblical traditions do not make *ḥesed* a legal obligation, but that *ḥesed* has a distinctively voluntary character. The one doing *ḥesed* acts to assist an endangered person, providing emergency assistance for those unable to help themselves. Thus, the *ḥesed* of God's active assistance both for individuals and for the community became a central term for expressing God's relationship to Israel (Ps 106:45).

Within the stream of the Sinai or Mosaic covenant tradition, *ḥesed* highlights the freedom of God within the covenant relationship, including the possibility of forgiveness as an act of divine *ḥesed* (Exod 34:6b-7; Pss 86:15; 103:8). In another stream of Israelite covenant tradition, God's irrevocable commitment to David's line is described as God's *ḥesed* to David (2 Sam 7; Ps 89). Psalm 89 praises the incomparable Creator of the universe, whose throne is founded on justice and righteousness, before whom stand *ḥesed* and faithfulness as divine attendants (v. 14). Even if disobedient rulers must be chastised, God promises the relationship with his people will endure through his *ḥesed, steadfast love* (vv. 24, 28, 33-34).

The many references to divine *ḥesed* in the Psalter most frequently associate *steadfast love* with a plea for deliverance from enemies (17:7; 143:12) or thanksgiving for such deliverance (138:2, 7). There are also petitions for general divine protection (40:11). In the context of the exile and its aftermath, when both the Mosaic and Davidic theologies were in need of reinterpretation, the emphasis on God's divine commitment continued. God's forgiveness is seen as the surprising gift of *ḥesed* from the One who is free to end the relationship with Israel. As the refrain of Psalm 136 insists, God's *steadfast love* endures forever.

It is the nation Israel that experiences first of all the LORD's *steadfast love* (118:2-4). However, forgiveness of individual supplicants through God's *ḥesed* is also affirmed (6:1, 4-5; 26:3, 6-7; 51:1).

The psalms most frequently use this term of God's relationship toward his people; yet they can also use it to describe relationships between humans. In 109:21-31, for example, it seems to be used both for God and also some form of human solidarity that is lacking, which prompts the call for God's *ḥesed* to make up for the vacuum.

In summary, God's *steadfast love* is his liberating, saving, helping, healing mercy extended to Israel and to the poor in Israel. It implies action that changes destiny: *ḥesed* is God's readiness to help and save in every situation and every place of distress and suffering. Thus, the LORD's *steadfast love* is the object and constant ground of great trust (13:5; 52:8). In the psalms, *steadfast love* and *faithfulness* are linked eleven times as descriptive of the character of God (25:10; 40:11; 61:7; 89:14; 138:2; etc.). The basic meaning of faithfulness is "to be firm, reliable." In this sense *ḥesed*, *steadfast love*, has been understood as God's covenant love, love that is boundless and loves no matter what the circumstance or response.

References: Glueck; Kraus, 1986:43-44; Roop, 2002:268-69; Sakenfeld, 1978:44-45, 78-82; Sakenfeld, *ABD*, 4:375-81.

SUPERSCRIPTIONS Superscriptions are the statements prefixed to individual psalms as titles or headings. In translations such as NRSV and NIV, they are set off in italics or smaller print to indicate they are not part of the psalm text. With these literary accretions to older prayers and songs, the scribes or collectors sought to indicate the nature, authority, and use of the psalm.

Of the 150 psalms, 116 have superscriptions, ranging from one word (98) to a lengthy comment (Ps 18). The 34 psalms that do not have titles are 1; 2; 10; 33; 43; 71; 91; 93-97; 99; 104-107; 111-119; 135-137; and 146-150. Psalms 10 and 43 are attached to the preceding psalms through literary structure, and 33 and 71 appear to be connected thematically to the psalms preceding them. Psalms 111-113, 117, 135, and 146-150 all begin with the cultic cry "Praise the LORD!" which also may serve as a title. In books I–III of the Psalter, only six psalms are without superscriptions, while books IV–V have 28 such psalms.

The superscriptions include notations of attribution, classification of categories of psalms, instructions for performance, and occasions for a psalm's use in worship.

Personal names and groups include the following: David (73 psalms), Korahites (Pss 42-49; 84-85; 87-88) and Asaph (50; 73-83) *[Asaph; Korah]*. Additional individuals associated with psalms are Solomon (72; 127); Heman (88); Ethan (89); Moses (90); and Jeduthun (39; 62; 77; 1 Chron

25:1-2; 2 Chron 5:12). Scholars continue to debate the nature of the references to persons. For example, the designation *Of David* could mean "to," "for," "of," or "belonging to." Although in some cases it is possible that these names indicate authorship, it is more likely that they originated in the process of collection. The biblical tradition depicts David as a composer of psalms (2 Sam 1:17) and as a musician (1 Sam 16:16-23; 2 Sam 23:1; 1 Chron 16:7-43). Some psalms may have been attributed to David as a result of this memory rather than as a result of Davidic authorship. With the passage of time, the tendency was to ascribe more psalms to David, as illustrated in the LXX's added association of Psalms 33; 43; 71; 91; 93–99; 104; and 137 with David (though omitting mention of David in the titles of 122 and 124), for a total of 85 Davidic psalms (Limburg, *ABD*, 5:528). Thirteen psalms associate the psalm with an event in David's life (3; 7; 18; 34; 51; 52; 54; 56; 57; 59; 60; 63; 142). We need not construe these references as necessarily historically accurate, but rather as illustrative of narrative settings in which the psalm is to be heard and interpreted. The significant Korahite and Asaphite collections probably point to a process of both authorship and collection of psalms within Levitical guilds (McCann, 1996:656).

Some superscriptions identify ancient categories of psalms. The most frequent designation, *psalm* (*mizmôr*), 57 times (as for Ps 3), may describe both singing and the musical accompaniment to singing. It may indicate music associated with liturgy and the guilds. A second designation, *song* (*šîr*), 30 times (as for Ps 30), also points to the musical performance of the poem. In certain contexts it seems to indicate a body or a particular type of religious music (as in 120–134). The distinction between *mizmôr* and *šîr* is lost to us, and in thirteen titles both terms occur.

Additional terms include *maśkîl* (13 times, as for Ps 52), which may refer to a didactic or artistic song (from *śākal*, "teach, instruct"); *miktām* (6 times, as for Ps 16), always of David, but with uncertain meaning; *šiggayôn* (Ps 7), perhaps meaning "lamentation"; *tĕhillâ*, "praise" (145), used in expressing thanksgiving (22:25); and *tĕpillâ*, "prayer" (17; 86; 90; 102; 142).

Many superscriptions offer instructions for musical performance and are addressed 55 times to "the leader" (NRSV) or "the director of music" (NIV). Most of these occur in books I–III of the Psalter and may refer to "oversight" of the music or choir (Ezra 3:8-9). There are references to the instruments to be used, such as "stringed instruments" (Pss 4; 6; 54; 55; 61; 67; 76; cf. 1 Sam 16:16, 23; Ps 33:2-3), and "flutes" (Ps 5). *The Sheminith* (*šemînît*; Ps 6; 12; 1 Chron 15:21) means (lit.) "according to/on the eighth," possibly referring to the eighth musical pattern (or low notes sung by men) or to an eight-string instrument *[Musical]*.

Some of the musical directions may refer to melodies, such as *according to the Gittith* (*gittît*; 81; 84), which might have also been a musical instrument. *According to Mahalath* (53; 88) could refer to a tune or a dance. The following appear to be well-known tunes: *Do Not Destroy* (57–59; 75); *The Deer of the Dawn* (22); *The Dove on Far-off Terebinths* (56); *Lilies* (45; 69); *Lily of the Covenant* (60); and *Lilies, a Covenant* (80). *According to Muth-labben* (9) is unexplained, as are others of the above. All these songs are long forgotten, their melodies lost.

Finally, some superscriptions identify occasions for the psalm's use in worship. Psalm 92 is assigned to the Sabbath (and in the LXX, Ps 24 is designated for Sunday, 94 for Wednesday, and 93 for Friday). Other designations are *for the memorial offering* (38; 70), *for the thank offering* (100 RSV), and *for the dedication of the temple* (30). Psalms 120–134, the "Songs of Ascents," are pilgrim songs associated with the opportunity to "go up" to Jerusalem and worship in the sanctuary at Zion (Exod 23:16-17; Deut 16:16-17).

Although the superscriptions were likely not part of the original psalms, these psalm titles provide important clues to the history of interpreting the psalms and their use in the lives of the people individually and in the community. The activity of collecting and annotating the psalms, perhaps during the fourth and third centuries BC, may have been guided by a desire to connect the psalms with their history. David as poet and singer provides the origin and goal in terms of which we must ultimately understand the psalms. As stated by Patrick Miller, "When these psalms were given to us from the lips of David, they are given to us from one who lived and felt and responded as one of us, whose hatred could run deep, whose agony could be unbearable, who cried out to God in confidence that he had tried to serve God faithfully, and who could fear the judgment of God because of the terrible weight of his own sinfulness. In the psalms of David we see our own image" (Miller, 1986:27).

In summary, though the psalm titles may be obscure as to the technical musical references and may not provide accurate historical information for a given psalm, they serve an interpretive purpose. They suggest a circumstance in which the intended psalm could be appropriate and provide an illustrative clue to interpretation. Transmitted as the sacred psalms of David, "they testify to all the common troubles and joys of ordinary life in which all persons participate" (Childs, 1979:521).

References: Gerstenberger: 256; Holladay: 70-75; Kraus, 1986:175-176; 1988:21-32; Limburg, *ABD*, 5:527-528; McCann, 1996:655-657; Miller, 1986:26-27; Wilson, 2002:78-81.

THEOPHANY Theophany is a compound term combining the Greek words *theos* (God) and *phainein* (to appear or show oneself). The OT theophanies usually refer to God's self-disclosure in dramatic and awe-inspiring means such as fire, storms, and earthquakes (Exod 3:2-5; 19:16-25; 24:15-18; Job 38:1; Ps 18:7-15; Ezek 1:27-28; etc.), but could include dreams (Gen 28:11-19; 32:22-32).

These theophanies are often connected with mountains, which were considered sacred sites (Exod 19:2-9, 16-25; Ps 48:1-8). The most prominent were Mt. Sinai (Deut 33:2-4, 26-29; Judg 5:1-5; Ps 68:7-8, 17-18; Hab 3:3, 7) and Mt Zion (Jerusalem), which from the time of David onward was referred to as God's sacred mountain (Pss 2:6; 48:1-3; 87:1-3). In a typical theophany, the LORD appears on Mt. Zion (in a thunderstorm image) going into war against Israel's enemies to protect Zion and the Davidic king (18:7-19; 29:1-11; 97:1-5; 144:1-11). Apocalyptic writers regarded Mt. Zion as the site where the divine warrior would one day appear in a decisive battle against the nations, to permanently remove any threat to Zion's security (Isa 66:15-23; Ezek 38–39; Joel 3:1-3, 9-18; Zech 9:1-17). God's self-disclosure could also come at other places, such as a spring, well, or river (Ps 46:1-5; Ezek 47:1-12; Joel 3:18; Zech 14:8).

The most vivid form for theophany in the psalms is the thunderstorm, with thunder representing God's voice and lightning bolts God's weapons (Exod 19:16, 19; Pss 18:14-15; 29:3-10; Hab 3:8). Although much of the language and imagery of OT theophany is borrowed from Israel's ancient neighbors (Keel: 212-30), the thunderstorm represents the LORD's destructive power over Israel's enemies, and also the blessings of fertility on the land as described in the theophany psalms (18; 29; 50; 68; 77; 80; 83; 97; 104; 114; 144).

In addition to theophany as a natural phenomenon such as the thunderstorm, the deity is at the same time depicted with human characteristics, with God having ears, nose, mouth, hands, and feet (18:6, 8, 9, 15). Especially prominent in the psalms is the reference to God's face, which is associated with divine favor (27:7-9; 80:3, 7, 19; Hiebert, *ABD*, 6:510).

The intention of theophanies is to bear testimony to the LORD's appearing to his people. These descriptions are found in hymns of triumph (Deut 33:2-5, 26-29; Ps 18:7-19) and constitute a verbal witness to the activity and reality of God's manifestation. In prayers the people would beseech the LORD for a theophany (Ps 80:2-3). A theophany in the sanctuary gave assurance that the LORD was present and had the power to save.

References: Hiebert, *ABD,* 6:505-11; Jeremias, *IDB,* 5:896-98; Keel: 212-30; Kraus, 1986:36-39, 142.

TORAH The noun *torah* (*tôrâ*) is derived from the verb *yārāh*, meaning "to direct" or "point the way." Torah has become the OT term for "divine instruction and guidance." Though *torah* is often translated "law," it is more than inhibiting legalism. The word *torah* may refer to the story of the LORD's activity to create a people and guide them into the future. It may also refer to the precepts and commandments that shape the life of the people who tell and retell the story.

The term appears to have developed from priestly instruction provided on the basis of oracles and traditional understandings of the requirements of the LORD. By the time of the later monarchy, "torah" refers to the basic instruction and direction provided to Israel by the LORD, especially the legal materials. By the time of Ezra in the postexilic period, "torah" means the substance of the book of Moses (Ezra 7:6; Neh 8:1, 8). Finally, "Torah" (capitalized in this use) becomes the standard term for the Pentateuch (first five books of the OT) in its entirety.

Three psalms can specifically be identified as Torah Psalms (1; 19; 119). Here too, Torah is instruction rather than rigid legalistic law. On the contrary, torah is a living, active word through which one's life is revived and one's heart rejoices (19:7-8). Light shines forth from the Torah (119:105, 130). The relation of individuals to torah is characterized by joy, love, and eagerness (1:2-3). The Torah Psalms celebrate the revelation of the LORD's will as the source of all knowledge and as an indispensable guide in life. Torah instruction, as experienced by the individual, suggests that the primary mode of faithfulness and knowing God is obedience (1). Psalm 1 provides an important key for reading the psalms. As an introduction to the Psalter, Psalm 1 announces that the torah of the LORD, God's instruction, applies to everything. The godly are those whose "delight is in the torah of the LORD," an expression understood as all the "teaching" that follows in the book of Psalms. Thus, to be flourishing as a tree by the water requires attention to the teachings laid out in the psalms.

Torah is an inclusive term. For the Hebrew people, it has always meant both the story of God's gracious acts in creating and preserving a people for himself, and also God's will for the way people should shape their lives in the light of those acts. Hence, zeal for the torah gave rise to the oral torah in later Judaism. When the written Torah no longer seemed relevant to some aspects of life, oral traditions were collected and expanded to help make it relevant to changing contexts and to address the question of identity of God's people.

References: B. Anderson, 1983:219-22; Kraus, 1986:161-62; McCann, 1993:25-40; Peterson, 1989:25, 144; Rad, 1962:221-22; Sanders, *IDB*, 5:909-11; Tate, 2004:455-56.

VENGEANCE Contrary to common understandings of vengeance as retaliatory punishment inflicted in return for an injury or an offense, the Hebrew word usually translated "vengeance" has a positive connotation, that of restoring wholeness and integrity to the community. The biblical idea of vengeance is rooted in the belief that God is sovereign and dependable and that vengeance belongs to the moral order of the universe (Jer 51:56; Ezek 17:19).

The Hebrew word *nāqam*, "vengeance," "vindicate," or "avenge," comes out of a judicial context. Vengeance was understood to be a necessary means for healing a breach made in the solidarity of the family or the community (see Pitard, *ABD*, 6:786-87, in response to Mendenhall, chap. 3, regarding *nāqam*). Seldom, however, does this word's use carry the connotation of "vindictiveness" or "revenge." The extreme violence that could develop from unrestrained personal vengeance is illustrated in the song of Lamech (Gen 4:24) and the story of Samson (Judg 14–16). In contrast, the Hebrew word *nāqam* accents the element of "save" in the OT. The language presupposes the view that God has entered into covenant relationship with the people Israel and acts as its vindicator to defend and uphold justice (B. Anderson, 1983:91).

The Bible is clear that vengeance belongs to God (Deut 32:35; Ps 94:1; Isa 63:4). Indeed, the LORD is Israel's vindicator and avenger (Isa 41:14; 43:1, 14; 44:6). Thus, in the psalms the call for vengeance takes on special importance (79:10-12; 83:9-12; 137). The cry for vengeance proceeds from the fact that the LORD is being treated with contempt and his honor is defiled (79:12). In these psalms, Israel does not set out to take revenge, but prays to the LORD and calls on him to respond. The prayer is that the LORD will not allow his enemies free rein or let their rage go unanswered, but that he will bring about a total restoration (80:3, 7, 19).

In psalms of imprecation, we are not to equate the speech of vengeance with human acts of vengeance (109; 137). Rather, worshippers offer and yield to God these prayers, often full of bitterness and rage (Brueggemann, 1982:69-71). Such calls for God's vengeance are not to be construed as calls for vindictive action by God, but as appeals for justice, which may well entail punishment of evildoers (9:18; 12:5-7; 34:6; 35:10; 64:7-8; 79:10; 94:1-3, 6, 10; Isa 35:4-6; Jer 51:34-37).

This motif of vengeance on behalf of the poor is carried into the NT (Luke 1:51-53; 4:18-19). Human vengeance is discouraged, and reliance on God's action is emphasized. The theme of forgiveness and renunciation of human vengeance becomes a major theme in the words of both Jesus and Paul (Matt 5:38-48; Luke 17:3-4; 23:34; Rom 12:17-21). The persecuted church strengthened its conviction that God would avenge the suffering of the faithful witnesses (Luke 18:3-8), and gave poignant context to the ancient words

Essays

"Vengeance is mine, and recompense. . . . For he will avenge the blood of his children" (Deut 32:35, 43; Rom 12:19; Heb 10:30).

References: Anderson, B., 1983:90-93; Brueggemann, 1982:67-80; Harrelson, *IDB*, 4:748; Pitard, *ABD*, 6:786-787; Zenger, 1996:69-73. Also see the essays *Imprecation; Wrath of God*.

WAR AND WAR IMAGES War and war images play a prominent role in the literature of the OT. How do we understand these stories of war and God's role in them?

God's sovereignty is affirmed throughout the OT, and the language of war is one of the ways of speaking about God's sovereignty. The OT accepts war as a fact of human life; although it presents some wars as God's, the OT extols the desirability of peace even for its own day.

In recent years, biblical scholars have come to use the term "holy war" to describe God's involvement in some of the OT wars. The term is problematic because of its connections with Christian crusades or Islamic jihads. People fought/fight in crusades not so much with God's help as on God's behalf; the term implies spreading a certain religion by force of arms. A jihad was/is directed at the conversion of pagans or the subjection of Christians and Jews under Muslim rule. "Holy war," as articulated by Gerhard von Rad (1951) and others, focuses on wars in which the LORD (Yahweh) fights the battle without help or with only minimal help from human warriors (see Rad, 1991:1-33, Ollenburger's "Introduction"). In this commentary, we use the term "Yahweh war" to describe this understanding (Janzen, 2000:464).

Israel's earliest literature, a group of poems, describes divine activity in terms of war. These poems (Exod 15; Deut 33; Judg 5; Hab 3) are hymns of victory recording Israel's early military successes or reporting a theophany. They describe God as fighting on behalf of or alongside Israel's tribal militia, and thus representing the determining factor in the victory. The oldest of these poems introduces Israel's deity with "The LORD [Yahweh] is a warrior" (Exod 15:3). Such faith in a God who has the power to win victories is later declared as "the battle is the LORD's" (1 Sam 17:47). In this manner, Israel's earliest poets expressed their confidence that the LORD would preserve his people's life from all threats against it.

During the early tribal confederacy, the warfare of Israel has been described as primarily defensive (Rad, 1951), primarily offensive (Miller, 1973), or as a popular struggle for liberation from an oppressive city-state regime (Gottwald, 1976). In these early battles, the divine power is portrayed as determining the outcome (Exod 14–15; Judg 5:12-18, 23). Yahweh war was conducted with the full support of the priests and involved ritual preparation (Deut 20:2-4; 23:14; 1 Sam 10:1).

With the coming of centralized administration during the monarchy, the concept of Yahweh war lost much of its power. The text indicates that David tested his plans with God, and the LORD is said to have given approval numerous times for war (2 Sam 2:1–5:25). Increasingly, it appears, warfare was transformed into an instrument of national policy declared at the wish of the king to serve his purposes (2 Sam 10:6-19; 11:1, 14-25; 1 Kings 4:20-28; 10:26–11:40).

The prophets considered the LORD to be king of the universe, executing divine will through the practice of divine warfare (Isa 6:11-13; Joel 2:1-11; Mic 1:2-4; Zeph 1:14-18). However, their concern for justice led them to warn the Israelite ruling class and state apparatus against oppressing others. Indeed, Yahweh war could include the divine warrior attacking Israel itself (through the armies of its enemies) as judgment for the corruption in its own society (Isa 5:20-30; 63:10; Jer 9:7-11; Hos 9:1, 5-6; Amos 2:4-8; Mic 1:1-7). The prophets associated the warfare of God with God's justice, which would eventually abolish war and bring the reign of peace (Isa 2:2-11; Jer 31:1-14).

The Deuteronomistic history (from the time of Josiah) represented a reform movement. It included teaching Yahweh war as God's demand that the nearby enemy, with its idols and possessions, be completely annihilated (Deut 20:10-18; Josh 6–7) to protect the Israelites from learning "abhorrent things." This history emphasized God's demand for obedience to the law and rejection of idolatry (2 Kings 17:34-40).

After the exile, the concept of Yahweh war took the form of apocalyptic literature in which the appearance of the divine warrior was understood as someone leading an attack made up of heavenly forces, which would destroy existing political institutions oppressing God's faithful people. The result would be establishment of an unending divine government (Dan 7–12; Rev 19:11-21).

Millard Lind has traced the history and theology of Yahweh war from the exodus events to the sixth century BC. Lind contends that Israel's calling was to serve God in a nonviolent manner, allowing itself to be led by the prophetic word and by God's own miraculous intervention. He sees the increased participation of Israel in military conflict through the monarch as a falling away from God's command to establish a new and peaceful theopolitical society in the world based on obedience to God, rather than on the use of military power. Thus, Yahweh war is not the endorsement of OT violence in the name of God, but rather a restriction on warfare and violence. It is God's command to Israel to hold back and let God deal with the enemies (Ps 46:10-11; Lind, 1971; 1980:23-113; Janzen, 1982:173-211).

In psalms written to honor the rule of God and the Davidic king on Mt. Zion, the imagery of the divine warrior is prominent (Pss 2; 18; 24; 46; 48; 76; 89; 97; 132; 144). These poems depict the LORD as warrior who has vanquished primordial chaos and become king in the universe, ruling on Zion and ensuring the failure of any natural or historical threat to Israel's security and well-being.

The psalms also express open criticism of earthly kings who take upon themselves oppressive power and set themselves against the LORD (Ps 2:1-4, 10-12). While the emphasis in Psalm 18 is on arming the king and conquest of the enemy, limits to kingly power are suggested (18:22, 35). Psalm 20 offers a similar caution about pride in military might (vv. 7-8). Psalm 33 underscores the truth that force does not have the last word. Even the most formidable weapons are nothing more than a lie in terms of security (33:13-19). Psalm 46 speaks of a God who "makes wars to cease" and invites the people: "Be still, and know that I am God!" (vv. 9-10). Midway through the Psalter is found the prayer for a just king who will "defend the cause of the poor of the people" (72:4) and the conjunction of peace and righteousness (85:10-13). At the end of this collection of psalms, the warning is sounded once again not to place undue trust in princes and their armies (146:3; 147:10).

The imagery and terminology of battle have strongly influenced the language of the OT. The protection of the LORD is compared to that of a shield (Ps 5:12), but his help against the wicked is expressed by the offensive power of the sword (Deut 33:29). This is metaphorical language. All our language about God is borrowed from some realm of human life. The references to God as warrior and king are intended to highlight metaphorically God's sovereign authority and power to establish justice rather than violence. The warrior metaphor used for God does not command or sanction human warfare (Janzen, 2000:465).

References: Gottwald, *IDB*, 5:942-44; Hiebert, *ABD*, 6:876-79; Janzen, 1982:173-211; 2000:463-65; Lind, 1971; 1980:23-113, 169-74; McDonald: 73-97; Rad, 1962:17, 59-60, 307; 1991:1-33; Toombs, *IDB*, 4:796-801.

WAYS OF READING THE PSALMS The history of reading and interpreting the psalms, briefly sketched here, has interesting twists and turns. Initially, many of the psalms appear to have been developed for use in the liturgical worship of the temple, giving voice to the people's prayers and praise. With the Babylonian exile of 587 (or 586) BC, their use in the temple came to an end. But their preservation beyond this crisis is evidence that the words of these liturgies were rescued as sacred literature on scrolls. When the temple was rebuilt (515 BC), the psalms were again used as liturgies, but also continued as sacred literature, to be read for meditation and instruction (Broyles: 4-6).

For a long time people assumed that David wrote all of the psalms or at least most of them. Since David was "a man after [the LORD's] own heart" (1 Sam 13:14), his prayers became exemplary for the people of God. Yet the superscriptions of the psalms themselves demonstrate a more complex process of authorship, composition, and use. Scholars have alerted us to the traditional tendency to associate major sections of the Hebrew Bible with a single character (e.g., Moses, David, Solomon), and to the ambiguity of such statements as "of David" in regard to authorship [*Superscriptions*].

Uriel Simon points to a range of Jewish approaches in reading the psalms by recounting the controversy that raged from the tenth to the twelfth centuries regarding the theological status and literary genre of the Psalms. Saadiah Gaon (ca. AD 1000), who initiated the controversy, claimed that the Psalter was a second Torah—the Lord's word to David—and not human prayer to God. Salmon ben Yerucham and Yefet ben Ali insisted that the book of Psalms was the prophetic common prayer book of Israel. Opposing both of these concepts, Rabbi Moses Ibn Giqatilah regarded the Psalms as nonprophetic prayers authored by different poets, beginning with David and ending with captive Levites in the Babylonian exile. Finally, Rabbi Abraham Ibn Ezra (AD 1092-1167) reverted to the belief held by the talmudic sages—that the Psalms were Israel's divinely inspired and most sacred poetry.

In the NT, as in Jewish tradition, David was taken to be the chief author, referring beyond his own life to Christ and his followers. Jesus Christ now became the new David of the Psalms, as one who was both human and the anointed king or messiah. The NT writers quote the psalms, for they exemplify a noble royal figure that finds its ultimate representative in Jesus the Christ. In this sense, the psalms became messianic prophecies (Luke 24:44-47; Matt 21:42; John 19:24, 28, 36; cf. Pss 118:22; 22:15, 18; 34:20; Broyles: 6-7).

The church read the psalms christologically, as though Jesus was the subject of the psalms or was speaking. For Origen (AD 185-253), the dominant commentator on the psalms in the third century, Scripture had both a plain and mystical sense, the latter being given the most attention. Many commentators drew on the work of Origen, including Jerome (342-420). However, where Origen would draw a philosophical conclusion from a psalm, Jerome preferred to draw theological and ethical conclusions from the same text (Holladay: 169-73). Theodore of Mopsuestia (350-428) represented the school of Antioch, whose exegesis placed more stress on the plain meaning, with emphasis on the text, grammatical sense, and historical setting. Augustine (354-430), whose conversion was aided by listening to psalms being sung, read them in constant recollection of Christ, while David receded from view (Eaton, 1999:325). More than a millennium later, Augustine's writings continued to influence Protestant reformers, such as Martin Luther.

For Luther, the standard four levels of sense (literal, symbolic, moral, and mystical) tended to flow into the principal sense of Christ the Word. In its sense of history, John Calvin's commentary is more akin to modern historical-critical works than to the interpretations of his sixteenth-century contemporaries. Calvin was determined to find the truth of the passage at hand, with emphasis on the plain sense of the reading. Both Luther and Calvin tended to depict the psalms as doctrine and admonition (Eaton, 1999:325-26).

With the rise of historical consciousness in the Enlightenment of the eighteenth century, interest moved to identify the historical situation in which a psalm arose. Robert Lowth's (1753) analysis of Hebrew poetry was directly important for psalms study *[Hebrew Poetry]*. This was also the era of textual and philological study, when much knowledge was gained concerning the ancient world and literary development of the Hebrew Bible. By the early nineteenth century, the tendency was to date psalms late, most as composed after the exile of the sixth century BC. Not all readers followed the lead of these scholars, and their conclusions were controversial among both laypeople and other scholars.

Present-day studies in the psalms owe much to Hermann Gunkel (1862-1932), whose form-critical approach called attention to the setting in life from which characteristic speech forms arose. Gunkel's work resulted in classifying psalms according to genre or type. Gunkel's major categories included hymns, community laments, songs of the individual, thank-offering songs, laments of the individual, as well as a number of minor types (Gunkel, 1967:5-39) *[Psalm Genres]*. Gunkel concluded that most of these types had their origin in the worship of the preexilic Israelite community, but that they had been adapted and edited to be more personal in outlook. Sigmund Mowinckel (1962) challenged this individualized approach to the psalms, emphasizing that these religious texts were shaped within worship. Thus, with Mowinckel, form criticism took account not only of patterns of expression, but also of the function in society that had molded these texts. Mowinckel sought to relate many of the psalms to a yearly reenactment of the enthronement of the LORD (Yahweh) as king of Israel and of the cosmos. No clear evidence of such a ritual is found in the Psalms, though modified proposals of possible festivals giving rise to these psalms and their liturgical character are found in the commentaries by Weiser (1962) and Kraus (1988; 1989).

Claus Westermann followed Gunkel in further developing categories of psalms. With Luther's translation of the NT and Psalms as his only reference tool, Westermann worked out the basic ideas for his book *The Praise of God in the Psalms* (German, 1954; English, 1965) while interred in a German prison camp during World War II. Westermann concluded that lament and praise are the two dominant tonalities characterizing the psalms of Israel, and that psalms of praise and lament correspond to the rhythm of joy and grief that characterizes human life. Calling attention to the principal form of lament, Westermann demonstrated how lament moves from plea to praise, from deep alienation to profound trust, confidence, and gratitude (1965:152-62; 1974:20-38; 1980:23-26; 1989:10-11). Another line of interpretation for many of the lament psalms, following H. Birkeland and S. Mowinckel, was that of John H. Eaton (1967), who placed emphasis on the ideas and language of royal interpretation, favoring a much larger group of royal psalms than the usual eleven so classified (J. Day: 21-24).

In 1968, James Muilenberg called for biblical scholarship "to venture beyond the confines of form criticism into an inquiry into other literary features" (1969:4). This invitation to what is called rhetorical criticism summoned attention to the literary features that lead to appreciation of each psalm as a unique poetic creation (McCann, 1996:652).

Mitchell Dahood explores the impact of Canaanite Ugaritic texts on the language and thought patterns of the psalms in his three-volume commentary in the Anchor Bible (1965-70). Some of his suggestions are highly contentious and out of favor with Psalms scholars today. Walter Brueggemann (1984:9-11), drawing on the work of Paul Ricoeur, utilizes the grid of *orientation, disorientation,* and *new orientation.* Brueggemann's commentary on selected psalms, *The Message of the Psalms,* organizes psalms on the basis of those that came out of the ordered life experiences, those stimulated by life's disruptions, and those reflecting a new orientation (thanksgivings, "the LORD is king" psalms, and doxologies of praise).

Brevard Childs has articulated the need to take seriously the canonical form of the Psalter and "to profit from the shaping which the final redactors gave the older material in order to transform traditional poetry into Sacred Scripture for the later generations of the faithful" (Childs, 1976:385). A century earlier, conservative scholar Franz Delitzsch published a commentary (1859-60) that gave considerable attention to the arrangement and order of the psalms in the Psalter. This "intertextual" approach has grown in popularity over the past thirty years as Psalms commentators shift from the exegesis of psalms as purely discrete compositions toward attempts to interpret them in the context, and contexts, of the Psalter (Tate, 2004:443-45). This canonical approach, seeking to take seriously the editorial shaping of the Psalter, is illustrated in the commentary by James Mays (1994b), and particularly in the work of Gerald L. Wilson (1985; 2002) and J. Clinton McCann (1996).

Marvin Tate, reviewing recent developments in the interpretation of the Psalter, calls for teams to work on the psalms: "We need more commentaries that give exposition of groups of psalms. . . . At the same time, the exegesis of individual psalms must go forward. . . . The interpretation of individual psalms is essential for the task of reading them as groups." He concludes, "The Psalms can be read starting at any point and moving backward and forward as long as it seems appropriate to the reader's good judgment" (Tate, 2004:471-72).

The above are but a few of the many interpreters on whose contributions we draw. Readers can find a bibliography of works cited at the end of this commentary, as well as an annotated list of resources. Scholarly study of the Bible continues. It is not static; there are always new discoveries that can increase our understanding. We draw on studies in archaeology, the history of traditions, literary forms, and theology to help illuminate the texts.

References: Broyles: 4-8; Brueggemann, 1984:9-11, 16-19; Childs, 1976:385; J. Day: 21-24; Eaton, 1999:324-29; Gunkel: 5-39; Holladay: 166-74; McCann, 1996:651-52; Muilenberg, 1969:4; Simon: vii-xi; Tate, 2004:443-45, 471-72; Westermann, 1965:152-62; 1974:20-38; 1980:23-26; 1989:10-11).

WICKED The term "wicked" (rāšaʿ) is used 102 times in the book of Psalms. The wicked or evildoers are those who destroy community, ignore the duties of kinship and covenant, exercise falsehood and violent force, and trample the rights of others.

The wicked, those who do not acknowledge the covenant or foolishly doubt the existence of the LORD (Pss 10:4, 13; 14:1; 53:1-3), are often set in contrast to the righteous. The righteous, who do not swear falsely and who uphold their oath, will receive blessing and will never be moved (15:4-5; 24:4). The psalms declare that the one who trusts in the LORD will fear neither the sun nor the moon (121:6) nor serpents nor lions (91:13). The wicked, on the other hand, have no stability (1:4-6; 9:3, 15-16; 14:5; 34:21; 37:13, 17, 20-21, 34-38). They are without standing and will be destroyed, either by their own crimes or through God's direct judgment (5:6; 11:5-6; 12:2-3; 28:3-5; 37:22). The failure of the wicked may come at the intervention of God or through the operation of the order established by God at creation (7:16; 34:21; 37:15).

An example of the wicked can be seen in the OT view of the magician or sorcerer (Pss 31; 57; 59). These "workers of iniquity" transgressed by declaring the LORD to be insufficient and by making use of powers that the LORD did not wish to grant (Deut 18:9-14). The influence of the wicked spreads like poison and issues in violence and mischief (Ps 55:9-11). Such a concern is the reason for imprecation against the wicked (109; 139). The psalms leave no doubt that "the way of the wicked will perish" (1:6; 145:20; 146:9; 147:6). Wisdom psalms often describe the two ways, with reflection on the blessings of those who fear the LORD and on the emptiness of the life of the wicked (32:10; 37:1-2, 20-21, 35-36; 73:27-28; 112:9-10).

References: Grayston, 1950:227-228; Keel, 1978:95-100; Maillot, 1958:447-449. See also essays on *Enemies; Imprecation; Sin; Wrath of God*.

WRATH OF GOD The OT describes God's attitude toward sin in terms borrowed from the human emotions of anger, indignation, and wrath. However, we are not to think of the wrath of God as irrational, irresponsible action on the part of God, but as manifestation of the aversion to sin that derives from God's holiness, an element of his character. Biblical literature sees the wrath of God operating as part of the final judgment in the end time, and also in particular historical and natural catastrophes, as well as in personal disasters.

The OT uses a variety of terms to designate God's wrath. Nahum 1:6 lists ʾap, "anger"; ḥēmâ, "wrath"; ḥărôn, "rage"; and zaʿam, "indignation." Deuteronomy 29:18-28 also provides a catalogue of words and images associated with divine wrath. The expression most frequently used to represent the wrath of God is the noun ʾap, meaning "anger" (Ps 90:7). The noun is also the Hebrew word for "nose" (Amos 4:10), which the ancient Hebrews considered to be the seat of anger. Thus, in God's wrath *smoke went up from his nostrils* (Ps 18:8). Another synonym for *anger* (*'ap*) is *ḥēmâ*, "rage" or "heat" (Jer 4:4). In addition, at least half a dozen more words are used for the wrath of God (*ḥărôn*, "rage"; *qeṣep*, "ire"; *'ebrâ*, "fury"; *za'am*; "indignation"; *ka'as*, "aggravation"; and *za'ap*, "vexation"). God's wrath is also suggested through metaphors drawn from the vocabulary of flood, famine, and conflagration, or from the language of cursing, devouring, reaping, demolishing, slaughter, refining, military siege, and battle.

While some OT stories convey a picture of God as bordering on cruel caprice (Exod 4:24; 19:21; Judg 13:22), usually God's wrath is related to deliberate human attempts to thwart his will and purpose. A recurring theme is Israel's repeated apostasy, the abandonment of the LORD to go after other gods (Deut 13:2, 6, 13). Israel's rebellion against the kingship and rule of the LORD is the major cause of divine wrath in the OT (Deut 1:26-36; Josh 7:1; 2 Chron 36:15-16; Ps 78:21-22). The destruction of Israel means not only the fearsome experience of encountering the wrath of God (80:4), but also the feeling of being forsaken and rejected by God (60:1-3; 74:1). Nations incur the wrath of God because they oppress God's people (1 Sam 15:2-3; 28:18; Ps 2:1-6) and practice self-idolatry (Isa 10:5-19; Jer 27:7-14).

The prevalence of injustice led to notions about God's decisive and climactic intrusion when God's saving purpose would finally be accomplished. The prophets and apocalyptic writers point toward such a day of the LORD's wrath (Ps 110:5; Isa 2; Amos 5:18-20). The psalmists invoke this eschatological wrath upon the nations as well as upon apostates in their own community, while they count on their own piety shielding them from the divine wrath in that day (Pss 7:6-8; 11:5-7; 56:7, 9; 79:5-13; 94:1-2, 12-15). Even so, the righteous worshipper is not without anxiety as God's judgment is anticipated (22:1-21; 30:8-10; 139:1-12, 19-24).

This language of the day of wrath is carried over into the book of Revelation. The wrath of God to be poured over the hostile nations is characterized by OT metaphors. The *cup of wrath* (Pss 69:24; 75:8) appears in Revelation 14:10 and 16:1. The apocalyptic terrors of God's judgment are portrayed in Revelation 16:4, 6 in terms of the events of the exodus and the plagues that fell on Pharaoh (Pss 78:44; 79:3). Here also is found the judgment doxology "The LORD is just in all his ways, and kind in all his doings" (Ps 145:17; Rev 15:3; 16:5).

In summary, the biblical writers view God's wrath as righteous because it destroys the wickedness that impedes deliverance (Isa 34:2). For that reason, the psalmists yearn for God to apply that wrath (Pss 59:13; 79:6). God's wrath represents his reaction to evil; God's basic stance is one of grace (Exod 34:6-7). So there is trust in the grace and power of God to bring deliverance in the end time (Pss 17:15; 22:4; 42:2; Rev 22:4).

References: Dahlberg, *IDB*, 4:903-8; Herion, *ABD*, 6:989-96; Kraus, 1986:99, 203; Zenger: 72-73. See also the essays *Vengeance; War*.

ZION The name "Zion" occurs thirty-nine times in the Psalter. The name originally referred to the fortified hill of pre-Israelite Jerusalem, which was conquered by David (cf. "stronghold of Zion," 2 Sam 5:6-10). With transfer of the ark to Solomon's temple, the name Zion came to designate the temple area as the dwelling place of the LORD (Pss 48:1-2; 74:2; 84:7). Zion also became an equivalent for the city of Jerusalem as the religious capital (Ps 51:18; Isa 40:9). Finally, Zion, like Jerusalem, came to refer to the people of Jerusalem, indeed, the people of all Israel, whose destiny lay in God's hands (Pss 97:8; 149:2).

The "hymns of Zion" (Pss 46; 48; 76; 84; 87; 122) celebrate Zion as the abode of the LORD and the principal locale of Israelite worship. These songs of praise have roots in the time of the monarchy as well as in pre-Israelite traditions (Kraus, 1986:83). In their reuse after the exile, they reflect the theology of the early Hebrew community in dispersion and its worship oriented toward the spiritual center, Jerusalem (Gerstenberger: 258).

In the Zion tradition we can identify at least four motifs that glorify Zion/Jerusalem as the LORD's royal city, God's earthly abode, from where his worldwide rule is exercised. First, Zion is the divine mountain (Pss 48:1-2; 68:15-18). Mount Zion is to the LORD what Mt. Zaphon (present-day Mt. Casius, just north of Ugarit) is to Canaanite religion, the dwelling of God and the most hallowed spot of the land. Theologically, Mount Zion is Israel's equivalent to the highest of all mountains of the world (Isa 2:2-3; Ezek 5:5).

A second motif is the conquest of chaos (Pss 46:1-5; 68:21-23). Because the LORD is in the city, Zion/Jerusalem cannot be shaken by the threatening waters of chaos. Those privileged to dwell in Zion live under the power of the LORD, who can master all assaults (65:7-8). In contrast to the angry chaotic waters, there is "a river whose streams make glad the city of God" (46:4), referring to a paradisiacal river bringing fertility and healing and joy to God's city (Ezek 47:6-12; Zech 13:1; 14:8).

A third motif is the invincibility of Jerusalem and defeat of the nations (Pss 46:6-11; 68:11-14). The LORD saves the holy city by his conquest of the foreign kings and their forces who attack Jerusalem (76:3-6; Isa 17:13-14). The result is the abolition of war and an era of peace (Pss 2:1-3, 10-12; 18:43-45; 48:4-8; 72:8-11). Jerusalem, the city of God, is the abode of peace (72:3, 7; 85:11; 122:6-7).

Finally, a motif of the Zion tradition declares Zion as a destination for pilgrims (84:5, 7; 120–134). This includes the pilgrimage of the nations who acknowledge the LORD's sovereignty and go up to Jerusalem to worship and pay tribute (68:29-31; 76:11-12; Isa 2:2-4).

After the fall of Judah and destruction of the temple in 587/586 BC, Zion became a symbol of national disgrace (Ps 137:1-3). However, the faithful retained the Zion ideology and projected it into the future through eschatological and apocalyptic writings, with Jerusalem as the place where the Messiah shall appear at the end of time. In the NT, Zion became the equivalent of the heavenly Jerusalem (Isa 60:14; Heb 12:22; Rev 14:1).

References: Gerstenberger: 258; Kraus, 1986:78-84; Levenson, *ABD*, 6:1099-1102; Ollenburger; Roberts, *IDB*, 5:985-87.

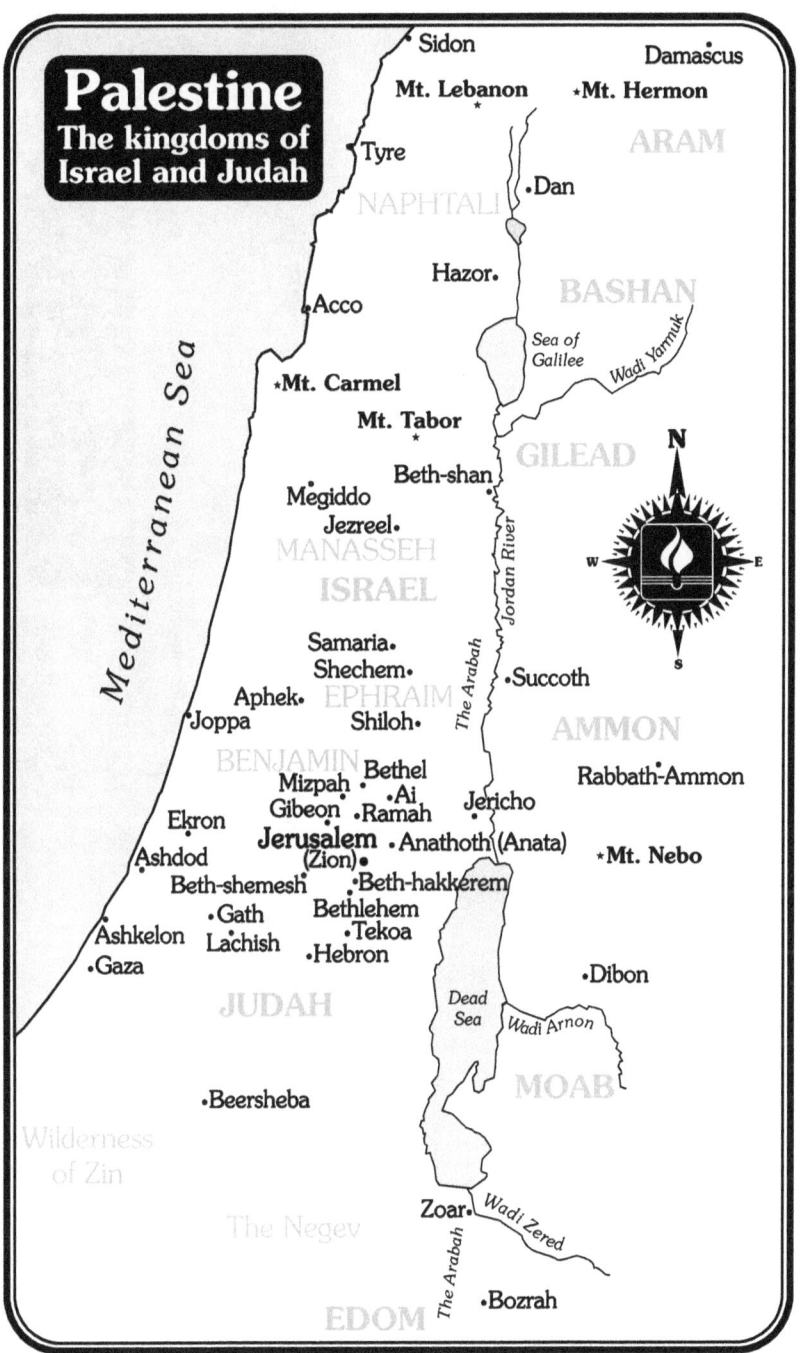

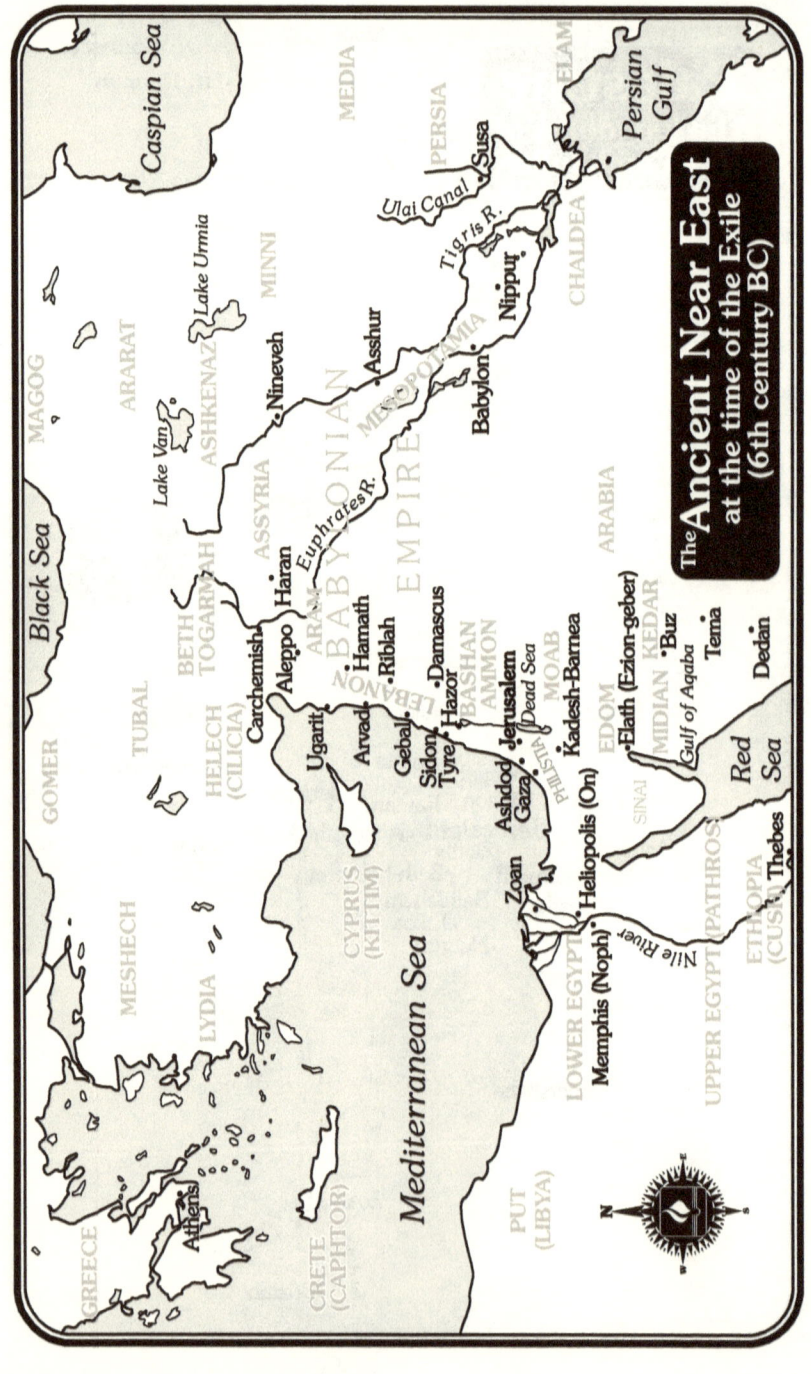

Appendix I

The Psalms Arranged by Literary Genre (Type)

We can identify some psalms by several genres. The following psalms are listed twice, once each in two categories: 12; 14; 19; 26; 32; 53; 60; 68; 75; 78; 115; 135; 136; 139. Note Appendix II.

Lament (61): The lament is an individual or communal complaint song articulating the distress threatening the worshipping group or individual. In the lament, the petitioner cries out to God for deliverance and a better future.
  Individual (45): Pss 3; 4; 5; 6; 7; 9–10; 13; 14; 17; 22; 25; 26; 28; 31; 35; 36; 38; 39; 42–43; 51; 53; 54; 55; 56; 57; 59; 61; 64; 69; 70; 71; 77; 86; 88; 102; 109; 120; 130; 139; 140; 141; 142; 143.
  Community (16): Pss 12; 44; 58; 60; 74; 79; 80; 83; 85; 90; 94; 108; 123; 126; 129; 137.

Thanksgiving (21): Thanksgiving psalms originated as grateful response to God for a specific deliverance such as healing, liberation from enemies, or rescue from trouble. Thanksgiving psalms may have individual or communal dimensions. Historical reviews offer thanksgiving or warning and usually have a teaching purpose.
  Individual (8): Pss 30; 32; 34; 40; 41; 92; 116; 138.
  Community (8): Pss 65; 66; 67; 75; 107; 118; 124; 136.
  Historical (5): Pss 78; 105; 106 (also 135, a hymn; and 136, thanksgiving of the community).

Praise (45): The hymn gives expression to praise as Israel's response to God. Psalms of trust assert God's protective help. "The LORD is King" psalms proclaim the sovereignty of the LORD. Songs of Zion celebrate the choice of Mt. Zion as the earthly center of the LORD's presence.
  Hymns (21): Pss 8; 19; 29; 33; 68; 100; 103; 104; 111; 113; 114; 115; 117; 134; 135; 145; 146; 147; 148; 149; 150.

Trust (11): Pss 11; 16; 23; 27; 62; 63; 91; 115; 121; 125; 131.
The LORD is King (7): Pss 47; 93; 95; 96; 97; 98; 99.
Zion (6): Pss 46; 48; 76; 84; 87; 122.

Liturgies (14): Entrance liturgies functioned for entrance into the temple area. Prophetic liturgies had an instructional intent.
Entrance (4): Pss 15; 24; 26; 68.
Prophetic (10): Pss 12; 14; 50; 52; 53; 60; 75; 78; 81; 82.

Royal (11): Likely composed for an event connected with the life of a Davidic earthly king, the faithful later reinterpreted these psalms as descriptions of an ideal king to come.
Royal: Pss 2; 18; 20; 21; 45; 72; 89; 101; 110; 132; 144.

Wisdom/Torah (12): Wisdom psalms offer reflection on the possibilities and problems of life before God and advice on how best to live that life. Torah psalms focus on the importance of instruction in the way of the LORD.
Wisdom (9): Pss 32; 37; 49; 73; 112; 127; 128; 133; 139.
Torah (3): Pss 1; 19; 119.

For additional description of each type, see the essay *Psalm Genres*.

Appendix II

Index of Psalms According to Genre (Type)

We can identify some psalms by several types: various genres may appear in a particular psalm. The following list is suggestive rather than definitive. For similar lists see B. Anderson (1983:239-42; 2000:219-22).

BOOK I
1 Torah
2 Royal
3 Individual lament
4 Individual lament
5 Individual lament
6 Individual lament (penitential)
7 Individual lament
8 Hymn (creation)
9–10 Individual lament
11 Trust
12 Community lament (also prophetic liturgy)
13 Individual lament
14 Individual lament (also prophetic oracle of judgment)
15 Entrance liturgy
16 Trust
17 Individual lament
18 Royal
19 Torah (also creation hymn, vv. 1-6)
20 Royal
21 Royal
22 Individual lament
23 Trust
24 Entrance liturgy
25 Individual lament
26 Individual lament (perhaps also entrance liturgy)
27 Trust
28 Individual lament
29 Hymn
30 Individual thanksgiving
31 Individual lament
32 Individual thanksgiving (penitential, with wisdom characteristics)
33 Hymn
34 Individual thanksgiving
35 Individual lament
36 Individual lament (also wisdom and hymn elements)
37 Wisdom
38 Individual lament (penitential)
39 Individual lament

40	Individual thanksgiving (with plea for a new deliverance, vv. 11-17)	78	Historical (also prophetic in using history as the basis of warning)
41	Individual thanksgiving	79	Community lament
		80	Community lament

BOOK II

42–43	Individual lament	81	Prophetic liturgy
44	Community lament	82	Prophetic liturgy
45	Royal	83	Community lament
46	Song of Zion	84	Song of Zion
47	The LORD is King	85	Community lament
48	Song of Zion	86	Individual lament
49	Wisdom	87	Song of Zion
50	Prophetic liturgy	88	Individual lament
51	Individual lament (penitential)	89	Royal

BOOK IV

52	Prophetic liturgy	90	Community lament
53	Individual lament (also prophetic liturgy)	91	Trust
		92	Individual thanksgiving
54	Individual lament	93	The LORD is King
55	Individual lament	94	Community lament
56	Individual lament	95	The LORD is King
57	Individual lament	96	The LORD is King
58	Community lament	97	The LORD is King
59	Individual lament	98	The LORD is King
60	Community lament (also prophetic liturgy)	99	The LORD is King
		100	Hymn
61	Individual lament	101	Royal
62	Trust	102	Individual lament (penitential)
63	Trust (but also lament)		
64	Individual lament	103	Hymn
65	Community thanksgiving	104	Hymn (creation)
66	Community thanksgiving	105	Historical
67	Community thanksgiving	106	Historical
68	Hymn (and possibly processional liturgy)		

BOOK V

69	Individual lament	107	Community thanksgiving
70	Individual lament	108	Community lament
71	Individual lament	109	Individual lament
72	Royal	110	Royal
		111	Hymn

BOOK III

73	Wisdom	112	Wisdom
74	Community lament	113	Hymn
75	Prophetic liturgy (also thanksgiving of the community)	114	Hymn
		115	Hymn (also community trust song)
76	Song of Zion	116	Individual thanksgiving
77	Individual lament	117	Hymn
		118	Community thanksgiving

Appendix II

119	Torah	137	Community lament
120	Individual lament	138	Individual thanksgiving
121	Trust	139	Individual lament (with wisdom characteristics)
122	Song of Zion		
123	Community lament	140	Individual lament
124	Community thanksgiving	141	Individual lament
125	Trust	142	Individual lament
126	Community lament	143	Individual lament (penitential)
127	Wisdom		
128	Wisdom	144	Royal
129	Community lament	145	Hymn
130	Individual lament (penitential)	146	Hymn
		147	Hymn
131	Trust	148	Hymn (creation)
132	Royal	149	Hymn
133	Wisdom	150	Hymn: doxology to conclude the Psalter
134	Hymn		
135	Hymn (also historical)		
136	Community thanksgiving (also historical)		

Bibliography of Works Cited

Achtemeier, Elizabeth R.
    1962   "Righteousness in the Old Testament." *IDB* 4:80-85.
Allen, Leslie C.
    1982   "Psalm 73: An Analysis." *Tyndale Bulletin* 33:93-118.
    1983   *Psalms 101–150*. Rev., 2002. Word Biblical Commentary 21. Waco: Word Books.
    1987   *Psalms*. Word Biblical Themes. Waco: Word.
Alter, Robert
    1985   *The Art of Biblical Poetry*. New York: Basic Books.
Anderson, Arnold A.
    1981   *The Book of Psalms*. 2 vols. New Century Bible. Grand Rapids: Eerdmans.
Anderson, Bernhard W.
    1983   *Out of the Depths*. Revised and expanded ed. Philadelphia: Westminster.
    2000   *Out of the Depths*. 3d ed., revised and expanded with Steven Bishop. Louisville: Westminster John Knox.
Anderson, James
    1948-49   *Calvin's Commentaries: Psalms*. Grand Rapids: Eerdmans.
Appleton, George, ed.
    1985   *The Oxford Book of Prayer*. New York: Oxford University Press.
Attridge, Harold W., and Margot E. Fassler, eds.
    2003   *Psalms in Community: Jewish and Christian Textual, Liturgical, and Artistic Traditions*. Atlanta: Society of Biblical Literature.
Bainton, Roland H.
    1950   *Here I Stand*. New York: New American Library.
Barrois, Georges A.
    1962   "Debt, Debtor." *IDB* 1:809.

Barth, Markus
    1974   *Ephesians 4–6*. AB 34A. Garden City, NY: Doubleday.
Barton, John
    1992   "Form Criticism." *ABD* 2:838-41.
Bellinger, W. H., Jr.
    1990   *Psalms: Reading and Studying the Book of Psalms*. Peabody, MA: Henrickson.
Berlin, Adele
    1992   "Parallelism." *ABD* 5:155-62.
    1996   "Introduction to Hebrew Poetry." *NIB* 4:301-15.
Blackman, Edwin C.
    1962   "Justification, Justify." *IDB* 2:1027-30.
Braght, Thieleman J. van
    1938   *Martyrs Mirror*. Translated by Joseph F. Sohm from the 1660 Dutch original. Scottdale, PA: Mennonite Publishing House.
Brandt, Leslie F.
    1973   *Psalms/Now*. St. Louis: Concordia.
Braude, William G.
    1959   *The Midrash on the Psalms*. Vol. 1. New Haven: Yale University Press.
Bright, John
    1960   *A History of Israel*. London: SCM.
Broyles, Craig C.
    1999   *Psalms*. New International Biblical Commentary. Peabody, MA: Hendrickson.
Brueggemann, Walter
    1982   *Praying the Psalms*. Winona, MN: Saint Mary's Press.
    1984   *The Message of the Psalms*. Augsburg Old Testament Studies. Minneapolis: Augsburg.
    1985   "Psalm 109: Three Times 'Steadfast Love.'" *Word and World* 5/2:144-54.
    1988   *Israel's Praise*. Philadelphia: Fortress.
    1989   *Finally Comes the Poet: Daring Speech for Proclamation*. Minneapolis: Fortress.
    1991   "Bounded by Obedience and Praise: The Psalms as Canon." *Journal for the Study of the Old Testament* 50:63-92.
    1995   *The Psalms and the Life of Faith*. Minneapolis: Fortress.
    2002   *The Land: Place as Gift, Promise, and Challenge in Biblical Faith*. 2d ed. Minneapolis: Fortress.
Buber, Martin
    1953   *Good and Evil*. New York: Scribner.
Caird, George B.
    1980   *The Language and Imagery of the Bible*. Philadelphia: Westminster. Reprint, Grand Rapids: Eerdmans, 1997.
Cardenal, Ernesto
    1981   *Psalms*. New York: Crossroad.
Childs, Brevard S.
    1976   "Reflections on the Modern Study of the Psalms." In *Magnalia Dei: The Mighty Acts of God; Essays in Memory of G. Ernest Wright*. Edited by F. M. Cross, W. E. Lemke,

Bibliography of Works Cited

        and P. D. Miller Jr. Garden City, NY: Doubleday.
   1979   *Introduction to the Old Testament as Scripture.* Philadelphia: Fortress.

Clifford, Richard J.
   1981   "In Zion and David a New Beginning: An Interpretation of Psalm 78." Pages 127-29 in *Traditions in Transformation.* Edited by F. M. Cross. Winona Lake: Eisenbrauns.
   1986   *Psalms 1–72.* Collegeville Bible Commentary. Collegeville: Liturgical Press.
   1986   *Psalms 73–150.* Collegeville Bible Commentary. Collegeville: Liturgical Press.
   2002   *Psalms 1–72.* Abingdon Old Testament Commentaries. Nashville: Abingdon.
   2003   *Psalms 73–150.* Abingdon Old Testament Commentaries. Nashville: Abingdon.

Clinton, Hillary Rodham
   2003   *Living History.* New York: Simon & Schuster.

Consultation on Common Texts
   1992   *The Revised Common Lectionary.* Nashville: Abingdon.

Cover, Robin C.
   1992   "Sin, Sinners." *ABD* 6:31-40.

Craigie, Peter C.
   1983   *Psalms 1–50.* Word Biblical Commentary. Waco: Word Books.
   2004   *Psalms 1–50.* 2d ed., with supplement by Marvin E. Tate. Word Biblical Commentary. Nashville: Nelson.

Craven, Toni
   1992   *The Book of Psalms.* Collegeville: Liturgical Press.

Dahlberg, B. T.
   1962   "Wrath of God." *IDB* 4:903-908.

Dahood, Mitchell J.
   1966   *Psalms I.* AB 16. Garden City, NY: Doubleday.
   1968   *Psalms II.* AB 17. Garden City, NY: Doubleday.
   1970   *Psalms III.* AB 17A. Garden City, NY: Doubleday.

Dante Alighieri
   1932   *The Divine Comedy.* Carlyle-Wicksteed translation. New York: Random House.

Davidson, Robert
   1990   *Wisdom and Worship.* Philadelphia: Trinity Press International.
   1998   *The Vitality of Worship.* Grand Rapids: Eerdmans.

Day, Dorothy
   1952   *The Long Loneliness.* New York: Harper & Row.

Day, John
   1990   *Psalms.* Old Testament Guides. Sheffield: JSOT Press.

De Vries, S.J.
   1962   "Sin, Sinners." *IDB* 4:361-76.

Delitzsch, Franz, and Keil, C. F.
   1976   *Psalms.* Vol. 5 of Keil and Delitzsch's *Commentary on the Old Testament.* Translated by James Martin. Reprint, Grand Rapids: Eerdmans.

Eaton, John H.
    1967   *Psalms: Introduction and Commentary*. Torch Bible Commentary. London: SCM.
    1999   "Psalms, Book of." Pages 324-29 in vol. 2 of *Dictionary of Biblical Interpretation*. Edited by John Hayes. Nashville: Abingdon.

Enz, Jacob J.
    1972   *The Christian and Warfare*. Scottdale, PA: Herald Press.

Freedman, David Noel
    1971   "The Structure of Psalm 137." Pages 187-205 in *Near Eastern Studies in Honor of William Foxwell Albright*. Edited by Hans Goedicke. Baltimore: Johns Hopkins University Press.

Friedmann, Robert
    1957   "Lord's Supper." *ME* 3:394.

Gammie, John
    1989   *Holiness in Israel*. Minneapolis: Fortress.

Geiser, Samuel
    1959   "Psalms as Hymns." *ME* 4:226-27.

Gerstenberger, Erhard S.
    1988   *Psalms, Part 1*. Vol. 1 of *Psalms and Lamentations*. Forms of the Old Testament Literature 14. Grand Rapids: Eerdmans.

Glueck, Nelson
    1967   *ḥesed in the Bible*. Translated by A. Gottschalk from German (1927). Cincinnati: Hebrew Union College Press.

Gottwald, Norman
    1976   "War, Holy." *IDB* 5:942-44.

Goulder, Michael D.
    1982   *The Psalms of the Sons of Korah*. JSOTSup 20. Sheffield: JSOT Press.

Grayston, Kenneth
    1950   "Sin." *A Theological Word Book of the Bible*. Edited by Alan Richardson. NewYork: Macmillan.

Guenther, Allen R.
    1998   *Hosea, Amos*. Believers Church Bible Commentary. Scottdale, PA: Herald Press.

Guenther, Margaret
    2000   *My Soul in Silence Waits: Meditations on Psalm 62*. Cambridge, MA: Cowley Publications.

Gunkel, Hermann
    1967   *The Psalms: A Form-Critical Introduction*. Translated by Thomas M. Horner. Philadelphia: Fortress.

Guthrie, Harvey H., Jr.
    1981   *Theology as Thanksgiving*. New York: Seabury.

Haas, David
    1994   *Psalm Prayers*. Cincinnati: St. Anthony Messenger Press.

Harrelson, W. J.
    1962   "Vengeance." *IDB* 4:748.

Harrisville, Roy A.
    1985   "Paul and the Psalms: A Formal Study." *Word and World* 5/2:168-79.

Hays, Richard B.
    1996   *The Moral Vision of the New Testament.* San Francisco: HarperSanFrancisco.

Healey, Joseph P.
    1992   "Repentance." *ABD* 5:671-672.

Henry, Kathleen M.
    1987   *The Book of Enneagram Prayers.* Jamaica Plains, MA: Alabaster Jar Liturgical Arts.

Herion, Gary A.
    1992   "Wrath of God." *ABD* 6:989-96.

Hiebert, Theodore
    1992   "Theophany in the OT." *ABD* 6:505-511.
    1992   "Warrior, Divine." In *ABD* 6:876-80.

Holladay, William Lee
    1993   *The Psalms Through Three Thousand Years: Prayerbook of a Cloud of Witnesses.* Minneapolis: Fortress. Reprint, 1996.

Huck, Gabe, ed.
    1995   *Psalms for Morning and Evening Prayer.* Chicago: Liturgy Training Publications.
    1995   *Proclaim Praise: Daily Prayer for Parish and Home.* Chicago: Liturgy Training Publications.

Janzen, Waldemar
    1982   *Still in the Image.* Newton, KS: Faith & Life Press.
    2000   *Exodus.* Believers Church Bible Commentary. Scottdale, PA: Herald Press.

Jeremias, Joachim
    1976   "Theophany in the OT." *IDB* 5:896-98.

Jeschke, Marlin
    2005   *Rethinking Holy Land.* Scottdale, PA: Herald Press.

Jones, Ivor H.
    1992   "Musical Instruments." *ABD* 4:934-39.

Jonge, Marinus de
    1992   "Messiah." *ABD* 4:777-88.

Keel, Othmar
    1978   *The Symbolism of the Biblical World: Ancient Near Eastern Iconography and the Book of Psalms.* Translated by Timothy J. Hallett. New York: Seabury.

Kenik, Helen Ann
    1976   "Code of Conduct for a King: Psalm 101." *Journal of Biblical Literature* 95:391-403.

Kidner, Derek
    1973   *Psalms 1–72.* Tyndale Old Testament Commentaries. Downers Grove, IL: InterVarsity.
    1975   *Psalms 73–150.* Tyndale Old Testament Commentaries. Downers Grove, IL: InterVarsity.

Koehler, Ludwig
    1957   *Old Testament Theology.* Philadelphia: Westminster.

Knight, George A. F.
    1982-83   *Psalms.* 2 vols. Daily Study Bible. Philadelphia: Westminster.

Kraus, Hans-Joachim
    1986   *Theology of the Psalms*. Translated by Keith R. Crim. Minneapolis: Augsburg.
    1988   *Psalms 1–59*. Translated by Hilton C. Oswald. Minneapolis: Augsburg.
    1989   *Psalms 60–150*. Translated by Hilton C. Oswald. Minneapolis: Augsburg.

Kugel, James
    1981   *The Idea of Biblical Poetry: Parallelism and Its History*. New Haven: Yale University Press.

Levenson, Jon D.
    1992   "Zion Traditions." *ABD* 6:1098-1102.

Lewis, C. S.
    1961   *Reflections on the Psalms*. London: Collins.
    1967   *Letters to an American Lady*. Grand Rapids: Eerdmans.

Lewis, Theodore J.
    1992   "Dead, Abode of the." *ABD* 2:101-5.

Limburg, James
    1985   "Psalm 121: A Psalm for Sojourners." *Word and World* 5/2:180-87.
    1992   "Psalms, Book of." In *ABD*, 5:522-36.
    2000   *Psalms*. Louisville: Westminster John Knox.

Lind, Millard
    1971   "Paradigm of Holy War in the Old Testament." *Biblical Research* 16:16-31.
    1980   *Yahweh Is a Warrior*. Scottdale, PA: Herald Press.

Lohfink, Norbert
    2003   "Peace Poetry in Israel: Psalm 46." Chapter in *In the Shadow of Your Wings: New Readings of Great Texts of the Bible*. Collegeville: Liturgical Press.

Longman, Tremper, III
    1988   *How to Read the Psalms*. Downers Grove, IL: InterVarsity.

Luther, Martin
    1956   *Selected Psalms II*. Vol. 13 of *Luther's Works*. Edited by Jaroslav Pelikan. St. Louis: Concordia.
    1974   *Lectures on the Psalms I*. Vol. 10 of *Luther's Works*. Edited by Jaroslav Pelikan. St. Louis: Concordia.

Mafico, Temba L. J.
    1992   "Just, Justice." *ABD* 3:1127-29.

Maillot, A.
    1958   "Wicked." Pages 447-49 in *A Companion Bible*. Edited by H. H. Rowley. New York: Oxford University Press.

Mannes, Marya
    1958   *More in Anger*. Philadelphia: J. P. Lippincott.

Martens, Elmer
    1983   "Psalm 73: A Corrective to a Modern Misunderstanding." *Direction* 12/4:15-26.
    1986   *Jeremiah*. Believers Church Bible Commentary. Scottdale, PA: Herald Press.
    1988   "Mashakh." In *Theological Wordbook of the Old Testament*. Edited by R. L. Harris. Chicago: Moody Press.

  1998 *God's Design*. 3d ed. North Richland, TX: Bibal Press.
  2002 "The Christian and Old Testament Law." *Bulletin for Biblical Research* 12/2:119-216.
Marty, Martin E.
  1983 *A Cry of Absence*. San Francisco: Harper & Row.
  1992 "Look for Your Immortality Closer to Home." *Context: A Commentary on the Interaction of Religion and Culture,* May 15, page 6.
Matthews, Victor H.
  1992 "Abimelech." *ABD* 1:21.
  1992 "Music and Musical Instruments." *ABD* 4:930-34.
Mays, James Luther
  1980 "Psalm 13." *Interpretation* 34:279-83.
  1985a "Prayer and Christology: Psalm 22 as Perspective on the Passion." *Theology Today* 42:322-31.
  1985b "Psalm 29." *Interpretation* 39:64.
  1994a *The Lord Reigns: A Theological Handbook to the Psalms*. Louisville: Westminster John Knox.
  1994b *Psalms*. Interpretation: A Bible Commentary for Teaching and Preaching. Louisville: John Knox.
McCann, J. Clinton, Jr.
  1992 "Preaching on Psalms for Advent." *Journal for Preachers* 16/1:11-13.
  1993 *A Theological Introduction to the Book of Psalms: The Psalms as Torah*. Nashville: Abingdon.
  1996 "The Book of Psalms." *NIB* 4:639-1280.
McDonald, Patricia M.
  2004 *God and Violence*. Scottdale, PA: Herald Press.
Mendenhall, George E.
  1973 *The Tenth Generation*. Baltimore: Johns Hopkins University Press.
Menno Simons
  1956 *The Complete Writings of Menno Simons*. Translated by Leonard Verduin. Edited by John C. Wenger. Scottdale, PA: Herald Press.
Merton, Thomas
  1986 *Bread in the Wilderness*. Collegeville: Liturgical Press.
Miles, Carol Antablin
  1994 "'Singing the Songs of Zion' and other Sermons from the Margins of the Canon." *Koinonia* 6:151-75.
Milgrom, J.
  1976 "Leviticus." *IDB* 5:543-44.
  1976 "Repentance." *IDB* 5:736-38.
Miller, Patrick D., Jr.
  1973 *The Divine Warrior in Early Israel*. Cambridge, MA: Harvard University Press.
  1986 *Interpreting the Psalms*. Philadelphia: Fortress.
  2004 "The Hermeneutics of Imprecation." Pages 193-202 in *The Way of the Lord*. Tübingen: Mohr Siebeck.
Morgan, G. Campbell
  1946 *Notes on the Psalms*. London: Henry E. Walter.

Morschauser, Scott
    2003   "Potters' Wheels and Pregnancies: A Note on Exodus 1:16." *Journal of Biblical Literature* 122:731-33.

Mowinckel, Sigmund
    1962   *Psalms in Israel's Worship.* 2 vols. Translated by D. R. Ap-Thomas. New York: Abingdon.

Muilenberg, James
    1962   "Holiness." *IDB* 2:616-22.
    1969   "Form Criticism and Beyond." *Journal of Biblical Literature* 88:4.

Murphy, Roland E.
    1993   *The Psalms Are Yours.* New York: Paulist Press.

Ollenburger, Ben C.
    1987   *Zion: The City of the Great King.* JSOTSup 41. Sheffield: JSOT Press.

Parkander, Dorothy J.
    1985   "Exalted Manna: The Psalms as Literature." *Word and World* 2:122-31.

Paterson, John
    1950   *The Praises of Israel.* New York: Scribner.

Peterson, Eugene H.
    1989   *Answering God: The Psalms as Tools for Prayer.* San Francisco: Harper & Row.
    1994   *The Message: Psalms.* Colorado Springs: NavPress.

Pidoux, G.
    1958   "Judgment." In *A Companion to the Bible.* Edited by J. J. von Allmen. New York: Oxford University Press.

Pitard, Wayne T.
    1992   "Vengeance." *ABD* 6:786-87.

Pleins, J. David
    1993   *The Psalms: Songs of Tragedy, Hope, and Justice.* Maryknoll, NY: Orbis Books.

Quell, Gottfried
    1967   "Struktur und Sinn des Psalms 131." Pages 173-85 in *Das Ferne und Nahe Wort: Festschrift Leonard Rost.* Edited by Fritz Maass. BZAW 105. Berlin: Topelmann.

Rad, Gerhard von
    1962   *Old Testament Theology.* Translated by D. M. G. Stalker. Vol. 1. New York: Harper & Row.
    1977   *Biblical Interpretations in Preaching.* Translated by John E. Steely. Nashville: Abingdon.
    1991   *Holy War in Ancient Israel.* First German ed., 1951. Translated from the 3d German ed. (1958) and edited by Marva J. Dawn. Grand Rapids: Eerdmans. Reprint, Eugene, OR: Wipf & Stock, 2000.

Reardon, Patrick Henry
    2000   *Christ in the Psalms.* Ben Lomand, CA: Conciliar Press.

Reid, Stephen Breck
    1997   *Listening In: A Multicultural Reading of the Psalms.* Nashville: Abingdon.

  2001 Ed. *Psalms and Practice: Worship, Virtue, and Authority.* Collegeville: Liturgical Press.
Reumann, John H.
  1974 "Psalm 22 at the Cross." *Interpretation* 28:39-58.
Reuter, Rosemary Radford
  1985 *Women—Church: Theology and Practice of Feminist Liturgical Communities.* San Francisco: Harper & Row.
Revised Common Lectionary. See Consultation
Rhodes, Arnold B.
  1960 *The Book of Psalms.* Richmond: John Knox.
Rienstra, Marchiene Vroon
  1992 *Swallow's Nest: A Feminine Reading of the Psalms.* Grand Rapids: Eerdmans.
Rivkin, Ellis
  1976 "Messiah, Jewish." *IDB* 5:588-91.
Roberts, J. J. M.
  1976 "Zion Tradition." *IDB* 5:985-87.
Rogers, J. S.
  1992 "Asaph." *ABD* 1:471.
Roop, Eugene F.
  2002 *Ruth, Jonah, Esther.* Believers Church Bible Commentary. Scottdale, PA: Herald Press.
Rose, Martin
  1992 "Names of God in the OT." *ABD* 4:1001-11.
Sabourin, Leopold
  1974 *The Psalms: Their Origin and Meaning.* New York: Alba House.
Sakenfeld, Katherine Doop
  1978 *The Meaning of ḥesed in the Hebrew Bible: A New Inquiry.* Harvard Semitic Museum 17. Missoula: Scholars Press.
  1992 "Love." *ABD* 4:374-81.
Sanders, James A.
  1976 "Torah." *IDB* 5:909-11.
Scullion, John J.
  1992 "God in the OT." *ABD* 2:1041-48.
  1992 "Rightousness." *ABD* 5:724-36.
Seybold, Klaus
  1990 *Introducing the Psalms.* Translated by R. Graeme Dunphy. Edinburgh: T&T Clark.
Simon, Uriel
  1991 *Four Approaches to the Book of Psalms.* Translated by Lenn J. Schramm. Albany: State University of New York Press.
Soll, Will
  1991 *Psalm 119: Matrix, Form, and Setting.* Catholic Biblical Quarterly Monograph Series 23. Washington, DC: Catholic Biblical Association.
Stevens, Marty
  2003 "Between Text and Sermon." *Interpretation* 57:187-89.

Stuhlmueller, Carroll
- 1983   *Psalms 1*. Old Testament Message 21. Wilmington: Michael Glazier.
- 1983   *Psalms 2*. Old Testament Message 22. Wilmington: Michael Glazier.
- 2002   *The Spirituality of the Psalms*. Edited by Carol J. Dempsey and Timothy Lenchak. Collegeville: Liturgical Press.

Tate, Marvin E.
- 1990   *Psalms 51–100*. Word Biblical Commentary 20. Dallas: Word Books.
- 2004   "Rethinking the Nature of Hebrew Poetry" and "Rethinking the Nature of the Psalter." In Peter C. Craigie's *Psalms 1–50*. 2d edition, with supplement. Nashville: Nelson.

Taylor, Vincent
- 1952   *The Gospel According to St. Mark*. London: Macmillan.

Taylor, William R.
- 1955   *The Book of Psalms*. In vol. 4 of *The Interpreter's Bible*. Nashville: Abingdon.

Thompson, Henry O.
- 1992   "Yahweh." *ABD* 6:1011-12.

Toombs, Lawrence E.
- 1962   "War, Ideas of." *IDB* 4:796-801.

Trible, Phyllis
- 1976   "God, Nature of, in the OT." *IBD* 5:368-69.

Vancil, Jack W.
- 1992   "Sheep, Shepherd." *ABD* 5:1187-90.

VanderKam, James C.
- 1992   "Weeks, Festival of." *ABD* 6:895-97.

Weiser, Artur
- 1962   *The Psalms*. Translated by Herbert Hartwell. Old Testament Library. Philadelphia: Westminster.

Wells, Jo Bailey
- 2000   *God's Holy People: A Theme in Biblical Theology*. JSOTSup 305. Sheffield: Sheffield Academic Press.

Werner, Eric
- 1962   "Music." *IDB* 3:457-76.

Westermann, Claus
- 1965   *The Praise of God in the Psalms*. Translated by Keith R. Crim. Richmond: John Knox.
- 1970   *The Old Testament and Jesus Christ*. Minneapolis: Augsburg.
- 1974   "The Role of Lament in the Theology of the Old Testament." *Interpretation* 20:38.
- 1980   *The Psalms: Structure, Content, and Message*. Translated by Ralph D. Gehrke. Minneapolis: Augsburg.
- 1981   *Praise and Lament in the Psalms*. Translated by Keith R. Crim and R. N. Soulen. Edinburgh: T&T Clark.
- 1989   *The Living Psalms*. Translated by J. R. Porter. Grand Rapids: Eerdmans.

White, Reginald E. O.
    1984   *A Christian Handbook to the Psalms.* Grand Rapids: Eerdmans.
Wieder, Laurance
    1995   *The Poets' Book of Psalms.* San Francisco: HarperSanFrancisco; Oxford: Oxford University Press, 1999.
Wilson, Gerald Henry
    1985   *Editing of the Hebrew Psalter.* Society of Biblical Literature Dissertation Series 76. Chico, CA: Scholars Press.
    1992   "The Shape of the Book of Psalms." *Interpretation* 46:129-142.
    2002   *Psalms.* Vol. 1. NIV Application Commentary. Grand Rapids: Zondervan.
Wood, Lawrence
    2004   "A Wandering Faith." *Christian Century* 121/15 (July 27, 2004): 21.
Wright, David P.
    1992   "Holiness." *ABD* 3:236-49.
Wyrtzen, Don
    1988   *A Musician Looks at the Psalms.* Grand Rapids: Daybreak Books, Zondervan.
Yoder, Sanford Calvin
    1948   *Poetry of the Old Testament.* Scottdale, PA: Herald Press. Reprint, 1952.
Zenger, Erich
    1996   *A God of Vengeance? Understanding the Psalms of Divine Wrath.* Translated by Linda M. Maloney. Louisville: Westminster John Knox Press.
Zijpp, N. van der
    1956   "Hymnology of the Mennonites in the Netherlands." *ME* 2:873-75.
    1959   "Psalms as Hymns." *ME* 4:226-27.

Selected Resources

Commentaries
*Recommended for pastors and Sunday school teachers
*Allen, Leslie C. *Psalms 101–150*. Word Biblical Commentary 21. Waco: Word Books, 1983; revised, 2002. One of the better scholarly commentaries, noting form, structure, and setting with constant reference to contemporary literature. Gives the author's translation as well as theological reflection.
Anderson, Arnold A. *Psalms 1–72* and *Psalms 73–150*. New Century Bible. Grand Rapids: Eerdmans, 1981. A technical collection of notes on the psalms. Valuable for the meaning and impact of important Hebrew words. Less helpful at getting a sense of the whole.
*Broyles, Craig C. *Psalms*. New International Biblical Commentary. Peabody, MA: Hendrickson, 1999. Based on the NIV, it presents section-by-section exposition with key terms and phrases highlighted. Draws on the latest scholarly work on Psalms. Giving attention to the context of worship, it explores the contemporary word of the psalms to believers and the church as a whole.
*Brueggemann, Walter. *The Message of the Psalms*. Augsburg Old Testament Studies. Minneapolis: Augsburg, 1984. Organized by a contemporary typology (orientation, disorientation, new orientation), this commentary on fifty-eight psalms is rich in literary and theological insights and the relevance of the psalms to our life and times.
Clifford, Richard J. *Psalms 1–72* and *Psalms 73–150*. Collegeville Bible Commentary. Collegeville: Liturgical Press, 1986. Brief comments identify the genre, themes, and movement in each psalm.
*———. *Psalms 1–72* and *Psalms 73–150*. Abingdon Old Testament Commentaries. Nashville: Abingdon, 2002-3. Concisely and clearly treats each psalm with literary, exegetical, theological, and ethical analysis. Views psalms in their biblical context and the context of the early Christian community. Seeks to make the psalms available as a book of prayer for contemporary believers.
*Craigie, Peter C. *Psalms 1–50*. Word Biblical Commentary 19. 2d ed., with supplement by Marvin E. Tate. Nashville: Nelson, 2004. One of the bet-

ter scholarly commentaries. Oriented to form criticism. Provides helpful elaboration of the meaning of each psalm against the background of the OT context. A helpful supplement on the nature of Hebrew poetry, recent developments in exegesis of the Psalter, and the nature of the Psalter.

Dahood, Mitchell. *Psalms I, 1–50*; *Psalms II, 51–100*; and *Psalms III, 101-150*. Anchor Bible. Garden City, NY: Doubleday, 1965-70. A technical commentary, drawing on the background of the Ugaritic (ancient Northwest Semitic) language. The original translation suggests many modifications of the MT. Though presenting significant insights, many of Dahood's proposals are controversial and no longer endorsed by Psalms scholars.

*Davidson, Robert. *The Vitality of Worship*. Grand Rapids: Eerdmans, 1998. Focuses on the place the psalms originally had in the worship of ancient Israel and highlights the continuing relevance of the psalms for worship today. Reflects sound exegetical work and offers many theological insights.

Gerstenberger, Erhard S. *Psalms, Part 1*. Vol. 1 of *Psalms and Lamentations*. Forms of the Old Testament Literature 14. Grand Rapids: Eerdmans, 1988. A form-critical commentary on Psalms 1–60, with an introduction to cultic poetry. Proposes that psalms be understood as rituals originally set in small primary groups, such as the family or the local synagogue.

*Kidner, Derek. *Psalms 1–72* and *Psalms 73–150*. Tyndale Old Testament Commentaries. Downers Grove, IL: InterVarsity Press, 1973-75. A brief commentary analyzing each psalm. Packed with helpful insights for the lay reader. Section outline headings provide helpful summaries of content.

Knight, George A. F. *Psalms*. 2 vols. Daily Study Bible. Philadelphia: Westminster, 1982-83. Aids laypeople by applying insights from the psalms for today.

Kraus, Hans-Joachim. *Psalms 1–59* and *Psalms 60–150*. Translated by Hilton C. Oswald from 5th German edition (1978). Minneapolis: Augsburg, 1988-89. One of the most thorough studies of the Psalms in recent years. Presents each psalm according to text and translation, literary form, rule in Israel's life and worship, principal words, and applications. Uses a form-critical approach. Offers many helpful theological insights.

*Limburg, James. *Psalms*. Louisville: Westminster John Knox Press, 2000. Written for lay readers. Comments are brief but based on solid scholarship. Includes helpful contemporary examples of application.

*Mays, James Luther. *Psalms*. Interpretation: A Bible Commentary for Teaching and Preaching. Louisville: John Knox, 1994. Draws on the disciplines of form, literary, and canonical criticism and offers many helpful theological insights. An excellent commentary for teachers and preachers.

*McCann, J. Clinton, Jr. "The Book of Psalms." *NIB* 4:639-1280. Nashville: Abingdon, 1996. Moves beyond form and literary criticism to focus on the canonical shape of the Psalter. Sees the psalms affirming God's reign as a present reality, even though many psalms came out of circumstances seeming to deny God's universal reign. Introduction contains helpful arti-

cles on the study of the psalms, genres, Hebrew poetry, composition, and theology of the Psalter.
Sabourin, Leopold. *The Psalms: Their Origin and Meaning.* New York: Alba House, 1974. Contains a sketchy treatment of each psalm. Arranges the psalms by their type or genre. Many references to contemporary literature. Most useful to one who knows Hebrew.
Stuhlmueller, Carroll. *Psalms 1* and *Psalms 2.* Old Testament Message 21-22. Wilmington: Michael Glazier, 1983. Written for laypeople. Examines each psalm for origin and later modification in Israel's worship, literary form and structure, key words and phrases, and impact of the psalm today in public worship, private devotion, and social-moral questions. Enables readers to pray the psalms more devoutly.
*Tate, Marvin E. *Psalms 51–100.* Word Biblical Commentary 20. Dallas: Word Books, 1990. A thorough commentary offering the author's translation, a survey of scholarly treatment, and helpful theological reflection. Gives attention to the shaping of the Psalter.
Weiser, Artur. *The Psalms.* Translated by Herbert Hartwell from 5th German ed. (1959). Old Testament Library. Philadelphia: Westminster, 1962. A widely used theological commentary. Comments are generally nontechnical and of an expository character. Draws illustrative insights from classical Lutheran sources and hymnody. Based on the theory of a covenant renewal festival, a theory not widely accepted today.
Westermann, Claus. *The Living Psalms.* Translated by J. R. Porter from *Ausgewalte Psalmen* (1984). Grand Rapids: Eerdmans, 1989. Organized according to form-critical categories. Offers commentary on forty-six psalms and concludes with examples of how the psalms are connected to the work of Christ.
*Wilson, Gerald Henry. *Psalms.* Vol. 1. NIV Application Commentary. Grand Rapids: Zondervan, 2002. Based on the NIV. Speaks to the original meaning and the biblical and theological context. Gives attention to the contemporary significance and application of each psalm. Takes into account canonical concerns that grow out of the shaping of the Psalter. Helpful introduction to the origin and historical use of the psalms, Hebrew poetry, and types of psalms.

Other Studies on the Psalms

Anderson, Bernhard W. *Out of the Depths: The Psalms Speak for Us Today.* Revised and expanded ed. Philadelphia: Westminster, 1983. 3d ed. with Steven Bishop. Louisville: Westminster John Knox, 2000. A popular study guide to the Psalms, organized on the basis of the major psalm types. Treats selected psalms. Helpful appendixes list the psalms by genre and list NT quotations of OT psalms.
Attridge, Harold W., and Margot E. Fassler, eds. *Psalms in Community: Jewish and Christian Textual, Liturgical, and Artistic Traditions.* Atlanta: Society of Biblical Literature, 2003. Twenty-five essays by scholars and leaders of local faith communities, from presentations at the January 2002 Yale University Conference "Up with a Shout: Psalmody in the Jewish and Christian Traditions." Gives attention to how the psalms have inspired music and art; tries to understand the explosion of psalmody taking place in American religious life today. Extensive bibliography.

Bellinger, W. H., Jr. *Psalms: Reading and Studying the Book of Psalms.* Peabody, MA: Hendrickson, 1990. Brief introduction aimed at preparing persons to engage in their own informed study of the psalms. Examples in each chapter illustrate the reading of different types of psalms.

Craven, Toni. *The Book of Psalms.* Collegeville: Liturgical Press, 1992. Focuses on topics related to spirituality in the psalms. Explores the questions Who is God? What does it mean to be faithful, individually and communally? A key chapter and two appendixes explore the names of God in the book of Psalms.

Davidson, Robert. *Wisdom and Worship.* Philadelphia: Trinity Press International, 1990. Focuses on the relationship between faith and doubt. Examines how Israel's worship integrated the insights of wisdom. Asks how the worshipping community today relates to what happens in the world around us.

Day, John. *Psalms.* Old Testament Guides. Sheffield: JSOT Press, 1990. A concise introduction identifying the major types of psalms. The final chapters focus on the theology of the psalms and the history of their interpretation by the Jewish community and in the Christian church. Includes annotated bibliographies assessing recent scholarship.

Gunkel, Hermann. *The Psalms: A Form-Critical Introduction.* Translated by Thomas M. Horner from *Die Religion in Geschichte und Gegenwart* (1930). Philadelphia: Fortress, 1967. Makes available in English the basis of Gunkel's classical work on psalm types.

Guthrie, Harvey H., Jr. *Theology as Thanksgiving.* New York: Seabury, 1981. Helpful on the relationship of psalms to liturgy. Proposes that the liturgical norm underlying the Bible is eucharistic.

Holladay, William Lee. *The Psalms Through Three Thousand Years: Prayerbook of a Cloud of Witnesses.* Minneapolis: Fortress, 1993. Offers an informative overview of the psalms and illustrates how they have functioned throughout history. Addresses contemporary theological issues in interpreting and using the psalms. Preachers and teachers will find illustrative material drawn from a wide range of sources.

Keel, Othmar. *The Symbolism of the Biblical World: Ancient Near Eastern Iconography and the Book of Psalms.* Translated by Timothy J. Hallett. New York: Seabury, 1978. Provides a visual commentary on the psalms arranged by theme and topic. The text and illustrations illuminate the psalms' imagery from ancient Near Eastern iconography, with an index to track illustrations pertaining to any particular psalm.

Kraus, Hans-Joachim. *Theology of the Psalms.* Translated by Keith Crim. Minneapolis: Augsburg, 1986. Kraus analyzes the central themes of the psalms in their ancient setting—God, people, Zion, the king, the enemies, and the individual. Concludes with a chapter on "The Psalms in the New Testament."

Lewis, C. S. *Reflections on the Psalms.* London: Collins, 1961. Informed reflections that came to Lewis while reading the Psalms. He relates them to the ancient Judaic religion that produced them, to the age of Christ when they took on new meanings, and to daily experiences in the modern world.

Longman, Tremper, III. *How to Read the Psalms.* Downers Grove, IL: InterVarsity, 1988. Concise, clear. Provides a helpful guidebook into the psalms, their use in Hebrew worship, and their relationship to the rest of the OT. Suggests how Christians can appropriate their message and insights today, interpreting the psalms on their own.

Mays, James Luther. *The Lord Reigns: A Theological Handbook to the Psalms.* Louisville: Westminster John Knox Press, 1994. Offers essays exploring theological issues involved in the ongoing use of the psalms as both Scripture and liturgy. Serves as a helpful companion to this author's commentary *Psalms.*

McCann, J. Clinton. *A Theological Introduction to the Book of Psalms: The Psalms as Torah.* Nashville: Abingdon, 1993. Interprets the psalms in the context of their final shape and canonical form. Focuses on hearing the psalms in the contemporary context as Scripture, giving instruction about God, humanity, and the faithful life. An appendix deals with singing the psalms and offers help for using psalms in worship.

Miller, Patrick D., Jr. *Interpreting the Psalms.* Philadelphia: Fortress, 1986. An excellent handbook on interpreting the psalms. Introductory essays on contemporary issues in interpretation are followed by expository essays on ten psalms.

Peterson, Eugene H. *Answering God: The Psalms as Tools for Prayer.* San Francisco: Harper & Row, 1989. Drawing on twenty-five years of pastoral experience in teaching others to pray, Peterson writes about how the psalms train people of faith in speech that answers God. An excellent guide to the use of the psalms in contemporary prayer.

Pleins, J. David. *The Psalms: Songs of Tragedy, Hope, and Justice.* Maryknoll, NY: Orbis Books, 1993. Hears the psalms as "poetry of justice." The final section addresses the history of salvation, wisdom instruction, and prophetic admonition.

Reardon, Patrick Henry. *Christ in the Psalms.* Ben Lomand, CA: Conciliar Press, 2000. Meditations written by a parish priest within the Orthodox Church. Offers a Christian look at each psalm and draws on the rich history of the church's use of the psalms through the centuries.

Reid, Stephen Breck. *Listening In: A Multicultural Reading of the Psalms.* Nashville: Abingdon, 1997. Uses recent scholarship on the Psalms and combines it with an imaginative reading of African-American, Latino, Asian-American, and other nondominant cultural materials. Provides a compelling glimpse of the promise in a multicultural reading of the psalms.

―――, ed. *Psalms and Practice: Worship, Virtue, and Authority.* Collegeville: Liturgical Press, 2001. Fifteen essays from a three-day conference of Protestant and Roman Catholic pastors and biblical scholars, focusing on the psalms and their use in worshipping congregations. The essays suggest ways to locate the psalms in prayer, liturgy, preaching, and in living the Christian life.

Rienstra, Marchiene Vroon. *Swallow's Nest: A Feminine Reading of the Psalms.* Grand Rapids: Eerdmans, 1992. An invitation to pray the psalms, arranged in a four-week cycle, with different themes for each day of the week. Includes prayers and meditations from women of Christian antiquity and other classic hymns and prayers.

Seybold, Klaus. *Introducing the Psalms.* Translated by R. Graeme Dunphy. Edinburgh: T&T Clark, 1990. A good general introduction to the Psalms: historical background, literary form, classification, and parallels in other ancient literature. The final chapters deal with how the psalms have been interpreted and used in worship over the last two thousand years.

Stuhlmueller, Carroll. *The Spirituality of the Psalms*. Edited by Carol J. Dempsey and Timothy Lenchak. Collegeville: Liturgical Press, 2002. Published posthumously; the author was professor of Old Testament at the Catholic Union in Chicago. Through the use of contemporary biblical scholarship, Stuhlmueller describes how readers might apply the psalms to their spiritual lives.

Westermann, Claus. *The Psalms: Structure, Content, and Message*. Translated by Ralph D. Gehrke. Minneapolis: Augsburg, 1980. An excellent brief introduction to the psalms in terms of their basic types.

———. *Praise and Lament in the Psalms*. Translated by Keith R. Crim and Richard N. Soulen. Atlanta: John Knox, 1981. Investigates these two major types of psalms and their meaning for prayer and worship. Demonstrates how the psalms move from supplication to praise.

Wieder, Laurance, ed. *The Poets' Book of Psalms*. San Francisco: Harper San Francisco, 1995; Oxford: Oxford University Press, 1999. Compiles poetic renditions of all 150 psalms from poets of the last five centuries. A shorter collection of poems based on psalms appears in *Chapters into Verse: Poetry in English Inspired by the Bible*, vol. 1, *Genesis to Malachi*, edited by Robert Atwan and Laurance Wieder (Oxford: Oxford University Press, 1993), 290-338.

Wyrtzen, Don. *A Musician Looks at the Psalms*. Grand Rapids: Zondervan, 1988. Composer-musician Don Wyrtzen has compiled a book of personal devotions for the year based on the book of Psalms. Throughout, he has tied in musical analogies.

Zenger, Erich. *A God of Vengeance? Understanding the Psalms of Divine Wrath*. Translated by Linda M. Maloney. Louisville: Westminster John Knox, 1996. Contends that the psalms crying out against violence and injustice in the world have great relevance to people of faith today. Helpful suggestions on how to incorporate these psalms of enmity and lament into the worship of the church.

Index of Ancient Sources

OLD TESTAMENT
Genesis
1 . . . . . 63, 502, 648
1–3. . . . . 63, 443
1–11. 444
1:1 . . . . . . 259, 503
1:1-31 . . . . . 63, 454
1:2 505
1:6-8. 705
1:6-10. 175
1:7-8. 503
1:9-10. 503
1:9-11. 701
1:11-12. 504
1:26 63
1:26-28 . . . 135, 401
1:31 502
2–3. 190
2:1-3. 63
2:1-4. 454
2:7 663
2:8 190
2:10-14. 235
2:24 232
3 . . . . 444, 445, 770
3:1-7. 64
3:11-13. 200
3:17-19. 616
3:19 . . . . . . 443, 696
3:22 117
3:22-24. 63
4. 444
4:7 260
4:10 68
4:12-14. 200
4:15 389
4:17 276
5:24 248
6:1-8. 444
6:5-7. 63
7:17-24. 503
8:1-5. 503
8:21 . . . . . . 258, 681,
770
9:5 68
9:14 701
9:20-27. 444
10:2 591
10:6 510
11:1-9. 444
11:9 274
12. 508
12:1-3 326,
351, 567
12:14-17. 510
13. 636
14:18-19. 538
14:18-24. 536
15:1 280
15:6 172
15:18 508
16 . . . . . . 404, 551
16:7 180
18:14 544
18:16-33. 276
18:19 671
18:25. 73,
359, 757
19:1-29. 276
19:17 73
19:24 73
20:4-7. 144
20:7 510
22:1 321
22:18-19. 351
24. 564
24:7 448
25:30 404
26:26-28. 326
27. 436
27:1-41. 144
27:28 637
27:41-46. 636
28:11-19. 774
28:20-22 300,
321
30:27 326
32:3-32. 636
32:22-32. 774
32:24-30. 113
33:1-16. 636
35:9-15. 113
36:6-8. 636
36:9 404
37 . . . . 510, 636
37:20-28. 207
37:25-28. 404
37:34 162
39–50. 510

39:1-12. 144
39:3-5. 326
39:9 770
39:20-23. 678
39:21-23. 326
40. 678
41:1-14. 678
41:42 162
48:15 128
48:20 326
49:1-33. 204
49:8 118
49:24 . . . . 128, 633
50:20 493
50:21 149
50:22-23. 519
50:24 509

Exodus
1:11-14. 622
2:13 308
2:23-24 . . . . 56, 406
2:23-25 . . . . 77, 287,
  290, 300, 352,
  535, 558, 605
2:24 509
3:2 . . . . 180, 473
3:2-5. 774
3:6-17. 760
3:8 526
3:13-15 . . . . 62, 369
3:13-16. 279
3:14 760
3:15 . . . . . . 113, 642
3:16 526
3:18 526
3:20 420
4:15-17. 280
4:16 286
4:23 516
4:24 783
5:22 125
6:1-8. 113
6:2-8. 760
6:3 447
6:3-5. 509
6:6 478
6:6-7. 397
6:12 516
6:18-21. 758
7–11. 510
7–12. 383
9:27 771
10:2-3. 397
11–14. 331
11:31-35. 516
12:12 347
12:21 526
12:26-27. 382
13:18 554
13:21-22. 473
14–15. 777
14–16. 696
14:10-12. 516
14:15-18. 482
14:21 554
14:21-22 . . 320, 516
14:29 . . . . 364, 105,
  452, 456,
  711, 777
15:1-18 . . . 185, 243,
  332, 482,
  516, 573, 605
15:1-19 . . . 320, 373
15:2 . . . . . . 570, 572
15:11. 187,
  346-47, 372,
  382, 420, 435,
  464, 544, 551
15:12 570
15:13 . . . . 126, 128,
  383, 421, 483
15:16 478
15:17 128
15:17-18. 388
15:18 . . . . . 448, 697
15:20. 162,
  425, 711
15:20-21. 715
15:21 373
15:22-25. 292
15:22-27. 308
15:3 . . . . . . 134, 777
15:6 . . . . . . 477, 570
16. 383
16:1-3. 292
16:3 524
17:1-4. 292
17:1-6. 308
17:1-7. 465
17:1-7. 517
17:3 524
17:6 555
18:10 166
18:10-12. 326
18:11 . . . . . 642, 644
19:1-8. 255
19:2-9. 774
19:4-5. 767
19:5 . . . . . 139, 642,
  643, 645
19:5-6. 755
19:6 . . . . . 123, 181,
  483, 511, 754
19:16 774
19:16-18. 252
19:16-25. 774
19:18 . . . . . 473, 555
19:19 774
19:21 783
19:23 483
20. 714
20:2 509
20:2-3. 465
20:2-4. 397
20:2-6. 271
20:3 . . . 93, 133, 229
20:5 . . . . . . 388, 620
20:7 . . . 78, 133, 272
20:16 . . . . . . 52, 78
21:30 249
22:21 512
22:21-22. 697
22:21-24 . . . 77, 214
22:25 89
22:27 625
22:31 483
23:1-3. 287
23:2-3. 757
23:4 750
23:4-5. 751
23:6 671
23:6-8 142,
  287, 757
23:9-11. 671
23:14-17 396,
  597
23:16 314
23:16-17. 774
23:20 448
23:32-33. 518
25:10-22. 633
24:15-18. 774

Index of Ancient Sources

25:18-20 103	16:21 170	12:5 483
26:33 483	16:30 261	13:25-29 517
28:41 . . . . . . 36, 745	18:21 518	14:4 517
29:38-42 673	19:2 89,	14:18 . . . . . 419, 420,
29:39-40 454	483, 754	499, 692
31:18 577	19:15 757	15:1-10 . . . . 271, 564
32–34 . . . . . 414, 444	19:18 390,	15:14-16 512
32:1 292	484, 754	15:34 676
32:1-35 517	19:33 512	16 516
32:11-13 517	19:33-34 214	16:1-35 219
32:30-35 482	19:34 . . . . . 484, 754	16:3-35 275
32:31-32 517	19:9-10 754	16:30 769
32:32 425	20:2-11 308	16:41-50 482
32:32-33 664	20:26 754	18:20 . . . . . 580, 678
33:7 221	22:18-30 271	19:11-16 388
33:9 483	22:29-30 525	20:1-13 517
33:11 221	23:34-36 324,	20:8-13 465
33:13 221	396	20:11 . . . . . 364, 555
33:20 73	23:39-43 396	20:13 397
33:23 221	23:40 571	21:1-3 321
34:6 . . . . . . 377, 420,	24:12 676	21:21-35 . . . 644, 648
421, 499,	25 . . . . 93, 135	22:22 180
563, 566	25:23 204	23:11 533
34:6-7 . . . . 419, 434,	25:35-37 89	25 517
483, 489, 500,	26:4-6 326	25:7-8 520
625, 659, 690,	26:9 139	25:9 517
692, 771, 783	26:9-11 219	25:11-13 517
34:6-9 260	26:12-13 139	26:55-56 608
34:10 . . . . . 316, 420	26:14-39 339	29:12-38 396
34:11-17 518	26:17 200	31:8 709
34:22 314	26:18 389	32:11 509
34:29-35 73	26:21 . . . . . 200, 389	35:9-15 300
	26:24 200	
Leviticus	26:33 517	**Deuteronomy**
2:1-2 673	26:40-42 200	. . . . 101, 576
2:1-10 197	27:32 129	1:8 508-9
5:12 341	29:12-38 324	1:16 508
6:14-15 673		1:26-36 783
7:11-15 . . . . 525, 564	**Numbers**	1:31 629
7:11-18 271	3:3 410	1:41 771
7:11-20 487	6:1-21 344	2:5 299
7:12-13 630	6:22-26 640,	2:9 . . . . 299, 404
8:12 637	325, 392,	2:19 299
9:22 640	571, 594	2:26-37 644
11:44-45 754	6:25 47	3:1-11 644
13:1-8 429	10:35 . . . . . 328, 401	4:1 511
13:2-17 204	11 383	4:1-8 702
13:45-46 429	11:4-6 516	4:2 577
14 197	11:11-15 630	4:9 516
16:1-34 421	11:33-34 383	4:11 473
16:12-13 673	12:3 113	4:11-12 252

4:12 148	10:12 . . . . . 166, 486	25:5-10 636
4:19 . . . . . . 409, 504	10:17 647	25:9 616
4:21-24 462	10:17-18 287	25:19 465
4:24 388	10:17-19 671	26:1-11 224
4:27 . . . . . . 244, 517	10:18 70	26:5-9 508
4:29 576	10:19 204	26:5-10 . . . . 325, 421
4:31 508	10:21 531	26:9 526
4:35 486	10:21-22 316	26:12-13 70
4:39 486	11:2 463	26:17-18 511
4:40 . . . . . . 463, 511	11:11-12 326	26:17-19 643
4:44 577	11:11-14 308	26:19 484
5:3 463	11:13-17 315	27–28 682
5:7 93	11:13-21 595	27:11-26 144
6:3 508	11:17 . . . . . 326, 414	27:15-26 339
6:4 486	12:5 508	28 225
6:4-7 385	12:9-10 465	28:6 595
6:4-9 140,	12:11 370	28:15-68 339
395, 595	12:17-19 123	28:20-22 200
6:5 . . . . . . 164, 166	12:31 518	28:26 388
6:6 463	13:2 783	28:45-46 346
6:6-9 . . . . . 208, 382	13:6 783	28:49 299
6:10 276	13:13 783	28:58-59 385
6:10-11 . . . . 308, 512	14:2 . . . . . . 484, 643	28:60 200
6:13 486	14:28-29 214	29:18-28 782
6:16 449	15:4 214	30:15-20 . . . 193, 712
6:17 577	16:8-9 314	31:7-8 148
6:20 577	16:13 396	31:9-13 . . . . . 455, 576
7:1-6 711	16:13-15 . . . 314, 324	31:26 577
7:2 518	16:16 . . . . . 589, 593	32–33 443
7:6 . . . . . . 642, 645	16:16-17 . . . 597, 774	32:1 252
7:6-7 643	16:18-20 287	32:2 308
7:7 508	17:2-7 144	32:3 508
7:9 508	17:3 504	32:4 165
7:11 463	17:8-9 577	32:4-5 381
7:16 518	17:8-11 96	32:5-6 382
7:18 508	17:8-13 757	32:6 486
8:1 508	17:16 113	32:7 381
8:2-3 321	17:18-20 577	32:8-9 702
8:3 703	18:7 640	32:9 508
8:5 54	18:9-10 518	32:10-11 97
8:7 308	19:21 43	32:11 . . . . . . 153, 448
8:11-20 291	20:2-4 777	32:12 . . . . . . 397, 443
8:15 308	20:10-18 . . . 711, 778	32:15 486
8:15-16 648	20:1 653	32:18 . . . . . 165, 630
8:16 321	20:16-18 518	32:23 198
9:3 463	21:5 640	32:31 165
9:8-21 517	21:6-7 143	32:35 . . . . . . 43, 154,
9:25-29 517	23:14 777	288, 312, 339,
10:8 640	23:20 89	390, 460, 462,
10:8-9 93	24:17-21 512	655, 664, 712,
10:9 . . . . . . 580, 678	24:19-22 . . . 214, 697	756, 776-77

Index of Ancient Sources

32:36 ..... 381, 642
32:39 346
32:40 687
32:41 460
32:43 ..... 460, 777
32:51-52 517
33 777
33:1-5 711
33:2 ...... 252, 392
33:2-4 774
33:2-5 775
33:26 ..... 187, 316
33:26-29 ...... 711, 774, 775
33:28 637
33:29 779
34:23 598

Joshua
.... 225
1:6-9 148
1:8 31
1:11-15 299
1:13 465
3:11 364
3:14-17 320
3:16 554
4:19-24 320
6 701
6-7 778
6:1-21 373
6:21 653
7:1 783
7:7-9 125
8:31-35 577
10:24 ..... 118, 537
10:24-27 709
13:14 580
13:14-33 93
18:1 384
18:2-7 93
18:6 608
21:44 465
23:1 ...... 465, 750
23:14-16 512
24:2-13 508
24:6-13 224
24:11 750
24:17 486

Judges
.... 225
1:6-7 709
1:21-36 518
2:1-5 518
2:12-23 383
3:3 331
3:7-9 648
3:14 622
4-5 405
4:2-3 622
4:15-16 373
5 .... 105, 456, 777
5:1-5 774
5:4-5 ..... 103, 473
5:5 555
5:12-18 777
5:23 777
5:28-30 330
6-7 648
6-8 405
6:6 622
7:2-25 113
7:19-22 373
7:25 405
8:1-32 648
8:21 405
9:33 118
9:48 330
10:9 622
11:30-31 ... 301, 321
11:34 711
11:34-35 301
12:3 583
13:22 783
14-16 776
16:23 750

Ruth
1:16-17 232
2:4 622
3-4 636
4:8-9 296
4:11 616

1 Samuel
.... 225, 745
1 551
1:11 ...... 301, 321
1:15 304

1:17 773
1:21 301
2:1-10 ..... 630, 696
2:2 .... 483, 754
2:5 551
2:8 .... 369, 551
2:12-17 85
2:35 616
3:1 364
3:3-14 483
3:17 591
3:21 384
4-6 633
4:3-4 409
4:3-5 633
4:4 481
5-6 633
6:18 276
7:1-2 633
7:5 616
7:6 771
7:8-9 482
7:9 112
7:10 243
7:11 616
7:14 47
8:4-18 483
10:1 777
10:7 118
11:2 622
12:15 483
12:19-25 482
12:25 483
13:9-12 112
13:14 779
14:45 249
15:2-3 783
15:22 208
16:1-35 758
16:6 745
16:12 229
16:16 ..... 715, 773
16:16-23 773
16:19 ..... 126, 276
16:23 773
17:45 ..... 113, 409
17:47 ..... 224, 777
18:6 162
18:7 447
18:25-27 570
18:29 750

19:11-17 289	7:5-16 631	1:49-53 345
20:1 770	7:6 89	1:50 102
20:8 770	7:8 276	2:19 537
21:2 179	7:13-16 490	2:23 591
21:7-23 . . . . 263, 265	7:14 . . . . 37, 39,	3–4 354
21:10-15 . . . 179, 278	436, 538	3–10 615
22:1 268	7:14-17 745	3:4 538
22:1-2 677-78	7:16 435	3:5-14 616
22:1-23 . . . . 263, 265	7:22 435	3:13 347
23 . . . . 96, 268	7:26-29 616	3:14 117
23:14-15 307	8:3-8 294	3:16-28 350
23:19-29 . . . 269, 282	8:11-12 296	4:20-28 . . . . 353, 777
24:1 307	8:13-14 294	4:31 . . . . . . 428, 434
24:1-7 . . . . 282, 677,	8:15 . . . . . . 350, 598	6:29 453
678	9–20 105	7:2 453
24:6 . . . . 36, 436	10:6-19 777	7:7 453
24:10 36	11–12 491	8 . . . . 160, 632
24:11 117	11 256	8:1-11 331
24:17-19 751	11:1 777	8:10-11 415
24–26 57	11:14-25 777	8:14 538
25 . . . . 85, 268,	11:27 258	8:16 631
609	12 256	8:22 152
25:22 591	12:13 . . . . . 256, 770	8:22-53 118
25:26 390	12:13-16 259	8:31-32 142
26 268	12:25 615	8:31-34 . . . . . 57, 345
26:1-5 269	15:6 41	8:33-36 314
26:9-11 758	15:7-8 321	8:47 516
26:23-24 117	15:10 . . . . . 240, 478	8:55-56 538
28:18 783	15:13 41	8:59 677
	15:30-31 211	8:62-63 538
2 Samuel	15–18 668	9:11 453
. . . . 105, 225,	15–19 41	9:15 538
745, 758	16:15-23 273	9:25 396
2–5 777	21:17 634	9:26-28 526
3:9 591	22 . . . . . . 101-2, 105	9:28 230
5:6-9 384	22:2-3 686	10:2 351
5:6-10 783	22:11-13 481	10:10 351
6 631-33	23:1 773	10:11 230
6:1-15 633	23:1-2 397	10:26-29 . . . 113, 777
6:2 481	23:1-7 351	11–12 350
6:5 . . . . 425, 715	23:5 634	11:1 228
6:6-15 633		11:1-40 777
6:12-19 132,	**1 Kings**	11:28 353
239, 538	 225	11:36 634
6:14-15 711	1–2 105	11:38 616
6:15 239	1–12 349	12:4 354
6:16 425	1:23 464	15:4 634
6:21 425	1:34 478	16:2 551
7 . . . . 38, 354	1:38 539	16:31 228
7:2 . . . . 331, 632	1:39 478	17:18 770
7:4-17 . . . . . 105, 433	1:39-40 239	18:27 559

Index of Ancient Sources

18:27-28 595
18:39 486
19 125
19:1-18 . . . . 276, 678
19:10 77
19:16 . . . . . . 36, 510
21:1-14 462
21:19 331
22:19-23 400
22:38 331
22:39 . . . . . 228, 230
22:49 526

2 Kings
. . . . 225
2:9-11 248
6:20-23 655
7:6-7 267
8:12 653
8:18 228
8:26 228
9:13 240
9:26 98
9:36 331
10:14 526
11:12 240
14:23 228
15:29 223
15:29-30 225
16:3-4 518
16:12-15 538
17 225
17:34-40 778
18 381
18–20 102
18:13-37 371
18:33-35 559
18:35-37 233
19:1-37 371
19:14-19 118
19:22 483
19:32-35 372
19:32-36 . . . 373, 701
19:32-37 242
19:35 447
19:35-36 . . . 235, 267
20:1-21 205
21:16 518
22–23 381
22:8-20 32
23:1-3 32
23:3 488
23:5 594
23:29-30 433
24:2 653
24:8-15 437
24:8-17 433
25:8-12 653
25:8-21 387
25:9 362

1 Chronicles
. . . . 515, 692
6 758
6:31-32 . . . . 357, 746
6:33 428
6:39 . . . . . . 357, 746
9:1 . . . . . 219, 758-59
9:31 . . . . . . 219, 758
9:33 640
15–16 758
15:16 715
15:16-19 . . . 357, 746
15:17 . . . . . 434, 758
15:19 . . . . . 434, 715,
758
15:20 234
15:21 . . . . . . 53, 773
16:4-7 . . . . . 357, 746
16:5 758
16:7 . . . . . . 747, 758,
759
16:7-43 773
16:8-22 508
16:23-33 467
16:34 . . . . . 524, 647
16:34-36 514
16:41-42 302,
377, 428
16:42 203
23:30 640
25 758
25:1 . . . . . 203, 377,
758
25:1-2 . . . . 252, 357,
746, 758,
773
25:1-8 758
25:3 377
25:6 377
28:2 . . . . . . 481, 633
28:5 537

29:3 643
29:15 204
29:23 537

2 Chronicles
. . . . 515, 692
5–7 160
5:11-12 377
5:12 . . . . . . 357, 773
5:13 647
6 632
6:13 640
6:41-42 633
7 758
7:1-3 647
7:1-6 647
7:6 747
7:14 . . . . 98, 147
15:8-15 255
20:1-19 114
20:1-23 224
20:1-30 403
20:19 . . . . . 218, 747,
758-59
20:21 . . . . . 647, 649
21:7 634
24:27 543
26:20-21 429
28:8-15 655
28:17 653
29:11 640
29:30 . . . . . 252, 746
35:14-19 758
36:15-16 783
36:23 649

Ezra
. . . . 107, 576
1:1-4 413
1:2 649
2:1 589
2:41 759
2:65 759
3:7-13 160
3:8-9 773
3:10-11 759
3:11 . . . . . . 570, 647
4:1-5 608
4:4-5 336
4:23-24 336
5:2-3 336

6:22 405	2:10 55	15:15-16 681
7:1-10 747	3:8 .... 236, 504	16:12-13 198
7:1-26 587	4:7-9 212	16:22 430
7:6 775	4:8 613	17:12-13 665
7:7-9 589	4:17 258	17:16 769
8:8 775	4:17-21 .... 681, 770	19:13-15 337
8:15-20 747	5:10 .... 308, 701	19:13-22 429
9 .... 171, 771	5:11 551	19:23-24 494
9:5 673	5:11-16 ... 370, 526,	19:25 113
10:3 687	698, 702	19:25-26 .... 94, 769
10:8 526	5:17 461	20:12-16 400
10:19 687	5:27 662	21:26 769
	6:4 198	22:15-22 182
Nehemiah	7:6-10 246	23:8-9 378
.... 403	7:7 686	25:4 ...... 258, 681,
1:4-5 649	7:9 .... 430, 769	770
1:9 700	7:11-21 62	25:6 .... 63, 122
2:10 608	7:16 492	26:6 663
2:17 260	7:17 686	26:12 243
2:17-19 600	7:17-18 .... 63, 203,	26:12-13 236
2:19 608	661	27:5 .... 144, 378
4:1-8 600	7:19 204	28:3 662
4:10-23 709	7:21 430	28:6 144
5 193	8:5 677	28:16 230
5:1-5 608	9:2 681	28:27 662
5:1-19 214	9:6 369	28:28 ..... 194, 544
7:73 587	9:8 243	29:3 575
8:1 775	9:11 378	29:7-29 757
8:1-18 587	9:25-26 246	29:22 538
8:9 747	10:8-11 665	30:9-23 ..... 81, 429
9 ..... 166, 171, 771	10:8-12 663	31:6 144
9:2 686	10:20 204	31:29 751
9:8 767	10:20-22 .... 54, 769	31:34 601
11:22-24 746	10:21 430	33:6 663
12:27-43 ... 570, 699	10:21-22 280	33:14-30 200
	11:20 677	33:23-25 249
Esther	12:10 505	36:5-23 493
.... 692	12:17-25 370,	36:27-31 701
	526, 698,	37:15 252
Job	702	38 .... 503, 707
...... 54, 55, 192,	12:21 526	38:1 774
197, 200, 202,	12:24 526	38:4 648
454, 548, 576,	13:4 469	38:4-6 369
766	13:4-7 462	38:8-11 456
1:6-7 531	13:9 661-62	38:8-12 243
1:6-12 400	14:1-2 246	38:25 316
1:22 55	14:4 ...... 681, 770	38:28 538
2:1-2 531	14:6 204	38:29-30 700
2:1-6 400	14:10-12 246	38:39-41 700
2:3 144	14:18-21 430	38:41 701
2:9 144	15:14-16 770	39:19-25 701

41:1 236	10:24-25 192	26:27 283
42:1-6 .... 195, 200, 359	10:29-31 181	28:13 170
	10:30 548	30:15-31 304
42:3 629	10:31-32 77	31:5 287
	11:3 144	31:8-9 214
Proverbs	11:4-11 616	
.... 153, 576, 665, 766	11:5 153	**Ecclesiastes**
	11:19 195	.... 202, 444, 766
1:2-3 253	11:20 489	
1:4 578	11:21 195	1:2 204
1:7 .... 181, 248, 253, 544	11:28 195	2:8 643
	11:30-31 181	3:16-21 246
1:8 578	12:21 357	3:20 663
1:10 578	12:28 94	5:12 617
1:12 604	13:3 673	5:13-17 246
1:15 578	13:9 347	9:10 118
1:18-19 283	13:18 347	10:11 286
2:1 578	13:19 194	10:18 283
2:19 94	13:20 85	11:5 663
2:21 609	14:1 615	12:7 168
3:1 .... 381, 578	14:32 144	
3:5 .... 381, 560	15:5 253	**Isaiah**
3:10 347	15:11 663	 576
3:11-12 .... 461, 571	15:16-17 194	1:2 252
3:12 54	15:24 94	1:4 .... 481, 483
3:16 347	15:26-32 674	1:10-17 .... 214, 254
3:19 648	15:32-33 253	1:11-17 208
3:34-35 411	16:1 616	1:12-17 ..... 90, 352
3:35 85	16:5 629	1:13 673
4:1-9 182	16:9 616	1:15-17 762
4:11 97	16:18 291	1:15-26 518
4:18-19 181	16:20 207	1:16-17 469
4:26 97	17:20 591	1:17 .... 70, 459, 762
5:6 94	17:23 287	
5:21 97	18:17 662	1:18 258
6:4 633	18:21 266	1:21-26 214
6:12-15 189	19:21 616	1:23 459
6:16 304	20:7 144	1:25 77
6:16-19 77	20:26 490	2 783
6:31 389	21:6 304	2:1-4 236
7:2 97	22:1 578	2:2-11 778
8:24-31 504	22:4 ...... 347, 578	2:2-3 ...... 243, 784
8:27-29 705	22:8 613	2:2-4 ..... 240, 352, 425-26, 494, 598, 784
9:1 615	22:22-23 671	
9:1-11 182	23:17-18 193	
10:1 85	24:1 193	2:2-5 756
10:9 489	24:3 615	2:4 .... 241, 374
10:11 181	24:19-20 193	2:5 575
10:16 195	25:2 662	2:6-22 629
10:17 94	25:21-22 ... 751, 756	3:10 357
10:22 195	26:3 171	3:13-15 77

4:3 425	17:12-13 457	37:33-38 233
5:1-7 214	17:13-14 ... 405, 784	38:10 769
5:13-16 757	18:4-6 374	38:10-20 161
5:14 769	19:23-25 352	38:18 429
5:16 ...... 482, 754, 768	19:25 423	38:18-19 769
	21:16-17 591	40:1-5 326
5:19 481	22:15-19 263	40:1-11 414
5:20-30 778	23 406	40:2 ...... 172, 413, 414
5:23 287	24:1-6 401	
5:24 481	24:18-20 401	40:3-5 566
5:26 299	25:4 300	40:5 ...... 472, 477
5:29 199	25:6 191	40:6-7 622
6:1-2 156	25:10 258	40:6-8 ..... 444, 498
6:1-4 473	26:4 560	40:8 ...... 576, 582
6:1-5 307	26:19 ...... 94, 769	40:9 ...... 280, 468, 784
6:1-13 400	27:1 ...... 236, 457	
6:3 ..... 481-82, 754	28:16 572	40:10 ..... 244, 478
6:5 .... 258, 770	29:5-6 118	40:11 ..... 128, 153, 394
6:8 208	29:6 252	
6:11 390	29:13 ..... 762, 770	40:12-14 629
6:11-13 777	29:15 311	40:15 304
7:1-17 117	30:3 612	40:18-19 469
7:14 ..... 234, 236	30:7 425	40:18-20 559
8:5-8 234	30:8 577	40:18-25 420
8:6-10 235	30:15 236	40:18-26 467
8:7 457	30:15-17 113	40:25 754
8:8 236	30:18 ..... 601, 612, 757	40:26 700
8:14-15 572		40:26-29 697
9:1-7 ...... 21, 746	30:23 308	40:28-31 134
9:5 .... 241, 374	30:27-33 378	40:29 701
9:5-6 778	31:1-3 ..... 113, 177	40:31 499
9:6 114	31:4 31	40–55 414
10:1-2 70	31:23 612	40–66 ..... 319, 481, 498, 658
10:1-4 ..... 214, 254	32:6 86	
10:11 559	32:9-14 601	41:10 ..... 149, 280
10:22 757	33:2 51	41:13 ..... 149, 280
10:5-19 783	33:7-12 76	41:14 ..... 762, 776
10:8-9 559	33:11 258	41:17-18 410
11:1-9 .... 130, 353, 746, 756	33:13-16 90	41:18 526
	33:15 ..... 478, 762	41:23-24 467
11:1-10 21	33:21 ..... 235, 316	42:6 757
11:4 490	34 653	42:6-7 635
12:3 ...... 308, 425	34:2 783	42:7 676
12:3-4 509	35:4 ...... 280, 460	42:10 ..... 468, 472, 710
13:12 230	35:4-6 ..... 697, 776	
14:31-32 234	35:7 308	42:10-12 207
14:32 ..... 424, 608	36–37 371	42:11 591
15:16 258	36–39 102	42:13 ..... 243, 472
16:2 73	37:16-17 697	42:17 472
16:5 598	37:23-36 113	42:24 757
16:9 258	37:33-37 242	42:25 149

Index of Ancient Sources

43:1 . . . . 81, 486, 762, 776	51:9-11 364	59:16-17 712
43:1-2 . . . . . 280, 605	51:10 625	59:17 669
43:1-3 129	51:17 . . . . . . 73, 295	60:1 . . . . . . 411, 472
43:3 249	51:22 295	60:1-3 . . . . 240, 322, 469, 475
43:5 149	51:23 . . . . . 537, 622	60:1-4 467
43:5-6 524	52:7 . . . . . . 468, 702	60:2 415
43:6 299	52:7-10 . . . . 240, 479, 711	60:3 326
43:14 776	52:10 . . . . 244, 478, 612	60:3-7 . . . . . 230, 494
43:19 468	53 . . . . 431, 493	60:10 686
43:21 486	53:1 477-78	60:14 784
44:2 . . . . . . 486, 762	53:1-12 225-26	60:21 658
44:6 776	53:1-9 177	61:1-2 70
44:6-8 467	53:4 113	61:1-3 519
44:9-20 . . . . 559, 644	53:4-6 260	61:3 . . . . . . 229, 551
44:23 469	53:6 . . . . . 464, 586	61:5 686
44:28 130	53:10 448	61:8 . . . . 73, 177, 482, 757
45:1 130	54:1 424	62:1-2 757
45:8 416	54:1-5 551	62:1-5 231
45:13 415	54:10 81	62:1-12 424
45:16 472	55:1 397	62:2 415
45:20-25 . . . 326, 469	55:1-2 308	62:8 686
45:22 . . . . . . 322, 425	55:3 . . . . . . 634, 686	62:10-12 524
45:22-23 420	55:3-5 105	62:12 484
46:3 102	55:6 512	63:1-3 185
46:3-4 629	55:6-7 172	63:1-6 . . . . . 103, 378
46:9 551	55:8-9 663	63:3-6 287
46:13 757	55:10-11 703	63:4 . . . . . . 462, 756, 776
47 653	55:11 525	63:5 478
47:3 460	55:12 469	63:6 296
48:5 664	56:1 477	63:7-19 . . . . 387, 519
48:13 133	56:1-7 322	63:9 153
49:1-6 125	56:3 686	63:10 778
49:6 . . . . . . 322, 426, 635, 702	56:6-8 . . . . . 240, 467	63:11 130
49:8-9 697	56:8 700	63:14 244
49:8-12 696	57:13 607	64:1-12 . . . . 387, 519
49:9-13 128	57:15 . . . . 552, 658, 754	64:8 . . . . . . 282, 367, 658
49:10 . . . . . 244, 595	57:16 498	64:10-11 362
49:12 524	57:19-21 415	65:6 208
49:13 . . . . . 469, 472	58:6-7 254	66:2 658
49:15 . . . . . 501, 630	58:6-10 214	66:8 551
49:22-23 240	58:8 475	66:13 . . . . . 257, 630
49:22-26 326	58:10 472	66:15-16 118
50:2 526	58:13-14 454	66:15-23 774
50:4-9 125	59 519	66:18-23 . . . . . . 315, 317, 322
51:5 . . . . . 415, 472	59:4 86	66:23 420
51:9 478	59:9-15 260	
51:9-10 . . . . . . 236, 435, 457, 503, 706	59:13 69	
	59:16 478	

Jeremiah

...... 164, 576, 665
1:5 664
1:9 397
2:1 516
2:1-3 231
2:6 648
2:11 517
2:12 252
2:13 191
2:30-32 231
3:23 594
4:4 783
5:1 73
5:1-13 86
5:15-18 335
5:24 47
5:24-25 414
6:6-7 274
6:14 415
6:25 167
7:1-15 .... 90, 245, 254, 335
7:2 577
7:5-7 ...... 461, 519
7:11 73
7:12 384
7:21-28 208
7:31 518
7:33-34 388
7:34 ...... 229, 258
8:1-2 388
8:1-12 267
8:2 405
8:11 415
8:17 286
9:2 .... 273, 274
9:3-6 52
9:7 661
9:7-11 778
9:8 591
9:22 ...... 388, 405
9:23-24 247
9:24 768
10:1-5 559
10:6 551
10:13 ..... 642, 644
10:25 388
11:1-13 125
11:19 ..... 404, 669
11:20 768
12:6 273
13:10-11 373
14:1-6 219
14:14 469
15:11 754
15:15 336
15:16 583
15:21 270
16:9 229
17:7-8 264
17:8 453
17:9 ...... 311, 770
17:10 661
17:11 86
17:13 191
17:14 531
17:14-18 ... 335, 532
17:17 677
18:18-20 207
18:20 576
18:21-23 335
18:22 207
18:23 584
19:7 388
19:13 504
20:2 273
20:3 167
20:7-13 82
20:8 335
20:9 203
20:10 167
20:11 ..... 185, 352
21:11-12 697
21:12 ..... 461, 598
22:3 ...... 352, 461, 518, 697
22:13-19 541
22:15-16 697
22:18-19 388
23:1 363
23:1-6 746
23:1-8 ..... 21, 128
23:3 128
23:9 335
23:23-24 663
24:7 260
25:1-14 388
25:10 229
25:15 73
25:35 677
26:6 384
26:13 762
27:7-14 783
29:11 345
29:14 612
30:2-3 494
30:3 86
31:11 249
31:1-14 778
31:4 711
31:8-14 128
31:12 180
31:13 167
31:23 414
31:31-34 ... 208, 413
31:33 ..... 210, 260, 366, 487
31:35 134
31:38 260
32:18 134
32:33-41 420
32:39 260
33:2 369
33:9 326
33:11 .... 230, 524, 570
37:11-21 678
38:1-28 678
38:6 ...... 335, 525
40:11-12 295
41:5 673
45:3 335
46:5 167
46:7-8 457
46:22-23 363
46:27-28 149
48:15 134
49:7-22 653
49:29 167
49:35 372
49:39 86
50:6 586
50:29 754
50:34 134
51:1-58 653
51:5 ...... 483, 754
51:16 ..... 642, 644
51:19 134
51:34-37 776
51:51 335
51:56 776
51:57 134

Index of Ancient Sources

Lamentations
.... 197
1–2 224
1:8 634
1:17 682
1:18 634
2:9 364
2:19 ..... 152, 304
2:22 167
3 .... 335, 431
3:6-9 676
3:12-13 198
3:22-23 439
3:23 51
3:42 516
4–5 224
4:20 438
5:6 405
5:7 388

Ezekiel
.... 576, 746
1:27-28 774
3:3 .... 575, 583
3:15 652
5:5 .... 243, 784
6:5 267
7:2-4 405
7:23 274
7:26 364
10:1-5 103
10:1-19 415
11:19-20 420
12:19-20 274
13:9 425
16 516
16:8-63 231
16:9 673
17:18 687
17:19 776
18:8 89
18:31 573
19:10-14 393
20:23 517
22:3-13 519
22:23-29 519
22:30 517
23:1-49 231
25:14 711
25:14-17 460
27:13 591

27:25-36 243
27:34 625
28:1-19 .... 406, 425
28:2 629
28:17 629
28:22 754
28:25 754
28:25-26 405
29:3 364
29:21 634
32:2-4 364
32:18-32 769
34 354
34:11-16 464
34:15 128
34:16 586
34:23-25 130
34:26-27 326
35 653
35:1-5 653
36:25-28 ... 208, 260
36:26 ..... 259, 366
36:36 612
37:28 484
38 243
38:1-4 591
38:12 243
38:23 754
38–39 774
39 243
39:7 ...... 483, 754
39:25-27 754
41:18-20 481
43:2-5 494
44:7 686
44:9 686
47:1-12 .... 235, 774
47:6-12 784
47:12 425
48:35 ..... 551, 599

Daniel
.... 692
2:18 649
3:19-23 678
6:16-26 678
7–12 778
7:14 567
8:13 390
9 171
9:20-24 260

9:21 673
10:14 456
11:31 362
12:1 664
12:2 .... 94, 769
12:6 390
12:7 687
12:11 362

Hosea
.... 484
1 231
1–3 518
1:5 372
2 231
2:18 ...... 372, 374
2:19-20 434
3 231
3:1-5 625
4:1-3 ...... 76, 401
5:14 253
5:15 .... 98, 147
6:6 208
6:11 612
7:11 330
7:14 762
8:7 613
9:1 778
9:16 653
11:1 622
11:4 629
11:9 ...... 483, 754
13:1 573
14:5 637

Joel
1:2-20 613
2:1-11 777
2:1-17 613
2:12-13 762
2:17 558
2:18-32 613
3:1 613
3:1-3 774
3:1-21 613
3:9-18 774
3:16 300
3:18 ...... 316, 774

Amos
1:2 401

1:3 414
1:6 414
1:9 414
1:12 414
2:4-8 778
2:6-8 214
2:10 648
2:14 677
3:1-2 712
3:15 230
4:1-2 214
4:10 783
4:13 409
5:2 573
5:7 400
5:8 369
5:10-12 214
5:12 . . . . . . 287, 400
5:14-15 . . . . 352, 762
5:15 181
5:18-20 783
5:21-24 . . . . . 70, 90,
144, 208,
254, 757
5:21-25 673
5:24 . . . . 352, 671
6:1 600
6:1-7 601
6:6 637
6:12 400
7:1-3 625
8:1-3 712
8:4-8 214
9:2 663
9:5 . . . . 409, 505
9:6 369
9:11 166
9:14 612

Obadiah
. . . . 529
1:1-21 653
1:8-14 653
1:14 295

Jonah
1:4-6 526
1:9 649
2:2-3 625
2:5-6 625
4:2 . . . . 499, 692

Micah
1:1-7 778
1:2-4 777
1:3-4 473
2:1-5 214
3:1-3 518
3:1-4 461
3:8 98
3:9-11 287
3:12 622
4:1-3 240
4:1-4 . . . . . . 236, 598
4:1-5 756
4:5 144
4:13 711
5:2 746
5:2-6 21
5:10 372
5:15 460
6:6-8 . . . . 70, 90,
208, 214,
254, 757
6:8 671
6:15 637
7:2-3 86
7:2-4 76
7:3 287
7:8 . . . . 147, 149
7:10 558
7:12 494
7:16-17 104

Nahum
1:5 473
1:6 782
3:10 653

Habakkuk
. . . . 454
1 84
1:2 390
1:2-4 76
1:4 369
1:6-11 359
1:12 483
1:12-13 369
1:12-17 634
2:1-4 634
2:3-5 369
2:5 769
2:12 74

2:15-16 369
2:17 74
3 777
3:2-19 359
3:3 774
3:3-15 . . . . . 103, 332
3:6-16 473
3:7 774
3:8 . . . 316, 555, 774
3:10 555
3:14-15 378

Zephaniah
1:14-18 777
2:7 612
3:5 768
3:12 300
3:13 591
3:20 612

Haggai
1:5-11 413
2:5 149
2:16-17 413
2:20-23 434

Zechariah
1:1-15 601
1:7-17 400
1:12 390
1:12-17 413
2:7-12 608
2:10-11 425
3:1-5 400
4:6 177
4:6-14 434
6:9-14 632
6:9-15 434
7:2-7 389
7:3 337
8:8 768
8:18-23 389
8:20-23 . . . . 240, 351
9:1-17 774
9:9-10 . . . . . . 21, 746
9:10 . . . . . . 241, 372
9:11 525
10:10 405
12 243
12:2 295
12:6 711

Index of Ancient Sources

12:8 286
13:1 . . . . . . 260, 784
14 243
14:8 . . . . . 774, 784
14:16 . . . . . 455, 494
14:16-17 351
14:16-19 409

Malachi
3:1 135
3:5 . . . . 460, 671
3:10 324
3:13-15 460
3:16 664
3:16-17 279
3:17 643
4:2 411

APOCRYPHA
Additions to Daniel
Bel and the Dragon
. . . . 559
Song of the Three Jews
. . . . 707

1 Maccabees
1:16-24 362
1:36-40 365
1:54 362
1:59 362
2:7-13 365
2:42 709
3:45 365
3:50-53 365
4:24 709
4:33 709
4:52-59 . . . . 160, 572
7:16-17 389
7:46-49 709
9:27 362

2 Maccabees
6:4-5 362
7:27 629

Wisdom of Solomon
13:10-19 559

NEW TESTAMENT
Matthew
1:16 746
1:20 280
1:21 . . . . 82, 477
1:21-23 272
1:23 552
2:2 746
2:9-11 353
3:1 276
3:17 . . . . 25, 39
4:1 276
4:1-11 466
4:4 703
4:5-7 449
5–7 . . . . 90, 511
5:3 366
5:3-10 360
5:3-12 . . . . . . 33, 182
5:4 . . . . 56, 613
5:5 . . . . 195, 366
5:6 . . . . 221, 308
5:7 214
5:8 . . . . 260, 360
5:9 375
5:10 614
5:10-11 187
5:16 . . . . . . 327, 549
5:17 33
5:22-24 254,
. . . . 465, 638
5:24 90
5:33-37 78
5:37 52,
. . . . 266, 312
5:38-39 534
5:38-48 271,
. . . . 655, 776
5:43-44 751
5:43-45 756
5:44 . . . . 99, 187
5:45 548
5:48 . . . . . . 549, 756
6:9 272,
. . . . 484, 602
6:9-10 . . . . . 159, 693
6:9-13 . . . . . 421, 650
6:10 . . . . 284, 354,
. . . . 402, 711
6:12-15 172
6:13 674

6:19-21 305
6:24-33 360
6:25-31 . . . . . 506, 617
6:25-34 . . . . . 48, 136,
. . . . 195, 277
6:26 703
6:33 . . . . 241, 415,
. . . . 474, 549,
. . . . 693
7:13-14 . . . . . 33, 665
7:15-20 491
7:24 398
7:24-27 . . . . . 33, 254
8:12 549
8:16-17 697
8:19 140
9:15 231
9:27 602
9:35-36 130
9:37-38 327
10:26-31 281
11:2-6 678
11:5 697
14:13-21 527
14:43-45 277
16:13-20 . . . . . 21, 635
16:18 245
16:26 249
16:27 305
17:5 . . . . 25, 39
17:15 595
18:1-5 629
18:3-8 776
18:15-17 90
18:15-20 14
18:20 . . . . . 145, 638
20:28 . . . . . 249, 609
21:5 746
21:9 . . . . 25, 165,
. . . . 571-73
21:16 . . . . 62, 64
21:42 . . . . . . 25, 572,
. . . . 779
22:1-10 191
22:2-14 231
22:34-40 90
22:37 166
22:41-46 540
23:1-12 144
23:12 370
23:34 623

23:37 448	4:26-29 616-17	1:46-55 177,
23:37-39 427	4:35-41 . . . . 458, 526	187, 370,
24:30 474	4:39 527	526, 552
25:1-13 231	5:21-43 163	1:48 659
25:30 549	6:17-29 678	1:49-54 479
25:31-33 130	6:34 130	1:50 500
25:31-46 . . . . 60, 86,	6:41 130	1:51-53 462,
214, 402,	7:21-23 519	474, 776
462, 479,	8:27-30 21	1:51-54 70
671, 682	8:29 746	1:53 . . . . . . 181, 697
25:40 130	8:34 366,	1:57-58 552
26:1-5 292	458, 623	1:68 519
26:2-4 312	9:7 39	1:69-79 635
26:14-49 277	9:24 . . . . . . 205, 417	1:72-73 511
26:30 552,	9:33 629	1:80 276
558, 572	9:37 629	2:10 280
26:38 221	10:13-16 629	2:11 746
26:52 60,	10:17 140	2:13-14 707
177, 712	10:38-39 370	2:32 635
27:1 . . . . . . 106, 347	10:43-45 65	2:41-42 615
27:11 746	10:45 249	2:41-51 598
27:24-26 143	11:9-10 25,	2:9-11 149
27:27-30 540	572-73	3:12 140
27:34 . . . . . . 25, 339	11:23-26 119	3:22 . . . . 25, 39
27:35 . . . . . . 25, 124	11:25 214	4:4 703
27:39 25,	12:1-11 572	4:9-12 449
124, 533	12:10-11 25	4:16-21 . . . . . 70, 697
27:43 . . . . . . 25, 124	12:30 166	4:18 527
27:44 439	12:35-37 . . . 353, 540	4:18-19 462,
27:46 . . . . . . 25, 124,	14:1 167	474, 484,
205, 432	14:10-21 277	552, 776
27:48 339	14:18 215	4:43 693
28:5 280	14:24 255	5:16 276
28:10 280	14:26 552,	5:20-26 172
28:18-20 471	572, 697	6:23 288
28:19 426	14:34 221	6:29 532
28:19-20 . . . . 39, 317	14:36 370	6:35-36 288
28:20 131,	14:50 167	7:11-17 163
496, 670	14:55-59 167	7:18-23 697
	14:62 25	9:18-22 21
Mark	15:24 . . . . . . 25, 124	9:33 635
1:11 39	15:29 . . . . . . 25, 124	9:35 . . . . 25, 39
1:14-15 . . . . 26, 240,	15:29-32 167	10:30 594
366, 458,	15:34 . . . . . . 25, 124	11:1-13 119
623, 398	15:36 . . . . . . 25, 339	11:2-4 421
1:15 . . . . . . 693, 698		11:11-13 501
2:1-12 172,	**Luke**	11:28 32
200, 527	1:5-25 552	11:31 353
2:5 258	1:13 280	12:4-7 281
3:6 167	1:30 280	12:13-21 . . 203, 249,
4:3-9 703	1:32-33 353	277, 617

Index of Ancient Sources

12:24 . . . . . 701, 703	1:14 . . . . . . 177, 245,	12:13 . . . . . . 25, 272,
12:32 241	411, 416,	573, 746
12:48 511	475, 703	12:24-25 613
13:28 549	1:17 . . . . . . 416, 500	12:35-36 149
13:34 519	2:1-11 231	12:46 149
14:7-24 231	2:5-13 423	13:2 277
15:1-7 394	2:8-20 130	13:13-14 . . . 140, 635
15:8-10 630	2:17 339	13:18 215
15:11-32 484,	2:17-36 25	13:21 312
501, 552,	2:21 272	14:6 140,
638	2:25-33 94	144, 703
15:20-23 625	2:30 439	14:13-14 272
15:21 260	2:30-36 635	14:27 610
16:19-31 249,	2:34-36 540	15:4 412
462, 552	2:38 272	15:10 412
17:3-4 776	2:43-47 671	15:1-11 394
18:9-14 552	2:47 617	15:1-12 638
18:14 659	3:3 693	15:18 592
18:32 439	3:16 260,	15:25 . . . . . 187, 339
19:1-8 462	500, 659	16:20 613
19:9 573	3:29 231	17:20-21 412
19:38 25,	4:6-7 308	17:21 638
573, 573	4:10 191	18–19 671
19:41-42 . . . 427, 598	4:13-14 308	18:1-5 277
19:44 755	4:15 221	18:33-37 471
20:17 25	4:23-24 254	18:36 . . . . . 592, 712
20:41-44 540	4:35-38 327	19:24 25,
20:45-47 462	5:17 506	124, 779
21:1-4 462	5:18 292	19:28 779
22:1-6 277	6:1-14 703	19:29 . . . . . . 25, 339
22:30 . . . . . . 64, 620	6:25-35 191	19:30 25
22:47-53 277	6:31 . . . . . 385, 511	19:36 779
23:2 746	6:35 221	20:19-22 280
23:34 . . . . . . 25, 51,	6:48-51 703	20:26 280
214, 258, 271,	7:1 292	20:31 626
339, 407, 682,	7:37-38 309	21 163
756, 776	7:38 191	21:15-17 153
23:35 25	8:32 144	
23:36 25	8:43-47 144	**Acts**
23:42 205	9:1-3 . . . . 55, 200	1:8 . . . . 39, 276
23:46 25,	9:5 . . . . 431, 475	1:15-26 534
167, 205	10 248	1:20 . . . . . . 339, 534
23:49 432	10:1-30 130	3:16 272
24:36 280	10:10-16 153	3:25 326
24:44-47 779	10:11-15 595	4:10 272
	10:11-16 635	4:11 . . . 25, 572, 573
John	10:11-18 394	4:23-24 697
1:1-18 . . . . . 110, 587	10:14 464	4:25-26 39
1:4 191	10:16 240	4:32-37 214
1:4-9 475	10:22 . . . . . 160, 572	5:12-26 678
1:5 431	10:27-30 595	6:7 549

7:42-43 398	2:4 683	11:20 629
7:59 167	2:6 305	11:22 519
7:59-60 205	3:4 261	11:32-36 261
7:60 . . . . 99, 258, 757	3:9-20 519	11:33 . . . . . 454, 665
	3:10-13 86	12:1 . . . . . . 261, 484
8:21 385	3:10-18 . . . . 191, 626, 670	12:1-13 254
8:27-40 335		12:1-21 416
9:2 . . . . 33, 94, 140	3:14 70	12:3 629
	3:20 . . . . 258, 626, 683	12:3-13 638
9:19-30 292		12:6-8 140
13:16-41 25	3:22-23 191	12:9 475
13:22 439	3:24 670	12:14 756
13:22-23 438	3:24-26 519	12:14-21 . . . 214, 271
13:32-39 438	4 511	12:17 655
13:33 39	4:3 172	12:17-21 . . . 75, 154, 265, 776
13:33-35 94	4:7-8 172	
14:15 560	5:1 549	12:18-21 756
14:15-17 . . . 327, 487	5:1-2 519	12:19 . . . . . . 43, 339, 462, 756, 777
14:17 317	5:1-10 416	
16:16-40 678	5:6-8 626	
16:25 581	5:8 . . . . . . 501, 519	12:19-20 534
16:25-40 525	5:20-21 626	12:19-21 . . . 99, 312, 366, 390, 406, 609, 712
17:7 746	6:4 . . . . 94, 178	
17:24-28 327	7:6 178	
18:25 140	7:14-25 519	
19:9 . . . . 33, 94, 140	8:18 574	12:20 . . . . 655, 670, 751
	8:18-25 708	
19:23 . . . . 33, 94	8:22 471	13:1-7 300
20:24 309	8:22-25 431	15:11 567
22:4 . . . . 33, 94, 140	8:26-27 309	15:9 105
	8:28 . . . . . 237, 366, 373, 511	16:26 549
23:1 145		
24:14 140	8:28-30 665	**1 Corinthians**
24:16 145	8:28-39 205	1:17-18 406
24:22 . . . . 94, 140	8:31 . . . . 56, 149, 449	1:18-25 626
26:19-23 292		1:18-31 552
27:6-44 526	8:31-34 534	1:25 . . . . . . 375, 501
	8:31-39 . . . . 90, 119, 222, 226, 281, 366, 605	1:30 416
Romans		3 638
1–2 445		3:6-9 617
1:16-17 . . . . 416, 479	8:33-35 670	3:16-17 458
1:18-28 519	8:34 540	5:7 650
1:19-20 110	8:35-39 94	8 519
1:20 327	8:36 226	8:5-6 402
1:22 86	8:38-39 . . . . 360, 596, 665	10:1-13 650
1:22-23 559		10:4 511
1:23 519	9:4-5 426	10:9 385
1:24 398	9:14 454	10:11 496
1:25 . . . . 86, 560	9:33 572	10:11-13 519
1:26 398	10 110	10:13 623
1:28-32 191	11:9-10 339	10:14-21 519

Index of Ancient Sources

11:23 277	3:6-14 511	2:6-11 . . . . 135, 177, 305
11:23-26 130	3:7-9 240	
11:25-28 370	3:8 326	2:7-9 552
11:27-32 91	3:28 . . . . . . 317, 426	2:8-11 406
11:29 277	3:29 511	3:9-10 221
12:3 660	4:21-31 426	3:10 200
12:12-13 638	4:26 620	3:20 426
12:28-29 140	5:1 398	4:4 173
13:12 665	5:16-25 684	4:4-7 487
15 444	6:15-16 620	4:7 . . . . 305, 595, 630
15:25-26 540	6:16 . . . . . . 599, 610	
15:27 64		4:9 638
15:33 674	**Ephesians**	4:11 630
15:35-38 613	1:3 620	
15:42-44 613	1:20 540	**Colossians**
15:54-55 94	1:20-21 241	1:13-14 605
15:54-57 564	1:20-23 540	1:15-20 708
16:1-3 214	1:22 64	1:16 402
	2:4-22 703	1:19 416
2 Corinthians	2:6 241	2:9 416
1:12 145	2:10 . . . . . . 487, 665	2:10 300
1:19-22 635	2:13 301	2:15 402
2:17 144	2:14 . . . . . . 416, 592	3:1 540
3:7-18 73	2:19-20 426	3:12-17 . . . . 254, 713
3:18 73	2:20 572	3:15 630
4:2 145	3:3 426	3:16 177
4:6 . . . . 73, 149, 416, 475	3:6 426	3:16-17 487
	3:9 426	3:17 370
4:8-9 623	3:20 659	
4:11-12 83	4–6 144	**1 Thessalonians**
5:17-21 178	4:1 144	1:4 645
5:19 491	4:8-10 333	2:4 665
6:2 . . . . 466, 573	4:13 587	4:7 483
6:11 588	4:23-24 261	5:15 265
9:8-15 703	4:25 312	
9:9 549	4:26 48	**1 Timothy**
10:4 712	4:31 671	2:1-2 353
11:2 231	5:15 144	2:2 . . . . 114, 548
11:21-33 . . . 292, 605	5:19-20 . . . . 713, 717	2:5-6 249
11:24 385	5:22-33 231	2:8 675
12:9 . . . . . . 390, 501	5:31 232	6:4 671
12:20 671	6:10-17 . . . . 373, 712	6:6 548
13:8 312	6:12 406	6:6-10 249
13:11 638	6:15 712	6:7-10 305
		6:17 249
Galatians	**Philippians**	
1:8-9 755	1:6 659	**2 Timothy**
2:10 671	2 638	1:10 431
2:16 . . . . 258, 626, 683	2:1-11 682	2:12 64
	2:5-8 65	2:14 645
2:20 309	2:5-11 . . . . . 527, 659	3:1-2 300

3:11 623
4:14 305

Hebrews
1:2-4 708
1:3 . . . 149, 327, 540
1:5 . . . . 39, 746
1:7 506
1:8 231
1:10-12 746
1:14 506
2:6-9 64
2:10 125
2:12 124
2:17 125
3:11-18 519
3:12-19 466
4:1-13 466
4:9 466
4:12-13 712
4:13 665
5:5 . . . . 39, 746
5:6 25
5:10 25
6:20 25
7 540
7:11 25
7:15 25
7:15-22 540
7:17 25
7:19 301
7:21 25
8:1 540
8:10 487
9:11-12 754
9:15 249
10:1-10 209
10:5 209
10:10 209
10:12 540
10:12-13 540
10:14 209
10:19-25 484
10:21-22 301
10:25 398
10:30 . . . . . 288, 462,
              756, 777
10:30-31 . . . 390, 712
10:31 375
11:13 205
12:2 540

12:6 623
12:22 . . . . . 245, 784
12:22-24 426
12:29 . . . . . 375, 475
13:1 638
13:15 673
13:17 130
13:20 . . . . . 153, 394
13:20-21 130

James
1:12-16 674
1:19 591
1:19-26 674
1:26–27 214,
              266, 402
1:27 671
2:1-7 . . . . . . 214, 671
2:1-26 402
2:14-26 254
3:5-8 670
3:5-10 52
3:5-12 266
3:8 591
4:6 659
4:13-14 203
5:8-9 370
5:12 78

1 Peter
1:1 592
1:1-9 623
1:6 . . . . 592, 614
1:6-7 200
1:15-16 484
1:18-19 249
2:4-5 411
2:4-10 635
2:5 484
2:6 245
2:6-8 . . . . 25, 572
2:9 . . . . 431, 484
2:9-10 496,
              511, 645
2:11 205
2:12 592
2:20 592
2:23 592
2:25 130,
              394, 595
3:9 265

3:10 266
3:10-12 182
3:14-15 182
3:21 95
4:14 614
5:2 . . . . 130, 394
5:4 . . . . 130, 394
5:5 659
5:7 . . . . 277, 617

2 Peter
3:7 496
3:8 445
3:10 496

1 John
1:1-4 . . . . . . 385, 626
1:2 411
1:3 665
1:5 665
1:5-10 431
1:7 665
1:9 . . . . 172, 261
1:9-10 145
2:23-25 412
4:11-12 638
4:18 149
4:20-21 254

Revelation
. . . . 623
1:5 439
1:6 693
1:7 474
1:8 587
1:9 678
1:16 . . . . . . 491, 712
2–3 491
2:12 712
2:14 519
2:26-27 . . . . . . 39, 64
3:5 337
4:2 241
4:8 755
4:9 241
4:17 241
5:5-10 471
5:9 26
5:9-10 . . . . . 177, 713
5:10 64
5:11-13 717

Index of Ancient Sources

5:13 708	20:12 425	Theodore of Mopsuestia
6:7-11 534	21:1 496	. . . . 39, 125
6:9-10 390	21:1-4 417	
6:9-11 287,	21:1-5 708	
654, 755	21:2 . . . . . 231, 276,	**OTHER JEWISH**
6:11 390	426, 620	**TEXTS**
6:12-17 375	21:2-4 599	**Mishnah**
7 56	21:3 635	*Middot* 2:5 589
7:10 241	21:5 . . . . . . 178, 241	*Sukkah* 4:2-7 571
7:12 56	21:6 . . . . . . 191, 587	4:4 589
7:17 130,	21:10 276	*Tamid* 7:4 . . . 454, 457
191, 308	21:22 635	
8:3-4 674	21:27 664	**Qumran/Dead Sea**
9:11 430	22:1-2 425	**Scrolls**
9:20 559	22:1-5 . . . . . 605, 708	. . . . 196, 693
10:9-10 575	22:4 . . . . 99, 783	*Psalm Scroll* 11Q5
11:15 . . . . . . 26, 693	22:12 305	(11QPs^a) 586
12:10 26	22:13 587	1QH 9.25 = 1.25
14:1 . . . . . . 245, 784	22:17 . . . . . 231, 309	 261
14:1-3 177	22:20 471	
14:3 . . . . . . 26, 713		
14:6 567		**OTHER ANCIENT**
14:10 . . . . . 370, 783	**OTHER CHRISTIAN**	**TEXTS**
14:13 564	**TEXTS**	"Akkadian Creation
14:18-20 374	Apostles' Creed . . . 421,	Epic" 435,
15:3 . . . 26, 693, 783	540, 595	457, 503
15:3-4 . . . . 323, 484,	*Apostolic Const.* 2.59	Egyptian mythopoetic
713, 755	 309	text 663
15:4 . . . . . . 496, 567	Athanasius 167	El-Amarna inscription
16:1 . . . . . . 339, 783	Augustine of Hippo	 181
16:4 783	 545	"Hymn to Shamash"
16:4-6 . . . . . 385, 390	*Confessions* 1.1 . . . 309	 108
16:5 . . . . . . 693, 783	*1 Clement*	"Hymn to the Aton"
16:6 783	16.15-16 125	 504
16:7 110	18 261	"Onomasticon of
16:19 370	36.4 39	Amenemope" 707
17:9 276	52.4 261	Ugaritic texts 133,
17:18 276	Cassian, John 245	155, 234,
18:2-24 276	*Didache* 12.1 573	435, 452,
18:6 . . . . . . 295, 370	Hippolytus 545	456, 555
19:1 305	Jerome 39	
19:1-6 645	Justin Martyr . . 39, 125	
19:2 110	*Martyrdom of Polycarp*	
19:6 . . . . . . 698, 717	9.3 348	
19:7-9 231	19.2 130	
19:11-21 778	Nicene Creed 462	
19:13 587	Origen of Alexandria	
19:15 39	 39	
19:16 439	*Shepherd of Hermas*	
20:6 64	 130	
20:11 496		

The Author

James H. Waltner, a pastor, has strong interests in biblical studies, preaching, and pastoral care. His pastorates have included Tabor Mennonite, Newton, Kansas (1958-67); First Mennonite, Upland, California (1967-72); First Mennonite, Normal, Illinois, and after a merger, Mennonite Church of Normal (1972-86); and College Mennonite, Goshen, Indiana (1986-96).

Waltner was born near Freeman, South Dakota, grew up on a farm there, and was baptized in the Salem Mennonite Church. His educational studies include Freeman Junior College in South Dakota; Bethel College in North Newton, Kansas; and Mennonite Biblical Seminary in Chicago, graduating in 1958. In 1971, he completed a DMin program with a focus on Old Testament Studies and Preaching from Claremont School of Theology in California.

Waltner wrote a number of Bible study guides for youth and adult Sunday school classes. In 1967 he wrote *This We Believe,* a catechism for young people, still in print; and in 1979, *Baptism and Church Membership.* He has served his denomination in numerous assignments, including being on the Membership Committee (1998-99), which helped to develop Mennonite Church USA and Mennonite Church Canada. He was Interim Executive Secretary for Mennonite Board of Congregational Ministries (2000-2002) and Interim Executive Secretary for the Commission on Education (2001-2). He continues to serve as a pastoral overseer for four northern Indiana Mennonite congregations.

James and his wife, Lenore, are members of College Mennonite Church, Goshen, Indiana. They have three adult children—Rachel Waltner Goossen, Tim Waltner, and JoAn Waltner Thieszen—and three grandchildren.

"This book is refreshing! It is a readable and inspirational study of the psalms and how they intersect with contemporary Christian life. The scholarship is quite good and respectful of a variety of viewpoints. To borrow James Waltner's own phrase, the psalms are 'literature of astonishment' and that comes through in this study. One senses that ultimately, Waltner's purpose in writing the book is to assist people of faith in worship. He provides very helpful analysis and much to ponder. Be sure to read the essays at the end! They contain a wealth of information that will help the reader understand those odd words such as 'selah' and the identity of persons mentioned in the superscriptions such as 'Korah,' the structure of the book and troubling aspects of the psalms such as the calls for vengeance." —*Wilma Ann Bailey, Christian Theological Seminary, Indianapolis, Indiana*

"Like the Psalms themselves, Waltner's commentary should inspire a deeper learning of God's ways and a deeper devotion to the God who listens. Quite readable and clear, Waltner's style keeps the reader's interest and provides the reader with a deep respect for the sublime poetry of the Psalms." —*Craig Broyles, Trinity Western University, Langley, British Columbia*

"James Waltner's immense study of the Psalms merits close attention and wide use. Well informed on critical issues, but, more importantly, it is alive and alert to theological, pastoral concerns. Waltner reads the Psalms in and for the church, and makes connections that will serve the pastoral, liturgical, devotional life of the church. We can be grateful for this important contribution." —*Walter Brueggemann, Columbia Theological Seminary, Columbia, South Carolina*

"James Waltner comes to the biblical text with the heart of a pastor, and the mind of a scholar. This is always a good combination, but is especially advantageous for bringing to life the Psalter, the prayer book and instruction book for Israel. The pastor is most evident when he deals with the difficult passages where psalmists express their rage at God, or their enemies.

The scholar writes clear and helpful explanatory essays which provide a rich resource of valuable background for interpreting these prayers to God. The result is a lucid commentary able to inspire and inform pastor or layperson." —*Gerald Gerbrandt, Canadian Mennonite University, Winnipeg, Manitoba*

"James Waltner has written a very usable, accessible commentary on the Psalms that will be helpful to the pastor and layperson as they begin their encounter with these prayers. This commentary provides short, introductory explanations of the concerns of the individual psalms without getting bogged down in wearisome, tedious details.

His comments about the way the different psalms have been used in the church, and many times by the early Anabaptist martyrs, are a valuable reminder about the way the psalms have been used to carry persons through times of great trouble and distress."
—*Ron Guengerich, Zion Mennonite Church, Archbold, Ohio*

"James Waltner's commentary provides a rich treasury of resources for preachers and teachers of the Psalms. He expounds and interprets each Psalm with warmth and spiritual depth, yet in a straightforward, clear and crisp style. With great care, Waltner sets the Psalms in their canonical context and in the context of the life of the church. This is a resource of immeasurable worth to serious students of the Bible and to those seeking spiritual direction from the Psalms." —*Helmut Harder, Mennonite Church Canada, Winnipeg, Manitoba*

www.ingramcontent.com/pod-product-compliance
Lightning Source LLC
Chambersburg PA
CBHW020911020526
44114CB00039B/100